BRAZIL

THE ROUGH GUIDE

542 80 80

THE ROUGH GUIDES

OTHER AVAILABLE ROUGH GUIDES

MEXICO, PERU, BRITTANY & NORMANDY, VENICE, SICILY, IRELAND, ITALY, WEST GERMANY, BERLIN, SPAIN, PORTUGAL, GREECE, CRETE, YUGOSLAVIA, HUNGARY, EASTERN EUROPE, AMSTERDAM, SCANDINAVIA, MOROCCO, TUNISIA, KENYA, ISRAEL, CHINA, NEW YORK, CALIFORNIA, FRANCE, PROVENCE and **PARIS**

FORTHCOMING

TURKEY, WEST AFRICA, EGYPT, ZIMBABWE & BOTSWANA, GUATEMALA & BELIZE, NEPAL, HONG KONG, THE PYRENEES, HOLLAND, BELGIUM & LUXEMBOURG and **MEDITERRANEAN WILDLIFE**

ROUGH GUIDE CREDITS

Series Editor: Mark Ellingham
Editorial: Martin Dunford, John Fisher, Jack Holland, Jonathan Buckley
Production: Susanne Hillen, Greg Ward, Kate Berens, Andy Hilliard
Typesetting: Gail Jammy
Series Design: Andrew Oliver

Thanks to all the regional and local offices of the **Brazilian National Tourist Board** who helped with the research of this book: in particular, Maria Mhlongo (*EMBRATUR*), Walter Firmo (Director; *FUNARTE*), Alexandro at *TURISRIO*, *EMCETUR*, *BAHIATURSA*, Alfredo Spinola de Mello Neto at *PAULISTUR*, Amilcar Garcia at *PARANATUR*, Mario do Carmo Werner at *SANTUR*, Tamara Pereira and Carlos at *CR-TUR* and Sêve and Senhora de Oliveira at *EMPETUR*. And, **in Brazil**, many thanks to Monica and José Manoel, Luciá da Silva, Marcus and Maria Palacios, Raimundo Pereira, Circe Monteiro, Betânia Pessoa, Sergio and Mundicarmo Ferretti, Fabiana Migliari, Lúcia Lamounier.

Many thanks, too, to the *Rough Guides* team: Kate Berens, Dan Richardson, Mick Sinclair, Helen Lee, Pol Ferguson-Thompson. And to the South American Explorers' Club.

Published by Harrap Columbus, Chelsea House, 26 Market Square, Bromley, Kent BR1 1NA

Typeset in Linotron Univers and Century Old Style
Printed by Cox & Wyman, Reading, Berks

© David Cleary, Dilwyn Jenkins, Oliver Marshall and Jim Hine 1990

576pp
includes index

British Library Cataloguing in Publication Data

Cleary, David
Brazil: the rough guide

1. Brazil. Visitors' guides
I. Title II. Jenkins, Dilwyn III. Marshall, Oliver IV. Hine, Jim
918'.0463

ISBN 0–7471–0127–2

BRAZIL

THE ROUGH GUIDE

written and researched by

**DAVID CLEARY, DILWYN JENKINS,
OLIVER MARSHALL and JIM HINE**

edited by

JULES BROWN and JOHN FISHER

HARRAP COLUMBUS ■ LONDON

CONTENTS

PART ONE   BASICS

PART TWO   THE GUIDE

PART THREE   CONTEXTS

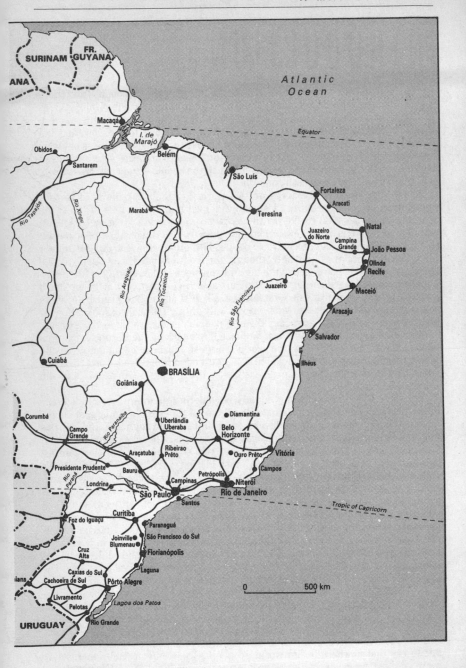

INTRODUCTION

B
razilians often say they live in a continent rather than a country, and that's an excusable exaggeration. The landmass is bigger than the United States if you exclude Alaska: the journey from Recife in the east to the western border with Peru is longer than that from London to Moscow, and the distance between the northern and southern borders is about the same as between New York and Los Angeles. Brazil has no mountains to compare with its Andean neighbours, but in every other respect it has all the scenic – and cultural – variety you would expect from so vast a country.

Despite the immense expanses of the interior, roughly two-thirds of Brazil's **population** live on or near the coast; and well over half live in cities – even in the Amazon. In Rio and São Paulo, Brazil has two of the world's great metropolises, and nine other cities have over a million inhabitants. Yet Brazil still thinks of itself as a frontier country, and certainly the deeper into the interior you go, the thinner the population becomes. In reality, though, the frontiers have been rapidly disappearing since the construction of the highway network in the Amazon in the 1960s.

Other South Americans regard Brazilians as a **race** apart, and language has a lot to do with it – Brazilians understand Spanish, just about, but Spanish speakers won't understand Portuguese. More importantly, though, Brazilians look different. They're one of the most ethnically diverse peoples in the world: in the extreme south, German and Italian immigration has left its mark on the European features of the people; São Paulo has the world's largest Japanese community outside Japan; there's a large black population concentrated in Rio, Salvador and São Luis; while the Indian influence is most visible in the people of Amazonia and the Northeastern interior.

Alongside this ethnic mix run equally bewildering **economic** contradictions. Rapid postwar industrialisation made Brazil one of the world's ten largest economies and put it among the most developed of Third World countries. But this has not improved the lot of the vast majority of Brazilians. The cities are dotted with *favelas*, shanty towns which crowd around the skyscrapers, and the contrast between rich and poor is one of the most glaring anywhere. There are wide **regional differerences**, too: Brazilians talk of a "Switzerland" in the south, centred along the Rio–São Paulo axis, and an "India" above it; and although this is a simplification, it's true that the level of economic development tends to fall the further north you go. This throws up facts which are hard to swallow: Brazil is the industrial powerhouse of South America, but cannot feed and educate its people; in a country almost the size of a continent, the extreme inequalities in land distribution have led to land shortages but not to agrarian reform; and while Brazil has enormous natural resources, their exploitation so far has benefited just a few. The IMF and the greed of First World banks must bear some of the blame for this situation – Brazil's debt stands at $120 billion and rising – but institutionalised corruption and the reluctance of the country's large middle class to do anything that might jeopardise its comfortable lifestyle are also part of the problem.

These difficulties, however, rarely seem to overshadow everyday life in Brazil, and the positive aspects of the Brazilian character and culture are well known. It's fair to say that nowhere in the world do people know how to enjoy themselves more – most famously in the annual orgiastic celebrations of **Carnaval**, but reflected, too, in the lively year-round nightlife that you'll find in any decent-sized town. This national hedonism also manifests itself in Brazil's highly developed **beach culture**; the country's superb **music** and dancing; rich regional **cuisines**; and in the most relaxed and tolerant attitude to **sexuality** – gay and straight – that you'll find anywhere in South America. And if you needed more reason to visit, there's a strength and variety of **popular culture**, and a genuine friendliness and humour in the people that is tremendously welcoming and infectious.

Where to go

The most heavily populated and economically advanced part of the country is **the South**, where the three largest cities – **São Paulo, Rio de Janeiro** and **Belo Horizonte** – form a triangle around which the economy pivots. All are worth visiting in their own right, though **Rio**, one of the world's most stupendously sited cities, stands head and shoulders above the lot. The South stretches down to the borders with Uruguay and northern Argentina, and westwards to Paraguay, and includes much of the enormous **Paraná** river system, where the spectacular falls of **Foz do Iguaçú** (at the point where Brazil, Paraguay and Argentina meet) are one of the great natural wonders of South America.

The vast hinterland of the South is often called the Centre-West and includes an enormous central plateau of savanna and rock escarpments, the **Planalto Central**. In the middle stands **Brasília**, the country's space-age capital, built from nothing in the late 1950s and still developing today. The capital is gateway to a vast interior, the **Mato Grosso**, only fully charted and settled over the last three decades: it includes the mighty **Pantanal** swampland, the richest wildlife reserve on the continent. North and west, the Mato Grosso shades into the **Amazon**, a mosaic of jungle, rivers, savanna and marshland that also contains two major cities – **Belém**, at the mouth of the Amazon itself, and **Manaus**, some 1600km upstream. The tributaries of the Amazon, rivers like the Tapajós, the Xingu, the Negro, the Araguaia or the Tocantins, are virtually unknown outside Brazil, but each is a huge river system in its own right, far larger than any in Europe.

The other major sub-region of Brazil is the **Northeast**, the part of the country that curves out into the Atlantic Ocean. This was the first part of Brazil to be settled by the Portuguese and colonial remains are thicker on the ground here than anywhere else in the country – notably in the cities of **Salvador** and **São Luis** and the lovely town of **Olinda**. It's a region of dramatic contrasts; a lush, tropical coastline with the best beaches in Brazil, slipping inland into the *sertão*, a semi-arid interior plagued by drought and appallingly unequal land distribution. All the major cities of the Northeast are on the coast – the two most famous are **Salvador** and **Recife**, both magical blends of Africa and the Americas.

When to go

Although Brazil is the size of a small continent, with a variety of weather to match, the country splits into four distinct **climatic** regions. The coldest part – in fact the only part of Brazil which ever gets really cold – is **the south**, the inland region roughly from central Minas Gerais to Rio Grande do Sul, which includes Belo Horizonte, São Paulo and Porto Alegre. Here, there's a distinct winter between June and September, with occasional cold, wind and rain. Although Brazilians complain, however, it's all fairly mild. Temperatures rarely hit freezing overnight, and when they do it's featured on the TV news. The coldest part is the interior of Rio Grande do Sul, in the extreme south of the country, but even here there are many warm, bright days in winter and the summer (Dec–March) is hot.

The **coastal climate** is exceptionally good. Brazil has been called a "crab civilisation" because most of its population lives on or near the coast – with good reason. Seven thousand kilometres of coastline, from Paraná practically to the equator, basks under a warm tropical climate. There is a "winter", when there are cloudy days and sometimes the temperature dips below 25°C (77°F), and a rainy season, when it can really bucket down. In Rio **the rains** run from October through to January, but they come much earlier in the Northeast, lasting about three months from April in Fortaleza and Salvador, from May in Recife. However, even in winter or the rainy season, the weather will be excellent much of the time.

The **Northeast** is too hot to have a winter. Nowhere is the average monthly temperature below 25°C (77°F) and the interior, semi-arid at the best of times, often soars beyond that – regularly to as much as 40°C (104°F). Rain is sparse and irregular, although violent. **Amazonia** is stereotyped as being steamy jungle with constant rainfall, but much of the region has a distinct dry season – apparently getting longer every year in the most deforested areas of east and west Amazonia. And in the large expanses of savanna in the northern and central Amazon basin, rainfall is far from constant. Belém is closest to the image of a steamy tropical city; it rains there an awful lot from January to May, and merely quite a lot for the rest of the year. Manaus and central Amazonia, in contrast, have a marked dry season from July to October.

Average temperatures (°C) and rainfall

The first figure is the average **maximum** temperature; the second the average **minimum**; and the third the average number of rainy days per month

	Jan	Feb	Mar	Apr	May	Jun	Jul	Aug	Sep	Oct	Nov	Dec
Belém	31	30	30	31	31	32	32	32	32	32	32	32
	23	23	23	23	23	23	22	22	22	22	22	22
	24	26	25	22	24	15	14	15	13	10	11	14
Belo Horizonte	27	27	27	27	25	24	24	25	27	27	27	26
	18	18	17	16	12	10	10	12	14	16	17	18
	15	13	9	4	4	2	2	1	2	10	12	14
Brasília	27	28	28	28	27	26	26	28	30	29	27	27
	18	18	18	17	15	13	13	14	16	18	18	18
	19	16	15	9	3	1	0	2	4	11	15	20
Manaus	30	30	30	30	31	31	32	33	33	33	32	31
	23	23	23	23	24	23	23	24	24	24	24	24
	20	18	21	20	18	12	12	5	7	4	12	16
Porto Alegre	31	30	29	25	22	20	20	21	22	24	27	29
	20	20	19	16	13	11	10	11	13	15	17	18
	9	10	10	6	6	8	8	8	11	10	8	8
Recife	30	30	30	30	29	28	27	27	28	29	30	30
	25	25	24	23	23	22	21	22	22	23	24	24
	7	8	10	11	17	16	17	14	7	3	4	4
Rio de Janeiro	30	30	27	29	26	25	25	25	25	26	28	28
	23	23	23	21	20	18	18	18	19	20	20	22
	13	11	9	9	6	5	5	4	5	11	10	12
Salvador	29	29	29	28	27	26	26	26	27	28	28	29
	23	23	24	23	22	21	21	21	21	22	23	23
	6	9	17	19	22	23	18	15	10	8	9	11
São Paulo	28	28	27	25	23	22	21	23	25	25	25	26
	18	18	17	15	13	11	10	11	13	14	15	16
	15	13	12	6	3	4	4	3	5	12	11	14

PART ONE

THE
BASICS

GETTING THERE

FROM BRITAIN AND EUROPE

Two airlines operate direct flights from Britain to Brazil, *Varig* (Brazilian Airlines) and *British Airways*. Their fares are generally identical, currently starting at £540 for a ninety-day return to Rio in low season, £595 high season. On these the return dates are fixed, although once in Brazil *Varig* will allow you to change the date (within the ninety days) for a fee of around £50. Flying direct to São Paulo, reckon on paying £10–20 more.

These fares are pretty competitive if you're prepared to live with the restrictions, and certainly the direct flights are quicker and less hassle than any of the alternatives. But they can be fully booked at peak times, and if you want more flexibility, or you're determined to find the absolute cheapest option, there are plenty of others. The way to find the best deal is to look in the travel classified pages of national newspapers like the *Guardian* or *Observer*, or in London listings magazines such as *Time Out* or *LAW*, and to ring as many of the agents as you have patience for. Start, though, with some of the specialist operators we've listed here to get an idea of what you should be aiming at: *Journey Latin America* generally have the widest range, and the first few companies listed under packages will also offer flight-only prices.

The cheapest fares are often offered on *TAP* (Air Portugal), via Lisbon, currently around £530 for a ninety-day fixed date return, and also the best deal on an open ticket – £610 for a return ticket valid for a year. Others include *Iberia* via Madrid, with good value one-way tickets (£306 low season, £326 high) and ninety-day returns for around £600; *Air France* via Paris (£615 ninety days, around £700 yearly open); *Pan Am*, which offers a stopover in the States (ninety days for £557 low season, £577 high); *KLM* via Amsterdam (ninety days £580–635, yearly open £670–780); and *Viasa* via Caracas.

Students and anyone under 26 may also find a better deal from a specialist youth/student operator like *STA* or *Campus Travel*, both of whom also deal with regular flights and have offices around the country.

If you are heading for the northeast of Brazil or the Amazon, it is possible to go direct. *Varig* fly from **Miami to Belém** or **Manaus**, for example, for US$535 one-way and anything from $610 (low season, thirty-day fixed date) to $810 (high season ninety days) return. If you can find a very cheap ticket to Miami, which is often possible, this can be worth doing; otherwise it's probably cheaper to go to Rio and take an internal flight north. *Air France* also fly direct to **Recife**, although, again, this is rarely the cheapest way of getting there.

When buying your ticket to Brazil, you should consider the possibility of adding an **air pass** for travel within Brazil. *Varig/TransBrasil* currently offer 21 days unlimited air travel for US$330, which is excellent value – though it's rumoured that the price may go up considerably, and that the pass may in future be restricted to people flying to Brazil with *Varig*. Bear in mind also that having a pass doesn't guarantee you a seat on a plane. Some routes, especially to and from the Amazon, are always busy, and at Carnaval time virtually all flights are oversubscribed.

Flying to Brazil on a scheduled airline from anywhere else in **Europe** is usually more expensive – to the extent that it is often cheaper to fly to London first. However, before taking such a radical step it is certainly worth checking out local possibilities: *Nouvelles Frontières* often have competitively priced flights, as – if you qualify – do many student travel offices. There are also **charters** from many places, but these have the usual problem of tight restrictions on when you can travel, and usually allow you less than a month in Brazil.

OPERATORS TO BRAZIL FROM THE UK

Airlines

British Airways 156 Regent Street, London W1 (☎071-897 4000).

Varig Brazilian Airlines 16–17 Hanover Street, London W1 (☎071-629 9408).

Flight Specialists

Journey Latin America 14–16 Devonshire Road, London W4 (☎081-747 3108).

STA 74 Old Brompton Road, London SW7 (☎071-937 9962). Other offices throughout England.

Campus Travel 52 Grosvenor Gardens, London SW1 (☎071-730 3402). Offices throughout the UK and Ireland.

Packages and Tours

Journey Latin America 14–16 Devonshire Road, London W4 (☎081-747 8315).

Steamond Travel 23 Eccleston Street, London SW1 (☎071-730 8646).

Dellstar Travel 98 Field End Road, Eastcote, Pinner, Middlesex (☎081-868 2968).

Abreu 109 Westbourne Grove, London W2 (☎071-229 9905).

Lamington Travel 54 Shepherds Market, Curzon Street, London W1 (☎071-408 1477).

Twickers World 23 Church Street, Twickenham, Middlesex (☎081-892 8164).

Exodus 9 Weir Road, London SW12 (☎081-675 5550).

Explore Worldwide 7 High Street, Aldershot, Hants (☎0252-319448).

Encounter Overland 267 Old Brompton Road, London SW5 (☎071-370 6845).

Shipping Companies

Strand Cruise Centre Charing Cross Shopping Concourse, The Strand, London WC2 (☎071-836 6363).

Blue Star Line Albion House, 20 Queen Elizabeth Street, London SE1 (☎071-407 2345).

Gdynia America Shipping Lines 238 City Road, London EC1 (☎071-251 3389).

Grimaldi Lines Eagle House, 109–110 Jermyn Street, London SW1 (☎071-930 5683).

PACKAGES AND TOURS

If your trip is not a long one, and certainly if you plan simply to visit Rio for a couple of weeks, then **package holidays**, with flight and accommodation included, can be exceptionally good value. A week in a four-star hotel in Copacabana can cost less than £800. Trouble is, you won't see much of Brazil. These packages can be found in the brochures at any travel agent – *Thomson*, *Thomas Cook* and the like – and also through some of the specialists listed here. If you hope to go for **Carnaval** you'll need to book months in advance.

More likely to be of interest are the **tours** offered by specialist operators and upmarket package companies. *Journey Latin America* have 22- and 29-day guided tours of Brazil (£895 and £1125 respectively, excluding transatlantic flights), as well as larger scale overland options which also take in Paraguay, Bolivia and Peru, or Chile and Argentina. They can also design individual itineraries, and make the bookings for you. *Twickers World* specialise in wildlife and ecology tours, though with prices starting at almost £2000 (including flights) for fifteen days they're not cheap. Other overland trips are offered by *Exodus* (22 days for around £2000 inclusive), *Explore Worldwide* (Paraguay–Brazil–Peru, 22 days from £1695 inclusive) and *Encounter Overland* (Rio–Lima or Quito, upwards of ten weeks from around £1700 excluding flights). Up-market tour operators like *Kuoni* or *Voyages Jules Verne* (details from travel agents) also offer tours of Brazil in slightly more comfort for a great deal more money.

BY SHIP

It is still just about possible to get to Brazil **by ship**, though it's an expensive and slow way to get there. You'll travel by cargo boat, most of which have room for about twelve passengers travelling in some luxury. They take about three weeks to cross the Atlantic, depending on where they call en route. *Gdynia America Shipping Lines*, a Polish company, depart Hamburg every couple of weeks via Bremen, London and the Canaries to Santos and Montevideo (Uruguay), returning through Santos and on up the Brazilian coast. The cheapest one-way berth on this is about £830, sharing a cabin. *Blue Star* have a departure from London approximately every seven weeks for a seven-week round trip, again calling at various points on the Brazilian coast. The round trip costs £2950 – and you can spend seven weeks in Brazil and catch the next ship back if you want – one-ways start at £1400 to Santos (again, the first port of call). *Grimaldi Lines* have two departures a month from Italy (Genoa, Livorno and Salerno; from about $1000) to Brazil, and just over once a month from London to Hamburg, Rotterdam, Antwerp, West Africa and Brazil (from about £800).

A good first stop for information on all the seaborne options is the *Strand Cruise Centre*.

FROM AUSTRALIA AND NEW ZEALAND

Flights from Australasia to South America are never cheap, and Brazil is no exception. The most direct routings are on *Aerolineas Argentinas* who have a weekly flight Sydney–Auckland–Buenos Aires–Rio over the South Pole, and *LAN Chile* who fly Sydney–Fiji–Santiago–Rio. However it is almost always cheaper to fly via the States: *Qantas* for example connect with *Varig* flights at Los Angeles, and you can make similar connections with *Air New Zealand*, *United* and *Continental*. None of these will cost less than US$2000. A good place to start is *STA*, with offices at 1a Lee Street, Railway Square, Sydney 2000 (☎02/212 1255); 10 O'Connell Street, Auckland (☎09/399 191); and also at Adelaide, Brisbane, Canberra, Christchurch, Hobart, Melbourne, Perth, Townsville and Wellington.

RED TAPE AND VISAS

Britons and citizens of all western European nations except France need a valid passport and either a return ticket, or evidence of funds to pay for one, to enter Brazil. You fill in an entry card on arrival and will get a tourist visa allowing you to stay for ninety days. Australian, New Zealand, French, US and Canadian citizens need visas in advance, available from the relevant embassies.

Do not lose the carbon copy of the entry card the police staple into your passport on arrival, as you may be fined when you leave if you don't present it. A sensible precaution is to photocopy it: otherwise, say it was in a stolen bag.

A tourist visa can be **extended** for another ninety days if you apply at least fifteen days before it expires, but it will only be extended once: if you want to stay longer you'll have to leave the country and re-enter. There's nothing in the rule book to stop you re-entering immediately, but it's advisable to wait at least a day. For anything to do with visas you deal with the federal police, the ***Policia Federal*** (see "Police and Thieves", below). Every state capital has a federal police station with a visa section: ask for the *delegacia federal*. A $10 charge, payable in local currency, is made on tourist visa extensions.

LONGER STAYS: ACADEMIC VISITS

Academic visitors and researchers making a short trip or attending a conference are best advised to enter on a tourist visa, which cuts down on the bureaucracy. If you're staying for a longer period, or intend to do research, before you leave home you need to get a special visa, known as an "Item IV". To obtain this, you'll need to present a letter from a Brazilian Institute of Higher Education saying it knows about, and approves, your research, and you will be formally affiliated to the institution while you do it. Visas are issued either for six months, a year or two years: if in any doubt about exactly how long you're going to stay, apply for the two-year visa. One-year visas can be extended for a further year inside Brazil, but only after months of chasing up the police, and often involving a trip to the Ministry of Justice in Brasília.

On arrival, you must **register** at the *seção dos estrangeiros* office in the nearest federal police station to where you are based. Take some passport photographs, and you'll be issued with an identity card; you can expect registering and getting the card to take at least a day of mindless drudgery, sitting in queues and chasing around, but it has to be done. If your work involves taking samples out of Brazil, a whole new bureaucratic ballgame begins; you will need to get in touch well in advance with the Brazilian Embassy and with the Brazilian institution in question.

WORKING

Working in Brazil is illegal for people entering on a tourist visa, although some do, either clandestinely or leaving and re-entering every three months. It is possible to make a living in a large city **teaching English**: scan the noticeboards of universities, where schools advertise for English teachers, no questions asked. You'll need to be able speak at least some Portuguese first. There are very few other possibilities.

COSTS, MONEY AND BANKS

Despite its exotic reputation Brazil is a fairly cheap country and even the jet-set glamour of somewhere like Rio turns out considerably easier on your pocket than anywhere in Europe. However, inflation is rampant and confusion about the monetary system rife, though the details given below **should help you through the maze. Prices throughout the book are given in US dollars ($), a far more stable medium of exchange**.

Staying in good hotels, eating out, travelling by comfortable coaches and not stinting on the extras, you'll still have change from **$30 a day**. And you could shoestring it for half that, and still cover food, transport and basic accommodation. Many of the essentials of life are, by European standards, extremely cheap; and as the economy slips into hyperinflation, with a rising demand for dollars pushing exchange rates upwards, it looks like Brazil will become even cheaper in real terms. Nevertheless, some things are much more **expensive**, and should be brought with you, like anything to do with cameras, especially film, and suntan lotion (inexplicably, in such a sun-and-body obsessed culture). And sending anything other than a letter by airmail proves costly, too.

MONEY AND PRICES

Brazil's economy has been teetering on the edge of **hyperinflation** for several years now, and this makes **money** confusing. The name of the currency changes roughly every two years, prices change constantly, with inflation at over 1000 percent in 1989 (that's thirty to forty percent *a month*), banknotes are often worth a few noughts less than they say, and there are not one but three rates of exchange! Impossible though it seems at first, it's surprising how quickly most people get used to it.

CURRENCY

At the moment, the Brazilian **currency** is the *cruzado novo*, written as NCz$, made up of one hundred *centavos*. This replaced the *cruzado*, which in turn replaced the *cruzeiro*: both *cruzado* and *cruzeiro* notes are still in circulation, and you knock off three and six noughts respectively to arrive at the value in NCz$. So the 10,000 *cruzado* note is worth NCz$10, and the 100,000 *cruzeiro* note ten *centavos*. Triangular Central Bank stamps on higher denomination notes, which convert them into *cruzados novos* for you, make life slightly easier.

The parallel circulation of all these notes has a paradoxical result: the higher the number on the note, the less it tends to be worth. There's no point in listing the notes in circulation: new ones come out every six months or so, and no guidebook could hope to keep pace with Brazilian inflation.

It is unlikely, at present, that the upward trend of inflation will be reversed – it got steadily worse every year during the 1980s – and so, on past form, the *cruzado novo* will probably be replaced in 1990 or 1991; banknotes will be overstamped again; and the cycle goes on.

PRICES

Prices displayed in shops, hotels and restaurants can also be confusing. Although *centavos* are rarely used, they often appear as two extra noughts on the end of the price: a steak marked NCz$1000 on a menu really costs NCz$10. Strictly speaking it should be written NCz$10.00, but the point is usually left out. Inflation means that the price of most things changes at least once a month, often by as much as fifty percent. You will also find that **change** becomes a problem. Small denomination notes may seem worthless to you, but you need a large stock to pay for things like local buses, telephone tokens and cups of coffee. Newspaper stands, small shops and street stalls will refuse payment in even quite small notes if it cleans them out of change.

THE BLACK MARKET

Changing cash and travellers' cheques is much easier now with the effective legalisation of the *paralelo*, the **black market** in dollars. The black market kept the street price of dollars at roughly twice the bank rate and as a result, in 1988 foreign tourists changed the miserly sum of $19,000 in banks – the dollar-starved government realised something had to be done. So it set up three rates, which you see quoted simultaneously: the *oficial*, the rate Brazilians have to pay to buy air tickets and foreign currency, which visitors to Brazil can ignore; the *dólar turismo*, worth about twice as much, and the rate paid by banks and hotels; and the *dólar paralelo*, the true black market rate.

The effect of all this has been to make life a lot easier for the tourist. Previously, you had to search out the black market, never difficult in Rio or São Paulo but inconvenient elsewhere. Now, as the *dólar turismo* is pegged only slightly below the *paralelo*, you can get an acceptable rate of exchange everywhere that money is changed. A word of caution though: *turismo* and *paralelo* rates only operate for the dollar. Other currencies have to be changed in banks at official rates, which means visitors **must bring dollars** (cash or travellers' cheques): anything else and you lose about fifty percent of the real value.

CHANGING MONEY

In large cities, only the head offices of major **banks** (the state *Banco do Brasil, Banco Itaú* and *Banespa* are the largest) will have an exchange department offering the *turismo* rate (ask for *Câmbio*): whether changing cash or travellers' cheques, you'll need your passport. You can also change cash and travellers' cheques at *turismo* rates in smart hotels, large travel agents, and airline offices. The **best rates** are usually to be found in a *casa de câmbio*, which generally pay the full *paralelo* rate, but these only operate on any scale in Rio and São Paulo. And in large cities, bookshops, record shops and travel agents will often give you a rate even higher than the *paralelo* if you pay in cash dollars: they set a minimum purchase level at around $50.

Outside large cities it can sometimes be difficult to change money. There's always an exchange department in the head office of the *Banco do Brasil* in a state capital, and· smart hotels will usually change cash, too, though you may have problems with travellers' cheques. If you get stuck, travel agents are worth a try: if they don't buy themselves they will know who does. If you plan to travel outside major cities, to small towns and rural areas, don't forget to stock up on currency.

The main **credit cards** have Brazilian affiliates, but can only be used in smarter parts of Rio and São Paulo: you *cannot* get cash with them.

To **change Brazilian currency back into dollars** when you leave, you need to show bank exchange receipts to the value of what you want to change. These receipts are called *comprovantes*, and banks will type one out for you on request when you buy Brazilian currency – a *casa de câmbio* does not issue them.

In such an unstable economic climate, learning how to **manage your money** is vital: you have to do as Brazilians do and play the system to protect against erosion by inflation. The dollar rate changes enough for you to notice most days, and occasionally jumps several percentage points overnight, so it makes sense to change money in small amounts rather than all at once. If you're staying for a month, and change all your money when you arrive, you're effectively kissing goodbye to a real value percentage equal to that month's inflation rate – an amount that will make an awful lot of difference to your stay, even if you exchange for *paralelo* rates.

INFORMATION AND MAPS

You'll find tourist information fairly easy to come across once in Brazil, though it won't do any harm to visit an office of the Brazilian National Tourist Board (*EMBRATUR*) before you leave home. Their offices are generally none too efficient, but they do have plenty of glossy brochures.

Outside Brazil, they are generally attached to an embassy (see "Red Tape and Visas" for addresses): in Britain it's part of the trade section at 15 Berkeley Street, London W1 (☎071-499 0877).

TOURIST OFFICES

In Brazil, facilities vary greatly. Popular destinations like Rio and Salvador have efficient and helpful **tourist offices**, but anywhere even slightly off the beaten track has nothing at all.

All state capitals have tourist information offices, open during office hours, in bus stations and airports – look for signs saying *Informações Turísticas*. Most provide free city maps and booklets, usually all in Portuguese, although you occasionally see atrociously mangled English. As a rule, only airport tourist offices have hotel booking services, and none of them are very good on advising about cheaper accommodation. There are *EMBRATUR* offices in many major centres, but local tourist offices are usually more helpful: these are run by the different state and municipal governments, so you have to learn a new acronym every time you cross a state line. In Rio, for example, you'll find rival national (*EMBRATUR*), state (*Flumitur*) and city (*Riotur*) offices. See the *Guide* for assessments of how useful they are in specific places.

MAPS

We've provided **maps** of all the major towns and cities and various other regions. More detailed maps are surprisingly hard to get hold of outside Brazil, and are rarely very good: there are plenty of maps of South America, but the only widely available one that is specifically of Brazil seems to be the *Bartholomew Brazil & Bolivia* (1:5,000,000) which is not very easy to read.

Much better are the six regional maps in the *Mapa Rodoviário Touring* series (1:2,500,000) which clearly mark all the major routes. These should be available from offices of *EMBRATUR*, or in London they're stocked by *Stanfords* (12–14 Long Acre, London WC2; ☎071-836 1231).

In Brazil, a useful compendium of city maps and main road networks is published by *Guias Quatro Rodas*, a Brazilian motoring organisation, who also have guides to Rio, Salvador and São Paulo. These are easy to find in bookshops, newsagents and magazine stalls. Very clear maps of individual states are published by *Polimapas*, and usually available on the spot. At 1:1,000,000 these are the largest scale of all, though they actually have less detail than some of the above.

HEALTH AND INSURANCE

Although there are no compulsory vaccinations required to enter the country, certain precautions should be taken, certainly if you're staying for any length of time or visiting the more remote regions. Taking out travel insurance is vital, and you should take all possible precautions to guard against AIDS, a major worry in Brazil.

INOCULATIONS AND DISEASES

A **yellow fever** jab is advisable if you are going to Amazonia. Cars and buses en route to western Amazonia are stopped on the roads, and anyone who can't produce a certificate has to be vaccinated on the spot. **Malaria**, too, is endemic in

many parts of Amazonia, and again you should take precautions. These take the form of a course of pills, which usually begins before you enter the country and continues after you leave, so it's something you need to take advice about beforehand, preferably at a specialist hospital of tropical medicine (see box below). Even when taking the pills, you may still get malaria as there are resistant strains. The only comforting factor is that malaria treatment is the one public health area where Brazil can take some credit. Dotted everywhere around Amazonia are small malaria control posts and **clinics**, run by the anti-malaria agency *SUCAM* – ask for the *posto da SUCAM*. They may not look like much, but the people who staff them are very experienced and know their local strains better than any city specialist. Treatment in a *posto* is free, and if you do catch malaria you should get yourself taken to one as quickly as possible: don't shiver in your hammock and wait for it to pass. It often does, but it can also kill.

The other infectious disease you should guard against is **Chagas' disease**. This is endemic in parts of the Northeast and Amazonia and, although it is difficult to catch, it can be serious, leading to heart and kidney problems that appear twenty years after infection. The disease is carried in the faeces of beetles which live in the cracks of adobe walls, so if sleeping in an adobe hut, make sure nothing can crawl into your hammock; either use a mosquito net or sling the hammock as far from walls as you can. The beetle bites and then defecates next to the spot: it itches and you rub infected faeces in when you scratch it. So before scratching a bite you know wasn't caused by a mosquito, bathe it in alcohol. If you are infected, you will have fever for a few days which will then clear up, and though the disease can be treated in its early stages, it becomes incurable once established. If you travel through a Chagas area and get an undiagnosed fever, have a blood test as soon as possible afterwards.

Wherever you go, protection against **hepatitis** is also a sensible precaution. This consists of gammaglobulin injections, one before you go and boosters every six months. If you plan to spend much time in Amazonia or the Northeast, or if you know that you will be travelling rough, these shots are essential. In Britain, supplies of gammaglobulin for these shots are free: they must be kept in a fridge. If you have had jaundice, you may well have immunity and should have a blood test to see if you need the injections.

DIARRHOEA AND DYSENTERY

Diarrhoea is something everybody gets at some stage, and there's little to be done except drink a lot (but not alcohol) and bide your time. You can minimise the risk by being sensible about what you eat, and by *not drinking tapwater* anywhere – and especially not outside large cities. This isn't difficult, given the extreme cheapness and universal availability of soft drinks and *agua mineral*, while Brazilians are great believers in herbal teas, which often help alleviate cramps.

Rather more serious is **dysentery**, which you can easily pick up from infected food or water in rural areas. The symptoms are violent diarrhoea accompanied by painful cramps, and some fever. If you find youself passing blood, it's likely you have it and you should seek medical attention: if there is none, take 500mg of tetracyclin or ampicillin every six hours (travel with a supply if you know you are going off the beaten track for a while). You will also need to replace salts and body liquid: boil up a litre of water with a teaspoon of salt and two tablespoons of sugar for

five minutes, let it cool, and drink all you possibly can. Keep doing this as long as the symptoms persist, and when you finally get to civilisation have a stool sample taken to see if you need more treatment. The symptoms disappear without the disease going away, and you can get serious liver complications later if you forget about it.

CHEMISTS, MEDICAL TREATMENT AND INSURANCE

Standard drugs are available in **chemists**, *farmácias*, which you'll find everywhere – no prescriptions are necessary. A chemist will also provide injections (you need a tetanus jab if you get bitten by a dog) and free medical advice, and they're a good first line of defence if you fall ill.

If you are unlucky enough to need **medical treatment** in Brazil, forget about the public hospitals – as a foreigner you have virtually no chance of getting a bed unless you have an infectious disease, and the level of health care offered by most is appalling. You can get reasonably good medical and dental care privately: North Americans will think it cheap, Europeans used to state-subsidised health care will not. A doctor's visit will cost on average about $30; drugs are relatively inexpensive. Local tourist offices and smart hotels in big cities will have lists of English, French and German speaking **doctors**; ask for a *médico*. Outside the larger centres, you will probably have to try out your Portuguese.

Given all this, it makes sense to take out some kind of **travel insurance policy** which covers medical costs. This is easiest bought when you buy your ticket, but any local travel agent or bank can also sell you a policy which covers not only medical expenses but also loss or theft of baggage, expenses for delays or cancellations, and so on. Prices start from around £40 a month.

AIDS

Brazil has the world's third highest number of **AIDS** sufferers, surpassed only by the USA and Uganda. There are many reasons for this: a scandalous lack of screening of either blood donors or supplies; the level of gay sex between Brazilian

---

men, amongst whom bisexuality is common; the popularity of anal sex, not least amongst heterosexual couples; and the sharing of needles, both amongst drug users in large cities and when giving injections. There are high profile public education campaigns on TV and billboards, but there is still widespread ignorance of how the disease is transmitted, and fear and persecution of its victims. Things have not been helped by the Catholic church, in Brazil usually so liberal on many issues, which has taken a firmly conservative stance on the use of condoms.

A non-exaggerated knowledge of the disease and how it is transmitted is the best defence against it. It is especially important not to be stampeded by the hysteria which surrounds AIDS in Brazil. Firstly, AIDS is not evenly distributed throughout Brazil. A large majority of sufferers and HIV carriers are concentrated in Rio and São Paulo, where you should take extra care. Wherever you are, make sure that if you have an injection it is with a needle you see being removed from its packaging. (It is now possible to buy travellers' medical packs which contain sterile needles, attachments for intravenous drips and the like: they're available, among other places, from the *British Airways* immunisation

centre.) **Avoid blood transfusions unless absolutely neccessary**. Aid agencies in Brazil now provide their staff with bloodbanks, so worried are they about the lack of screening of blood used in both the private and the public hospital networks. If you need blood, repatriate yourself or get your embassy to do it.

Finally, **use a condom**. Only a tiny minority of Brazilian men carry them as a matter of course. They are widely available in chemists, where you should ask for a *camisinha* or a *camiseta de Vênus*. There are often local shortages, however, and Brazilian condoms are not as durable nor as reliable as condoms in the developed world. Take a good supply along with you: you can always give them away if you don't use them.

It's worth stressing that the large Brazilian gay community is working hard to raise public awareness, lobbying for research money and fighting against prejudice. Even taking into account the ugly eruptions of homophobia, the level of popular acceptance and tolerance of gays is still much higher in Brazil than anywhere else in South America, in the cities at least. The gay scene has certainly quietened over recent years, but it's still there – Rio is still very popular with gay tourists, who have a special duty to act responsibly.

GETTING AROUND

Local travel in Brazil is always easy. Public transport is generally by bus or plane, though there are a few passenger trains, too. However you travel, services will be crowded, plentiful and cheap.

BUSES

The **bus system** in Brazil is excellent, as good as anywhere in the Americas, and makes travelling around the country easy, comfortable and economical, despite the distances involved. Intercity buses leave from a station called a **Rodoviária**, usually built on city outskirts.

Buses are operated by hundreds of private companies, but **prices** are standardised, even when more than one firm plies the same route, and are very reasonable: Rio to São Paulo is around $4, Rio to Belo Horizonte $15, São Paulo to Brasília $22, Recife to Salvador $16 and Fortaleza to Belém $34. Long distance buses are comfortable enough to sleep in, and have on-board toilets (which can get smelly on long journeys): the lower your seat number, the further away from them you'll be. Buses stop every two to three hours at well-supplied *postos* where prices are low, so you don't need to stock up on food and drink. There are luxury coaches, too, called **leitos**, which do nocturnal runs between the major cities – worth taking once for the experience, with fully reclining seats in curtained partitions, freshly ironed sheets and an attendant plying insomniacs with coffee and conversation. They cost about a third of the price of an airticket, and between twice and three times as much as a normal long-distance bus; they're also less frequent and need to be booked a few days in advance.

A **ticket** is called a *passagem*: going any distance, it's best to buy it at least a day in advance, more if it's a long journey. An exception is the Rio to São Paulo route, where a shuttle service means you can turn up without a ticket and never have to wait more than fifteen minutes. You buy a numbered seat: if you want a window ask for *janela*. If you cross a state line you will get a small form with the ticket, which asks for the number of your seat (*poltrona*), the number of your ticket (*passagem*), the number of your passport (*identidade*) and your destination (*destino*). You have to fill it in and give it to the driver before you'll be let on board. Buses have **luggage** compartments, which are safe: you check pieces at the side of the bus and get a ticket for them. Keep an eye on your hand luggage, and take anything valuable with you when you get off for a halt.

PLANES

It's hardly surprising that a country the size of Brazil relies on **air travel** a good deal: in some parts of Amazonia air links are more important than either the roads or rivers. Any town has at least an airstrip, and all cities have airports, usually some distance from the city but not always: Santos Dumont in Rio, Guarulhos in São Paulo and Guararapes in Recife are all pretty central. The main domestic carriers are **VASP**, **Varig** and **Transbrasil**. VASP is a notoriously bad timekeeper. Most of their planes are relatively modern jets: the only major exception is the "air bridge" shuttle service between Rio and São Paulo, still plied by Lockheed Electra turbo-props, more because they're popular rather than for lack of anything to replace them with – they may be old, but they have a lot of character.

Flights tend to be booked up in advance (with the exception of the Rio–São Paulo shuttle, though here the flights at the beginning and end of the working day get crowded) and you need to book a *passagem* as far ahead as you can. **Prices**, again, are reasonable: Rio to São Paulo $32, Rio to Belém $140, Rio to Salvador $80, for example. There are cheap rates for flights that leave in the dead of night: ask about the *vôo*

coruja. If you plan on flying a lot in a relatively short time, then consider buying an **air pass** before you leave for Brazil – see "Getting There". Flying to the Northeast or Amazonia from southern Brazil can be tiresome, as many long-distance routes are no more than glorified bus runs, stopping everywhere before heading north again. On scheduled domestic flights you should check-in an hour before take-off, but expect delays if the plane you're catching is arriving from elsewhere.

For all internal flights you have to pay **airport tax**: $6 payable in local currency at the airline desk of the company you're travelling with (not the check-in desk, except at Rio and São Paulo): airline desks are usually in the entrance hall of the airport. If you are doing a lot of air travel it's convenient to buy several airport tax slips at once: they can be used at any airport, where you hand them in when you check in.

A word of **warning**: in many parts of Amazonia air travel in small planes, or an *aero-taxi*, is very common – the regional word for these flights is *teco-teco*. Before taking one, you should be aware that the airstrips are often dangerous, the planes routinely fly overloaded and are not reliably maintained, and no checks are made on the qualifications of pilots – some don't have any. It's up to you . . .

TRAINS AND FERRIES

You probably won't be taking many **trains** in Brazil. Although there's an extensive rail network, much of it is for cargo only, and even where there are passenger trains they're almost invariably slower and less convenient than the buses. Exceptions are a few tourist journeys worth making for themselves – in the south and Minas Gerais especially – and one or two specific routes, especially in and out of São Paulo. The trains worth taking are all discussed in the Guide.

Water travel and ferries are also important forms of transport in parts of Brazil. Specific details are included in the relevant parts of the *Guide*, but look out for the ferry to Niterói, without which no journey to Rio would be complete; **Salvador**, where there are regular services to islands and towns in the huge bay on which the city is built, and most of all in **Amazonia**. Here rivers have been the main highways for centuries, and the Amazon itself is navigable to ocean-going ships as far west as Iquitos in Peru, nearly 3000 kilometres upstream from Belém.

In all the large riverside cities of the Amazon – notably Belém, Manaus and Santarém – there are *hidroviárias*, ferry terminals for waterborne bus services. **Amazon river travel** is slow and can be tough-going, but it's a fascinating experience. On longer journeys there are a number of classes; in general it's best to avoid *primeiro* or *cabine*, where you swelter in a cabin, and choose *segundo* instead, sleeping in a hammock on deck. Take plenty of provisions, and expect to practice your Portuguese.

CITY TRANSPORT

Shoals of **local buses** clog city streets: you enter at the back – where route details are posted – and move through a turnstile as you pay your fare. **Fares** are all flat rate, and rarely more than a few cents. Buses often get unbelievably crowded, and in large cities are favourite targets for pickpockets. It's safer to go through the turnstile even when there are seats at the rear, as *assaltantes* prefer the backs of buses where they can make a quick getaway through the rear door. There are also good modern **Metro** systems in Rio, São Paulo, Belo Horizonte and Recife. Again, they're cheap and efficient, and they're also relatively safe – but since they weren't built with tourism in mind, their routes are not always the most useful.

There are enormous numbers of **taxis** in Brazilian cities, all very cheap by European standards. Generally, the larger the city, the cheaper they get. In cities fares are metered, but the meters always lag way behind inflation. On the windscreen is a sticker for a *UT* (*unidade taxímetro*), showing by what fraction or multiple you should reduce or increase the meter figure. This gives you a rough idea of what you're paying, though the exact fare is determined by the *tabela*, the card with price readjustments to which the driver will refer at the end of the journey – ask to see it if you suspect overcharging.

Taxis in small towns and rural areas do not have meters, and you need to agree the fare in advance – they'll be more expensive than in the cities. Most airports and some bus stations are covered by taxi co-operatives, with a slightly different system: attendants give you a coupon with fares to various destinations printed on it – you pay either at a kiosk in advance, or the driver. Tipping is not obligatory, but appreciated.

DRIVING AND CAR HIRE

Driving standards in Brazil hover between the abysmal and the appalling: in 1988 over 20,000 people died on Brazilian roads, easily the highest toll in the world, and on any journey you can see why, with thundering lorries and drivers treating the road as if it were a Grand Prix racetrack. City driving would make even an Italian blanch, and takes a lot of getting used to. Fortunately, coach drivers are the exception to the rule: they are usually very good, and many coaches have devices fitted that make it impossible for them to exceed the speed limit.

Road quality varies according to region: the south has a good paved network; the Northeast has a good network on the coast but is poor in the interior; while roads in Amazonia are by far the worst, with even major highways closed for weeks or months at a time as they are washed away by the rains. Over half of Brazilian cars now run on *álcool* – a mixture of petrol and alcohol – which is half the price of *gasolina*, petrol.

HIRING A CAR

Hiring a car in Brazil is relatively straightforward, as long as you're confident that you can handle the drivers. *Hertz*, *Avis* and other big-name international companies operate here, and there are plenty of local alternatives – *Nobre* and *Localiza* are the biggest. Often, though, you'll find the cheapest rates are offered by smaller, local companies. Renting a car can be a useful way of seeing a small area which would take days to see on public transport, or of getting to places otherwise entirely inaccessible. An **international driving licence** (available in Britain from the *AA*) is useful, but it's not compulsory as most foreign licences are accepted for short visits.

Prices start from around $30 a day for a Beetle or similar: when you're quoted a price, make sure that it includes insurance (which is compulsory) and any other hidden "extras". **Parking**, especially in the cities, can be tricky, and it may be worth paying extra for a hotel with some kind of lock-up garage – on the street you'll often be approached by someone offering to "guard" your car, and it's usually worth a few cents to prevent your self-appointed guardian from doing any damage. In any event, never leave anything visible inside the car if you don't want to lose it.

Car rental offices (*locadoras*) can be found at every airport and in most towns of any size.

HITCHING

Hitching – *carona* – is a surprisingly tricky proposition, and as a serious means of long-distance travel it can be virtually ruled out. In the past there have been incidents of assaults by hitchhikers on drivers, and there was actually a government campaign to discourage people from giving lifts. If you do want to find a long ride, the best way to do so is to wait at a petrol station or truck stop and approach drivers directly – but it's not easy.

Having said this, hitching can be useful over short distances – to get to a beach not served by public transport for instance. To get a ride of this kind, simply stick out your thumb.

SLEEPING

Accommodation in Brazil comes in various guises, from hostels and basic hotels clustered around bus stations to regular hotels. You can find places to sleep for as little as $1–2 a night, but more realistically, a clean double room in a one-star hotel will set you back about $10.

DORMITORIES AND HOSTELS

At the bottom end of the scale, in terms of both quality and price, are *dormitórios*, small and very basic (to put it mildly) hotels, situated close to bus stations and in the poorer parts of town. They are extremely cheap – $1–2 a night – but usually unsavoury and sometimes positively dangerous.

You could stay for similar prices, in far better conditions, in a **youth hostel**, an *albergue de juventude*, also sometimes called a *Casa de Estudante*. There's an extensive network of these, with at least one in every state capital, and they are very well maintained, often in restored buildings. It helps to have an *IYHF* card with a recent photograph – you're not usually asked for one, but every so often you'll find an *albergue* which refuses entry unless it's produced. Cards are available in Britain from the *YHA* (14 Southampton Street, London WC2; ☎071-836 8542), who also have guides to official youth hostels throughout the world; the equivalent organisation in Brazil is the *Federeção Brasileira dos Albergues de Juventude* (Praça Ana Amélia 09 8°–11°, CEP20020 Castello, Rio de Janeiro; ☎021/220 7123).

Demand for places far outstrips supply at certain times of year – December through to Carnaval, June, August to September – but if you travel with a **hammock** you can often hook it up in a corridor or patio. A major advantage that hostels have is to throw you together with young Brazilians, the main users of the network: they are friendly and intensely curious about life abroad, as they don't meet many foreigners this close up.

PENSOES AND POUSADAS

In a slightly higher price range are the small, family-run hotels, called either a **pensão** or a *Hotel Familiar*. These vary a great deal: some are no more appealing than a *dormitório*, while others are friendlier and better value than many hotels. They tend to be better in small towns than in large cities, but are also usefully thick on the ground in some of the main tourist towns, where hotels are generally more expensive: Olinda and Ouro Preto are two good examples.

You will also come across the **pousada**. This can just be another name for a *pensão*, but can also be a small hotel, running up to luxury class but usually cheaper than a hotel proper. The tourist information offices will tell you in what parts of town you will find a *pensão*, but won't usually recommend anything other than an upmarket *pousada*, as they expect foreigners to go for the better class accommodation. In southern Brazil, many of the *postos*, highway service stations on town outskirts, have cheap **rooms**, and showers, that are usually well kept and clean.

HOTELS

Hotels proper run from dives to luxury apartments. There is a Brazilian classification system, from one to five stars, but the absence of stars doesn't necessarily mean a bad hotel: they depend on bureaucratic requirements like the width of liftshafts and kitchen floorspace as much as on the standard of accommodation – many perfectly good hotels don't have stars.

Hotels offer a range of different rooms, with significant price differences: a *quarto* is a room without a bathroom, an *apartamento* with (actually a shower – Brazilians don't use baths); an *apartamento de luxo* is normally just an *apartamento* with a fridge full of (marked-up) drinks; a *casal* is a double room; and a *solteiro* a single. In a starred hotel, an *apartamento* upwards would normally come with telephone, air conditioning (*ar-condicionado*) and a TV; a *ventilador* is a fan. Rooms start at around $10 in a one-star hotel, around $15 in a two-star hotel, and around $20 in a three-star place. Anything above three stars and you'll pay "international" – ie exorbitant – prices. Generally speaking, though, for $15–20 a night you could expect to stay in a reasonable mid-range hotel, with bathroom and air conditioning. Many hotels in this range in Brazil are excellent value for the standard of accommodation they offer.

Most hotels – although not all – will add a ten percent **service charge** to your bill, the *taxa de serviço*: those that don't will have a sign at the desk saying *"Nos não cobramos taxa de serviço"*, and it's very bad form to leave them without tipping the receptionist. The price will almost invariably include breakfast – gargantuan helpings of fruit, cheese, bread and coffee – but no other meals, although there will usually be a restaurant. Hotels usually have a **safe deposit box**, a *caixa*, which it's advisable to ask about when you check in: they are free to use and, although not invulnerable, anything left in a *caixa* is safer than in your room or on your person.

Finally, a **motel**, as you'll gather from the name and decor, is strictly for couples. This is not to say that it's not possible to stay in one if you can't find anything else – since they're used by locals they're rarely too expensive – but you should be aware that most of the other rooms will be rented by the hour.

CAMPING

There are a fair number of **campsites** in Brazil, almost all of them on the coast near the bigger beaches – mostly they're near cities rather than in out-of-the-way places. They will usually have basic facilities – running water and toilets, perhaps a simple restaurant – and are popular with young Brazilians; a few fancier sites are designed for people with camper vans or big tents in the back of their cars. In all cases, however, the problem is **security**, partly of your person, but more significantly of your possessions, which can never really be made safe.

FOOD AND DRINK

It's hard to generalise about Brazilian food, largely because there is no single national cuisine but several very distinct regional ones. Nature dealt Brazil a full hand, too, for these regional cuisines to work with: there's an abundant variety of fruit, vegetables and spices, as you can see for yourself walking through any food market.

REGIONAL CUISINE

There are four main **regional cuisines**: *comida mineira* from Minas Gerais, based on pork, vegetables (especially *couve*, a relative of spinach) and *tutú*, a kind of refried bean cooked with manioc flour and used as a thick sauce; **comida baiana** from the Salvador coast, the most exotic to gringo palates, using fish and shellfish, hot peppers, palm oil, coconut milk and fresh coriander; **comida do sertão** from the interior of the Northeast, which relies on rehydrated dried or salted meat and the fruit, beans and tubers of the interior of the Northeast; and **comida gaúcha** from Rio Grande do Sul, the most carnivorous diet in the world, revolving around every imaginable kind of meat grilled over charcoal. *Comida do sertão* is rarely served outside its homeland, but you'll find restaurants serving the others throughout Brazil, although – naturally – they're at their best in their region of origin.

Alongside the regional restaurants, there is a **standard fare** available everywhere that can soon get dull unless you cast around: steak (*bife*) or chicken (*frango*), served with *arroz e feijão*, rice and beans, and often with salad, chips and *farinha*, dried manioc flour that you sprinkle over everything. *Farofa* is toasted farinha, and usually comes with onions and bits of bacon mixed in. In cheaper restaurants all this would come on a single large plate: look for the words *prato feito*, *prato comercial* or *refeição completa* if you want to fill up without spending too much.

Feijoada is the closest Brazil comes to a national dish: a stew of pork, sausage and smoked meat cooked with black beans and garlic, garnished with slices of orange. Eating it is a national ritual at weekends, when restaurants serve it all day, but it is delicious any weekday.

Some of the **fruit** is familiar – *manga*, mango, *maracujá*, passion fruit, *limão*, lime – but most of it has only Brazilian names: like *jaboticaba*, *fruta do conde*, *sapotí* and *jaca*. The most exotic fruits are Amazonian: try *bacurí*, *açaí*, and the extraordinary *cupuaçú*, the most delicious of all. These all serve as the basis for juices and **ice cream**, *sorvete*, which is excellent; keep an eye out for *sorvetarias*, ice-cream parlours.

SNACKS, FAST FOOD AND STREET FOOD

You can get food at a growing number of **fast food** outlets in cities, which look garishly American but take the hamburger or hot dog and "Brazilianise" it, much improving it in the process. All sorts of things are added, and the menus are easy to understand because they are in mangled but recognisable English, albeit with Brazilian pronunciation. A hamburger is a *X-burger* (pronounced "sheezboorga"), a hot dog a *cachorro quente*; a *baurú* is a club sandwich with steak and egg; a *mixto quente* a toasted cheese and ham sandwich.

On every street corner in Brazil you will find a **lanchonete**, a mixture of café and bar. They sell beer and rum, snacks, cigarettes, soft drinks, coffee and sometimes small meals. **Bakeries** – *padarias* – often have a *lanchonete* attached, and they're good places for cheap snacks: an *empada* or *empadinha* is a small pie, which has various fillings (*carne*, meat, *palmito*, palm heart and *camarão*, shrimp, the best); a *pastel* is a fried, filled pasty; an *esfiha* a savoury pastry stuffed with spiced meat; and a *coxinha* is spiced chicken rolled in manioc dough and then fried. In central Brazil try *pão de queijo*, a savoury cheese snack that goes perfectly with coffee. All these savoury snacks go under the generic heading *salgados*.

If you haven't had **breakfast** (*café da manhã*) at your hotel, then a bakery/*lanchonete* is a good place to head; and for a more substantial meal *lanchonetes* will generally serve a *prato commercial* too. In both *lanchonetes* and *padarias* you usually pay first at the till, and then take your ticket to the counter to get what you want.

Food sold by **street vendors** in Brazil should be treated with caution, but not dismissed out of hand. You can practically see the hepatitis bugs and amoebas crawling over some of the food you see on sale in the streets, but some vendors have proper stalls and can be very professional, with a loyal clientele of office workers and locals. Some of the food they sell has the advantage of being cooked a long time, which reduces the chance of picking anything up, and in some places – Salvador and Belém especially – you can get good food cheaply in the street; just choose your vendor sensibly. In Salvador try *acarajé*, only available from street vendors – a delicious fried bean mix with shrimp and hot pepper; and in Belém go for *maniçoba*, spiced sausage with chicory leaves, or *pato no tucupí*, duck stewed in manioc sauce.

RESTAURANTS

Restaurants – *restaurantes* – are ubiquitous, portions are very large and prices are extremely reasonable. A *prato comercial* is around $2, while a good full meal can usually be had for $6–8, even in expensive-looking restaurants. Cheaper restaurants, though, tend only to be open for lunch. Specialist restaurants to look out for include a **rodízio**, where you pay a fixed charge and eat as much as you want; all **churrascarias** operate this system, too, bringing a constant supply of meat on huge spits to the tables.

In many restaurants you will be presented with unsolicited food the moment you sit down. This is the **couvert**, which can consist of anything from a couple of bits of raw carrot and an olive to quite an elaborate and substantial plate. Although the price is generally modest, it still has to be paid for. If you don't want it, don't touch it.

Brazil also has a large variety of **ethnic restaurants**, thanks to the generations of Portuguese, Arabs, Italians and Japanese who have made the country their home. The widest selection is in São Paulo, with the best Italian, Arab and Japanese food in Brazil, but anywhere of any size will have good ethnic restaurants, often in surprising places: Belém, for example, has several excellent Japanese restaurants, thanks to a Japanese colony founded fifty years ago in the interior. Ethnic food may be marginally more expensive than Brazilian, but it's rarely exorbitant.

The bill normally comes with a ten percent service charge, but you should still tip, as waiters rely more on tips than on their very low wages.

VEGETARIAN FOOD

Being a vegetarian – or at least a strict one – is no easy matter in Brazil. Many Brazilians are unwilling vegetarians, of course, surviving on the staple diet of rice, beans and *farinha* – and there's wonderful fruit everywhere – but this is not food that you'll find in restaurants, except as side dishes.

If you eat fish there's no problem, especially in the Northeast and Amazonia where seafood forms the basis of many meals; and in the larger cities there are occasional **vegetarian restaurants** (usually described as *Restaurante Natural*). But elsewhere you're up against one of the world's most carnivorous cultures. In the south and centre-west, *churrasco* is king – served at restaurants where you eat as many different cuts of meat as you can manage, and where requests for meals without meat are greeted with astonishment.

DRINK

Coffee is the great national drink, served strong, hot and sweet in small cups and drunk quickly. There is little to say about it, except that it's simply the best there is anywhere. You are never far from a *cafézinho* (as these small cups of coffee are known; *café* refers to coffee in its raw

state). Coffee is sold from flasks in the street, in *lanchonetes* and bars, and in restaurants, where it comes free after the meal. The best way to start your day is with *café com leite*, hot milk with coffee added to taste.

The great variety of fruit in Brazil is put to excellent use in **sucos**, where the fruit is popped into a liquidiser with sugar and crushed ice to make a deliciously refreshing drink. Made with milk rather than water it becomes a **vitamina**. Most *lanchonetes* and bars sell *sucos* and *vitaminas*, but for the full variety you should visit a specialist **casa de sucos**, found in most town centres. Widely available, and the best option to quench a thirst, are *suco de maracujá*, passion fruit, and *suco de limão*, lime. In the North and Northeast, try *graviola*, *bacurí* and *cupuaçú*. Sugar will always to be added to a *suco* unless you ask for it *sem açúcar*: some, notably *maracujá* and *limão*, are undrinkable without.

Soft drinks are the regular products of corporate capitalism and all the usual brands are available. Outshining them all, though, is a local variety, **guaraná**, a fizzy version of the herb southerners make tea out of and you come across occasionally in health shops in the developed world.

ALCOHOL

Beer is mainly of the lager type and excellent. Brazilians drink it ice-cold and it comes mostly in litre bottles: ask for a *cerveja*. Many places only serve beer on draught – called *chop*. Generally acknowledged as the best brands are the regional beers of Pará and Maranhão, *Cerma* and *Cerpa*, but the best nationally available beer is *Antártica*. *Brahma* is also good, *Kaiser* a little watery.

Wine, *vinho*, is mostly mediocre and sweet, though some of those produced in the south aren't too bad. Among the better ones are *Almaden*, *Chateau Chandon*, *Baron de Lantier* and *Cotes de Blancs* (white – *branco*) and *Forestier*, *Conde de Foucaud*, *Chateau Duvalier* and *Baron de Lentier* (red – *tinto*). Imported wines from Chile and Argentina (or Europe) are generally better but far more expensive.

As for spirits, you can buy **Scotch** (*uisque*), either *nacional*, made up from imported whisky essence and not worth drinking, or *internacional*, imported and extremely expensive. Far better to stick to what Brazilians drink, **cachaça**, or sugar cane rum. The best *cachaça* is produced in stills on country farms; it is called *cachaça da terra*, and has a smoothness and taste the industrially

A LIST OF FOODS AND DISHES

Food (*Comida*)

açúcar	sugar	*legumes/*	vegetables	*pão*	bread
arroz	rice	*verduras*		*peixe*	fish
azeite	olive oil	*manteiga*	butter	*pimenta*	pepper
carne	meat	*mariscos*	seafood	*queijo*	cheese
farinha	dried manioc flour	*molho*	sauce	*sal*	salt
feijão	beans	*ovos*	eggs	*sopa/caldo*	soup

Seafood (*Frutas do Mar*)

agulha	needle fish	*lagosta*	lobster	*pescada*	seafood stew, or hake
atum	tuna	*lula*	squid	*pitú*	crayfish
camarão	prawns, shrimp	*moqueca*	seafood stewed	*pirarucú*	Amazon river fish
carangueijo	crab		in palm oil and	*polvo*	octopus
filhote	Amazon river		coconut sauce	*siri*	mussels
	fish	*ostra*	oyster	*sururú*	a type of mussel

Meat and Poultry (*Carne e Aves*)

bife	steak	*costeleta*	chop	*veado*	venison
bife a cavalo	steak with egg	*fígado*	liver	*vitela*	veal
	and *farinha*	*leitão*	sucking pig	*frango*	chicken
cabrito	kid	*lingulça*	sausage	*pato*	duck
carne de porco	pork	*milanesa*	breaded escalope	*perú*	turkey
carneiro	lamb	*picadinha*	stew	*peito*	breast
costela	ribs	*salsicha*	hot dog, salami	*perna*	leg

Fruit (*Frutas*)

abacate	avocado	*goiaba*	guava	*maracujá*	passion fruit
abacaxí	pineapple	*graviola*	cherimoya	*melancia*	watermelon
ameixa	plum, prune	*laranja*	orange	*melão*	melon
cajú	cashew fruit	*limão*	lime	*morango*	strawberry
carambola	star fruit	*maçã*	apple	*pera*	pear
cerejas	cherries	*mamão*	papaya	*pêssego*	peach
côco	coconut	*manga*	mango	*uvas*	grapes
fruta do conde	custard apple (also *ata*)				

Vegetables and Spices (*Legumes e Ervas*)

alface	lettuce	*coentro*	parsley	*mandioca*	manioc
alho	garlic	*cravo*	clove	*milho*	corn
arroz e feijão	rice and beans	*dendê*	palm oil	*palmito*	palm heart
azeitonas	olives	*ervilhas*	peas	*pepinho*	cucumber
batatas	potatoes	*espinafre*	spinach	*repolho*	cabbage
canela	cinnamon	*macaxeira*	roasted manioc	*tomate*	tomato
cebola	onion	*malagueta*	very hot pepper,		
cenoura	carrot		looks like red or		
cheiro verde	fresh coriander		yellow cherry		

Useful Terms

acarajé	fried bean cake stuffed with *vatapà* (see below)	*mal passado/bem passado*	rare/well done (meat)
alho e óleo	garlic and olive oil sauce	*médio*	medium grilled
almoço	lunch	*na chapa/na brasa*	charcoal grilled
assado	roasted	*sobremesa*	dessert
bem gelado	well chilled	*sorvete*	ice cream
café de manhã	breakfast	*suco*	fruit juice
conta/nota	bill	*taxa de serviço*	service charge
cozido	boiled, steamed	*tucupí*	fermented manioc and chicory sauce used in Amazonian cuisine
cozinhar	to cook		
entrada	hors d'oeuvre	*vatapá*	Bahian shrimp dish, cooked with palm oil, skinned tomato and coconut milk, served with fresh coriander and hot peppers
feijoada	black bean, pork and sausage stew		
garçom	waiter		
grelhado	grilled		
jantar	dinner, to have dinner	*vitamina*	fruit juice made with milk

produced brands lack. You won't find it in shops, but it's often on sale in markets. There are scores of brands of industrially produced rum: some of the better ones are *Velho Barreiro, Pitú* and *51*.

Brazilians drink *cachaça* either neat or mixed with fruit juice. Neat, it's very fiery, but in a cocktail it can be delicious. By far the best way to drink it is in a **caipirinha**, along with football and music one of Brazil's great gifts to world civilisation. This is rum mixed with fresh lime, sugar and crushed ice: it may not sound like much, but it is the best cocktail you're ever likely to drink. You should stir it regularly while drinking, and treat it with healthy respect – it is much more powerful than it tastes. Variants are the *caipirosca* or *caipiríssima*, the same made with vodka. Waiters will often assume foreigners want vodka, so make sure you say *caipirinha de cachaça*. You can also get *batidas*, rum mixed with fruit juice and ice, which flow like water during Carnaval: they also pack quite a punch, despite tasting like a soft drink. A *cuba libre* is a rum and Coke.

There are no **licensing laws** in Brazil, so you can get a drink at any time of day or night.

COMMUNICATIONS: POST AND PHONES

Postal services within Brazil are very cheap, though sending airmail abroad is expensive. The phone network, too, is impressive, especially considering the size of the country: public phones are everywhere, most places can be dialled direct and rates are very cheap.

TELEPHONES

Public telephones are called *orelhões*, "big ears", after their distinctive conch-shaped covers. They come in two varieties: red for local calls and blue for inter-urban. Inflation has long since made coin-operated phones obsolete, and instead they

DIALLING CODES AND NUMBERS

If you're dialling from abroad, the international code for Brazil is 55. Calling direct out of Brazil, dial 00 followed by the relevant country code:

Australia 61	**Ireland** 353	**UK** 44
Canada 1	**New Zealand** 64	**USA** 1

SOME USEFUL NUMBERS

International operator ☎000111.   **Reverse charge international calls** ☎000333.

are operated by tokens called *fichas*, on sale everywhere – from newspaper stands, streetsellers' trays and most cafés. For local calls you need a *ficha local*, which costs practically nothing; for long distance a *ficha interurbano*, costing about ten cents. Lift the phone from the hook and get a dialling tone before inserting the token. *Interurbano* tokens are more difficult to find, and are best bought at a **public telephone exchange**, a *posto telefónico*: once you have them you'll find over half the public inter-urban phones out of order. You save time calling from a *posto*, although outside large cities they shut at 10pm. There are no cheap rates on local calls, but **long distance calls** are cheaper after 8pm.

The **dialling tone** is a single continuous note, **engaged** is rapid pips, and the **ringing tone** is regular peals, as in the United States. **International calls** can be dialled direct from a *posto telefónico* (see below), or via operators, who speak all major languages.

USING A *POSTO TELEFÓNICO*

Calling from a **posto telefónico** is the best option for long distance and international calls. They are run by the various state phone companies, but all work the same way: you ask at the counter for a *chave* and are given a numbered key. You go to the booth, insert the key and turn it to the right, and can then make up to three completed calls. You are billed when you return the key – something like $2 a minute to the USA

or Europe. To make an inter-urban call you need to dial the trunk code, the *código DDD* (pronounced "daydayday"): they are listed at the front of phone directories. For international calls, ask for *chamada internacional*; a reverse charge call is a *chamada a cobrar*. Except in the most remote parts of Amazonia and the Northeast, everything from a small town upwards has a *posto*.

POST OFFICES AND LETTERS

A **post office** is called a *correio*: they have bright yellow postboxes and signs. An imposing *Correios e Telégrafos* building will always be found in the centre of a city of any size, and from here you can send telegrams as well; but there are also small offices and kiosks scattered around which only deal with post. Because post offices in Brazil deal with other things besides post, **queues** are often a problem. Save time by queueing for a franking machine rather than for stamps; the lines move much more quickly. **Stamps** (*selos*) lag far behind inflation, to the point where fitting them all onto the envelope or postcard becomes a problem. You have to glue them on from pots or rollers provided on the counter.

Post within Brazil takes three or four days, longer in the North and Northeast, while airmail letters to Europe and North America usually take about a week. **Surface mail** takes about a month to North America, and three to Europe. It is not advisable to send valuables by post.

OPENING HOURS AND HOLIDAYS

Basic hours for most shops and businesses are from 9am to 6pm, with an extended lunch hour from around noon to 2pm. Banks don't open until 10am but stay open all day; they're closed at weekends and on public holidays. Museums and monuments more or less follow office hours but most are closed on Monday.

Although plane and bus **timetables** are kept to when possible, in the less developed parts of the country – most notably Amazonia but also the interior of the Northeast – delays often happen. Brazilians are very Latin in their attitude to time, and if ever there was a country where patience will stand you in good stead it's Brazil. Turn up at the arranged time, but don't be surprised if you're kept waiting. Waiting times are especially long if you have to deal with any part of the state bureaucracy, like extending a visa. There is no way out of it: take a good book.

BRAZILIAN PUBLIC HOLIDAYS

On the following days everything will be closed:

January 1	Corpus Christi
Carnaval – the five days leading up to Ash Wednesday	September 7 – Independence Day
	October 12 – Nossa Senhora Aparecida
Good Friday	November 2 – *Dia dos Finados*, the Day of the Dead
April 21 – Remembrance of Tiradentes	November 15 – Proclamation of the Republic
May 1 – Labour Day	December 25

There are also local and State holidays, which vary from place to place.

FESTIVALS

Carnaval is by some way the most important festival in Brazil, but there are other holidays, too, from saints' days to celebrations based around elections or the World Cup.

CARNAVAL

When **Carnaval** comes – Brazil's famous carnival – the country gets down to some of the most serious partying in the world. A Caribbean carnival might prepare you a little, but what happens in Brazil goes on longer, is more spectacular and on a far larger scale. Everywhere in Brazil, large or small, has some form of Carnaval, and in three places especially (Rio, Salvador and Olinda) Carnaval has become a mass event, involving almost the entire populations of the cities and drawing visitors from all over the world.

When exactly Carnaval begins depends on the ecclesiastical calendar: it starts at midnight of the Friday before Ash Wednesday and ends on the Wednesday night, though effectively people start partying on Friday afternoon – over five days of continuous, determined celebration. It usually happens in the middle of February, although very

---

A CARNAVAL WARNING

Wherever you go at Carnaval, take care of your possessions: it is high season for **pickpockets and thefts**. Warnings about specific places are given in the text, but the basic advice is – if you don't need it, don't take it with you.

---

occasionally it can be early March. But in effect the entire period from Christmas is a kind of run-up to Carnaval. People start working on costumes, songs are composed and rehearsals staged in school playgrounds and back yards, so that Carnaval comes as the culmination of something rather than a sudden burst of excitement and colour.

In the couple of weekends immediately before Carnaval proper there are carnival balls, *bailes carnavalescas*, which get pretty wild. Don't expect to find many things open or to get much done in the week before Carnaval, or the week after it, when the country takes a few days off to shake off its enormous collective hangover. During Carnaval itself, shops open briefly on Monday and Tuesday mornings, but banks and offices stay closed. Domestic airlines, local and inter-city buses run a Sunday service during the period.

Three Brazilian carnivals in particular have become famous, each with a very distinctive feel. The most familiar and most spectacular is in **Rio**, dominated by samba and the parade of samba schools down the enormous concrete expanse of the gloriously named *Sambódromo*. It is one of the world's great sights, a production beyond even Cecil B. De Mille, and is televised live to the whole country. However, it has its critics. It is certainly less participatory than Olinda or Salvador, with people crammed into grandstands watching, rather than down following the schools.

Salvador is, in many ways, the antithesis of Rio, with several focuses around the old city centre: the parade is only one of a number of things going on, and people follow parading schools and the *trio elétrico*, groups playing on top of lorries wired for sound. Samba is only one of several types of music being played, and if it's music you're interested in, Salvador is the best place to hear and see it.

Olinda, in a magical colonial setting just outside Recife, has a character all its own, less frantic than Rio and Salvador, and musically is dominated by *frevo*, the fast, whirling beat of Pernambuco.

Some places you would think are large enough to have an impressive Carnaval are in fact notoriously bad at it: cities in this category are São Paulo, Brasília and Belo Horizonte. On the other hand, there are also places which have much better Carnavals than you would expect: the one in **Belém** is very distinctive, with the Amazonian food and rhythms of the *carimbó*, and **Fortaleza** also has a good reputation. There are full details of the events, music and happenings at each of the main Carnavals under the relevant sections of the *Guide*.

OTHER FESTIVALS

The third week in June sees the *festas juninas*, mainly for children, who dress up in straw hats and checked shirts and release paper balloons with candles attached (to provide the hot air), causing anything from a fright to a major conflagration when they land.

Elections and the **World Cup** are usually excuses for impromptu celebrations, too, while official celebrations, with military parades and patriotic speeches, take place on September 7 (Independence Day) and November 15, the anniversary of the declaration of the Republic.

In towns and rural areas you may well stumble across a *dia de festa*, the day of the local patron saint. It is all very simple: the image of the saint is paraded through the town, with a band and firecrackers, a thanksgiving mass is celebrated, and then everyone turns to the secular pleasures of the fair, the market and the bottle.

In **Belém** this tradition reaches its fullest expression in the *Cirio* on the second Sunday of October, when crowds of over a million follow the procession of the image of Nossa Senhora de Nazaré, but most *festas* are small-scale, small town events.

CARNAVAL DATES IN THE 90s	
1990 Feb 28	1995 Feb 25
1991 Feb 9	1996 Feb 17
1992 Feb 29	1997 Feb 8
1993 Feb 20	1998 Feb 21
1994 Feb 12	1999 Feb 13

FOOTBALL

To those numbed by the permanent state of crisis in British soccer, football in Brazil comes like an oasis in the desert. It's not just that the mix of brilliant attack and fragile defence that makes Brazilian international sides so enthralling is to be found at all levels of Brazilian football, but also the lack of crowd problems – fans from different clubs mingle peacefully inside the grounds – the fine stadiums, and above all the sheer love of games that is universal in Brazil. The parallel that springs to mind is the hold cricket has over hearts and minds in the Caribbean.

Football was introduced into Brazil by Scottish railway engineers round about the time of World War I, and Brazilians took to it like a duck to water. By the 1920s the Rio and São Paulo leagues which dominate Brazilian football had been founded, and Brazil became the first South American country to compete in the World Cup, sending a squad to Italy in 1938. Getúlio Vargas was the first in a long line of Brazilian presidents to make political capital out of the game, building the beautiful Pacaembú stadium in São Paulo and then the world's largest stadium, the Maracanã in Rio, for the 1950 **World Cup**, which Brazil hosted.

In that competition they had what many older Brazilians still think was the greatest Brazilian side ever, hammered everybody, and then in the final, with the whole country already celebrating, came up against Uruguay. Unfortunately the Uruguayans hadn't read the script and won 2–1 – a national trauma that still haunts popular memory forty years on.

Yet success was not long in coming. A succession of great teams, all with **Pelé** as playmaker, won the World Cup in Stockholm in 1958 (the only World Cup won by a South American team in Europe), Chile in 1962 and, most memorably of all, **1970 in Mexico**. Mexico saw the side that is now widely regarded as the greatest in football history, with Pelé playing alongside such great names as Jairzinho, Rivelino, Carlos Alberto, Gerson and Tostão. As three-time winners, Brazil also got to keep the Jules Rimet Trophy, the original World Cup. Since then the ultimate prize has eluded Brazil, but (with the exception of the dull 1974 team) they have stayed true to their ball-

playing, attacking traditions, delighting audiences around the world. Further success can only be a matter of time.

Going to a football match is something which even those bored by the game will enjoy purely as spectacle: the stadiums are sights in themselves, and a big match is watched behind a screen of tickertape and waving flags to the accompaniment of massed drums and thousands of roaring voices. The best grounds are the temple of Brazilian football, Maracanã in Rio, and the Art Deco Pacaembú in São Paulo, one of the most beautiful football stadiums in the world. Tickets are cheap – less than $1 to stand on the terraces (*geral*), $3–4 for stand seats (*arquibancada*); championship and international matches are a little more. Grounds are large, and stadiums usually well below their enormous capacities except for important matches, which means that you can almost always turn up and pay at the turnstile rather than having to get a ticket in advance. Most stadiums are two-tier, with terracing at the bottom surrounding the pitch, and seats on the upper deck. Even small cities have international-class stadiums: they're a municipal virility symbol.

The number of regional championships and national play-offs means there is football virtually all the year round in Brazil – the **national championship** is a complicated mix of state leagues and national sudden-death play-offs. Even though many major Brazilian stars play in Europe these days, there is still enough domestic talent to support very high quality football.

Good teams are thickest on the ground in Rio and São Paulo. In Rio, **Flamengo** and **Fluminense** annually play out the most intense rivalry in Brazilian club football, meeting several times a year in local derbies that are good fixtures to go for; together with **Botafogo** they dominate *carioca* football. In São Paulo there is similar rivalry between **São Paulo** and **Corintians**, whose pre-eminence is challenged by **Guaraní**, **Portuguesa** and **Santos**, the latter now a shadow of the team that Pelé led to glory in the 1960s. The only clubs elsewhere that come up to the standards of the best of Rio and São Paulo are **Internacional** and **Grêmio** in Porto Alegre, **Atlético Mineiro** in Belo Horizonte, **Salvador** and **Bahia** in Bahia, and **Sport** in Recife.

POLICE AND THIEVES

Brazil has a reputation as a rather dangerous place, both for people and their possessions. It's not entirely undeserved, but it's a subject that is often treated hysterically, and many visitors arrive with a wildly exaggerated idea of the perils lying in wait for them. While you would be foolish to ignore them, don't allow worries about safety to interfere with your enjoyment of the country. Certainly, if you take the precautions outlined below, you are extremely unlikely to come to any harm – although you might still have something stolen somewhere along the way.

ROBBERIES, HOLD-UPS AND THEFTS

Remember that while being a gringo can attract unwelcome attention, it is also an important protection. The Brazilian police can be extremely violent, and law enforcement tends to take the form of periodic crackdowns. Therefore, criminals know that any injury to a foreign tourist is going to mean a heavy clampdown, which in turn means no pickings for a while. So unless you resist, nothing will happen to you. That said, having a knife or a gun held on you, as anyone who's had the experience will know, is something of a shock: it's very difficult to think rationally. But if you are unlucky enough to be the victim of an **assalto**, a hold-up, try to remember that it's your possessions rather than you that's the target. Your money and anything you're carrying will be snatched, your watch will get pulled off your wrist, but within a couple of seconds it will be over. *On no account resist*: it isn't worth the risk.

As a rule, *assaltos* are most common in the larger cities, and are rare in the countryside and towns. Most *assaltos* take place at night, in ill-lit streets with few people around, so stick to busy, well-lit streets; in a city, it's always a lot safer to take a taxi than walk. Also, prepare for the worst by locking your money and passport in the hotel safe (see below) – if you must carry them, make sure they're in a moneybelt or a concealed internal pocket. Only take along as much money as you'll need for the day, but do take at least some money, as the average *assaltante* won't believe a gringo could be skint, and might cut up rough. Don't wear an expensive watch or jewellery: if you need a watch you can always buy a cheap

plastic digital one on a street corner for a couple of dollars. And keep wallets and purses out of sight – pockets with button or zips are best.

More common than an *assalto* is a simple **theft**, a *furto*. Bags that look like they come from the First World are an obvious target, so go for the downmarket look. You're at your most vulnerable when travelling and though the luggage compartments of buses are pretty safe – remember to get a baggage check from the person putting them in and don't throw it away – the overhead racks inside are less so; keep an eye on things you stash there, especially on night journeys. On a city beach, never leave things unattended while you take a dip: any beachside bar will stow things for you. Most hotels (even the cheaper ones) will have a safe, a *caixa*, and unless you've serious doubts about the place, you should lock away your most valuable things: the better the hotel, the more secure it's likely to be. In cheaper places, where rooms are shared, the risks are obviously greater. Some people take along a small padlock for extra security and many wardrobes in cheaper hotels have latches fitted for this very purpose. Finally, Carnaval is a notorious time for pickpockets and thieves, so heed the warnings given in the appropriate places in the text and be careful.

THE POLICE

If you are robbed or held up, it's not necessarily a good idea to go to the **police**. Except with something like a theft from a hotel room, they're very unlikely to be able to do anything, and reporting something can take hours even without the language barrier. You may have to do it for insurance purposes, when you'll need a local police report: this could take an entire, and very frustrating, day to get, so think first about how badly you want to be reimbursed. If your passport is stolen, go to your consulate first and they'll smooth the path. Stolen travellers' cheques are the least hassle if they're *American Express*: in Rio and São Paulo they take your word they've been stolen, and don't make you go to the police.

If you have to deal with the police, there are various kinds. The best are usually the **tourist police**, the *polícia de turismo*, who are used to tourists and their problems and often speak some English or French, but they're thin on the ground outside Rio. In a city, their number should be displayed on or near the desk of reasonable hotels. The most efficient by far are the **Polícia Federal**, the Brazilian equivalent of the American FBI, who deal with visas and their extension: they have offices at frontier posts, airports and ports, and state capitals. The ones you see on every street corner are the **Polícia Militar**, with blue uniforms and military helmets. They look mean – and often are – but they generally leave gringos alone. There is also a plain-clothes **Polícia Civil**, to whom thefts are reported if there is no tourist police post around – they are overworked, under-paid, and extremely slow. If you decide to go to the police in a city where there is a consulate, get in touch with them first and do as they tell you.

DRUGS

You should be very, very careful about **drugs**. **Marijuana** – *maconha* – is common, but you are in serious trouble if the police find any on you.

You'll probably be able to bribe your way out of it, but it will be an expensive business. Foreigners sometimes get targeted for a shakedown and have drugs planted on them – the area around the Bolivian border has a bad reputation for this. The idea isn't to lock you up but to get a bribe out of you, so play it by ear. If the bite isn't too outrageous it might be worth paying to save the hassle, but the best way to put a stop to it would be to deny everything, refuse to pay, and insist on seeing a superior officer and telephoning the nearest consulate – this approach is only for the patient. **Cocaine** is not as common as you might think as most of it goes for export, although the home market has grown in recent years.

Be careful about taking anything illegal on buses: they are sometimes stopped and searched at state lines. The most stupid thing you could do would be to take anything illegal anywhere near Bolívia as buses and trains heading in that direction get taken apart by the *federais*.

SEXUAL HARASSMENT & THE WOMEN'S MOVEMENT

Despite the nation's ingrained *machismo*, sexual harassment is less of a problem than you might expect in Brazil. Wolf-whistles and horn-tooting are probably less common than they would be in Spain or Italy, and while you do see a lot of men cruising, more than you might think aren't looking for women, which spreads what hassle there is more evenly between the sexes for a change. Blondes (men as well as women) bring out the stares, but attention which can seem threatening is often no more than curiosity combined with a language barrier.

Chances of trouble depend, to an extent, on where you are: the stereotype of free-and-easy cities and small towns and rural areas that are formal to the point of prudishness often holds good – but not always. Many interior Amazon towns have a frontier feel and a bad, *machista* atmosphere. Also bear in mind that in any town of any size the area around the *rodoviária* or rail-way station is likely to be a red-light district at night; not somewhere to hang around. The transport terminals themselves, though, are usually policed and fairly safe at all hours.

Women travelling alone will arouse curiosity, especially outside the cities, but the fact that you're a crazy foreigner explains why you do it in most Brazilian eyes; it shouldn't make you a target. **Hitching** is not something you'd do in Brazil anyway – truck drivers have a bad reputation.

There is no national **women's movement** in Brazil, but there are loosely linked organisations in big cities and some university campuses, and a growing awareness of the issues: the more important or accessible ones are listed in the *Guide. Mulherio* is a national feminist paper.

GAY BRAZIL

Gay life in Brazil still thrives in the large cities, despite the long shadow cast by the AIDS problem (see "Health and Insurance"). The scene benefits from a relaxed tolerance in attitudes towards sexuality.

There are large numbers of gays in Brazil, and while homophobia does exist it is much less of a factor in Brazil than, say, Britain. Gay life is highly visible: female impersonation and transvestism scale heights unseen anywhere else. Some *travestis* have become sought-after models, while many nationally respected musicians and artists are open about their sexuality in a way that would be unthinkable in Britain or the United States.

Again, both scene and attitudes vary from region to region: rural areas and small towns, especially in Minas Gerais and the south, are deeply conservative; the medium-sized and larger cities are not. The two most popular **gay destinations** are Rio, one of the great gay cities of the world, and Salvador. Pointers to gay life for specific places are given in the *Guide*. A refreshing point to bear in mind is that in Brazil the divide between gay and straight nightlife is very blurred: in the overlap you will find many places popular with both gays and straights. There is as yet no national **gay organisation** in Brazil.

DIRECTORY

ADDRESSES Trying to find an address can be confusing: streets often have two names, numbers don't always follow a logical sequence, and parts of the address are often abbreviated. The street name and number will often have a floor, apartment or room number tacked on: thus R. Afonso Pena 111-3° s.234 means third floor, room 234. S. is short for *sala*, and you may also come across *andar* (floor), *Ed.* (*edifício*, or building) or *s/n* (*sem número*, no number), very common in rural areas and small towns. All addresses in Brazil also have a five digit postcode, or *CEP*, often followed by two capital letters for the state; leaving it out causes delay in

postage. So a full address might read:
Rua do Sol 132 3 andar, s.12
65000 São Luís – MA.

Brasília is a special case: it is divided into sections, which all get an acronym, and everyone lives in apartment blocks called *superquadras*. It seems impossible at first, but with practice enables you to locate an address with great accuracy:
SQN 208
Bloco H – 304
70000 Brasília DF
means *superquadra* north 208, block H, apartment 304.

BRING Useful things to bring with you include a torch and alarm clock, for early morning buses, insect repellent, suntan lotion and film, all of which are available but expensive.

CONTRACEPTIVES Condoms – *camisinhas* or *camisetas do Vénus* – are widely available at chemists, though there are occasional local shortages and doubts about quality. They should always be used (see "Health and Insurance"). The pill – *pílula concepcional* – is also readily available at *farmácias* in Rio or São Paulo without prescription, but you'd be much better advised to bring your own, as Brazil is one of the dumping grounds of unscrupulous drug companies. If you do have to buy, stick to a brand you know is available at home.

DISABLED TRAVELLERS Brazil is not geared at all towards disabled people and their needs, and makes few concessions to them. You are likely to face more than the usual problems.

ELECTRICITY Electricity supplies vary – sometimes 110V and sometimes 220V – so check before plugging anything in. It's a fair bet that you'll blow the fuses anyway. Plugs have two round pins.

EMERGENCIES Emergency phone numbers vary from place to place, but you'll always find them listed in phone boxes – look for *Bombeiros* or *Polícia Civil*.

KIDS Travelling with children is relatively easy in Brazil, but not cheap. They pay full fare on buses if they take up a seat, and full airfares over the age of twelve. The up side is that Brazilians love children, and that travelling as a family will bring you into contact with people you might not otherwise meet, as well as saving you from hassle: the Latin stereotype of respect for family life holds good here. In smaller hotels you'll usually find someone to baby sit or produce special foods for you.

LAUNDRY There are hardly any launderettes in Brazil, but even the humblest (especially the humblest) hotel has a *lavadeira* who will wash and iron your clothes. Agree a price beforehand, but don't be too hard – livelihoods are at stake.

LEFT LUGGAGE Most *Rodoviária* will have a *guarda volume* where you can leave bags. In cities it's usually a locker system, open 24 hours – there's a booth where you buy a key, and a token for every day that you want to leave things; you leave the tokens inside the locker. In smaller places it will usually be a lock-up room operated by a bus company, so check the opening hours before you leave anything. All are safe enough to leave your bags for short periods while you look for a hotel, but don't check money or anything really valuable, especially if you are leaving them for longer periods.

PHOTOGRAPHY Only regular 35mm 100 ASA Kodacolor film is easily available in Brazil and even this is likely to be poorly kept and past its "use by" date. If you use anything else, bring it

with you. Small batteries are also hard to get hold of. A polarizing filter is essential if you have an SLR camera. If possible try to keep the film at a constant temperature before and after use.

STUDENT CARDS An international student card, or a *FIYTO* youth card (available from the student travel operators listed under "Getting There" to anyone under 26), is well worth carrying. It will get you occasional reductions at museums and the like, but more importantly it serves as extremely useful ID for bus drivers and hotels, saving you from having to keep your passport available at all times. Any official-looking card with a picture and number on it will serve almost as well.

TAMPONS *Toalhas Sanitárias* are readily available in supermarkets and *farmácias*; they're cheap, but generally poor quality.

TIME ZONES Brazil is large enough to have different time zones. Most of the country is three hours behind GMT, but the states of Amazonas, Acre, Rondônia, Mato Grosso do Norte and Mato Grosso do Sul are four hours behind – that includes the cities of Manaus, Corumbá, Rio Branco, Porto Velho, Cuiabá and Campo Grande. Clocks go forward an hour on the second Sunday in November for summer time, and go back on the second Sunday in March.

TIPPING Bills usually come with ten percent *taxa de serviço* included, in which case you don't have to tip – ten percent is about right if it is not included. Waiters and some hotel employees depend on tips, so don't be too mean. You don't have to tip taxi drivers (though they won't say no!), but you are expected to tip barbers, hairdressers, shoeshine kids, self-appointed guides and porters. It's useful to keep change handy for them and for beggars.

TOILETS Public toilets are not very common and often disgusting. The words to look for are *Banheiro* or *Sanitário*: where they're marked (less often than you might hope) *Cavalheiros* means men, *Senhoras* or *Damas* women.

WATER Don't drink tapwater – bottled drinks, juices or *agua mineral* are always available.

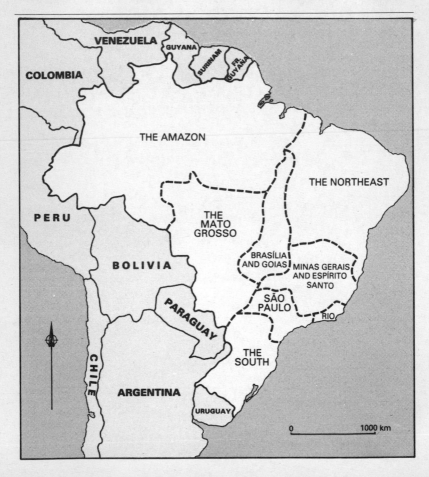

VENEZUELA

GUYANA

SURINAM

FR. GUYANA

COLOMBIA

THE AMAZON

THE NORTHEAST

PERU

THE MATO GROSSO

BRASÍLIA AND GOIAS

MINAS GERAIS AND ESPÍRITO SANTO

BOLIVIA

SÃO PAULO

RIO

PARAGUAY

CHILE

THE SOUTH

ARGENTINA

URUGUAY

0   1000 km

CHAPTER ONE

RIO

T he citizens of the ten-million-strong city of **Rio de Janeiro** call it the *Cidade Marvilhosa* – and there can't be much argument about that. It sits on the southern shore of a landlocked harbour within the magnificent natural setting of Guanabara Bay. Extending for twenty kilometres along an alluvial strip, between an azure sea and jungle-clad mountains, the city's streets and buildings have been moulded around the foothills of the mountain range which provides its backdrop; while out in the bay there are innumerable rocky islands fringed with white sand. The panoramic view over Rio is breathtaking, and even the concrete skyscrapers which dominate the city's skyline add to the attraction.

Although riven by inequality, Rio de Janeiro has great style. Its international renown is bolstered by a series of symbols that rank as some of the greatest landmarks in the world, the **Corcovado** ("hunchback") mountain supporting the great statue of Christ the Redeemer; the rounded incline of the **Sugar Loaf** mountain, standing at the entrance to the bay; and the famous sweep of **Copacabana beach**, probably the most notable length of sand on the planet. It's a setting enhanced by the annual, frenetic sensuality of **Carnaval**, an explosive celebration which – for many people – sums up Rio and her citizens, the **cariocas**. The major downside in a city given over to conspicuous consumption is the rapacious development which is engulfing Rio de Janeiro. As the rural poor, escaping drought and poverty in other regions of Brazil, flock to swell Rio's population, the city is being squeezed like a toothpaste tube between mountains and sea, pushing its human contents out along the coast in either direction. The city's rich architectural heritage is being whittled away and, if the present form of economic development is sustained, the natural environment will eventually be destroyed, too. It's a process unwittingly hastened by Rio's citizens who look forward optimistically to the future, most with the hope of relief from poverty, some with an eye to the main chance and greater wealth.

The **State of Rio de Janeiro**, surrounding the city, is a fairly recent phenomenon, established in 1975 as a result of the amalgamation of Guanabara State and Rio city. Fairly small by Brazilian standards, the state is both beautiful and accessible, with easy trips either east along the **Costa do Sol** or west along the **Costa Verde**, taking in unspoilt beaches, washed by a relatively unpolluted ocean. **Inland** routes make a welcome change from the sands, especially the trip to **Petrópolis**, the nineteenth-century mountain retreat of Rio's rich.

The best time to visit both city and state, as least as far as the **climate** goes, is between May and August, when the region is cooled by trade winds and the temperature remains at around 22–32°C. Between December and March, the rainy season, it's more humid, the temperature more like 40°C; but even then it's never as oppressive as it is in the north of Brazil. Nevertheless, you shouldn't underestimate the sun: don't try for a quick tan in the midday heat, and drink plenty of liquid.

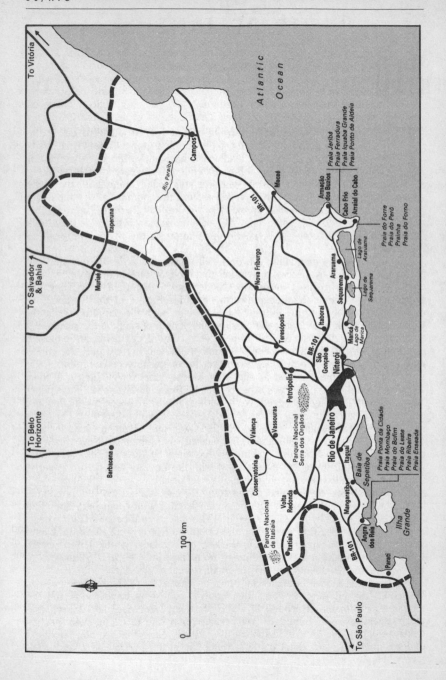

RIO DE JANEIRO

Nearly five hundred years has seen **Rio de Janeiro** transformed from a fortified outpost on the rim of an unknown continent into one of the world's great cities. Its recorded past is tied exclusively to the legacy of the colonialism on which it was founded. No lasting vestige survives of the civilisation of the **Tamoios** tribe, who inhabited the land before the Portuguese arrived, and the city's history effectively begins on January 1, 1502, when a **Portuguese** captain, André Gonçalves, steered his craft into Guanabara Bay, thinking he was heading into the mouth of a great river. The city takes its name from this event – Rio de Janeiro means the "River of January". In 1555, the French, keen to stake a claim on the New World, established a garrison near the Sugar Loaf mountain, and the Governor General of Brazil, Mem de Sá, made an unsuccessful attempt to oust them. It was left to his son, Estácio de Sá, finally to defeat them in 1567, though he fell – mortally wounded – during the battle. The city then acquired its official name, São Sebastião de Rio de Janeiro, after the infant king of Portugal, and Rio began to develop on and around the Morro do Castelo – in front of where Santos Dumont airport now stands.

With Bahia the centre of the new Portuguese colony, initial progress in Rio was slow, and only in the 1690s, when gold was discovered in the neighbouring state of Minas Gerais, did the city's fortunes look up, as it became the control and taxation centre for the gold trade. During the seventeenth century the **sugar cane** economy brought new wealth to Rio, but despite being a prosperous entrepot, the city remained poorly developed. For the most part it comprised a collection of narrow streets and alleys, cramped and dirty, bordered by habitations built from lath and mud. However, Rio's strategic importance grew as a result of the struggle with the Spanish over territories to the south (which would become Uruguay), and in 1763 the city replaced Bahia (Salvador) as Brazil's capital city. By the eighteenth century, the majority of Rio's inhabitants were **African** slaves. Unlike other foreign colonies, in Brazil miscegenation became the rule rather than the exception – even the Catholic Church tolerated procreation between the races, on the grounds that it supplied more souls to be saved. As a result, virtually nothing in Rio remained untouched by African customs, beliefs and behaviour; a state of affairs that clearly influences today's city, too, with its mixture of Afro-Brazilian music, spiritualist cults and cuisine.

In March 1808, having fled before the advance of Napoleon Bonaparte's forces during the Peninsular War, **Dom João VI** of Portugal arrived in Rio, bringing with him some 1500 nobles of the Portuguese Royal Court. So enamoured of Brazil was he, that after Napoleon's defeat in 1815 he declined to return to Portugal and instead proclaimed "The United Kingdom of Portugal, Brazil and the Algarves, of this side and the far side of the sea, and the Guinea Coast of Africa" – the greatest **colonial empire** of the age, with Rio de Janeiro as its capital. During Dom João's reign the Enlightenment came to Rio, the city's streets were paved and lit, and Rio acquired a new prosperity based on coffee.

Royal patronage allowed the arts and sciences to flourish, and Rio was visited by many of the illustrious European names of the day. In their literary and artistic work they left a vivid account of contemporary Rio society – colonial, patriarchal and slave-based. Yet while conveying images of Rio's street-life, fashions and natural beauty, they don't give any hint of the heat, stench and squalor of life in a tropical city of over 100,000 inhabitants, without a sewage system. Behind the

Imperial gloss, Rio was still mostly a slum of dark, airless habitations, intermittently scourged by outbreaks of yellow fever, its economy completely reliant upon human **slavery**.

However, by the late nineteenth century, Rio had lost much of its mercantilist colonial flavour and started to develop as a modern city: trams and trains replaced sedans, the first sewage system was inauguarated in 1864, a telegraph link was established between Rio and London; and a tunnel was excavated which opened the way to Copacabana, as people left the crowded centre and looked for new living space. Under the administration of the engineer **Francisco Pereira Passos**, Rio underwent a period of urban reconstruction that all but destroyed the last vestiges of its colonial design. The city was torn apart by a period of frenzied building between 1900 and 1910, its monumental splendour modelled on the Paris of the Second Empire. Public buildings, grand avenues, libraries and parks were all built to embellish the city, lending it the dignity perceived as characteristic of the great capital cities of the Old World.

During the **1930s** Rio enjoyed international renown, buttressed by Hollywood images and the patronage of the first-generation jet set. Rio became the nation's commercial centre, too, and a new wave of modernisation swept the city, leaving little more than the Catholic churches as monuments to the past. Even the removal of the country's political administration to the new federal capital of Brasília in 1960 did nothing to discourage the developers. Today, with the centre rebuilt many times since colonial days, most interest lies not in Rio's buildings and monuments but firmly in the **beaches** to the south of the city. For sixty years or so these have been Rio's heart and soul, providing a constant source of recreation and income for cariocas.

The favelas

There's another side to Rio that says much about the divisions within the city – the **favelas**. Although not exclusive to the capital, these slums are all the more stark in Rio because of the plenty and beauty that surrounds them. In a low-wage economy, and without even half-decent social services, life is extremely difficult for the majority of Brazilians. During the last twenty years the rural poor have descended on urban centres in search of a livelihood. Unable to find accommodation, or pay rent, they have established shanty towns on any available empty space, which in Rio usually means the slopes of the hills around which the city has grown.

They start off as huddles of cardboard boxes and plastic sheeting, and slowly expand and transform as metal sheeting and bricks provide more solid shelters. Clinging precariously to the sides of Rio's hills, and glistening in the sun, they can from a distance appear not unlike a medieval Spanish hamlet, perched secure atop a mountain. It is, however, a spurious beauty. The *favelas* are creations of need, and their inhabitants are engaged in an immense daily struggle for survival, worsened by the prospect of landslides caused by heavy rains, tearing their dwellings from their tenuous hold on precipitous inclines. The people who live there are denied public services, and are forced to live in conditions which promote ill-health – little better in fact than the squalor that typified Rio de Janeiro in the seventeenth century. Bound together by their shared poverty and exclusion from effective citizenship, within their communities the *favelados* display a great resourcefulness and co-operative strength in their struggle to force the authorities to meet their needs.

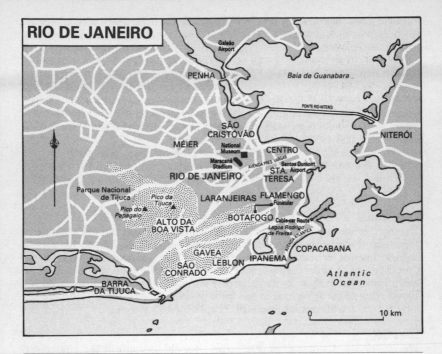

RIO DE JANEIRO

Galeão Airport

PENHA

Baia de Guanabara

PONTE RIO-NITERÓI

SÃO CRISTÓVÃO

NITERÓI

MÉIER

National Museum

CENTRO

Maracanã Stadium

AVENIDA PRES. VARGAS

Santos Dumont Airport

RIO DE JANEIRO

STA. TERESA

Parque Nacional de Tijuca

Pico da Tijuca

LARANJEIRAS

FLAMENGO

Funicular

Pico do Papagaio

ALTO DA BOA VISTA

BOTAFOGO

Cable-car Route

Lagoa Rodrigo de Freitas

AVENIDA ATLÂNTICA

COPACABANA

GAVEA

LEBLON

IPANEMA

SÃO CONRADO

BARRA DA TIJUCA

Atlantic Ocean

0   10 km

Orientation

Arriving in a big city can be a daunting experience, and many people come to **RIO DE JANEIRO**, scramble their way to Copacabana, and go no further, except on an occasional foray by guided tour. The beaches, though, are only one facet of Rio. The city is divided into three parts – centre, north and south – and the various *bairros* (neighbourhoods) have retained their individuality and characteristic atmosphere. So, while you'll certainly want to get a good dose of the beaches, you may prefer to put up in a quieter quarter and explore the rich history of the centre as well. Rio's layout is straightforward and the transport system makes it easy to get around – just buy a **map** (a *Planta do Rio*) from any city kiosk.

Centro

Centro is the commercial and historic centre of Rio, and though the elegance of its colonial and Neoclassical architecture has become overshadowed by the towering office blocks, it has by no means yet been swamped. It's an effective grid, cut by two main arteries at right angles to each other, **Avenida Presidente Vargas** and **Avenida Rio Branco**. Presidente Vargas runs west from the waterfront and the Candelária church to Dom Pedro II **train station** and on to the **Sambódromo**, where the Carnaval procession takes place. Rio Branco crosses it in front of the Candelária church, running from **Praça Mauá** in the dockland area, south through **Praça Mahatma Ghandi** to the **Avenida Beira Mar**. On the west side of Avenida Rio Branco is **Largo da Carioca**, which provides access to the hilly suburb of **Santa Teresa**, whose leafy streets wind their way upwards and westwards towards the Corcovado (see below). At the foot of the slope on which Santa Teresa is built lies **Lapa**, just south of Centro, an inner-city residential and red-light district, its past grandeur reflected in the faded elegance of the **Passeio Público** park.

On the east side of Rio Branco, **Rua da Assembléia** contains the *Turisrio* tourist office, and runs into **Praça XV de Novembro**: the square near the water where you'll find the **ferry station** for boats and hydrofoils to Niterói (across the bay) and the Ilha de Paquetá (to the north).

Both Avenida Rio Branco and Praça XV de Novembro are good places to catch a **bus to the southern beaches**, an area known as the Zona Sul – any bus with the name of a distant beach, like Leblon, passes along the coastline, or parallel to it.

Zona Norte

The northernmost part of Rio, the **Zona Norte**, contains the city's industrial areas and the major working-class residential *bairros* with little in the way of historic interest or natural beauty. However, the **National Museum** in the Quinta da Boa Vista park is a splendid collection well worth making time for. This apart, you're not likely to go much further north than Praça Mauá (see "Centro", above), exceptions being trips to and from the international airport, inter-city bus terminal and the **Maracanã Stadium**, Brazil's football Mecca.

Zona Sul

The **Zona Sul**, the name used to cover everything south of the city centre, though generally taken to mean just the *bairros* shouldering the coastline, has much more to attract you.

Following the Avenida Beira Mar south from Centro, the zone is heralded by the **Parque do Flamengo**, an extensive area of reclaimed land transformed into a public recreation area and beach. First up is the *bairro* of **Glória**, where the whitewashed church of Nossa Senhora da Glória do Outeiro, high on a wooded hill, makes an unmistakable landmark. Beyond, Beira Mar becomes Avenida Praia do Flamengo, which leads into the *bairros* of **Catete** and **Flamengo** – together with Glória, areas where you'll find innumerable cheap hotels. On the other side of Flamengo is the **Largo do Machado**, whose central position, between the centre and the beach areas, makes it a useful place to base yourself. From the square you can reach the *bairros* of **Laranjeiras** and **Cosme Velho**, to the west. The latter is the site of the **Corcovado** and the famous hilltop statue of Christ the Redeemer.

Further south, the bay of **Botafogo** is overshadowed by the famous **Sugar Loaf** mountain, looming above the *bairro* of **Urca**. From Botafogo, the **Pasmado Tunnel** leads to **Leme**, a small *bairro* whose three kilometres of beach, bordered by **Avenida Atlântica**, sweep around to **Copacabana**. Now one of the world's most densely populated areas, Copacabana is less classy than it once was, losing ground to its western neighbours, **Ipanema** and **Leblon**, which provide another four kilometres of sand and surf. These areas are the most chic of the residential *bairros*, with clubs and restaurants sitting amidst the stylish homes of Rio's more prosperous citizens.

TROUBLE – A WARNING

Although it sometimes seems that one half of Rio is constantly being robbed by the other, don't let paranoia ruin your stay. It's true that there is a lot of petty theft in Rio: pockets are picked and bags and cameras swiped. But use a little common sense and you'll encounter few problems, certainly since none of the real, drug-industry-related violence will touch you. That said, there are certain **areas that should be avoided**.

In **Centro**, contrary to popular belief, Sunday is not the best time to stroll around – the streets are empty, which means you can be more easily identified, stalked and robbed. And with nobody about, there is little hope of immediate assistance. The area around **Praça Mauá**, just to the north of Centro, should be avoided after nightfall, too. Along the Avenida Atlântica in **Copacabana**, the areas in front of the *Help Discoteque* and the *Rio Othon Palace Hotel* are also likely places to encounter trouble. Copacabana's record, though, has been much improved since the authorities started to floodlight the beach at night. Around the **Praça do Lido** in Leme, a red-light district, gringos are fair game; nor is it advisable to wander unaccompanied around the darker corners of the **Parque do Flamengo** after nightfall. Finally, tourists who choose to walk between **Cosme Velho** and the **Corcovado** are increasingly being subjected to robbery and assault – something that can be best avoided by taking the train, which is more comfortable anyway.

Ipanema and Leblon are situated on a thin strip of land, only a few hundred metres wide, between the Atlantic Ocean and the **Lagoa Rodrigo de Freitas**, a lake tucked beneath the green hills of the **Tijuca National Park**. On the north side of the lake are the **Botanic Gardens** (*Jardim Botânico*) and Jockey Club racecourse and, just to the west, the *bairro* of **Gávea**. Further south, through Gávea, the *Auto-Estrada Lagoa-Barra* leads into **São Conrado** and its southern neighbour, **Barra de Tijuca**, the preserve of Rio's middle classes. São Conrado, in particular, shows up the great contradictions in Brazilian society: overlooking the elegant *Gávea Golf Club* and the prosperous residences that surround it is the **Favela Roçinha**, a shanty town clinging to the mountainside and reputedly home to 200,000 people.

Arriving – and leaving Rio

You're most likely to fly in to Rio or arrive by bus, though there is a train station, too. Details about handling your arrival and departure are given below, but one thing to bear in mind concerns each of the various methods of transport: opportunistic thieves are active at all points of arrival, so don't leave baggage unattended or valuables exposed; be especially careful of dangling cameras and wallets stuffed into back pockets.

Arriving by bus

All inter-city bus services arrive at the **Novo Rio Rodoviária** (☎291-5151), three kilometres north of Centro in the São Cristovão *bairro*, close to the city's dockside at the corner of Avenida Rodrigues Alves and Avenida Franscisco Bicalho. International buses from Santiago, Buenos Aires, Montevideo and Ascunción, among others, use this terminus, too. The *Rodoviária* has two sides, one for departures, the other for arrivals: once through the gate at arrivals, either grab a taxi ($2.50 to Centro, $4–6 to the Zona Sul), or cross the road to the bus terminal in Praça Hermes. Alternatively, ask at the **tourist office** desk (daily 8am–8pm) at the bottom of the stairs, in the middle of the foyer in front of the main exit – they'll help with hotels, and advise which buses to catch. Ask, too, about the *executivo* **air-conditioned buses** that leave from directly outside the arrivals side of the station and run along the coast towards Copacabana and Leblon; they leave every half-hour or so, are cheaper than taxis, and more secure than the ordinary buses.

By air

Rio de Janeiro is served by two airports. The one at **Santos Dumont** (☎210-2457) deals mainly with the **shuttle service to São Paulo**, and is at the end of the Parque de Flamengo, immediately south of Centro. From here, taxis or the air-conditioned *executivo* bus will take you through the Zona Sul; a taxi to Copacabana will cost about $2.50. Alternatively, cross the road and catch an ordinary bus from Avenida Marechal Câmara, which you can reach by crossing the pedestrian walkway in front of the airport terminal: #438 to Ipanema and Leblon via Botafogo; #442 to Urca; #472 to Leme; for Copacabana, #484 goes from Avenida General Justo, over which the walkway crosses.

The **international airport** at GALEÃO lies on the Ilha do Governador in Guanabara Bay, 14km north of the city. On arrival make sure that your passport is stamped and that you retain your immigration form, as failure to do so can cause problems come the moment of departure. **Customs** are fairly strict on the subject of electronic equipment and anything to do with computers (especially if they think that you're going to sell them in the country): if there's a problem, leave the goods with the customs officer, make sure you get an official receipt, and collect them when you leave. Walk through the green "nothing to declare" channel and you'll be asked to press a button, a random selection method: if the light flashes green, you're home and dry; if it's red, be prepared to expose the contents of your bags to customs officials. In the arrivals hall, ignore the hotel and taxi touts and consult one of the official **tourist information** desks – *Flumitur/Turisrio* or *Embratur*. You'll get useful and relevant information here, but avoid the desks which represent private concerns, trying to pass themselves off as official agencies. You'll be offered a tourist pack for $15, but ask instead for a list of hotels. The desk will check for vacancies for you, but not at the very cheapest places.

To reach your hotel, catch the air-conditioned *executivo* bus, which runs every half-hour via Centro to Santos Dumont; another, every twenty minutes, runs along the coast, via Centro, to Copacabana and on to São Conrado. The buses stop at midnight, after which a **taxi** ride is the only alternative, worth the cash to make your entry into Rio that little bit easier. Buy a ticket at either the *Cootramo* or *Transcoopass* desks, near the arrivals gate, and give it to the driver at the taxi rank; to Flamengo costs $5, Copacabana $7. Use the air-conditioned taxis operated by the airport; it's best not to take the ordinary taxis (yellow with a blue stripe), and don't accept a lift from one of the unofficial drivers hanging about in the airport. It's about half an hour into the centre, unless you meet the rush hour, and the drive will take you through one of Rio's industrial sectors, past the docks – so don't worry if it looks a bit grim at first; you're going the right way.

By train

The main **train station**, the Dom Pedro II Ferroviária, is halfway along Avenida Presidente Vargas in Centro, almost opposite the Campo de Santana park; easy to spot with its high clock tower. Services from São Paulo and Belo Horizonte, and from Vitória and the North stop here, as well as suburban trains running to and from the outlying northern districts of Rio.

There's a taxi rank outside the station and the journey to the Zona Sul isn't expensive (around $3–5); if you want to get to Flamengo, Botafogo or Copacabana, the taxi will run through Centro and out along the coast; to reach Ipanema or Leblon, the driver may go via the *bairro* of Cosme Velho and through the Antônio Rebouças tunnel, emerging on the north side of the Lagoa Rodrigo de Freitas. Otherwise, the Estação Central Metro stop (see below for details of the Metro) is next to the station (in Praça Duque de Caxias), and the Metro will take you as far as Botafogo; or, on the other side of Avenida Presidente Vargas, there are no shortage of buses running down into Centro and beyond; #438 or #464 to Leblon; #474 or #475 to Ipanema; #455 or #456 to Copacabana; #442 to Urca; #472 to Leme; #498 to Largo do Machado.

Tourist information

Apart from the information you pick up at your point of arrival from the posts there (see above), at some stage you'll probably want to make use of the **tourist offices** in the city. There are three official agencies, all of which have recently been reorganised after much talk of corruption – even now none of them are particularly efficient.

Information about Rio itself is from *Riotur*, Rua da Assembléia 10 (8th floor; Mon–Fri 9am–6pm; ☎242-8000), which distributes maps and brochures and has a helpful multilingual telephone information service (on the above number). Most of *Riotur*'s information can also be picked up at the *Rodoviária*, the Cinelândia Metro station and at the Sugar Loaf. Information about the state of Rio is from *Flumitur*, at the same address on the seventh floor (☎252-4512); and about the rest of Brazil from *Embratur*, on the way to the Maracanã stadium at Rua Mariz e Barros 13, in Praça da Bandeira (☎273-2212).

Note that if you're going to stay in Brazil for over six months, you are obliged to **register** at the *Registro de Estrangeiros*, Polícia Federal, Avenida Venezuela 2 (Mon–Fri 11am–4pm; ☎263-3747).

Leaving Rio: a few details

Leaving Rio **by bus** and travelling out of the state, it's best to book two days in advance. The same goes for popular in-state destinations, like Búzios or Paratí, services to which fill up at weekends; or for travelling anywhere immediately before or after Carnaval. Most **tickets** can be bought from travel agents all over the city, while inside the *Rodoviária*, on both sides, upstairs and down, you'll find the ticket offices of the various bus companies. There are places to buy food and reading material inside the bus station, so you can stock up for the journey, though the buses stop for refreshments every couple of hours or so on long trips, anyway. You can reach the *Rodoviária* on bus #104 from Centro, #127 or #128 from Copacabana, and #456, #171 or #172 from Flamengo.

To reach the **international airport**, arrange for a fixed-fare taxi to pick you up from your hotel (get reception to do it or phone *Transcopass* ☎270-4888, *Coopertramo* ☎260-2022 or *Cootramo* ☎270-1442), or take the air-conditioned bus which follows the coastline and can be picked up on Avenida Delfim Moreira (Leblon), Avenida Vieira Souto (Ipanema), Avenida Atlântica (Copacabana), Avenida Beira Mar (Flamengo), or on the Avenida Rio Branco in Centro. Inside Galeão, departure desks are split into three sections: internal Brazilian flights from Sector A; Sectors B and C for international flights. And remember that there's a departure tax of $8, payable in either US currency or cruzados.

The **night-train to São Paulo** leaves at 11pm, takes nine hours, and has sleeper and lounge-car facilities; from about $10 for a seat to $45 for a double cabin. Book at least three days in advance for mid-week travel, and two weeks in advance if you want to go at the weekend. The rail journey takes longer than the bus, but it's a good choice for those who want a bit of comfort and room to relax. There is also a Friday, Saturday and Sunday service for **Belo Horizonte**, which takes eleven hours and leaves at 9pm. The station is also the terminal for suburban trains running to the outlying northern districts – they are regular and extremely cheap, if a tad uncomfortable and slow. To reach Dom Pedro II station, catch any bus marked *E. Ferro*, or take the Metro to Estação Central in the Praça Duque de Caxias, adjacent to the station.

Getting around the city

Rio's **public transport** system is cheap and effective; most places can be reached by Metro, bus or taxi, or a combination of these; while for getting about the state you might want to hire a car – though driving in the city itself is not recommended unless you are Ayrton Senna.

The metro

The safest and most comfortable way to travel is by using Rio's **Metro** system, in operation since 1979. At present it's limited to two lines, which run from Monday to Saturday, 6am to 11pm: **Line 1** runs from Botafogo, north through Centro and then out to the Sãens Pena station in the *bairro* of Maracanã (though this last is not the stop for the Maracanã stadium); **Line 2** comes in from Maria de Graça, to the north of the city, via the Maracanã stadium, and meets line 1 at Estação Central, by Dom Pedro II train station.

The system is well-designed and efficient, the stations bright, cool, clean and secure. And the trains are air-conditioned, a relief if you've just descended from the scorching world above.

Tickets, which cost a few cents, are bought as singles (*ida*) or returns (*ida e volta*), or are valid for ten journeys. The latter can save time, but it costs the same and you can't share a ten-journey ticket, as the electronic turnstiles only allow entrance at eight-minute intervals.

You can also buy integrated bus/Metro tickets, useful to make the link between the final Metro station at Botafogo and Ipanema or Leblon. You catch the buses directly outside the Botafogo station: they both run circular routes between Botafogo and Leblon; the #M21 going via the *Jóquei Clube*, the #M22 via Copacabana.

Buses

It's sometimes suggested that it's irresponsible to encourage tourists to use the **city buses** because they're badly driven, will probably end up getting you lost, and are the scene of much petty theft. But, while it's true that some of Rio's bus drivers have a somewhat erratic driving style – to say the least – it's well worth mastering the system: with over 300 routes and 6000 buses, you never have to wait more than a few moments for a bus, they run till midnight and it's not that easy to get lost.

Numbers and **destinations** are clearly marked on the front of buses, and there are plaques at the front and by the entrance detailing the route. You **get on at the back**, pay the seated conductor (the price is on a card behind his head) and then push through the turnstile and find yourself a seat. Buses are jampacked at rush hour, so if your journey is short, start working your way to the front of the bus as soon as you're through the turnstile; you alight at the front. If the bus reaches the stop before you reach the front, haul on the bell and the driver will wait. This kind of confusion really only occurs during **rush hour**, which is 5pm to 7pm in the evening. In the beach areas of the Zona Sul, especially along the coast, **bus stops** are not always marked. Stick your arm out to flag the bus down, or look for groups of people by the roadside facing the oncoming traffic, as this indicates a bus stop.

To avoid **being robbed** on the bus, don't leave wallets or money in easily accessible pockets, or flash cameras around. If there's a crush, carry any bags close to your chest. Have your fare ready so that you can pass through the turnstile easily, and don't let the turnstile come between you and anything you don't want to lose.

RIO: SOME USEFUL BUS ROUTES

From Avenida Rio Branco: #119, #121, #123, #127, #173 and #177 to Copacabana; #128 (via Copacabana), #132 (via Flamengo) and #172 (via Jóquei Clube) to Leblon.

From Praça XV do Novembro: #119, #154, #413, #415 to Copacabana; #154 and #474 to Ipanema.

From Avenida Beira Mar, in Lapa, near the Praça Deodoro: #158 (via Jóquei Clube), #170, #172 (via Jardim Botânico), #174 (via Praia do Botafogo), #438, #464, #571 and #572 to Leblon; #472 to Leme; #104 to Jardim Botânico.

From Copacabana: #455 to Centro; #464 to Maracanã.

From Urca: #511 (via Jóquei Clube) and #512 (via Copacabana) to Leblon.

From the Menezes Cortes terminal, adjacent to Praça XV: air-con buses along the coast to Barra de Guaratiba, south of Rio; on the return journey, these buses are marked *Castelo*, the name of the area near Praça XV.

To Novo Rio Rodoviária: #104 from Centro, #127 or #128 from Copacabana, and #456, #171 or #172 from Flamengo.

To the train station: any bus marked *E. Ferro*.

Parque do Flamengo: any bus marked *via Aterro* passes along the length of the Parque do Flamengo without stopping.

Between Centro and the Zona Sul, most buses run along the coast as far as Botafogo; those for Copacabana continue around the bay, past the RioSul shopping centre; and through the Pasmado Tunnel; those for Leblon, via the Jóquei Clube, turn right at Botafogo and travel along Avenida São Clemente.

Taxis

Taxis in Rio come in two varieties: **yellow** ones with a blue stripe, often none too luxurious, which cruise the streets; or **radio cabs**, white and with a red and yellow stripe, ordered by phone. Both have meters, but they don't adjust them to keep up with Brazil's inflation. Instead, the drivers use regularly up-dated price sheets which show the inflation-adjusted equivalent of the meter price: at the end of every journey, the driver will consult the sheet and you should do the same. *Always* check that the cards are printed in red and black columns, and are not photocopies – a common dodge. Also, when you get into a cab, make certain that the meter has been cleared after the last fare. The flag, or *bandeira*, over the meter denotes the tariff. Normally this will read "1", but after 10pm, and on Sundays, holidays and throughout December, you have to pay twenty percent more; then the *bandeira* will read "2".

Generally speaking, Rio's taxi service is cheap and it is not in the cabbies' interest to alienate tourists by ripping them off. However, late at night, drivers often quote a fixed price that can be up to three times the normal fare. Whether you accept this depends on the availability of other cabs and how badly you need to travel. Radio cabs are thirty percent more expensive than the regular taxis, but they are reliable; companies include *Coopertramo* (☎260-2022), *Cootramo* (☎270-1442) and *Transcoopass* (☎270-4888).

Ferries, hydrofoils and trams

From Praça XV de Novembro **ferries** transport passengers across Guanabara Bay to the city of Niterói (see "Rio de Janeiro State" below) and to Paquetá Island, a holiday resort to the north of Guanabara Bay. The ferries are extremely cheap and the view of Rio they afford, especially at sunset, is well worth the effort, even if you don't set foot in Niterói. Crossings are very frequent and cost about ten cents; just turn up and buy a ticket. The *Conerj* company ferries run Monday to Saturday, every fifteen minutes from 5am to 11pm; Sunday and public holidays, every thirty minutes from 7am to 11pm. Also from Praça XV de Novembro, *Transtur* operates **hydrofoils** to the island of Paquetá; departures every thirty minutes from 7am to 10pm.

Rio's last remaining electric **trams**, the *bondes* (pronounced "bonjis"), climb from near Largo Carioca, across the eighteenth-century Aqueduto da Carioca, to the inner suburb of Santa Teresa and on to Dois Irmãos. An open tram, it still serves its original purpose of transporting locals, and hasn't yet become a tourist service. The views of Rio are excellent, but beware of the young chaps who jump onto the tram and attempt to relieve you of your possessions. It's not really a big deal, as there are guards on all the trams, but keep your wits about you. The tram station is adjacent to the Nova Catedral and waiting passengers queue up in eight lines, one for every row of seats on the tram; the fare is just a few cents which you pay on board.

Driving in Rio

If you're hiring a **car** then you must understand what you're letting yourself in for. Rio's road system is characterised by a confusion of one-way streets, tunnels, slip-roads and fly-overs, and **parking** is not easy. **Lane markings**, apart from lending a little colouring to the asphalt, serve no apparent practical purpose (though it seems to be regarded as bad luck to allow your vehicle to remain between the lines demarcating any lane for more than a second or two). **Overtaking** on the inside appears to be mandatory and, after nightfall, obeying **traffic lights** is optional. Rio's motorists are very good at some things – but driving isn't one of them. (See "Listings" for details of car hire in Rio.)

Finding a place to stay

There's no shortage of choice of accommodation in Rio, but it's as well to bear in mind two things. From November to February (inclusive) is **high season**, so if you arrive then without an advance booking, either make one through a tourist office or leave your luggage in the *guarda volumes* (baggage offices) at the *Rodoviária* or at Santos Dumont airport while you look; there's no point lugging heavy bags around Rio's hot thoroughfares, and it makes you vulnerable to theft. Also, be prepared for **prices** to rise from one week to the next, in line with Brazil's hyperinflation, and note that most hotels stick a ten percent service charge on your bill, too, so make allowances for this as well. One other period when prices tend to fluctuate wildly is at Carnaval, when accommodation becomes that much harder to find.

Unless otherwise stated, all the hotels listed below start at around $7–8 for a single room, double that for two people. It is unusual for a hotel not to have air conditioners in each room; and, unless otherwise indicated, hotels serve some form of breakfast included in the price. The highest concentration of budget places is in Glória, Catete and Flamengo, but reasonably priced accommodation can be found just about anywhere. If you have any problems with unscrupulous hotel owners, call *SUNAB* (Mon–Sat 8am–6pm; ☎262-0198), the government's consumer affairs agency.

There are no **campsites** within easy reach of Rio.

The city centre: Centro, Saúde and Lapa

Most of the cheap *pensões* are in the north of the city, or near Dom Pedro II train station, but they're mostly inhabited by full-time residents, usually single men, who are working in Rio. It's hard to find a vacancy, and you will be looking in areas that are not particularly safe. Lapa, in the southern corner of the city centre, is a far better bet. There are countless small hotels in this down-at-heel red-light area, and – surprisingly – most of them are clean and cheap enough.

Around Praça Mauá: *Internacional*, Rua Senador Pompeu 82, and *Rio Grande*, Rua Senador Pompeu 220, are both cheap and friendly. Generally, though, neither Saúde nor Praça Mauá itself are recommended.

Rua São Joaquim da Silva: near the Passeio Público park, and well placed for walking access to Centro and buses to the Zona Sul. Try the *Americano* at no. 69 and the *Ipiranga* at no. 87, both friendly and comfortable; at no. 99 is the *Marajó*, around $7 for a single room and, with comfy beds and efficient showers, probably the best choice in the area.

Avenida Mem de Sá: the *Novo Mundo* at no. 85 (clean, cheap and air-conditioned); and the *Bragança* (☎242-8116) at no. 115 (bigger and better equipped; with bar, telephones and TVs) – both tend to be busy.

Avenida Gomes Freire (the road which intersects Mem de Sá across from the Cathedral): *Marialva* (☎221-1187) at no. 430, a good hotel with singles starting at around $5.

Rua Resende: the *Estadual*, no. 31, is generally good, clean and friendly, though the (optional) pornographic videos may not be to everyone's taste.

Glória

Glória, too, is not without its share of prostitution of an evening, but the *bairro* has a faded grandeur that's worth getting to know, and it's not a dangerous area.

Ladeira da Glória (from opposite the Estação Glória, climb up round to the right of the Igreja de N.S. Outeiro da Glória, through the Lago da Glória): the *Hotel Turístico* (☎225-9388) at no. 30 is highly recommended; friendly, clean and cheap, with bath, breakfast and a place to leave valuables. Around $6 single, it's a favourite budget traveller's haunt and consequently usually busy, so try and book ahead.

Rua Cândido Mendes (on the other side of the Metro station, to the left): the *Alameda* at no. 112, *Cândido Mendes*, no. 117, and *Monte Castelo* at no. 201 are all fine, inexpensive and clean, with the *Alameda* the pick of the bunch. Prices at all three start at about $5 for a single.

Rua Catete: further south, at Rua Catete 36, check out the friendly, basic and very cheap *Casa da Hospedagem*; for more places on Rua Catete, see "Catete and Flamengo", below.

Catete and Flamengo

Catete and Flamengo, centred around the Largo do Machado and once the chic residential *bairros* of the middle classes, are well served by hotels – all a good bit cheaper than the ones at Copacabana. It's a convenient place to stay, too, handily placed between the centre and the beach zone, with buses, taxis and the Metro providing easy access. Apart from the ones on the streets around the square (the first two listed below), the rest of the hotels are all along or off Rua Catete, which runs north from the square.

Rua Paissandú: at no. 23 is the *Hotel Paysandú* (☎225-7270), a recommended establishment, from $7 single and $15 double, with bathroom and TV; there's a decent restaurant on the ground floor, too, and though the front doors close at midnight, there is a night porter on duty. On the other side of the street, the *Venezuela* (☎205-2098) is clean and safe, too, though a bit poky, and costs the same.

Rua Gago Coutinho (to the right of the Igreja de N.S. da Glória, facing Largo do Machado): the *Hotel Serraro*, at no. 22, is fairly comfortable.

Rua Artur Bernardes (second left up from Largo do Machado): the *Rio Lisboa* (☎265-9599) at no. 29, and the *Monterrey* at no. 39 are both cheap (singles start at $3) with a pleasant atmosphere.

Rua Catete: *Rio Claro* at no. 233 starts at $7 single; double rooms are good, but singles lack air conditioning. Further up are the cheap but adequate *Hotel Vitória*, no. 172, and the slightly more expensive *Monte Blanco* at no. 160 (☎225-0121); around $6 a single, very clean and friendly.

Rua Buarque de Macedo (right off Rua Catete): the *Rondônia*, with rooms from a very cheap $2.50.

Rua Correia Dutra: several hotels here, the *Caxambú*, no. 22, and the *Cambuquira*, no. 19, the best.

Rua Ferreira Viana: the *Hotel Ferreira Viana* (☎205-7396), at no. 58, is inexpensive but a little cramped and with a communal shower room. The *Flórida*, nos. 69–81, comes highly recommended, $9 a single, spacious rooms, private showers, nice and clean and with a safety deposit box.

Rua Silveira Martins (where the Catete Metro station is): turn left off Rua Catete for the *Hispânico Brasileira* (☎225-7537), no. 135, which is pleasant and airy ($8 single); and right for the *Hotel Inglês* at no. 20 (down near the Praia do Flamengo), a bit snooty and $15 for a double with TV, and only $9 for one without; obviously good televisions.

Copacabana and Ipanema

Although the bulk of Rio's high-class, expensive hotels are located by the beaches in the Zona Sul, it is possible to find reasonably priced accommodation here, too.

COPACABANA

Avenida N.S. de Copacabana: the *Copa Linda* (2nd floor; ☎255-0938), at no. 116, provides good, basic accommodation, from $11 single. A block away (just down a sidestreet at Travessa Angarense no. 25) the *Hotel Angarense* (☎255-3875) offers safe, rather dull rooms from $8 single. The recently restored *Cánada*, no. 687 (☎257-1864), is good value at $20 a double room.

Rua Aires Saldanha: the *Biarritz* (☎255-6552), no. 54 (one block back from Avenida Atlântica), is located in a quiet backstreet, and is clean and friendly. Prices start at $12 for a single room.

Rua Sá Ferreira: the popular *Martinique*, no. 30 (☎521-4552), is near the western end of Copacabana, towards the fort – around $17 single, $30 double.

Rua Domingos Ferreira: the pleasant *Toledo* (☎257-1990), no. 71, is extremely comfortable; halfway down Copacabana, just one block from the beach and excellent value at $20 single, $25 double.

Rua Décio Vilares (away from the sea, up Rua Anita Garibaldi, past Praça Edmundo Bittencourt): the *Santa Clara*, at no. 316 (☎256-2650), is recommended; it's close to the Velho Tunnel which, if it isn't shut for repairs, provides a shortish walk to Botafogo's restaurants and museums, past the St John the Baptist Cemetery.

Copacabana's luxury hotels: there's nothing at all reasonable about these, which start at around $100 for a single room. If you're holding the folding, though, the *Meridian* (☎275-9922), *Rio Palace* (☎521-3232) and *Rio Othon Palace* (☎255-8812) are all along the Avenida Atlântica – handy for the beach and dripping with facilities. *The* place to stay is the *Copacabana Palace* (☎255-7070), Avenida Atlântica 1702: built in the 1930s, it marked the arrival of Copacabana as the international playground for the rich, and has been host to kings, queens and personalities aplenty – Orson Welles stayed here regularly.

IPANEMA

Rua Visconde de Pirajá: the *San Marco* (☎239-5032), no. 524, is a good deal at around $20 a night for a double room; at no. 254 the *Vermont* (☎247-6100) comes at a similar price. Both are only two blocks from the beach.

Rua Francisco Otaviano: slightly more expensive is the *Arpoador Inn* (☎247-6090), at no. 177.

Rua Maria Quiteria: the *Ipanema Inn* (☎287-6092), no. 29, is tucked in behind the five-star *Caesar Park Hotel* (☎287-3122; Avenida Vieira Souto, 460) so at least you'll have some nice neighbours.

Hostels and rooms to rent

There are a couple of options for those with youth hostel or *ISIC* cards, but remember that the universities are on holiday between December and March and then the places mentioned below will be packed out.

Casa do Estudante, Praça Ana Amélia, towards the southern end of Avenida Presidente Antônio Carlos, near Santa Luzia church: on the eleventh floor there's an inexpensive youth hostel (around $1.50 a night), but you share small dormitories, and there is a midnight curfew.

Women's Youth Hostel, Rua Almirante Gomes Pereira 86, in Urca, near the Praia da Urca, facing Flamengo: women only.

Rented Rooms: if you're stopping in Rio for a while, check out the classified ads in the *Jornal do Brasil* – "vaga" (vacancy) and "quarto" (room) signify space in someone's home; "conjugado", abbreviated to "conj", means a bedsitter.

Apartments: try *Rio Star Imóveis Ltda* in Copacabana (☎275-8393/8147; English and French spoken) or *Rio Flat Service* (☎274-7222 during business hours), which has three apartment blocks in the Copacabana area – from $35 a day for a small apartment, with breakfast and swimming pool.

The City Centre

Much of historical Rio is concentrated in **Centro**, with pockets of interest, too, in the **Saúde** and **Lapa** quarters of the city. And you'll find you can tour the centre fairly easily on foot. It's worth repeating, though, that the real interest of Rio lies elsewhere – at the beaches of the Zona Sul, and the heights of Urca and Corcovado – and it's not the most exciting city in Brazil to explore. Lots of the old historical squares, streets and buildings have disappeared this century under a torrent of redevelopment, and fighting your way through the traffic – the reason many of the streets were widened in the first place – can be a daunting prospect.

Nonetheless, if you have the time, there is still a lot to see, and a quite different side to Rio than that of the beaches and spectacular viewpoints. The cultural influences that shaped the city through its five centuries of existence – the austere Catholicism of the city's European founders, the squalor of colonialism and the grandiose design of the Enlightenment – are all reflected in the surviving churches, streets and squares. And although a lot of what remains is decidedly low-key, there are enough churches and interesting museums to keep anybody happy for a day or two. Above all, a walk around Rio – old and new – gives you an idea of the wealth generated by the rich lands that the Portuguese conquerors appropriated 500 years ago.

The sections following deal with Santa Teresa and the Corcovado, the Zona Norte, the Zona Sul and Tijuca National Park respectively.

Praça XV de Novembro and around

Praça XV de Novembro is the obvious place to start. Once the hub of Rio's social and political life, it takes its name from the day (November 15) in 1899 that Marshall Deodoro de Fonseca proclaimed the Republic of Brazil, of which he was the first president. The square was originally called the Largo do Paço, a name that survives in the imposing **Palácio Imperial** (Tues–Sun 10am–6.30pm) – at various times, the Governor's Palace, the headquarters of the Portuguese government in Brazil until 1791 and, later, of the Department of Post and Telegraph. It was here, in 1808, that the Portuguese monarch, Dom João VI, established his court in Brazil (later shifting to the Palácio da Quinta da Boa Vista, now the National Museum; see "Zona Norte"), and the building continued to be used for Royal receptions and special occasions: on May 13, 1888, Princess Isabel proclaimed from the palace the end of slavery in Brazil. It's been tinkered with over the years, undergoing numerous structural modifications, but has lately been restored to its original state and provides an interesting example of colonial architecture. Right on the square, too, is the seventeenth-century **Faculdade Cândido Mendes** (Mon–Fri 8am–9pm), the first Carmelite convent to be built in Rio. Used between times as a royal residence (after 1808 the Queen Mother, Dona Maria I, lived here), it has also been altered several times, and is still awaiting final renovation to its original condition.

The **Arco de Teles**, on the northern side of the square, was named after the judge and landowner, Francisco Teles de Meneza, who ordered its construction upon the site of the old *pelourinho* (pillory) in around 1755. It's really an arcade, linking the Travessa do Comércio to the Rua Ouvidor (this latter street was previously the *Beco do Peixe* and site of the first free fish market in Rio), and originally the Arco contained three houses. One of these was home to the Menezes family, but all were severely damaged by fire in 1790. More engaging than the building itself, is the social history of the Arco de Teles and its immediate vicinity. In the luxurious apartments above street level lived families belonging to Rio's wealthy classes, while the street below was traditionally a refuge for "beggars and rogues of the worst type; lepers, thieves, murderers, prostitutes and hoodlums" – according to Brasil Gerson in his *History of Rio's Streets*. In the late eighteenth and early nineteenth century, one of the leprous local inhabitants – **Bárbara dos Prazeres** – achieved notoriety as a folk devil: it was a common belief that the blood of a dead dog or cat applied to the body provided a cure for leprosy, and Bárbara is supposed to have earned her reputation around the Arco de Teles by attempting to enhance the efficacy of this cure by stealing new-born babies and sucking their blood.

Before you leave the square, it's worth noting that one of Rio's oldest **markets** is held here on Thursday and Friday (8am–6pm). The stalls are packed with typical foods, handicrafts and ceramics; and there are paintings and prints, too, as well as a brisk trade in stamps and coins. Nearby in the Praça Marechal Ancora, by the *Alba Mar* restaurant, there is an expensive antiques market (Saturday 8am–5pm) – a laid-back affair, selling everything from *Melrose*'s tea tins to eighteenth-century French clocks, nearly all the antiques European in origin.

At the back of Praça XV de Novembro, on the corner where Rua VII de Setembro meets Rua I de Março, stands the old **Cathedral of São Sebastião do Rio de Janeiro**, with the image of Saint Sebastian, Rio's patron saint, high on the front of the church. Building started in 1749 and, to all intents and purposes, continued right into the twentieth century as structural collapse and financial difficulties necessitated several restorations and delays: the present tower, for example, was built as late as 1905 by the Italian architect Rebecchi. Inside, the high altar is detailed in silver and boasts a beautiful work by the painter Antônio Parreires, representing *Nossa Senhora do Carmo* seated amongst the clouds and surrounded by the sainted founders of the Carmelite Order. Below, in the **crypt**, are what are said to be the mortal remains of Pedro Alvares Cabral, Portuguese discoverer of Brazil.

Museu Naval e Oceanográfico

Close to Praça XV de Novembro, down Rua Dom Manuel, is the **Museu Naval e Oceanográfico** (daily noon–4.45pm; free). Housed in what was originally the naval headquarters, the museum's excellent collection (laid out in ten rooms on two floors) shows the chronology of Brazil's naval history – from sixteenth-century nautical charts and scale replicas of European galleons, to paintings depicting scenes from the Brazil-Paraguay War and exhibits of twentieth-century naval hardware. It's all very well presented, the museum watched over by naval ratings in formal, starched white uniforms who hand out felt overshoes to protect the highly polished, parquet floor. Above all, the collections provide an insight into the colonial nature of Brazilian history: the exhibits show that Brazilian naval engagements were determined by the interests of the Portuguese Empire until the nineteenth century, while as a primarily slave-based plantation economy until 1888, Brazil's military hardware came from the foundries of industrialised Europe – like the brass and copper expansion valve made by *Benjamin Hobson and Son*, engineers of Bolton. The most impressive items, though, must be the hand-crafted replicas of sixteenth-century galleons – the *São Felipe* (1690) complete with its 98 cannons – and the first map of the New World, drawn by Pedro Alvares Cabral between 1492 and 1500.

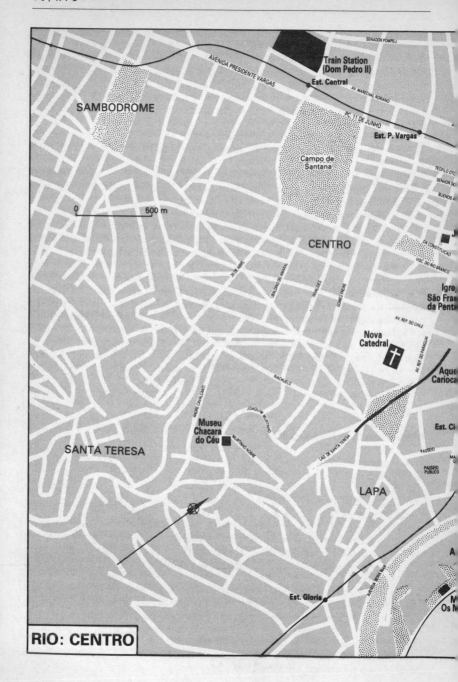

SENADOR POMPEU

AVENIDA PRESIDENTE VARGAS

Train Station
(Dom Pedro II)
Est. Central

AV. MARECHAL RORIANO

PC 11 DE JUNHO

Est. P. Vargas

SAMBODROME

Campo de
Santana

TEOFILO OTC

SENHOR DO

BUENOS A

0   500 m

CENTRO

DA CONSTITUIÇÃO

VISC. DO RIO BRANCO

Igre
São Fra
da Penti

AV. REP. DO CHILE

Nova
Catedral ✝

AV. REP DO PARAGUAI

20 DE ABRIL

DIRUNINO DO AMARAL

INVALIDES

GOMES FREIRE

Aque
Carioca

BIACHUELO

ANDRE CAVALCANTI

JOAQUIM MURTINHO

Est. Ci

Museu
Chacara
do Céu

MURTINHO NOBRE

LAD. DE SANTA TERESA

PASSEIO

SANTA TERESA

PASSEIO
PUBLICO

MA
O

LAPA

A

AVENIDA BEIR MAR

Est. Gloria

M
Os M

RIO: CENTRO

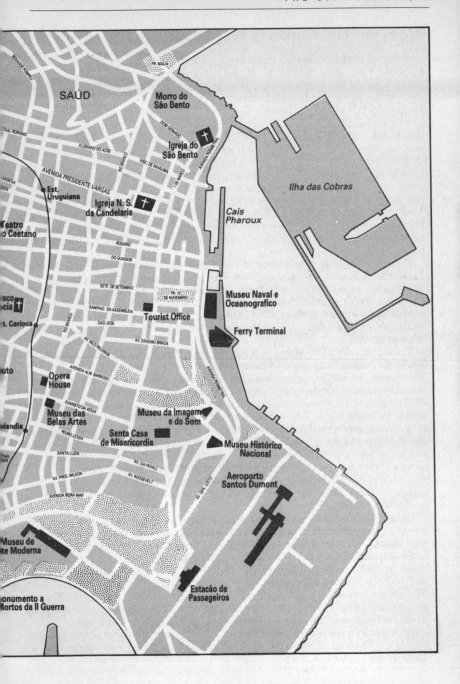

SAÚD

Morro do
São Bento

Igreja do
São Bento

Est.
Uruguiana

Igreja N. S.
da Candelaria

Teatro
o Caetano

sco
cia

t. Carioca

Tourist Office

Opera
House

uto

Museu das
Belas Artes

elandia

Museu da Imagem
e do Som

Santa Casa
de Misericordia

Museu Histórico
Nacional

Museu de
te Moderna

Aeroporto
Santos Dumont

onumento a
lortos da II Guerra

Estacão de
Passageiros

Ilha das Cobras

Cais
Pharoux

Museu Naval e
Oceanografico

Ferry Terminal

Along Rua I de Março: to Praça Pio X

Heading up **Rua I de Março** from the Praça you'll pass the museum and church of **Santa Cruz dos Militares** (Mon–Fri 8am–6pm, Sat 8am–2pm), its name giving a hint of its curious history. In 1628, a number of army officers organised the construction of the first church here, on the site of an early fort. It was used for the funerals of serving officers until, in 1703, the Catholic Church attempted to take over control of the building. The proposal met stiff resistance, and it was only in 1716 that the Fathers of the Church of São Sebastião, which had become severely dilapidated, succeeded in installing themselves in Santa Cruz. Sadly, they were no more successful in the maintenance of this church either, and by 1760 it had been reduced to a state of ruin – only reversed when army officers again took control of the reconstruction work in 1780, completing the building that survives today. It's built from granite and marble and inside, the nave, with its stuccoed ceiling, has been skilfully decorated with plaster relief images from Portugal's imperial past. The two owners long since reconciled, there's a **museum**, with a dual collection of military and religious relics, on the ground floor.

Further along Rua I de Março is the eighteenth-century **Igreja da Ordem Terceira do Monte do Carmo** (Mon–Fri 7am–4pm, Sat 7–11am), whose seven altars each bear an image symbolising a moment from the Passion of Christ, from Calvary to the Crucifixion, sculpted by Pedro Luiz da Cunha. The high altar itself is beautifully worked in silver. The church and adjacent convent are linked by a small public chapel, dedicated to Our Lady of the Cape of Good Hope, and decorated in *azulejos*.

At the end of Rua I de Março you emerge onto **Praça Pio X**, dominated by the **Igreja de Nossa Senhora da Candelária** (Mon–Fri 7am–noon & 2–4.30pm, Sat 7am–noon), an interesting combination of Baroque and Renaissance features. It owes this variety of style to the financial difficulties which delayed the completion of the building for more than a century after its foundation in 1775. Inside, the altars, walls and supporting columns are built from variously coloured marble – grey, white, green, yellow, red and black – admirably combined and sculpted. Eight pictures in the dome, measuring roughly twice the size of a human figure, represent the three theological virtues (Faith, Hope and Charity), the cardinal virtues (Prudence, Justice, Strength and Temperance) and the Virgin Mary – all the work of João Zeferino da Costa. There's more grand decoration in the two pulpits, luxuriously worked in bronze and supported by large, white angels sculpted in marble.

Until 1943 the church was hemmed in by other buildings, but it was appointed its own space when the **Avenida Presidente Vargas** was opened, opening up new vistas. The avenue runs west for almost three kilometres and has fourteen lanes of traffic, and when work started on it in 1941 there was considerable opposition from the owners of houses and businesses which were demolished in its path – not to mention clerical dissent at the destruction of a number of churches. The avenue was inaugurated with a military parade in 1944, watched by Vargas himself in the year before he was deposed by a quiet coup. Until the construction of the Sambódromo, the main Carnaval procession took place along here.

Back towards the waterfront, turn into Rua Visconde de Itaborai and you will pass the **Alfândega Antiga**, the old Customs House, which was constructed in 1820 by the French architect Grandjean de Montigny, in Neoclassical style.

Unfortunately it's closed for restoration, but it's been home to a bizarre array of organisations in its time, from the English merchants who arrived after the opening of the port to free trade in 1808, through the Mauá Gas Company and the Brazilian Society for the Protection of Animals, to the Socialist organisers of Rio's 1918 general strike.

From São Bento to the Largo da Carioca: Saúde

Heading north, on the continuation of Rua I de Março, the Ladeira de São Bento leads to the **Igreja e Mosqueiro de São Bento** (daily 8am–5pm), in the *bairro* of **Saúde** overlooking the Ilha das Cobras. The monastery was founded by Benedictine monks who arrived in Rio in 1589 by way of Bahia. They had been offered a piece of ground in the corner of Praça XV de Novembro, by Rua VII de Septembro, which they declined because of the noise emanating from the adjacent fish market, and started building instead on the present site in 1633, finishing nine years later. The facade displays a pleasing architectural simplicity, its twin towers culminating in pyramid-shaped spires, while the interior is richly adorned. The altars and walls are covered by images of saints, and there are statues representing various popes and bishops, work executed by the deft hand of Mestre Valentim. The panels and paintings particularly, late-seventeenth-century work, represent valuable examples of colonial art, while six lateral altars, illuminated by lamps fashioned from silver, add texture to the interior's atmosphere. There is not much else to grab your attention in the area. The monastery is next to **Praça Mauá** and the docklands, a seedy and run-down part of the city that you'd do best to avoid at night.

Largo Santa Rita

Instead, head along Rua Dom Gerardo, which will lead you to the north end of Avenida Rio Branco, on the far (west) side of which (off Visconde de Inhaúma) is **Largo Santa Rita** and its church, the **Igreja da Santa Rita** (Mon–Sat 8am–noon & 2–5pm). Built on land previously used as a slaves' burial ground, the building dates from 1721, its bell tower tucked to one side giving it a lopsided look. It's not one of Rio's more attractive churches, but the interior stonework is a fine example of Rococo style, and is magnificently decorated with a series of panels, three on the high altar and eight on the ceiling, painted by Ananias Correia do Amaral and depicting scenes from the life of Santa Rita.

Rua Uruguaiana: Sahara and Largo de São Francisco de Paula

To return south, to the Largo da Carioca in Centro, cross Avenida Presidente Vargas and continue down **Rua Uruguaiana**. In the streets to your left (between Uruguiana and I de Março) lies the most interesting concentration of shops in Rio, in the area known as **Sahara**. Traditionally the cheapest place to shop, it was originally peopled by Jewish and Arab merchants, who moved into the area after a ban prohibiting their residence within the city limits was lifted in the eighteenth century. In the maze of narrow streets you'll find everything from basic items of beachware and handicrafts to expensive jewellery. The streets are lined with stalls selling trinkets and are thronged with street traders and folk musicians, so it's always a lively place to visit: particularly good buys here include sports equipment, musical instruments and records and tapes.

Halfway down Rua Uruguaiana is **Largo de São Francisco de Paula**, whose church, the **Igreja de São Francisco de Paula** (Mon–Sat 9am–2pm), has hosted some significant moments in Brazil's history. Behind the monumental, carved wooden entrance door the Te Deum was sung in 1816 to celebrate Brazil's promotion from colony to kingdom; in 1831, the Mass celebrating the "Swearing-in" of the Brazilian Constitution was performed here. More tangibly, the chapel of *Nossa Senhora da Vitória*, on the right as you enter, was dedicated by Pope Pius X to the victory of the Christian forces over the Turkish in the naval battle of Lepanto in 1571. The meticulous decoration is attributed to Mestre Valentim, who spent thirty years working on the chapel; while the paintings on the walls were done by a slave who called himself Manoel da Cunha. With the consent of his owner, Manoel travelled to Europe as the assistant of the artist João de Souza, and on his return bought his own freedom with money earned from the sale of his artwork.

To Largo da Carioca

From Largo de São Francisco de Paula, if you follow Rua Ramalho Ortigão for the short distance to **Rua Carioca**, you can stop for a well-earned **beer** in Rio's oldest *cervejaria*, the *Bar Luiz* at no. 39. It's been here since 1887, changing its original name – the *Bar Adolfo* – following World War II, for obvious reasons. The bar was once a favourite watering hole for Rio's Bohemian and intellectual groups and though it's a little faded these days, it's still a bustling, enjoyable place to be – the beer's cold and you can get *wurst* if you want it.

The **Largo da Carioca** itself has undergone considerable transformation since the turn of the century, many of its buildings demolished to allow widening of the square and the improving of nearby streets. Today street traders selling leather goods dominate the centre of the square, while a couple of things of interest remain, most notably the **Igreja e Convento de Santo Antônio** (Mon–Sat 7am–6pm), standing above the Largo. It's known as Saint Anthony of the Rich (to differentiate it from Saint Anthony of the Poor, which is located elsewhere in the city). A tranquil, cloistered refuge, built between 1608 and 1620, it's the oldest church in Rio and was founded by Franciscan monks who had arrived in Brazil in 1592. A popular saint in Brazil, Saint Anthony's help was sought during the French invasion of 1710: he was made a captain in the Brazilian army and in a startling lack of progress through the ranks it was 1814 before he was promoted to Lieutenant-Colonel, retiring from service in 1914. More improbably still, the tomb of **Wild Jock of Skelater** lies in the crypt. A Scottish mercenary who entered the service of the Portuguese Crown during the Napoleonic Wars, he was later appointed commander-in-chief of the Portuguese army in Brazil.

This aside, the interior of the church boasts a beautiful sacristy, constructed from Portuguese marble and decorated in *azulejos* depicting the miracles performed by Saint Anthony. Notice, too, the rich wooden ornamentation throughout, carved from jacaranda, including the great chest in the sacristy. The image of Christ, adorned with a crown of thorns, came from Portugal in 1678 – a remarkable piece of work of great skill and spiritual perception.

Praça Tiradentes and Campo de Santana

Leave Largo da Carioca by turning left along Rua Carioca, and you're soon in **Praça Tiradentes**, named after the leader of the so-called Minas Conspiracy of

1789, a plot hatched in the state of Minas Gerais to overthrow the Portuguese regime (for more see the *Minas Gerais and Espirito Santo* chapter). This nationalist struggle, partly inspired by the American War of Independence, came to nothing and Tiradentes was captured and executed as an example to other anti-Imperialists. His resurrection as a national martyr came only with Brazilian independence in the nineteenth century.

In the square stands the **Teatro João Caetano**, after João Caetano dos Santos, who based his drama company in the theatre from 1840. He also notches up a bust which stands in the square, a reward for producing shows starring such theatrical luminaries as Sarah Bernhardt. The original theatre on this site, the *Teatro Real*, erected in 1813, had a much more political history: it was here in 1821 that Dom João VI swore obedience to the Constitution promulgated in Lisbon after the Porto Revolution. Three years later, at the end of the ceremony proclaiming Dom Pedro I Emperor of Brazil, a fire razed the old theatre to the ground.

Campo de Santana and around

Three blocks west of Praça Tiradentes, along Rua Visconde do Rio Branco, you'll enter the **Praça da República** in the **Campo de Santana**. Until the beginning of the seventeenth century this area was outside the city limits, which extended only as far as Rua Uruguaiana. Its sandy soils made it unsuitable for cultivation and the only building here was the Chapel of St Domingo, sited in the area now covered by the asphalt of Avenida President Vargas, and used by the Fraternity of Saint Anne to celebrate the festivals of their patron saint – hence the name, Campo de Santana (field of Saint Anne).

By the end of the eighteenth century the city had spread to surround the Campo de Santana, and in 1811 a barracks was built to house the Second Regiment of the Line, who used the square as a parade ground. From here, Dom Pedro I proclaimed Brazil's independence from the Portuguese Crown in 1822, and after 1889 the lower half of the square became known as Praça da República. The first president of the new republic, Deodoro de Fonseca, lived at no. 197 Praça da República. At the start of this century, the square was landscaped, and today it's a pleasant place for a walk, with lots of trees and small lakes ruled by swans. In the centre lies the **João Furtado Park**, worth visiting in the evening, when small, furry shapes can be seen scuttling about in the gloom – gophers, happily, not rats.

Directly across Avenida Presidente Vargas is the Praça Duque de Caxias and the **National Pantheon**, on top of which stands the equestrian statue of the Duque de Caxias, military patron and general in the Paraguayan War – his remains lie below in the Pantheon. Nearby, the **Dom Pedro II train station** is an unmistakable landmark, its tower rising 110 metres into the sky and supporting clock faces measuring seven and a half by five and a half metres, all linked to a central winding mechanism. In front of the station, at Avenida Marechal Floriano 196 (running parallel to Avenida Presidente Vargas), the **Palácio do Itamarati** is one of Rio's best examples of Neoclassical architecture. Completed in 1853, as the *pied-à-terre* of the great landowner Baron of Itamarati, it was bought by the government and was home to a number of the Republic's presidents before being handed over as a museum. Sadly, it's closed for restoration, although it's worth checking to see if the work's finished yet.

From the Nova Catedral to Cinelandia and Praça Floriano

Back behind the Largo da Carioca, the unmistakable shape of the **Nova Catedral** (Mon–Sat 7am–4pm, Sun 9am–noon) rises up like some futuristic teepee. It's an impressive piece of modern architecture and a considerable engineering feat, whatever you think of the style: the Morro de Santo Antônio was levelled to make way for the cathedral's construction, and the thousands of tons of resulting soil were used for the land reclamation project that gave rise to the Parque de Flamengo. Similar in style to the blunt-topped Mayan pyramids found in the Yucatán region of Mexico, the cathedral is 83 metres high and, with a diameter of 104 metres, has a capacity of 25,000 people. Inside it feels vast, a remarkable sense of space enhanced by the absence of supporting columns. Four huge stained-glass windows dominate, each measuring twenty by sixty metres and corresponding to a symbolic colour scheme – ecclesiastical green, saintly red, Catholic blue and apostolic yellow. From outside, you'll be able to see the **Aqueduto da Carioca**, which carries trams up to Santa Teresa, the *bairro* on the hill opposite (see "Santa Teresa", below): the tram terminal is between the cathedral and the Largo da Carioca.

Retrace your steps along Avenida República de Chile, turn right down **Avenida Rio Branco**, and a couple of blocks later you're in Praça Marechal Floriano (see below) and the area known as **Cinelândia**, named after long-gone movie houses built in the 1930s. Today it's a bustling location whose bars fill up with thirsty office workers at the end of the day. Rio Branco, originally named Avenida Central, must once have been Latin America's most impressive urban thoroughfare. Old photos show it bordered by Neoclassical-style buildings of no more than three storeys high, its pavements lined with trees, and with a promenade that ran right down the centre. Nowadays, however, the once graceful avenue has been swamped by ugly office blocks and traffic pollution.

Praça Floriana

The **Praça Floriana** is the one section of Avenida Rio Branco that still impresses. In the centre of the square is a bust of **Getúlio Vargas**, still anonymously decorated with flowers on the anniversary of the ex-dictator's birthday, March 19. At the north end of the square the **Teatro Municipal**, opened in 1909 and a dramatic example of Neoclassical architecture, was modelled on the Paris Opera – all granite, marble and bronze, with a foyer decorated in the white and gold characteristic of Louis XV style. There has been talk of initiating English-language tours around the building, which is worth checking out; the theatre has its own restaurant and bar, the *Assyrian Room* (open till 7pm), which is richly adorned with mosaics.

On the opposite side of the road, the **Museu das Belas Artes** (Tues & Thurs 10am–6.30pm, Wed & Fri noon–6.30pm, Sat & Sun 3–8pm; free) is a grandiose construction, demanding a visit for its extensive and well presented collection. The European dimension includes Boudin, Tournay and Franz Post amongst many others, but it's the **Brazilian** collection which is really interesting. Organised in chronological order, each room shows the various stages in the development of Brazilian painting as a result of the influences imported from Europe – the years of diversification (1919–28); the movement into modernism and eclecticism (1921–49); and the consolidation of modern forms between 1928 and 1967, especially in the works of Cândido Portinari, Djanira and Francisco Rebolo.

The last building of note on the Praça Floriano is the **Biblioteca Nacional** (Mon–Fri 9am–8pm, Sat noon–6pm), whose stairway was decorated by some of the most important artistic names of the nineteenth century, including Modesto Brocas, Eliseu Visconti, Rodolfo Amoedo and Henrique Bernadelli. If you speak Portuguese and want to use the library, the staff are very obliging.

South to the Passeio Público: Lapa

Continuing south down Avenida Rio Branco from Cinelândia, you pass on the right-hand side the Praça Mahatma Ghandi which borders the **Passeio Público** park (daily 7.30am–9pm), well into Lapa *bairro*. A little past its best, and neglected by the authorities these days, the park is, nevertheless, a green oasis away from the hustle and bustle of the city. Opened in 1783, it was designed in part by Mestre Valentim, its trees providing shade for busts commemorating famous figures from the city's history; including Mestre Valentim de Fonseca e Silva himself. One of the most recent busts to be placed in the park is that of Chiquinha Gonzaga, who wrote the first recorded samba for Carnaval – "Pelo Telefone". Other diversions include Valentim's fountain, the *Chafariz dos Jacarés*, fashioned as a group of alligators cast in bronze. Sunday morning is a good time to wander through the Passeio Público, when a stroll can be combined with a visit to the stamp and coin **market** held inside the park.

On the Rua do Passeio, which runs under the *Teatro Mesbla*, the **Museu Instrumental Delgado de Carvalho** (no. 98; Mon–Fri 8am–5pm; free) is in the entrance to the Federal University's School of Music. The collection, initially organised by the composer Delgado de Carvalho in 1901, contains musical instruments from various parts of the world, combined with a more interesting selection of indigenous exhibits.

The rest of **Lapa** has much the same faded charm as the park, attractive enough to want to explore – though it would be wise not to wander the streets unaccompanied at night. It's an old *bairro*: Brasil Gerson, writing in his *History of Rio's Streets*, notes that it was traditionally known as an "area of 'cabarets' and bawdy houses, the haunt of scoundrels, of gamblers, swashbucklers and inverteds and the 'trottoir' of poor, fallen women" – evidently a place to rush to, or avoid, depending upon your taste in entertainment. Until the mid-seventeenth century, Lapa was a beach, known as the "Spanish Sands", but development and land reclamation have assisted its slide into shabby grandeur.

From Lapa you can walk or take the Metro down to Praça Paris, below which runs the Avenida Beira Mar, where the **Monument to the Dead** of World War II is a clearly visible landmark. Next to the monument, at the north end of the Parque do Flamengo (see "Zona Sul" below) is the ugly **Museu de Arte Moderna** (☎210-2188), designed in 1954 by Burle Marx – as was the whole of the Parque do Flamengo – and presently closed for renovation after a fire in 1978 that devastated its collection. However, its re-opening is imminent so a phone call to check might be worthwhile.

East to the Museu Histórico Nacional

Heading east from the Passeio Público, along Rua Santa Luzia, you'll pass the **Igreja de Santa Luzia** in the Praça da Academia, an attractive eighteenth-century church whose predecessor stood on the seashore – hard to believe today, when it's overwhelmed by the surrounding office blocks. On December 13 every year, devotees enter the "room of miracles" at the back of the church and bathe their eyes in water from the white marble font – reputedly a miraculous cure for eye defects.

When you reach the busy Avenida Presidente Antônio Carlos, turn left and pass the imposing **Fazenda Federal**, the Federal Treasury. Directly across the road, the **Santa Casa de Misericórdia**, a large colonial structure dating from 1582, was built by the Sisterhood of Misericordia, a nursing order dedicated to the care of the sick, and the provision of asylum to orphans and invalids. It was here in 1849 that, for the first time in Rio, a case of yellow fever was diagnosed, and from 1856 to 1916 the building was used as the University's Faculty of Medicine.

The Santa Casa is not open to the public, but you can visit the attached church, the **Igreja de Nossa Senhora de Bom Successo** (Mon–Sat 8–10.30am & 2–3.30pm), which contains finely detailed altars, a collection of Bohemian crystal and an eighteenth-century organ.

Close by, in Praça Rui Barbosa, is the **Museu do Imagem e Som** (Mon–Fri 1–6pm; 50¢), whose purpose is to explain Rio's social history using records, tape recordings, books and film. There's also a fascinating photographic collection (numbering some 10,000 prints, though sadly only a fraction are displayed), documenting the city's life from the turn of the century until the 1940s.

Museu Histórico Nacional

From Praça Rui Barbosa, it's only a short distance to the **Museu Histórico Nacional** (Tues–Fri 10am–5.30pm, Sat & Sun 2.30–5.30pm; free), uncomfortably located in the shadow of the Presidente Kubitschek flyover that runs into the Parque do Flamengo. Built in 1762 as an arsenal, it later served as a military prison where escaped slaves were detained. In 1922 the building was converted into an exhibition centre for the centenary celebrations of Brazil's independence from Portugal; it has remained a museum ever since.

The large **collection** contains some pieces of great value – from furniture to nineteenth-century firearms and locomotives – but it's not very well organised at present and awaits a much-needed restructuring. Nevertheless, the displays on the second floor, a documentation of Brazilian history since 1500, make this museum a must. Artefacts, charts and written explanations trace the country's development from the moment of discovery to the proclamation of the Republic in 1889 – a fascinating insight into the nature of Imperial conquest and subsequent colonial society. Clearly demonstrated, for example, is the social structure of sixteenth-century Brazilian society, including the system of *sesmarias*, or royal land grants of enormous dimensions, which provided the basis for the highly unequal system of land tenure that endures today. Through the use of scale models and imaginatively arranged displays, the agrarian and cyclical nature of Brazil's economic history is explained, too, organised around a slave-labour plantation system which produced – at different times – sugar cane, cattle and cotton, rubber and coffee. The story continues into the eighteenth and nineteenth centuries, following the impact of the English industrial revolution, and the spread of new ideas following the French Revolution – and the extension of this story into the twentieth century is well underway and should be completed by the time this book is out.

Santa Teresa, Cosme Velho and the Corcovado

Before you hit the beaches of the Zona Sul, two of the most pleasant city excursions are to *bairros* just west of Centro. **Santa Teresa** offers an excellent respite from the steamy hubbub of Rio's main thoroughfares, while visiting Rio without making the tourist pilgrimage up the **Corcovado** is unthinkable.

Santa Teresa

Santa Teresa, a leafy *bairro* composed of labyrinthine, cobbled streets and steps (*ladeiras*), and with stupendous vistas of the city and bay below, makes a refreshing contrast to the city centre. Although it clings to the side of a hill, Santa Teresa is no *favela*: it's a slightly dishevelled residential area dominated by the colonial mansions and walled gardens of a prosperous community that still enjoys something of a Bohemian reputation. The attractions are enhanced by an absence of the kind of development that is turning the rest of Rio into a cracked, concrete nightmare. There is not a great deal of traffic on the roads up here, which are dominated instead by ageing trams hauling their human load up and down the hill.

You take the **tram** from Centro, from the terminal adjacent to the Nova Catedral and Largo do Carioca. Two lines run every fifteen minutes from 5am to midnight: the one for Dois Irmãos permits you to see more of Santa Teresa.

The tram takes you across the seventeenth-century **Aqueduto do Carioca**, over Lapa, and past the **Carmelite Convent of Santa Teresa**, which marks the spot where a French force was defeated by the city's inhabitants in 1710. As you climb, the panoramic view of Guanabara Bay drifts in and out of view between the trees which line the streets. On your right, you'll pass the *Bar Arnaudo*, worth considering for **lunch**: once the tram reaches the terminus at the top, you can stay on (and pay again) to descend for something to eat. From the bar, it's a pleasant, well-signposted walk downhill to the **Museu Chácara do Céu** (Tues–Sat 2–5pm, Sun 1–5pm; $1) at Rua Murtinho Nobre 93, in a pleasing stone building set in its own grounds – one of Rio's better museums. It holds a good eclectic collection, favourite amongst which are counted Picasso's *Le Danse* and a grouping of 21 crayon sketches by Cândido Portinari, all scenes from Cervantes' *Don Quixote*. In the upper hall, two screens depict the life of Krishna and there are twin seventh-century iron-sculptured horses from the Imperial Palace in Beijing; on the second floor there's artwork from Brazilian painters Djanira and Heitor dos Prazeres.

The Corcovado

The most famous of all images of Rio de Janeiro is that of the vast statue of Christ the Redeemer gazing across the bay from the **Corcovado** hill, arms outstretched in welcome, or as if preparing for a dive into the waters below. The **statue** (daily 8am–7pm), thirty metres high and weighing over one thousand metric tons, was first planned to be completed in 1922 as part of Brazil's independence centenary celebrations. In fact it wasn't finished until 1931 – the French sculptor Paul Landowski responsible for the head and hands, and the rest erected by the engineers Heitor Silva Costa and Pedro Viana.

Fear no anticlimax: climbing the statue is a stunning experience by day, and nothing short of miraculous at night. In daylight the whole of Rio and Guanabara Bay is laid out before you; after dark the floodlit statue can be seen from everywhere in the Zona Sul, seemingly suspended in the darkness that surrounds it, and often shrouded in eerie cloud. Up on the platform the effect of the clouds, driven by warm air currents, and the thousands of tiny winged insects clustering round the spotlights, help give the impression that the statue is careering through space out into the blackness that lies beyond the arc of the lights – dramatic, and not a little hypnotic.

Using the **view** from the statue of Christ the Redeemer for **orientation** purposes is a smart move if you've just arrived in Rio. On a clear day, you can see as far as the outlying districts of the Zona Norte, while on the south side of the viewing platform you're directly over the Lagoa Rodrigo de Freitas, with Ipanema on the left, Leblon on the right; on the near side of the lake Avenida São Clemente is clearly visible, curving its way through Botafogo, towards the Jardim Botânico and the racecourse; and on your left, the small *bairro* of Lagoa can be seen tucked in beneath the Morro dos Cabritos, on the other side of which is Copacabana.

It is, of course, a thoroughly exploited tourist experience. There are the usual facilities for eating, drinking and buying souvenirs. On the walk up to the statue, someone will probably take your photograph clandestinely and, when you descend, a saucer, complete with your photograph superimposed on it, will be thrust before your face: if you don't want the saucer, no-one is going to twist your arm.

Back down at the bottom, if you have the time and inclination, a five-minute walk from the train station will take you to **Largo do Boticário**, named after the nineteenth-century apothecary to the royal family, Joaquim Luiz da Silva Santo, who lived here. A picturesque little corner of Rio, the houses here (some with fronts decorated with *azulejos*) are built in the colonial style, while roundabout are pebbled streets and a fountain in a small square.

Getting to Corcovado

All major hotels organise **excursions** to the Corcovado. Alternatively, if you want to get there yourself, the easiest way is to take a **taxi** and from anywhere in the Zona Sul the cost won't be prohibitive. **Buses** run to the *bairro* of **Cosme Velho** – take the #422 or #497 from Largo do Machado, the #583 from Leblon or the #584 from Copacabana – and stop at the **Estação Cosme Velho**, at Rua Cosme Velho 513. From there you take a cog-train, a thirty-minute ride to the top, where only 220 steps remain between you and the viewing platform. You can also **drive** up to a car park near the top if you wish, but if you want to **walk** go in a group, as reports of assaults and robberies are becoming ever more frequent.

Zona Norte

The parts of the **Zona Norte** you'll have seen on the way in from the transport terminals aren't very enticing, and they're a fair reflection of the general tenor of northern Rio. But there are a couple of places well worth making the effort to come back out of the centre for – especially the National Museum in the Quinta da Boa Vista, which you reach by Metro (get off at Estação São Cristovão) or by bus #472, #474 or #475 from Copacabana or Flamengo, or #262 from Praça Mauá.

The Quinta da Boa Vista

The area covered by the **Quinta da Boa Vista** park (daily 7am–7pm) was once incorporated in a *sesmaria* held by the Society of Jesus in the sixteenth and seventeenth centuries. The Jesuits used the area as a sugar plantation, though it later became the *chácara* (country seat) of the royal family when the Portuguese merchant Elias Antônio Lopes presented the Palácio de São Cristovão (today the National Museum; see below) and surrounding lands to Dom João VI in 1808. The park, with its wide open expanses of greenery, tree-lined avenues, lakes, sports areas and games tables, is an excellent place for a stroll, best during the week as weekends can get very crowded. You may as well make a day of it, and see all the sights once you're here.

The Museu Nacional

In the centre of the park, on a small hill, stands the imposing Neoclassical structure of the **Museu Nacional** (daily 10am–4.45pm), the oldest scientific institution in Brazil and certainly one of the most important, containing extensive archaeological, zoological and botanic collections, an excellent ethnological section, and a good display of artefacts dating from classical antiquity; altogether, an estimated one million pieces exhibited in twenty-two rooms.

The **archaeological** section deals with the human history of Latin America, displaying Peruvian ceramics, the craftsmanship of the ancient Aztec, Mayan and Toltec civilisations of Mexico, and mummies excavated in the Chiu-Chiu region of Chile. In the Brazilian room, exhibits of Tupi-Guarani and Marajó ceramics lead on to the indigenous **ethnographical** section, uniting pieces collected from the numerous tribes that once populated Brazil. The genocidal policies of Brazil's European settlers, together with the ravages of disease, reduced the indigenous population from an estimated six million in 1500 to the present-day total of less than two hundred thousand. And while the destruction of Indian culture was once the result of the plundering greed of private adventurers, the Brazilian state must now shoulder the blame for the dispersal of the remnants of tribal society. Policies facilitating land speculation in the Amazon have led to the theft of the very source of the Indians' physical and spiritual sustenance – the land itself – and though Brazil was a signatory to the Geneva Convention of Human Rights, its politicians have apparently failed to read the text of the charter.

The ethnology section also has a room dedicated to Brazilian folklore, centred around an exhibition of the ancient Afro- and Indo-Brazilian **cults** that still play an important role in modern Brazilian society – *macumba*, *candomblé* and *umbanda*.

On a different tack, the mineral collection's star exhibit is the **Bendigo Meteorite**, which fell to earth in 1888 (the year slavery was abolished for sign-seekers) in the state of Bahia. Its original weight of 5360kg makes it the heaviest metallic mass known to have fallen through the Earth's atmosphere. And beyond the rich native finds you'll also come across Etruscan pottery, Graeco-Roman ceramics, Egyptian sarcophagi and prehistoric remains – all in all, a good half-day's worth.

Museu da Fauna, Jardim Zoólogico and the Feira do Nordeste

Also in the Quinta da Boa Vista is the **Museu da Fauna** (Tues–Sun noon–4.30pm), which has organised a collection of Amazonian birds; worth a look on the way to the **Jardim Zoólogico** (Tues–Sun 8am–6pm), close by. What was once a run-down and dirty zoo is reported to have been transformed recently – the animals look happier and the grounds are now kept scrupulously clean by zealous functionaries – but it's still basically an old-fashioned place where animals are kept in small cages to be stared at.

The **Feira do Nordeste**, held every Sunday (6am–1pm) in the Campo de São Cristovão, close to the Quinta da Boa Vista, is probably the best of Rio's regular **outdoor markets**. A replica of the great Northeastern markets, with stalls run by people in traditional costume, there are typical handicrafts, food, caged birds, tropical fish – while music from the parched Northeastern backlands fills the air. Best buys are beautifully worked hammocks, leather bags and hats, folk medi-cines and spices. Go as early as you can, on any bus marked *São Cristovão* – #469 from Leblon, #461 from Ipanema, #462 or #463 from Copacabana.

Maracanã Stadium

To the west of Quinta da Boa Vista, a short walk across the railway line, over the Viaduto São Cristovão, stands the **Maracanã Stadium**, more formally known as the *Mario Filho* stadium. Built in 1950 for the World Cup, it's the biggest stadium of its kind in the world, holding nearly 200,000 people – in the final match of the 1950 tournament, 199,854 spectators turned up here to watch Brazil lose to Uruguay. Well over 100,000 fans still come to attend a local derby, like the Flamengo v Fluminense fixture, and during November and December games are played here three times a week, as many of Rio's teams have followings that exceed the capacity of their own stadiums; kick-off is at 5pm.

Attending a **game** is one of the most extraordinary experiences Rio has to offer, and even if you don't like football, it's worth going for the theatrical specta-cle. The stadium looks like a futuristic colosseum, its upper stand (the *arquiban-cadas*) rising almost vertically from the playing surface. Great silken banners wave across the stand, shrouded by the smoke from fireworks, while support for each team is proclaimed by the insistent rhythm of massed samba drums which drive the game along. Carioca supporters are animated to say the least, often near hysterical, but their love of the game is infectious.

Depending on your interest, the Maracanã is open, too, for **guided tours** (Mon–Fri 9am–5pm). You'll be shown through an interesting **sports museum**, see the view from the Presidential box, reached by lift, get to wander through the changing rooms and – an extra treat if you want to display your own silky skills – have a chance to tread on the hallowed turf itself.

Getting there . . . and seeing a game

The Maracanã is an easy and inexpensive destination to reach by **taxi**, but if you come by **Metro**, get off at the Maracanã station and walk southeast, along Avenida Osvaldo Aranha. By **bus**, it's the #464 from Leblon (Ataúlfo Paiva) via Ipanema (on Visc. de Pirajá), Copacabana (Avenida N.S. de Copacabana) and Flamengo (Praia do Flamengo).

The **entrance** is on Rua Prof Eurico Rabelo, Gate 18 (☎264-9962). Arrive in plenty of time (at least a couple of hours before kick-off for big games) and buy your entrance card at any of the **ticket offices** set in the perimeter wall – a ticket for the *gerais* (lower terracing) costs about 75¢, the *arquibancadas* (all-seated upper terracing) about $2.50. Then go round to the entrance and pass your card through a machine at the turnstile. It gets frantic around the ticket offices before big games and if you're not there early enough you may get stranded outside, as the kiosk attendants leave their positions as soon as the starting whistle blows so as not to miss an early goal.

After the game, it's a bit tedious getting back into town as transport is packed. Watch your belongings in the thick crowds.

Zona Sul: the beaches and the sights

From Rio's Bay of Guanabara to the Bay of Sepetiba, to the west, there are approximately ninety kilometres of sandy **beaches**, including one of the world's most famous – Copacabana. Uniquely, Rio's identity is closely linked to its beaches, which shape the social life of all the city's inhabitants, who use them as a source of recreation and inspiration. For many, the beach provides a source of livelihood and a sizeable service industry has developed, providing for the needs of those who regard the beach as a social environment – as significant, say, as the pub is in England.

Rio de Janeiro's sophisticated **beach culture** is entirely a product of the twentieth century. The 1930s saw Rio's international reputation emerge, as Hollywood started to incorporate images of the city in its productions, and film stars started to grace the Copacabana. Rio was one of the first destinations for the newly established jet-set: "flying down to Rio" became an enduring cliché, celebrated in music, film and literature for the last fifty years.

The most renowned of the beaches, **Copacabana**, was originally an isolated area, cut off from the city by mountains, until 1892 when the *Túnel Velho* link with Botafogo was inaugurated. The open sea and strong waves soon attracted beachgoers, though Copacabana remained a quiet, sparsely populated *bairro* until the splendid Neoclassically styled *Palace Hotel* opened its doors, its famous guests publicising the beach, and alerting enterprising souls as to the commercial potential of the area. Rapid growth followed and a land fill project was undertaken, along which the two-lane **Avenida Atlântica** now runs.

Prior to Copacabana's rise, it was the beaches of **Guanabara Bay** – Flamengo, Botafogo, Urca and Vermelha – that were the most sought after. Today, the most fashionable beaches are those of **Ipanema** and **Leblon**, residential areas where the young, wealthy and beautiful have only to cross the road to flaunt their tans.

The beaches are described in the order you come across them as you head south out of the city – from Flamengo to Leblon and beyond. And as well as full details of the sand and surf, you'll also find coverage of the other sights in the Zona Sul, as most of the beach areas are backed by a *bairro*, with its own character and amenities.

Glória, Catete and Flamengo

The nearest beach to the city centre is at Flamengo (see below), and although it's not the best in Rio, you might end up using it more than you think since the neighbouring *bairros*, Catete and Glória are useful and cheap **places to stay**. The streets away from the beach – especially around Largo do Machado and along Rua do Catete – are full of inexpensive hotels, and there's a pleasant atmosphere

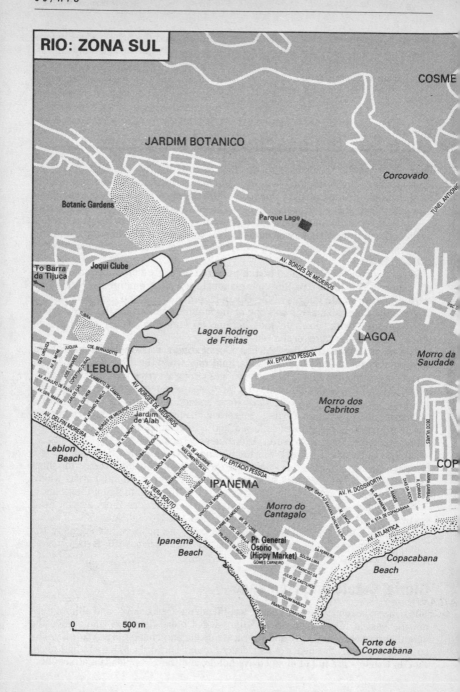

RIO: ZONA SUL

COSME

JARDIM BOTANICO

Corcovado

Botanic Gardens

Parque Lage

TUNEL ANTONIO

AV. BORGES DE MEDEIROS

To Barra
da Tijuca

Joqui Clube

VISC D

Lagoa Rodrigo
de Freitas

LAGOA

AV. EPITACIO PESSOA

Morro da
Saudade

GEN. URQUIZA
AV. E. MITRE
JOSE LINHARES
JUQUIA
COE. BERNADOTTE
COSUTTO GUAS
AV. ATAULFO DE PAIVA
CARLOS GOIS
DO GALEÃO
JUMBERTO DE CAMPOS
AV. GEN. MARTIN

LEBLON

AV. BORGES DE MEDEIROS

Morro dos
Cabritos

DECO VILARES

AV. DELFIN MOREIRA

Jardim
de Alah

N. BORGES DE MEDEIROS
AV. VISCONDE DE MELO
R. P. DUMONT
ANIBA MENDONÇA
GARCIA D'AVILA
MARIA QUITERIA
COUSA ANGELICA
BR. DE JAGUARIBE
NASCIMENTO SILVA

COP

Leblon
Beach

AV. VIERA SOUTO

AV. EPITACIO PESSOA

IPANEMA

PROF. GASTÃO BAHIANA
QUEBRA DEÇA
AV. H. DODSWORTH

C. LLANES
DIAS DA ROCHA
DE PANEMA
ANIBA GUEBALD
R. DORADO

VINICUS DE MORAES
FAME DE AMEDO
BR. DE TORRE
VISC DE PIRAJA
PILORTE DE MORAIS

Morro do
Cantagalo

AV. N. STA. DE COPACABANA
M. LEMOS

AV. ATLANTICA

Ipanema
Beach

Pr. General
Osorio
(Hippy Market)

SOUSA LIMA
SA FERREIRA
FRANCISO SA
GOMES CARNEIRO

Copacabana
Beach

JULIO DE CASTILHOS

JOAQUIM NABUCO
FRANCISCO OTAVIANO

0   500 m

Forte de
Copacabana

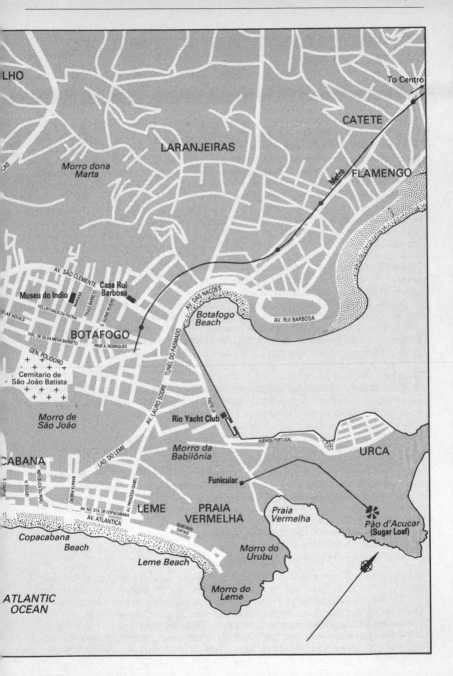

LHO

LARANJEIRAS

Morro dona Marta

CATETE

Metro FLAMENGO

To Centro

AV. SÃO CLEMENTE

Casa Rui Barbosa

Museu do Índio

MENA

PAULO BARRETO

VOLUNTÁRIOS DA PATRIA

G. DENE FEREYRO

TELAS NOVAIS

VISC. DE SILVA MENA BARRETO

BOTAFOGO

PROF. A. RODRIGUES

AV. DAS NAÇÕES

Botafogo Beach

AV. RUI BARBOSA

GEN. POLIDORO

+ + +

Cemitario de São João Batista

+ + +

+ + + +

Morro de São João

TUNEL DO PASMADO

AV. LAURO SODRE

Rio Yacht Club

AVENIDA PORTUGAL

URCA

CABANA

S. CAMPOS

N. SOUVEL

REPUBLICA DO PERÚ

BARATA RIBEIRO

PRINCESA ISABEL

LAD. DO LEME

Morro da Babilônia

Funicular

LEME

PRAIA VERMELHA

Praia Vermelha

Pão d'Açucar (Sugar Loaf)

AV. NO. STA. DE COPACABANA

AV. ATLANTICA

GUSTAVO SAPAO

Copacabana Beach

Leme Beach

Morro do Urubu

Morro do Leme

ATLANTIC OCEAN

BEACH BEHAVIOUR: SURVIVING IN STYLE

Sport, food and fashion

Maintaining an even tan and tight musculature is still the principal occupation for most of Rio's beachgoers. Joggers swarm up and down the pavements, bronzed types flex their muscles on parallel bars, located at intervals along the beaches, while the tradition of **beach football** is as strong as legend would have it on the Copacabana – certainly, there's no problem getting a game, though playing on loose sand amidst highly skilled practitioners of Brazil's national sport has the potential for great humiliation. There's lots of volleyball, too, as well as the ubiquitous **batball**, a kind of table-tennis with a heavy ball, and without the table. It's extremely popular with the kind of people who wait till you've settled down on your towel, and then run past spraying sand in all directions – taking an electric cattle-prod to the beach is the only way to keep them off.

A lot of people make their living by plying **food** – fruit, sweets, ice cream – and beach equipment along the sea shore, while dotted along the beaches are make-shift canopies, from which you can buy cold drinks. Like bars, most of these have a regular clientele and deliver a very efficient service – remember to return your bottle when you've finished. Coconut milk, *côco verde*, is sold everywhere, and is a brilliant hangover cure. You don't need to be wary of the edibles either: if the traders were to start poisoning their customers, they'd soon lose their hard-won trading space on the beach and their livelihood.

Beach fashion is important, too, and you'll come across some pretty snappy seaside threads. Over the last few years, women have favoured the *fio dental*, or dental floss, a two-piece arrangement of scant proportions; while it's the standard posing-pouch, or bermudas, for men. Fashions change regularly, though, so if you're really desperate to make your mark, you should buy your swimming togs in Rio.

Beaches: the bad news

● Many of the beaches are **dangerous**. The seabed falls sharply away, the waves are strong, and currents can pull you down the beach. Mark your spot well before entering the water, or you'll find youself emerging from a paddle twenty or thirty metres from where you started – which, when the beaches are packed at weekends, can cause considerable problems when it comes to relocating your towel and coco-nut oil. Copacabana is particularly dangerous, even for strong swimmers. However, the beaches are well served by **lifeguards**, whose posts are marked by a white flag with a red cross; a **red flag** indicates that bathing is prohibited. Constant surveillance of the beach fronts from helicopters and support boats means that, if you do get into trouble, help should arrive quickly.

In an **emergency**, telephone the following numbers:
Copacabana, Leblon and Ipanema ☎287-2121.
Barra de Tijuca ☎399-0340.
Botafogo, Urca and Flamengo ☎275-7444.

● Giving your passport, money and **valuables** the chance of a sun tan, rather than leaving them in the hotel safe, is madness. Take only the clothes and money that you'll need; it's quite acceptable to use public transport while dressed for the beach. Don't be caught out either by the young lad who approaches you from one side, distracting your attention with some request, while his mate approaches from the other side and whips your bag: it's the most common and efficient method of relieving you of things you shouldn't have brought with you in the first place.

to this part of town. Until the 1950s, Flamengo and Catete were the principal residential zones of Rio's wealthier middle classes, and although the mantle has now
passed to Ipanema and Leblon, the *bairros* still have a pleasantly relaxed appeal.
Busy during the day, the tree-lined streets are alive at night with residents eating
in the local restaurants; and though the nightlife is nothing special, it's tranquil
enough to encourage sitting out on the pavement at the bars, beneath the palm
trees and apartment blocks.

Glória

Across from the **Glória** Metro station, on top of the Morro do Glória, stands the
Igreja de Nossa Senhora da Glória do Outeiro (Mon–Fri 8am–noon & 1–
5pm, Sat & Sun 8am–noon), decorated with excellent seventeenth-century *azulejos* and nineteenth-century marble masonry. It's an attractive church, worth the
twenty-minute detour, and behind it you'll find the **Museu da Imperial
Irmandade de N.S. da Glória**, which has a small collection of religious relics,
ex-votos and the personal possessions of Empress Tereza Cristina.

Catete

On the Rua do Catete, adjacent to the **Catete** Metro station, stands the *Palácio do
Catete*, home to the **Museu do República**, presently shut for restoration. The
palace was used as the presidential residence until 1960, and it was here in 1954
that Getúlio Vargas turned his gun on himself and took his own life, believing he
was betrayed. There is a possibility that the building will be open to the public
quite soon. In the meantime, two buildings here, one inside the palace grounds
and the other adjacent, house the **Museu de Folclore Edison Cruz** (Tues–
Thurs 11am–6pm, Sat & Sun 3–6pm), a fascinating collection which unites pieces
from all over Brazil – leatherwork, musical instruments, ceramics, toys, Afro-
Brazilian cult paraphernalia, photographs and ex-votos; an enjoyable diversion.

Behind the palace lies the **Parque do Catete** (daily 8am–6pm), whose birdlife,
towering palms and calm walks are useful for a few moments' cool recuperation.

Flamengo

If you follow Avenida Beira Mar away from Centro you enter the **Parque do
Flamengo**, the biggest land reclamation project in Brazil, completed in 1960.
Sweeping round as far as Botafogo Bay, it comprises 1.2 square kilometres of
prime seafront. You'll pass through the park many times by bus as you travel
between Centro and the beach zone and it's popular with local residents who use
it mostly for sports – there are countless tennis courts (open 9am–11pm) and
football pitches.

The **beach** at Flamengo runs along the park for about a kilometre and offers
excellent views across the bay to Niterói. Unfortunately, it's not much cop for
swimming as the water here is polluted. Instead, you might want to take a look at
the quirky **Museu Carmen Miranda** (Tues–Fri 11am–5pm, Sat & Sun 1–5pm;
50¢), located in Avenida Rui Barboso near the *Hotel Glória*, at the southern end of
the park. Carmen was born in Portugal, made it big in Hollywood in the 1940s
and become the patron saint of Rio's Carnaval transvestites. The museum
contains a wonderful collection of kitsch memorabilia, as well as some of the
star's costumes and personal possessions – fruit-laden hats, posters and
"Chattanooga Choo-Choo" in Portuguese.

Botafogo

Botafogo curves around the 800 metres between Flamengo and Rio's yacht club. The name derives, reputedly, from the first white Portuguese settler who lived in the area, one João Pereira de Souza Botafogo. The bay is dominated by the yachts and boats tethered near the club, and again the beach doesn't have much to recommend it to bathers.

However, there's plenty to see in the *bairro* itself. From the Botafogo Metro station, walk away from the ocean along Avenida São Clemente, and you'll find the **Museu Casa de Rui Barbosa** at no. 134 (Tues–Fri 10am–4.30pm, Sat & Sun 2–5pm; guided tours at 10am, 2pm & 4pm), set amidst the lush bowers of a garden with well kept paths and borders. Built in 1849, it became the home of Rui Barbosa, jurist, statesman and author, in 1893, and the federal government established a museum here after his death. Born in Bahia state, Barbosa (1849–1923) graduated as a lawyer in São Paulo and, later, working as a journalist and critic of the monarchy, founded the newspaper *A Imprensa*. He became senator of Bahia and in 1905, and again in 1909, made unsuccessful attempts to be elected as the country's president. A liberal, he made an excellent opposition politician, earning himself exile between 1893 and 1895, years he spent in Argentina and England – perhaps where he bought the copy of Courbey's *The Working Constitution of the United Kingdom*, found in the library. The museum is basically a collection of his possessions – beautiful Dutch and English furniture, Chinese and Japanese porcelain (including the first plumbed bathroom in Rio), and a library of 35,000 volumes, amongst which are two hundred works penned by Rui himself. Barbosa conferred a title on each room in the house – the *Sala Bahia*, *Sala Questão Religiosa*, *Sala Habeau Corpus*, *Sala Codigo Civil* – all of them identified with some part of his life.

Four blocks further down Avenida São Clemente, turn left down Avenida Sorocaba to discover the **Museu Villa-Lobos** at no. 200 (Mon–Fri 9am–5.30pm). Established in 1960 to celebrate the work of the Brazilian composer, Heitor Villa-Lobos, it's again largely a display of his personal possessions and original music scores, but you can also buy tapes and records of his music here.

Botafogo's museums are completed in the next street along, at Rua das Palmeiras 55, with the **Museu do Índio** (Thurs & Fri 10am–6pm, Sat & Sun 1–5pm). Housed in an old colonial building, the museum was inauguarated on April 19, 1953, the commemoration of Brazil's "Day of the Indian" – not that there were many around by then to celebrate. It's a broad and interesting collection, containing utensils, musical instruments, tribal costumes and ritual devices from many of Brazil's dwindling indigenous peoples. There's a good photographic exhibition, too, and an accessible anthropological explanation of the rituals and institutions of some tribes. The ethnographical section of the National Museum (see "Zona Norte", above) probably provides you with more information, but this museum is still being developed and is worth a look to check on progress – certainly since they've started to build examples of indigenous housing in the grounds.

Urca and the Sugar Loaf

The best bet for swimming this close to the centre are the small beaches on each side of the promontory on which stands **Urca**, a middle-class *bairro* whose name is an acronym of the company that undertook its construction – *Urbanizador Construção*. Facing Botafogo here the **Praia da Urca**, only a hundred metres long, is frequented almost exclusively by the small *bairro*'s inhabitants; while in front of the cable car station (see below), beneath the Sugar Loaf mountain, **Praia Vermelha** is a cove sheltered from the South Atlantic, whose relatively gentle waters are popular with swimmers.

You should come to Urca at least once during your stay, anyway, to climb the **Pão de Açúcar**, which rises where Guanabara Bay meets the Atlantic Ocean. In Portuguese the name means "Sugar Loaf", but it also resembles the Tupi-Guarani Indians' word *Pau-nh-Acuqua*, or "high hill" – a more apt description. The first recorded non-indigenous ascent to the summit was made in 1817 by an English nanny, Henrietta Carstairs. Today, mountaineers are a common site scaling the smooth, precipitous slopes, but the cable car ride to the summit is easier, even if you do leave your stomach behind you.

The **cable car** system has been in place since 1912; sixty years later the present Italian system, which can carry 1360 passengers every hour, was installed. It's in Praça General Tibúrcio (reached by buses marked *Urca* or *Praia Vermelha* from Centro, or #511 and #512 from Zona Sul) and operates daily from 8am to 10pm, with departures every half-hour. The 1400m journey is made in two stages, first to the summit of **Morro da Urca** (215m), where there is a theatre, restaurant and shops, and then on to the top of Pão de Açúcar itself (394m). The cable cars have glass walls and once on top the view is as glorious as you could wish. Facing inland, you can see right over the city, from Centro and the Santos Dumont airport all the way through Flamengo and Botafogo; face Praia Vermelha and the cable car terminal, and to the left you'll see the sweep of Copacabana and on into Ipanema; while back from the coast, the mountains around which Rio was built rise to the Tijuca National Park. Try and avoid the busy times between 10am and 3pm: it's best of all at sunset on a clear day, when the lights of the city are starting to twinkle.

On the lower hill, the *Beija Flor* **samba school** performs every Monday at 10pm, a touristy affair that costs about $15 for dinner and the glitzy floor show; while on Thursday and Friday live music shows start at 10pm, and you can eat and drink till 2am – check in the *Jornal do Brasil* for what is going on. This hill is also the location of the expensive Carnaval ball (see "Rio's Carnaval").

Leme and Copacabana

Leme and **Copacabana** are different stretches of the same four-kilometre beach. The **Praia do Leme** extends for a thousand metres, between the Morro do Leme and Avenida Princesa Isabel, at which point there's the first lifeguard post. From there, the **Praia de Copacabana** runs for a further three kilometres to the military-owned Copacabana Fort. Along the way, concrete lifeguard stations with toilets and showers have recently been installed.

Copacabana is amazing, the over-the-top atmosphere apparent even in the mosaic pavements, designed by Burle Marx to represent images of rolling waves. The seafront is backed by a line of prestigious, high-rise hotels and luxury apartment blocks that have sprung up since the 1940s, while a steady stream of noisy traffic patrols the two-lane **Avenida Atlântica**. Families, friends and lovers cover the palm-fringed sand – at weekends it's no easy matter to find space on which to lay your towel – the bars and restaurants along the avenue pulsate, while the busy **Avenida N.S. de Copacabana** is lined with assorted shops, containing everything your heart could desire.

Copacabana is dominated to the east by the Pão de Açúcar and circled by a line of hills that stretch out into the bay. A popular residential area, the *bairro*'s expansion has been restricted by the Morro de São João, which separates it from Botafogo, and the Morro dos Cabritos, which forms a natural barrier to the west. Consequently, it's one of the world's most densely populated areas, and a frenzy of sensual activity, most of which takes place in a thoroughly impressive, though hardly natural, setting. Some say that Copacabana is past its best and certainly it's not as exclusive as it once was. You'll be frequently accosted by a stream of the dispossessed young and old – who want money, or the scraps off your plate, while the street traders work into the night, selling t-shirts, lace tablecloths and plastic Rio car numberplates. It's still an enjoyable place to sit and watch the world go by, though, and at night on the floodlit beach football is played into the early hours.

Ipanema and Leblon

On the other side of the point from Copacabana Fort, the lively waters off the **Praia do Arpoador** are popular with surfers. From here, as far as the unkempt and balding greenery of the Jardim de Allah, a couple of kilometres away, you're in **Ipanema**; while thereafter lies **Leblon**. There are few apartment blocks in either *bairro* that don't have their own pistol-toting guard, eyes alert to anyone who looks out of place in this rich person's hangout. A bit calmer than Copacabana, the beaches here are stupendous, though there's not much in the way of bars and restaurants near the beach: in fact, the only bar/restaurant on the front is *Caneco*, at the far end of Leblon, a good spot to aim for anyway. On Sunday, the seafront roads – Avenida Vieira Souto in Ipanema, Avenida Delfim Moreira in Leblon – are closed to traffic, and much skateboarding and the like takes place.

Ipanema has a reputation as a fashion centre second to none in Latin America. It's hard to say whether in fact that's true, but certainly the place is packed with bijou little boutiques, flogging the very best names in fine threads. If you do go shopping here, go on Friday and take in the large **food and flower** market on the Praça de Paz. More realistically, you're likely to be able to afford something at Leblon's so-called **Hippie Market**, held between 9am and 6pm on Sunday in Praça General Osório. Once, the traders here hawked their wares in the streets of Copacabana, but now they gather together and wait for the tourists to come to them. Artisans from all over Brazil sell a variety of goods – leather, interesting jewellery, hammocks and crocheted table cloths, shawls and cushion covers. Not a hash pipe in the place, though.

Jardim Botânico and Gávea: the Jóquei Clube

Back from the plush beaches, north of the Lagoa Rodrigo Freitas, lies **Jardim Botânico** *bairro*, whose **Parque Lage** (daily 9am–5pm) consists of half a million square metres of forest, with a labyrinthine path network and seven small lakes – just the spot for a little shady relaxation. A little further on is the **Jardim Botânico** itself (daily 8am–5pm), half natural jungle, half laid-out in impressive avenues lined with immense Imperial Palms that date from the garden's inauguration in 1808. Dom João used the gardens to introduce foreign plants into Brazil –

tea, cloves, cinnamon and pineapples among them – and there are now 5000 plant species, amongst which live monkeys, parrots and other assorted wildlife. There are also a number of sculptures to be seen throughout the garden, notably the *Ninfa do Eco* by Mestre Valentim. Above all, though, the garden offers you an insight into the nature of tropical rainforest (albeit a tame one as the garden is well patrolled by uniformed officers), and the feel and smell of the vegetation provide a welcome contrast to the exhaust fumes polluting the streets outside. The **entrance** is at Rua Jardim Botânico 1008, where there's a car park and the garden's library with English-language literature about the plants inside.

Gávea and the Jóquei Clube

On the **Gávea** side of Lagoa Rodrigo de Freitas lies the **Jóquei Clube**, also known as the *Hipódromo da Gávea*, which can be reached on any bus marked *via Jóquei* – get off at Praça Santos Dumont at the end of Rua Jardim Botânico. Racing in Rio dates back to 1825 though the *Hipódromo* wasn't built until 1926. Today, **races** take place four times a week, every week of the year (Mon & Thurs night, Sat & Sun afternoon), with the international *Grande Prêmio Brazil* taking place on the first Sunday of August. A night at the races is great fun and foreigners can get into the palatial members' stand for just $1. You don't have to bet to enjoy the experience – it's not very easy to understand the tote system they use anyway. But it's an entertaining place, especially during the midweek racing under floodlights, when the air is balmy and you can eat or sip a drink as you watch the action.

Also in Gávea is the **Parque** and **Museu da Cidade** (Tues–Sun noon–4.30pm), at the end of Estrada de Santa Marinha: bus #591, #593 or #594 from Copacabana; #179 or #178 from Centro. The museum is contained within a two-storey nineteenth-century mansion once owned by the Marquis de São Vicente, and the collection is all related to the history of Rio from its foundation until the end of the Old Republic in 1930. The exhibits – paintings, weapons, porcelain, medals – are arranged in chronological order; the first salon deals with city's foundation, the rest with the colonial period.

West: Vidigal, São Conrado and Barra de Tijuca

Further to the west lies kilometre after kilometre of white sand. **Praia do Vidigal**, tucked under the Morro Dois Irmãos, is only about five hundred metres long, and used to be the preserve of the inhabitants of the **Favela do Vidigal**, one of the biggest shanty towns in Rio. They lost their beach with the construction of the *Rio Sheraton Hotel*, the sands appropriated for the use of hotel guests.

The beach at **São Conrado**, dominated by high-rise hotels, is becoming ever trendier: frequented by the famous and packed with hang-gliders and surfers at weekends, its star is in the ascendant – and it's certainly a beautiful beach. Before you get carried away, though, enormous inequality is close at hand. Above São Conrado, on the slopes between the Tijuca mountains and the peak of Pedra dos Dois Irmãos, sits **Favela Roçinha** – spuriously picturesque and glistening in the tropical sun. Here, over 200,000 Brazilians live, for whom a salary of $60 a month is about as much as an entire family can expect. Bus #500 from Urca will take you to São Conrado via Avenida Atlântica (Copacabana), Avenida Viera Souto (Ipanema) and Avenida Delfim Moreira (Leblon).

The last area within the city limits is **Barra de Tijuca**, with clean waters and white sands that run for over sixteen kilometres. The first four kilometres are hard by the residential area, where there's no shortage of facilities; after that, the beach is deserted and you'll need a car to reach the extreme stretches, though the whole length is popular at weekends with the beach party and barbecue set. You can reach Barra de Tijuca by bus from Copacabana (#553), or from Botafogo Metro station (#524).

Tijuca National Park and Alta da Boa Vista

When the Portuguese arrived, the area which is now the city of Rio was covered by dense, green tropical forest. As the city grew the trees were felled and the timber used in construction or for charcoal. However, if you look up from the streets of Zona Sul today, the mountains running south from the Corcovado are still covered with exuberant forest, the periphery of the **Tijuca National Park** which covers an area of approximately 120 square kilometres, and is maintained by Brazil's State Institute of Forestry (*IBDF*). By the nineteenth century much of the area enclosed within the park had been deforested to make way for coffee plantations and small-scale agriculture, and it wasn't until 1857 that a reafforestation project was initiated: by 1870 over 100,000 trees had been planted and the forest was reborn.

The park offers lots of walks and some excellent views of Rio, and though areas of it have been burnt, it remains an appealing place to get away from the city for a few hours. Buses don't enter the park so a **car** is useful if you plan to do an extensive tour: you can go in via Cosme Velho *bairro*, near the **Entrada dos Caboclos**, and follow Estrada Heitor da Silva Costa. (Areas of the park are used as *terrenos*, places where *candomblé* and *umbanda* ritual ceremonies are performed: *caboclos* is the collective name for the spirits involved in these cults.) An alternative entrance is at Rua Leão Pacheco, which runs up the side of the Jardim Botânico (off Rua Jardim Botânico), and leads to the **Entrada dos Macacos** and on to the **Vista Chinesa**, above the Museu da Cidade in Gávea. From here there's a marvellous view of Guanabara Bay and the Zona Sul. Both of these entrances lead to different roads that run through the park, but they converge eventually in the *bairro* of **Alta da Boa Vista**. If you're intent upon **walking**, you should be warned that even the shorter trip from the Entrada dos Macacos will mean a hot, dehydrating climb for more than twenty kilometres.

If you don't have your own transport, it's much easier to aim for the area to the north of the park known as the **Floresta de Tijuca** (daily 7am–9pm). Take a bus to Alto da Boa Vista (#221 from Praça XV de Novembro; #233 or #234 from the *Rodoviária*; #133 or #334 from Rua Jardim Botânico) and get off at Praça Alfonso Viseu near the **Entrada da Floresta**, with its distinctive stone columns – where you'll notice an old British telephone kiosk next to the *Robin Hood* bar. A few hundred metres after the entrance (where you can buy a **map** for 75¢), you'll pass a 35-metre-high waterfall and, further on, the **Capela do Mairynk**, built in 1860. The lush forest is full of secluded grottos and waterfalls, but do use the map as it's possible to wander off the beaten track. If you have the energy, you can climb all the way to the **Pico da Papagaio** (975m) or **Pico da Tijuca** (1021m) peaks in the far north of the forest, above the popular picnic spot known as **Bon Retiro**.

The whole park is a good place for a picnic, but there are also two decent **restaurants**, *A Floresta* and *Os Esquilos*, neither of which are expensive.

Eating and drinking

As one of the world's most exotic tourist resorts and with (for Brazil) a relatively large middle-class population, Rio is well served by reasonable restaurants offering a wide variety of cuisine – from traditional Brazilian to French and Japanese. Don't be afraid to experiment. Apart from a handful of extremely expensive exceptions, it's cheap to eat out in Rio's restaurants. There's no shortage either of minimally priced places to grab a lunchtime meal, or just a snack and a drink: either at a *galeto*, where you eat, diner-style, at the counter; or a *lanchonete*, the ubiquitous Brazilian café, which serves very cheap combined plates of meat, beans and rice, as well as other snacks. Cariocas dine late, and restaurants don't start to fill up until after 9pm. Generally, last orders will be taken around midnight in most places, but there are others where you can get a meal well after 2am.

The suggestions below are listed alphabetically under the city *bairros*, with other self-explanatory sections, too, on particular types of eating and drinking.

Fast food, snacks, cakes and ice cream

There's no shortage of **hamburger** joints in Rio, though it's worth bearing in mind that there's a good chance that the ground beef used comes from the Amazon, where immense ranches are displacing Indians, peasants and trees at a criminal rate. You'll get better, more authentic, food at any *galeto* or *lanchonete* – there are plenty in the Centro or at Copacabana, though most are closed at night. You won't really need any guidance to find these; the places given below deal in more specialised fare.

If you're just peckish, then it's nice to take **tea and cakes** at *Confeitaria Colombo*, which has two branches, in Copacabana at Avenida N.S. de Copacabana 890 and in the Centro at Rua Gonçalves Dias 32. Founded in 1894, the *Colombo* recalls Rio's *belle époque*, with its ornate interior decoration and air of tradition; the branch in Copacabana has a decent restaurant upstairs, too. Also in Copacabana, and good for **sandwiches**, is *Cervantes*, Avenida Prado Junior 335 (near Leme); while at Leblon you'll get a fresh, crisp **salad** at *Gulla Gulla* in the *Hotel Marina Palace*, Avenida Delfim Moreira – a bit pricier than usual, but recommended. There are more cakes at the *Bonbon d'Or* in Ipanema (Rua Visc. de Pirajá 351), or at any branch of *Kopenhagen*. For a choice of **ice cream**, aim for *Mr Ice*, Rua Ayres e Saldanha 98, Copacabana, or a branch of *Babuska* – at Rua Aníbal de Mendonça 55, Ipanema, and Rua Rainha Guilhermina 90, Leblon. Also in Leblon, there's a particularly good place for a *suco*, fresh, iced fruit juice: the *Polis* bar on Avenida Ataúlfo Paiva.

A NOTE ON DRINKING

The lists given below are for both eating and drinking. Many bars serve food and lots of restaurants allow a night's drinking, too, so you should be able to find somewhere that suits you. Two things to note: in most regions of Brazil, **beer** comes to your table in a bottle, but in Rio draught beer – or *chopp*, pronounced "shopee" – predominates; and a good place to sample Brazil's national drink, **cachaça**, is at the *Academia da Cachaça*, Rua Cde. Bernadotte 26, Leblon, a small bar where there are three hundred available brands to sample – treat it with respect at all times.

Check the **fruit markets** for something exotic and healthy: at Botafogo on Wednesday by Praça Canoinhas; Flamengo on Sunday in Largo do Machado; Copacabana on Thursday near Praça do Lido.

Centro and Santa Teresa

The restaurants in the city centre cater largely for people working in the area, and at lunchtime the service is rushed. Around the Praça Tiradentes, particularly, there are lots of cheap eating places, bakeries and bars, while Santa Teresa has a couple of specialist restaurants.

Alba Mar, Praça Marechal Ancora 184 (☎240-8378); a short walk from Praça XV de Novembro. Founded in 1933 and housed in the remaining tower of the old municipal market, this cool, green, octagonal building provides a superb view of Guanabara Bay. Stick with the seafood, served by serious-looking waiters in white uniforms.

Adega do Pimenta, Rua Almirante Alexandrino 296, Santa Teresa. German cuisine – lots of sausage and sauerkraut, and very pleasant for lunch or dinner. The Santa Teresa tram passes the restaurant.

Bar do Arnaudo, Rua Almirante Alexandrino 316; just up from the *Adega do Pimenta*. An excellent place to sample traditional food from Brazil's Northeast; *carne do sol* (sun-dried meat), *macaxeira* (sweet cassava), and *pirão de bode* (goat meat soup). Again, the tram passes the restaurant.

Bar dos Estudantes, Praça Tiradentes. Basic food and friendly service for next to nothing.

Caldeirão, Rua do Ouvidor 26. Open at lunchtime for good, cheap seafood, with a pleasant atmosphere. The raw materials land near Praça XV de Novembro and from there head towards your plate – try *badejo* (a type of fish) or *capixaba* (seafood stew).

Entrecote, Rua Gonçalves Dias 82; a block west of Avenida Rio Branco. A steak house, popular and inexpensive, with a friendly atmosphere.

Miako, Rua do Ouvidor 45 (☎222-2397); north side of Praça XV. One of the first Japanese restaurants in Rio. Sushi, sashimi, teppan-yaki and *filé na chapa*; good, and reasonably priced.

Rio Minho, Rua do Ouvidor 10 (☎231-2338). Tasty Brazilian food at fair prices in a restaurant that's been going for 92 years. The kitchen concentrates on seafood – try *badejo* fish, lobster in butter, prawn in coconut milk or the fried fish with red peppers, rice and broccoli.

Flamengo

There are numerous restaurants, *galetos* and *lanchonetes* around the Largo do Machado, as well as the places listed below.

Adega Real, Rua Marques de Abrantes; a few doors along from the *Cafe Lamas* (see below). No haughty nouvelle cuisine here, just piles of good basics – if you like decent quality food in large quantities, this place is recommended as the friendly waiters serve up tasty portions that are sufficient for at least two people. The restaurant opens onto the street, and on Friday you can hang on to the bar and swallow draught beer until 4am; the *bolinhas de bacalhau* (cod balls) are worth testing.

Alho & Óleo, Rua Barque de Macedo 13; down at the bottom near Praia do Flamengo. Tasty homemade pasta and good food (try the salami flavoured with pepper and lemon) in an upmarket atmosphere, but reasonably priced.

Café Lamas, Rua Marques de Abrantes 18. This 120-year-old restaurant serves well-prepared food to members of the art and journalism worlds. Always busy, with a vibrant atmosphere, it's a good example of carioca middle-class tradition, and highly recommended; open until 4am, too.

Churrascaria Majorica, Rua Senador Vergueiro 11. Nice pieces of meat in a popular, local restaurant. Packed out with families and gossip on Sunday, also an air-conditioned room.

Botafogo

Botafogo undoubtedly hosts some of Rio's most interesting restaurants, often overlooked because they lie a bit off the beaten track, hidden away in back streets.

Adega do Valentim, Rua da Passagem 178 (☎295-2748). A comfortable restaurant (especially the front salon) serving up good Portuguese food. Not especially cheap, but easily affordable at about $4 for a satisfying munch through cod, onions, potatoes and smoked ham.

Botequim-184, Rua Visconde de Caravelas 184; at the Lagoa end. Good, varied food in a lively establishment; next door, the *Overnight Bar* is a friendly place for a few drinks afterwards.

Café Pacífico, Rua Visconde Silva 14. Average Mexican food in a relaxed atmosphere; tables upstairs or outside on an enclosed patio. Go for the trendy ambience rather than the food and the run-of-the-mill cocktails.

Cochrane's, Rua das Palmeiras 66. Food and drink in a lively atmosphere reminiscent of an English wine bar. Live music, too, and the patronage of some of Rio's gay community.

Comidinhas 46, Praça Joia Valansi, Rua Muniz Barreto. Brazilian cooking, with inexpensive dishes from the state of Minas Gerais. Not at all bad – and with some of the best cheese in Rio.

La Mole, Praia de Botafogo 228. Inexpensive, palatable Italian food, with similar deals, too, at *Bella Blu*, Rua da Passagem 44, and *Bella Roma*, Rua General Gois Monteiro 18.

Madrugadas, Rua Sorocabana 305. More homemade pasta, this time including one with a sauce made with figs and nuts. It's not expensive and the service is friendly; quite a cosy place.

Maria Tereza Weiss, Rua Visconde de Silva 152 (☎286-3098). A pricey choice, sited in an old colonial house and named after its owner, who is the author of a number of books about Brazilian cuisine. Order *pirão*, *vatapá* or any of the seafood dishes, which come in wonderful sauces. Best to book a table.

Rajmahal, Rua General Polidoro 29 (☎541-6999). An Indian restaurant that is English-owned, and extends itself well beyond the basic curry. Let the waiter know how well seasoned you want your dish, as the restaurant tends to cater for the local preference for mild curries; a little more expensive than usual (around $5), but not frightening. Closed Monday.

Copacabana and Leme

It comes as no surprise that Copacabana is riddled with restaurants, but that doesn't mean that the choice is particularly good – unless you enjoy sitting in a restaurant swamped with holidaymakers being shuttled about by tour companies. For this reason, one to avoid is the *Palace*, Rua Rudolfo Dantas. Steer clear, too, of places like *Le Pre Catalan*, in the *Rio Palace Hotel*, or *Le Saint Honore*, in the *Hotel Meridien* – unless you're convinced that nouvelle cuisine supplies sufficient calories to sustain human life, and have an irresistible desire to pay through the nose.

A Marisqueira, Rua Barata Ribeiro 232 (☎237-3920). A good spot for seafood. The restaurant has been around for over thirty years and the owners have just opened a new branch in Ipanema, in Rua Gomes Carneiro. The food is well prepared, though perhaps a little unimaginative and a touch on the pricey side – a main dish will set you back about $5.

A Polonesa, Rua Hilário de Gouveia 116 (☎237-7378). Polish food in a tiny restaurant, presided over by Dona Josefa for the last four decades. An undoubtedly different menu for Rio – herring with apple and onion, chachlik kebab and goulash. Again, about $4.50–7 for a main dish.

Arataca, Rua Figueiredo Magalhaes 28 (☎255-7448); halfway along Copacabana. Brazilian food dominates the menu, in particular traditional dishes from the Amazonian state of Para: try *surubim*, *tucunaré* or *pirarucú*, fish from the waters of the Amazon Basin, served grilled, in stews (*caldeirada*) or in coconut sauce; *pato no tucupí* is duck in *tucupí* sauce; and for dessert, have a go at the exotic *cupuaçú* fruit.

Ouro Verde, Avenida Atlântica (☎542-1887); just after Praça de Lido. Part of a hotel (go through the lobby and use the lift), the restaurant serves international cuisine featuring some snappy French cooking and a gracious maitre d'; don't go in shorts. It's well worth it for a treat, as the food is good and the dishes are creative; nice desserts too. Two people can eat, and drink a bottle of wine, for about $22.

Shirley, Rua Gustavo Sampaio 610, Leme. Stuffed away in a side street behind the *Hotel Meridien*, this is not one of Rio's classiest eateries, but the Spanish food served up is both good and inexpensive.

Lagoa

Most of the restaurants in Lagoa are on the Avenida Epitácio Pessoa, which runs along the east side of the lake: generally plush, pricey, air-conditioned and boastful of their views over the lake – which are usually obscured by trees.

Café Lagoa, Avenida Epitácio Pessoa 1674; tucked into the southern corner of the lake by Ipanema. The cheapest and oldest of the lakeside restaurants, it's usually full of families from the adjacent neighbourhoods; white-coated waiters deliver beer, German sausage and smoked pork chops the size of football boots to your table. Arrive by 9pm and grab a seat on the patio, from where there's a good view of the lake. Inexpensive and definitely recommended.

Lagoa Charlie, Rua Maria Quitéria 136. Mexican food, eaten outside on the terrace, or inside where you'll be charmed or annoyed by serenading musicians who stroll between the tables. About $5 for a main dish.

The Queen's Legs, Avenida Epitácio Pessoa 5030. A facsimile Victorian pub, good for a beer and a game of darts downstairs – but don't bother with the upstairs restaurant, which is overpriced and overestimated.

Ipanema

There are lots of expensive restaurants in Ipanema, but budget eating choices are fairly limited. There are, however, some great, late-opening **bars** where you can sample a taste of the high life.

Alô-Alô, Rua Barao de Torre 368; below the *Sal e Pimenta* (see below). A piano bar with live jazz until 4am, this is a smart place to lounge on sofas and listen to faultlessly executed music. Cover charge.

Baroni Fasoli, Rua Jangadeiras 14; near Praça General Osório. Reasonably priced Italian place in an area otherwise brimming with expensive choices.

Barril 1800, Avenida Viera Souto 110. Together with *Alberico's* at no. 236, both more bars than restaurants, well frequented by the young and beautiful, and good places to fill your face with cold beer after a hot day on the beach.

Cabeça Feita, Rua Barão de Torre 655. Drink, dance and chew to live music until 3am. There is a cover charge, but it's not extortionate.

Del Mare, Rua Paul Redfern. Seafood in comfortable surroundings, though some of the prawn dishes are more expensive than they should be.

Garota de Ipanema, Rua Vinícius de Morais 49. Always busy, this bar has entered the folk annals of Rio de Janeiro since the song of the same name ("The Girl from Ipanema") was written in here one night when the muse came to Tom Jobim, the song's composer. Few better places in Rio for a beer.

Lord Jim, Rua Paul Redfern. An English boozer serving steak and kidney pie, fish and chips and High Tea. Downstairs, there's a dart board amongst the horse brasses and fake half-timbering. It opens at 5pm and is busy with English ex-pats bemoaning the number of "foreigners" in Brazil.

Saideira, Rua Gomes Carneiro, near Praça General Osório. Eating and drinking through the night, until 8am. The term *saideira* means "one for the road" and it's a place that the night-people stop off at after strenuous entertainment in the clubs roundabout. Worth considering for a late – or early – snack.

Sal e Pimenta, Rua Barão de Torre 368 (☎521-1460); above the *Alô-Alô*. A gold *American Express* card joint; you'll need to make a reservation, and the fifteen percent service charge is outrageous – but it's gracious international cuisine served in pleasant surroundings overlooking a courtyard.

Satiricon, Rua Barão de Torre 192. Good seafood in pink-coloured surroundings. This is a smart place that doesn't overcharge ($5), and is worth visiting.

Trattoria Torna, Rua Maria Quiteria 46. Italian, with man-and-guitar-type live music. The pasta is pretty good, and the atmosphere lively.

Leblon

Many of Leblon's restaurants are situated along the Avenida Ataulfo de Paiva, also where you'll find a lot of the late-opening bars. Another popular food and drink venue is around Rua Dias Ferreira, which is very lively at the weekend.

Alta Munchen, Avenida Ataúlfo de Paiva 410 (☎294-4197). A varied menu of German and Swiss dishes; on a hot evening the veranda is a pleasant place to eat. Open until 3am and reasonably priced.

Arataca, Avenida Ataúlfo de Paiva 135 (☎274-1444). Sister branch of the regional Brazilian restaurant in Copacabana – food from the Amazonian state of Pará, excellent fruit juices. There is not much to choose between the two branches; both are simple, not too many frills.

Caneco 70, Avenida Delfim Moreira 1026; at the very end near the Praça Atahualpa. The only restaurant serving the beach in Leblon, the terrace upstairs provides a nice view of the scenery; open 10am–3am.

Degrau, Avenida Ataúlfo de Paiva 517. Extensive international cuisine; doesn't figure in Rio's gourmet guides, but it's always busy, and the food is satisfactory and affordable.

Le Coin, Avenida Ataúlfo de Paiva 658. Reasonable international cuisine; inexpensive and no complaints.

Le Tarot, Rua General Urquiza 104. Popular with young people, fairly standard international cuisine, and not expensive.

Pizzeria Guanabara, Avenida Ataúlfo de Paiva 1228. Good if nothing special, and they keep serving pasta and pizza until 5am.

Gávea

Not an obvious choice for restaurants but a night at the races and a dip into the food available there is fun.

Jóquei Clube, Praça Santos Dumont. There's racing on Monday and Thursday night, and at the weekend, and you can enjoy the palatial surroundings and a decent, inexpensive meal in the restaurant overlooking the race track.

Guima's, Rua José Roberto Macedo Soares 5 (☎259-7996); on the opposite side of Praça Santos Dumont from the *Jóquei Clube*. A small, intimate restaurant with a happy atmosphere, catering for artists and intellectuals; the food is delicious, and even the *couvert* of wholemeal bread and paté is worth the price. Steak in a mustard and pear sauce will set you back $5, so even if you indulge in one of the brilliant desserts to follow, you aren't going to spend a fortune. One of Rio's best.

Vegetarian food

Vegetarians won't have any serious problems in Rio. While beans and rice are always available for basic sustenance, don't be shy of asking the waiter in any restaurant to have the kitchen prepare something a little more tasty: if nothing else, you'll get a plate of fresh vegetables. Specific options include:

Associacão Macrobiótica, Rua Emb. Regis Oliveira 7, Centro (11am–4.30pm only). An inexpensive macrobiotic restaurant – busy and, strangely enough, with some dishes which include fish.

Café Bohemia, Avenida Santa Luzia; off Avenida Rio Branco. A bit different: a decent vegetarian restaurant by day, and at night a mixture of comedy store and transvestite revue, with a bit of dancing thrown in; entry is about $2 and it starts after midnight.

Natural; branches of this restaurant in Botafogo (Rua 19 de Fevereiro 118) and in Ipanema (Rua Barão de Torre 171) – not strictly vegetarian as fish can be had too, but the food is good and cheap.

Vegetarian food: for down-the-line veggie food the following restaurants are all in Centro – *Health's*, Rua dos Beneditinos 18; *Greens*, Rua do Carmo 38; *Le Bon Menu*, Rua Araújo Porto Alegre 71; and *Zan*, Travessa do Ouvidor 25.

Definitely not vegetarian

A number of Rio's *churrascarias* (barbecue houses) serve their meats **rodízio** style. For a set price (approximately $4–6), a selection of salads, beans and potatoes is laid out before you, followed by the repeated arrival of the waiter bearing roast meats skewered on a sword. You choose the piece that takes your fancy, and the waiter deftly transfers it from skewer to plate – cuts of filet mignon, pork, chicken, ham, sausage, brisket of beef, and anything else that's had its head over a gate. Take your time, as the waiter will always come back when you're ready for more.

The following *churrascarias* are all recommended.

Estrela do Sul, Avenida Reporter Nestor Moreira, Botafogo. This place has a long history and a good reputation.

Gaúcha, Rua das Laranjeiras 114; near Largo do Machado. A bit of a barn, but with live music and a dance floor.

Mariu's, Avenida Atlântica 290; at the top end of Leme's beach. Probably the most popular *rodízio* in Rio, it seats over three hundred, and what it lacks in elegance it makes up for in service and atmosphere.

Plataforma, Rua Adalberto Ferreira 32, Leblon. Upstairs, tourists are entertained by a samba show, downstairs you mingle with cariocas (and afterwards you can always stagger to the *Academia de Cachaça*, around the corner, and sample a few with the benefit of a good lining on the stomach).

Nightlife and Entertainment

The best way to find out what's on and where in Rio is to consult *Caderno B*, a separate section of the *Jornal do Brasil*, which lists cinema, arts events and concerts; *O Globo*, too, details sporting and cultural events in the city. You shouldn't be stuck: there's no end of things to do come nightfall in the city whose name is synonymous with Carnaval, samba and jazz.

Samba

Samba shows are inevitably tourist affairs, where members of Rio's more successful samba schools perform glitzy music and dance routines. Still, some are worth catching. Every Monday night at 10pm, the *Beija Flor* school performs at the *Morro da Urca*, halfway up Pão d'Açúcar; $15, which includes dinner from 8pm, a well executed show and spectacular views, if a tad snooty.

Of the **clubs**, try *Clube do Samba*, Estrada de Barra 65 in Barra de Tijuca, with lots of dancing and a nice open-air bar. Dedicated just to samba, Saturday often sees shows by big names like Beth Carvalho, Alcione, João and Giza Nogeuiral; check in the *Jornal do Brasil*; entrance costs about $3 which is typical for this type of set-up. More big names, too, at *Canecão*, Avenida Wenceslas Bras 215, Botafogo, which can get pleasantly rowdy of an evening. For cheaper, early evening entertainment there are the *Seis e Meia* **shows** (at 6.30pm, as the name suggests): in Centro try the *Teatro João Caetano*, Praça Tiradentes, or the *Paço Imperial*, Praça XV de Novembro.

Discos, live music and jazz

Although Rio's discos and piano bars attempt sophistication, the product is generally bland and unpalatable. Discos, particularly, too often pump out a steady stream of British and American hits, interspersed with examples from Brazil's own dreadful pop industry.

Most of the big **discos** are private clubs, but if you're staying in one of the five-star hotels, and promise to spend a minimum of $20 per person, you can usually arrange temporary membership. Soft options for the wealthy and unadventurous are *Hippopotamus*, Rua Barre de Torre 354, in Ipanema, and *Studio C*, Rua Xavier da Silveira 7, under the *Hotel Rio Othon Palace* in Copacabana. Halfway along Avenida Atlântica, *Help* is a massive disco which gets mobbed at weekends: it only admits couples, so if you're approached in a bar outside, your partner is merely looking to get in; entrance is about $2.50. Other *boates* (disco clubs) are: *Caligula*, Rua Prudente de Morais 129, Ipanema, which costs $4 entrance and attracts some famous types; and *Biblos*, Avenida Epitácio Pessoa 1484, Lagoa, with good popular Brazilian home-grown music and jazz (Tues) – open until about 5am it's a more tranquil place. *Peoples*, Avenida Bartolemeu Mitre 370, Leblon, is one of the trendiest spots in Rio: upstairs the city's fashion-conscious middle class listen to live music of varying quality; downstairs (invitation only) in the private club, chemically assisted rich-kids sustain a funky posture till dawn. All pretentious nonsense, but a bit of a laugh, though with a $6 cover charge, it's not a cheap night out.

For **live rock music**, give the *Crespúsculo de Cubatão* (Rua Barata Ribeiro 543) a whirl. Part-owned by Ronnie Biggs, its atmosphere, when busy, is curiously in keeping with the club's name, "Cubatão Twilight" – Cubatão being an industrial area near São Paulo which pollution has made virtually uninhabitable. Entrance is about $2. *Let It Be*, Rua Siqueira Campos 206, also has live rock combined with taped music that, not surprisingly, favours old stuff from the Fab Four.

Another option is for live **reggae** at *Casa Branca*, Rua do Catete 112, near Largo do Machado; sessions every Sunday until 4am, a lively crowd, lots of students, and cheap entrance.

Jazz

Rio de Janeiro has a tradition of **jazz music** that extends well beyond "The Girl from Ipanema" and which is celebrated in the **Free Jazz Festival**, usually around September, based in the theatre in the *Hotel Nacional*: for more information, contact *Dueto Productions*, Rua Visconde de Pirajá 146 in Ipanema. In past festivals, Brazilian musicians like Egberto Gismonti, Hermeto Pascoal, Airto Moreira and Flora Purim have combined with the likes of Art Blakey, Sarah Vaughan, Ray Charles and Stan Jordan – an important event on the international jazz circuit.

Amongst the clubs that specialise in **live jazz** and tend to have consistently good programmes are *Jazzmania*, Rua Rainha Elizabeth 769, in the corner between Copacabana and Ipanema, and *Peoples*, Avenida Bartolomeu Mitre 370, Leblon (see above). The latter is very trendy, but make sure you go on the right night and avoid the dreadful Country and Western band that has a regular Tuesday spot.

Brazilian Dancing

Brazilians can dance, no question about that. The various regionally rooted traditions in folk music remain alive and popular, and if you'd like to get into a bit of Brazilian swing, go in search of the more traditional dance halls.

Gafieiras

Gafieiras originally sprung up in the 1920s as ballrooms for the poorer classes, and today they remain popular because they are places where cariocas can be assured of traditional dance music. The most famous – both highly recommended – are *Estudantina*, Praça Tiradentes 79 (1st floor; Thurs 10pm–3am, Fri & Sat 11pm–4am), and *Elite*, Rua Frei Caneca 4 (1st floor; Fri & Sat 11pm–4am, Sun 9pm–3am), both in Centro. *Estudantina*'s decor recalls an earlier age, and with live bands on the stage busying the dancers along, and a small veranda to cool off on, it's a good place to go; *Elite* is smaller, more traditional and has a famous ball during Carnaval.

Asa Branca, Avenida Mem de Sá 17, in Lapa (Tues–Sun 10pm–3am), is another good option for a jig, principally samba, and next door is *Arcos de Velha*, a dance hall where the band play *fundo do quintal* style – around a table rather than on the stage. Under the viaduct in Lapa, there's also *Circo Voador*, housed under a big top on some evenings, with open-air dancing and drinking on others. It puts on *forró* (see below), samba and *trio elétrico* music, is inexpensive and has some excellent Northeastern bands.

Forró

For some accordion-driven swing from Brazil's Northeast, look for a **forró** club. The term *forró* (pronounced "fawhaw") originates from the English "for all", a reference to the dances financed by English engineering companies for their manual labour forces, as opposed to the balls organised for the elite. As drought and poverty have forced the *nordestino* to migrate south in search of employment in Brazil's large urban centres, so the culture has followed. At Rua Catete 235, *Forró Forrado* (Fri–Sun 10pm–late) has an excellent band and a mixed clientele that spans Rio's social scale. On Saturday nights, there's also the *Forró da Praia*, on Avenida Nações Unidas near the Botafogo recreation ground.

Gay Rio

The best introduction into Rio's male gay society is *The Club*, in fact a bar in the Travessa Cristiano Lacorte, just off Rua Miguel Lemos, at the Ipanema end of Copacabana. Opposite this, the *Teatro Brigitte Blair* hosts a gay transvestite show from around 10pm, as does the *Teatro Alaska*, inside the *Galeria Alaska* at Avenida N.S. de Copacabana 1241. Up in Lagoa, *Papagaio* disco (Av. Borges de Medeiros 1426) has a gay night on Friday. In Botafogo the bar *Cochranes*, Rua das Palmeiras 66, is a civilised and relaxed venue favoured by gay society, though is not exclusively gay; and in Copacabana *Encontros*, on Praça do Lido set back from Avenida N.S. de Copacabana, is also popular.

Tradition has it that some bars around Cinelândia in the city centre are popular meeting spots for gay men, though tradition doesn't indicate exactly which establishments are appropriate, while in Copacabana, the beach area in front of the *Copacabana Palace Hotel* is frequented by gay bathers; as is the strip of beach between Rua Farme de Melo and Rua Vinícius de Morais in Ipanema.

See the "Carnaval" section, below, for information about Rio's gay balls.

Cinema, classical music and exhibitions

Brazil is one of the world's largest film markets. Most European and American films are quickly released in Brazil and play to large audiences on big screens with their original soundtracks. **Cinemas** are very cheap (75¢) and among the best are the *Largo do Machado I & II* and the *São Luiz I & II*, both in Largo do Machado; the *Ricamar* and the *Roxy*, along Avenida N.S. de Copacabana; and *Condor Copacabana* in Rua Figueiredo Magalhães. *Jornal do Brasil* lists what's on and where.

Since 1984 Rio de Janeiro has hosted **Festrio**, an international festival of film that includes some TV and video productions as well, and ranks alongside those of Cannes, Montreal and Moscow. It takes place over ten days in November, and is based in the Convention Centre of the *Hotel Nacional*: contact the organisers at Rua Paissandú 362 (☎285-7649), in Flamengo. Cariocas love the cinema, have very catholic tastes and their festival lacks the snobbery that has marred Cannes. Over three hundred films are shown during the festival, with parallel screenings in cinemas all over Rio. Obscure foreign films can play to packed houses that charge minimal entrance fees.

Classical music, ballet and opera

Rio is the home of the **Brazilian Symphony Orchestra**, and the orchestra of the *Teatro Municipal* – the theatre which is home to the city's **ballet** troupe and **opera** company. This is the venue for almost everything that happens in terms of "high culture", with four or five major productions a year. All kinds of events attract famous names, and prices are cheap; again, check the *Jornal do Brasil*.

Exhibitions and recitals

For musical, photographic and fine art **exhibitions**, it's worth checking at the headquarters of *Funarte*, around the corner from the Museu das Belas Artes in Rua Araújo de Porto Alegre; either go and get a copy of their programme, or keep an eye on the newspapers. Particularly good are the photographic exhibitions under the direction of Walter Firmo, and the musical **recitals** that take place in the Sidney Millar room on the first floor of *Funarte*.

Rio's Carnaval

Carnaval is celebrated in all of Brazil's cities, but Rio's is the biggest and most flash. From the Friday before Ash Wednesday to the following Thursday, the city shuts up shop and throws itself into the world's most famous manifestation of unbridled hedonism. Its greatest quality is that Rio's Carnaval has never become stale, something to do with its status as the most important celebration on the Brazilian calendar, easily outstripping either Christmas or Easter. In a city riven by poverty, Carnaval represents a moment of freedom and release, when the aspirations of cariocas can be expressed in music and song.

The background

The direct origins of Carnaval in Rio can be traced back to a fifteenth-century tradition of Easter revelry in the Azores, that caught on in Portugal and was exported to Brazil. Anarchy reigned in the streets for four days and nights, the festivities often so riotous that they were formally abolished in 1843 – although the street celebrations have remained the most accessible and widely enjoyed feature of Carnaval ever since. In the mid-nineteenth century, **masquerade balls** – *bailes* – were first held by members of the social elite, while processions, with carriages decorated in allegorical themes, also made an appearance; thus marking the ascendancy of the procession over the general street melée. Rio's masses, who were denied admission to the balls, had their own music – *jongo* – and they reinforced the tradition of street celebration by organising in *Zé Pereira* bands, named after the Portuguese tambor which provided the basic musical beat. The organisational structure behind today's samba schools (*escolas da samba*) was partly a legacy of those bands sponsored by migrant Bahian port workers in the 1870s. Theirs was a more disciplined approach to the Carnaval procession: marching to string and wind instruments, using costumes and appointing people to co-ordinate different dimensions of the parade.

Music written specifically for Carnaval emerged in the early twentieth century, by composers like Chiquinho Gonzaga, who wrote the first recorded **samba** piece in 1917 ("Pelo Telefone"), and Mauro de Almeida e Donga. In the 1930s, radio and records began to spread the music of Rio's Carnaval, and competition between different Samba schools became institutionalised: in 1932 the *Estação Primeira Mangueira* school won the first prize for its performance in the Carnaval parade. The format has remained virtually unchanged since then, except for the emergence – in the mid-1960s – of the **bandas**; street processions by the residents of various *bairros*, who eschew style, discipline and prizes and give themselves up to the most traditional element of Carnaval – street revelry, of which even the principal Carnaval procession in the Sambódromo is technically a part.

Carnaval – all the action

Rio's street celebrations centre around the **evening processions** that fill **Avenida Rio Branco** (Metro to Largo do Carioca or Cinelândia). Be prepared for the crowds and beware of pickpockets: even though the revellers are generally high-spirited and good-hearted, it's as well to keep the little cash you should take in inaccessible places (like your shoes), wear only light clothes and leave your valuables locked up at the hotel.

Most of what's good takes place down the Avenida Rio Branco. The processions include Samba schools (though not the best; see below), *Clubes de Frevo*, whose loudspeaker-laden floats blast out the frenetic dance music typical of the Recife Carnaval, and the *Blocos de Empolgacão*, including the *Bafo da Onça* and *Cacique de Ramos* clubs, between which exists a tremendous rivalry. There are also *rancho* bands, a traditional carioca carnival music that predates samba.

Bandas

In whatever *bairro* you're staying there will probably be a **banda** organised by the local residents; ask in your hotel. Starting in mid-afternoon, they'll continue well into the small hours, the popular ones accumulating thousands of followers as they wend their way through the neighbourhood. They all have a regular starting point, some have set routes, others wander freely; but they're easy to follow – there's always time to have a beer and catch up later.

Some of the best *bandas* are: the *Banda da Glória*, which sets off from near the Estação Glória Metro station; the *Banda da Ipanema* (the first to be formed, in 1965), which gathers behind Praça General Osório in Ipanema; and the *Banda da Vergonha do Posto 6*, starting in Rua Francisco Sá in Copacabana. There are dozens of others, including several in each *bairro* of the Zona Sul, each providing a mix of music, movement and none-too-serious cross-dressing – a tradition during Carnaval that even the most macho of men indulge in.

Carnaval balls

It's the **Carnaval balls** that really signal the start of the celebrations, warm-up sessions in clubs and hotels for rusty revellers, which are quite likely to get out of hand as inhibitions give way to a rampant eroticism. They all start late, normally after 10pm, and the continual samba beat supplied by live bands drives the festivities into the new day. At most of the balls, *fantasia* (fancy dress) is the order of the day, elaborate costumes brightening the already hectic proceedings – but don't worry if you haven't got one; just dress reasonably smartly. At some of the balls your clothes might not stay on for too long anyway . . .

You'll often have to pay an awful lot to get in to these affairs, as some of the more fashionable balls attract the rich and famous. If you've got the money and the silly costume, then those worth checking out include the *Pão de Açúcar*, on the Friday before Carnaval, halfway up the famous landmark – spectacular views, exotic company and about $70 a head, but a trifle snobby (☎541-3737 for details). The *Hawaiian Ball*, hosted by the Rio Yacht Club, opens the season on the Friday of the week before Carnaval: it takes place around the club's swimming pool, amid lavish decorations, and is popular and expensive (about $45); tickets from the Yacht Club, on Avenida Pasteur, a few hundred metres before the Sugar Loaf cable car terminus. The Friday immediately before Carnaval (which doesn't officially start until Monday) is a big occasion, too, with the *Baile de Champagne* and the *Baile Vermelho e Preto* taking place. The latter (the "Red and Black Ball") has developed a particular reputation as a no-holds-barred affair. Named after the colours of Rio's favourite football team, Flamengo, it's a media event with TV cameras scanning the crowds for famous faces – exhibitionism is an inadequate term for the immodest goings-on at the Red and Black celebrations. In Leblon the *Monte Libano* (☎239-0032 for details) hosts a number of "last days of Rome" festivities – the *Baile das Gatas*, *Baile Fio Dental*, even *Bum Bum Night* – sexually charged exercises all, though safe to attend and reasonable at around $17 a ticket.

There are a number of **gay balls**, too, which attract an international atten-
dance. The *Grande Gala G* is an institution, usually held in the *Help* disco on
Copacabana's Avenida Atlântica. Another is the *Baile dos Enxutos*, hosted by the
Hotel Itália on Praça Tiradentes, Centro.

Over the last few years, the *Scala* club in Leblon has become an important
centre for balls, and has hosted the *Baille Vermelho e Preto* amongst others. You
can confirm venues by phoning the *Scala* (☎274-9148), or by asking at the box
office, Avenida Afriano de Melo Franco 292, Leblon.

Samba schools and the Desfile

The **samba schools**, each representing a different neighbourhood or social club,
are divided into three leagues, each allowing promotion and relegation. Division 1
schools play in the Sambódromo, Division 2 on Avenida Rio Branco and Division
3 on Avenida 28 de Setembro, up in Aldeia Campista, near the Maracanã Stadium.

Until 1984, the main procession of Division 1 schools – the Desfile – took place
along Avenida Presidente Vargas. It has since been shifted to the purpose-built
Sambódromo, further along the avenue beyond the train station, a concrete
structure 1700 metres long which can accommodate 90,000 spectators. On the
Sunday and Monday nights of Carnaval week, some 50,000 others, divided up
into the various Samba schools, take part in a spectacular piece of theatre: no
simple parade, but a competition between schools attempting to gain points from
their presentation composed of song, story, dress, dance and rhythm.

It all starts in the year preceeding Carnaval, as each samba school mobilises
thousands of supporters who will create the various parts of the school's display.
A theme is chosen, music written, costumes created, while the dances are chore-
ographed by the **carnavelesco**, the school's director. By December, rehearsals
have begun and, in time for Christmas, the sambas are recorded and released to
record stores.

At the **Desfile** itself, the schools pass through the *Passarela do Samba*, the
Sambódromo's parade ground, and the judges allocate points according to a
number of criteria. Each school must parade for between 85 and 95 minutes, no
more and no less. The **bateria**, the percussion section, has to sustain the cadence
that drives the school's song and dance; the *samba enredo* is the music, the
enredo the accompanying story or lyric. The **harmonia** refers to the degree of

---

SAMBA SCHOOLS

If you can't make Carnaval, you can get a taste of the samba schools at the **ensaios**
below. They take place from August to February, Friday to Sunday at about 10pm.

Beija-Flor, Rua Pracinha Wallace Paes Leme 1652, Nilopolis (founded 1948; blue
and white).

Estação Primeira de Mangueira, Rua Visconde de Niterói 1072, Mangueira
(founded 1928; green and pink; winners 1984, 1985 & 1986).

Portela, Rua Clara Nunes 81, Madureira (founded 1923; blue and white).

Mocidade Independente de Padre Miguel, Rua Cel. Tamarindo 38, Padre
Miguel (founded 1952; green and white).

Império Serrano, Avenida Ministro Edgar Romero 114, Madureira (founded 1947;
green and white; winners 1982).

SAMBÓDROMO PARADES

The starting dates for the Sambódromo parades for the next few years are as follows:

1990 Feb 25	1995 Feb 26
1991 Feb 10	1996 Feb 18
1992 Mar 1	1997 Feb 9
1993 Feb 21	1998 Feb 22
1994 Feb 13	1999 Feb 14

synchronicity between the *bateria* and the dance by the thousands of **passistas** (samba dancers); the dancers conducted by the **pastoras**, who lead by example. The **evolução** refers to the quality of the dance, and the choreography is judged on its spontaneity, the skill of the *pastoras* and the excitement that the display generates. The costumes, too, are judged on their originality; their colours always the traditional ones adopted by each school. The **carros alegóricos** (no more than ten metres high and eight wide) are the gigantic, richly decorated floats, which carry some of the **Figuras de Destaque** ("prominent figures"), amongst them the **Porta-Bandeira** ("flag bearer") – a woman who carries the school's symbol, a potentially big point scorer. The **Mestre-Sala** is the dance master, also an important symbolic figure, whose ability to sustain the rhythm of his dancers is of paramount importance.

The **Comissão da Frente**, traditionally a school's "board of directors", marches at the head of the procession, a role often filled these days by invited TV stars or sports teams. The bulk of the procession behind is formed by the **alas**, the wings or blocks consisting of hundreds of costumed individuals each linked to a part of the school's theme.

Traditionally, every school has in addition to parade an **Ala das Baianas** – hundreds of women dressed in the flowing white costumes typical of Salvador – in remembrance of the debt owed to the Bahian emigrants, who introduced many of the traditions of the Rio Carnival procession.

The **parade** of schools starts at 7.30pm, with eight schools parading on each of the two nights, and goes on to noon the following day. Two stands (7 & 9) in the Sambódromo are reserved for foreign visitors and **seats** cost about $75–85 per night. Though much more expensive than other areas, they are more comfortable and have good catering facilities. Other sections of the Sambódromo cost from $5 to $20 and the seating options are: the high stands (*arquibancadas*), lower stands (*geral*) and the ringside seats (*cadeiras de pista*; $16) – these last the best, consisting of a table, four chairs and full bar service.

Unless you have a very tough backside you will find sitting through a ten-hour show to be an intolerable test of endurance. Most people don't turn up until 11pm, by which time the show is well underway and hotting up considerably. **Tickets** are available from *Turisrio*, Rua da Assembléia 10 (☎297-7117), or through the *Banco do Brasil*, with offices in most major capital cities. Tickets should be booked well in advance, so contact the Brazilian Embassy in the UK for details (See *Basics*).

All phone numbers in Rio are prefixed ☎021.

Listings

Airlines *Aerolineas Argentinas*, Rua S. José 40a, Centro (☎224-9242); *Aeroperu*, Praça Mahatma Gandhi 2, Centro (☎240-1622); *Air Canada*, Avenida Mal. Câmara 160, Centro (☎220-9888); *Air France*, Avenida Rio Branco 257a, Centro (☎220-8661/3666); *American Airlines*, Rua da Assembléia 10, Centro (☎221-9455); *British Airways*, Avenida Rio Branco 108, Centro (☎242-6020); *KLM*, Avenida Rio Branco 311, Centro (☎210-1342); *Mexicana*, Rua Uruguaiana 10, Centro (☎221-7373); *Pan Am*, Avenida Pres. Wilson 165, Centro (☎240-6662); *TAP*, Avenida Rio Branco 311, Centro (☎210-2414) and Avenida Princ. Isabel, Copacabana (☎275-3744); *Transbrasil*, Avenida Atlântica 1998, Copacabana (☎236-7475) and Avenida Calógeras 30, Centro (☎297-4442); *Varig-Cruzeiro*, Avenida Rio Branco 128, Centro (☎222-2535), Rua Rodolfo Dantas 16, Copacabana (☎541-6343) and Rua Visc. de Pirajá 351, Ipanema (☎287-9440/9040).

Airports *Galeão* international airport is situated on the Ilha do Governador, 14km north of Centro. For general enquiries ☎398-5050; international flights ☎398-4133; domestic flights ☎398-6060. Domestic flights use sector A, international sectors B and C. *Santos Dumont*, for shuttle flights to São Paulo, is at Praça Senador Salgado Filho at the north end of the Parque do Flamengo. ☎262-6311 for general enquiries, ☎262-6212 for flight information, and ☎220-7728 for reservations. There is a direct bus link between the two airports.

Banks Banks are listed in the Yellow Pages (*Lista Telefonica Classificada*) under *Bancos*: main branches are concentrated on Avenida Rio Branco in Centro, and Avenida N.S. de Copacabana in Copacabana. Foreign banks in Rio include: *Chase Manhattan*, Rua Ouvidor 98, Centro (☎216-6112)); *Citibank*, Rua da Assembléia 100, Centro (☎276-3636); *Lloyds*, Rua da Alfândega 33, Centro (☎211-2332); *Royal Bank of Canada*, Rua Ouvidor 90, Centro (☎231-2145); *Standard Chartered*, Avenida Rio Branco 110, Centro (☎222-5090).

Books For English-language books, branches of *Unilivros* are all over Rio, including ones at the Largo do Machado (Flamengo), Avenida Ataúlfo de Paiva 686 (Leblon) and Rua Visconde de Pirajá 207 (Ipanema). Branches, too, of *Siciliano* at Avenida Rio Branco 158 (Centro), Avenida N.S. de Copacabana 830 (Copacabana) and Rua Visconde de Pirajá 511 (Ipanema).

Buses The main inter-city and state bus station is the *Novo Rio Rodoviária*, at Avenida Francisco Bicalho 1 in São Cristovão (☎291-5151). A more central terminal, the *Menezes Cortes Rodoviária* in Rua São José (☎224-7577), has departures to the suburbs and Zona Sul, as well as to some in-state destinations such as Petrópolis and Teresópolis.

Car rental *Arcos*, Avenida Mem de Sá 49, Lapa (☎224-9120); *Avis*, Avenida Princ. Isabel 150, Copacabana (☎542-4249); *Budget*, Avenida Princ. Isabel 350, Copacabana (☎275-3244); *Hertz*, Avenida Princ. Isabel 334, Copacabana (☎275-3245); *Interlocadora*, Avenida Princ. Isabel 186, Copacabana (☎275-6546); *Localiza*, Avenida Princ. Isabel 214, Copacabana (☎275-3340); *Nobre*, Avenida Princ. Isabel 150 (☎541-4646) and Rua da Passagem 29/47, Botafogo (☎295-9547). Prices start at about $20 per day (the Brazilian companies are often cheapest); you'll need an International Driving Licence.

Chemist 24-hour service from *Farmácia do Leme*, Avenida Prado Junior 237, Leme (☎275-3847); and *Farmácia Piauí*, Avenida Ataulfo de Paiva 1283, Ipanema (☎274-7322).

Consulates *Australia*, Rua Voluntários da Pátria 45, Botafogo (5th floor; ☎286-7922); *Canada*, Rua Dom Gerardo 35, Centro (3rd floor; ☎233-9286); *Denmark*, Praia do Flamengo 284/101, Flamengo (☎552-6149); *Eire*, Rua Fonseca Teles 18, São Cristovão (☎248-0215); *France*, Avenida Pres. Antônio Carlos 58, Centro (☎220-4529 or ☎210-1272); *Netherlands*, Avenida Sorocaba 570, Botafogo (☎246-4050); *Sweden*, Praia do Flamengo 344, Flamengo (9th floor; ☎552-2422); *UK*, Praia do Flamengo 284, Flamengo (2nd floor; ☎552-1422); *USA*,

Avenida Presidente Wilson 147, Centro (☎292-7117); *West Germany*, Rua Pres. Carlos de Campos 417, Laranjeiras (☎285-2333).

Dentists Hellishly expensive in Brazil, but if the pain is too great to bear try one of the following clinics: *Assistência Dentária*, Avenida das Américas 2300, Barra de Tijuca (☎399-1603); *Dentário Rollin*, Rua Cupertinho Durão 81, Leblon (☎259-2647); *Clínica de Urgência*, Rua Marquês de Abrantes 27, Botafogo (☎226-0083).

Exchange You can get *turismo* rates for your dollars at the 24-hour bank at the airport on arrival: avoid the blandishments of the porters, whose rates are lower. In Rio itself, the *Banco do Brasil* and international banks have *câmbio* sections but you can do better (for cash only) at a *casa de câmbio*. These pay full *paralelo* rates: they are clustered on Avenida Rio Branco in Centro.

Ferries and hydrofoils The *Companhia de Navegação do Estado de Rio de Janeiro* (*CONERJ*; ☎231-0388) runs regular ferries from Praça XV de Novembro to the Ilha de Paquetá (Mon–Sat 5.30am–11.30pm, Sun 7am–11pm, hourly; Estação 1) and Niterói (24-hour service Mon–Sat 5am–11pm every 15min, Sun & Mon–Sat 11pm–5am every 30min; Estações 2 & 3). *TRANSTUR* (☎231-0339) runs hydrofoils from Praça XV de Novembro to Paquetá (Jan–April & July Mon–Sat 7am–5pm, Sun 8am–5pm, hourly; rest of the year hourly 2–6pm) and to Niterói (constantly 6.15am–8.15pm).

Festivals and events February (Carnaval); March (Brazilian Grand Prix); May (International Festival of Dance, Grande Prêmio Jóquei Clube Brasileiro, Festa de São Pedro and maritime procession in Guanabara Bay); August (Brazilian Sweepstake, Rio Cine Festival, Rio Marathon and Free Jazz Festival); November (FestRio international festival of cinema, TV and video); December (Festival de Iemanjá).

Health matters Best bet for any problems is the *Rio Health Collective*, which has an information and referral system for physical and mental health problems. A non-profit making organisation, its phone-in service is free, and provides names of qualified professionals who speak foreign languages; ☎325-9300 ext. 44. There's an office, open during normal business hours, in the *Banco Nacional* building, next to the *Barra Shopping*, Avenida das Américas 4430 (room 303), Barra de Tijuca. Or your consulate should have a list of professionals who speak an appropriate language. If you speak Portuguese, call *Golden Cross* – the national health insurance service – which operates a 24-hour referral service in Rio; ☎286-0044; outside Rio ☎021/800-3070.

Laundry *Laundromat*, Avenida N.S. de Copacabana, 1226, Copacabana; and Rua Marquês de Abrantes 82, Flamengo. Large hotels have a laundry service, too.

Maps Most kiosks (*bancas*) sell reasonable maps of Rio. *Guia Quatro Rodas* do a good one.

Markets Ad hoc markets are advertised in the *Jornal do Brasil*. And see the *Guide* for details of weekly and permanent markets throughout the city.

Medical emergencies English-speakers should try a private clinic: *Sorocaba Clinic*, Rua Sorocaba 464, Botafogo (☎286-0022); *Centro Médico Ipanema*, Rua Anibal Mendonça 135, Ipanema (☎239-4647). Normally, they'll send an ambulance, but if they haven't got one, phone *Clinic Saviour* (☎227-5099/6187) or *Pullman* (☎236-1011 & ☎257-4132).

Newspapers There are several 24-hour kiosks where foreign-language newspapers are available, including ones on Rua Lauro Muller (Botafogo), at junctions along Avenida N.S. de Copacabana (Copacabana), and on Rua Visc. de Pirajá/Praça Gen. Osório (Ipanema); kiosks, too, along Avenida Rio Branco in Centro. English-language newspapers published in Brazil are the *Brazil Herald* and the *Latin American Daily Post*.

Police Emergency number ☎190. The beach areas have Police Posts located at regular intervals, and there are police stations at Rua Hilário de Gouveia 102, Copacabana (☎257-1121); Rua Bambina 140, Botafogo (☎226-0227); Rua Humberto de Campos 315, Leblon (☎239-6049); Rua Maj. Rubens Vaz 170, Gávea (☎279-5096); Praça Mauá 5, Centro (☎263-6080); and Praça da República 24, Centro (☎242-5518).

Post Office Post offices (*correios*) are open Mon–Fri 8am–6pm, Sat 8am–noon. There's a *Central de Informações* at Avenida Presidente Vargas 3077, Centro (☎293-0159). Main post offices are at Rua Primeiro do Março (corner of Rosario) in Centro; Avenida N.S. de Copacabana 540 in Copacabana; Rua Visconde de Piraja 452, Ipanema; Avenida Ataúlfo de Paiva 822, Leblon.

Public holidays Most places will close on the following days: Jan 1; Jan 20 (Dia de São Sebastião); Carnaval; Ash Wednesday; March 1 (Founding of the City); Good Friday; April 21 (Remembrance of Tiradentes); May 1 (Labour Day); June 2 (Corpus Christi); Sept 7 (Independence Day); Oct 12 (Nossa Senhora Aparecida); Nov 2 (Finados); Nov 15 (Proclamation of the Republic); Dec 25.

Records Records are a good bit cheaper in Rio than in Europe. Try *Bilboard*, with branches in Copacabana (Rua Barata Ribeiro 502) and Ipanema (Rua Visconde de Pirajá 602), and *Gabriela* with several branches including one in the *RioSul* shopping centre and another at Avenida Ataúlfo de Paiva 467, Leblon. If you want to experiment with Brazilian music, ask one of the attendants for a selection to listen to. For secondhand records, go to *Toc Discos*, Rua Uruguaiana 18 and Rua Sete Setembro 139, both branches in the Centro. Buying tapes, the more expensive the recording, the more likely it is to last.

Shopping Purpose-built shopping centres – *Shoppings* – have mushroomed over Rio during the last decade. The best known and most central of them is *RioSul*, before the Pasmado Tunnel at the end of Botafogo. Apart from branches of department stores, like *C&A*, there are also supermarkets, fashion boutiques, record stores and lots of places to grab a snack; air-conditioned, too, which is a blessing. Others are at Gávea (Rua Marquês de São Vicente) and Leblon (Avenida Ataúlfo de Paiva), the latter specialising in those little items of interior decoration that turn a house into a gold-plated bordello.

Trains Daily departures for São Paulo and Belo Horizonte from Estação Ferroviária Dom Pedro II, Praça Cristiano Ottoni in Centro (☎233-3277).

Women's Groups *Associação Brasileira de Mulheres Universitárias* (University Women's Group), Praça Mahatma Gandhi 2 (☎220-6085); *Faculty of Women's Studies* (Catholic University), Rua Mqe. de São Vicente 225, Gávea (☎274-9922 ext 288); *Black Women's Collective*, Avenida Mem de Sá 208 (2nd floor; ☎252-7459); *Rio Women's Collective* (☎259-9226 & ☎266-7459). Also, *Delegacias da Mulher*, women's police stations, are being established in various locations – Avenida Pres. Vargas 1248 (5th floor) is the first fully operational one.

RIO DE JANEIRO STATE

It's easy to get out of Rio city, something you'll probably want to do at some stage during your stay. There's a good bus service to all the places mentioned below, while the easiest trips are by ferry to the **Ilha de Paquetá** or **Niterói**, just over the bay. After that, the choice is a simple one: either head east along the **Costa do Sol** to Cabo Frio and Búzios, or west along the **Costa Verde** to Ilha Grande and Parati; both coasts offer endless good beaches and little holiday towns, developed to varying degrees. Or strike off **inland** to Petrópolis and Teresópolis, where the mountainous interior provides a welcome, cool relief from the frenetic goings-on back in Rio.

If you fancy **hiring a car**, this is as good a state as any to brave the traffic: the coasts are an easy drive from the city and stopping off at more remote beaches is easy; while your own wheels would let you get to grips with the extraordinary scenery up in the mountains. There are a number of **bus** companies, each one serving a different region – *1001* deals with routes north along the Costa do Sol to Búzios and beyond; *Eval* runs along the Costa Verde and down to Parati; *Fácil* and *Única* go up into the mountains to Petrópolis and its environs; while *Cidade do Aço* carts its passengers to the steel town of Volta Redonda.

Ilha de Paquetá

The **ILHA DE PAQUETÁ** is a large island to the north of Guanabara Bay, an easy day trip that is very popular with cariocas at weekends. It was first occupied by the Portuguese in 1565, and later was a favourite resort of Dom João VI, who had the São Roque chapel built here in 1810. During the naval revolt of 1893 against the government of Floriano Peixoto, the island was the insurgents' principal base: their HQ, the Chácara dos Coqueiros, still stands, though it's not open to the public. Nowadays, however, the island is almost entirely given over to tourism. About 2000 people live here, but at weekends that number is multiplied several times by visitors from the city. They come for the tranquillity – the only motor vehicle is an ambulance – and for the beaches, which sadly are now heavily polluted. Still, it makes a pleasant day's excursion – with colonial-style buildings that retain a certain shabby charm – and the trip is an attraction in itself: if possible time your return to catch the sunset over the city as you sail back. Weekdays are best if you want to avoid the crowds, or in August come for the wildly celebrated **Festival de São Roque**.

The way to get around is by **bike**, thousands of which are available for hire very cheaply; you can also take a ride in a small horse-drawn cart (*charrete*) or hire one by the hour (about $2.50) if you want to take your time and stop off along the way. Not that there's a great deal to see. When you disembark, head along the road past the Yacht Club and you'll soon reach the first **beaches** – Praia da Ribeira and Praia dos Frades. **Praia da Guarda**, a few hundred metres on, has the added attraction of the *Lido* restaurant and the **Parque Duque de Mattos**, with exuberant vegetation and panoramic views from the top of the Morro da Cruz, a hill riddled with tunnels dug to extract china clay.

Boats (see "Listings" for schedules) take around an hour and cost about ten cents; the hydrofoil is twice as quick and ten times as expensive.

East: Niterói and the Costa do Sol

Across the strait at the mouth of Guanabara Bay lies **Niterói**, founded in 1573 and until 1975 the capital of the old state of Guanabara. Though lacking the splendour of the city of Rio, Niterói, with a population of half a million, has a busy commercial centre and lively nightlife – well worth a visit, certainly, as it's the gateway to the **Costa do Sol** to the east.

Niterói

You reach **NITERÓI** either by car or **bus** across the fourteen kilometres of the **Ponte Costa e Silva**, the Rio–Niterói bridge (bus #999 from the Menezes Cortes bus terminal); or, much more fun, by catching the extremely cheap **ferry**, every twenty minutes from the *Conerj* docks, close to Praça XV de Novembro. **Hydrofoils** leave from the same dock every few minutes, too. On arrival, pick up a map of Niterói at the **tourist office** (daily 9am–6pm) in the ferry terminal.

An historic city in its own right, Niterói has a couple of buildings worth seeing if you have time. The church of **São Francisco Xavier**, built in 1572, is near the São Francisco beach; that of **Nossa Senhora da Boa Viagem** (1663) on the Ilha da Boa Viagem, connected to the mainland by a causeway leading from Icaraí beach. A short distance along the coast, through JURUBA, the **Fortaleza de Santa Cruz** dates from the sixteenth century. It's still in use as a military establishment, but you can visit daily between 9am and 4pm. Check out the archaeology museum as well if you have time, the **Museu de Arqueologia de Itaipú**, in the ruined Santa Maria convent near Itaipú beach. Around here, to the east of Niterói, there are loads of **restaurants, bars and hotels**, all of which fill up with cariocas at weekends.

Along the Costa do Sol: lakes and beaches

Buses out of Niterói head east along the **Costa do Sol**, which is dominated by three large **lakes** – Maricá, Saquerema and Araruama, separated from the ocean by long, narrow stretches of white sandy beach – and flecked with small towns bearing the same names as the lakes. Approximately 10km directly south of Niterói are a number of smaller lakes, too, collectively known as the **Lagos Fluminenses**, though these aren't really worth the effort to get to as the water is polluted. However, the evil-smelling sludge which surrounds them is purported to have medicinal properties. The main lakes are also muddy, but at least the water here is clean and much used for watersports of all kinds. The brush around the lakes is full of wildlife (none of it particularly ferocious), while the fresh, salty air makes a pleasing change from the city streets.

Maricá and Saquerema

MARICÁ, 40km from Niterói, is the first stop, standing on the north bank of the lagoon, its peaceful waters only narrowly separated from the ocean surf by the **Barra de Maricá** and **Ponta Negra** beaches. From Ponta Negra the view of the coast is breathtaking, while the atmosphere here is more laid-back than in Rio de Janeiro's Zona Sul. Nearby, in **UBATIBA**, the colonial farm of Rio Fundo has been turned into a museum exhibiting relics from the centuries of slavery.

SAQUEREMA, 100km to the east of Rio, is a larger town in a beautiful natural setting, squeezed between the sea and its sixteen-kilometre-long lagoon, retaining vestiges of its origins as a fishing village. Local anti-pollution legislation means that the environment still sustains much wildlife, including the *micro-leão* monkey which you may be able to glimpse on a walk into the nearby forests. Saquerema has a healthy agricultural sector, too, based on fruit cultivation, and orchards surround the town. The main business nowadays, though, is holidaymaking: you'll find holiday homes, art and craft shops and young *brasileiros* with surfboards here in abundance. The **Praia de Itaúna**, 3km north of the town, is favourite with the surfers, who gather every year for the National Championship. A strong undertow makes its waters potentially dangerous for the casual breaststroker. If you want to swim without struggling against the currents head instead for the **Praia da Vila**, where a seventeenth-century church stands on the rocky promontory. For fishing, the **Praia de Jaconé** is a popular haunt, stretching 4km west of Saquerema.

All in all, if you're looking for a place to stop awhile, there's a lot to recommend Saquerema; a relaxed atmosphere, plenty of bars and restaurants, and lots of action at the weekend. Places **to stay** near the centre of town include the inexpensive *Sol e Mar*, and the *Caxanga* which has a pool and costs about $8 for a single room.

Araruama and around

Fourteen kilometres further along the coast, **ARARUAMA** stands at the western end of one of the largest lakes in Brazil. The lake – of the same name as the town – covers an area of 192 square kilometres, its highly saline water fringed with white sand that is purported to be effective in treating rheumatic and dermatological illnesses. The water is clean and the white, sandy banks shine as bright as snow under the tropical sun.

The town itself has started to sprawl a bit as holiday homes, campsites and hotels have been built to accommodate the growing numbers of cariocas who come here at the weekend. Nonetheless it's still relatively small-scale and there's no shortage of unpolluted beaches within walking distance – bathed most evenings in the warm glow of sunsets so beautiful that they evoke tranquillity in the breasts of even the most boisterous of weekenders. While there are **beaches** all round the town, the most popular ones are located some distance away – **Praia Seca**, the nearest of these, is some sixteen kilometres away, part of the much larger **Maçambaba** beach, which continues all the way to Arraial do Cabo (see below). The road between Araruama and Cabo Frio passes alongside these beaches; there's an occasional bus or you can take a taxi, though either way it can be hard to get transport back.

Accommodation choices in Araruama include the beachside *Hotel Senzala*, 10km from the centre in the district of Iguabinha (☎24-2230), and the *Parque Hotel Aruarema* (☎65-2129), nearer the centre at Rua Argentina 502, with rooms starting at about $12 a night. The *Hotel Carrateiro*, on the outskirts of town on the intersection of Rua Dom Pedro I and Rua Martin Alfonso, is your cheapest bet – $2.50 single and $4 double.

Around Araruama is one of Brazil's most important **salt producing** regions, and the windmills that pull the saline solution up to the surface dominate the skyline. The saltpans into which the solution emerges are of various sizes, but are always square and arranged juxtaposed like a great patchwork quilt, speckled with small piles of salt brushed into heaps from the surface of the pans. At the north end of Araruama lake, the small town of **SÃO PEDRO DA ALDEIA**, a 22-kilometre bus ride east of Araruama on the way to Cabo Frio, is built around a Jesuit church which dates back to 1617. Perched on a hill above the shores of the lake, the town provides a marvellous view over the saltpans and surrounding area.

To Cabo Frio

Instead of reaching Araruama along the coast there's a **direct bus** from Rio's *Rodoviária*, useful if your final destination is either Cabo Frio or Búzios (see below). Buses leave every hour and tickets are from the *1001* bus company at their office in the *Rodoviária*.

The route leaves Niterói by the BR-101, heading inland towards SÃO GONÇALO, then takes the BR-104 to ITABORAÍ, turning towards the coast again at Rio Bonito. After Itaboraí, the bus enters a wide valley, ringed by mountains rising either side in the distance. At **RIO BONITO**, the road rises into a tumbling mountain range, whose fertile, verdant slopes and valleys are taken up by **coffee** plantations; everywhere, thousands of coffee bushes stand in neat, well-tended rows. Once through the mountains, you descend to the sea, with the corrupt odour of the saltworks assaulting your nose as you speed between the saltpans into Araruama and on to Cabo Frio.

During the summer months, and especially at weekends, **CABO FRIO** is at a pitch of holiday excitement, generated by the out-of-towners who come here to relax in the fresh sea breezes. The town was founded in 1815, but it's only really in the twentieth century that it's developed, thanks to the salt and tourist industries. Cabo Frio is built around sand dunes and there are **beaches** everywhere: indeed, this is the only attraction, since the town is neither attractive nor well planned, but it is a relaxed place and the bars are full of happy holidaymakers at night.

The closest beach to town is the popular **Praia do Forte**, near the centre, with its fort of **São Mateus** (Tues–Sun 10am–4pm) built by the French in 1616 for protection against pirates. The best beaches, though, all lie outside Cabo Frio, a taxi ride or decent walk away on the route to Arraial do Cabo, another small town a few kilometres to the south (see below). Six kilometres north in the direction of Búzios, near Ogivas, lies **Praia Pero**, a good surfing spot, peaceful and deserted on weekdays, and further on lies the particularly popular **Praia das Conchas**, with its clear blue waters.

Arriving, it's a three-kilometre walk in from the bus station to the centre, along Avenida Julia Kubitschek. There are lots of **hotels** and *pensões* in Cabo Frio. The *Malibu Palace* (☎43-3131) on the Praia do Forte is the most expensive, while the *Colonial*, near the centre, offers low-cost accommodation, and the *Pousada Portoveleiro* (☎43-3081), by the Canal da Ogiva, is a comfortable mid-range choice. Cheaper alternatives are located on Rua José Bonifácio.

Arraial do Cabo

Six kilometres south of Cabo Frio, **ARRAIAL DO CABO** nestles amongst more sand dunes, surrounded by hills. It's home to the Institute of Marine Research, based on Cabo Frio island (4km east of the town), whose object is to increase the level of marine life in the region. The aim is a laudable one, though it's uncertain whether the purpose is ecological or has to do with replenishing stocks for next season's marine sports. The **beaches** around Arraial do Cabo are good: the main ones – Grande, Prainha and Pontal – can be reached on foot, while Forno can only be reached by boat from the town. You might be interested, too, in the local lace-bone works, and the **Manoel Camargo Centre for Popular Arts**, on Avenida Liberdade, has an excellent collection of arts and crafts on display.

Búzios

Keep time free for **ARMAÇÃO DOS BÚZIOS**, or Búzios as it's more commonly known: direct buses run from Rio twice a day, or every half-hour from Cabo Frio. A place of great natural beauty, it's a bit like taking a step out of Brazil and into some high-spending Mediterranean resort: built in the Portuguese colonial style, its narrow cobbled streets are lined with restaurants, bars and chic boutiques where you can buy beach gear at extortionate prices. Búzios has been nicknamed "Brazil's St Tropez", and it comes as little surprise to find that it was "discovered" by none other than Brigitte Bardot, who stumbled upon it by accident while touring the area in 1964. Despite being transformed overnight from humble fishing village to playground of the rich, Búzios didn't change much until, during the last decade, some serious property development took hold. Now, during the high season, the population swells from eight to thirty-eight thousand, the fishing boats that once ferried the catch back to shore take pleasure-seekers island-hopping and scuba diving, and the roads connecting the town with the outlying beaches have been paved.

In walking distance of the centre are seventeen white-sand **beaches**, cradled between rocky cliffs and promontories, and bathed by crystal blue waters. It doesn't matter which you choose – Brava, Ossos, Ferradura, Geribá – as each is charming, the ocean offshore studded with little islands covered in luxuriant vegetation. The Brava, Ferradura and João Fernandes beaches all have *barracas*, which serve cold beer and fried fish. You can rent kayaks or pedalos, or indulge in a little windsurfing or diving. And in the evening, bars and restaurants fill up after 9pm and stay open till late, while the streets are the venue for some designer strolling – Ray Bans in hand and designer knitwear draped over shoulders.

Accommodation is pretty expensive and even in low season double rooms are $15–40. Some ideas are: *Bons Ventos* and *Aquarius* pousadas, which will do you a room for less than $20, although both get very busy at weekends between November and March; and *Pousada do Arco Íris* (☎23-1256), Rua Manoel Turibe de Farias 182, which charges $15 a double in low season ($25 high season).

Most restaurants serve tolerably priced **food**. *O Gostinho Natural* is one cheap place where the food is good; *Le Streghe* and *Au Cheval Blanc* are expensive restaurants with good reputations. For **drinks**, the beautiful people hang out at *Estalagem*, or at *Chez Mixou*, where the atmosphere is a tad less sophisticated. If you want to see the dawn come up, *cachaça* in hand, try *Marulle*.

Northeast to Campos

The next town of any size is **MACAÉ**, a substantial place on the edge of a large sugar cane producing region. Again you'll find excellent beaches here, but the city is more industrial than what has gone before, and the arrival of offshore oil drilling seems unlikely to increase its attractions. From here the main road heads northeast, inland around the Lagoa Feia, to **CAMPOS**, on the River Paraíba some fifty kilometres before it flows into the sea. Again it's predominantly a sugar cane producing town, and its primarily agro-industrial nature makes it a less than attractive target given the local alternatives.

If you're not yet tired of beaches, you'll find more beautiful examples on the coast downstream from Campos, around **BARRA DE SÃO JOÃO** and **RIO DAS OSTRAS**. Near the latter, the iodised waters of the **Lagoa da Coca Cola** (yes, really) boast more medicinal qualities – everyone must be very healthy in this neck of the woods. If you want to stay round here, you'll find nondescript *pensões* in most of these places, but no hotels.

West: the Costa Verde

The mountainous littoral and calm green waters of the aptly-named **Costa Verde** ("Green Coast") provide a marked contrast to the sand and surf of the coastline east of Rio. One of Brazil's truly beautiful landscapes, the Costa Verde has been made much more accessible by the new **Rio–Santos BR-101 Highway** – something, however, that has led to an increase in commercial penetration of this region. The fate of this 280-kilometre stretch of lush vegetation, rolling hills and tropical beaches hangs in the balance between rational development and ecological destruction, and so far the signs augur badly. Ecologists are already predicting that fish stocks in the Bay of Sepetiba, which covers almost half the length of the Costa Verde, will be destroyed within five years because of pollution. Enjoy your trip; you may be amongst the last to have the privilege.

There are two ways to reach the Costa Verde from Rio. By **car**, drive through the Zona Sul by way of Barra de Tijuca, to BARRA DE GUARATIBA. The road runs past kilometre after kilometre of white sand, but you'll need to be mobile to reach any of it. Alternatively, take the **bus** from Rio's *Rodoviária*, which leaves the city by the Zona Norte and follows the BR-101 to Itacuruçá.

To Itacuruçá and Mangaratiba

ITACURUÇÁ, around ninety kilometres from Rio, is a tranquil hamlet that attracts wealthy yachting types. The attraction here is obvious: the village nestles between rolling hills and a malachite-coloured sea, its offshore **islands** – Jaguanum and Itacaruçú, with their pleasant walks and beaches – easily reached by boat. Tours of the islands can be arranged with the **tourist office** at Praça da Igreja 130, in Itacuruçú, or are operated direct from Rio; ask at *Passamar Turismo*, Rua Siqueira Campos 7 (☎021/233-8835).

Both islands have **hotels**, though they are a bit pricey – *Hotel Pierre* (☎021-521-1546 for bookings) on Itacuruçú, and *Hotel Jaguanum* (☎021/235-2893; or enquire at *Sepetiba Turismo*, Avenida N.S. de Copacabana 605, Rio).

Mangaratiba

Muddy beaches and the incongruous industrial presence of the *Terminal de Sepetiba* put off many people from stopping at MANGARATIBA which lies 25km west of Itacuruçá along the BR-101. **Ferries** from here make the hour-and-forty-minute trip to Ilha Grande (daily at 9am & 2pm, a return ferry at 4pm; see below), and there are also some very good beaches within walking distance – Saco, Cação, São Bras, Ibicui and Praia Brava are the main ones. Anyone will tell you where to find them but on the whole the initial impression is the correct one; there are better spots further along the coast. Five **buses** a day run from Rio to Mangaratiba – currently at 6am, 9am, 12.30pm, 3pm and 7pm – and if you catch the earliest bus you'll make the morning ferry to Ilha Grande. If you do need to **stay** there are numerous *pensões*, easy enough to locate in a place of this size: none stand out.

Angra dos Reis

From Mangaratiba, the road continues to hug the coast as it wends its way westwards, rising and falling between towering, green-clad mountains and the ocean. Roughly sixty kilometres west of Mangaratiba lies ANGRA DOS REIS, a shabby little town at first sight, but nevertheless, one with a history. The lands around here were "discovered" by the navigator André Gonçalves in 1502, though it wasn't until 1556 that a colonial settlement was established. The port first developed as an entrepot for the exportation of agricultural produce from São Paulo and Minas Gerais. Fifteen slave-worked sugar refineries dominated the local economy which, with the abolition of slavery at the end of the nineteenth century, suffered a dramatic collapse. The 1930s saw the economy regenerated, with the construction of a new port, and shipbuilding remains an important local trade – although the latest venture is the work that's underway on Brazil's first nuclear power station, to be located nearby.

The main reason to come here is to get out to the thirty or so islands in the bay, but the town itself is worth a look on the way, and it's easy enough to tour on foot. There are guided tours (daily 10am–5pm) around the late-sixteenth-century church and convent of **Nossa Senhora do Carmo**, in Praça Gal. Osório, as well as around the later convent of **São Bernardino de Sena** (daily 8–11.30am & 1–5pm), on the Morro de Santo Antônio. Best use of time, though, is to take in the old **town hall** and jail, in Praça Nilo Peçanha, an interesting colonial building dating from the beginning of the seventeenth century and still in use today as the municipal seat of government. For all the historical interest, however, Angra dos Reis suffers from its rather unprepossessing aspect and in the end most people usually can't wait to get out.

Boat trips and beaches

Boat and fishing trips are Angra's stock in trade, and a tour of the local islands – Cataguazes, Pitanguí, Duas Botinas, Senhor do Bonfim, Gipóia and Do Maia (amongst others) – is an absorbing experience. Numerous leisurely cruises around the bay are on offer, and most yachts have a bar at which you can fill the time between stops for swimming at beaches penned in between clear waters and tropical forest. Visiting **Gipóia** by boat, for instance, allows you a couple of hours to splash about and get something to eat in the *Luiz Rosa* bar – all very relaxing.

Various companies run trips, so it's best to ask at the tourist information in Largo do Lapa, right across from the bus station and next to the **Cais de Santa Luzia**, from where the boats depart. Trips can also be arranged on the quay with independent operators, but check on the noticeboard for those boatowners who have been authorised to carry tourists. If you want an organised trip, try *Iate Delta*, Praça Lopes Trovão, or *Escuna Frademar*, in the foyer of the *Hotel do Frade*: most trips leave around 10am and return in the late afternoon. Prices with independent boat operators are negotiable but on average you'll pay around $4 a head.

Beaches in the town are nothing special. Better ones are found by following the Estrada do Contorno (by car), or catching a **bus** from the bus terminal (*Vila Velha* line; buses leave hourly) to the beaches of Bonfim, Gordas, Grande, Tanguá, Tanguazinho, Ribeira or Retiro. There are other beaches within reach, too: along the main BR-101 highway, in the direction of Rio, good spots for bathing and free camping are Garatucaia and Monsuaba.

Angra practicalities

Back in Angra dos Reis the bus terminal, tourist information and ferry dock are all located within a few steps of each other. There's no shortage of **hotels** if you're planning to stay around for the beaches and islands. Avoid the *Hotel Porto Rico*, which is dark, dirty and depressing and try instead the modest, but comfortable *Hotel Londres*, Avenida Raul Pompeia 75, in the centre (it's a good idea to make reservations while in Rio on ☎021/223-3252 ext 7). Alternatively, if you're feeling rich, there's the four-star *Hotel do Frade*, Praia do Frade (reservations in Rio on ☎021/267-7375).

There'll be no trouble **eating and drinking** either, with lots of restaurants and bars: try *Cheiro Verde*, Rua Pereira Peixoto 53, which has Arab cuisine.

The **ferry** from Angra dos Reis to Abraão on Ilha Grande leaves on Monday, Wednesday and Friday at 3.30pm, a ninety-minute trip (returning at 10.15am the following day). You can hire a fishing boat to make the same journey, but it will cost you about $25.

Ilha Grande

Ilha Grande comprises 193 square kilometres of mountainous jungle, historic ruins and beautiful beaches (amongst which Praia Lopes Mendes is outstanding) – excellent for some scenic, tropical rambling. The only real drawback is the ferocity of the local mosquitoes, so come equipped with repellent.

Islands like this deserve a good pirate story and Ilha Grande is no exception. According to legend, the pirate Jorge Grego was heading for the Straits of Magellan when his ship was sunk by a British fleet. He managed to escape with his two daughters to Ilha Grande, where he became a successful farmer and merchant. In a fit of jealousy he murdered the lover of one of his daughters and, shortly afterwards, a terrible storm destroyed all his farms and houses. From then on, Jorge Grego passed his time roaming the island, distraught, pausing only long enough to bury his treasure before his final demise. If there is any treasure, though, it's in the island's wildlife: parrots, exotic hummingbirds, butterflies and monkeys abound in the thick vegetation. To the west of the island there's an **ecological reserve** where it's all easily observed for free.

Around the island

As you approach the low-lying, whitewashed colonial port of **VILA DO ABRAÃO**, the mountains rise dramatically from the sea, and in the distance there's the curiously shaped summit of *Pico do Papagaio*. On the opposite side of the island from Vila Abraão are the ruins of the **Antigo Presídio**. Originally built as a hospital, it was converted to a prison for political prisoners in 1910 and was finally dynamited in the early 1960s. Among the ruins, you'll find the *cafofo*, the containment centre where prisoners who had failed in escape attempts were immersed in freezing water. Nearer to Vila do Abraão, and overgrown with vegetation, stands the **Antigo Aqueduto** which used to channel the island's water supply. There's a fine view of the aqueduct from the **Pedra Mirante**, a hill near the centre of the island, and, close by, a waterfall provides the opportunity for a cool bathe on a hot day. The island offers lots of beautiful walks, but it is large and the sun gets very hot: take a guide or a map if you can.

The **beaches** can be reached by either **hiring a boat** ($5–6 per hour) and circumnavigating the island's coast, or **on foot** across the many trails that network the interior. The hike from Abraão to Parnaioca (see below) will take about three hours, so it's no jaunt, and a guide would be a good idea for those with limited energy and a poor sense of direction – there are no official guides but local lads will usually oblige if you cough up the necessary recompense. For the most part the beaches – Canto, Júlia, Comprida, Crena or Morcegoare, to name a few – are still wild and unspoilt. By the **Praia da Parnaioca** is a ghost town, an old fishing village abandoned by its inhabitants because of their fear of escaped prisoners.

Accommodation and other practical details

Accommodation is mostly around Vila do Abraão, and when you arrive you'll probably be approached by youths intent on taking you to a room. One of the best places, though, is in Praia Grande (two hours' walk or twenty minutes' boat ride) on the trail to Praia Lopes Mendes: the *Hotel Fazenda Paraíso do Sol* (make reservations in Rio on ☎021/252-9158). Another good, inexpensive hotel is the *Mar da Tranquilidade* (reservations in Rio on ☎021/288-4162) in Vila do Abraão, for which you'll need to book ahead during the high season, November to March.

There are privately owned **campsites** around Abraão, too, like *Camping Gilson*, but they are not much cop and camping rough is prohibited by the police.

Nightlife lovers are reasonably well catered for by seafood restaurants and bars, while the *Calango da Jovina* bashes out some eminently danceable *forró* music. Locals say that **Carnaval** is well celebrated here, much more relaxed and less intense than the Rio experience; and watch, too, for the festival of São João (Jan 20) and the Pirate Regatta, which takes place some time in February.

You will notice that the **police** are thick on the ground when you arrive in Vila do Abraão. This is because there is still a small, high-security prison on the island, and prisoners sometimes escape and hide on the island until they can find a boat. It's not quite Devil's Island, but it might be as well to enquire if the Brazilian version of Jack the Ripper has legged it before you go swanning off across the island with your rucksack on your back.

The **return trip** to Angra dos Reis leaves daily (Mon–Sat) at 10.15am, and to Mangaratiba at 8.30am.

Parati

Back on the mainland, the road west rises amidst the most exhilarating scenery that the whole coast has to offer. About 300km from Rio on the BR-101 is the Costa Verde's main attraction, the town of **PARATI**. Inhabited since 1650, Parati has remained fundamentally unaltered since its heyday as a staging post for the eighteenth-century trade in Brazilian gold, passing from Minas Gerais to Portugal. Before white settlement, the land had been occupied by the **Guaianá Indians**, and the gold routes followed the old Indian trails down to Parati and its sheltered harbour. Inland raids and pirate attacks necessitated the establishment of a new route linking Minas Gerais directly with Rio de Janeiro, and as trade was diverted to Rio the result was a decline in Parati's fortunes. Apart from a short-lived coffee-shipping boom in the nineteenth century, Parati remained hidden away off the beaten track, quietly stagnating but intact. Nowadays, though, *UNESCO* considers Parati to represent one of the world's most important examples of colonial architecture, and the entire city has been elevated to the status of a national monument.

Today, Parati is very much alive, with its population of 15,000 involved in fishing, farming and tourism. The town centre was one of Brazil's first planned urban projects, and its narrow cobbled streets, out of bounds to motorised transport, are bordered by houses built around courtyards, adorned with brightly coloured flowers and alive with hummingbirds. The cobblestones of the streets are arranged in channels to drain off storm water and allow the sea to enter and wash the streets at high tides and full moon. There's an air of prosperity in Parati, as there is in Búzios (see above), yet it has a much more democratic feel to it, and by and large provides a more satisfying experience than its chic counterpart on the Costa do Sol.

The **bus station** is about half a kilometre from the old town known officially as *Vila de Nossa Senhora dos Remédios de Paraty*; turn right out of the station and walk straight ahead. The best way to orientate yourself is to head for the **Antiga Cadeia**, the old jail, at the end of Rua Santa Rita, facing the sea. There's a shop selling local crafts and the **Secretaria de Turismo e Cultura** (daily 9am–6pm; ☎71-1256), which supplies literature in English, and a guidebook called *Paraty Para Você*, with a map of the town and details of the sights of historical interest. There is also a **tourist office** (daily 8am–10pm; ☎71-1186) on Avenida Roberto Silveira, the road in from the bus station, at the old town end.

Keeping yourself amused should be no problem, even if you quickly exhaust the possibilities of the town itself. From the **Praia do Pontal** on the other side of the Pereque-Açu River from the town, and from the **port quay**, *baleiras* and *saveiros* (whaling and fishing boats) leave for the excellent **beaches** of Paraty-Mirim, Jurumirim, Lula and Picinguaba. In fact, there are 65 islands and about 200 beaches to choose from, and anyone can tell you which are the current favourites. The **Boa Vista distillery** is worth a visit, too (boats from the quay). Home of the famous *Quero Esse* brand of *cachaça*, the old colonial house here was once the residence of Thomas Mann's grandfather, Johan Ludwig Brown, before he returned to Germany in around 1850. The caretaker, and master distiller, will give guided tours of the *alambique* before plying you with a liquor that has distinctly invigorating properties.

Around Parati

Another good way to see a bit of the landscape is to catch a bus from the bus station, headed for CUNHA, and get off after about 8km at the **Cachoeira das Penhas**; a waterfall up in the mountains that offers a chance to bake on the sun-scorched rocks of the river gully and then cool off in the river. From here you can descend from rock to rock for a few hundred metres before scrambling up to the road above you, which you follow for 2km, crossing a small bridge into **PONTE BRANCA**. At the end of the village, overlooking the river, is a restaurant, the *Ponte Branca*, where you can take a break and have a cold beer. The walk from the waterfall takes you amongst the hills, up and down dale, and past tropical fruit plantations, all very pleasant. You'll probably manage to get a lift back to Parati from the restaurant when you're sufficiently refreshed.

Parati: some details

You might well have been offered **accommodation** by people waiting at the bus station, but it's easy to track down yourself: the standard is high, and not particularly expensive. Most of the best **pousadas** are in the old Portuguese colonial centre, five minutes' walk from the bus station, and often young lads will guide you to the ones with vacancies. Once again, though, remember that between November and March this entire area is packed and hotel space becomes hard to find. The *Pousada Fortaleza* (☎71-1338), Rua Abel de Oliveira 31, has double rooms starting at $11, and the *Hotel Estalagem* (☎71-1626), Rua Mal Santos Dias 9, charges $6 per person. *Coixo* (☎71-1370), Rua Tenente Francisco Antônio 74, is very pleasant with a garden setting at $18 for a double, and *Hotel Porto Rio*, Rua Coronel Carvalho, is cheap and excellent (but not very well marked). More upmarket is the *Pousada do Ouro* (☎71-1311), Rua da Praia 145, which costs from $35 for a double. There's a **campsite** on the way into town, and another on the Praia do Pontal, on the other side of the Pereque-açu river from the town centre.

The town has plenty of good **restaurants**, too, charging an average of $3 for a meal – the *Galeria de Engenho*, Rua de Commercio 40, is recommended, as is the *Vagalume*, Rua Comadore José Luis 5. Fresh fish, fruit and vegetables can be bought daily on the pier from where the boats leave. There's **live music** at the *Art Café*, and plenty of other watering holes to keep you amused into the evening.

In May, June and July **festivals** celebrating local holidays are frequent occasions, and in the square the folk dances – *Cerandis*, *Congadas* and *Xibas* – demonstrate the European and African influence on Brazilian culture.

Inland: North to the Mountains

Excellent bus services from Rio de Janeiro make the **interior** of the state easily accessible, and its mountainous wooded landscape and relatively cool climate are a pleasant contrast to the coastal heat. There's not a great deal in the way of historical interest, but the scenic beauty of the countryside, studded by small towns still bearing their colonial heritage, is an attraction in itself.

Northwest to the River Paraíba: Volta Redonda, Itatiaia and around

From Rio, the *Cidade do Aço* bus company takes you along the BR-116 to **VOLTA REDONDA** and the heartland of Brazil's steel industry. Situated on the banks of the **River Paraíba**, the city is dominated by steel mills, and though it may once have been a picturesque little village, it's now an expanding industrial monster.

If you want to visit the **steel mill**, you can – but you need to arrange the guided tour about a week in advance, either with the headquarters of the *Companhia Siderúrgica Nacional* (Avenida XIII de Maio, Rio de Janeiro), or locally at the *Hotel Bela Vista*. Tour buses leave from Rio and travel direct to the mills; the journey takes about three hours and the price is negligible. Although your visit probably won't be as momentous, mine coincided with the city's invasion by a division of the Brazilian army, sent to quell a steel workers' strike. Tanks and assorted military personnel patrolled the streets and confronted 23,000 foundry workers whose wages had been hopelessly eroded by Brazil's hyperinflation. In the ensuing conflict between military, police and strikers, which lasted for days, three workers were killed and large numbers seriously injured.

Volta Redonda, in fact, serves as a textbook example of the (often disastrous) way that Brazil is developing, economically and socially. To all intents and purposes, the city has been a company town since 1941 and the urban structure represents the priorities of the company – slums for the poor and nice neighbourhoods for the management sprawl on opposite sides of the river, the water so polluted by industrial and domestic effluence that its plant and animal life has been almost completely destroyed. Apart from industrial conflict and pollution, according to a report in the *Jornal do Brazil* the citizens of Volta Redonda also have to cope with the highest incidence of arterial hypertension and deaths caused through cardiovascular disease in the country. All this in what four decades ago must have been one of the healthiest climates in Brazil.

If you're not remotely interested in steel production then don't waste your time in Volta Redonda, but press on along the BR-116 Highway the forty kilometres to Itatiaia park.

Itatiaia park

Nestling in the northwest corner of the state, 165km from Rio, between the borders with São Paulo and Minas Gerais, the **National Park of Itatiaia** is the oldest in Brazil, founded in 1937 and covering 120 square kilometres of the Mantigueira mountain range. People come here to climb – favourites are the **Pico das Agulhas Negras** (2787m) and the **Pico de Prateleira** (2540m), and the park is also an important nature reserve.

The town of **ITATIAIA**, on the BR-116, is surrounded by beautiful scenery and makes a good base: it has plenty of hotels, mainly found along Via Dutra and the road to the park, which is within walking distance. There's also **cabin** accommodation in the park, but it has to be booked about two weeks in advance at the *Administração do Parque Nacional de Itatiaia* in Itatiaia town. You can get **information** and maps at the park office located near the entrance; and before you come it's worth contacting the *Clube Excursionista Brasileira*, Avenida Almirante Barroso 2, in Rio (8th floor; ☎021-220-3695). The other possible base for the park is the small town of **PENEDO**, which was settled in the 1930s by Finnish immigrants. It's popular with weekenders from São Paulo and Rio, who come for the horseriding, and to buy the various jams, preserves and local liquors which are produced in the town.

Itatiaia park is a nature reserve comprising waterfalls, primary forest, wildlife and orchids – which makes it all the more depressing to have to report that a fire in September 1988 ravaged some twenty percent of the park's area. In the area affected by the fire, forest and pasture land were devastated, rare orchids and native conifers (*Podocarpus lamperti* and *Araucaria angustifolia*) destroyed; the fire reached areas of the Serra da Mantiqueira, 2500m above sea level, wiping out forty kilometres of mountain pathways. In the areas most favoured by biologists, who come to study the rich fauna and flora, the once beautiful alpine scenery now resembles a lunar landscape. Also severely affected were the many natural springs and streams which combine to form the Bonito, Preto, Pirapitinga and Palmital rivers: these supply the massive hydrographic basin of the Paraíba plate, giving much needed oxygenation to the Paraíba watercourse in one of its most polluted stretches. Ecologists reckon that it will take more than twenty years to repair this environmental disaster. For the casual walker, however, there's still plenty of unaffected park to be seen.

Vassouras, Valença and Conservatória

Northeast of Volta Redonda are a few other small towns which make good targets if you have a car and a few spare days. All are picked out by their colonial architecture and attractive natural settings.

The BR-393 leads to **VASSOURAS** and **VALENÇA**, both university towns, and both considered as national historical monuments, whose essentially agricultural economies produce cattle and coffee. Around Vassouras particularly, there are a number of **colonial farmhouses** worth seeing: *Fazenda Santa Eufrásia* and *Fazenda Dom Carlos* are within walking distance (4km) from the town, and the *Chácara da Hera* (Tues–Sun 1–4pm) has a small museum dealing with local history. The problem with **accommodation** hereabouts is that it is rather pricey. The *Mara Palace* in Vassouras (Rua Chanceler Raul Fernandes 121; ☎71-1993), for example, starts at around $18 for a good double room, the *Santa Amelia* (☎71-1346) is similarly priced. Both are easily located near the centre.

About thirty kilometres to the west of Valença on the BR-143, the little town of **CONSERVATÓRIA**, 518m above sea level, is much visited for its fresh climate. It's a very tranquil place, though perhaps a bit self-conscious of its status as a tourist attraction. There are four **hotels** in the town if you should wish to stay for a night – all much the same, starting at around $10 a single. At night, one or two of the local citizens indulge in a spot of public serenading, maintaining an old and nowadays rare tradition: the music combines well with the warm breezes, a pleasant background to an evening's relaxation. And not far from the town is the

Fazenda Santa Clara, considered a fine example of a colonial-style mansion house.

Petrópolis

Sixty-six kilometres directly to the north of Rio de Janeiro, high in the mountains, stands the Imperial city of **PETRÓPOLIS**. The route there is a busy one, with *Fácil* and *Única* company buses leaving Rio every fifteen minutes, but even so you may have to wait a day or two for a bus with available seats. It's worth the hassle, for the journey there is a glorious one. On the way up, sit on the left-hand side of the bus and don't be too concerned with the driver's obsession with over-taking heavy goods vehicles on blind corners, bordered by naked rock on one side, and a sheer drop on the other – it's a one-way road, and the return to Rio is made by a different route which also snakes its way through terrifying mountain passes. The scenery is dramatic, climbing among forested slopes which give way suddenly to ravines and gullies, while clouds shroud the surrounding mountains.

In 1720, Bernardo Soares de Proença opened a trade route between Rio and Minas Gerais, and in return was conceded the area around the present site of Petrópolis as a royal land grant. Surrounded by stunning scenery, and with a gentle, alpine summer climate, it had by the nineteenth century become a favour-ite retreat of Rio's elite. The arrival of German immigrants contributed towards the development of Petrópolis as a town, and has much to do with the curious European Gothic feel to the place. Dom Pedro II took a fancy to Petrópolis and in 1843 designated it the summer seat of his government. He also initiated an agri-cultural colony, which failed because of the unsuitability of the soil, and then in 1849 – with an epidemic of yellow fever in Rio – the emperor and his court took refuge in the town, thus assuring Petrópolis' prosperity.

You can easily do a tour of Petrópolis in a day, returning to Rio in the evening (or heading inland somewhere else – see below). Simply strolling around is as good a way to pass the time as any, with plenty of interest in the buildings, like the mansions that border **Avenida Koeller**, which has a tree-lined canal running up its centre. The **Museu Imperial** on Avenida VII de Setembro (Tues–Sun noon–5.30pm) is another fine structure, set in beautifully maintained gardens. Once a royal residence, it now houses a fascinating collection of the royal family's bits and bobs. On entry, you're given felt overshoes with which to slide around the polished floors and inside there's everything from Dom Pedro II's crown (639 diamonds, 77 pearls; all set in finely wrought gold) to the regal commode. The Cathedral of **São Pedro de Alcântara** in town blends in with the rest of the architecture around, but is much more recent than its rather overbearing Neo-Gothic style suggests – it was only finished in 1939. Inside, on the walls, are ten relief sculptures depicting scenes from the Crucifixion; while in the mausoleum lie the tombs of Dom Pedro himself, Princess Regent Dona Isabel and several other royal personages. If you need more direction to your strolling, then other grand buildings to track down are the **Palácio de Cristal**, Rua Alfredo Pacha (daily 8am–6pm); **Casa Santos Dumont** on Rua do Encanto, an alpine chalet built in 1918 (Tues–Sun 9am–5pm); and **Quitandinha** on the Estrada de Quitandinha, just outside of town. Once the *Quitandinha Casino*, this last build-ing stopped receiving the rich and famous when the Brazilian government prohib-ited gambling in 1946, and today serves as a sports club.

Some practicalities

If you want to stay put for a while, Petrópolis has some decent **hotels**, plenty of restaurants, and easy access to some lovely climbing country. The *Hotel Dom Pedro*, Praça Dom Pedro 26 (☎43-7170) is reasonably priced, from $6 a single, and the *Casablanca Center Hotel*, Rua General Osório 28 (☎42-2612) is cheap and reliable, too. Also cheap and clean is the *Hotel Comércio* (☎42-3500), Rua Dr. Porciúncula 56, in front of the bus station – around $3.50 a single.

For information there's a *Petrotur* **tourist office** at Rua Barão do Amazonas 98 – at the opposite end of the main Avenida do Imperador from the bus station; turn right up Rua João Pessoa and left at Praça Rui Barboso. Most of the **restaurants** are found along this route as well. If you're going to do any **hiking** around Petrópolis, contact the *Centro Alpinista*, Rua Irmãos d'Angelo 28: it's an amateur association, so go after 8pm.

When it's time to **move on**, bear in mind that you'll want to undertake the journey to Teresópolis (below) during the day, so as not to miss the scenery.

Teresópolis

While **TERESÓPOLIS** can be reached directly from Rio by bus, the best route is from Petrópolis. It's not a long journey, no more than forty kilometres, but the road to this highest town in the state (872m) passes through the **Serra dos Órgãos**, much of which is a national park – dramatic rock formations here resemble rows of organ pipes (hence the range's name), dominated by the towering **Dedo de Deus** ("God's Finger") peak. Teresópolis, like Petrópolis, owed its initial development to the opening of a road between Minas Gerais and Rio during the eighteenth century. It, too, was a favoured summer retreat (for the Empress Teresa Christine, for whom the town was named) and though smaller than Petrópolis it also shares some of its Germanic characteristics, including a benevolent alpine climate. The town itself is not wildly exciting, built along one main street which changes its name every couple of blocks, and the real interest lies in the surrounding countryside. There are, however, magnificent views from almost anywhere in town – especially from **Soberbo**, where the Rio highway enters Teresópolis, with its panoramic view of Rio and the Baixada Fluminense.

Around Teresópolis

There's plenty to do in the surrounding countryside, so get your walking boots on. Lakes (the Iaci lake) and waterfalls – the **Cascata dos Amores** and the **Cascata do Imbuí** – provide good swimming; there's the **Mulher de Pedra** rock formation; and interest, too, in the birdlife around the **Granja Comary** (on the BR-495), and in the **Von Martinó** natural history museum.

The main attraction, though, is the **National Park of the Serra dos Órgãos**, where favourite peaks for those with mountain goat tendencies are the Agulha do Diabo (2050m) and the Pedra do Sino (2263m): the latter has a path leading to the summit, a relatively easy three-hour trip (take refreshments). The highest local peak is the **Pedra Açu**, but at 2400m and with no apparent path to the top, you may end up doing what I did – go for a beer instead. It costs about fifty cents to enter the park and the State Forestry Institute rents out basic **accommodation** for climbers in hostels that cost about $5 for full board. There are some campsites, too, but equipment is not for hire, so you'll need to come prepared.

For more **information** about all these places, visit either the tourist office (Mon–Fri 1–5pm) on Avenida Lúcio Meira, or the office in the bus station (daily 8am–11pm). **Guidebooks and trail maps** can be purchased in front of the Igreja Matriz at the *Cupelo Banco de Jornais* – maps are a must because, while there are walks all over the place, they are not signposted. In the national park, you'll also be able to hire guides inexpensively.

Some practicalities

Teresópolis doesn't have many **hotels**. The best of them is the rather pricey *São Moritz* chalet, on the Nova Friburgo road: slightly cheaper alternatives are the *Philips*, Rua Duval Fonseca, and (at $15 a single) the *Hotel Center* (☎742-5890), Rua Sebastião Teixeira 245; while inexpensive choices are the *Várzea Palace*, (Rua Sebastião Teixeira 41), which is a beautiful white building that offers amazing value starting at $4 a double, and *Flórida*, Avenida Lúcio Meira 467. There is also a **youth hostel** at Rua Farjadi 171.

In January, Teresópolis hosts the **Curso Internacional PRO-ARTE**, with live classical music performances (information from the tourist office).

Nova Friburgo

NOVA FRIBURGO, to the northeast of Teresópolis, was founded by a hundred Swiss immigrant families from the canton of Friburg, transferred to the region by royal decree in 1818, and whose only other activity of note was that they introduced the first sauna into Brazil. The Germanic influence remains, principally in the architecture of the **Conego** area of this attractive town of 90,000 people, which lies in a valley surrounded by mountains. During the summer, Nova Friburgo's many hotels and campsites are brimming with city folk who come to enjoy the waterfalls and wooded trails or take on the local peaks – like **Caledonia**, a favourite with hang-gliders. Less of a hike, the dramatic rock formations of the **Furnos da Catete** forestry reserve on the road to BOM JARDIM (23km north on the BR-492) offer an excellent walk; and for an easy view of the world a cable car (9am–5.30pm) from Praça dos Suspiros in town takes you up to the summit of **Morro da Cruz**, some 1800m up.

You could easily stay awhile in this peaceful town and there are a number of good **hotels**. Some, like *Buksky* (☎22-5052), 4km along the Niterói road and $30 a double, lie a short distance outside of town; nearer the centre is the *Hotel São Paulo*, Rua Monsenhor Miranda 41. Cheap options include *Hotel Montanus* (☎22-1235), Rua Fernando Bizotto 26, at $6 a double, or the similarly priced *Hotel Fabris* (☎22-2852), Avenida Alberto Braune 148 (the same street as the bus station).

For **eating**, try the *Oberland* delicatessen on Rua Fernando Bizotto, which doubles as a restaurant with good, cheap Swiss and German food – veal sausage, sauerkraut and the like. The *Churrascaria Majórica*, Praça Getúlio Vargas 74, is good, too. And in the same square you can buy homemade preserves and liqueurs.

To reach Nova Friburgo from Rio takes about three hours by bus (departures from *Novo Rio Rodoviária* every half-hour). You'll head across the Rio–Niterói bridge, and out on Highways 101, 104 and 116. It's also possible to get a bus from Teresópolis.

travel details

Buses

Frequent departures from *Novo Rio Rodoviária* to all parts of Brazil. Main **out-of-state** destinations include: São Paulo (3 daily; 6hr); Brasília (2; 18hr); Belo Horizonte (3; 7hr); Vitória (1; 9hr); Salvador (2; 27hr); Recife (2; 38hr); Fortaleza (1; 43hr); São Luis (1; 50hr); Belém (1; 52hr); Campo Grande (1; 21hr); Ouro Preto (1; 8hr).

International departures daily to Buenos Aires (50hr), Asunción (30hr), Montevideo (37hr) and Santiago (70hr).

Main **in-state** services include Petrópolis (half hourly; 90min); Teresópolis (half hourly; 2hr); Angra dos Reis (hourly; 2hr 30min); Paratí (5; 4hr 30min); Cabo Frio (5; 2hr 30min); Búzios (2; 4hr).

Trains

Departures from Dom Pedro II Ferroviária to **São Paulo** (daily 11pm sleeper; 9hr) and **Belo Horizonte** (Fri, Sat & Sun 9pm; 11hr).

Planes

Frequent **domestic** flights from Sector A of Galeão airport on Ilha do Governador to all state capitals and other internal destinations. **Rio–São Paulo** shuttle from Santos Dumont, downtown, half hourly from 6.30am to 10.30pm (55min).

MINAS GERAIS AND ESPIRITO SANTO

The French geologist Gorceix summed up **Minas Gerais** 150 years ago, when he wrote that the state had "a breast of iron and a heart of gold". Its hills and mountains contain the richest mineral deposits in Brazil, and led to the area being christened "General Mines" when gold and diamonds were found at the end of the seventeenth century. The gold strikes sparked a

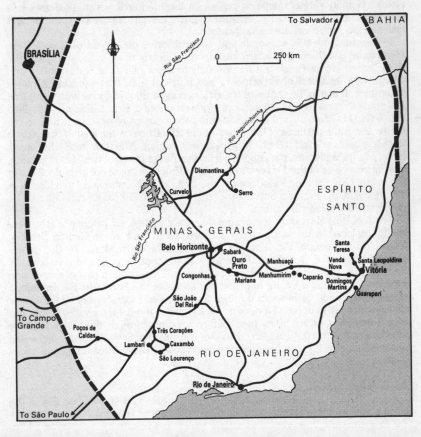

wave of migration from Rio and São Paulo, which lasted a century and shifted the centre of gravity of Brazil's economy and population from the northeast decisively to the south, where it has remained ever since. In the nineteenth century new metals, especially iron, steel and manganese, replaced gold in importance, while the uplands in the west and east proved ideal for coffee production. Land too steep for coffee bushes was converted to cattle pasture, and the luxuriant forests of southern Minas were destroyed and turned into charcoal for smelting. The bare hills are a foretaste of what parts of Amazonia might look like a century from now and only their strange beauty – sea-like, as waves of them recede into the distance – saves them from seeming desolate. Mineral wealth still flows from Minas' hills, but iron, bauxite, manganese and steel have superseded the precious metals of colonial times.

In more recent times, too, Minas Gerais has been at the centre of Brazilian history. *Mineiros* have a well deserved reputation for political cunning, and have produced the two greatest post-war Brazilian presidents: **Juscelino Kubitschek**, the builder of Brasília, and **Tancredo Neves**, midwife of the rebirth of Brazilian democracy in 1985. It was troops from Minas who put down the São Paulo revolt against Getúlio Vargas's populist regime in the brief civil war of 1932 and, less creditably, the army division in Minas which moved against Rio in 1964 and ensured the success of the military coup.

In keeping with this economic and political force, the capital of Minas, **Belo Horizonte**, is a thriving, modern metropolis of nearly three million people – the third largest city in Brazil and second only to São Paulo as an industrial centre, which, with its forest of skyscrapers and miles of industrial suburbs, it rather resembles. It lies in the centre of the rich mining and agricultural hinterland that has made the state one of the economic powerhouses of Brazil. This area is called the *Triângulo Mineiro*, and runs from the coffee estates of western Minas to the mines and cattle pastures of the valley of the **Rio Doce**, in the east of the state; a thickly populated and relatively prosperous region. You can read the area's history in its landscape, the jagged horizons a direct result of decades of mining. The largest cities of the *Triângulo* apart from Belo Horizonte are **Juiz de Fora** in the south, **Governador Valadares** to the east, and **Uberaba** and **Uberlândia** in the west – all modern and unprepossessing; only Belo Horizonte can honestly be recommended as worth visiting.

North of Belo Horizonte, the grassy slopes and occasional patches of forest are swiftly replaced by the stubby trees and savanna of the Planalto Central (leading to Brasília and central Brazil proper); and in northeastern Minas, by the cactus, rock and perennial drought of the *sertão* – as desperately poor and economically backward as anywhere in the Northeast proper. The northern part of the state is physically dominated by the hills and highlands of the **Serra do Espinhaço**, a range which runs north–south through the state like a massive dorsal fin, before petering out south of Belo Horizonte. To its west is the flat river valley of the **Rio São Francisco**, which rises here before winding through the interior of the Northeast. And to the east, the **Rio Jequitinhonha** flows through the *sertão mineiro* – life in the parched landscapes of northeastern Minas depends on its waters.

As Cidades Históricas

Despite the cities, all *mineiros* would agree that the soul of the state lies in the rural areas, in the hill and mountain villages of its vast **interior**. The eighteenth-century mining settlements, in particular, are now quiet and beautiful colonial towns, with a fraction of the population they had 200 years ago. They're called *as cidades históricas*, "the historic cities", and are the only colonial survivals in southern Brazil that stand comparison with the Northeast. Most importantly, they're the repository of a great flowering of Baroque **religious art** that took place here in the eighteenth century: *arte sacra mineira* was the finest work of its time in the Americas, and Minas Gerais can lay claim to undisputably the greatest figure in Brazilian cultural history – the mulatto leper sculptor, **Aleijadinho**, whose magnificent work is scattered throughout the historic cities. The most important of the *cidades históricas* are **Ouro Preto**, **Mariana** and **Sabará**, all within easy striking distance of Belo Horizonte, and **Congonhas**, **São João del Rey**, **Tiradentes** and **Diamantina**, a little further afield.

In the southwest of Minas, in fine mountainous scenery near the border with São Paulo, are a number of **spa towns** built around mineral water springs: **São Lourenço**, **Caxambú** and **Lambarí** are small and quiet, but **Poços de Caldas** is a large and very lively resort. Perhaps the most scenically attractive part of Minas Gerais – certainly the least visited – is the **eastern** border with Espírito Santo. There's some spectacular walking country in the **Caparaó** national park, where the highest mountain in southern Brazil, the 3000-meter high **Pico da Bandeira** is more easily climbed than its height suggests.

Espírito Santo

Espírito Santo, the small coastal state that separates eastern Minas from the Atlantic, is the kind of place that you rarely hear about, even within Brazil. It's completely off the tourist map. This is hard to understand, as the interior has some claim to being the most beautiful part of Brazil. Settled mostly by Italians and Germans, it has a disconcertingly European feel – Jersey cows graze in front of German-looking ranches, and if it weren't for the heat and the hummingbirds darting around, you might imagine yourself somewhere in Switzerland. Vast numbers of *mineiros* head for Espírito Santo for their holidays, but are only interested in the beaches, the one thing landlocked Minas lacks. This has the fortunate effect of cramming all the crowds into an easily avoidable coastal strip, leaving the interior free for you to explore.

The only place of any size is **Vitória**, a rather grimy city saved by a fine location, on an island surrounded by hills and granite outcrops. It was one of the few spots on the coast that could be easily defended, and the **Botocudo Indians** were able to restrict the Portuguese to scattered coastal settlements until the last century. This is one of the reasons the interior is relatively thinly settled: the other is the sheer difficulty of communications in the steep, thickly forested hills that rear up into mountains along the border with Minas. The semi-deciduous tropical forest that once carpeted much of the southern coast of Brazil still survives relatively unscathed here – and is what southern Minas would have looked like before the gold rushes. To a degree, the forest resembles Amazonian jungle but if you look closely during winter you'll see that many of the trees have shed their leaves. The best way to view the region is to make the round of the towns which began as German and Italian colonies: **Santa Teresa**, **Santa Leopoldina**, **Campinho** and **Venda Nova** – the last near the remarkable sheer granite face of **Pedra Azul**, one of the least known but most spectacular sights in the country.

COMIDA MINEIRA

Minas Gerais' delicious **regional food**, *comida mineira*, is one of Brazil's most distinctive; based mainly on pork, the imaginative use of vegetables, *couve*, a green vegetable similar to spinach, and the famous *tutú*, a thick bean sauce made by grinding uncooked beans with manioc flour and cooking the mixture. Many of the dishes originate from the early mule trains and *bandeirante* expeditions of the eighteenth century, when food had to keep for long periods (hence the use of salted pork, now replaced by fresh) and be easily prepared without elaborate ingredients.

Comida mineira is not difficult to find: in fact, outside Belo Horizonte it is rare to find restaurants that serve anything else. It's said that it is only in the interior that you can find authentic *comida mineira*, but this is quite untrue, provided you know where to look in Belo Horizonte (see p.000). There are also small shops everywhere serving Minas Gerais' *doces* – cakes and sweetmeats. Among the **typical dishes** are:

Tutú a mineira Most typical of all dishes, found on every menu; roasted pork served with lashings of *tutú*, garnished with steamed *couve* and *torresmo* (an excellent salted pork crackling).

Feijão tropeiro ("Mule driver's beans") A close relative to *tutú a mineira*, with a name that betrays its eighteenth-century origins; it features everything in a *tutú* but also has beans fried with *farinha*, (manioc flour) and egg, often with onion, thrown into the mix.

Frango com quiabo Chicken roasted with okra and served sizzling with a side-plate of *anjú*, a corn porridge that *mineiros* eat with almost anything.

Carne picadinha A straightforward, rich stew of either beef or pork, cooked for hours until tender.

Costelinha Stewed ribs of ham.

Dobradinha Tripe stew cooked with sweet potatoes. The stews (including the two above) often include the excellent Minas sausages, smoked and peppery.

Doce de leite A rich caramel sludge.

Brigadeiro The ultimate in chocolate snacks, so rich it should come with a health warning.

BELO HORIZONTE

The best way to approach **BELO HORIZONTE** is from the south, over the magnificent hills of the Serra do Espinhaço, on a road that winds back and forth before finally cresting a ridge where the entire city is set out before you. It's a spectacular sight: Belo Horizonte sprawls in an enormous bowl surrounded by hills, a sea of skyscrapers, *favelas* and industrial suburbs. From the centre, the jagged rust-coloured skyline of the Serra do Espinhaço which gave the city its name, is always visible on the horizon – still being transformed by the mines gnawing away at the "breast of iron".

Despite its size and importance, Belo Horizonte is less than a century old. It was the first of Brazil's planned cities, laid out in the 1890s on the site of the poor village of Curral d'El Rey, of which nothing remains. As late as 1945 it had only 100,000 inhabitants: now it has almost thirty times that number, an explosive rate of growth even by Latin American standards. It rapidly became the most important pole of economic development in the country, after São Paulo, thanks to the wealth of the *Triângulo Mineiro* and the energy of its inhabitants. And while it may not be as historic as the rest of the state – only a few public buildings survive from its early days – it's difficult not to be impressed by the city's scale and energy. Moreover, its central location and proximity to some of the most important *cidades históricas* (Sabará is only just outside the city, Ouro Preto and Mariana less than two hours away by road) make it a good base.

Orientation and arrival

The **central zone** of Belo Horizonte consists of the large area within the inner ring road, **Contorno**; the centre is laid out in a diamond-shaped grid pattern that makes it easy to find your way around. The spine of the city is the broad **Avenida Afonso Pena** and the *Rodoviária* is in the heart of the downtown area, on the corner of Afonso Pena and Contorno. Accommodation of all standards is nearby. A good landmark is the obelisk in the **Praça Sete**, just up from the *Rodoviária*, the middle of the hotel and financial district and the city's busiest part; while a few blocks further up Afonso Pena are the trees and shade of the **Parque Municipal**. A short city bus ride south is the chic area of **Savassí**, with its nightlife, boutiques and art cinemas, and the **Praça da Liberdade**, Belo Horizonte's main square – dominated by a double row of Imperial palms and important public buildings.

The two places **outside the centre** you're most likely to visit are the artificial lake and Niemeyer buildings of **Pampulha**, to the north, and the rambling nature reserve of **Mangabeiras**, on the southern boundary of the city.

Points of arrival

Belo Horizonte has two **airports**: *Pampulha*, eight kilometres from the centre, now only takes short-haul flights and you're more likely to arrive at the new *Aeroporto Tancredo Neves*, over thirty kilometres away, but linked by frequent buses that leave you either at the *Rodoviária* or at the tourist centre, *Terminal Turístico JK* (see below). The latter is further from the main hotel area than the *Rodoviária*. **Buses to the airport** leave every half-hour from both the *Rodoviária* and the *Terminal Turístico*: make sure you know which airport you are leaving from; if it's *Tancredo Neves*, allow at least an hour for the journey. You can shorten your journey by about twenty minutes if you take the air-conditioned airport coaches (*executivos*), though these run only from the *Terminal Turístico*: they cost $2, as opposed to fifty cents for the *convencional* bus.

The tropical Edwardian **train station**, the finest building in the city, is on Praça Rui Barbosa, very near the **Rodoviária**. There are two trains weekly to Rio and one interminably slow, but fascinating, link to the badlands of northern Minas, heading first to Montes Claros and then Monte Azul, deep in the *sertão mineiro* on the border with Bahia (see "Listings" for details).

Information and getting around

The municipal *BELOTUR* organisation are very knowledgeable about the city and the rest of the state. Their **tourist offices** are open office hours – you'll find them at both airports, at the *Rodoviária* and in a booth on Praça Sete. If you arrive at the **Terminal Turístico** in Praça Olegário Maciel, take advantage of the *TURMINAS* (Minas state) information post, which hands out free brochures with a perfectly serviceable map of the central zone. They can also help with planning routes for journeys in the interior.

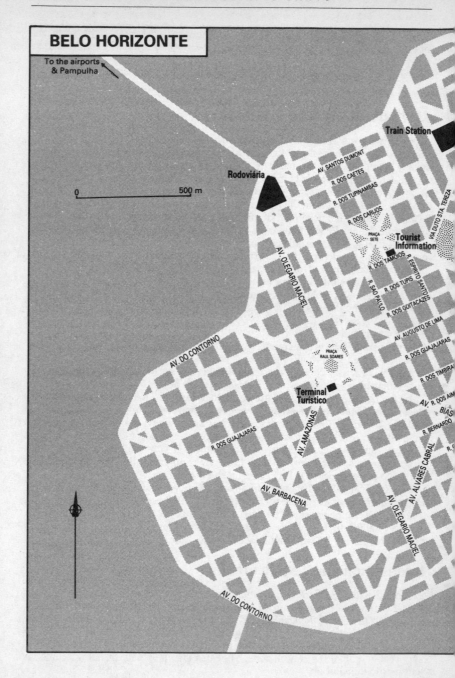

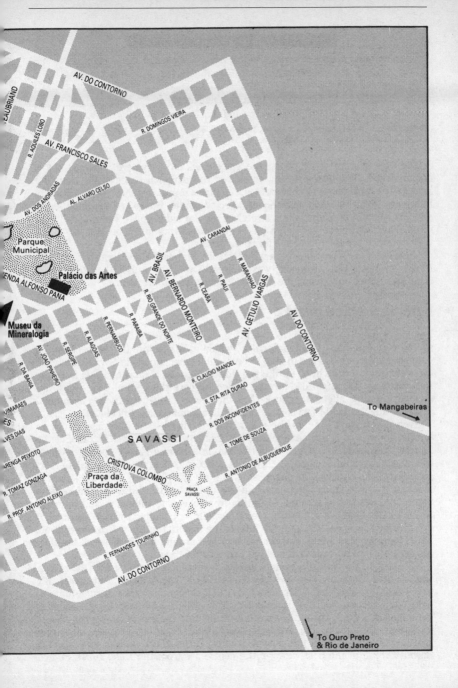

USEFUL BUS ROUTES

Yellow SCO2: from the *Rodoviária* to Praça Sete and Savassí, via Liberdade.
Blue 1202: from Avenida Afonso Pena, down the tree-lined Avenida Amazonas and out to *Pampulha* airport.
Blue 2003: from Avenida Afonso Pena to Liberdade.
Blue 3002: from the Parque Municipal to Praça Sete and the *Rodoviária*.
Blue 6001: from the Parque Municipal to Savassí.

The **bus system** works along the same lines as elsewhere in Brazil but is colour coded: blue buses run up and down the diagonal roads of the diamond grid, yellow buses have circular routes, red buses only serve the centre and white buses are "express", stopping only at selected points. Buses are also numbered, and virtually all routes include a stretch along Avenida Afonso Pena, usually the most convenient place to catch a bus if you are staying in the centre. Buses are very frequent; see the box above for route details.

Otherwise, **taxis** are cheap, even by Brazilian standards, and there's a new city **Metro system**. This, however, was built with workers rather than tourists in mind and serves only to link the industrial suburbs with the centre.

Finding a place to stay

You don't need to stray far from the centre for **accommodation**. There are scores of hotels, most fairly reasonable, within easy reach of the *Rodoviária*: the only alternative options are to stay in one of the smart hotels in Savassí (only for the well-heeled), or to head for the two **youth hostels**, a short taxi ride from the *Rodoviária* in the *bairro* of Floresta, which borders the central zone. Both are popular, so ring ahead to check that they have space: *Albergue Pousadinha Mineira*, Rua Araxá 514 (☎442-2049) and at Rua Januária 206 (☎444-8205).

Even if you can't get into the youth hostels, there is no shortage of **cheap hotels** downtown. Very inexpensive, but a little grimy, is *Hotel Macedo*, at the bottom of Avenida Amazonas. Better is the *Sul America Palace* opposite, where rooms start at around $8 and the friendly staff come free: the only problem is its popularity, which means the cheapest rooms are often booked up at weekends. A block up towards Praça Sete, turn right for the *Hotel BH Centro*, at Rua Espírito Santo 284, which has a range of rooms from cheap to middling, and is clean. Around here, there's a whole string of other hotels, including the *São Salvador* at no. 227, the *Lux* at no. 220 and, the best of the bunch, the *Hotel Magalhães* at no. 237. There are also lots of *dormitórios* bunched around the *Rodoviária*, but they are insecure and the area is a red-light district after dark.

The best of the **middle range hotels** is undoubtedly the *Hotel Amazonas*, almost next door to the *Sul America Palace*, at Avenida Amazonas 121 (☎201-4644): rooms start at around $15, the inclusive breakfast is something to write home about, and the German-Brazilian owners and staff are an island of Teutonic efficiency – try and get a room facing onto the street for a great view of the palms that make the Avenida spectacular. A little cheaper, with front apartments looking onto the railway station, is the *Hotel Itatiaia* at Praça Rui Barbosa 187. But the best views of the centre are from the *Hotel Brasil Palace*,

Rua Carijós 269 (overlooking Praça Sete), a fine 1940s building that still looks like the cinema it once was. Cheaper, but still central, are the *Hotel Gontijo*, Rua Tupinambas 731, and *Hotel São Domingos*, Rua São Paulo 566. The *Hotel Cecília* at Rua Carijós 454 used to be one of the nicest and most reasonably priced central hotels, but has now been taken over by the *Estoril* next door and become much more expensive.

Around the City

Even the most patriotic *mineiro* would make few claims for the **architecture** of Belo Horizonte. Old buildings are thin on the ground (some of the oldest, the 1930s concrete churches particularly, are positively hideous anyway) and there is little you could call beautiful. All the same, if you stand in the heart of the city, in **Praça Sete**, and look around you, it's hard to call it ugly: Avenida Afonso Pena is broad enough not to be dwarfed even by the huge skyscrapers that line it, the pavements are thronged with people, and the graceful lines of palms add a touch of elegance to Avenida Amazonas, stretching away downhill.

Something is always happening in the Praça. It's the traditional destination of demonstrations – visitors in August 1989 were driven from their hotel balconies by teargas, as police laid into protesting students – and the venue of street draughts tournaments, when rows of hustlers set up boards on the pavement and play all comers for money. Life in the Praça never stops. The bars and *lanchonetes* stay open until midnight, even later at weekends, and when the rest of the city has gone home to sleep, the square is the base for scores of homeless people, huddling around fires on deserted pavements, in front of the plush skyscrapers of international banks.

A stroll in the Parque

A few minutes' walk up **Avenida Afonso Pena** from Praça Sete brings you to the only relief from the traffic and noise that you'll find downtown: the green and shade of the **Parque Municipal**. Other than this park, if you want greenery in Belo Horizonte, you have to leave the city boundaries at Mangabeiras (see below) or be content with views of distant hills. Beautifully laid out, the park encompasses a boating lake, two thousand species of tree, shaded walks much patronised by courting couples, aviaries, a permanent fairground and exercise yards where Brazilian men make their sweaty sacrifices to the national cult of the body beautiful. It also contains the main **arts complex** in the city, the Palácio das Artes.

The Palácio das Artes
The **Palácio das Artes** is one of the few really fine buildings in the city, very modern, and well laid out inside. There are a number of **galleries** with exhibitions concentrating on modern art, a couple of small **theatres** and one big one, the **Grande Teatro**, on which no expense has been spared, and where the big names in Brazilian music play when they come to town.

Though it's hard to believe in such a large city, the Palácio is also the only place in Belo Horizonte where you'll come across a good display of the distinctive *artesanato* of the state, in the **Centro de Artesanato Mineiro***. A large shop rather than a gallery proper, it's nevertheless a place you can wander around and look without being pressured to buy. Although there's a lot of dross here, there is also some excellent pottery – stubby figurines and realistic clay tableaux. Distinctive though it is, you wouldn't be wrong in thinking that the best work looked Northeastern: it comes from the valley of the Rio Jequitinhonha, in the *sertão mineiro*, and contains elements of both traditions. There are also some good textiles. Cotton grows in northern Minas, and the roughly woven hammocks, clothes, wall hangings and even rugs are of a high quality, although the best work – the striking collage wall hangings, for example – is too bulky to be transported easily. Despite the sleek surroundings, the prices here are reasonable; not more than twice what you'd pay where the work comes from.

Museums: minerals and the city

Minas Gerais has some of the best museums in Brazil: the problem is that none of them are in Belo Horizonte. There's a sample, nothing more, of the tradition of religious art in Minas at the **Museu Mineiro** (Tues–Fri 12.30–6.30pm, Sat & Sun 10am–4pm), near the Parque Municipal at Avenida João Pinheiro 342.

More interesting – certainly wackier – is the **Museu de Mineralogia** (Mon–Sat 8.30am–5.30pm), three blocks down towards the Parque at Rua da Bahia 1149. Although it tries hard to be a fusty old museum, consisting solely of every mineral substance from amethyst to zirconite, displayed in glass cases, it's enjoyable despite itself. Partly this is due to the building, a bizarre, concrete Gothic monstrosity painted a bilious yellow, but some of the exhibits are actually fairly interesting, too. There is something elemental about precious stones and metals, and they are here in abundance, mostly on the top floor, all diligently labelled with their point of origin. There is gold – powdered and nuggets – and diamonds; cut glass replicas of the world's largest, but genuine Minas diamonds, too, (marked *cascalho diamantífero*), presented as they look scooped out of river beds, which is more like gravel than jewels. And there are precious and semiprecious stones by the score – topaz, malachite, aquamarine, emeralds, sapphires, huge chunks of rock crystal and bits of meteor.

The Museu Histórico Abílio Barreto

For the best museum in the city, you need to take the #2902 bus (marked *São Cristovão/Santo Antônio via Lourdes*); the most convenient stop is along Avenida Afonso Pena, between Rua Espírito Santo and Rua Tupis. Ask the conductor for the *Museu Histórico* and you'll be dropped on Contorno, a block away, from where there are signs to the **Museu Histórico Abílio Barreto** on Rua Bernardo Mascarenhas (Wed–Mon 10am–5pm). The area is called Cidade Jardim, and is rapidly becoming one of the most fashionable, upper class parts of the city, with new skyscrapers sprouting like weeds. It's an ironic location for the oldest building in the city, the only one that predates 1893 when construction of the new capital began.

---

*A *Museu de Folclore* is marked on most city maps, on Rua Felipe dos Santos near Savassí, but it was demolished in 1989 and replaced by an office block. The fine collection will most likely gather dust for years until a new home is found for it. That it was, by some way, the most interesting museum in the city doesn't seem to have been a factor.

The museum looks exactly like what it once was – a *fazenda* (estate house) built in 1883, comfortable but not luxurious, and typical of the ranches of rural Minas. It has been perfectly preserved and, though now swamped by the burgeoning city, it once stood on its own, a couple of miles away from the church and hovels of the hamlet of Curral d'El Rey, which straggled along what is now the stretch of Avenida Afonso Pena opposite the Parque Municipal. The most interesting part of the museum is the **photograph gallery**, juxtaposing the sleepy village before it was obliterated – mules, mud huts and oxcarts – with views of the modern city through the decades; there are a couple of well designed maps to help you get your bearings. The last remnant of Curral d'El Rey, the eighteenth-century Igreja Matriz, was flattened in 1932: these photographs, and carved bits of the church piled in a shed in the garden, are all that remain of the vanished community.

Equally remarkable are the series of photographs that record the building of Belo Horizonte and its early years: a trashed building site becomes the Parque Municipal, the railway station stands in glorious isolation (it's now dwarfed by the surrounding buildings); and the Praça Sete is shown as it was in the 1930s, ringed by trees and fine Art Deco buildings, of which only the *Cine Brasil* (now the *Hotel Brasil Palace*, see "Finding a place to stay", above) – is still standing. Like Rio, urban architecture in Belo Horizonte was at its peak in the 1930s and 1940s, when the city was an elegant, political capital, rather than an economic centre, and it has suffered since at the hands of the developers. A classic demonstration of this is the wonderful Art Deco market building, the *Feira de Amostras Permanentes*, which you can now only appreciate here in the museum. It was demolished in 1970 and replaced by the *Rodoviária*.

There are other things here, too, including the usual collection of old furniture and mediocre paintings, upstairs, and in the garden an old tram and turn-of-the-century train used in the construction of Belo Horizonte. But far better is the rustic wooden veranda at the front, where you can sit with your feet up and imagine yourself back in the 1880s, directing operations below.

Pampulha

Some distance north of the centre is the luxurious district of **PAMPULHA**, built around an artificial lake which is overlooked by the finest modern buildings in the city – the Museu de Arte, the modernist Igreja de São Francisco and the Casa do Baile. They are instantly recognisable as the work of architect **Oscar Niemeyer**, creator of Brasília, and landscape designer **Burle Marx**, both Communists and presumably horrified by the subsequent development of the area: it's become a rich residential district, where cars do not so much drive as swish and rich kids don't know where the bus stops are.

The construction of the **Igreja de São Francisco** (Mon–Fri 8am–1.30pm & 2–6pm), with its striking curves and *azulejo* frontage, provides a roll-call of the greatest names of Brazilian modernism: Burle Marx laid out its grounds, Niemeyer designed the church, Cândido Portinari did the tiles and murals and João Ceschiatti (best known for his gravity-defying angels in Brasília's cathedral) contributed the bronze baptismal font. It was decades ahead of its time and it's astonishing to realise that it dates from the 1940s. The best time to see it is on Sunday, when it's used for Mass at 10.30am and 6pm. To get there, take bus #2004 (marked *Bandeirantes/Olho d'Agua*) from Avenida Afonso Pena, between Rua Rio de Janeiro and Rua Tupinambas.

The **Museu de Arte** (daily 8am–6pm) is more difficult to reach: take the #2004 bus and get off on Avenida Portugal, shortly after Pampulha airport, when you see a sign for the Museu to the left – you then have to walk down to the lakeside Avenida Otacílio Negrão de Lima, turn right, and the museum is on a small peninsula jutting out into the lake. It's worth the trip, although the small collection of modern art it holds wouldn't be at all compelling if it weren't for the building and its setting. The building, however, is a product of two geniuses at the height of their powers. Niemeyer constructed a virtuoso building, all straight lines and right angles at the front but melting into rippling curves at the back, with a marvellous use of glass; check out the light inside the gallery. And Burle Marx set the whole thing off beautifully, with a sculpture garden out back and an exquisite garden framing the building in front.

Directly opposite, on the other side of the lake, the **Casa do Baile** is by the same duo. It's a great shame that these fine buildings are so under-used. The Casa do Baile, once a concert hall, is now closed completely, and only a fraction of the art museum is actually used – this doesn't include the main part of it, fenced off, empty and forlorn.

Soccer in Pampulha

Belo Horizonte's main football stadium, the **Mineirão**, is also in prestigious Pampulha – an instructive contrast with Britain, where old soccer stadiums are usually situated in run-down, industrial suburbs. With a capacity of 140,000, the *Mineirão* is a world class stadium, but it's rarely more than half-full, and usually much less. One of Brazil's better teams, *Atlético Mineiro*, play here and they're worth catching if you're in Belo Horizonte on a Sunday when they are playing at home. The #2004 bus passes by, but like all bus journeys to Pampulha, you should allow an hour to travel from the centre. Entrance costs around $1, $3 for the *arquibancada* (stands).

Mangabeiras: walks and views

Unlikely as it may seem amid the skysrapers of Avenida Afonso Pena, the city limits are only a short bus ride away to the south. Here, the urban sprawl is abruptly cut off by the steep hills of the **Serra do Curral**, a natural barrier that forces the city to expand in other directions. The views of the city from its slopes are spectacular, and it's also the site of of a huge 1500-acre nature reserve, the **Parque Florestal de Mangabeiras** (Tues–Sun 8am–6pm; 25c), where you can walk along forest paths that open out now and again to reveal the city below. To get there, catch the blue #2001-A or #2001-C bus, both marked *Aparecida*, from Avenida Afonso Pena between Avenida Amazonas and Rua Tamoios: it takes about fifteen minutes' hard climbing to arrive at the terminus above the park entrance.

The park is so big it has its own **internal bus service**; buses leave every thirty minutes from the left of the entrance, and end up there again after making a circuit of the park. It's worth taking the twenty-minute trip to appreciate the size of the place. Near the entrance is a well kept leisure area, with fountains, rows of *lanchonetes* and an open-air amphitheatre, the **Teatro de Arena**, where something often happens at weekends. The best view of the city is from the **Mirante da Mata** viewing platform, a twenty-minute walk from the entrance; while the finest walks are along the nature trails and streams of the **Parque Florestal**, a little further along. **Maps** of the park are available from the park office near the entrance.

Mirante da Cidade

The single most spectacular view of the city is from the **Mirante da Cidade**, outside the park, largely hidden by trees behind the palatial Governor's residence. Contrary to what the tourist brochures say, buses do not stop there: it's simplest to get a **taxi**, which will cost you $1–2 from the centre. The view is splendid. Too high up for the grime and *favelas* to register – although pollution can obscure things on a bad day – it makes Belo Horizonte seem like Los Angeles, an impression reinforced if you go by night, when the carpet of lights below really is magnificent. You can get back to the centre by bus easily enough if you walk down the steep Rua Bady Salum, turn right at the bottom onto Praça Israel Pinheiro (where, incidentally, the Pope celebrated Mass in 1982), and catch the #2001 from there.

Eating, drinking, nightlife and entertainment

Outside the immediate downtown area, **restaurants** tend to be upmarket and expensive: this is especially so in Savassí, where the bars are fine but the restaurants are mostly mediocre and vastly overpriced. If air conditioning and servile waiters are what you want, you'll find them in abundance in places along the lower reaches of Rua Alagoas and Rua Sergipe. People say that **nightlife** in Belo Horizonte is concentrated in Savassí, too, but this is a little misleading: chic nightlife certainly is, but there is no single area where all the entertainment is concentrated. Belo Horizonte boasts an excellent weekly **market**, too, where there's scope for all kinds of entertainment – from buying to drinking to watching the world go by.

Eating: snacks, street food and restaurants

The best area for **cheaper eating places** is downtown, around Praça Sete, where, often, sandwich bars and *lanchonetes* serve better food than many of the pricier restaurants in other parts of town. You can get a good meal for $2–3 (less for club sandwiches and hamburgers) at *Lanches Praça Sete*, on the corner of Avenida Amazonas and Praça Sete; at *Lanches Tuim* nearby, at Avenida Afonso Pena 723; and at *Café Nice* next door, whose excellent coffee also deserves a mention. *Acaiaca Lanches* has branches on the corner of Avenida Afonso Pena and Rua Espírito Santo, and opposite the Parque Municipal – both have a rather 1950s feel to them, the food is fast but good, and there is a mouthwatering range of *mineiro* desserts for you to choose from.

Street food is worth trying, too. On Thursday nights and Sunday mornings food stalls go up in the Praça de Liberdade as the square gets taken over by revellers and marketgoers; the food can be good and is always cheap. It's also worth keeping your eyes open around Praça Sete, where *doceiros*, sweetsellers, often set up stalls in the late afternoon and early evening, hoping to tempt homebound office workers.

Other central choices include an excellent **ice cream parlour**, on the corner of Rua Goiás and Rua Guajajaras, near the Palácio das Artes. It's a block behind a good **pizza** place, *Rococo*, Afonso Pena 1537, where the cool dudes hang out before and after concerts. **Vegetarians** could try the *Via Natural* at Afonso Pena 941. And there is also a good **Chinese** restaurant on Avenida Afonso Pena, near the *Rodoviária*, the *Dragão Chinêsa* – the nearest available good food if you have a couple of hours to kill while changing buses.

Wholeheartedly recommended, despite the $10 price tag, the *Petisqueira do Galo* (only open lunchtime Mon–Sat) is the best place in the city for **comida mineira**: it's at Avenida Olegário Maciel 1536; blue bus #8902 from Praça Sete, get off at the *Olympia* disco and walk up three blocks. For the set price you can fill your plate as many times as you can manage from a wonderful hot buffet of regional food – easily as good as anything you could get in the interior. If you don't waddle rather than walk out, you haven't eaten enough.

Drinking and nightlife

Nightlife in the **centre** varies according to the day of the week. The best is on Thursday nights, when the **Praça de Liberdade** is taken over by stalls and tables and there is a generalised *batucada*, with live music and impromptu singing and dancing until around midnight; very relaxed and enjoyable. On Friday, the bottom end of **Avenida Amazonas** is lively: the bars put out tables underneath the palm trees and the action goes on until the small hours. The area around the intersection of **Rua Rio de Janeiro and Avenida Augusto Lima** is more student-like. There are a couple of small theatres and cinemas close by, and a group of bars and restaurants: *Mateus* on the corner is a good one. In the same general area, don't forget the *Petisqueira do Galo* on Avenida Olegário Maciel (see above) – at night it becomes a very popular bar (closed Sun).

Savassí

The more sophisticated bars are in **Savassí**, which is a pleasant place to spend an evening. Drinks at least are no more expensive here than anywhere else, and the bars get very crowded at weekends. Good places include *Chantilly Chopparia* at Rua Alagoas 1283; further down are *Trianon* at no. 730 and *Portofino* next door, but avoid *Chez Bastião* and *Chico Mineiro*, glitzy and over-priced. *Bardô*, Rua Claudio Manuel 734, is one of the places where the fashionable try to be seen. One of the main attractions of Savassí is the **art cinema**, *Ciné Pathé* on Avenida Cristovão Columbus (and there's another in the Palácio das Artes), which combines an alluring location with imaginative and non-dubbed programming. The **pizzas** in the restaurant opposite are the best in town.

Discos and live music

The most popular current **nightspot** is the *Olympia* at Avenida Olegário Maciel 1206, which is hardly done justice by describing it as a disco; it has a disco, but also five separate bars, two dance floors and three video rooms, all kitted out in modern, tropical nightclub style and a snip at $4 for entry – the clientele is strictly brat pack, but enjoyable just the same.

Big names in **music** will either play at the Palácio das Artes or the *Cabaré Mineiro* at Rua Gonçalves Dias 54; luxurious but not as expensive as it looks. It operates a similar system to many upmarket Brazilian nightclubs, where you pay for seats at a table, or *mesa*, and order drinks and food during the performance. It can be a little difficult to get in if you're on your own, as tables have even numbers of seats and most people go in couples. The *Cabaré Mineiro* also costs

$4 entrance, but you don't have to order anything to eat – though it would look strange if you didn't drink either. It's always worth looking in the paper to see who is playing here at weekends, and there's a good house band; open daily from 9pm, but you will certainly need to book at weekends (☎227-5860/7237).

Sunday morning at the market

It's worth making an effort to be in Belo Horizonte on a Sunday morning, as the **Feira de Arte e Artesanato** is not to be missed. A massive affair, this is a huge market that takes over not only the whole Praça de Liberdade, but also sprawls into the streets around. It's always packed and if you're going to buy things there you need to arrive by 9am at the latest. After that the crowds come in earnest and moving through the narrow avenues between rows of stalls gets difficult; by noon, stallholders are packing up and leaving.

The market is a good place for bargains. Virtually anything is sold somewhere or other and it's split into sections, with related stalls grouped together – jewellery, leather goods, cane furniture, clothes, food, paintings and drinks, to name but a few. Prices of more expensive items and clothes are fixed – a lot of things on view are labelled – but otherwise there is some scope for **bargaining**. Highlights are the truly awful fluffy toys and sentimental paintings; very good jewellery and reasonably priced precious and semi-precious stones, cut and uncut; the cheap but cheerful knick-knacks in the "hippy" section; some good t-shirts (the ones protesting against the destruction of Amazonia are popular); and the wide variety of cheap but succulent food. There is no arts and crafts section as such: several of the stalls underneath the palms lining the centre of the square do have *artesanato*, but it's not as good as the stuff available outside Belo Horizonte.

As always with Brazilian markets, what's going on around you is just as interesting as what's on sale. Even if you have no intention of buying anything it's a fascinating place to walk around. Or sit down instead, if you can find a seat in the **bars** at the corner facing the Governor's palace, and watch the stallholders hustling, buyers negotiating, and people doing the same as you – just enjoying the action or listening to the buskers and serious musicians who play at the fringes of the crowds and sell tapes of their work.

> The **phone code** for Belo Horizonte is ☎031

Listings

Airlines *Alitalia*, Rua Pernambuco 1077, 9th floor, Savassí (☎226-9700); *KLM*, Avenida Cristóvão Colombo 519, Room 307, Savassí (☎221-9700); *SAS*, Avenida Cristóvão Colombo 515, Savassí (☎227-7600); *Transbrasil*, Rua Tamoios 86 (☎226-0622/3433); *Varig*, Rua Espírito Santo 643 (☎273-6595); *VASP*, Rua Carijós 279 (☎335-2955).

Airport Apart from some Rio and São Paulo flights, all destinations are served by *Tancredo Neves*; the airport is near the town of Confins, and is sometimes called after it, just to confuse you. Flight enquiries on ☎689-2700 (*Tancredo Neves*) or ☎441-2000 (Pampulha). And see "Orientation and arrival", above.

Car hire *Hertz*, at the airports and Avenida João Pinheiro 341 (☎224-5166 & ☎224-1279); *Interlocadora*, at the airports and Rua São Paulo 1670 (☎441-6555 & ☎275-3866); *Localiza-National*, at the airports and Avenida Bernardo Monteiro 1567 (☎273-3222).

Consulates *France*, Rua Professor Alexandre Aleixo 843, 5th floor (☎335-5563); *Netherlands*, Rua Alagoas 1460, 11th floor (☎221-0615); *Sweden*, Rua Dezenove 117, Cidade Industrial (☎333-4333 ext 20); *UK*, Avenida Afonso Pena 952, Room 500 (☎222-6318); *USA*, Avenida Cristóvão Colombo 400, 1st floor, Savassí (☎224-9339 & 224-9327); *West Germany*, Rua Carijós 244, 8th floor (☎222-3411).

Exchange Best done in the downtown financial zone around Praça Sete, where a cluster of banks give *turista* rates. There is a *câmbio* in Room 1402 of the Edifício Bradesco office building, Avenida Amazonas 298; and also on the 4th floor of the *Banco do Brasil*, Rua Rio de Janeiro 750, just off Praça Sete, the only bank exchange department that opens at 10am. Open an hour later is *Citibank*, Rua Espírito Santo 871 (exchange on 2nd floor) and *Lloyds*, Avenida João Pinheiro 580. Only the exchange department in the *Banco do Brasil* always stays open over lunch: the queues are mainly Brazilians buying dollars for trips abroad; go straight to the cashier and they deal with you first.

Post Office Main post office is at Avenida Afonso Pena 1270.

Telephone Trunk and international calls from *TELEMIG* offices at *Tancredo Neves* airport, the *Rodoviária*, Rua Caetés 467 in the centre and Rua Paraíba 1441 in Savassí – all open daily until 10pm.

Train to Rio If the journey wasn't almost entirely by night, the marvellous scenery of the trip to Rio would make it one of the great train rides of the world. As it is, you only get some three hours of daylight towards the end of the journey, and have to wake up at dawn to catch the best of it. See "Travel Details" at the end of this chapter.

THE CIDADES HISTÓRICAS

The **cidades históricas** of Minas Gerais are small – towns rather than cities – and were founded within a couple of decades of each other in the early eighteenth century. Rough and violent mining camps in their early days, they were soon transformed by mineral wealth into treasure houses, not merely of gold, but also of Baroque art and architecture. Well preserved and carefully maintained, together the towns form one of the most impressive sets of colonial remains in the Americas, comparable only to the silver-mining towns that flourished in Mexico at roughly the same time. In Brazil, they are equalled only by the remnants of the plantation culture of the Northeast, to which they contributed much of the gold you see in the gilded churches of Olinda and Salvador.

Although some have acquired a modern urban fringe, all the historic cities have centres untouched by modern developers – and a couple, like **Tiradentes**, look very much as they did two centuries ago. All have colonial churches – **Ouro Preto** has thirteen – at least one good museum, steep cobbled streets, ornate mansions and the particular atmosphere of places soaked in history. It was in them that the **Inconfidência Mineira**, Brazil's first bungling attempt to throw off the Portuguese yoke, was played out in 1789. And here the great sculptor Antônio Francisco Lisboa, **Aleijadinho** or the "little cripple", spent all his life, leaving behind him a body of work unmatched by any other figure working in the contemporary Baroque tradition (see the box below for an account of his life).

The nearest town to Belo Horizonte is **Sabará**, only a local bus ride away; the furthest is **Diamantina**, six hours by bus from the capital, in the wild scenery of the Serra do Espinhaço, and the only important one north of the capital. Two hours from Belo Horizonte, Ouro Preto is the ex-capital of the state and the largest of the historic cities, with **Mariana** a short distance away. And also two hours from Belo Horizonte, but not on the same route, is **Congonhas**, where the church of Bom Jesus do Matozinhos is considered to be Aleijadinho's masterpiece. Further to the south, another six-hour coach ride, are **São João Del Rey** and **Tiradentes**.

Only in Sabará is **accommodation** difficult. All the others are well supplied with places to stay, and are worth more than a quick day trip. If you only have a little time to spare, the best option from Belo Horizonte is probably Ouro Preto: you can easily get there and back in a day, and although everyone has their own favourites, it is the most classically beautiful of all.

ALEIJADINHO: A LIFE

Although little is known of his life, we do know roughly what Aleijadinho looked like. In the Museu de Aleijadinho in Ouro Preto is a crude but vivid portrait showing an intense, aquiline man, clearly what Brazilians call *pardo* – of mixed race. His hands are under his jacket, which seems a trivial detail unless you know what makes his achievement truly astonishing: the great sculptor of the *barroco mineiro* was a leper, and produced much of his best work after he had lost the use of his hands.

Despite being recognised as a master sculptor during his lifetime, only the barest outline of the life of **Antônio Francisco Lisboa** is clear. He was born in Ouro Preto in 1738, the son of a Portuguese craftsman; his mother was probably a slave. For the first half of his exceptionally long life he was perfectly healthy, a womaniser and *bon-viveur* despite his exclusively religious output. His prodigious talent, equally at home in wood or stone, human figures or abstract decoration, allowed him to set up a workshop with apprentices while still young, and he was much in demand. Although he always based himself in Ouro Preto, he spent long periods in all the major historic towns except Diamantina, working on commissions; but he never travelled beyond the state. Self-taught, he was an obsessive reader of the Bible and medical textbooks, the only two obvious influences in his work, one with its imagery, the other underlying the anatomical detail of his human figures.

In the late 1770s, his life changed utterly. He began to suffer from a progressively debilitating disease which seems to have been leprosy, although even this is not certain. As it got worse he became a recluse, only venturing outdoors in the dark, and increasingly obsessed with his work. His physical disabilities were terrible: he lost his fingers, toes and the use of his lower legs. Sometimes the pain was so bad his apprentices had to stop him hacking away at the offending part of his body with a chisel.

Yet despite all this he actually increased his output, working with hammer and chisel strapped to his wrists by his apprentices, who moved him about on a wooden trolley. It was under these impossible conditions that he sculpted his masterpiece, the twelve massive figures of the Prophets and the 64 lifesize Passion figures for the **Igreja de Bom Jesus de Matozinhos** in Congonhas, between 1796 and 1805. They were his swansong: failing eyesight finally forced him to stop work and he ended his life as a hermit in a hovel on the outskirts of Ouro Preto. The death he longed for finally came on November 18, 1814: he is buried in a simple grave in the church he attended all his life, Nossa Senhora da Conceição in Ouro Preto.

Aleijadinho's prolific output would have been remarkable under any circumstances: given his condition it was nothing short of miraculous, a triumph of the creative spirit. The bulk of his work is to be found in Ouro Preto, but there are also significant items in Sabará, São João Del Rey, Mariana and Congonhas. His achievement was to stay within the Baroque tradition, yet bring to its ornate conventions a raw physicality and unmatched technical skill that gives his work unique power.

Sabará

SABARÁ lies strung out over and between a series of hills, wound around the Rio das Velhas. It was here that the first alluvial gold strikes in Minas were made, on the banks of the river, and both Ouro Preto and Mariana are downstream. Many of the cobbled streets are so steep they have to be taken slowly, but ascents are rewarded with gorgeous churches, austere on the outside, choked with carving and ornamentation inside. The only drawback is the lack of accommodation. Sabará's proximity to Belo Horizonte would make it the ideal base for seeing the metropolis, but for some mysterious reason there are no hotels or *pensões*. Fortunately, the frequency of the **bus** link (every fifteen minutes from 4am to midnight) makes it an easy – and unmissable – day trip from the city: *Viação Cisne* buses leave from the local section of the Belo Horizonte *Rodoviária*, to the right of the main entrance. Start early; all the churches are open in the morning only.

The journey from Belo Horizonte takes just thirty minutes. Shortly after arriving in the town, the bus turns left into the colonial area and makes a stop at the fine Praça Santa Rita, where you should get off, before continuing to the bus station. There is a rudimentary **tourist office** before the turn-off, but it doesn't stock maps and isn't really worth bothering with. The main sights are all signposted, anyway, and the colonial zone is small enough to manage without a street plan. **Buses back to Belo Horizonte** are caught either from the bus station or on the main road leading out of town at the bottom of the colonial zone.

The Town

Standing in **Praça Santa Rita**, you're in the centre not just of the oldest part of Sabará, but of the oldest inhabited streets in southern Brazil. Sabará, founded in 1674, is the most venerable of the *cidades históricas*, and was the first major centre of gold mining in the state, although attention shifted southwards to Ouro Preto and Mariana by the end of the seventeenth century. It was founded by Borba Gato, a typical Paulista cut-throat who combined Catholic fervour – the town's first name was Vila Real de Nossa Senhora da Conceição de Sabarabuçú, later thankfully shortened – with ruthlessness: his determined extermination of the local Indians made gold mining possible in Sabará.

Not until forty years after its foundation were the mud huts and stockades of the early adventurers replaced by stone buildings, and it wasn't until the second quarter of the eighteenth century, when gold production was at its peak, that serious church building began, and the village began to acquire an air of permanence. A fair proportion of the local gold ended up gilding the interiors of the town's churches (insurance against the verse in the Bible that talks of rich men and the Kingdom of Heaven), but by the turn of the nineteenth century, all the alluvial gold had been exhausted and the town entered a steep decline. Sophisticated deep mining techniques, introduced by Europeans in the nineteenth century, failed to stop the decline and Sabará became a small and grindingly poor place – today, the colonial zone is fringed by *favelas*.

The very early days of Sabará are represented by the tiny **Igreja de Nossa Senhora de Ó**, one of the oldest, and certainly one of the most unusual, colonial churches in Brazil. It's a couple of kilometres from Praça Santa Rita; a signposted walk, or you can take the local bus marked *Esplanada* from the square. It is extremely unusual since it doesn't look in the least Portuguese: an austere, irregularly shaped exterior is topped off by an unmistakably Chinese tower, complete with pagoda-like upturns at the corners. The cramped interior, dominated by a gilded arch over the altar, also shows distinct Oriental influences, but the church is so old – it was built in 1698 – that nobody knows who was responsible for its unique design. The most likely explanation is that the Portuguese, despairing of the local talent, imported a group of Chinese craftsmen from Macau. There were certainly artisans from Macau in Diamantina, to the north, where streets are named after them, but here no other trace of them survives.

There are three other **churches** worth seeing in town; two, including Sabará's main church, are vintage specimens from the (literally) Golden Age of Minas Baroque (see below), while the third – despite being left half-built and open to the elements – is just as fascinating in its own way. This, the church of **Nossa Senhora do Rosário dos Pretos**, fifteen-minutes' signposted walk from Praça Santa Rita, was built by slaves, who actually did the work in the gold mines: until the mines declined, a large majority of the population of all the historic cities was black. Organised into lay societies called *irmandades*, the slaves financed and built churches, but this one was begun late, in 1767, and with the decline of the mines the money ran out. Although sporadic restarts were made during the nineteenth century, it was never more than half-built and when slavery was abolished in 1888, it was left as a memorial.

Sabará's main church, **Nossa Senhora da Conceição** (also called the Igreja Matriz: Wed–Fri 10am–noon and for Mass on Sun) is signposted from Praça Santa Rita. Started by the Jesuits in 1720, it's a fine example of the so-called first and second phases of Minas Baroque*. Succeeding generations added features to the original layout and inside it's extremely impressive, with a double row of heavily carved and gilded arches, a beautifully decorated ceiling and, once again, Chinese influence in the gildings and painted panels of the door leading to the sacristy.

The church of **Nossa Senhora do Carmo**, a vintage third phase church, is a good contrast, while it's also a demonstration of the remarkable talents of Aleijadinho, who oversaw its construction and contributed much of the decoration between 1770 and 1783, a time when he was at the height of his powers. The interior manages to be elaborate and uncluttered at the same time, with graceful curves in the gallery, largely plain walls, comparatively little gilding and a beautifully painted ceiling. Aleijadinho left his mark everywhere: the imposing soapstone and painted wood pulpits, the banister in the nave, the flowing lines of the choir, and above all in the two statues of São João da Cruz and São Simão Stock. You can tell an Aleijadinho from the faces: the remarkably lifelike head of São Simão is complete with wrinkles and transfixed by religious ecstacy.

---

*There are three distinct phases of **Baroque church architecture** in Minas. The **first**, from the beginning of the eighteenth century to about 1730, was very ornate and often involved extravagant carving and gilding, but left exteriors plain; sculpture was formal, with stiff, rather crude statues. The **second phase** dominated the middle decades of the eighteenth century, with equally extravagant decorations inside, especially around the altar, and the wholesale plastering of everything with gold; the exteriors were now embellished with curlicues and panels in fine Minas soapstone, ceilings painted and sculpture noticeably more natural, although still highly stylised. The peak was the period from 1760–1810 and this **third phase** *barroco mineiro* can be stunning: the exterior decoration was more elaborate, but the interiors are less cluttered, with walls often left plain, and fine carving in both wood and stone. By now, too, the religious sculpture, with its flowing realism, had broken the stylistic bounds that confine most Baroque art.

Make the effort, too, to visit the **Museu do Ouro** (Tues–Fri noon–5pm), a short but steep signposted walk up from Praça Santa Rita. Built in 1732, this is the only royal foundry house remaining in Brazil. When gold was discovered in Minas Gerais, the Portuguese Crown was entitled to a fifth of the output, but had to collect it first. To do so, it put a military cordon around the goldmines, and then built several royal foundries, where gold from the surrounding area was melted down, franked, and the royal fifth deducted. The functional building that now houses the museum easily reveals its origins: it is built around an interior courtyard, overlooked by a balcony on three sides, from where the officials could keep an eagle eye on gold being melted into bars and weighed. Along with the other royal foundry in Ouro Preto, it was Brazil's most heavily guarded building.

Most of the museum is devoted to gold mining history. **Downstairs** there are rooms full of colonial scales, weights, pans and other mining instruments, and a strongroom where until 1986 you could see genuine eighteenth-century gold bars and jewels in the safe. Unfortunately, that year two men walked in, put a pistol to the guard's head, and walked off with the safe's contents, which have never been recovered: the bars on display now are plaster casts of the real thing, although they look authentic enough. **Upstairs** you'll find the usual collection of colonial furniture and some moderate *arte sacra*, but also some interesting prints and one very fine painted ceiling, representing the four continents known at the time it was built. In a room off the courtyard, to the right of the large wooden water-driven grinding mill, is a model of the **Morro Velho** mine in nearby Nova Lima, the deepest goldmine in the world outside South Africa. There's a commemorative photograph of the 44 Welsh mining engineers and single Brazilian lawyer who began it, all working for the wonderfully named *St John Del Rey Gold Mining Company*.

If you tire of colonial sightseeing, just wandering around the bars and cobbled streets near the Praça Santa Rita is very pleasant, too. There are lots of impressive buildings, notably the **Prefeitura** on Rua Dom Pedro II, and the nineteenth-century theatre on the same street: it was designed as an opera house and completed just as the gold ran out – the interior is open during the day from Tuesday to Friday. There are several **bars and restaurants**, which get lively at weekends: *Quinto do Ouro* does reliable *comida mineira*.

Ouro Preto

The drive to **OURO PRETO** from Belo Horizonte is spectacular in places, winding around hill country 1000m above sea level and passing several valleys where patches of forest survive: imagine the entire landscape covered with it and you have an idea of what greeted the goldseekers in the 1690s. On arrival, the first thing that strikes you is how small the town is, considering that until 1897 it was the capital of Minas – its population is still only around 40,000. That said, you can see at a glance why the capital had to be shifted to Belo Horizonte. The steep hills the town is built around, straddling a network of creeks, severely limit space for expansion: any larger than it is at present and you would need climbing gear to get around. Yet Ouro Preto's very existence is a sign of how rich the gold seams were, as you'd need a compelling reason to build on such irregular terrain. But the hills and vertiginous streets (some so steep they have steps rather than pavements) are vital ingredients in what is one of the loveliest towns in Brazil, an almost unspoilt eighteenth-century jewel.

Avoid coming on **Monday** if you want to see the sights, as all the churches and most of the museums close for the day. Also, buy your ticket **back to Belo Horizonte** as soon as you arrive (or the day before if you've stayed over) as buses fill up very quickly. Some people complain about Ouro Preto being touristy – and it is more commercialised than any other *cidade histórica* – but they miss the point: it's because there really is something to savour here that the visitors come. From the modern bus station on the outskirts of town where you arrive, or, even better, coming into Ouro Preto from the other side on the road from Mariana, the town is spread out below you, every hill crowned with a church, a sea of tiled roofs and straggling lines of colonial buildings. It's immediately obvious why this is one of the main tourist destinations in Brazil.

Arriving and finding a place to stay

It's an easy walk from the **Rodoviária** into town, providing you don't have much to carry. The road comes out in the main square, **Praça Tiradentes**, dominated by a statue of the martyr to Brazilian independence and lined with beautiful colonial buildings. On the left is the **municipal tourist office**, which sells an excellent city map: armed with it you can easily find any of the several cheap *pensões* nearby, all in colonial buildings. Ouro Preto does get crowded at weekends and holiday periods, but there are so many establishments that you can usually find somewhere to stay: the tourist office will ring round the more upmarket places for you if you have problems, or keep an eye on your luggage while you search.

If you're moving on later **to Mariana** (see below), the most convenient place to catch the local bus there is from the stop on Rua Conselheiro Quintiliano, by the side of the Escola de Minas: it runs every half an hour.

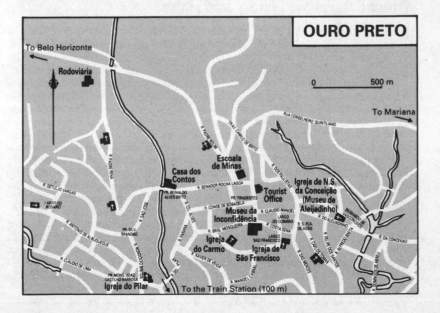

Accommodation

Recommended, **cheapish places to stay** are *Pousada América*, Rua Camilo de Brito 15, and *Pensão Vermelha* on Largo São Francisco, where some rooms overlook the magnificent façade of the São Francisco church. Down the other side of the hill are *Pensão D. Conceição*, a friendly family guesthouse at Rua Paraná 90, and *Pousada Solar do Barão*, Rua Coronel Alves 90. The *Pilão* is right on Praça Tiradentes; the place is fine but the square is often noisy at night. Cheap, but involving a steep walk up into the centre, is the *Hotel Aparecida*, opposite the (freight only) railway station on Praça Cesário Alvim. And the old *Hotel Tófolo* at Rua São José 76 has a fine location. These are only the pick of a crowded field: despite what people say about too many tourists driving prices up, you'll be able to get a reasonably cheap room in Ouro Preto.

There are also several **medium range places**, the best of which is undoubtedly the *Pouso Chico Rei* at Rua Brigador Mosqueira 90 (☎551-1274; only Portuguese spoken); a small eighteenth-century house converted into a comfortable *pensão*, filled with a collection of relics that would do credit to a museum, with a stunning view from a reading room on the first floor, excellent breakfasts and a tranquil, timeless atmosphere. The small number of rooms means you have to book in advance; five of the six rooms are doubles, starting at $20 a night, but there is a single for only $8, certainly the best deal in town if you can get it. On the road out to Mariana is the *Pousada Panorama Barroco*, perched at the best possible point for a view of the centre; it's at Rua Conselheiro Quintiliano 722 (☎551-3366) and is run by a US-Brazilian couple who are very good on suggestions about what to see. You could also try the *Hotel Grande*, Rua Senador Rocha 164, built by Niemeyer on one of his bad days – at least staying there you don't have to look at it.

Around the town: history and sights

A decade after gold was struck at Sabará, a Paulista adventurer called **Antônio Dias** pitched camp underneath a mountain the Indians called Itacolomí, with an unmistakable thumb-shaped rock on its summit. Panning the streams nearby, he found "black gold" – alluvial gold mixed with iron ore – and named his camp after it. It attracted a flood of people as it became clear the deposits were the richest yet found in Minas, and so many came that they outstripped the food supply. In 1700 there was a famine and legend has it that people died of hunger with gold nuggets in their hands. The early years were hard, made worse by a war started in 1707 between the Portuguese and Paulista *bandeirantes*, who resisted the Crown's attempts to take the area over. The war, the **Guerra das Emboabas**, lasted for two years and was brutal, with ambushes and massacres the preferred tactics of both sides. Ouro Preto was the Portuguese base, and troops from here drove the Paulistas from their headquarters at Sabará and finally annihilated them near São João Del Rey. From then on, Ouro Preto was the effective capital of the gold producing area of Minas, although it wasn't officially named as such until 1823. Indeed, compared to places like nearby Mariana, Ouro Preto was a late developer: all but two of its churches date from the second half of the eighteenth century, and several of its finest buildings, like the school of mining and the town hall on Praça Tiradentes, were not finished until well into the nineteenth century.

Ouro Preto is most famous in Brazil, though, as the site of the **Inconfidência Mineira**, the first attempt to free Brazil from the Portuguese. Inspired by the French Revolution, and heartily sick of the heavy taxes levied by a bankrupt

Portugal, a group of twelve prominent town citizens led by **Joaquim José da Silva Xavier** began in 1789 to discuss organising a rebellion: Xavier was a dentist, known to everyone as *Tiradentes*, "teeth-puller"*.

In the event the conspiracy was a fiasco and all were betrayed and arrested before any uprising was organised. The leaders were condemned to hang, but the Portuguese, realising that they could ill afford to offend the inhabitants of a state whose taxes kept them afloat, arranged a royal reprieve, commuting the sentence to exile in Angola and Mozambique. Unfortunately the messenger arrived two days too late to save Tiradentes, marked as the first to die. He was hanged where the column now stands in the square that bears his name, his head stuck on a post and his limbs despatched to the other mining towns to serve as a warning.

The gold gave out about the time that Brazil finally became independent in 1822, but for decades the town survived as an administrative centre and university town: a school of mining was founded in 1876. After the capital moved to Belo Horizonte, steady decline set in, though the populist government of Getúlio Vargas brought back the bodies of the *Inconfidentes* to a proper shrine, and sensitively restored the crumbling monuments.

Praça Tiradentes is the best place to start any **walking tour**. First stop should be the tourist office, to pick up a map and a card that gives the opening hours of the churches and museums. The size of the town is deceptive. There's enough to keep you going for days – thirteen colonial churches, seven chapels, six museums and several other sights – and if you want to explore in depth you should buy a copy of the **guidebook** on sale at the tourist office, *Passeio a Ouro Preto*, which has sections in English: better, but with only Portuguese text, is the *Guia de Ouro Preto* by Manuel Bandeira.

Praça Tiradentes and around

Right on the **Praça Tiradentes** stands the mining school, the **Escola de Minas**, now housed in the old governor's palace. It's still the best mining school in the country, and its students, with their bars and motorbikes, lend a Bohemian air to the town. The white turrets make the building itself look rather like a fortress: the exterior, with a fine marble entrance, dates from the 1740s, but the inside was gutted during the last century and not improved by it. Attached to the school is a **Museu da Mineralogia** (daily noon–5pm), most of whose exhibits are strictly of interest to the geologist, but there is one fascinating room where gold and precious stones are beautifully displayed, in contrast to the chaos of the rest of it. One stunning nugget comes from the Gurupí in Maranhão, way to the north – a delicate leaf of gold sprouting impossibly out of a lump of quartz.

Also in the square are the old city chambers, the **Paço Municipal** (Tues–Sun noon–5.30pm), a glorious eighteenth-century building that provides a perfect example of the classical grace of Minas colonial architecture. Its beautifully restored interior lives up to expectations: like many colonial town halls, it was also a jail, and many of the huge rooms, so well suited to the display of *arte sacra*, were once dungeons. The building contains the **Museu da Inconfidência**

---

*Another of the conspirators was **Tomas Gonzaga**, whose hopeless love poems to the beautiful **Marília Dirceu**, promised by her family to another, made the couple into the Brazilian equivalent of Romeo and Juliet. Time has not aged Gonzaga's work: *When you appear at dawn, all rumpled/like a badly wrapped parcel, no ribbons or flowers/how Nature shines, how much lovelier you seem.*

(Tues–Sun noon–5.30pm), interesting enough since the surrounding towns have been stripped of a great deal of their wealth to stock the museum: the only collection that compares with it is in Mariana. There are relics of eighteenth-century daily life, from sedan chairs and kitchen utensils (including the seal the bishop used to stamp his coat of arms on his cakes) to swords and pistols. A ground floor room is dominated by a vivid life-size effigy of Saint George, complete with spear, which was propped on a horse and paraded around during religious processions. And on the table opposite is the museum's highlight: four exquisite, small Aleijadinho statues that are a fitting introduction to the flowing detail of his best work.

Upstairs there's colonial furniture and more art, but the spiritual heart of the place is found at the rear of the ground floor, where the cell in which Tiradentes spent the last night of his life is now the **shrine to the Inconfidentes**. An antechamber holds documents, like the execution order and birth and death register of Tiradentes, reverently framed, and leads into a room containing the remains of the thirteen conspirators and Tiradentes himself – all in the vaguely Fascist style the Vargas era usually chose for its public monuments. Most of the conspirators died in Africa, some in Portugal: all were exiled for the rest of their lives and never returned to Brazil.

Next door to the Paço Municipal is one of the finest churches in Ouro Preto, the **Igreja de Nossa Senhora do Carmo** (Tues–Sun 8–11.30am & 1–5pm). It was designed by Antônio Francisco Lisboa, Aleijadinho's father, and construction began just before his death in 1766. Aleijadinho himself then took over the building of the church and finished it six years later. He contributed the carving of the exterior, and worked on the interior, on and off, for four decades: the baptismal font in the sacristy is a masterpiece, as are the carved doors leading to the pulpits. Two of the side chapels in the main church (*São João* and *Nossa Senhora da Piedade*) were among the last commissions he was able to complete; finished in 1809, the accounts book has Aleijadinho complaining he was paid with "false gold". Much the least cluttered of the major churches in Ouro Preto, it's the only one to have *azulejo* tiled panels, to make the Portuguese who patronised it feel at home.

To the side of the church is yet another **museum** of religious art, open the same hours as the church, and housed in an excellently restored mansion that was once the meeting house for the lay society attached to Nossa Senhora do Carmo. It's a high quality collection and very well displayed, the best part being the glittering array of gold and silver religious objects downstairs in the *Sala de Tesouro*.

Rua Brigadeiro Mosqueira, which runs downhill from here, is one of the quietest and most beautiful streets in Ouro Preto, almost every building worth savouring. Wander down, bear left at the bottom, and you come out onto one of the steepest streets in town, Rua do Pilar, from where you can glimpse the towers of the Igreja do Pilar (see below) well before the plunging, cobbled path deposits you in front of it.

From the Igreja do Pilar to the Casa dos Contos

The **Igreja do Pilar** (Tues–Sun noon–5pm), with an exterior ornate even by Baroque standards, is the finest example anywhere of early Minas Baroque architecture. The oldest of Ouro Preto's churches, it was begun in the 1720s and the interior is the opposite of Carmo's restraint, a wild explosion of glinting Rococo, liberally plastered with gold. The best carving was done by Francisco Xavier de

Brito, who worked in Minas from 1741 until his early death ten years later – and about whom nothing is known except that he was Portuguese and influenced Aleijadinho. He was responsible for the astonishing arch over the altar, where the angels supporting the Rococo pillars seem to swarm out of the wall on either side. In the sacristy, there's a small but interesting museum featuring enormous colonial wardrobes and a collection of gold and silver relics: the latter weakened by the theft of its most valuable items in 1973, which have never been recovered.

Leaving Pilar, turn right up Rua Rondolfo Bretos and round into **Rua São José** (also, confusingly, called Rua Tiradentes), whose many bars and restaurants make it a good place to take a breather. Crossing the small stone bridge, you come to the perfectly proportioned **Casa dos Contos**, the old treasury building, now a museum (Tues–Sun 12.30–5pm). Finished in 1787, it was built as a bank-cum-mansion by Ouro Preto's richest family, and in 1803 became the *Fazenda Real*, the place where the crown extracted its fifth of the gold and assembled armed convoys to escort it down to Rio for shipment to Portugal. The museum is no more than moderately interesting – the usual mixture of *arte sacra* and furniture – but the building is terrific; a magnificent colonial mansion built when Ouro Preto was at its peak. The entrance hall is dominated by an imposing staircase, four storeys high, and built around a beautiful courtyard, large enough for a dozen cavalry troopers. The most interesting places radiate off it: the huge furnace for melting the gold and shaping it into bars, the slave quarters, the stables (horses were definitely better accommodated than slaves), and even an eighteenth-century privy. And don't forget to go right up to the *mirante* on the top floor for one of the best views of Ouro Preto.

To the Museu do Aleijadinho

It's a steep toil back up to Praça Tiradentes, compensated by the lovingly kept buildings on either side. From there, take Rua Claudio Manoel, downhill to the left, lined with shops selling precious stones and jewellery which doesn't come from Ouro Preto (but from eastern Minas) and is rather expensive. Ahead, on the right, is arguably the most beautiful church in Ouro Preto, the **Igreja de São Francisco de Assis** (Tues–Sun 8–11.30am & 1–5pm; entrance ticket also valid for the Conceição church and Aleijadinho museum, below): the small square that sets it off is a food **market** in the morning and a mediocre arts and crafts market in the afternoon.

The church was begun in 1765, and no other contains more work by Aleijadinho. The magnificent exterior soapstone panels are his, as is virtually all of the virtuoso carving, in both wood and stone, inside; and to top it off, Aleijadinho also designed the church and supervised its construction. You would think the church commissioners would have left it at that, but in 1801 they contracted the best painter of the *barroco mineiro*, **Manuel da Costa Athayde**, to decorate the ceilings. It took him nine years, using natural dyes made from plant juices and powdered iron ore, and his work has stood the test of time far better than other church paintings of the period. The squirming mass of cherubs and saints are framed within a cunning *trompe l'oeil* effect, which extends the real Baroque pillars on the side of the nave into painted ones on the ceiling, making it seem like an open-air canopy through which you can glimpse clouds. There are also painted *azulejo s* which look remarkably like the real thing.

Returning to Rua Claudio Manuel, take the winding Rua Bernardo de Vasconcelos, to the left – this is the back way down to the last of the major churches in Ouro Preto, **Matriz de Nossa Senhora da Conceição** (Tues–Sun 8–11.30am & 1–5pm), and it's a steep descent. Coming this way, you're leaving the main tourist area and everything looks just as it did the day Aleijadinho died: the Matriz is famous as the church he belonged to and where he is buried. The one-time cut-throat Antônio Dias, who founded Ouro Preto and died old and rich in 1727, left his fortune to build this church on the spot of his first camp – so this is where it all began and, with the death of Aleijadinho, also where it can be said to have ended.

Despite Aleijadinho's connection with the church, he never worked on this one. All the same, it is an impressive example of mid-period Minas Baroque, and the painting and carving is very fine, especially the figures of saints in the side altars – look at the expression and movement of Saint Sebastian, on the left of the nave. Aleijadinho is buried in a simple **tomb** on the right of the nave, marked *Antônio Francisco Lisboa* and covered by nothing more elaborate than a plain wooden plank.

A side door by the main altar leads to the sacristy and the fascinating **Museu do Aleijadinho**, which is worth lingering over; not so much a museum of Aleijadinho's work as of his life and times. What work there is by him is in the basement, and is quite something – four magnificent lions which once served as supports for the plinth on which coffins were laid. Aleijadinho, never having seen a lion, drew from imagination and produced medieval monsters with the faces of monkeys. The ground floor is taken up by a high quality collection of religious art, but the highlight is upstairs, in a room dedicated not just to Aleijadinho but to all the legendary figures of Ouro Preto's golden age.

There are reproductions of the birth and death entries in the parish register for Aleijadinho, Marília Dirceu and Manuel Athayde. But even better are the riveting eighteenth-century ex-votos on the wall, a fascinating insight into the tribulations of bygone daily life. One shows a black slave on her sickbed: the inscription reads "Ana, slave of António Dias, had me made after finding herself gravely ill, without hope of life, but praying to Our Lord of the Slaves miraculously recovered". Opposite is a gruesome one from 1778 giving thanks for the successful setting of a broken leg, shown in graphic detail.

And also on the wall there's a small **portrait**, crude but priceless, of Aleijadinho in middle age. It doesn't flatter so is probably a good likeness; slightly hunched, sharp features, dark and intense.

Bars and restaurants
One of the nice things about Ouro Preto is the number of places where you can eat, drink, or just hang out: when the students are out in force at weekend nights, it doesn't have any of the quiet atmosphere of a small interior town that you might expect. During termtime, at the weekend, the steep Rua Conde de Bobadela, leading up to Praça Tiradentes, is chocked up with students spilling out of the **bars** and cafés; more congregate in the square itself, where there are even more bars.

There is no shortage of **restaurants**, either; the better-value ones are clustered at the bottom of the hill on Rua São José. The *Chafariz* does good *mineiro* food, and there are several good cafés with snacks and *sucos*. *Pastelzinho* does excellent, freshly fried *pasteis*. The cheapest places to eat are the bars on Praça Tiradentes – try *Lampeão*, *Forno do Barro* or the *Casa Grande*, all of which do good *caipirinhas*. If you prefer a quiet drink away from the crowds, *Espaço Final* on Praça Rio Branco, near the Pilar church, is worth checking out.

Mariana

MARIANA is one of the major colonial towns, and in the first half of the eighteenth century was grander by far than Ouro Preto. Today it's really no more than a large village, but although its churches are less grand, it has a fine museum and a perfectly preserved colonial centre, mercifully free of steep climbs, that is far less crowded and commercialised than Ouro Preto. It's only a short local bus ride away and if you can't stand crowds you could always stay here instead, and be within easy touch of Ouro Preto. If you want to unwind, Mariana is a good place to do it.

The **local bus** leaves you right in the centre, opposite an excellent **tourist information post**, the *Terminal Turístico*, which sells a good map with everything helpfully marked on it. If you arrive by coach, the **Rodoviária** is just over the small bridges that run over the Carmo stream and link the colonial centre with the newer part of town.

All the **places to stay** are within easy walking distance, except for the *Posto Mariana*, a highway service station on the Belo Horizonte road that the local bus stops at. It doesn't look promising but in fact has a fine *dormitório* attached, with clean rooms and showers. The best place to stay in town is the *Hotel Central*, a beautiful colonial building overlooking the main square, Praça Gomes Freire: like almost all the others it is cheap and good value. Other places include the basic and modern *Hotel Faisca*, which you can see up the street from the tourist office; *Hotel Muller*, across the bridge opposite the office at Rua Getúlio Vargas 34; and the *Providência*, along the road that leads up to the Basilica, overlooking the centre, at Rua Dom Silvério 51.

The Mine

If you've come on the local bus from Ouro Preto, through steep hills bearing clear traces of centuries of mining, it takes just twenty minutes to arrive on the outskirts of Mariana and at one of the area's more unusual sights – the ancient gold mine of **Mina da Passagem**, with a bus stop conveniently opposite.

One of the rare deep-shaft gold mines still operating in Minas, it's also by far the oldest. Gold has been dug out here since 1719, although most of the seventeen kilometres of galleries date from the nineteenth century. These days the mine is less successful, and all except one of the eight faces have been closed down. Nevertheless over 400 people still work here, and it tries hard to halt the decline by running delightfully ramshackle tours every day from 9am until 5pm; the $4 charge is steep, but it's an interesting trip.

Wandering through repair yards you arrive on a lip of land overlooking woods to find yourself face to face with what must be the oldest functioning machine in Brazil – a vintage 1825 British steam engine, now adapted to run on compressed air. It powers a drum cable that drives railcars into and out of the mine: safer than it looks, though you do need to be careful of bumping your head once you trundle into the galleries. The young guides are friendly, knowledgeable and speak reasonable English and French; there are bits of nineteenth-century mining equipment knocking around, and the dripping gallery opens out into a small, crystalline floodlit lake. Back up on the surface, the visit is rounded off with a demonstration of gold panning, with real gold – not as easy as it looks.

The history of the mine is a roll-call of economic imperialism. Sold by the Portuguese to the British in 1830, whose owners happily worked it with slaves at the same time as the Royal Navy was intercepting slavers in the Atlantic, it was then offloaded onto the French in 1883 – one of the very richest mines in Minas. Nationalised by Vargas in 1937, it was sold to the South Africans, of all people, in 1970 – a grotesque detail they wait until you're safely underground before revealing.

The Town

In Mariana itself, the wealth generated by the mine was transmuted into rows of fine houses. Most now have shops on the ground floor (and not all are colonial), but later builders have taken care to blend their work in with the colonial core, and everything is carefully maintained. If you're going to tour the sights, then **orientation** is fairly straightforward. The truly colonial area begins at Praça Claudio Manuel, in front of the large Catedral Basílica; from here Rua Frei Durão, with several of the noblest eighteenth-century public buildings, leads to the exquisite square of Gomes Freire, with its bandstand, trees and pond, lined on all sides by colonial *sobrados*, two-storey mansions. Nearby are the two finest churches in Mariana and a lovely *Prefeitura* building in Praça João Pinheiro, complete with *pelourinho*, the old stone whipping post to which slaves were tied and beaten.

The Museu Arquidiocesano
Founded by the usual band of Paulista adventurers a couple of years before Ouro Preto, Mariana was for several decades the more imposing of the two towns. The first governors of Minas had their residence here and the first bishops their palace. The core of the town is older than Ouro Preto, too: despite regular riots and the war between Paulistas and the Portuguese, Mariana was the administrative centre of the gold mines of central Minas until the 1750s. Although it has been overshadowed by its neighbour for over two centuries now, you can still get a good idea of Mariana's early flourish in one of the best museums in Minas Gerais, the **Museu Arquidiocesano** in the old bishop's palace, on Rua Frei Durão (Tues noon–5pm, Wed–Sun 9am–4.45pm).

The **building** itself is magnificent, with parts dating from the first decade of the eighteenth century, when it began life, bizarrely, as a prison for erring churchmen. The Franciscans were deeply involved in the Paulista expeditions and were notorious for being the worst cut-throats of all. Between 1720 and 1756 the jail was extended into a palace: the door and window frames are massive, built in beautifully worked local soapstone. Inside, the **collection** is predictable – *arte sacra* and colonial furniture – but is distinguished by its very high quality and its age, often predating the earliest material in Ouro Preto by two or three decades. It gives a vivid idea of how Mariana was thriving, with stone buildings and all the trappings of the early eighteenth-century good life, when Ouro Preto was still a collection of hovels.

On the ground floor there's a sobering collection of chains and manacles draped along the walls, and also the "treasure room", containing the ecclesiastical gold and silver. But the bulk of things to see are upstairs. The stairwell is dominated by a taste of things to come, a powerful painting of *Christ's Passion* by Athayde, his best known work. The stairs lead up to a number of graceful colonial rooms, including the luxurious private quarters of the bishops, which contain an excellent collection of religious art, notably the largest number of Aleijadinho figures anywhere outside a church. They are instantly recognisable: São João Nepomuceno, the bearded São Joaquim in religious ecstacy, and a marvellous São Miguel in the corner by the window.

The colonial furniture section, usually the dullest part of Minas museums, is actually worth seeing here: lovely writing desks and chests of drawers, all early eighteenth-century and most made of jacaranda wood – there was a glut on the market at the time, as the forests were felled to get at the gold. The most unusual exhibit is a false bookcase, with wooden "books" painted to resemble leather. You can also wander around the bishop's audience room – the throne is also by Aleijadinho, who was nothing if not versatile – and there's a separate gallery of their portraits, incongruously included amongst which are three, rather good, local landscapes by the German artist Nobauer.

Mariana's churches

Mariana's colonial churches are smaller and less extravagant than Ouro Preto's, though most are decorated with paintings by **Athayde**, who came from here and is buried in the Igreja de São Francisco (see below).

The oldest church is the **Catedral e Basílica da Sé** on Praça Claudio Manuel, begun in 1709 and choked with gilded Rococo detail. This is very much an Aleijadinho family venture: his father, Manuel Francisco Lisboa, designed and built it, while Aleijadinho contributed the carvings in the sacristy and a font. The interior is dominated by the massive German organ donated by the king of Portugal in 1751. Look closely and you can see Chinese-style decorations carved by slaves, who also worked the bellows.

The two churches on Praça João Pinheiro, around the corner, show how tastes had changed by the end of the century. Their ornate facades and comparatively restrained interiors are typical of the third phase of *barroco mineiro*. The **Igreja de São Francisco de Assis**, finished in 1794, has the finest paintings of any Mariana church, as befits the place where Athayde is buried. The numbers on the church floor are where members of the lay Franciscan brotherhood are buried; Athayde is no. 94. The elaborate interior contains much that is worth seeing: a fine sacristy, and an altar and pews by Aleijadinho, who also put his signature on the church in his usual way, by sculpting the sumptuous soapstone "medal" over the door. The **Igreja do Carmo**, on the other side of the square with a less elaborate exterior, is disappointing in comparison. The combination of the two churches with the equally graceful **Prefeitura** make the bare grass square a pleasant place to sit awhile.

From here, it's a short uphill walk via the unspoilt Rua Dom Silvério to the dull nineteenth-century **Basílica** which overlooks the town; you pass the strange, geometric **Igreja da Arquiconfraria** on the way. The object is not so much to view the Basílica, which is run down, but to enjoy the view of the town stretched out before you. And if you follow the dirt path along the top the views are even better.

Some eating places . . . and a little gold mining

Mariana is not stuffed with bars and restaurants, but **eating out** is cheaper than in Ouro Preto and the bars are as pleasant, if quieter. The nicest views are to be had from the places that look out onto Praça Gomes Freire; the *Portão da Praça*, where the *beirutes* (unleavened bread stuffed with meat and salad) make a cheap but tasty lunch and the *mineiro* food is good; the Italian *Pappina della Nonna*; and the *Hotel Central*. Just up the Travessia São Francisco there's a good regional restaurant, the *Tambaú*, while the nearby *Alvorada* is another restaurant where the food is reasonable, economical and the views come free. There are simple **bars** on most corners. With these surroundings, all you really need for a success-ful bar are chairs and a freezer.

If you've got time to kill, an interesting place to stroll to is the town *garimpo*, a small **mining camp**. Stand on the last of the bridges over the Carmo creek and you can see figures digging and panning upstream. They are *garimpeiros*, gold miners, and are using methods almost unchanged since gold was first found here in 1696 – the only difference now is that the pans are metal rather than wood. They dig channels into the stream bed, divert the flow, and sift through the gravel with pans. To take a closer look, you can get there easily from Rua Rosário Velho. The *garimpeiros* are friendly, if a little bemused that gringos should find what they are doing interesting.

Congonhas

Compared with what's gone before, **CONGONHAS**, a rather ugly, modern town, sits ill as one of the historic cities. In truth, there's only one reason for coming here, to see the pilgrimage church of Bom Jesus do Matozinhos. It's a long way to come just to see one thing, but this is no ordinary church: if one place repre-sents the flowering of *barroco mineiro*, this is it – the spiritual heart of Minas Gerais.

Getting to Congonhas can be a little awkward from anywhere except Belo Horizonte (from where there are several daily direct buses, a two-hour ride). **From São João Del Rey** (see below), take the bus to Belo Horizonte and get off at the official stop, a *Petrobras* service station on the crossroads with the highway to Belo Horizonte, two hours drive from São João. The village here is called MURTINHO, and opposite the crossroads is a local bus stop from where buses leave every half-hour to Congonhas. From **Ouro Preto**, you need to take the *Cristo Rei* company bus to CONSELHEIRO LAFAIETE, which leaves daily at 5am, 6am, 9am, noon, 2.40pm and 6pm; buy a ticket as far as Murtinho, ask the conductor to tell you when you arrive, get off at the crossroads and wait for a local bus to Congonhas. The ride from Ouro Preto takes about three hours and is a fascinating journey, much of it on country dirt roads through sleepy villages.

The **bus** from Murtinho goes right into Congonhas, but unless you want a stiff uphill walk to the church you should get off at the modern *Rodoviária* on the outskirts of town. From here take the local bus marked *Basílica*, which takes you all the way; Bom Jesus is impossible to miss.

Bom Jesus do Matozinhos

After all that, the church of **Bom Jesus do Matozhinos** is not in itself the main attraction. Built on a hill overlooking the town, with a panoramic view of the hills around it, it is set in a magnificent sloping **garden** studded with palms and what look like six tiny mosques with oriental domes. These are small **chapels** commemorating episodes of the Passion: each is filled with lifesize statues dramatising the scene in a tableau, 64 in all. Looking down on them from the parapets of the extraordinary terrace leading up to the church are twelve towering soap-stone **statues** of Old Testament Prophets. Everything, the figures and the statues, was sculpted by **Aleijadinho**, in what he must have known would be his last major commission. His leprosy was already advanced, and he could only work with chisels strapped to his wrists. The results are astonishing, a masterpiece made all the more moving by the fact it was also the farewell piece of a great artist suffering his own Calvary.

The whole complex is modelled on the shrine of Bom Jesus in Braga, in northern Portugal. The idea and money came from a Portuguese adventurer, **Feliciano Mendes**, who – towards the end of his life – planned to recreate the pilgrimage church of his native Braga, to house an image of the dead Christ he brought with him from Portugal in 1713. Mendes died in 1756, when work had only just begun, and it was forty years before the local bishop contracted Aleijadinho to produce the figures of the Passion and the Prophets. It seems likely that it was a conscious swansong on Aleijadinho's part: there is no other explanation for the way a seriously ill man pushed so hard to finish such a massive undertaking, whose theme was immediately relevant to his own suffering. Somehow, with his apprentices filling in fine detail, he managed to complete everything by 1805 – and the result defies belief that the project was executed by a man who had lost the use of his hands.

The Passion and the Prophets

There are always **guides** hanging around, who do know their stuff and can fill in a lot of interesting detail, but you're not obliged to go around with one.

Start at the bottom of the garden if you want to appreciate the deep religious mysticism that lies behind the design. The **slope** symbolises the ascent towards the Cross and governs the sequence of tableaux, the scenes leading you up from the Garden of Gethsemane through Christ's imprisonment, trial, whipping, the crown of thorns, and the carrying of the Cross to Calvary. On top, guarded by the Prophets, is the church, housing both the wooden image of Christ's body and the real body, in the communion host: built in the shape of a cross it represents both the Crucifixion and the Kingdom of Heaven.

Two of the chapels are empty as the **figures** are undergoing restoration (you can see them lined up in the museum by the side of the church), but the rest are still in place. Viewing isn't ideal: there are grilles to stop people getting in, and some of the figures are difficult or impossible to see. All are sculpted from cedar and were brightly painted by Athayde, using his preferred natural paints made from ox blood, egg whites, crushed flowers and vegetable dyes. They are marvellously lifelike: you can see Christ's veins and individual muscles, a soldier's cheeks bulge as he blows a trumpet, a dwarf leers as he carries the nail to crucify Christ with. Too savage and realistic to be Baroque art, there is nothing with which to compare it – it's as if Aleijadinho was driven to take his genius for realism to its logical conclusion, and finally shatter the restrictions of the Baroque tradition he had worked in all his life.

Things become even more interesting on the **symbolic** front when you look closely at the figures. Christ is more than once portrayed with a vivid red mark around his neck, which make many think he also represents Tiradentes. Support for the theory comes from the Roman soldiers, viciously caricatured, whom Aleijadinho gives two left feet and ankle boots – which only the Portuguese wore.

Although nothing is known of Aleijadinho's politics, he was a native Brazilian and lived through the *Inconfidência* in Ouro Preto. He would certainly have known Tiradentes by sight, and it is more than likely that Congonhas' Christ is meant to represent him.

If the cedar figures are outside the Baroque tradition, the statues of the **Prophets** are its finest expression in all Brazil: carved from blocks of soapstone they dominate both the garden they look down on and the church they lead to. They are remarkably dramatic, larger than lifesize, full of movement and expression; perched on the parapet, you look up at them against the backdrop of either hills or sky. Travellers have left pages of descriptions – Richard Burton, dreadful Victorian philistine that he was, thought them "grotesque and utterly vile" – but suffice it to say that they are one of the finest works of art anywhere in the world for their period.

The **church** is inevitably something of an anticlimax, but still interesting. The effigy of the dead Christ that Mendes brought over from Portugal is in a glass case in the altar, and through the door to the right of the altar is the cross which carried the image. The lampholders are Chinese dragons, yet more of the Macau influence also to be seen in Sabará and Diamantina.

Next to the church is a fascinating collection of **ex-votos**: it keeps irregular hours but the friendly uniformed guards will open it up for you – they're not around at lunchtime. The display will be familiar to anyone who has been to other pilgrimage centres in Brazil, and the photos, pictures and messages from grateful sufferers have a voyeuristic fascination. This collection is remarkable for the number of really old ex-votos, the earliest from a slave who recovered from fever in 1722. Others record in crude but vivid paintings things like being gored by a bull, being seriously burnt, or escaping from a coach crash. If you are lucky, you will also find a row of Aleijadinho's Passion figures being restored. The ex-votos room doubles as a workshop, and you get a better view of them here than in their chapels.

The **bus** to take you back to the *Rodoviária* leaves from the parking bay behind the church.

Staying over and moving on

The best place **to stay** in Congonhas is the *Colonial*, overlooking the church and gardens; good and cheap. The *Hotel Casarão* at the bottom of the hill is less pleasant. If you want to **eat**, the *Cova do Daniel*, next to Bom Jesus, is a good restaurant.

Most people see Congonhas as a **day trip**, as it's easily the least attractive of the historic cities to stay in. The nearest decent base is São João Del Rey (see below), but you'll need to get a bus back to the *Petrobras* service station in Murtinho and wait there for one of the Belo Horizonte–São João buses; Friday and Sunday are bad, as inter-city coaches tend to be full. Instead, you may find yourself having to hop local buses from the crossroads at Murtinho to LAGOA DOURADA, from where there is a local bus to São João, the last leaving at 8.10pm: or you could try hitching. It is possible to start out from Belo Horizonte or Ouro Preto, go to Congonhas with enough time to see Bom Jesus, and still get to São João in the evening, but only if you set out early; add on two hours to the departure times of the Belo Horizonte–São João buses for a rough idea of when buses leave Murtinho for São João.

São João Del Rey

SÃO JOÃO DEL REY is the only one of the historic cities to have adjusted successfully to life after the gold rush. It has all the usual trappings of the *cidades históricas* – gilded churches, well stocked museums, colonial mansions – but it's also a thriving market town; easily the largest of the historic cities, with a population of around 80,000. This modern prosperity complements the colonial atmosphere rather than compromising it and, with its wide central avenue, stone bridges, squares and trees, São João is a very attractive place, well worth lingering over. If possible, stay over a Friday, Saturday or Sunday when you can take the "Smoking Mary", a lovingly restored nineteenth-century steam train, to the nearby village of Tiradentes – a great day out.

Founded in 1699 on the São João River, the town had the usual turbulent early years, but distinguished itself by successfully turning to ranching and trade when the gold ran out early in the last century. There is still a textile factory, and São João's carpets were once famous. Tiradentes was born here, Aleijadinho worked here, and in more recent times the great *mineiro* politician, **Tancredo Neves**, shepherded Brazil out of military rule when he was elected President in 1985. Tragically, he died before he took office (see "History" in *Contexts*) and is buried in the nearest place the town has to a shrine in the cemetery of São Francisco.

Around the Centre

São João has two colonial areas, both off the broad Avenida Tancredo Neves that forms the spine of the city. Up the only hill is a small zone around the beautiful Igreja de São Francisco, linked to the other side of town by two eighteenth-century stone bridges; the Ponte da Cadeia at the bottom of Rua Gabriel Passos, and the Ponte do Rosário. The latter leads into the commercial centre, usually bustling with people, cars and the horse-drawn trailers of rural Minas. This commercial zone sprang up in the nineteenth century, and shields the colonial area proper, several blocks of cobbled streets which jumble together Baroque churches, elegant mansions and the pastel fronts of humbler houses. For once you have the luxury of wandering around without losing your breath, as São João is largely flat.

The colonial sections are complemented by some fine buildings of more recent eras, notably the end of the last century, when the town's prosperity and self-confidence was high. The 1920s and 1930s were also good times – some of the vaguely Art Deco buildings combine surprisingly well with the colonial ones. The main public buildings line **Avenida Tancredo Neves**, making it very grand for a town centre; there's a sumptuous French-style theatre, and a graceful town hall with an imposing *Banco do Brasil* building facing it. The relaxed atmosphere is reinforced by the number of bars and restaurants, and if you stumble across knots of people staring at walls, take a closer look: in São João two traditional "street newspapers" still survive, the *Jornal do Povão* and *Jornal do Poste*. Broadsheets rather than papers, they are posted on the streets for passers-by to catch up on local events, just as they were in the earliest days of the Brazilian press.

The most impressive of the town's colonial churches is the newest, the **Igreja de São Francisco de Assis** (Tues–Sun 8am–noon & 1.30–8pm), finished in 1774. Overlooking a square with towering palms – some more than a century old – the church is exceptionally large, with an ornately carved exterior by a pupil of Aleijadinho. The master himself contributed the intricate decorations of the side chapels, which can be seen in all their glory now that the original paint and gilding has been stripped off. From the plaques, you'll see that the church has been visited by some illustrious guests, including President Mitterand of France. They came to pay homage at the **grave of Tancredo Neves**, in the cemetery behind the church. Tancredo was a canny and pragmatic politician in the Minas tradition, but with a touch of greatness; the transition to civilian rule in 1985 would not have happened without his skills. He was born in and spent all his life in São João, where he was loved and is still very much missed. Eerily, to some, he died the day Tiradentes died, who was also born in São João. His black marble grave has a rather fine epitaph from one of his speeches: "You shall have my bones, land that I love, the final blending of my being with these blessed hills". It is significant to see several ex-votos placed upon the grave, plaques thanking him "for graces granted": when people call Tancredo a saint, they mean it literally.

Across the avenue renamed after Tancredo an excellent museum, the **Museu do SPHAN** (Tues–Sun noon–5.30pm), is housed in a magnificently restored colonial mansion and run by the Brazilian equivalent of the National Trust. Perhaps the most fascinating pieces here are the eighteenth-century ex-votos on the ground floor, their vivid illustrations detailing the pickles that both masters and slaves got themselves into – José Alves de Carvalho was stabbed in the chest while crossing a bridge on the way home in 1765; a slave called Antônio had his leg broken and was half buried for hours in a mine cave-in. (Happily, the fact they had an ex-voto made means that they all recovered.) On the first floor are several figures of saints made by ordinary people in the eighteenth century: they have a simplicity and directness that makes them stand out. There's a collection of furniture and relics, too, and one of the oddest items is on the top floor – a machine used until 1928 to select the draft numbers of unfortunate army conscripts.

A block away from Avenida Tancredo Neves lies the main street of the other colonial area, **Largo do Rosário**. One end is formed by the small Rosário church, which looks onto a cobbled square dominated by two stunning colonial mansions: the one nearest the church is the **Solar dos Neves**, the family home of the Neves clan for over two centuries, and the place where Tancredo was born and lived – you can't visit, as the family still lives there. Behind the church, on the corner of a humble street, there's a 1920s house which resembles an Art Deco radio. A couple of buildings along from the Solar dos Neves is an excellent **Museu de Arte Sacra** (Tues–Sun 9am–5pm), contained within another sensitively restored house. The collection is small but very good – highlights are a finely painted Saint George and a remarkable figure of Christ mourned by Mary Magdalene, with rubies representing drops of blood. As you go around, you're accompanied by Baroque church music, which complements the pieces perfectly. Incidentally, the museum also has a small gallery for exhibitions by São João's large artistic colony.

Almost next door is a magnificent early Baroque church, the **Catedral Basílica de Nossa Senhora de Pilar** (Tues–Sun 7–11am & 2–4pm), completed in 1721. The interior is gorgeous: only Pilar in Ouro Preto and Santo Antônio in Tiradentes are as liberally plastered with gold. The gilding is seen to best effect over the altar, a riot of Rococo pillars, angels and curlicues. The ceiling painting is all done with vegetable dyes, and there is a beautiful tiled floor. There are other churches, too, if you're enthusiastic, though none of the same standard as either São Francisco or Pilar. The **Igreja de Nossa Senhora das Mercês**, behind Pilar, dates from 1750, while the elegant facade of **Nossa Senhora do Carmo** forms the other end of Largo do Rosário.

All the practical details

Arriving at the *Rodoviária* you'll have to take a local bus into the centre: the stop isn't the obvious one immediately outside the main entrance – instead you need to turn left and take any bus from the stop on the other side of the road. It will leave you at the **Terminal Turístico** (daily 6am–6pm), right in the middle of town: pick up the very useful free booklet with a clear map of the centre and all the opening hours marked.

Finding somewhere to stay is not a problem as accommodation in São João is plentiful and often excellent value. There are several dirt cheap *dormitórios* within sight of the *Terminal Turístico*, but you would be much better off (for only a slight rise in price) at either the *Hotel Brasil* or the *Hotel Colonial*, nearby on Avenida Tancredo Neves: rooms at the front have great views. Of the medium range places, best value is the *Casarão Grande*, a converted mansion near São Francisco church, where rooms are a snip at $8, and an added attraction is a good collection of pottery from the Jequitinhonha valley. More expensive, but still very reasonable, are the lovely *Pousada Requinte* on Rua Padre José Maria, and the two smarter hotels on Avenida Tancredo Neves, *Porto Real* and *Lenheiro Palace*.

Eating and drinking

Across Avenida Tancredo Neves from the São Francisco church, close to the Museu do SPHAN, you'll find two of the best **restaurants** in town; the *Churrascaria Ramon*, which does a good value *churrasco*, and the *Quinta do Ouro*, for the best *mineiro* food in São João.

Interior towns are notorious for being dead at night, but São João is a very definite exception to the rule at the weekend. This is partly because it is a popular destination for trippers from Belo Horizonte, but is mainly down to the large numbers of young people from São João itself who flock into the centre to drink, go to the cinema, roar up and down on scooters and hang out in bars. Almost all of the action is concentrated on Avenida Tiradentes, which runs parallel to Avenida Tancredo Neves, one block in on the São Francisco side. It is lined with **bars**, several of them more than usually good. Look for *Kakitu's*, near the cinema, which does very good snacks (the *fígado acebolado*, chunks of tender liver fried with onions and speared on cocktail sticks, is delicious); also *Porão* and *Zilo*, nearer the São Francisco end. Many have live music at weekends and they get very crowded later on when large numbers of good-natured people start spilling out onto the pavements.

The train to Tiradentes

If you're in São João between Friday and Sunday, don't miss the half-hour **train ride** to the colonial village of TIRADENTES, fifteen kilometres away. There are frequent buses, too (from São João's *Rodoviária*), but they don't compare to the trip on a nineteenth-century steam train, with rolling stock from the 1930s, immaculately maintained and run with great enthusiasm. You may think yourself immune to the romance of steam, and be bored by the collection of old steam engines and railway equipment in the nineteenth-century station on Avenida Tancredo Neves – the **Estação Ferroviária** – but by the time you've bought your ticket you'll be hooked: the booking hall is right out of a Thirties movie, the train hisses and spits out cinders, and as you sit down in carriages filled with excited children, it's all you can do not to run up and down the aisle with them.

Built in the 1880s, as the textile industry took off in São João, this was one of the earliest railway lines in Brazil and the trains were immediately christened *Maria Fumaça*, "Smoking Mary". The service runs only on Friday, Saturday and Sunday, when **trains** leave São João at 10am and 2.15pm, returning from Tiradentes at 1pm and 5pm. If you want to stay longer, accommodation in Tiradentes is easy to find, or you could get one of the many **local buses** back to São João. Sit on the left leaving São João for the best views, and sit as far from the engine as you can: steam trains bring tears to your eyes in more ways than one.

The half-hour ride is very scenic, following the banks of the winding Rio Grande – here no wider than a large stream – and granting fine views of the slopes of the **Serra de São João**, which by the time it gets to Tiradentes has reared up into a series of rocky bluffs. You are travelling through one of the oldest areas of gold mining in Minas Gerais, and from the train you'll see clear traces of the eighteenth-century mine workings in the hills. In the foreground, the rafts on the river have pumps which suck up alluvium from the river bed, from which gold is extracted by modern *garimpeiros*, heirs to over two centuries of mining tradition.

Tiradentes

TIRADENTES was founded as early as 1702, but had already been overshadowed by São João by the 1730s and is now no more than a sleepy village. The core is much as it was in the eighteenth century, straggling down the side of a hill crowned by the twin towers of the **Igreja Matriz de Santo Antônio** (Tues–Sun noon–4pm). Completed in 1710, it's the earliest of the major Minas Baroque churches, and for over a decade was the largest and richest church in any of the mining towns. It was built with the special extravagance of the newly rich, using more gold, the locals say, than any other in Brazil save the Capela Dourada in Recife. Whether this is true or not – and Pilar in Ouro Preto is probably as rich as either – the glinting and winking of the gold around the altar is certainly impressive. You can tell how early it is from the comparative crudeness of the statues and carvings; formal, stiff and with none of the movement of developed Minas Baroque. The exterior already needed restoring by the time Aleijadinho was active, and he left his usual signature of beautifully carved soapstone panels on the facade.

From the steps of the church you look down an unspoilt colonial street – the old town hall with the veranda has a restored eighteenth-century gaol – framed by the crests of the hills. If you had to take one photograph to summarise Minas Gerais, this would be it. Before walking down the hill, check out the **Museu Padre Toledo** (Wed–Mon 9–11am & noon–4pm), to the right of Santo Antônio. Padre Toledo was one of the *Inconfidentes* and built the mansion that is now the museum. He obviously didn't let being a priest stand in the way of enjoying the pleasures of life: the two-storey *sobrado* must have been very comfortable, and the ceiling paintings might be dressed up as classical allegories but even so are not the sort of thing you would expect a priest to commission. The museum comprises the usual mixture of furniture and religious art, but the interesting part is the yard out back, now converted into toilets but once the old slave quarters.

A more substantial reminder of the slave presence is the **Igreja da Nossa Senhora do Rosário dos Pretos**, down the hill and along the first street to the right. There could be no more eloquent reminder of the harsh divisions between masters and slaves than this small chapel, built by slaves for their own worship. There is gilding even here – some colonial miners were freed blacks working on their own account – and two fine figures of the black Saint Benedict stand out, but overall the church is moving precisely because it is so simple and dignified.

Some accommodation

Tiradentes might have a placid and timeless air during the week, but it gets surprisingly lively at weekends as the bars and *pensões* fill up with people attracted by its relaxed atmosphere. Finding **accommodation** is never a problem, as a good proportion of the town's population have turned their homes into guesthouses or *pousadas*; just take your pick along the road leading into the village from the railway station, or around the lovely Praça das Mercês it leads into. On weekend nights the visitors duly shatter the calm they came to find in the many small **bars** – the *Lumiar* has the best atmosphere.

Diamantina and the Jequitinhonha Valley

DIAMANTINA, home town of Juscelino Kubitschek, the president who built Brasília, is the only historic city to the north of Belo Horizonte and, at six hours by coach, is by some way the furthest from it. Yet the journey itself is one of the reasons for going there, as the road heads into the different landscapes of northern Minas on its way to the *sertão mineiro*. The second half of the journey is much the most spectacular, so to see it in daylight you need to catch either the 9am or the 11.30am bus from Belo Horizonte.

Diamantina has a very different atmosphere to any of the other colonial towns. Still a functioning diamond-mining town, it is also the gateway to the **Jequitinhonha Valley**, the river valley that is the heart of the Minas *sertão*. The green hills of the southern half of Minas seem very distant in Diamantina, set in a rocky, windswept and often cold highland zone – take a sweater or jacket.

The journey

Diamantina itself, scattered down the steep side of a rocky valley, faces escarpments the colour of rust; the setting has a lunar quality you also come across in parts of the Northeastern *sertão*. In fact, at Diamantina you're not quite in the *sertão* – that begins roughly at ARAÇUAI, some 300km to the north – but in the uplands of the **Serra do Espinhaço**, the highlands that form the spine of the state. Almost as soon as you leave Belo Horizonte, the look of the land changes to the stubby trees and savanna of the Planalto Central, the inland plateau that makes up much of central Brazil. At the dull modern town of CURVELO, roughly half-way to Diamantina, the road forks – left to Brasília and the Planalto proper, right to Diamantina and the *sertão*.

You hit the highland foothills soon after Curvelo, and from then on the route is very scenic. The road winds its way up spectacularly forbidding hills, the granite outcrops enlivened by caetus, wild flowers and the bright yellow and purple ipê trees, until it reaches the upland plateau, 1300m above sea level. This heralds yet another change: windswept moorland with few trees and strange rock formations. Keep your eyes peeled on the left and you'll see traces of an old stone road, with flagstones seemingly going nowhere: this is the old slave road, which for over a century was the only communication line between southern Minas and the *sertão*.

The town

Even if it were not set in such a striking landscape, Diamantina's **history** would still mark it out from the other historic cities. The Portuguese crown had reason to feel bitter about the gold strikes in Minas Gerais: it was forced to expend blood and treasure in prising the gold from the hands of the Paulistas, and when diamonds were found here in 1720 the same mistakes were not repeated. *Arraial do Tijuco*, as Diamantina was called at first, was put under strict military control. People could only come and go with royal passes and the town was isolated for almost a century. This may have something to do with Diamantina's very distinctive atmosphere. Although it has few buildings or churches to rival the masterpieces of Ouro Preto or Congonhas, the passage of time has had little effect on the large colonial centre of the town, which is the least spoilt of any of the *cidades históricas*. The narrow stone-flagged streets with their overhanging Chinese eaves and perfectly preserved colonial houses are exactly as they have been for generations.

Arriving and sleeping

Diamantina takes the *mineiro* penchant for building on slopes to extremes. Although the **Rodoviária** is not far from the centre of town, the only way back to it once there is by taxi, unless you have the legs of a mountain goat. The streets are either too narrow or too steep even for Brazil's intrepid local bus drivers. Fortunately the place is small enough for you to **get your bearings** very quickly. The central square is Praça Conselheiro Matta, which has the Catedral de Santo Antônio built in the middle of it – everyone calls the cathedral and the square "Sé". All the **places to stay**, and most of the sights, are within a stone's throw of here. The largest, priciest and most comfortable hotel is another Niemeyer creation, the *Tijuco*, where rooms start at $10. The *Hotel Dália* is both nicer and cheaper, no frills but a lovely two-storey building with fine views over Praça J Kubitschek. Good value, location and views are also to be had at *Grande Hotel*, Rua Quitanda 7; at *Pensão Avenida*, Avenida Francisco Sá 243; and *Hotel São Luiz*, further on at no. 557. More basic than most is *Hotel Carvalho* on Rua Quitanda. You can see most of these places from the cathedral.

Maps are free from the **tourist office** in the *Casa de Cultura*, tucked away at Praça Antônio Eulálio 55. There's also a **tourist post** in the bus station (daily 8–11am & 1–6pm), but it's often shut because of staff shortages. The reception at the *Hotel Tijuco* or the Museu do Diamante also hand out maps.

Mining in Diamantina

Uniquely among the *cidades históricas*, large sections of Diamantina still depend on mining for a living, and diamonds and gold are mined in the whole area using pans and motorised suction pumps called *chupadeiras*. This small-scale mining is known as *garimpagem*, these days best known as a feature of the Amazon gold rush but also a feature of life in Minas since colonial times. Walk around the backstreets in the centre, Rua Rosário for example, and you'll find several **mining stores**, instantly recognisable by the display of zinc pans for gold, and wire mesh pans used to sift the gravel that diamonds are found in. At weekends the *garim-*

peiros come in, piling into battered taxis and pick-ups for a night on the town, and the centre hums into the small hours – they are on the whole friendly and curious, belying their fearsome media image.

How much longer Diamantina can survive as a mining town is, however, uncertain as the *chupadeiras* are altering the courses and muddying the waterways for miles around. In river-infested Amazonia this wouldn't be a problem, but Diamantina is at the headwaters of the Rio Jequitinhonha, the only river in the *sertão mineiro* which doesn't run dry. For the inhabitants of the *sertão* the issue is simple: if anything happens to the river, they either die or migrate. In 1989, the state government closed all the *garimpos* down, and despite a spirited campaign by the *garimpeiros* they are still closed. They may end up having to move out, leaving Diamantina to rely on the little cotton that can grow, and a trickle of tourists.

The **Museu do Diamante** (Tues–Sun noon–5.30pm) on the cathedral square is for the time being the best place to get an idea of what *garimpagem* has meant to Diamantina. It's one of the best museums in Minas, not so much for the glories of its exhibits but the effort it makes to give you an idea of daily life in old Diamantina. The room behind the entrance desk is devoted to the history of mining in Diamantina: old mining instruments, maps and prints. Dominating everything is an enormous cast-iron English safe, brought by ox-cart all the way from Rio in the eighteenth century – it took eighteen months to get here, if you were wondering. It contains a riveting display of genuine gold and diamond jewellery and cut diamonds which are replicas: the originals are stashed in the *Banco do Brasil* across the road. On the upper shelf is a (genuine) pile of uncut diamonds and emeralds, as they would appear to *garimpeiros* panning – only the occasional dull glint distinguishes them from ordinary gravel. More disturbing is an appalling display of whips, chains and brands used on slaves right up until the late nineteenth century, though the terrifying-looking tongs, underneath the chains, are in fact colonial hair-curlers, and not torture instruments. The rest of the museum is great to wander through, stuffed with memorabilia from mouldering top-hats to photos of long dead town bandsmen: Diamantina has strong musical traditions and still supports *serestas*, small bands of accordion, guitar and flute players who stroll through the streets and hold dances around Carnaval, or on the evening of September 12, the *dia da seresta*.

Around the churches

Despite the ugliness of the **Catedral de Santo António**, built in 1932 on the site of an old colonial church, the cathedral square is worth savouring. It's lined with *sobrados*, many of them with exquisite ornamental ironwork – look closely and you'll see iron pineapples on the balconies. Most impressive of all are the serried windows of the massive *Prefeitura*, and the ornate *Banco do Brasil* building next to it.

For the other churches, you're faced with two problems. Most are closed for restoration, which is taking years, and though the workmen are usually happy to let you in, you're not seeing them at their best. Also, in recent years, a rash of thefts of artworks from churches in and around Diamantina has made people very reluctant to open them up for visitors: the opening hours given on the back of the town map are long obsolete. Disgracefully, some of the thieves were foreigners, and this has made people even more suspicious, so unless you can wheedle in Portuguese you stand little chance of getting in: ask at the nearest house for the *zelador* (guardian), and try your luck.

Fortunately, with one exception, the exteriors are actually more interesting than the interiors. Diamantina churches are very distinctive, simple but very striking, with stubby towers and Chinese eaves: street names, like Rua Macau do Meio and Rua Macau de Cima, recall where the Chinese craftsmen imported by the Portuguese lived during the eighteenth century. The one church worth trying to see the inside of, if at all possible, is the **Igreja do Carmo** on Rua Bonfim. Built between 1760 and 1765, legend has it that Chico da Silva, an ex-slave who married the heiress of Diamantina's richest miner, made sure the tower was built at the back of the church rather than the front, as was usual, so the bells didn't disturb her beauty sleep. Inside is an atypically florid interior, whose two main features are a rich, intricately carved altar screen and a gold-sheathed organ, which was actually built in Diamantina.

On the cobbled street leading down the hill from here is a local curiosity. The church at the bottom, **Igreja do Rosário**, has a tree growing in front of it: look closely and you can see a large distorted wooden cross embedded in the trunk and lower branches. The story behind this reads like something from Gabriel García Márquez, but did really happen. The year the old Sé church was knocked down, in 1932, the padre of Rosário planted a wooden cross outside his church to commemorate the chapel that old Diamantina had originally been built around. A fig tree sprouted up around it so that at first the cross seemed to flower – there's a photo of it at this stage in the Museu do Diamante – and eventually, rather than knocking it down, the tree grew up around the cross and ended up absorbing it.

Juscelino Kubitschek in Diamantina

Juscelino Kubitschek was born and spent the first seventeen years of his life in Diamantina. His enduring monument is the capital he built on the Planalto Central, Brasília, which fired Brazil's and the world's imagination and which now houses his remains: he was killed in a road accident in 1976. The house he was born and lived in is preserved as a shrine to his memory (Tues–Sun noon–5.30pm), on the steep Rua São Francisco, uphill from his statue at the bottom.

Juscelino had a meteoric political career. His energy, imagination and utterly uncompromising liberal instincts make him one of the great postwar presidents. You can understand his lifelong concern with the poor from the small, unpretentious house where he spent the first part of his life in poverty. Restoration has rather flattered it, as the photos of how it was when he lived there make plain – no Brazilian president has yet come from a humbler background. He was of the second generation of poor Czech immigrants: you won't find many family possessions because they didn't have any. The photos and the simplicity of the house are very moving, a refreshing contrast to the pampered corruption of many of his successors.

If you're interested, the **Casa de Cultura** in Praça Antônio Eulálio has a folder of photographs and clippings about Juscelino, relaxing with his *seresta* group – he was an accomplished guitarist – and being feted by the proud inhabitants of the town he clearly never left in spirit. Most of the bars still display his photograph, many dating from before he became President in 1956. And many still don't believe his death was a genuine accident, just as few *mineiros* believe Tancredo really died of natural causes. The massive turnout for Juscelino's funeral in Brasília in 1976 was one of the first times Brazilians dared to show their detestation of the military regime.

The municipal market

Diamantina's other important economic role is as the market town for the Jequitinhonha Valley. It's here that the products of the remote *sertão* towns of northeastern Minas are shipped and stockpiled before making their way to Belo Horizonte. The old **municipal market** on Praça Barão do Guaicuí, just a block downhill from the cathedral square, is the focus of Diamantina's trade, and worth seeing for the building alone, an interesting tiled wooden structure built in 1838 as a trading station by the Brazilian army. Its frontage, a rustic but very elegant series of shallow arches, played a significant role in modern Brazilian architecture. Niemeyer, who lived in Diamantina for a few months in the 1950s to build the *Hotel Tijuco*, was fascinated by it, and later used the shape for the striking exterior of the presidential palace in Brasília, the Palácio da Alvorada.

The market itself has a very Northeastern feel, with its cheeses, blocks of salt and raw sugar, and mules and horses tied up alongside the pick-ups. The food at the stalls here is very cheap, but only for the strong-stomached: the rich *mineiro* sausages (*linguiça*) are worth trying. From the market you have a fine vantage point of a square which is, if anything, even richer than the Praça Conselheiro Matta, a cornucopia of colonial window frames and balconies and exquisite ironwork. Most of the ground floors are still ordinary shops.

There is no *artesanato* section in the market, which is unfortunate since the most distinctive products of the Jequitinhonha Valley are its beautiful clay and pottery figures. The *Casa de Cultura*, on Praça Antônio Eulálio, has a very good collection for you to get a grasp of what the Jequitinhonha potters do, but buying it is difficult. The most reliable place is a friendly and very reasonably priced specialist **shop**, *Relíquias do Vale*, on the same street as the *Hotel Tijuco*, at Rua Macau de Meio 401. Besides the pottery, they also have a good stock of the rough but very rugged cotton clothes, hammocks and wall hangings that are the other specialities of the region.

Eating

The streets around the Catedral are the heart of the town, and there's no shortage of simple bars and *mineiro* **restaurants** here, like the *Capistrana* on Praça Antônio Eulálio, *Renata* on Rua Quitanda and *Confiança* on the cathedral square itself. Best of all is *Cantinha do Marinho*: you can see the tables on the first floor from Rua Alecrim, but the entrance is tucked away in Beco da Motta, in front of the cathedral. The menu is painted up on plaques on the wall, the food is good, and the prices are the best value in town – try a *doce de limão* to round off your meal.

Into the Jequitinhonha Valley

If you want to get a clearer idea of where the Jequitinhonha *artesanato* comes from, you have to head out into the *sertão* proper, and Diamantina is the obvious place to start your journey. Travelling into the **Jequitinhonha Valley** is not something to be undertaken lightly: it is one of the poorest and remotest parts of Brazil, the roads are bad, there are no hotels except bare flophouse *dormitórios*, and unless you speak good Portuguese you are liable to be looked on with great suspicion. There have been problems in recent years with foreigners buying up mining concessions and kicking out *garimpeiros*, and unless you can explain yourself people will assume you have ulterior motives. The region is so poor and isolated it's difficult for people to understand why outsiders, especially foreigners, would want to go there anyway.

If you need reasons, though, you don't have to look much further than the scenery, which is spectacularly beautiful, albeit forbidding. The landscapes are stunning, and bear some resemblance to the deserts of the American Southwest: massive granite hills and escarpments, cactus, rock, occasional wiry trees, and people tough as nails speaking with the lilting accent of the interior of the Northeast. Here you're a world away from the developed sophistication of southern and central Minas.

It seems wrong to call somewhere as off the beaten track as **ARAÇUAÍ** easy to get to, but it is the most accessible Jequitinhonha destination from Diamantina. You have to be up early – there is one bus a day at 7am (booking the day before is essential) – and the journey is hard; twelve hours of bouncing around on dusty dirt roads, hot as hell during the day and cold at night. The *dormitório* by the bus station is your only option for **accommodation**: take a hammock to avoid having to sleep in one of their beds. Araçuaí is no more than a large village, but it has the best place for buying *artesanato* in the whole region; a producers' co-operative called *Centro de Artesanato*, open Tuesday to Saturday but best to catch on a Saturday morning, when craft workers come in from surrounding villages to market.

From Araçuaí, if time were no object, you could hop local buses to ITINGA and then on thirty kilometres to the good quality BR-116 highway into Bahia state. Once you get to VITÓRIA DA CONQUISTA there are ready connections to all Bahian cities, but it could well take you a couple of days to get that far. It is often quicker to take the bus that leaves every other day to Belo Horizonte and make your connections there: or taking the daily bus to Diamantina and connections to Belo Horizonte is also a possibility.

Serro

A much easier trip from Diamantina is the day's outing to the even sleepier colonial village of **SERRO**. It takes over two hours to get there, so you'll have to start early: there are only two buses from Diamantina, one at 6am and the other at 3pm; and there are two daily buses back to Diamantina, one at 5.30am and the other at 3.30pm; if you want to return to Diamantina the same day, buy your ticket for the return journey when you arrive. The ride there is always interesting, especially in the early morning when the granite hills loom eerily out of the mist and the clouds seem only a few feet above the ground: warm clothing to keep out the morning cold is essential.

Serro is set in beautiful hill country, dominated by the pilgrimage church of **Santa Rita** on a rise above the centre, reached by steps cut into the slope. Little-visited, this is not so much a place to do and see things in, as somewhere peaceful to unwind and appreciate the leisurely pace of life in rural Minas. There are six colonial churches, but they are impossible to get to see: a spate of thefts has made the keyholders reluctant to let you in, even once you locate them. Founded in 1702, when gold was discovered in the stream nearby, Serro was at one time a rather aristocratic place. Across the valley, easily recognisable from the clump of palms, is the old house of the Barão do Serro which now houses a small **museum**, mostly composed of prints and old newspaper cuttings: the more valuable artefacts are all in storage waiting for the inevitable museum of sacred art: it's currently being constructed in the **Igreja do Bom Jesus do Matozinhos** and is scheduled to open at the end of 1990, finances permitting, just along the road from the museum.

From the front of the museum you get a good view of the finest buildings in the village, namely the the enormous **Casa do Barão de Diamantina**, clinging to the hillside, beautifully restored and now a school, and the twin Chinese towers of the **Igreja do Matriz**. The church forms one end of a main street that is completely unspoilt; at the other is the Santa Rita hill.

At the foot of the hill is the best **place to stay**, *Hotel Itacolomí*, which has a solid *mineiro* restaurant open to non-residents. Also on the main street is a good *pousada*, *Vila do Príncipe*, a cheap *churrascaria* of the same name nearby, and four cheap *pensões*. The **bus station** is almost in the centre: ignore the attentions of the taxi drivers, walk uphill for some thirty metres, and you're in the heart of the village.

SOUTHERN MINAS: THE SPA TOWNS

The drive **south** from Belo Horizonte to Rio turns into one of the most spectacular in Brazil once you cross the state border and encounter the glorious scenery of the Serra dos Órgãos, but there is little to detain you in Minas along the way. The route passes through Juiz de Fora, one of the larger interior cities, but it's an ugly industrial centre, best seen from the window of a coach.

The route **southwest to São Paulo**, however, is altogether different. The hills, rising into mountains near the state border, make it one of the most attractive parts of Minas.

Six or seven hours from Belo Horizonte there's a cluster of resort towns, each with a very distinctive look and feel, built around mineral water springs: **Cambuquira**, **São Lourenço**, **Caxambú**, **Lambarí** and, most importantly, the lively city of **Poços de Caldas**. With the exception of Poços de Caldas, they are all small, quiet and popular with older people, who flock there to take the waters and baths. They each revolve around a *parque hidromineral*, a park built around the springs, incorporating bath-houses and fountains, and are stuffed with hotels and guesthouses. Poços de Caldas is altogether different. Many times larger than the spa towns, it is a very lively city, set in spectacular volcanic mountains, and is a traditional place for couples to spend their honeymoon – so it's packed with young holidaymakers.

From Belo Horizonte to the Circuito das Aguas

It's five hours from Belo Horizonte before you hit the gateway to the *Circuito das Aguas*, the "Water Circuit", as the **spa resorts** are collectively known.

TRES CORAÇÕES is the first stop and although not a resort town itself, it is more famous, in Brazil at least, than any of the spas. This rather anonymous modern town was the birthplace of Edson Arantes do Nascimento, **Pelé** – the greatest footballer ever – and it's a holy place for any lover of the game. Keep an eye out on the left as the coach winds its way through the centre, and you'll see a bronze statue of him, holding aloft the World Cup, which Brazil (and Pelé) won in 1958, 1962 and 1970. Looking at the steep streets of the poor urban fringes he came from, you can understand why he developed such amazing ball control: one slip and it's a long chase to get the ball back.

After Tres Corações the hill country begins, although it's hardly got going before you run into the first and smallest of the spas, **CAMBUQUIRA**, a pleasant enough place but nothing to compare with the other resorts. It's much better to press on to the nearby cluster of spa towns, all within a relatively short distance of each other.

Caxambú

Just pipping São Lourenço (see below) for the title of nicest of the smaller spas, **CAXAMBÚ** was a favourite haunt of the Brazilian royal family in the nineteenth century. Dom Pedro II regularly took the waters here, which were meant to restore fertility as well as treating stomach, liver and kidney complaints: they certainly did the trick for his daughter, Princesa Isabel, who produced three children after only two visits and built the small **Igreja de Santa Isabel de Hungria**, overlooking the springs, in gratitude.

The **Parque Hidromineral** in the centre of town is delightful. Built in the last decades of the nineteenth century and the early years of the twentieth, it's dotted with eleven oriental-style pavilions sheltering the actual springs, and houses an ornate Turkish bath-house which is very reasonably priced – $3 gets you a Turkish bath in turn-of-the-century opulence, and there are also various kinds of sauna and massage available. The bath-house is open daily from 8.30am to noon for men, and 2pm to 5.30pm for women.

Even if you don't take the waters, wandering around the immaculately kept park, rich with the scent of pine and flowering trees, and overlooked by hills, is a pleasure. Even the bottling plant has an ornate Edwardian facade so that it complements its surroundings. And, next to the bowling track, concealed behind a curtain of pine, is what must be the most elegant urinal in Minas Gerais. As in all the mineral parks, once you've paid the nominal entrance fee you can sample any of the springs and bring bottles to fill up and take away, but drink the waters with caution: a mere mouthful is enough to produce intestinal rumblings and have you bolting to the toilets by the side of the bath-house. Brazilians swear by them for "cleaning out the system".

Next to the park is a good **market**, specialising in honey and homemade syrupy sweets, which leads on to a tree-shaded square, **Praça Dom Pedro**, with yet another oriental pavilion. If you're tired of walking, a new attraction is provided by the **chair-lift**, which runs from opposite the bus station up to the *Cristo Redentor* that overlooks the centre – hold tight, as it goes faster than you'd think. At the top there's a tremendous view, not only of the town and the park but also the lovely hill country in which it nestles. There's a restaurant, too, where the views are better than the food. The only drawback is that the chair-lift closes down at 4.30pm, which means you can't appreciate what would be a very spectacular sunset.

Some practicalities

The **Rodoviária** is on the far edge of town, but Caxambú is so small that it doesn't really matter. A **tourist information post** in the terminal building hands out free town maps, but again, you don't need them to find your way around. Basically, there's one main street, Wenceslau Braz, much of which is taken up by the Parque Hidromineral, and around which the town is built. Although walking is easy, it's fun to get one of the cheapish **horsedrawn cabs**, or *charretes*, that seem especially appropriate to Caxambú's turn-of-the-century surroundings.

For its size, Caxambú has a surprising range of **hotels**. Either of the luxury-class *Hotel Grande* and *Hotel Glória*, opposite the park, would make a great setting for a costume drama. The best middle-range place in town is the *Hotel Dom Pedro*, on Praça Dom Pedro, with rooms starting at $10; *Hotel Alex* and *Hotel Marquês*, near Praça Dom Pedro, are similarly priced. The cheapest places are the *Santa Cecília* on Wenceslau Braz (the *Video Hotel* next door is a video shop, not a hotel); *Hotel Lider*, nearby, and the *Jardim Imperial*, near the bus station on Rua Dr Viotti.

If you decide to **stay in São Lourenço** rather than Caxambú, the last bus is at 7.15pm, or a taxi there costs $12. If you're completely stuck, the midnight *Resendense* bus to São Paulo goes via São Lourenço, although you will probably have to stand for the forty minutes it takes to get there.

São Lourenço

If Caxambú is the last word in Edwardian elegance, **SÃO LOURENÇO** rivals it with its displays of Art Deco brilliance. Its *Parque das Aguas* is studded with striking 1940s pavilions and has a stunning bath-house that looks more like a film set for a Hollywood high society comedy. The most upmarket and modern-looking of the small spas, the town is popular with young and old alike.

It's built along the shores of a beautiful lake, a large chunk of which has been incorporated into the **Parque** (daily 7am–5.30pm; the pavilions with the mineral water fountains open daily 7–11.30am & 2–5.15pm), and during the day it's here that everything goes on. Much larger than the one in Caxambú, and much more modern, the park is kept to the same immaculate standard: again, a lovely place for a stroll, with its brilliant white pavilions, forested hillside, clouds of butterflies and birds – though steer clear of the black swans on the lake, which have a nasty temper. There are **rowing boats** for hire, and an ornamental, artificial island. The **Balneário** itself (daily 8.30am–noon & 2.30–5pm) is unique for its *banho carbogasoso*, a fizzy mineral water bath that is a kind of natural jacuzzi. Unfortunately, you can only have a go with a doctor's prescription; it's meant to be good for hypertension. There are ordinary baths (*duchas*), though, and saunas, available for $3–5 (a massage costs $10) and it's worth paying for the surroundings: marbled floors, mirror walls and white-coated attendants. There are separate sections for men and women.

Staying and moving on

The **Rodoviária** is half a block away from the main street, Avenida Dom Pedro II, which is lined with bars, hotels and restaurants. There is a **youth hostel** at no. 468, and cheap but clean **hotels** are the *Hotel Miranda* at no. 545 and *Aliança* at no. 505. A little more expensive, but a lot quieter, are the *Hotel Ponto Chic* and *Hotel Colonial*, by the square where the Parque is. The *Hotel Brasil* which dominates the square is luxury class.

Buses to Lambarí, next town on the circuit, take about ninety minutes – take the bus to VARGINHA. **Buses to Caxambú** leave at 7am, 10am, 2pm, 3.50pm and 6pm, or take a taxi from the post in front of the Parque, where there is a **tourist information kiosk** which has free town maps. There's no direct bus to Poços de Caldas: you need to get the 11.45am to Pouso Alegre and make a connection there – total journey time is around six hours.

Around São Lourenço: Cristina

Easily reached by local services from the São Lourenço *Rodoviária*, the small town of **CRISTINA** is forty minutes' drive away. Even by the high standards of the region the journey is spectacularly beautiful, and though Cristina is a traditional farming village rather than a spa town, it has a setting that would be hard to beat – surrounded and overlooked on all sides by rolling hills and farmland. It's very typical of the interior, with a main square where people sit under the trees, and where little new seems to have been built since the 1920s. Unaccustomed to visitors, the people are exceptionally friendly. It makes a good day trip from São Lourenço, and if you want to stay there are two cheap but perfectly adequate **hotels** on the main square, the better the *Hotel Cristina*. There are several simple bars and restaurants, too.

Lambarí

LAMBARÍ is the nearest you get to a downmarket spa town on the *Circuito das Aguas*. It has a beautiful lake and the obligatory spa-park, but lacks the prosperous feel of Caxambú and São Lourenço. The **Rodoviária** is on the main square, which also houses the **Parque das Águas**, small and scruffy, with only one fountain. The water, though, is rather better than elsewhere; gassy and less chemical, you can drink it without worrying about the effect it will have on your insides.

A couple of blocks uphill from the centre are the main – in fact the only – sights in Lambarí, the lake and an elegant 1940s building. All colonnades and courtyards, this was originally built as a luxury casino and is now partly used as a town hall and library. It's a shame to see such a magnificent building so underused – much of it simply lies empty, and nobody stops you wandering around – but at least it isn't an exclusive hotel. Next to it is a pleasant park with bars, a waterfall and a surprisingly well-kept public swimming pool; the lake itself is rather polluted. The *Cascata* **restaurant**, overlooking the waterfall, has the best location in town.

Several cheap **hotels** are either on or near the square, and in the nearby Rua G. Stockler are two places worth checking out. The *Amigão* at no. 37 is a simple but good *mineiro* restaurant whose enormous portions are excellent value. And at *Prince*, a block before, on the shelves marked "*Pinga da Roça*", you will find a good selection of rums distilled, in the traditional way, on the ranches hereabouts; much smoother and less fiery than the industrially produced varieties.

Poços de Caldas

POÇOS DE CALDAS is the easiest of the Minas spa resorts to get to. Rich Brazilians from the large cities of southern Brazil like to take breaks here, and there are daily bus services to and from Rio and São Paulo as well as from Belo Horizonte. It's some distance from the smaller spa towns, and is an altogether different place; definitely a city rather than a town, it is the liveliest spot in Minas after Belo Horizonte.

If possible, you should make the journey in daylight, because the countryside is something special and shouldn't be missed: mountainous rather than hilly, it would look rather like the spectacular border zone with Espírito Santo in eastern Minas, if it weren't for the type of forest, an uplands mixture of pine, eucalyptus and monkey-puzzle.

On the way, after the ugly modern town of POUSO ALEGRE, there is one of the more spectacular climbs into mountains that Brazil has to offer, with superb views of hills and plains laid out like sheets behind and beneath the road. It is easy to see why the whole region became a resort area.

The city itself, almost on the state line with São Paulo, nestles in the crater of an extinct volcano – you can trace the rim of what must once have been an enormous crater along the broken horizons. The centre is mostly modern, laid out in a grid pattern with a few skycrapers, but made very pleasant by huge tree-studded squares, an enormous but elegant bath-house, and the closeness of the thickly forested slopes of Alto da Serra, the hill crowned with the obligatory *Cristo Redentor* overlooking the city.

Arriving and finding a place to stay

If first impressions counted on arrival, you'd probably take one look at the dirty and decrepit **Rodoviária** and catch the next bus out: its sole redeeming feature is that it is very central, a short distance from the huge central square, Praça Pedro Sanchez, easily recognisable by the large Edwardian style bath-house set in gardens and fountains.

There is a **tourist office** in a Chinese-style kiosk on the corner of Avenida Francisco Salles and the main square: it hands out free, good quality town maps with places of interest numbered, though a hitch at the printers means that the key has been left out! This is not the drawback it seems, as everything goes on around the square and in the blocks to the east of it, and the grid pattern makes it easy to get your bearings.

You will find a *TELEMIG* office just up from the square, on Rua Minas Gerais, where you can make international **telephone** calls.

Accommodation will be the least of your worries. The entire city is geared to catering for visitors and even during holiday periods, when people flock from as far afield as Rio and São Paulo, capacity is never really stretched. Rua Paraná, behind the bath-house, has an over priced hotel named after the city but the *Hotel Serra Verde* nearby is very reasonable. Similar good medium-range hotels are the *Imperador*, looking onto the square on Avenida Francisco Salles, and the *Continental*, nearby on the corner with Rua Goiás. The best cheaper places are on Rua São Paulo: try *Hotel Guarany* at no. 106 or the *Hotel Serra* opposite; *Hotel Aparecida* is cheaper and nearer the bus station at Avenida Francisco Salles 113, but it's also rather grimier.

Around the town: taking the waters and up the cable car

Poços de Caldas doesn't have a single mineral water park that congregates all the springs, along the lines of Caxambú or São Lourenço; they are scattered all over the city and somehow don't seem as impressive when not set in a garden. The nearest, within easy walking distance of the centre, is **Fonte Frayha**, on the corner of Rua Amazonas with Rua Pernambuco. You can, however, take the waters in style in the opulent bath-house, the **Termas Antônio Carlos** (Mon, Wed & Fri 8am–noon & 4–6pm, Thurs & Sat 8am–noon & 4–8pm, Sun 8am–noon), whose Edwardian bulk looms over the main square. It specialises in sulphur baths, meant to be good for stomach ulcers, but also offers the usual range of saunas and massages: less personal than the *balneários* in the smaller resorts, but the increase in scale makes a Turkish bath in such splendid surroundings an experience.

On one side of the Praça, not far from the bath-house, is a **cable car** station, from where you're whisked up to the Alto da Serra and the Christ statue overlooking the city. It's a must: the views at the top are tremendous, there is the usual restaurant with panoramic views, and it's the starting point for an exceptionally scenic walk back down – although, sneakily, you can only buy a return ticket for the cable car. It doesn't run on Tuesday, otherwise between 8.30am and 11am, and 1pm and 6pm; tickets are $3.

The initial stretch carries you just above rooftop level over part of the city, and then rears up over the forest, before trundling into the station at the top of the hill ten minutes later; there is no better way to see Poços de Caldas. A viewing platform is built around the *Cristo Redentor*: take a jacket, because the wind can really blow at this altitude. In front sprawls the city – it's from here that you can best make out the remaining bits of the volcanic crater in which it is built – and behind, a beautiful view frames hills, ranches and even a lake.

If you have time and it isn't raining, try returning by the dirt road that winds down from the top. It brings you out a short distance from the centre and is an extremely scenic stroll through thick forest, with the bends offering you alternate glimpses of city and countryside.

Eating, drinking and nightlife

As you would expect in a place so popular with young couples, the nightlife here is very animated, especially at weekends. There are scores of bars and restaurants, many of which put their tables out on the pavement, thronged until late with people seeing and being seen, talking, drinking and listening to music.

Liveliest of all is the stretch of **Rua São Paulo** leading down to the square: there is a very good upstairs bar here, *Verde Amarelo*, which has high quality, live Brazilian music for free on Friday and Saturday nights; and possibly the best juice bar in Minas Gerais, *Casa de Sucos*, on the corner of São Paulo and Assis Figueiredo. It has an amazing variety of freshly made *sucos*, which come in jugs that run to three glassfuls, and also an excellent range of sandwiches and desserts – the *doce de arroz* translates literally as "rice pudding", but that doesn't begin to convey how delicious it is, flavoured with vanilla, lemon and cinnamon.

The more expensive **restaurants** are on Assis Figueiredo: a good rule is to avoid the air-conditioned ones, which are vastly overpriced. A recommended place is *Fenícia*, a serious meat restaurant where the portions are enormous and the beef good enough to satisfy even Argentinians – it has a *lanchonete* attached to the restaurant proper which does good burgers and sandwiches, and is the only place that rivals the *Casa de Sucos* for a snacky lunch.

EASTERN MINAS: CAPARAÓ NATIONAL PARK

Eastern Minas Gerais is the least visited part of the state and, travelling along the BR-262 highway leading to Espírito Santo state and the Atlantic, it seems very clear why. Although the *mineiro* hill country is pretty enough, the towns scattered along it are ugly industrial centres, steel mills belching fumes common even in the gaps between the towns. However, if you persevere right to the border with Espírito Santo, you enter the most beautiful part of Minas, where lush hills are covered with coffee bushes in terraced rows, like contour lines on a map. These hills gradually give way to the craggy, spectacular mountains of the **Parque Nacional do Caparaó** and the highest peak in southern Brazil, the **Pico da Bandeira**. The best time to go is from June to August as at other times of year the mists and rain make it difficult to see the marvellous scenery.

Getting to Caparaó: Manhuaçú and Manhumirim

Getting to the park can be complicated, and the fact that Caparaó is the name of both the national park and a village just outside it (whose full name is Alto do Caparaó; see below) makes things more confusing. But as you need to head for the village to get to the park the distinction is, for all practical purposes, irrelevant.

You can make the journey to Caparaó from either Belo Horizonte or Vitória, the capital of Espírito Santo – Vitória is considerably nearer – but there are no direct buses and you can bank on spending most of the day to get there, and possibly longer, wherever you start from. Initially, you should head for the two interior towns in the general region. **MANHUAÇÚ** is served by one daily direct bus from both Belo Horizonte and Vitória, and it's also a stopping point for the Belo Horizonte–Vitória express buses. From here, local services run the twenty kilometres to MANHUMIRIM (see below), much closer to Caparaó and a far nicer place to spend the night if necessary. There are two direct buses a day to Manhumirim from Belo Horizonte, and two from Vitória; all are run by the *Aguia Branca* company – the Belo Horizonte departure times are 10am and 5pm, and from Vitória at 9.30am and 3.30pm. Journey time from either place is about five hours; the afternoon bus from Vitória is the one to CARANGOLA, and fares are $3. Wherever you start from you'll need to book your **ticket** the day before if possible, as these routes fill up quickly, especially on Friday and Sunday.

Manhumirim

Once you get to **MANHUMIRIM**, your next destination will be Alto do Caparaó, 25km further on. It's an exceptionally scenic ride, so it's worth staying the night if you arrive after dark. Manhumirim is, in any case, a pleasant place, a very typical interior town where foreigners rarely appear and the people are curious and friendly. The bars in the centre get surprisingly lively on weekend evenings, and the best (but still basic) **hotel** is the *São Luis*, a short taxi ride from the *Rodoviária*. The only alternative, on the same street, is the much worse *Hotel Manhumirim*.

On to Alto do Caparaó

The easiest way to reach Alto do Caparaó is by **taxi** from the *Rodoviária*, which costs about $10. There are two direct local **buses** a day, too, leaving from the *Rodoviária* at around 8am and noon – check the exact times when you arrive, as they change frequently. If you miss a direct bus, then get one of the nine daily buses to PRESIDENTE SOARES, and either ask the conductor to let you off at *a estrada para Caparaó*, or walk up to the main road from the village and hitch up to Caparaó from the signposted turn-off: there is not much traffic but what there is usually obliges, and you would be unlucky to wait more than an hour. The journey to Presidente Soares is scenic enough, but from the turn-off to Caparaó the drive gets very spectacular, through glorious hill country. The gradients are steep, and the buses grind slowly uphill allowing you plenty of time to savour the view.

Alto do Caparaó

ALTO DO CAPARAÓ is a small village that lines the sloping asphalted road: wait until the bus makes its final stop opposite the bar at the top of the village before getting off. There is no hotel as such in the village, but locals do rent out **rooms** here – if you are on a tight budget, ask at the bar for a *casa familiar*, which will cost about $5. Otherwise, a winding signposted road leads a kilometre from the bus stop to the *Caparaó Parque Hotel* (☎032/741-2559), a beautiful place with stunning mountain views out back, good food and friendly staff. Rooms are on the steep side at $20 single, $25 double, but the location makes it worthwhile and the national park entrance is only a short walk on from the hotel.

Opposite the hotel you can **hire horses** for the day ($20) if you feel like exploring the park on a saddle rather than on foot. And there is also a simple, but very friendly, unnamed **bar** in a rustic wooden house with fantastic views back down the valley – a wonderful place from which to watch the sunsets.

Alternative accommodation for serious hikers is **camping in the park**, where there are two official campsites that you can use as a base for walking. You need your own equipment and you'll have to reserve a place at least a week in advance by ringing the Belo Horizonte branch of *IBAMA*, the national parks authority (☎031/275-4266; only Portuguese spoken), or by personal visit to *IBAMA* at Avenida Contorno 8121, in the *bairro* of Cidade Jardim, near the centre of Belo Horizonte. You won't be allowed to camp inside the park unless you've reserved a place in advance.

Leaving Caparaó

There are two **buses** a day from Alto do Caparaó to Manhumirim, at 6.45am and 12.30pm, taking about ninety minutes. Otherwise, there are always jeeps outside the entrance of the *Caparaó Parque Hotel* (see above) which will take you to Manhumirim for $10.

Direct buses from Manhumirim to Belo Horizonte leave at 11am and 10pm – there are four others during the day, but they arrive from other starting points and you may not be able to get a seat. If you want to go direct to the historic cities of Minas Gerais, you can get off any of these buses at Mariana rather than continuing all the way to Belo Horizonte.

Exploring the Parque Nacional do Caparaó

The official **park entrance** (daily 7am–5pm; $2) is the only way to get into the park. Here you will be handed a useful brochure, also given out free at the reception of the *Caparaó Parque Hotel*, which has a very clear **map** on the back: you'll need it, as the park is huge – 25,000 hectares of some of the most spectacular scenery in Brazil. The *Centro de Visitantes* marked on the map is only half-built and progressing very slowly, but the main thing you need to know is that the park covers two **ecological zones**. The lower half is extremely beautiful; thickly forested valleys, hills and mountain streams giving way, as the hills lead into mountains proper, to treeless alpine uplands strewn with wild flowers, heather and rock formations. The main **trails** are marked on the map and are just about passable by jeep: there is an (unmapped) maze of smaller trails off these, which you can only explore on foot or horseback.

Some twenty minutes into the park, the **main trail** forks: left to the mountains (see below), and right to **Vale Verde**, an enchanting forested valley where a mountain stream forms a series of small waterfalls and shallow pools. A picnic site here is a good base for exploring the several trails leading off into the forest. If you carefully pick your way downstream, after about a hundred metres you come to a natural viewing platform looking back down Caparaó valley, framed by forest trees – a wonderfully peaceful spot.

Climbing Pico da Bandeira

Despite being more than 3000m high, the **Pico da Bandeira** is not difficult to climb and the hike takes you through some truly spectacular scenery. That is not to say you shouldn't treat the mountain with the respect it deserves. You will need a thick sweater or jacket to guard against the wind, a packed lunch, a water-bottle or a few drinks, and a good pair of walking or training shoes – the climb isn't steep enough for boots to be necessary. Be careful, too, not to be caught out after dark. Even with a good torch the path is treacherous in places, and you shouldn't attempt it once the light has gone: let the rangers at the park entrance know you are going and roughly when you expect to return, so they can come after you if something goes wrong.

Exact timing depends on how you make **the climb**. There are two official **campsites** along the way, with piped spring water, a basic shelter and toilets. The first is called *Tronqueira* and is eight kilometres from the park entrance – uphill all the way, a hike that will take you the best part of a day. You're rewarded by stunning views, as the road winds its way out of forest into the alpine zone, with panoramic views of the Caparaó valley below. The trail culminates at *Tronqueira* itself, where a viewing platform has been built to allow you to appreciate one of the finest views in the country, as the hills far below recede to the jagged horizon. Just before you get to *Tronqueira*, a fork to the left takes you to **Cachoeira Bonita**, where the José Pedro stream, which incidentally is the state border between Minas Gerais and Espírito Santo, plunges eighty metres down a rockface into a thickly forested gorge; another viewing platform allows full appreciation of the spectacle.

The lazy way to do the Pico, but the only method that allows you to get back to Caparaó the same day, is to get a **jeep** to take you as far as *Tronqueira*. There are usually jeeps hanging around the entrance of the *Caparaó Parque Hotel*: if not, the reception will ring for you even if you're not a guest. You need to arrange it the day before, as you have to set out by 8am at the latest to be back the same day. The jeep leaves you at *Tronqueira*, taking about thirty minutes to get there, and returns at 4pm to pick you up – return fare is around $20. If you're staying at the hotel, let them know the day before and they'll prepare a packed lunch for you.

The path up to the mountains starts at *Tronqueira*, at the opposite end of the campsite from the viewing platform. The **round trip** to the summit is almost twenty kilometres, about six hours' walking time, with another couple of hours for rests and lunch along the way. The very first stretch up from *Tronqueira* is extremely steep, but don't be discouraged: it soon flattens out into a pleasant stroll along a mountain valley, with the path hugging a crystalline mountain stream that forms swimmable pools at a couple of points. There is evidence of a forgotten episode in modern Brazilian history along the way, in the shape of bits of a military transport plane that crashed here in 1965. After the 1964 coup a group of left-wing militants took to these hills hoping to foment a Cuban-style popular rebellion, but were either hunted down or driven away: the plane that crashed was supplying the army patrols combing the area.

Halfway to the summit you come to the second official **campsite**, *Terreirão*, a good spot for lunch. A path to the right leads to a point overlooking a valley dominated by two mountains, the rocky crags of **Pico do Calçado** to the left, and **Pico do Cristal** to the right, both only a hundred metres shorter than Pico da Bandeira, and with trails leading up them if you felt so inclined – though only to be attempted if you are camping at *Terreirão*, or you will find yourself still on the mountain at nightfall. Fill your water bottle at *Terreirão*, as there is none between here and the summit. The path up to Pico da Bandeira continues from the opposite end of the campsite. After the first stretch it hits rocky, treeless moorland where the exact path is sometimes difficult to see, especially when cloud closes in. There are painted arrows to help you get your bearings, but often you only have to follow the trail of rusting cans and plastic rubbish instead: the thoughtlessness of some of the people using the trail is remarkable.

The only really steep part of the climb is right at the end, when you need to scramble up a rocky path to get to the **summit** itself. The arrows disappear, but by now you can get a bearing on the tower that marks the peak. Once there, on a clear day you are rewarded with an absolutely superb 360-degree panorama of the mountains and hills of Espírito Santo and Minas Gerais. On the way back, take special care on the first stretch down from the summit: it's a steep descent and there are many points where undue haste could leave you with a sprained ankle or worse.

ESPÍRITO SANTO

Espírito Santo is one of the smallest states in Brazil, but as Minas Gerais' outlet to the sea it is strategically very important. More iron ore is exported through its capital, **Vitória**, than any other port in the world. Not surprisingly the preponderance of docks, railway yards and smelters limits the city's tourist potential, despite a fine natural location. To a *mineiro*, Espírito Santo means only one thing: **beaches**. The coastline is basically one long beach, and during weekends and holiday seasons they flock to take the waters, tending to concentrate on the stretch immediately south of Vitória, especially the resort town of **Guaraparí**. However, while the coast here is a pleasant one, it really doesn't compare with the state of Rio to the south or Bahia to the north, where serious beach fiends would be better advised to head.

The hinterland of Vitória, far less visited, is exceptionally beautiful, a spectacular mix of lush forest, river valleys, mountains and granite hills. It's here that the state's real pleasures lie. The soils of this central belt are fertile, and since the latter part of the nineteenth century the area has been colonised by successive waves of Italians, Poles, Germans and Russians: their descendants live in a number of small, very attractive country towns which combine a European feel and look with a thoroughly tropical landscape. All are easy to get to from Vitória, not more than an hour or two over good roads, with very frequent buses. You can easily spot where the first immigrants came from: the houses and churches of **Santa Teresa** look as Italian as those of **Campinho** and **São Leopoldina** look German. The smallest of these towns, **Venda Nova**, is the most spectacular of all, not so much for itself as for the remarkable sight of **Pedra Azul**, a grey granite finger almost 2000 metres high, one of the unsung natural wonders of Brazil.

Around the towns, the lack of mineral deposits and the sheer logistical difficulties in penetrating such a hilly area has preserved huge chunks of the *Mata Atlântica*, the lush semi-deciduous forest that once covered all the coastal parts of southern Brazil. And credit should also go to the local Indians, notably the *Botocudo*, whose dedicated resistance pinned the Portuguese down throughout the colonial period. To this day inhabitants of the state are called *capixabas*, a backhanded tribute to the now exterminated Indian tribe around Vitória, whose ferocity dictated the future urban geography of the city by forcing the Portuguese to build it on a defensible island rather than the mainland proper.

Vitória

As a city, **VITÓRIA** does not live up to its impressive location: somewhat remnisicent of Rio with its combination of sea, steep hills, granite outcrops and irregularly shaped mountains on the horizon. Founded in 1551, it's one of the oldest cities in Brazil, but few traces of its past remain and nowadays most of the centre is grimy, urban sprawl. The heart of Vitória is an island connected to the mainland by a series of bridges, but the city has long since broken its natural bounds, spreading onto the mainland north and south: the beach areas are on these mainland zones, **Camburí** to the north and **Vila Velha** with its beach **Praia da Costa** to the south.

Arrival

The **Rodoviária** is not far from the centre and, outside, all **local buses** from the stop across the road run into town: returning from the centre, most buses from Avenida Jerônimo Monteiro pass the *Rodoviária* and will have it marked as a destination on the route cards displayed on the windscreen or by the door. If you're heading straight for the **beaches** on arrival, any bus that says *Aeroporto*, *UFES*, *Eurico Sales* or *Via Camburí* will take you to Camburí; to the southern beaches you need *P. da Costa*, *Vila Velha* or *Itapoan* – all can be caught in the centre or at the cluster of stops outside the *Rodoviária*, which is the closest the city has to a local bus station. The **bus routes** to the south of the centre were being reorganised in late 1989 after the opening of a new bridge connecting Vila Velha directly with the city centre: ask around about the latest routes. **Taxis** are cheap, and a good option in a small city like this where the distances are short.

Information and orientation

You're more or less on your own as far as **tourist information** goes. There is a booth at the *Rodoviária* but it keeps very irregular hours and even if you catch it open the friendly staff can offer little help: the **map** in the free brochure is almost useless. The best available map is the one in the centre pages of the local direc-tory of bus routes, but don't bother carrying one around as the **central layout** is easy to cope with. The city is built into a steep hillside overlooking the docks, but the main streets are all at shore level – the two closest to the sea are Avenida Beira Mar and Avenida Governador Bley, where you catch the buses to the beach districts. Behind them is Avenida Jerônimo Monteiro, the main shopping street, where the colonial Palácio de Anchieta, now the state governor's palace, is the main landmark. Just down from here the pleasant, tree-shaded Praça Costa Pereira is the heart of the downtown area.

Accommodation

The choice for **accommodation** is between the beach zones and the centre. Vitória has fewer cheap places than you'd expect for a city of its size, and what there is is almost exclusively concentrated in the centre. The many beach hotels are all medium range rather than cheap.

Around the *Rodoviária* is the best bet for really **cheap** places. There's a row of hotels opposite the main entrance, the cleanest and best being the *Spala* – keep an eye on your bags all the same. In the centre, *Pouso Real* on Avenida Jeronimo Monteiro, near the Governor's palace, is the best bet, grotty but cheap. If you can afford $10–12 a night, much better are the cheaper rooms at the *Real Escoril*, nearby.

There are perfectly adequate **medium range hotels** in the centre, too, like the *São José* at Avenida Princesa Isabel 300, and *Hotel Cannes* at Avenida Jerônimo Monteiro 111, but if you're going to spend that much money you might as well be on the **beach**. In terms of price and location there is little to choose between Camburí and Praia da Costa, both only a short drive from the centre. Best value are the *Hostess* at Avenida Antônio Gil Veloso 412 in Praia da Costa, and *Hotel Praia*, Avenida Dante Michelini 207 in Camburí. And between the two beaches is the best hotel in the city, *Hotel SENAC* on Ilha do Boi, but it is luxury class and correspondingly expensive.

Changing money

Changing money can be a problem in Vitória. There is a *Banco do Brasil* on Avenida Jeronimo which has an exchange department, but it keeps irregular hours and is often shut altogether: not enough foreigners pass through to make it worth their while staying open. You can get equally good rates, much more conveniently, at the *Vitória* souvenir shop, next to the *Bar Escandinavo* on Avenida Beira Mar, about 200 metres up from the main dock entrance.

Around the City

The only truly historic building in the centre of Vitória is the very fine governor's palace, the **Palácio de Anchieta**, which dates from the 1650s but is closed to visitors. The one part you can see – the **tomb of Padre Anchieta**, in a side entrance (Tues–Fri 3–5pm) – is something of a curiosity. Anchieta was the first of a series of great Jesuit missionaries to Brazil, and is most famous for being one of the two founders of São Paulo, building the rough chapel the town formed around in the sixteenth century and giving his name to one of the city's main avenues, the Via Anchieta. He was a stout defender of the rights of Indians, doing all he could to protect them from the ravages of the Portuguese and pleading their case several times to the Portuguese Crown: he was the first to produce a grammar and dictionary of the Tupí language. Driven out of São Paulo by enraged Portuguese settlers, he retired to Vitória, died in 1597 and was finally canonised. The tomb is simple, set off by a small exhibition devoted to his life.

The only **museum** in the city is the **Museu Solar Monjardim** (Tues–Fri 2–5pm) on Avenida Paulino Muller, in the *bairro* of Jucutuquara to the north of the centre; take the bus marked *Circular Maruipe* or *Joana d'Arc* from Avenida Beira March. It's a restored seventeenth-century mansion filled with a predominantly nineteenth-century collection of furniture and household utensils, and it gives a good idea of the layout and domestic routines of a colonial estate. But if you're used to the fine displays of colonial artwork in the museums of Minas Gerais you'll find it disappointing.

The Convento da Penha

The one reminder of Vitória's colonial past really worth seeing is on the southern mainland in Vila Velha – the chapel and one-time **Convento da Penha**. Perched on a granite outcrop towering over the city, it is worth visiting not so much for the convent itself, interesting though it is, as for the marvellous panoramic views over the entire city. It is a major pilgrimage centre and, in the week after Easter, thousands come to pay homage to the image of Nossa Senhora da Penha, the most devout making the climb up to the convent on their knees. It also marks the southernmost point the Dutch managed to reach in the sugar wars of the seventeenth century; an expedition arrived here in 1649 and sacked the embryonic city, but were held off until a relief force sent from Rio drove them out – you can see how the 154-metre hill must have been almost impregnable.

You have a choice of **walks** up to the top. The steepest and most direct is the fork off the main road to the left, shortly after the main entrance, where a steep cobbled path (extremely treacherous – take care, especially coming down) leads up to the convent. Less direct, but considerably safer and with better views, is to follow the winding main road up – a very pleasant thirty-minute walk. Once at the top, the city is stretched out below you, the centre to the north framed by the silhouettes of the mountains inland and, to the south, by the golden arcs of Vila Velha's beaches. The builders of the **chapel** thoughtfully included a viewing platform, which you reach through a door to the left of the altar. More interesting than the chapel itself is the **Sala das Milagres**, next door to the café; a collection of photos, ex-votos, artificial limbs and artefacts from grateful pilgrims.

To **get to the convent** from the centre, take the bus marked *T. Carapina – Vila Velha* from Avenida Jerônimo Monteiro, which passes directly by the entrance at the bottom of the hill; while any bus to Praia da Costa will leave you within easy walking distance. To get back to the centre, turn right onto the main road coming out of the entrance, walk down a couple of blocks to the stop on Rua Luciano das Neves, and take the yellow bus.

Entertainment: beaches and food

Both the main city **beaches** look good, with palm trees and promenades in the best Brazilian tradition, but you can only swim at **Praia da Costa**. The **Camburí** beach is overlooked by the port of TUBARÃO in the distance, where iron ore and bauxite from Minas is either smelted or loaded onto supertankers, benefitting the economy but ruining the water: if you swim you'll have oil and chemicals for company. Nevertheless, Camburí still has the largest concentration of **restaurants and nightspots** in the city. Local cuisine is based around seafood and is pretty good – lobster is plentiful and cheap, tastiest *na brasa* or charcoal-grilled, and also worth trying is the *moqueca capixaba*, a seafood stew where the sauce is less spicy and uses more tomatoes than the better known Bahian variety. All the main restaurants in Camburí serve it, but the best in town is to be found in the centre, at the *Moqueca Capixaba* on Escada Maria Ortiz, the steep street leading up from Jerônimo Monteiro and ending in a flight of steps heading up to the cathedral.

As a beach, Praia da Costa has the edge over Camburí but bars and restaurants are thinner on the ground. Still, it does have the advantage of being the place where shrimp boats land their catches; enterprising street-sellers grill them immediately and sell them at several points along the beach – delicious, especially when washed down with the chilled fresh coconut milk, also available everywhere.

Campinho

The closest of the inland towns to Vitória is **CAMPINHO**, 42km away or an hour by bus. Confusingly, it has two names: Campinho is the most common, but Domingos Martins is also used. Strictly speaking the latter is the name of the municipality Campinho is part of, but it is used to refer to the town as well.

The drive there manages to pack a remarkable amount of scenery into a very short distance – sit on the right-hand side of the bus leaving Vitória for the best views. Almost as soon as the bus leaves the city limits the road starts to climb into the highlands, and very quickly becomes extremely scenic, with wonderful views of hills and forest. Campinho is high enough to be bracingly fresh by day and distinctly cold at night: it looks like a German mountain village, with its triangular wooden houses modelled after alpine chalets.

Get off at the first stop in the town, rather than continuing to the **Rodoviária**. The cheap *Hotel Campinho* is near the bus stop, but if you continue the few yards to the immaculately manicured main square there's a wonderful hotel, the *Hotel Imperador*, built in German style. Rooms are $15 single, $18 double – good value for the quality of accommodation – and at weekends you may well have to ring ahead to reserve a room (☎027/268-1115).

There's not much to Campinho, just a small museum, the **Casa de Cultura**, almost opposite the bus stop, which has some old documents and artefacts dating from the colony's early days after it was founded by Pomeranians in 1847. The main pastime, in decent weather, is walking in the surrounding forest and hills. A short bus or taxi ride out of town is the *Restaurante Vista Linda*, where the food is no more than moderate but the view out across a mountain valley is tremendous. The local bus to the neighbouring village of MARECHAL FLORIANO passes by – catch it from the Campinho *Rodoviária*.

It is possible to get a bus **direct to Manhumirim and Caparaó** from here without having to trek into Vitória. Take the local bus or taxi ($4) to Marechal Floriano, and catch the *Aguia Branca* bus to Manhumirim that passes by at 10.30am. You have to trust to luck there's a seat – weekdays you'll probably be lucky, otherwise go into Vitória and get a ticket on the 3.30pm coach to CARANGOLA, which stops at Manhumirim.

Santa Teresa

SANTA TERESA is only seventy kilometres from Vitória but the hills between are steep, reducing buses to a crawl for significant stretches, and padding the journey out to a good two hours. The initial run to the pleasant hill town of FUNDÃO (*Hotel Casarão*, opposite the *Rodoviária*, if you want to stay) is pretty, but the winding road that takes you the thirteen kilometres from here to Santa Teresa is something special, with great views from either side of the bus. The soils are rich, and dense forest is interspersed with coffee bushes and intensively cultivated hill farms, framed by dramatic granite cliffs and escarpments.

The closer you get to Santa Teresa, the more insistent the echoes of Europe become. The tiled hill-farms look more Italian and less Brazilian, you see vines, and signs advertising local wines, and when you finally pull into the village you might be arriving somewhere in the hills of northern Italy. The first colonists, mainly Italian but with several families of Polish and Russian Jews, arrived here in 1875: the last shipload of Italians docked in Vitória in 1925.

The town has grown very little in more recent times, and is still laid out along two streets in the shape of a cross. You go right down the main artery to arrive at the **Rodoviária** at the far end of the village, passing the *Hotel Globo*, basic but clean and very reasonably priced. Go down the street that runs by it and you come to a beautifully tended square, full of flowers, trees and hummingbirds darting around. At the far end, next to the school, is Santa Teresa's main attraction: the Museu de Biologia Professor Mello Leitão, a twenty-acre natural history museum and nature reserve.

The Museu de Biologia and Augusto Ruschi

Santa Teresa is full of flowers, and of hummingbirds feeding off them, and early this century they aroused the interest of one of the first generation of Italians to be born here, **Augusto Ruschi**. He turned a childhood fascination into a lifetime of study, and became a pioneering natural scientist and ecologist decades before it was fashionable. Specialising in the study of hummingbirds, he became the world's leading expert in the field and was also a stout defender of the environment. In the later years of his life he was almost single-handedly responsible for galvanising the state government into action to protect the exceptional beauty of the interior of Espírito Santo; that so much forest remains is due in no small measure to him. He died in 1986, at the age of 71, after being poisoned by the secretions of a tree-frog he collected on one of his many expeditions into the forest.

The **Museu de Biologia** represents his life's work, designed and laid out by him since the early 1930s. It contains his library and all his collections of animals, birds and insects as well as a small zoo, a snake farm, a butterfly garden and the richest park in the state, with thousands of species of trees, orchids, flowers and cacti. Underfunding has reduced this exceptional scientific and natural treasure to opening on only one day a week, Saturday from 9am to 5pm – and even this much wouldn't be possible were it not for the dedication of its staff. It is worth timing your journey to catch it open, a beautiful place to wander around and a fine memorial to an extraordinary man.

The first colonists . . . and on to São Leopoldina

Back on the square by the museum, go up the steps cut into the hillside. If you continue along the ridge, five minutes' walk leads to an unmistakably Italian **Igreja Matriz**, complete with roundels and cupola: the names of the first colonists are engraved on a plaque on its outside wall. The street leading uphill from here is the oldest in the village, now lined with solid, colonial-looking houses built in the early years of this century. Continue up it for about 300 metres and you come to the surviving two-storey wattle and daub houses put up by the first wave of Italians and Poles; oldest of all is the farmhouse opposite the tiny chapel.

A **trip** worth making from Santa Teresa is to the nearby German town of SÃO LEOPOLDINA (see below), 45 minutes by local bus from the Santa Teresa *Rodoviária*. Timing is important since accommodation is easy in Santa Teresa but not in Leopoldina, and although it's simple to get back to Vitória from Leopoldina, buses back to Santa Teresa are much less frequent. You could **hike** back, though. The whole area is wonderful walking country, and the twelve kilometres to Santa Teresa takes about five hours – there are some steep sections. If you decide to do the circuit of the hill villages this way around, get an early bus to Leopoldina from Vitória (hourly from the *Rodoviária*) and aim to end up in Santa Teresa. **From Santa Teresa**, there are buses to Leopoldina at 10am and 2pm, but, as on all country bus routes, it's advisable to check the times as soon as you arrive in Santa Teresa.

São Leopoldina

The drive to **SÃO LEOPOLDINA** (most people shorten it to Leopoldina) is fabulous, along a country dirt road winding through thickly forested hills and gorges. There are a few hair-raising drops, which the bus drivers – who know every stone and curve – negotiate with aplomb, grinding gears and holding shouted conversations with the passengers, mostly blonde peasants clutching string bags and chickens. At one point you pass a spectacular waterfall in a gorge choked with forest to the left; even on foot the descent is too steep for you to get close to it. Despite the temporary look of the road and the small settlements you pass through – clearings in the forest uncannily like Amazon highway settlements – these are long-established communities dating from 1919, when the road was finished.

Ironically, the road's completion meant the end of the line for São Leopoldina. Founded in 1856 by 160 Swiss colonists, who were followed over the next forty years by over a thousand Saxons, Pomeranians and Austrians, São Leopoldina was the first European colony in Espírito Santo and also the most successful: coffee grew well on the hills and found a ready market on the coast. Built on the last navigable stretch of the river Santa Maria, inland from Vitória, Leopoldina was the main point of entry for the whole region. Once the road was finished, however, Santa Teresa swiftly outgrew it, leaving only a street lined with solid German houses and trading posts as a reminder of earlier prosperity.

The bus leaves you at one end of the main street, **Rua do Comércio**, and if you walk back along it you soon come to the interesting **Museu da Colônia** (Wed–Sun 9–11am & 1–5pm), housed in the mansion of what used to be the leading German family in town. The museum documents the early decades of German settlement with photographs – including some fascinating ones of the construction of the road to Santa Teresa in 1919 – relics and documents. In a sense the whole village is a museum, with the gables and eaves of the buildings much as they were at the turn of the century, perfectly preserved by the twist of fate that turned the village into an economic backwater so many decades ago. Resting quietly in its beautiful river valley, it is a peaceful place to wander around, and there are some fine nineteenth-century buildings on the Rua do Comércio. Several of them are now **bars** or **restaurants**, including one next to the bridge with a great setting overlooking the river. Unfortunately, there is nowhere to **stay** and it's either back to Santa Teresa or to Vitória – buses to the latter leave every couple of hours from the stop on Rua do Comércio, with the last one going at 6pm.

Venda Nova and Pedra Azul

VENDA NOVA DO IMIGRANTE, to give it its full name, is an Italian village some 100km from Vitória and, even by the standards of the state, the landscape in which it is set is extraordinary, an alpine mix of forests, valleys and escarpments. A few kilometres outside the village is the most remarkable sight in Espírito Santo, a towering bare granite mountain, shaped like a thumb, almost 1000m high – the **Pedra Azul**, or "blue stone". Its peak is actually 2000m high, the other thousand accounted for by the hill country it sprouts out of. It's like an enormous version of the Sugar Loaf in Rio, except that no vegetation growns on its bare surface, which rears up from thick forest and looks so smooth that from a distance it appears more like glass than stone. During the day sunlight does strange things to it – it really does look blue in shadow – but the time to see it is either at dawn or sunset, when it turns all kinds of colours in a spectacular natural show.

Venda Nova itself is nothing more than a small village strung along the highway. There are three direct **buses** a day from Vitória, but any bus that goes to Minas Gerais also passes by, as it's on the highway to Belo Horizonte – *Aguia Branca* buses from Vitória are the best bet. There are two comfortable but rather pricey **hotels** outside the village in the rolling hills at the foot of the rock, *Pousada dos Pinhos* and *Pousada Pedra Azul*, both with rooms starting at around $20. And there is also a cheap place in Venda Nova itself, *Hotel Canal* on the main (and only) street. There are several **restaurants** – *Churrascaria Posso Fundo*, near the Prefeitura, is the best value, but better food is to be had either at the Portuguese *Lusitânia* or the *Peterle*. The countryside around here is excellent for walks and hiking: even if you don't stay there, the reception desks at the two *pousadas* give helpful advice on routes.

travel details

Bus company names are given below in italics.

Buses within the state

From Belo Horizonte to Caxambú (*Viação Ensa*; Fri & Sun at 7.30am & 11pm, Sat at 7.30am; also reachable via local service from São Lourenço; 6hr); Congonhas (*Viação Sandra*; daily every 2hr; 2hr); Diamantina (*Pássaro Verde*; daily at 5.30am, 9am, 11.30am, 3.30pm, 6.30pm, midnight; 6hr); Mariana (*Pássaro Verde*; daily at 6am, 8.30am, 10.30am, 1.15pm, 4pm, 6.15pm, 11pm; also reachable from Ouro Preto via local bus; 2hr); Ouro Preto (*Pássaro Verde*; daily roughly hourly; 2hr); Poços de Caldas (*Viação Ensa*; daily at 8am, 1pm, 4pm, 10.30pm, midnight; 8hr); Sabará (*Viação Cisne*; every 15 minutes 4am–midnight; 30min); São João del Rey (*Viação Sandra*; daily at 6.15am, 8.30am, noon, 1.30pm, 3pm, 4.45pm, 5.30pm, 7pm, Sun also at 9pm & 11pm; 6hr); São Lourenço (*Viação Ensa*; daily at 12.30pm, 3pm, 10.15pm, also Fri at 7pm; 6hr).

From Vitória to Campinho (13 daily; 1hr); Santa Teresa (roughly hourly; 2hr); São Leopoldina (roughly hourly; 2hr); Venda Nova (hourly; 3hr).

Buses out of the state

From Belo Horizonte to:

Campinas (13hr); *Viação Ensa* daily at 8.30am, 1.30pm, 9pm, 10pm, 11pm.

Brasília (14hr); *Itapemirim* daily at 8am, 7pm, 8pm, 8pm (*leito*), 10pm; *Penha* daily at 9pm (*leito*), 9.15pm, 10.15pm.

Rio (8hr); *Viação Útil* daily at 12.45am, 8am, 9am, 11am, 2pm, 4pm, 9pm, 11pm, 11pm (*leito*); *Viação Cometa* daily at 8.30am, 9.30am, 12.30pm, 1.30pm, 3.30pm, 9.30pm, 10.30pm, 11.15pm, 11.29pm, 11.30pm, 11.45pm (*leito*).

Salvador (24hr); *Viação Gontijo* daily at 7pm, *leito* 3pm Fri only; *São Geraldo* daily at 6pm, *leito* 2pm Tues only.

São Paulo (12hr); *Impala* daily at 6.15am, 9.15am, 11.15am, 6.15pm, 8.15pm, 8.30pm, 9pm, 9.15pm, 9.15pm (*leito*), 10pm, 10.15pm, 11.15pm, midnight; *Cometa* daily at 8.45am, 9.45am, 11.45am, 1.45pm, 6.45pm, 7.45pm, 8.45pm, 9pm, 9.30pm (*leito*), 9.45pm, 10pm, 10.30pm (*leito*), 10.45pm, 11.45pm.

Trains

From Belo Horizonte to Rio (2 weekly 8.15pm Fri & Sun; 13hr); Montes Claros (1 weekly at 7pm Sat; 14hr).

Planes

From Belo Horizonte to Brasília (6 daily; 1hr); Rio (13 daily; 1hr); São Paulo (15 daily; 1hr).

CHAPTER THREE

THE NORTHEAST

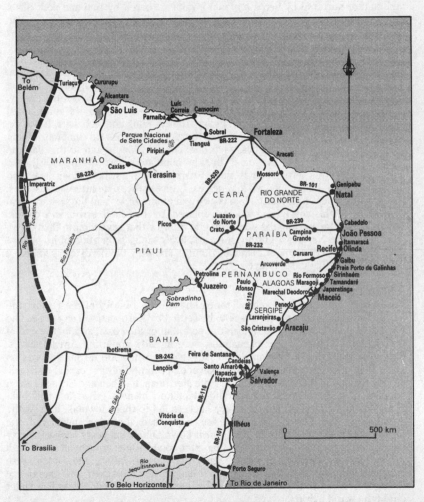

The **Northeast** (*nordeste*) of Brazil covers an immense area and features a variety of climates and scenery, from the dense equatorial forests of western Maranhão, only 200km from the mouth of the Amazon, to the parched interior of Bahia, some 2000km to the south. It takes in all or part of the nine **states** of Maranhão, Piauí, Ceará, Rio Grande do Norte, Paraíba,

Pernambuco, Alagoas, Sergipe and Bahia, which together form roughly a fifth of Brazil's land area and have a combined population of 36 million. When *nordestinos* living outside the region are included, they make up about a third of Brazil's total population. Within Brazil, the Northeast is notorious for its poverty, and it has been described as the largest concentration of poor people in the Americas. Yet it's also one of the most rewarding areas of Brazil to visit, with a special identity and culture nurtured by fierce regional loyalties, shared by rich and poor alike. You'll come across echoes of Northeastern culture all over Brazil – in the Amazon highway towns or the *favelas* of Rio and São Paulo – engendered by the millions of Northeasterners who migrate out of the region.

It is an identity forged by **geographical** contrasts, as most of the Northeastern states have three distinct areas. First is the flat coastal strip, the **zona da mata**, which literally means "forest zone". Little, apart from the name, is now left of the coastal jungle which greeted the first European settlers in the sixteenth century: at the same time as they marvelled at its beauty they cut it down and planted sugar cane, taking advantage of the heavy tropical rains and rich soils. It was on the coast that the first towns and cities of the Northeast grew up – not for nothing are all the region's state capitals, save one, coastal cities – and to this day the coastal strip is by far the most thickly populated part of the Northeast. Unfortunately, this fertile belt is rather narrow, and nowhere does it extend inland for more than a hundred kilometres. It gives way to an intermediate area, the **agreste**, where hills rear up into rocky mountain ranges and the lush, tropical vegetation of the coast is gradually replaced by highland scrub and cactus. Finally comes the **sertão**, the vast semi-arid interior that covers more than three-quarters of the Northeast but houses a relatively small proportion of its population. The soils here are poor, rainfall irregular, and only the hardy can scrabble a living out of the harsh landscape.

A little history

These very different geographical zones shaped the **history** of the region; the Northeast was the first part of Brazil to be settled by Europeans on any scale. The Portuguese were quick to recognise the potential of the coast, and by the end of the sixteenth century sugar plantations were already importing African slaves. **Salvador** and **Olinda** developed into large towns while Rio de Janeiro was no more than a swampy village. Indeed, Salvador became the first capital of Brazil, and by the end of the sixteenth century the Northeast had become Europe's main supplier of sugar. The merchants and plantation owners grew rich and built mansions and churches, but their very success led to their downfall. It drew the attention of the **Dutch**, who were so impressed that they destroyed the Portuguese fleet in Salvador in 1624, burnt down Olinda six years later and occupied much of the coast, paying particular attention to sugar growing areas. It took more than two decades of vicious guerrilla warfare before the Dutch were expelled, and even then they had the last laugh: they took their new experience of sugar growing to the West Indies, which soon began to edge Brazilian sugar out of the world market.

The Dutch invasion, and the subsequent decline of the sugar trade, proved quite a fillip to the development of the interior. With much of the coast in the hands of the invaders, the **colonisation** of the *agreste* and *sertão* was stepped up. The Indians and escaped slaves already there were joined by cattlemen, *vaqueiros*, as trails were opened up into the highlands and huge ranches carved out of the interior. Nevertheless, it took over two centuries, roughly from 1600 to 1800, before these regions were fully absorbed into the rest of Brazil. In the *agreste*, where some fruit and vegetables could be grown and cotton did well, market villages developed into towns. However, the *sertão* became, and still remains, cattle country, with an economy and society very different from the coast.

Life in the **interior** has always been hard. The landscape is dominated ·by cactus and dense scrub – *caatinga* – the heat is fierce, and for most of the year the countryside is parched brown. But it only takes a few drops of rain to fall for an astonishing transformation to take place. Within the space of a few hours the *sertão* blooms. Its plant life, adapted to semi-arid conditions, rushes to take advantage of the moisture: trees bud, cacti burst into flower, shoots sprout up from the earth and, literally overnight, the brown is replaced by a carpet of green. Too often, however, the rain never comes, or arrives too late, or too early, or in the wrong place, and the cattle begin to die. The first recorded **drought** was as early as 1710, and since then droughts have struck the *sertão* at ten or fifteen year intervals, sometimes lasting for years. The worst was in the early 1870s, when as many as two million people died of starvation; and the early 1980s were also a particularly bad time. The problems caused by drought were, and still are, aggravated by the inequalities in land ownership. The fertile areas around rivers were taken over in early times by powerful cattle barons, whose descendants still dominate much of the interior. The rest of the people of the interior, pushed into less favoured areas, are regularly forced by drought to seek refuge in the coastal cities until the rains return. For centuries, periodic waves of refugees, known as *os flagelados*, "the scourged ones", have poured out of the *sertão* fleeing droughts: modern Brazilian governments have been no more successful in dealing with the special problems of the interior than the Portuguese colonisers before them.

Around the region: some pointers

The contrast between the coast and the interior is the most striking thing about the region. You could have a fascinating time in the Northeast without ever leaving the *zona da mata*, but unless you make at least one foray into the interior you'll only get a partial view of what is the most varied region in Brazil. It is not just a difference in the way the country looks. Much of it also has to do with the **racial** mix, a product of the region's economic history. Blacks were imported to work on the coastal sugar plantations, and relatively few of them made it into the interior. The Northeast has the largest concentration of black people in Brazil, but most of them still live either on or near the coast, concentrated around **Salvador**, **Recife** and **São Luis**, where African influences are very obvious – in the cuisine, music and religion. In the *sertão*, though, Portuguese and Indian influences predominate in both popular culture and racial ancestry.

As far as specific attractions go, the region has a lot to offer. The **coastline** is over two thousand kilometres of practically unbroken beach, much of it just as you imagine tropical beaches to be: white sands, blue sea, palm trees – the stuff advertising campaigns are made of. The **colonial heritage** survives in the Baroque churches and cobbled streets of Salvador, Olinda and São Luis, often side by side with the modern Brazilian mix of skyscrapers and shanty towns. And in Salvador and Recife, with populations of around two million each, the Northeast has two of Brazil's great **cities**. Head **inland**, and the bustling market towns of the *agreste* and the enormous jagged landscapes of the *sertão* more than

THE NORTHEAST

APPROACHES . . .
You can reach the Northeast from almost any direction. Direct, there are **flights** to
Recife from Europe and North America, and frequent **buses** to the main
Northeastern cities from all parts of Brazil. From **southern and central Brazil**,
buses converge upon Salvador, although there are buses to other cities, too. From
the **Amazon**, buses from Belém run to São Luis, Teresina, Fortaleza and points
east. See *Basics* and the relevant chapters' "Travel Details" for more information.

. . . AND GETTING AROUND
Getting around is fairly straightforward in the Northeast's southern states and all
the details are given in the text. North and west of Pernambuco, though, things
start to get trickier: the main highways are usually good asphalt, but roads off them
are often precarious. This is especially true in the **rainy season**: in Maranhão the
rains come in February, in Piauí and Ceará in March, and points east in April, lasting for around three months – except in Maranhão where "rainy season" is a relative term, meaning that it pours down most of the time, rather than just raining
quite a lot, which it does throughout the year.

repay journeys. But above all, in both city and countryside, there's the force of a
richly diverse **popular culture** which you will find reflected not only in arts and
crafts, but in the texture of everyday life: what you eat, what you see happening
on the street, the music you hear, and what you see people doing.

We've covered the region starting from Recife, the largest city in the
Northeast, then dealt with the *agreste* and *sertão* of **Pernambuco** state, before
heading south, via the smaller states of **Alagoas** and **Sergipe**, to the vast state of
Bahia and its capital Salvador. The account of the northern half of the region, an
arc of land which stretches from the eastern tip of Brazil to the fringes of
Amazonia, begins with the state of **Paraíba** and heads east, via **Rio Grande do
Norte**, **Ceará** and its capital Fortaleza, and **Piauí**, ending in **Maranhão** state.
Maranhão marks the geographical and cultural limit of the Northeast: here the
dominant colour changes from brown to green, as the arid *sertão* yields to flat and
fertile river plains and palm forests, and the dry heat becomes steamily equatorial. Only a few hundred kilometres west of São Luis, capital of Maranhão, you
come to the fringes of the Amazon rainforest proper.

PERNAMBUCO

Recife, capital of the state of **Pernambuco**, shares with São Luis the distinction
of not having been founded by the Portuguese: when they arrived in the 1530s,
they settled just to the north, building the beautiful, colonial town of **Olinda** and
turning most of the surrounding land over to sugar. A century later, the Dutch,
under Maurice of Nassau, took Olinda and burned it down, choosing to build a
new capital, Recife, on swampy land to the south, where there was the fine natural harbour which Olinda had lacked. The Dutch, playing to their strengths,
drained and reclaimed the low-lying land, and the main evidence of the Dutch
presence today is not so much their few surviving churches and forts dotted up
and down the coast, as the reclaimed land on which the core of Recife is built.

Out of Recife, there are good beaches in both directions. The Portuguese first developed the coastline as far **north** as the island of **Itamaracá**, growing sugar cane on every available inch. This erstwhile fishing village still retains its Dutch fort, built to protect the new colonial power's acquisitions, but these days it's a fairly blighted weekenders' resort. Best is the **coastal route south**, where a succession of small towns and villages interrupt a glorious stretch of palm-fringed beach.

Head **inland** and the scenery changes quickly to the hot, dry and rocky land-scape of the *sertão*. **Caruarú** is the obvious target, home of the largest market in the Northeast, and close by is **Alto do Moura**, centre of the highly rated Pernambucan pottery industry. If you plan to go any further inland than this you'll need to prepare well for any kind of extended *sertão* journey, though it's straightforward enough to reach the twin river towns of **Petrolina** and **Juazeiro**.

Recife

Initial impressions are misleading and although **RECIFE** doesn't have the instantly definable atmosphere of Rio or Salvador, it's a very distinctive place all the same. The Northeast's largest city, it's lent a colonial grace and elegance by Olinda, so close that they're considered part of the same conurbation. Recife itself has long since burst its original, colonial boundaries and much of the centre is now given over to uninspired modern skyscrapers and office blocks. But there are still a few quiet squares, where an inordinate number of impressive churches lie cheek by jowl with the uglier, urban sprawl of the past thirty years. North of the centre are some pleasant leafy suburbs, dotted with museums and parks, and to the south there is the nearest the Northeast comes to Copacabana – the modern beachside district of **Boa Viagem**. Other beaches lie within easy reach, both north and south of the city, and there's also all the **nightlife** one would expect from a city of nearly two million Brazilians.

Arriving: orientation and getting around

The **airport** is fairly close to the city centre, at the far end of Boa Viagem: a taxi to Boa Viagem itself shouldn't be more than $5; or take the bus from right outside (marked "Aeroporto"), which will drive through Boa Viagem and drop you in the centre, in Praçinha (see below). The **Rodoviária**, though, is miles out and arriving here can give you the entirely wrong impression that Recife is in the middle of nowhere. This is not really a problem, since the new **Metro**, an over-ground rail link, whisks you very efficiently in to the centre, giving you a good introduction to city life as it glides through various *favelas*. The Metro is very cheap, but only serves industrial suburbs, so you're only likely to use it going to and from the Rodoviária. It will deposit you at the old train station, the **Estação Central**, from where the hotel district is only a short hop, by taxi or on foot; alter-natively you can get a bus to other parts of the city from Avenida Dantas Barreto, the wide avenue two blocks to the right as you come out of the train station.

Most **local city buses** arrive at and leave from two places in the centre: Praçinha do Comércio, a square which everyone calls Praçinha; and from in front of the large central Post Office, a convenient central landmark that locals call the *Correio*, on Avenida Guararapes. See "Getting Around", below, for more details.

Information

There's a **tourist information** post at the airport (open 24hr), run by the state tourist agency, *EMPETUR*, with English- and French-speaking staff, maps, calendars of events and itineraries. Pick up the **free map**, *Historical Circuit of the City of Recife* (in English), with places of interest clearly marked and a useful guide to the main sights on the back. Failing that, the *Itinerário* also has a reasonable city map, with a couple of sections in atrociously mangled English. *EMPETUR* will **book hotels** for you, but you'll be directed to the more expensive ones unless you ask: they're no good for the very cheapest places.

Other *EMPETUR* information posts are at the Rodoviária (daily 7am–9pm) and the Casa de Cultura (Mon–Sat 9am–8pm, Sun 3–8pm); there's an information trailer at the corner of Avenidas Guararapes and Dantas Barreto (daily 8am–7pm); while the **municipal tourist office** is at Loja 10, Pátio de São Pedro.

Orientation

The **central area** of Recife is by some way the dirtiest, and although it bustles with activity during the day it empties at night, when the enormous, largely deserted streets are a little spooky and forbidding. However, the centre does have the advantage of being cheap: all the most economical hotels are situated here. Although modern Recife sprawls onto the mainland, the heart of the city is three small **islands**, Santo Antônio, Boa Vista and Recife proper, connected with each other and the mainland by more than two dozen bridges over the rivers Beberibe and Capibaribe. This profusion of waterways has led to the inevitable description of Recife as the "Venice of Brazil" – a totally ludicrous idea.

Recife island is where the docks are and is the least interesting and salubrious part of town; certainly not somewhere to wander around after dark. **Avenida Dantas Barreto** splits the island of **Santo Antônio**, home to the central business district, together with many surviving colonial churches and such nightlife as there is in the centre. Just over the river is **Boa Vista**, linked to Santo Antônio by a series of small bridges; the brightly painted criss-cross girders of the **Ponte de Boa Vista** are a convenient central landmark.

Residential suburbs stretch to the north, but the bulk of the middle-class population is concentrated to the south, in a long ribbon development along **Boa Viagem** beach.

Getting around

Most **city buses** originate and terminate on Santo Antônio, in Praçinha and along Avenida Guararapes, with some stops overflowing into Avenida Dantas Barreto. **Bus routes** are given on signs at the stops, but the sheer number of them, combined with flyposters covering vital details, may mean you have to ask. This is even more true at the other local bus station, **Cais de Santa Rita**, at Santo Antônio docks, which most buses pass through before heading up to Praçinha. Far too many buses and people jam into the available space, but you may have to come to Cais de Santa Rita for buses to beaches north and south of the city, and to Itamaracá and Igaraçú – although these particular lines are regularly rerouted, so check with *EMPETUR* first.

Lots of buses head for **Boa Viagem**, passing through the centre; those marked "Aeroporto" and "Iguatemi" are the most common. If you can't stand the heat and the crowds, faster and more comfortable *frescões* go to Boa Viagem from Avenida Dantas Barreto, to the left of Praçinha, costing around fifty cents. And from about

4pm onwards you can get a cheap ($2) **shared taxi** there very easily, too: taxi drivers hustle customers from the bus stops, leaving when they've filled all the seats, which rarely takes more than a few minutes. **Olinda** is linked directly with Boa Viagem by buses #902 and #981, both marked *Rio Doce*; while any bus from the centre of Recife marked *Rio Doce* or *Olinda* takes you there as well.

Finding a place to stay

It's cheapest to stay right in the centre, and most expensive in Boa Viagem. The other obvious area to consider staying is Olinda, where prices fall somewhere between the two; hotels there are listed separately under "Olinda", below. If you're newly arrived, it may be better to make for Boa Viagem or the centre of Recife first, moving out to Olinda once you've had a chance to get your bearings.

The centre: Boa Vista and Santo Antônio

Most central hotels are concentrated around **Rua do Hospício**, over the bridges linking Santo Antônio with the neighbouring island of **Boa Vista**. At Rua do Hospício 51 the *Hotel do Parque* is cheap ($6 single) and a little grimy, but redeemed by high ceilings and a broad, curving staircase that survives from better days. Further down is the *Hotel Brasiliense*, at no. 179, but the best value is at two hotels almost next door to each other, right at the end of the street and fronting the greenery of the Parque 13 de Maio: the *Hotel 13 de Maio* at no. 659, whose rooms start at $4, is much favoured by Brazilian salesmen and has a pleasant tree-shaded yard out back; while the similarly priced *Hotel Suiça* at no. 687 has a noisy restaurant where tables are put outside in the evenings. Other reasonable places are the *Hotel Central* at Rua Manoel Borba 209, one of the few quiet and elegant streets left in Boa Vista, and the modern *Hotel América* on Praça Maciel Pinheiro, which, with rooms starting at $9, is not as expensive as it looks.

In **Santo Antônio**, try the *Hotel Praia* in Rua da Praia; the *Hotel Nassau* at Largo do Rosário (a good location); or the *Hotel Sete de Setembro* at Rua Matias de Albuquerque 318. They are all in the $7–10 range.

Boa Viagem

In **Boa Viagem** finding a hotel is the least of your problems: it sometimes seems as if they outnumber apartment buildings. The difficulty is finding a reasonably cheap one, as the majority cater for international tourists and rich Brazilians. Even so, you should be able to find somewhere for between $10 and $15 a night, certainly if you're prepared to stay a little way back from the seafront. If you can't bear to stay anywhere else, the cheapest **seafront** hotels (starting at $20) are at opposite ends of the Avenida Boa Viagem: the *Hotel 200 Milhas* at no. 864 and the *Hotel Canoa* at no. 106 are nearest the centre; at the airport end are the *Hotel Praia e Sol* at no. 5476 and the *Beira Mar* at no. 5426.

Cheaper, and very convenient for the airport, is the *Pousada Jequitinhonha*, at Rua General Luiz Mallet 49 (☎326-8338); while the *Hotel Galícia*, Rua Visconde de Jequitinhonha 301, is as cheap as you are likely to get in Boa Viagem. Good medium-priced hotels include the *Portal do Sol*, Avenida Conselheiro Aguiar 3217; the *Marazul*, Rua Professor José Brandão 135; the *Pousada da Praia*, Rua Alcídes Carneiro Leal 66; and the *Belmar*, Rua Raul Azedo 145. The *Pousada Aconchego*, Rua Félix de Brito 382 (☎326-2989), is small and comfortable, with a swimming pool and a good restaurant.

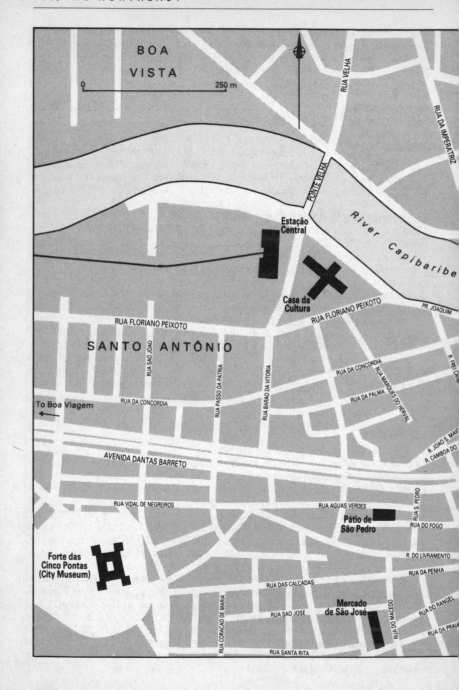

Around the city

There's no excuse for being bored in Recife. There are literally dozens of colonial churches in the city, at least one of which it would be criminal to miss; one excellent and several lesser museums; and some lovely public buildings. The churches tend not to have regular opening hours, but if the main door is shut you can often get in by banging on a side door – if there's anyone inside they'll be only too happy to let you in. Even for the less determined sightseer, there are parks, beaches, and a number of places where the most interesting thing to do is simply to drift about, absorbing the feel of the city and watching people get on with their lives – something that's particularly true of the city's markets.

Along Avenida Dantas Barreto to São Francisco

The broad **Avenida Dantas Barreto** forms the spine of the central island of Santo Antônio and, apart from the beach, is the area where you'll want to spend most time during your stay in the city. In southern Brazil, avenues like this are lined with skyscrapers, but although some have sprouted in Recife's financial district, generally the centre is on a human scale, with crowded, narrow lanes lined with stalls and shops opening out directly onto the streets. Dantas Barreto, the main thoroughfare, ends in the fine **Praça da República**, lined with majestic palms and surrounded by Recife's grandest public buildings – the governor's palace (not open to visitors) and an ornate theatre. One of the charms of the city, though, is the unpredictability of the streets and even off this main boulevard you'll stumble upon old churches sandwiched between modern buildings, the cool hush inside a refuge from the noise and bustle beyond.

Perhaps the most enticing of the central buildings is the seventeenth-century Franciscan complex known as the **Santo Antônio do Convento de São Francisco**, on Rua do Imperador a block down from Pracinha – a combination of church, convent and museum. Outside, you'll be besieged by crowds of beggars displaying sores and stumps, but negotiate your way through to the entrance of the museum (Mon–Fri 8–11.30am & 2–5pm, Sat 2–5pm), pay the nominal fee, and you'll find yourself in a cool and quiet haven. Built around a beautiful small cloister, the museum contains some delicately painted statues of saints and other artwork rescued from demolished or crumbling local churches. But the real highlight here is the **Capela Dourada** (same times as the museum), the "Golden Chapel", which has a lot in common with the churches in the old gold towns of Minas Gerais. Like them, it's a rather vulgar demonstration of colonial prosperity, from a time when conspicuous consumption often took the form of building grotesque churches. Certainly, this chapel is a classic example of nouveau riche Rococo: finished in 1697, it's the usual wall-to-ceiling-to-wall ornamentation, except that *everything* is covered with gold-leaf. If you look closely at the carving under the gilt you'll see that the level of workmanship is actually quite crude, but the overall effect of so much gold is undeniably impressive. What really gilded the chapel, of course, was sugar cane: the sugar trade was at its peak when it was built, and the sugar elite were building monuments to their wealth all over the city.

São Pedro and the Mercado de São José

The church of **São Pedro** (Tues–Fri 7–11am & 2–6pm, Sat 8–11am, Sun 10am– noon) is on the square of the same name, just off the Avenida. The impressive façade is dominated by a statue of Saint Peter that looks old but was in fact donated to the church in 1980 by a master sculptor from the ceramics centre of Tracunhaém in the interior. Inside there's some exquisite wood carving and a *trompe l'oeil* ceiling, but if you've missed the opening hours, content yourself with the exterior views, best seen with a cold beer in hand from one of the several bars which set up tables in the square outside.

Recife is probably the best big Brazilian city to find *artesanato*, popular art in all its varieties, and the area around São Pedro is the best place to look for it. If you shop around, even tight budgets can stretch to some wonderful bargains. There are stalls all over the city, but they coagulate into a bustling complex of winding streets, lined with beautiful but dilapidated early-nineteenth-century tenements, which begins on the **Pátio de São Pedro**. The streets are choked with people and goods, all of which used to converge on the ramshackle building of the market proper, the **Mercado de São José**. Tragically, this was almost completely destroyed by a fire in late 1989, which left the cast-iron girders that formed the skeleton of the nineteenth-century building twisted and buckled. Until the promised renovation, which is likely to take years, the traders and *artesanato* stalls lead a more precarious existence wherever they can set up shop on the streets around the ruin.

If you simply can't face the crowds, there's a very good **craft shop**, *Livraria Cordel*, on the corner of Pátio de São Pedro. It's the main city outlet for two excellent woodcut artists, Amaro Francisco and Jota Borges, who do extremely cheap prints on both cloth and paper. The shop takes its name from *literatura de cordel*, which are printed ballads illustrated by a woodblock print cover: in markets you see them hanging from string, *cordel*, hence the name. The usual themes are stock Northeastern stories about cowboys, devils, saints and bandits, although you also find *cordel* based on political events, and educational ballads about disease and hygiene: I found a verse poem about how AIDS is transmitted and the need to use condoms. Even if you don't understand a word of Portuguese, the printed covers are often worth having in their own right, and they're extremely cheap, around twenty-five cents each. Outside the shop, you can dig out *cordel* in a couple of stalls around the remains of the Mercado or in **Praça de Sebo**, next to the Mercado site, where the secondhand book sellers have stalls. You'll also find books in English here, though hardly any worth buying.

From Largo do Rosário to the Museu da Cidade

Another retreat from the crowds nearby is the **Igreja do Rosário dos Pretos** (daily 8am–noon & 2–5pm), just up Largo do Rosário from Pracinha. It's an interesting example of a colonial church which catered mainly for slaves, and which still has a high proportion of black worshippers. Determined culture vultures could also make the hop from here to Recife's most central museum, the **Museu da Cidade** (Tues–Fri 8am–6pm, Sat & Sun 2–6pm), in the star-shaped fort off the western end of Avenida Dantes Barreto; the best view of it is coming in by bus from Boa Viagem, and from the centre it's safest to go there by taxi as it's surrounded by main roads where the traffic is fast and furious. Built in 1630 by the Dutch, the fort was the last place they surrendered when they were expelled in 1654. The building is actually far more interesting than the museum itself, which is dedicated entirely to the history of the city, with old engravings and photographs.

Around the Estação Central: the Casa da Cultura

Right opposite the **Estação Central**, the forbidding **Casa da Cultura** (Mon–Fri 9am–9pm, Sat & Sun 3–8pm) was once the city's prison and is now an essential stop for visitors. It's cunningly designed, with three wings radiating out from a central point, so that a single warder could keep an eye on all nine corridors. The whole complex has been taken over by *EMPETUR* and turned into an arts and crafts centre, the cells converted into little boutiques. The quality of the goods on offer here is good, but the prices are a lot higher than elsewhere in the city, so go to look rather than buy. The other reason for visiting is to make use of the *EMPETUR* **information office**: it's the best place to find out what's on, and they often lay on events – dancing displays and the like – on weekend evenings, which are free and not at all bad.

Over in the Estação Central itself, the **Museu do Trem** (Tues–Fri 9am–noon & 1–5pm, Sat & Sun 2–6pm) is worth a look, too, tracing the history of the railways that played a vital role in opening up the interior of the Northeast. British visitors can wax nostalgic over the exploits of the *Great Western Railway of Brazil Limited*, one of whose engines looms over the forecourt of the station. It's a relic of the days when British companies dominated the Brazilian economy and did very well out of the Northeast – before the Brazilians did the sensible thing and nationalised them.

Out from the centre: the Museu do Homem do Nordeste

The **Museu do Homem do Nordeste** (Tues, Wed & Fri 11am–5pm, Thurs 8am–5pm, Sat & Sun 1–5pm) is one of Brazil's great museums and the best introduction there is to the history and culture of the Northeast. It's quite a way out of central Recife: take the "Dois Irmãos" bus from near the Post Office building or from Parque 13 de Maio, at the bottom of Rua do Hospício; there are two, the one marked "via Barbosa" is the one to get, a pleasant half-hour drive through leafy northern suburbs. The museum is not very easy to spot, on the left-hand side, so ask the driver or conductor where to get off.

Inside, you have to wait for a compulsory **guided tour**, in English, French or Portuguese, which for once is fairly worthwhile. It does go far too quickly, but as all the labelling is in Portuguese you need the commentary to orientate yourself. Afterwards, if you smile sweetly and ask, you can wander around at leisure. The museum is split into several galleries, each devoted to one of the great themes of Northeastern economy and society: sugar, cattle, fishing, popular religion, festivals, ceramics and so on. The historical material is well displayed and interesting, but the museum's strongest point is its unrivalled collection of popular art – there are displays not just of handicrafts, but also of cigarette packets, tobacco pouches, and, best of all, a superb collection of postwar bottles of *cachaça*, or rum. A look at the designs on the labels, very Brazilian adaptations of western 1950s and 1960s kitsch, leaves you with nothing but admiration for the imagination – and drinking capacity – of the people who put the display together.

The highlight of the museum is the **Galeria de Arte Popular** on the ground floor, largely devoted to the rich regional tradition of clay sculpture and pottery that still flourishes in the *agreste* and *sertão*, especially around Caruarú. **Mestre Vitalino**, a peasant farmer in the village of Alto do Moura, began in the 1920s to make small statues depicting scenes of rural life, of an astonishing vitality and power. The first display case in the gallery is devoted to him, and is worth lingering over – the feeling and expression in the faces is quite remarkable, for example in the leering devil appearing to a terrified drunk clutching a bottle of rum. As

Vitalino grew older, he began to incorporate the changes happening in the countryside around him into his work. There are statues of migrants, and urban
themes appear with a series of portraits of professionals; the lawyer, doctors and
dentists (very gruesome), the journalist and the secretary. These themes take
over in the work of the next generation of artists, the sons of Vitalino and other
pioneers, like the almost equally well-known **Zé Caboclo**, whose work fills the
next few cases. In the third generation the style changed, and it's interesting that
the best contemporary sculptors are women, notably the granddaughters of Zé
Caboclo. The statues remain true to the established themes, but they are miniaturised, and the effect comes from the extreme delicacy of detail and painting,
which contrasts with the cruder vigour of their male precursors. You'll see reproductions of many of the statues here on market stalls across Brazil, but
Pernambuco is the place to get the real thing: certainly, examples of the work of
many of the artists displayed in the Galeria can still be bought fairly cheaply if
you know where to look; see under "Alto do Moura", below.

The same bus ("Dois Irmãos; via Barbosa") is also the one to take for the
Museu do Estado (Tues–Fri 8am–5pm, Sat & Sun 2–5pm), a fine nineteenth-
century mansion at Avenida Rui Barbosa 1352. It's on the right-hand side about
twenty minutes after leaving the city centre, well before the Museu do Homem do
Nordeste, but again difficult to spot, so you might need to ask. Here you'll find
some fine engravings of Recife as it was in the early part of the last century, all of
them English, and upstairs there are good paintings by Teles Júnior, which give
you an idea of what tropical Turners might have looked like.

If the bus is crowded, or you can't make the driver understand where you want
to get off, don't worry: after the museums it runs on to the **Horto Zoobotânico**
(Mon–Sat 7am–5pm, Sun 7am–6pm), a combined zoo and botanical gardens. The
gardens are the best part, with outdoor cafés and shady paths to walk along: the
zoo, like most Brazilian zoos, is shockingly bad. The animals are confined in
concrete boxes far too small for them, where they're constantly taunted by children and adults who ought to know better.

The Olaria de Brennand

If you have time, try and round off your sightseeing with the bizarre **Olaria de
Brennand**, an industrial estate in the northern suburbs – there can't be anywhere
more impressively offbeat in the whole of Brazil. One of three brothers who inher-
ited a huge tile, ceramic and brickwork factory, Brennand became a very strange
kind of tycoon. Although already rich beyond the dreams of avarice, he was driven
to become an internationally famous ceramic artist and is also one of the most
prominent environmentalists in Brazil. His factory estate, far from being an industrial wasteland, nestles in the middle of the only part of the old coastal forest still
surviving in the metropolitan area. You can see the boundaries of the enormous
estate very clearly: the urban sprawl stops dead at the feet of gallery forest, and the
asphalt road suddenly becomes a dirt track winding through the jungle, lined with
young imperial palms. It's a very beautiful piece of land – and it's sobering to think
that without it, nothing at all would remain to show what the coast around Recife
looked like before the arrival of the Europeans.

Past the rows of workers' cottages and a brickworks, you come to the *oficina*,
an enormous personal gallery containing thousands of Brennand's sculptures,
decorated tiles, paintings and drawings. The collection is housed in a shed the
size of an aircraft hangar and very obsessive it is too, although a lot of the work is

very good, with strong erotic overtones – to say that genitals are a recurring theme is putting it mildly. Most remarkable of all is the space to the right of the gallery, which Brennand has transformed into something which almost defies description: a large area with a fountain, covered in ceramic tiles, dotted with columns and sculpture, and bounded by a huge tiled wall topped with a series of Egyptian-looking statues. It looks like nothing so much as the set for a bizarre film epic, except that everything is real and solid.

The gallery is a long way from the centre, but is definitely worth the effort. A taxi from Santo Antônio will set you back around $5 and if you don't want to walk back you'll have to arrange for it to pick you up again, because no taxis pass anywhere near. Or take any bus marked "Vargem", "Casa Forte" or "Dois Irmãos" from opposite the *Hotel 13 de Maio* to its terminus, and then get a taxi – say "a oficina de Brennand" to the driver. The gallery is open from 9am until noon and from 2pm to 4pm every weekday except Monday; it's free, and the staff are always pleased to see foreigners.

Boa Viagem: the beach

Regular buses make it easy to get down to **Boa Viagem** and the beach, an enormous skyscraper-lined arc of sand that constitutes the longest stretch of urbanised seafront in Brazil. As you'd expect of a city of islands, Recife was once studded with beaches, but they were swallowed up by industrial development, leaving only Boa Viagem within the city's limits – though there are others a short distance away to the north and south. In the seventeenth century, Boa Viagem's name was *Ilha Cheiro Dinheiro*, or "Smell Money Island" – as if whoever named it knew it would become the most expensive piece of real estate in the Northeast.

Much of Boa Viagem is only three or four blocks deep, so it's easy to find your way around. Take your bearings from one of the three main roads; the seafront **Avenida Boa Viagem**, with the posh hotels and a typically Brazilian promenade of palm trees and mosaic pavements; the broad Avenida Conselheiro Aguiar two blocks up; and then Avenida Engenheiro Domingos Ferreira.

The **beach** itself is longer and (claim the locals) better even than Copacabana, with warm natural rock pools to wallow in just offshore when the tide is out. It gets very crowded at the weekends, but weekdays are relatively relaxed. There's a constant flow of people selling everything the self-indulgent sunbather could possibly want: fresh coconut milk, iced beers, ready mixed *batidas* (rum cocktails), pineapples, watermelon, shrimp, crabs, oysters, ice creams, straw hats and suntan lotion. The usual cautions apply about not taking valuables to the beach or leaving things unattended while you swim.

Eating

Eating out in Recife follows the same pattern as accommodation: it's cheapest in the centre, most expensive in Boa Viagem, with Olinda somewhere in between. You'll find restaurant listings for Olinda under "Olinda", below.

Recifense **cuisine** revolves around fish and shellfish. Try *carangueijo mole*, crabs cooked in a spicy sauce until shells and legs are soft and edible, which solves the problem of digging out the meat; small crabs called *guaiamum*; and *agulhas fritas*, fried needle fish. As befits a sugar city, a favourite local drink is *caldo de cana*, the juice pressed from sugar cane by hypnotic Victorian-looking machines.

Daytime eating and snacks

Cheapest of all, but not to be scorned, are the **foodsellers** and *suco* **stalls** clogging the streets of the city centre, with the usual selection of iced fruit juices, kebabs, cakes, sandwiches and *pastel*. There's a row of stalls licensed by the city authorities on the pedestrianised **Rua da Palma**, across the road from the main post office, much patronised by office workers attracted by some very reasonably priced food.

Santo Antônio also has many cheap *lanchonetes* and restaurants, although as their clientele is mainly office workers they tend to close down in the early evening. At Avenida Dantas Barreto 666 try the *Papagaio*, while further down, at no. 712, the *Novo Brasileirinho* is something of a greasy spoon establishment that serves cheap and filling food. Over the bridges, on Boa Vista, there are several reasonable restaurants on **Rua do Hospício**: the best is *Le Buffet* at no. 147 (don't be deceived by the name – it's Japanese), and there's also the *Rex* and the *Viena*, opposite the *Hotel do Parque*.

O Vegetal, on the second floor of Avenida Guararapes 210 (Mon–Fri 11am–5pm) is a **vegetarian restaurant**: take a ticket as you go in, stuff yourself with all you can eat from the buffet, and pay on your way out; it's always crowded. Another vegetarian place, *Grande Vida* at Rua Riachuelo 581, is open until 8pm but isn't as good.

Evening eating

Eating out at night in the **city centre** is not so easy and you're probably better off in Boa Viagem or Olinda. If you are in the centre, the best place to head for is the cobbled square around São Pedro church, the **Pátio de São Pedro**, where there are some good regional restaurants: *Godofredo*, on the far corner, *Buraquinho*, and *Banguê*, with tables in the square and nice views of the church.

In **Boa Viagem** there are hundreds of restaurants, the best value being the seafood places on the promenade near the city centre end of the beach, and the dining rooms of the cheaper hotels (listed in the "Finding a place to stay" section), all of which are open to non-residents. If you can spend a little more, the *Futaba*, Rua Domício Rangel 101, is an outstanding Japanese restaurant, and *La Pinha*, Praça Boa Viagem 16, does good Northeastern food. There are two excellent **ice cream parlours** just off Praça Boa Viagem as well, the *Fri-Sabor* and *Eskimo* – go for the regional flavours, like *sapotí*, *jaboticara*, *renan* and *jaca*.

Nightlife and Carnaval

As elsewhere in Brazil, **nightlife** in Recife starts late, after 10pm. It's not every country in the world where half the population can dance better than the Temptations, and for sheer fun not many places can beat a good *dancetaria* on a weekend night. The variety of music and dances is enormous, and Recife has its own frenetic carnival music, the **frevo**, as well as **forró**, which you hear all over the Northeast. The dancing to *forró* can be really something, couples swivelling around the dancefloors with ballbearings for ankles.

The scene in Recife is concentrated in Boa Viagem, or in Olinda: there's very little in Recife itself. The Praça de Boa Viagem is easy to get to by bus, but some of the most interesting nightspots are in suburbs like Casa Forte and Graças – not so well served by public transport, especially in the late evenings. You'll have to take a taxi, around $3–4 return.

Bars and dancing

In the centre, virtually the only place with any zip to it is the **Pátio de São Pedro**, with its bars and restaurants. Occasionally something extra happens here, though: music and dance groups often appear at weekends, and it's one of the centres of Recife's Carnaval.

In **Boa Viagem**, bars open and close with bewildering speed, which makes it difficult to keep track of them. The liveliest area, though, is around Praça de Boa Viagem; the *Lapinha* bar and restaurant is a popular meeting place, as is *Caktos* bar, Avenida Conselheiro Aguiar 2328. Quieter and classier is the northern suburb of **Casa Forte**. A good place here is *Agua de Beber*, a gem of a bar at Praça de Casa Forte 661; a large house with an expensive restaurant upstairs, but a leafy courtyard in which you can sit and drink magical *caipirinhas*.

If you're looking to lay down a few steps, you need to head for a **casa de forró**; the best time to go is around midnight on a Friday or Saturday. In all of them you can drink and eat fairly cheaply, too. They often have rules about only letting in couples, but these are very haphazardly enforced, especially for foreigners. There's a small entry fee, and you may be given a coupon as you go in for the waiters to mark down what you eat: don't lose it or you'll have to pay a fine when you leave. Taxis back are rarely a problem, even in the small hours. Two good *casas de forró* are the *Belo Mar* on Avenida Bernardo Vieira de Melo, in Candeias *bairro*, and the *Casa de Festejo* on Praça do Derby in the *bairro* of Torre. Otherwise, look in local papers or ask *EMPETUR* for details; there are dozens of others. One place that mixes *forró* with samba is the lively *Cavalo Dourado* (Fri & Sat only), at Rua Carlos Gomes 390, in the *bairro* of Prado. More westernised, but still good, is *Over Point Dancing* at Rua das Graças 261 in Graças.

Carnaval

Carnaval in Recife is overshadowed by the one in Olinda, but the city affair is still worth sampling even if you decide, as many locals do, to spend most of Carnaval in Olinda. The best place for **Carnaval information** is the knowledgeable and helpful municipal tourist office, at Loja 10 in the Pátio de São Pedro, which publishes a free broadsheet with timetables and route details of all the Carnaval groups. You can also get a timetable in a free supplement to the local paper, the *Diário de Pernambuco*, on Saturday of Carnaval, but be warned that it's only a very approximate guide.

The *blocos*, or **Carnaval groups**, come in all shapes and sizes: the most famous is called *Galo da Madrugada*; the commonest are the *frevo* groups (trucks called *freviocas*, with an electric *frevo* band aboard, circulate around the centre, whipping up already frantic crowds); but most visually arresting are *caboclinhos*, who wear Brazilian ideas of Indian costume – feathers, animal-teeth necklaces – and carry bows and arrows, which they use to beat out the rhythm as they dance. It's also worth trying to see a *maracatú* group, unique to Pernambuco: they're mainly black, and wear bright costumes, the music an interesting (and danceable) hybrid of African percussion and Latin brass.

In Recife the **main events** are concentrated in Santo Antônio and Boa Vista. There are also things going on in Boa Viagem, in the area around the *Othon Palace* hotel (Avenida Boa Viagem 3722), but it's too middle class for its own good and is far inferior to what's on offer elsewhere. Carnaval in Recife officially begins with a trumpet fanfare welcoming *Rei Momo*, the carnival king and queen, on Avenida Guararapes at midnight on Friday, the cue for wild celebrations. At night, activities centre around the grandstands on Avenida Dantas Barreto, where the *blocos* parade under the critical eyes of the judges. The other central area to head for is the Pátio de São Pedro. During the day the *blocos* follow a route of sorts: beginning in the Praça Manuel Pinheiro, and then via Rua do Hospício, Avenida Conde de Boa Vista, Avenida Guararapes, Praça da República and Avenida Dantas Barreto to Pátio de São Pedro. Good places to hang around are near churches, especially Rosário dos Pretos, on Largo do Rosário, a special target for *maracatú* groups. The balconies of the *Hotel do Parque* are a good perch, too, if you can manage to get up there. The day is the best time to see the *blocos*; when the crowds are smaller and there are far more children around. At night it's far more intense and the usual safety warnings apply.

> The area telephone code for Recife and Olinda is ☎081.

Listings

Airlines *Air France*, Avenida Dantas Barreto 498, 7th floor (☎224-7944); *Air Portugal (TAP)*, Avenida Guararapes 111 (☎224-2700); *British Airways*, Avenida Conde de Boa Vista 1295 (☎222-4499); *Transbrasil*, Avenida Conde de Boa Vista 1546 (☎231-0522); *Varig-Cruzeiro*, Avenida Guararapes 120 (☎231-2037/224-8273); *VASP*, Avenida Guararapes 111 (☎222-3611). There are international connections to Paris (twice weekly), Miami (once weekly) and Orlando, Florida (twice weekly).

Airport Taxis from the centre to the airport cost $5; alternatively there's the *Aeroporto* bus or *frescão*, but allow at least an hour to get there.

Banks and Exchange Exchange (*câmbio*) departments are open 10am–4pm at *Lloyds*, Rua do Fogo 22; at the *Banco Comércio* branch on Rua Matias de Albuquerque; and (for dollars cash only) at *Lins Câmbio*, corner of Rua da Palma and Guararapes. You'll get reasonable rates for travellers' cheques and dollars in the seafront hotels in Boa Viagem; take your passport. Exchange rates tend to drop around Carnaval time, with the influx of dollars from foreign tourists, so, if you can, delay changing large amounts until afterwards. Don't at any time change money with people who approach you on the street.

Bookshops New books in all major European languages at *Livro 7*, Rua Sete de Setembro 329, in the city centre. Secondhand books in Praça do Sebo market, near Pátio de São Pedro.

Buses All interstate services now leave from the new *Rodoviária* outside the city, as do services to the interior of Pernambuco. The old bus station at the Cais de Santa Rita only takes local buses and a few coastal services to towns near Recife. Some of these – to Itamaracá, Igaraçú, Gaibú, Porto de Galinhas and São José de Coroa Grande – may well be relocated to the *Rodoviária* in the near future, so check with the tourist office.

Car Hire *Hertz* at the airport (☎800-8900) and at Avenida Conselheiro 4214, Boa Viagem (☎325-2907); *Avis* at the airport (☎800-8787) and next to the airport, at Avenida Mascarenhas de Morais 5174 (☎326-5730).

Consulates *France*, Av. Dantas Barreto 1200, 9th floor (Mon–Fri 8am–noon; ☎224-6722); *Netherlands*, Avenida Conselheiro Aguiar 600, Boa Viagem (Mon–Fri 2–5pm; ☎326-7206); *UK*, Avenida Marques de Olinda 200, Room 410, 4th floor (Mon–Thurs 9–11am & 2–4pm, Fri 9–11am; ☎224-0650); *USA*, Rua Gonçalves Maia 163, Boa Vista (Mon–Fri 9–11am; ☎221-1412/1413, 222-6577/6612); *West Germany*, Avenida Dantas Barreto 191, 4th floor (Mon–Fri 9am–noon; ☎224-3488). There are no Australasian or Scandinavian consulates in the Northeast: the nearest are in Rio. Australasians can ask the UK consulate to get in touch with the nearest relevant consulate on their behalf.

Post Office Main post office is the *Correio* building on Avenida Guararapes, in Santo Antônio.

Records *Disco 7*, Rua Sete de Setembro, next to the *Livro 7* bookshop (see above); small but the best record shop for Brazilian music in the Northeast.

Telephones Inter-urban telephone offices are located at Praçinha, Rua Diário de Pernambuco 38, and Rua do Hospício 148; open 24hr. International calls from the Praçinha office or the airport.

Olinda

OLINDA is, quite simply, one of the largest and most beautiful complexes of colonial architecture in Brazil: a maze of cobbled streets, hills crowned with brilliant white churches, pastel-coloured houses, Baroque fountains and graceful squares. Founded in 1535, the old city is spread across several small hills looking back towards Recife, but it belongs to a different world. In many ways Olinda is the Greenwich Village of Recife; it's here that many of the larger city's artists, musicians and liberal professionals live, and it's also the centre of Recife's gay scene. Olinda is most renowned, though, for its Carnaval, famous throughout Brazil, which attracts visitors from all over the country, as well as sizeable contingents from Europe.

A city in its own right, Olinda is far larger than it first appears. The old colonial centre is built on the hills, slightly back from the sea, but arching along the seafront and spreading inland behind the old town is a modern Brazilian city of over 300,000 people. Despite its size, Olinda has become effectively a neighbourhood of Recife: a high proportion of the population commutes into the city, which means that **transport links** are good, with buses leaving every few minutes.

Some practical details: arrival and accommodation

From Recife, a number of **buses** run to Olinda, marked "Rio Doce", "Casa Caiada", "Janga", "Pau Amarelo" or simply "Olinda". **Taxis** from the centre of Recife take around fifteen minutes and cost about $5. Buses follow the seafront road, where you get off and walk up to the old city: it's quite obvious where to go. After 6pm only residents are allowed to drive in, and all entrances are blocked off with chains and a police guard; one reason why the city is so well preserved.

A good **town map** is included in the Recife *Itinerário* distributed by *EMPETUR*; or pick one up from the **municipal tourist offices** at Rua de São Bento 233 (by the Governor's Palace in the centre) and by the central market, the *Mercado da Ribeira*, Rua Bernardo Vieira de Melo (no number, but it's down on the left); both are open from 8am to noon and between 2pm and 5pm, Monday to Saturday.

Finding a place to stay
There are dozens of **hotels** of all price ranges in Olinda. Staying in the old city is by far the most pleasant option, but places there are more expensive. You can get perfectly adequate accommodation instead, at a fraction of the price and within walking distance of the old city, by staying at one of the many hotels in the modern part of town, stretched out along the seafront – though, unfortunately, the seafront itself is an undistinguished urban sprawl, with no beach to speak of.

The best place in the **old city** is the *Pousada dos Quatro Cantos* at Rua Prudente de Morais 441 (☎429-0220/1845), a lovely converted mansion with an idyllic courtyard; rooms start at around $15, but they have a few without a bath-room which are much cheaper. Failing that, there's a small and cheap *pensão* just up the road on the other side, and the tourist office will have a list of others. There's even a **campsite** just inside the old city, at Rua do Bom Sucesso 262 (☎429-1365); watch your valuables.

Along the **seafront,** try the popular *Albergue da Olinda*, at Rua do Sol 537, first on the road from Recife. Others are stretched along the Avenida Beira Mar, start-ing with the conveniently placed *Pousada do Mar*, at no. 497, and the *Pousada da Praia* at no. 633. Further along is the *Hospedaria do Turista* at no. 989, *Pensionato Beira Mar* at no. 1103, *Hospedaria Olinda Beira Mar* at no. 1473 and the *Chalé da Praia* at no. 1835 – these are the cheaper ones, facing onto the beachless part of the seafront. Past the old city a beach of sorts reappears and hotel prices start climbing.

If you want to stay for a while, you could think of **renting a room** in some-body's house: they're expensive during Carnaval, but at other times of the year check with the tourist office to see what they have on their lists: try the municipal tourist office, Rua de São Bento 233, or ring the *Departamento de Turismo* (☎429-0397); there's normally somebody there who speaks French, though English is a little more difficult.

Around the town

Olinda's hills are steep, and you'll be best rewarded by taking a leisurely pace around the town. A good spot to have a drink and plan your attack is the **Alto da Sé,** the highest square in the town, not least because of the stunning view of

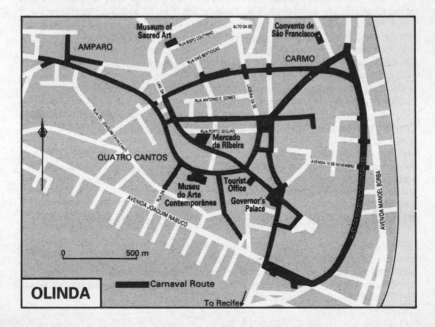

Recife's skyscrapers shimmering in the distance, framed in the foreground by the church towers, gardens and palm trees of Olinda. There's always an arts and crafts **market** going on here during the day, peaking in the late afternoon; a lot of the things on offer are pretty good, but the large numbers of tourists have driven prices up, and there's nothing here you can't get cheaper in Recife or the interior. Or just plonk yourself down at the tables and chairs set up in the square and drink in the views.

The **churches** you see are not quite as old as they look. The Dutch burnt them all down, except one, in 1630, built none of their own, and left the Portuguese to restore them during the following centuries. There are eighteen churches dating from the seventeenth and eighteenth centuries left today, seemingly tucked around every corner and up every street. Very few of them have set opening times, but they're usually open during weekdays and even when they're closed you can try banging on the door and asking for the *vigia*, the watchman. In front of all the more popular churches you'll be besieged by people selling things or offering themselves as guides; often over-insistent and always overpriced. All the same, it's impressive how many ragged children can recite the basic history of Olinda in French, English and German, as well as Portuguese, and it's worth the hassling to hear street cries like *queijo, tapioca, história de Olinda* . . . "cheese, candied tapioca, history of Olinda. . .".

If you're taken by the church buildings, there's a good sampling of religious art on display in the **Museum of Sacred Art** (Tues–Sat 9am–noon & 2–5pm), in the seventeenth-century Bishop's Palace on the Alto da Sé. The **Museu Regional** (same opening hours), at Rua do Amparo 128, is well laid out, too, although the emphasis is too much on artefacts and too little on history.

There's more contemporary interest in the colourful **graffiti** in which the old city is swathed. The local council commissions artists to adorn certain streets and walls, which has the twin advantage of keeping local talent in work and ensuring Olinda has the highest-quality graffiti in Brazil. Some is political, urging people to vote for this or that candidate, some is more abstract, illustrated poems about Olinda being especially popular; but it is all colourful, artistic, and blends in uncannily well with the colonial architecture. One of the best places to see it is along the municipal cemetery walls on the Avenida Liberdade, but there's good graffiti all over the old city, especially during elections and Carnaval.

More serious modern art is to be found in the **Museu de Arte Contemporânea**, on Rua 13 de Maio next to the market (Mon & Wed–Fri 8am–5pm, Sat & Sun 2–5.30pm): it's a fine eighteenth-century building that was once used as a jail by the Inquisition. The accent is on painting, and some of it is very good indeed, with local scenes and people in bright primary colours, executed with some style. If you're lucky, you might catch one of the occasional exhibitions of regional arts and crafts.

All the action: eating, drinking and nightlife

Olinda's relaxed atmosphere draws many Recifenses at night. Tables and chairs are set on squares and pavements, bars are tucked away in courtyards in spectacular tropical gardens – mix in a generous sprinkling of music, and, at weekends, a lot of young Brazilians out for a good time, and you have a pretty good recipe for enjoying yourself.

Eating and drinking

The best place to go for crowds and serious eating and drinking is the **Alto da Sé**. The good, cheap street food here, cooked on charcoal fires, can't be recommended too highly; try *acarajé*, which you get from women sitting next to sizzling wok-like pots – bean curd cake, fried in palm oil, cut open and filled with green salad, dried shrimps and *vatapá*, a yellow paste made with shrimps, coconut milk and fresh coriander. It's absolutely delicious and very cheap; fifty cents would be the top of the price range.

Behind the chairs and tables set in the square are several **bars**, built on the brow of the hill that directly overlooks the old city. The most famous is the *Bye-Bar Brasil* (after *Bye-Bye Brasil*, a Brazilian film of the 1970s). It has a reputation as a Bohemian hang-out, to some extent borne out by the quiet puffing of joints and picking at guitars; late on Friday and Saturday nights there's live music; and it's also a well-known gay rendezvous, although by no means exclusively so. There is another (unnamed) bar next to it which commands equally impressive views, and has the advantage of being open during the day. Just to the left, a short way down the Ladeira da Sé, is the *Cantinho da Sé*, almost always crowded and very lively indeed at night. Quieter, and set in beautiful tree-shaded courtyards, are the *Mourisco*, off the Praça do Carmo, which has a very good if rather pricey restaurant attached, and the *Pousada dos Quatro Cantos* on Rua Prudente de Morais, where the outdoor café and the restaurant are open to non-residents. The one disadvantage of most bars and cafés in Olinda is the constant procession of hippies trying to sell you jewellery and trinkets – it's unavoidable and you simply have to get used to it.

Most **restaurants** are concentrated along the seafront, where there is a mass of *churrascarias* and eating houses offering standard Brazilian fare at reasonable prices.

Best value is at *Sinha Maria*, on the seafront, at Avenida Beira Mar 953. It's not as expensive as it looks, and is especially good for dishes from the interior: try *buchadas*, a kind of Brazilian haggis, and *carne do sol*, rehydrated dried meat served with melted butter and roasted manioc. Many of the seafront restaurants specialise in lobster and *pitú* (crayfish), but as there's a lucrative export trade flying lobster and crayfish to the United States, local prices are disappointingly high. *Ostra*, oysters, are far better value, and are delicious in a *sopa de ostra*, stewed in coconut milk and palm oil.

Nightlife: clubs and dancing

Nightlife in Olinda can be very lively, especially at the end of the week. Places to check out, apart from the Alto da Sé, are the seafront restaurants and bars, many of which have *forró* groups on Friday and Saturday nights. If you get bored with *forró* – and the beat does get a bit monotonous after a while – try the *Clube Atlântico* on the Praça do Carmo, easily identifiable by its logo of a couple dancing on a crescent moon. Every Friday and Saturday night (starting at 11pm) it hosts the *Noites Olindenses*, dances to an eclectic variety of music, played very loudly by energetic groups or on record – *frevo, samba, forró, merengue*, and even non-Brazilian styles like salsa and tango. You pay an entrance fee of about $2, and both the music and the dancing can be quite superb. There are sometimes extras like magicians and *capoeira* displays going on outside, between and even during acts.

Carnaval in Olinda

Olinda's Carnaval is generally conceded to be one of the three greatest in Brazil, along with Rio and Salvador. It overshadows the celebrations in neighbouring Recife, and attracts thousands of revellers from all over the Northeast. It's easy to see why Olinda developed into such a major Carnaval: the setting is matchless, and local traditions of art and music are very strong. Like the other two great Brazilian carnivals, Olinda has a style and feel all of its own; not quite as large and potentially intimidating as in either Rio or Salvador, the fact that much of it takes place in the winding streets and small squares of the old city makes it seem more manageable. The music, with the local beats of *frevo* and *maracatú* predominating, the costumes and the enormous *bonecos*, papier-mâché figures of folk heroes or savage caricatures of local and national personalities, make this Carnaval unique.

Some practicalities: finding a bed and drunken driving

Inevitably, with so many visitors flocking into the city, **accommodation during Carnaval** can be a problem. It's easier to find a room in Recife but, unless you dance the night away, transport back in the small hours can be difficult: buses start running at around 5am, and before then you have to rely on taxis. This is not always easy, as many taxi-drivers stop work to enjoy Carnaval themselves. Even if you do find one, you either have to pay an exorbitant flat rate or three or four times the metered fare. Also, beware **drunken taxi drivers**: try to avoid travelling by road in the small hours during Carnaval as there are far too many legless drivers for comfort, and dozens of people are killed on the road every year.

In Olinda itself you might as well forget about **hotels**, as they're booked up months in advance. Many locals, though, rent out all or part of their house for Carnaval week: the municipal tourist office, Rua de São Bento 233, has a list of places and prices and will book one for you. Prices start at around $150 for the week, going up to as much as $800 – get a group together by leaving a note at the tourist office. If all the places on the tourist office lists are full – more than likely if you arrive less than a week before Carnaval starts – or if you fancy your chances of getting a cheaper and better deal on your own, wander round the side streets looking for signs saying "Aluga-se quartos"; knock on the door, and bargain away. (If you can pay in dollars you should be able to negotiate a reduction.)

Carnaval: the action

Carnaval in Olinda actually gets going on the Sunday before the official start, when the *Virgens do Bairro Novo*, a traditional *bloco* several hundred strong, parades down the seafront road followed by crowds that regularly top 200,000. By now the old city is covered with decorations: ribbons, streamers and coloured lanterns are hung from every nook and cranny, banners are strung across streets and coloured lighting set up in all the squares. Olinda's Carnaval is famous for the *bonecos*, huge papier-mâché figures that are first paraded around on Friday night and then at intervals during the days, and for the decorated umbrellas that aficionados use to dance the *frevo*. The tourist office has lists of the hundreds of groups, together with routes and approximate times, but you don't really need them as there is something going on all the time in most places in the old city. The most famous *blocos*, with mass followings, are *Pitombeira* and *Elefantes*; also try catching the daytime performances of *travestis*, transvestite groups, which have the most imaginative costumes: ask the tourist office to mark them out on the list for you.

Other festivals: the Torneio dos Repentistas

There are often **other festivals** of one kind or another besides Carnaval going on in Olinda; its location and cultural traditions make it a popular venue. Definitely worth catching if you happen to be around in late January is the **Torneio dos Repentistas**. A *repentista* is a Northeastern singer/poet who improvises strictly metered verses which are sung in a nasal voice accompanied only by a guitar. And they really do improvise, rather than repeat stock verses. Most *repentistas* make a living singing on streetcorners and in squares, or at markets, commenting wittily – and often obscenely – on the people going by or stopping to listen, or elaborating on themes shouted out by the audience. Even if you don't understand the lyrics, it's worth catching, especially if you can find a *cantoria*, a sing-off between two or more repentistas, who take alternate verses until a draw is agreed or until the audience acclaims a winner. The *Torneio dos Repentistas* in Olinda is one of the most famous events of its kind in the region, bringing in *repentistas* from all over the Northeast, who pair off and embark on singing duels while surrounded by audiences, who break into spontaneous applause at particularly good rhymes or well-turned stanzas. It's centred around the Praça da Preguiça, and lasts for three days.

North from Recife: Goiana and the coastal route to Itamaracá

North from Recife, the **BR-101 highway** runs a little way inland through low hills and sugar cane fields, a scenic enough route but one that offers little reason to stop off anywhere, save at the small town of **GOIANA** (six buses daily from the Recife *Rodoviária*). Parts of the town are still made up of rows of nineteenth-century terraced houses, built for workers in the local cotton mill, which has been long since bankrupted. Pottery has taken over as the main economic activity, and Goiana is one of the most important centres of the flourishing Pernambucan ceramics industry. The town centre is dotted with workshops, their wares spilling out onto the pavements, and there are some good bargains to be had. You can watch the potters at work in many places, like *Zé do Carmo* at Rua Padre Batalha 100. Opposite here, there's a good restaurant, the *Buraco de Giá*, where the trained crab which offers you a drink is perhaps the real highlight of any visit to the town.

If you want to stay in the area it's better to get out of Goiana and head the 30km over a country road to the coastal fishing village of **PITIMBÚ**, just over the border in Paraíba state. There are four buses a day from Goiana, the last around 2pm; it's a crowded and bumpy ride but Pitimbú is worth it. It has a good beach and friendly inhabitants, and while there's no hotel (although several are promised), camping on the beach is possible, or you can negotiate hammock space with local bar-owners. It's a quiet, sleepy place, ideal for a couple of days of doing nothing at all, with excellent fresh seafood available in several beachside bars. It's also a good place to see *jangadas* in action: the small fishing rafts with huge curving triangular sails, which look impossibly flimsy but are, in fact, well-designed to ride waves and surf. They go out at dawn and return in mid-afternoon, quite a sight, as they rear and plunge through the surf.

To Itamaracá

The **coast** north of Recife is, as you might expect, best explored along the smaller roads that branch off the highway. Nevertheless, it's as well to bear in mind that the Pernambuco coast is thickly populated by Brazilian standards. This isn't to say there aren't relatively peaceful spots, but what seems a deserted retreat during the week can fill up quickly at weekends, with Recifenses heading for the beaches, enlivening or destroying the rural atmosphere, depending on your point of view.

Rio Doce, Janga and Pau Amarelo

From Olinda, **local buses** continue along the coastal road to the beautiful palm-lined beaches of **RIO DOCE**, **JANGA** and **PAU AMARELO**. Until recently these were pretty much deserted, and although weekend homes are going up now, development, so far, is less obtrusive than in many places on the coast. The area gets busy at weekends, when in Janga especially there's music and dancing in the beachside bars at night. At Pau Amarelo you can still see one of several local star-shaped forts left behind by the Dutch, and if the original walls were their present height you can see why they lost.

Igarassú and Itapissuma

A more popular and even more scenic route north is through the pleasantly run-down colonial villages of Igarassú and Itapissuma to the island of Itamaracá (see below). Hourly **buses** to Igarassú, with easy connections to Itamaracá, leave from Avenida Martins de Barros in Recife, opposite the *Grande Hotel*. There are buses every half-hour from the *Rodoviária* to Itamaracá, stopping at Igarassú: they cost fifty cents and take around an hour, with a fair chance you'll have to stand. Another possibility is to go there **by boat**: every travel agency in Recife runs trips, stopping at beaches on the way, for around $10–15.

After turning off the highway past the ugly industrial suburb of PAULISTA, the road wends its way through a rich, green landscape of rolling hills and dense palm forest. The first town on the route is **IGARASSÚ**, an old colonial settlement built on a ridge rising out of a sea of palm trees: the name means "great canoe" in the language of the Tupi Indians, the cry that went up when they first saw the Portuguese galleons. The town was founded in 1535, when during a battle with the Indians the hard-pressed Portuguese commander vowed to build a church on the spot if victorious; and the **Igreja de São Cosme e Damião**, the oldest church in Brazil, is still there on the ridge. Down the hill the **Convento de Santo Antônio** is almost as old, built in 1588 and recently restored. Both are simpler and more austere than any of the churches in Recife or Olinda. There's a small museum in an old house near the convent with a dusty collection of nineteenth-century relics from sugar plantations.

Most of the houses in Igarassú are the rows of tied cottages characteristic of the old *engenhos*, or sugar estates. You can get a good idea of what a traditional *engenho* was like at the **Engenho Monjope**, an old plantation that has been taste-fully converted into a **campsite**. Minibuses back to Recife from Igarassú drop you at the turn-off (ask for "*o camping*"), and it's an easy ten-minute walk from there. The campsite is separate from the buildings, and you can ask at the entrance to look around even if you don't want to stay. The *engenho* dates from 1750; there's a decaying mansion, a chapel, water mill, cane presses and a *senzala*, the blockhouse where slaves lived.

The next town along is **ITAPISSUMA**, where a causeway leads from the main-land to Itamaracá island. Local legend says Itamaracá was once the site of the Garden of Eden, so it's a little ironic that the first building you see as you come off the causeway is an enormous open prison: all the fields are cultivated by prisoners, easily recognisable in blue and grey uniforms with ID cards pinned to their chests. They own and run a group of cafés and shops on the road just past the prison, selling bone carvings and jewellery made by prisoners whiling away the time. Some old lags still find it difficult to break old habits, overcharging and shortchanging shamelessly. These shops are built near another *engenho*, the **Engenho São João**, much better preserved than Monjope, with most of the original machinery used for pressing cane, boiling the syrup and refining sugar still intact.

Itamaracá

The short drive from Itapissuma to Itamaracá town promises much, passing through thousands of palm trees lapped by fields of sugar cane – the rich but sickly smell just before the harvest in March is enough to make you feel distinctly queasy. So it's a shame to have to say that the town of **ITAMARACÁ** is something of a disappointment. It's very crowded and increasingly scarred by the hundreds of weekend homes springing up in ugly rashes along the beaches – alongside the humble wattle huts roofed with palm leaves where the original islanders have managed to hold on.

The first part of Brazil to be settled by the Portuguese, Itamaracá was so prosperous as a sugar plantation that it was also the first part of Pernambuco to be occupied by the Dutch, who built a fort here. So rich is the soil, you can be reasonably sure that any field of sugar on the island has been there for over three centuries.

Nowadays Itamaracá has a reputation as an idyllic rural retreat, away from the pressures of life in Recife. This might have been true a decade ago, but it's stretching things a little now. Nonetheless, there are a couple of places of interest. A turn-off just before the town (walk or hitch – local buses exist but are very infrequent) leads 5km through tacky villas before rewarding you with the **Forte Oranje**, another star-shaped Dutch fort built in 1631 by Maurice of Nassau to protect the newly occupied sugar estates. There's a vicious enfilade at the front gate, where attackers were filtered through a zigzag corridor and exposed to musket fire from slits on all sides, and there are a few old cannons lying around on the ramparts with the makers' crests still visible. The souvenir shop inside is the most overpriced in Pernambuco, but the **beachside bars** opposite are really good value, with excellent food – highlight is the *casquinho de carangueijo*, crab-meat fried with garlic and onions, served in the shell and covered with roasted manioc flour. A couple of iced beers here, looking out across the bay, should be enough to make you feel more well-disposed towards the island, especially if you catch somebody selling the delicious local oysters out of a bucket. You buy them by the half-dozen, for around twenty-five cents: the seller flicks them open with a knife and supplies a lime to squeeze over them.

Otherwise, it's back to the town itself, which does have a small colonial section, the old port area called **Vila Velha**, where there's an ageing but otherwise unremarkable church, the Igreja do Matriz. There are the usual beachside bars and restaurants, and a couple of overpriced **hotels; camping** on the beach is technically illegal but possible, although not advisable with valuables. The best of the

restaurants is the *Sargaço*, which has fine seafood and a *ciranda* on Friday and Saturday nights, a circular dance to lilting, rhythmic music from flutes, guitars and drums.

The **beaches** are very good – wide and lined with palms – and they are a popular night venue for Carnaval celebrations, which attract hundreds of visitors. Unfortunately, however, stretches around the town and along as far as the Forte Oranje have been blighted by unregulated building. There are better, deserted beaches roundabout, but none less than a couple of hours walk along the shoreline in either direction.

There are *jangadas*, too, but they're a rather poignant symbol of what has happened to the town. A few years ago many families supported themselves by a combination of fishing and farming, and the *jangadas* were very much working fishing boats. A few *jangadeiros* still fish, but most of them now take weekenders and tourists out on trips; a couple of hours is usually around $1. *Jangada* trips are not advisable unless you're a reasonable swimmer, and even then you should be careful if the sea is at all rough; there's nothing to stop you being swept overboard, and no lifejackets are provided.

South from Recife

The coast south of Recife has the best **beaches** in the state and is fast realising its tourist potential – the sleepy fishing villages are unlikely to remain so for very much longer. Almost all **buses** to cities south of Recife take the BR-101 highway, which runs inland through fairly dull scenery, made worse by very heavy traffic: as this route eventually leads to the great cities of southern Brazil, lorries sometimes outnumber cars. The trick is to get a bus that goes along the much more scenic **coastal road**, the PE-60, or *via litoral*: they leave from Recife *Rodoviária* for the string of towns down the coast from CABO, through IPOJUCA, SIRINHAÉM, RIO FORMOSO, to SÃO JOSÉ DA COROA GRANDE. Before São José, where the road starts to run alongside the beach, you may need to get another local bus to get to the beachside villages themselves. In theory, you could hop from village to village down the coast on local buses, but only with time to spare. Services are infrequent – early morning is the usual departure time – and you might have to sleep on a beach or find somewhere to sling a hammock, as not all the villages have places to stay. As you move south, bays and promontories disappear, and walking along the beaches to the next village is often quicker than waiting for a bus.

Gaibú to Santo Agostino
The first stop out of Recife is the beach at **GAIBÚ**, some 20km south of Boa Viagem. There used to be a direct service from Recife's old Cais de Santa Rita bus station, a service which may reappear soon from the *Rodoviária* instead, so check first; otherwise, there are four buses a day from Cabo. Gaibú sports the familiar set-up – palm trees, bars and surf – and has a couple of cheap *pensões* and a **youth hostel**; a good base for village-hopping. It gets crowded at weekends, but there's a particularly beautiful stretch of coastline nearby, close enough to explore on foot. Just before Gaibú village, a turning in the dirt road heads off to the right, leading to the cape of **São Agostinho**, a pleasant walk uphill through palms and

mango trees, past the odd peasant hut in the forest. A couple of miles up is a ruined Dutch chapel, so overgrown it's almost invisible, and a path to the left leads out onto a promontory where the forest suddenly disappears and leaves you with a stunning view of the idyllic, and usually deserted, beach of **CALHETA**. You can clamber down to the beach, a ring of sand in a bay fringed with palm forest, the distant oil refinery at Suape providing the only jarring note.

If you continue on from the ruined chapel, you'll come to the sleepy hamlet of **SANTO AGOSTINHO**, where the present tranquillity masks a violent past. During the Dutch occupation there was vicious guerrilla fighting here, and an infamous massacre took place when Dutch settlers were herded into a church which was then burnt down. A small chapel still stands on the spot and there are the pulverised remains of a small fort. On the cape itself are burnt-out shells of Dutch buildings from the same campaign, and there's also a plaque commemorating the Spanish conquistador, Yanez Piñon, blown south by storms on his way to the Caribbean in 1500. He put in here for shelter a couple of months before Cabral "discovered" Brazil, and sailed off without knowing where he was – thus ensuring Brazil would end up speaking Portuguese rather than Spanish.

Porto de Galinhas to São Jose da Coroa Grande

From Cabo, or during the weekend direct from the Recife *Rodoviária*, buses head for another glorious beach, **PORTO DE GALINHAS**, deservedly popular but still quiet enough during the week. Good fresh fish is to be had in the beachside cafés here; fried needle fish, *agulhas fritas*, is a great snack with a cold beer as you wiggle your toes in the warm sand. There are two **campsites**, if you want to stay.

The sleepiest fishing villages of all are the ones around **ILHA DE SANTO ALEIXO**, reachable by local bus from Sirinhaém, but even here weekend houses for city slickers are going up, and it may well be ruined in the not too distant future. For the time being fishing still dominates, with *jangadas* drawn up on the beaches and men repairing nets. In **TAMANDARÉ** (local bus from Rio Formoso), as well as the usual stunning beach there are the ruins of the fort of Santo Inácio, destroyed in 1646, and a small hotel.

A little way south, in **SÃO JOSE DA COROA GRANDE**, where the *litoral* road finally hits the coast (and is thus reachable by a direct bus from Recife), there are bars, a huge beach, two large and expensive hotels, and one cheaper one (but still overpriced), the *Hotel Francês*. If you want to stay a night around here, it might be better to hop the 15km into Alagoas state by bus, to the even dozier village of **MARAGOGI**, where there is a cheap hotel, the *Hotel Gomes*. From here, you can catch a bus to MACEIÓ (see below).

Inland from Recife

In contrast to the gentle scenery of the coastal routes out of Recife, heading **inland** brings you abruptly into a completely different landscape, spectacular and forbidding. The people, too, look and speak differently; the typical *sertanejo* is short, wiry, and with the high cheekbones and thin nose of an Indian ancestor. They speak a heavily accented Portuguese, much ridiculed elsewhere, but really one of the loveliest Brazilian accents, irresistibly similar to a strong Welsh lilt.

Buses inland all leave from the Recife *Rodoviária*, and the best place to head for is Caruarú, 130km from Recife and the largest town in the *agreste*. The frequent buses there take two hours, cost $2, and are very comfortable: buy your ticket a day in advance. Seats on the right-hand side have the best view.

The route to Caruarú: Vitória, Gravatá and Bezerros

The BR232 highway heads directly away from the sea into gentle hills covered with enormous fields of sugar cane; the size of the estates gives you some idea of the inequality of land distribution in the Northeast, and explains why this part of Pernambuco has been in the forefront of the struggle for agrarian reform in Brazil. It was here in the late 1950s that the Peasant Leagues started, a social movement pressing for land reform through direct action, one of the factors that frightened the military into launching their coup in 1964. Most of the cane is destined for the first town en route, **VITÓRIA DE SANTO ANTÃO**, where, on the left-hand side of the road, is the factory which produces the most widely drunk rum in Brazil, *Pitú* – you can't miss the thirty-metre-high water tank cunningly camouflaged as an enormous bottle of *Pitú*.

After Vitória you begin to climb in earnest into the **Serra da Neblina**, threading into the hills of the *agreste* proper. Gradually the air becomes cooler, the heat drier, and highland plants replace the palms and sugar cane of the coastal strip. On a clear day the views are stunning, with rows of hills stretching into the distance on both sides and the coastal plain shimmering in the background. The fertile hills facing the sea get a lot of rain, cotton taking over from sugar as you climb, but deeper inland the hills are brown and parched and farming becomes more difficult. You begin to see cattle and strange-looking fields filled with neat rows of cactus. This is *palma*, and it's a foretaste of the harshness of *sertão* life: in times of drought, the cactus is chopped down and fed to cattle, thorns and all. It's a feed of last resource, but remarkably, the cactus contains enough water to keep cattle alive for a few more crucial months in the wait for rain.

The next town, 50km down the road, is **GRAVATÁ**, one of several *agreste* towns which has optimistically tagged itself "The Switzerland of Pernambuco", on the strength of its cool hill climate. There are lots of villas and a hotel built in Swiss chalet style, rather incongruous in a landscape that is parched brown as often as not. After Gravatá, it soon becomes obvious that you are nearing a major market from the activities at the roadside. Boys and men every few hundred yards stand as far into the road as they dare, leaping aside at the last moment, flourishing their wares at passing motorists: chickens, piglets, and the delicious fruit of the interior – pomegranates, *jaboticaba* (like a cross between a plum and a sweet grape), *mangaba*, a delicious red berry that stains the mouth black, and *umbú*, which looks like a gooseberry but doesn't taste like one. **BEZERROS**, the last town before Caruarú, is the home of a famous artist and printer, Jota Borges, some of whose work you may have seen in the Casa de Cultura and the *Livraria Cordel* in Recife. He has a roadside workshop on the left as you leave town, painted brilliant white with *Ateliê Jota Borges* in large letters across the front. Inside, you can see the carved wooden plates he makes to manufacture the prints on paper and cloth: the smaller ones are for the covers of *cordel*, a large library of which takes up one corner of the workshop. Borges himself is often at the market in Caruarú or delivering in Recife, but a family member is usually on hand to show visitors around. The absurdly cheap prints are simple but powerful depictions of peasant life.

Caruarú

As the home of the largest market in the Northeast, **CARUARÚ** is worth visiting in its own right, as well as being ideally placed for excursions into the *sertão*. It's important, though, to come on a market day: Saturday is the main one, but Wednesday and Friday are busy, too. As ever, the **bus station** is out of town, some four kilometres away; a local bus service (marked "Rodoviária") gets you to the centre in five minutes.

People come from all over the Northeast for the **market** here, which completely takes over the town, with stalls filling the squares and people clogging the streets. It's roughly divided into sections: around the bus station are clothes, the centre itself is devoted to food, and on the other side of the small river are arts and crafts, songbirds, and the famous *troca-troca*, where things are swapped rather than bought. Wandering around the **food market** introduces you to some characteristic sights and smells of the interior: the blocks of hard white *sertão* cheese, delicious with fruit; piles of leaves, roots and barks used in popular medicine; brown blocks of *rapadura*, a sweet made from unrefined sugar with a rich and sickly smell; and rows of mules having their teeth examined by prospective buyers. Across the small bridge is the **songbird market**, illegal but flourishing nonetheless, with dozens of species in small hand-made cages. And behind it is the most interesting part of all, the so-called **troca-troca**. Starting early on Saturday morning and finishing by noon, this patch of land is taken over by a crowd of people wandering around with whatever they want to swap: tapes and records, an old radio, used clothes, car parts – things which it would be difficult to sell for cash, which is why you don't see livestock or food being traded. It's fascinating to watch, but keep to the sidelines as locals don't appreciate wandering tourists getting in their way. It's also used by pickpockets unloading hot goods in a hurry, so if you don't want to see your own things being bartered, keep an eye on your bag.

The **arts and crafts market** (ask for the *mercado de artesanato*) is across the road from the songbirds, on a specially constructed site. It is becoming as near to a tourist trap as the interior ever gets, and there is some dross, but there's also a large amount of interesting work at prices far lower than in Recife. Again, it's divided into sections, straw, leather, pottery, and so forth, but most popular are the small clay statues for which this area is nationally famous, the *figurinhas de barro*. Caruarú is the main outlet for the renowned potters of Alto do Moura (see below), just up the road, and if you've seen the work of Mestre Vitalino in Recife you'll instantly recognise their vivid peasant style. The *figurinhas* are cheap, and come expertly wrapped in boxes.

A few places to stay

It's perfectly possible to see the market, make a trip out to Alto do Moura and get back to Recife in a day – which is what most people do. If you want to **stay over**, however, or intend to move on the next day further into the interior, there is no shortage of places to sleep. On a hill overlooking the town is a luxury class hotel, *Hotel do Sol*; more reasonably priced ($10 double) are the *Centenário* and *Expedicionário* on Rua Sete de Setembro in the centre. The cheapest places are clustered around the main square, Praça Getúlio Vargas: *Bela Vista* and *Sete de Setembro* are the cleanest of these.

Alto do Moura

To explore the tradition of *figurinhas* further, it's worth making the short journey to **ALTO DO MOURA**, 6km up the road from Caruarú: take a taxi or the marked bus from the main road that leads out from the food market. It's a dirt road to a small village that seems entirely unremarkable, except that every other house on the only street, **Rua Mestre Vitalino**, is a potter's workshop, with kilns like large beehives in the yards behind. The first house on the left was Mestre Vitalino's, and his widow and grandchildren still live in the simple hut next door. There's a plaque on the adobe wall and, inside, the hut has been kept as Vitalino left it, with his leather hat and jacket hanging on a nail. The only sign that Vitalino was somebody special are the framed photos of him being feted in Rio de Janeiro and introduced to the president. There's a visitor's book, and one of Vitalino's grandchildren is on hand to show you around. It's free, but do leave a donation: disgracefully, Vitalino's widow lives in penury next door without any kind of pension, a sad memorial to a man who brought fame and fortune to the town of his birth.

All the workshops are piled with pottery and *figurinhas* for sale, and are fascinating to browse around; each potter has a unique individual style. One of the most individual, and certainly the most eccentric, is Gaudino, on the corner opposite the solitary café. His inspiration comes to him in dreams, and much of his work consists of fantastic clay monsters, each with a poem, describing the dream that gave birth to them, stuffed into its mouth. Apart from his talents as a potter, Gaudino is a very skilled *repentista*: he can immediately improvise a stanza of welcome, rhyming your name to the last word of every line. Of the dozens of other workshops, the best are those of the children and grandchildren of Vitalino and his contemporaries: Manuel Eudócio at no. 151, who specialises in decorative pots; Luiz Antônio at no. 285; and Vitalino's son, Severino Pereira dos Santos, at no. 281. One more essential stopping point is the *Casa de Arte Zé Caboclo* at no. 63, one of the workshops of the large and extraordinarily talented family of Zé Caboclo, along with Vitalino the founder of the *figurinhas* tradition. A crowded cabinet holds a collection of his work that is more extensive even than that held by the Museu do Homem do Nordeste in Recife. His work is larger and cruder than Vitalino's, but has a vivid energy that many of the Alto do Moura potters rate even more highly than Vitalino's. Here you can also see his granddaughter Marliete's work, most of which is not for sale. She is the best of the younger generation: her delicate miniaturised figurines, superbly painted, show how the special skills of Alto do Moura are revitalised with each generation that passes, a tribute to the strength of popular culture in the interior.

Nova Jerusalém

In Easter week the market crowds are swollen by tourists and pilgrims heading for **NOVA JERUSALÉM**, in the heart of the *agreste*, 50km from Caruarú; the turn-off is on the right just after Caruarú, marked *Campina Grande*. After 24km another turn-off, to the left, leads to the small town of FAZENDA NOVA, just outside which is the site of Nova Jerusalém.

A granite replica of the old city of Jerusalem, it was built in the early 1970s by a local entrepreneur who cashed in on the deep religious feeling of the interior by mounting a Passion Play based on that of Oberammergau. Over the years, this *Paixão do Cristo* has become a new tradition of the *agreste*, attracting thousands of spectators to watch 500 costumed actors, mostly local amateurs, recreate the Passion and crucifixion. The "replica" of Jerusalem is in fact a third of the size of the original, and is basically a setting for the twelve stages on which the action takes place, each representing a Station of the Cross. There's an enjoyable sub-Cecil B. De Mille air of tackiness about the whole production, which is very free with the tomato ketchup in the whipping and crucifixion scenes. Next to the site is a sculpture park, where local artists have set up several impressively large granite statues of folk heroes done in the style of the interior, the largest versions you'll see of the *figurinhas de barro*.

Some practical details

The Passion is performed daily from the Tuesday before Easter to Easter Sunday inclusive, taking up most of the day. The most convenient way to see it is to go on one of the day **tours** which many travel agents in Recife – and other Northeastern cities – run there during Holy Week; about $10 a head. It's also easy to get there under your own steam, as there are **buses** to Fazenda Nova from Caruarú and Recife and a **campsite** when you get there, as well as several simple *dormitórios*. Entry to the spectacle used to cost $2, but there are strong rumours that *EMPETUR* will take it over in the near future and abolish the admission charge.

Into the Sertão

The **Pernambucan sertão** begins after Caruarú. There is no sudden transition: the hills simply get browner and rockier, dense thorny scrub takes over from the hill plants, and there are cacti every few yards, from tiny flowering stumps to massive tangled plants as large as trees. And, above all, it is hot, with parched winds that feel as if someone is training a hairdryer on your face. The Pernambucan *sertão* is one of the harshest in the Northeast, a scorched landscape under relentless sun for most of the year. This is cattle country, home of the *vaqueiro*, the Northeastern cowboy, and has been since the very beginning of Portuguese penetration inland in the seventeenth century; one of the oldest frontiers in the Americas.

Travelling in the sertão requires some preparation, as the interior is not geared to tourism. Hotels are fewer and dirtier; buses are less frequent, and you often have to rely on country services which leave very early in the morning and seem to stop every few hundred yards. A **hammock** is essential, as it's the coolest and most comfortable way to sleep, much better than the grimy beds in inland hotels, all of which have hammock hooks set into the walls as a standard fitting. The towns are much smaller than on the coast, and in most places there's little to do in the evening, as the population turns in early to be up for work at dawn. Far more people carry arms than on the coast, but in fact the *sertão* is one of the safest areas of Brazil for travellers – the guns are mainly used on animals, especially small birds, which are massacred on an enormous scale. Avoid **tap water**, by sticking to mineral water or soft drinks: dysentery is common, and although not dangerous these days it's extremely unpleasant.

But don't let these considerations put you off. People in the *sertão* are intrigued by gringos and are invariably very friendly. And while few *sertão* towns may have a lot to offer in terms of excitement or entertainment, the landscape in which they are set is spectacular. The Pernambucan *sertão* is more hilly than it is flat, and the main highway which runs through it like a spinal column winds through scenery unlike any you'll have seen before – an apparently endless expanse of cactus and scrub so thick in places that cowboys have to wear leather armour to protect themselves. If you travel in the rainy season here – March to June, although rain can never be relied upon in the interior – you may be lucky enough to catch it bursting with green, punctuated by the whites, reds and purples of flowering trees and cacti. Massive electrical storms are common at this time of year, and at night the horizon can flicker with sheet lightning for hours at a stretch.

To Petrolina

After Caruarú the highway passes through a number of anonymous farming towns. **ARCOVERDE**, 130km to the west, has a market on Saturdays and a reasonable **hotel**, the *Grande Majestic*, which doesn't quite live up to its name but is a cheap and handy place to break the journey. You may need to, because the best *sertão* towns to make for are buried deep in the interior, some eight or ten hours by bus from Caruarú. One is the pilgrimage centre of Juazeiro do Norte, just over the border in Ceará state, and dealt with below (see p.243). The others are the twin towns of Petrolina and Juazeiro, which have the enormous advantage of being built on the banks of the only river in the Northeast that never runs dry, the **Rio São Francisco**. There are three **buses** daily to Petrolina from Recife: they can be picked up at Caruarú, an $8 ride, for a journey that takes you through the heart of the Pernambucan *sertão*.

The last place that could reasonably be called a town is **SERRA TALHADA**, some 200km west of Arcoverde (the *Hotel Municipal* on the main square is reasonable). From then on, the road passes through a succession of flyblown villages, all of which would look vaguely Mediterranean – with their whitewashed churches, café, dusty square and rows of tumbledown cottages – if it weren't for the startling landscape in which they are set. Eighty kilometres beyond Serra Talhada, a turning leads north to Juazeiro do Norte, while one Petrolina bus turns south to follow an alternative route parallel to the São Francisco valley. The others continue for another 110km, across one of the most desolate semi-arid desert landscapes in the Northeast, before turning south along the BR-122, another 213km to Petrolina.

Petrolina

After the villages that have gone before, **PETROLINA** seems like a city. Certainly, by the standards of the *sertão*, it's a large, thriving and relatively prosperous town, thanks to the river trade to places downstream. Around the **Rodoviária**, which is quite central, there are a couple of *dormitórios*, while the best **hotel** in town – not that that means much – is the *Grande Rio*, on Rua Padre Fraga right in the centre. Nearby are the cheaper *Hotel Solar* on Praça Dom Malan, and the *Newman Hotel*, at Avenida Souza Filho 444.

Petrolina has a **waterfront**, where you can occasionally see river boats adorned with *carrancas*, carved wooden figureheads bolted onto the prow, brightly painted and with a grotesque monster's head, meant to frighten evil spirits lurking in wait for unwary mariners. It also has an interesting **Museu do Sertão** (Tues–Sun 8am–noon & 2–6pm), on the road to the airstrip: there's an infrequent local bus marked *Aeroporto*, otherwise take a taxi. Small but well put together, the museum documents *sertão* life and history through assorted relics and some fascinating photographs, including a couple of the bespectacled social bandit Lampião and his gang, popular heroes who roamed the *sertão* until they were shot in 1938. Lastly, Petrolina has a **market** on Friday and Saturday which brings people in from the *sertão* for miles around.

Juazeiro

Over the bridge that leads to Bahia state lies Petrolina's poorer sister town, **JUAZEIRO**, not to be confused with Juazeiro do Norte. Many of its inhabitants had their homes flooded when dams created the enormous **Sobradinho lake** just upstream in the 1960s. Subsequent plans to extend the lake and displace thousands more *sertanejos* have aroused fierce opposition and led to several violent clashes over the past few years, which is why there are a surprising number of uniforms around. There are several **hotels**, and an unusual attraction in the form of a nineteenth-century paddle steamer, the *Vaporzinho*, built in 1852 to ply the São Francisco river: it's been restored, turned into a **restaurant** and moored on the riverfront.

Juazeiro is the northern terminus for the **river services** of the *Companhia de Navegação do São Francisco*, which once ran frequent boats downriver as far south as Minas Gerais, but is now in decline. It still runs one monthly boat to Pirapora in Minas Gerais, from where there are bus connections to Brasília and Belo Horizonte, but its departure has become increasingly irregular: times and dates from tourist information offices in Recife and Salvador, or direct from the company (only Portuguese spoken; ☎075-811-2465). The journey takes three or four days. There are also smaller boats to towns both upstream and downstream leaving from the waterfront in Juazeiro, most of them river traders quite happy to take paying passengers – although always check when they return during negotiations, as it may not be for a couple of days.

It's remarkable how appealing the idea of even a short boat trip becomes after the heat and dust of the *sertão*, whose hills crowd right down to the Sobradinho lakeside. Tempting though it is, however, you should avoid **swimming** in still water, as schistosomiasis – also known as bilharzia – is endemic here.

ALAGOAS AND SERGIPE

Alagoas and **Sergipe** are, by some way, the smallest Brazilian states, but even so the two combined are a little larger than Switzerland. Sandwiched between Pernambuco to the north and Bahia to the south, they have traditionally been overshadowed by their neighbours and, to this day, still have a reputation for being something of a backwater. This isn't entirely fair. While it's true that there's nowhere remotely comparable to the cosmopolitan cities of Recife or Salvador, there are the two state capitals of **Maceió** and **Aracajú**, together with some well-preserved colonial towns, and exceptional beaches in Alagoas, which many rate as the best in the Northeast. Also, the harshness of the *sertão* here is much alleviated by the São Francisco river valley, which forms the border between the two states.

Alagoas is very poor, as you immediately discover from the potholes in the roads and its rickety local buses. Thousands of Alagoanos leave every year, looking for work as far afield as Rio, São Paulo and Amazonia, giving Alagoas the highest emigration rate of any state in Brazil. Sergipe was, for most of its history, in exactly the same position, but since the 1960s a minor offshore oil boom has brought affluence to parts of the coast. But Brazil being what it is, this doesn't mean the poor are proportionately any fewer: it's simply that the rich in Aracajú tend to be richer than the rich elsewhere in the Northeast.

Alagoas

There are two **routes into Alagoas** from the north: the highway from Recife, which runs inland through fairly dull country, and the indirect, but infinitely more scenic, continuation of the coastal (PE-60) road, running south from Recife. On this route, the first 20km is idyllic, alongside palm-lined tropical beaches, waves often lapping the sand within a few metres of the traffic. Broken lines of reefs offshore trap the sea in a series of calm, deep-blue and emerald-green lagoons, and even the occasional clump of hotels and weekend villas can't ruin a coastline like this – though you fear for it a decade from now. You may well find it impossible to resist hopping off the bus for a while at the **fishing villages**, all embryonic resorts as well these days, where locals often rent hammock space cheaply as a sideline: ask in the bars. Most places have a hotel or two, as well as a few *pensões* catering mainly for young Brazilians, who head here in droves during the holidays.

The coast to Maceió

From Maragogí (see "South of Recife", above) the more energetic can walk to the beautiful, isolated village of **JAPARATINGA** just down the coast: there's a turn-off on the left of the main road, just past the village (no signpost but anyone can direct you). It's a long but enjoyable walk, passing usually deserted beaches and, if you start early enough and take it easy, going for a couple of swims along the way, you should arrive by lunchtime. Take something to drink, and be careful not to overdo it when the sun is at its height. In Japaratinga, there's the cheap *Hotel Solmar* if you want to stay for a couple of days working on the tan.

Back at Maragogí, the road loops inland again, passing through low hills dotted with *engenhos* and small market towns, before re-emerging on the coast at the large fishing village of **BARRA DE SANTO ANTÔNIO** (local bus from Maragogí; also a stop for some of the Recife–Maceió interstate buses). Barra is quiet during the week but crowded at the weekend with people making the day trip from Maceió, only 40km down the road. It has a fine beach on a narrow neck of land jutting out from the coast a short canoe ride away, and good, fresh seafood in the small beachside **hotels**. And from here, it's only a short hop along a series of beaches to Maceió, the capital of Alagoas.

Maceió

Photos of **MACEIÓ** from the 1930s and 1940s show an elegant city of squares and houses nestling under palm trees. Today, while the city is still attractive in places, you can't help wishing the clock could be turned back. Some of the graceful squares and buildings remain, faded yet full of character, but the city as a whole has suffered in recent years from the attentions of planners. Their worst crime was the wrecking of a once famous waterfront parade, facing the harbour around which the city grew. An early-nineteenth-century customs house once stood here, framed by offices and the fine houses of traders – all now gone and replaced by grimy concrete boxes. The city's modern claim to fame is as the place where Brazil's first elected civilian president since 1960, **Fernando Collor de Melo**, cut his political teeth, becoming mayor and then state governor during the 1980s.

Arriving, orientation and information

By Brazilian standards the **Rodoviária** is not far from the centre, though it's still well beyond walking distance; buses marked *Ouro Preto* or *Serraria Mercado* connect it with the centre of town, or take a taxi. The **airport** is 20km from the city, and is irritatingly not served by a direct bus: a taxi will set you back around $10.

   Getting your bearings is easy enough. The small city centre is just inland from the modest harbour and, here, what remains of Maceió's past is to be found cheek by jowl with the cheap hotels and a central shopping area. The much larger and livelier area of **Pajuçara**, a few minutes away by bus to the north, is built along a spectacular beach, while to the south undistinguished urban sprawl conceals the enormous lagoon of **Mundaú**. It's here that the city ends, an ideal place to watch a sunset and eat cheaply at the simple bars and restaurants that dot its banks.

   Shoals of local buses make **getting around** very simple. All routes pass through the main squares in the centre, notably Praça Deodoro and Praça Dom Pedro II, names you'll often see on route cards propped in the front windows. Buses also run to *Ferroviária*, the decrepit **train station** on Rua Barão de Anadia, just before the waterfront. This is the stop for local routes south of the city, and you may use it to go to nearby Marechal Deodoro or the glorious beach of Praia do Francês.

   There's a **tourist information** booth at the small tourist market on the promenade, easily recognisable by the *jangadas* offering trips a mile out to the reef. There are other tourist information offices at the *Rodoviária*, the airport, and on Rua Senador Mendonça in the centre, next to the Livramento church. They are friendly and have excellent **free maps** of Maceió, but little else; staff shortages mean they keep very irregular hours.

Sleeping

Around the **Rodoviária** is a good bet for cheap but downmarket hotels – the *Reencontro* and *Hotel Sany* are cleaner than most. Otherwise, it's a choice between the centre and the district of Pajuçara, for which most people head. In the **centre**, try the *Hotel Flórida* at Rua Luiz Torres 126, the *Hotel California*, Rua Barão de Penedo 33, or the *Hotel Zumbi*, Rua Barão de Atalaia 67. (This last, incidentally, is the only reminder to be found in Maceió of Ganga Zumbi, seventeenth-century leader of the runaway slave kingdom of Palmares, in the interior of Alagoas – and a hero to Brazilian blacks.) A good medium-priced hotel, the *Hotel Parque*, on Praça Dom Pedro II, is the best value anywhere in the centre.

   It's only a short bus ride, though, to **Pajuçara**, where accommodation is more plentiful and of better quality than in the centre. Buses there are marked *Ponta Verde*, *Pajuçara* or *Ponta da Terra*, and run one block in from the beach, along **Avenida dos Jangadeiros Alagoanos**. Conveniently, this road is strung with a series of small hotels, two **youth hostels**, and *pensões* too numerous to name, with more down the sidestreets. The beach promenade is where the luxury hotels are, and there are good medium-priced hotels on Avenida Antônio Gouveia, the first stretch of promenade after the centre: the *Hotel Enseada* at no. 171 and *Verde Mar Hotel* nearby, with no number, are the pick of the bunch – not cheap but less expensive than they look.

The City

Maceió is not exactly bursting at the seams with museums and spectacular architecture, and the places worth seeing could all be rushed around in a morning if you were so inclined. There are two museums, but neither are in the same class as the one in nearby Marechal Deodoro (see below). However, it's worth visiting the waterfront **Museu Theo Brandão**, at Avenida Duque de Caxias 1490 (also called the Museu do Folclore; Mon–Fri 8am–noon & 2–5pm, Sat 2–5pm), for the fine nineteenth-century building that houses it, once part of the university and improving beyond measure as it decays. Inside you'll find the usual bundles of Indian arrows and motheaten feather ornaments. Judged strictly on exhibits, the **Instituto Histórico**, at Rua João Pessoa 382 (Tues–Fri 8am–noon & 2–5pm), has

the edge; worth seeing for the various relics and photographs of the bandit leader Lampião, including the famous "team photo" of his severed head, together with those of his wife, Maria Bonita, and his closest lieutenants. All were preserved in alcohol by the police detachment that shot them in 1938, so that they could be shown in market towns in the interior, the only way to make the people believe he really had been killed. His rifle, tunic, embroidered hat and revolver are also here.

The best place to get some sense of the old Maceió is **Praça dos Martírios**, the finest square in the city, and an object lesson to those who destroyed the waterfront. At one end is the eighteenth-century **Igreja Bom Jesus dos Martírios**, whose exterior, covered with well-preserved blue-and-white *azulejo* tiling, overshadows anything inside. At the other end the colonial **Governor's Palace** faces onto the palm-shaded square, brilliantly white during the day, floodlit at night.

From the square you can take a taxi, or a local bus marked *Mundaú* or *Ponta da Barra*, for the short ride to **Mundaú lagoon**. Have a *caipirinha* at a waterfront bar to accompany the routinely spectacular sunset. There are simple but excellent eating places here, too, selling fish and shrimp, and the early evening is a good time to watch prawn fishermen at work on punts in the lagoon, their silhouetted figures throwing out nets against the sunset.

The city's beaches

Maceió is most famous for its **beaches**, of which Alagoanos are justly proud. The main city beach is at **PAJUÇARA**, whose curving road and wide mosaic promenade is studded with palm trees. A series of bars, with numbers rather than names, are built around thatched emplacements at intervals along the beach. They mix excellent *caipirinhas* and serve cheaper food than you're likely to find in the seafront restaurants on the other side of the road, all much of a muchness. Seafood is, naturally, best: the *sopa de ostra* manages to get more oysters into a single dish than most gringos see in a lifetime; they're so common, you can even get an oyster omelette.

The bay then curves past the yacht club, into the even longer and less crowded beach of **JATIÚCA**, the first of a series of fine sands to the north. The best way to get to them is to take buses marked *Mirante* or *Fátima* from the centre, which take you along the coast as far as **PRATAGÍ** (also called Mirante da Sereia), 13km north, where there are coral pools in the reef at low tide. You can get off the bus anywhere that takes your fancy: the main beaches, in order of appearance, are JACARECICA, GARÇA TORTA and RIACHO DOCE, all of them less crowded than the city beaches during the week, but very popular at weekends.

South to Marechal Deodoro

Most visitors to Maceió flood north to the beaches, which leaves the coast **to the south** in relative calm. Hourly buses marked *Deodoro* leave from the bus stop in front of the old train station in Maceió, near the harbour, passing out of the city over the Trapiche bridge into a flat, swampy coastline. Sixteen kilometres south, the road swings left to a beach called **PRAIA DO FRANCÊS**, which even by Alagoano standards is something special. An enormous expanse of white sand, surf and thick palm forest, it even boasts a couple of small hotels; the *Hotel Cumarú* is the best value. Apparently there are plans to build a large luxury hotel here, but with any luck the recession in Brazil has put paid to that. The last bus back to Maceió leaves at 6pm.

Marechal Deodoro

Good though the beach is, it's overshadowed by the next stop, the beautifully preserved colonial town of **MARECHAL DEODORO**, 22km from Maceió. Basically it's no more than a small market town, built on rising ground on the banks of a lagoon, with streets that are either dirt or cobbled. But it's immaculately kept, with not a single building that looks as if it were constructed this century. Nor is it simply preserved for tourists to gawp at: the locals spit in the streets, gossip and hang about in bars as they would anywhere else, and there's a real air of small town tranquillity.

If you want **to stay**, there are a couple of simple *pensões* on the square where the bus ends up, or there's even a **campsite**, clean and with good facilities, half an hour's walk beyond the square – the road marked by a sign near the small bus company office.

The manicured **Praça João XXII**, where the bus drops you, is dominated by the imposing mid-eighteenth-century façade of the Igreja de Nossa Senhora da Conceição, with the older **Convento de São Francisco**, finished in 1684, attached. The Convento's plain exterior conceals an austere, yet strikingly beautiful interior, which is now turned over to the excellent **Museu de Arte Sagrada** (Tues–Sun 9am–1pm). Restoration has enhanced the character of the complex, preserving a cloistered calm, an appropriate setting for a high-quality collection of religious art; the museum's entrance is through the walled garden to the right. Once inside, you see that the convent is built around a silent and cool courtyard. The main galleries are on the first storey, where the floor is as interesting as many of the exhibits. It's made of rich brown *pau do brasil*, the tropical redwood that gave its name to the country, glistening in a protective coat of varnish: you have to wear the slippers the attendant provides to avoid damaging it. Everything on display is high Catholic religious art, with little concession made to the tropical setting save for the large number of portrayals of São Benedito, the black patron saint of the slaves who manned the *engenhos* all around and built most of Marechal Deodoro itself. The highlight of the collection, extracted from churches all over the state, is the group of seventeenth- to nineteenth-century statues of Saints and Virgins, in the first gallery to the right. Most are no more than a foot high, made of wood or plaster, and intricately painted. Look, too, for the couple of lifesize (and frighteningly lifelike) carved wooden bodies of Christ, with gruesome wounds. In comparison, the **Igreja de Nossa Senhora da Conceição** is not as impressive, a typical mid-eighteenth-century building, though less cloyingly Rococo than most, currently being restored. In front of a small side chapel, opposite the entrance from the museum, is a concealed entrance to a secret tunnel, a relic from the original chapel that stood on the site during the Dutch wars.

Down the road curving to the right past the museum is the modest house that was the birthplace of **Marshal Deodoro**, proclaimer and first President of the Republic in 1889; it's now preserved as a **museum** (Tues–Sun mornings only). Deodoro was the son of an army officer who served with distinction in the Paraguayan war, and rose to become head of the armed forces with the sonorous title "Generalissimo of the Forces of Land and Sea". He was the first Brazilian to mount a military coup, unceremoniously dumping the harmless old Emperor Dom Pedro II, but he proved an arrogant and inept president, the earliest in a depressingly long line of incompetent military authoritarians. Dissolving Congress and declaring a state of siege in 1891, he did everyone a favour by resigning when he couldn't make it stick. There's no hint, of course, of his disastrous political career in the museum, which is basically a mildly interesting collection of personal effects and period furniture.

In the streets around you'll find several **lacemakers**, with goods displayed in the windows. Marechal Deodoro is famous for its lace, which you see in any sizeable market in the Northeast. It is high quality stuff, and costs less than half the price you pay elsewhere when bought at source in the town.

Paulo Afonso

Inland from Maceió, 300km to the west, the most popular destination of all in Alagoas is the **Cachoeira de Paulo Afonso**, once the largest waterfall on the São Francisco river and the third largest in Brazil, but now largely emasculated by a hydroelectric scheme that diverted most of the flow – a spectacular piece of ecological vandalism surpassed only by the destruction of the even more impressive Sete Quedas waterfall in Paraná by similar means a few years ago. These days the only time a considerable amount of water passes over the falls is during the rains of January and February, but the whole surrounding area – a spectacular deep rocky gorge choked with tropical forest and declared a national park – is very scenic all year round.

You can get there by bus from Salvador, but the journey from Maceió is shorter, with two **buses** daily from the *Rodoviária* there. They leave you in the small river town of **PAULO AFONSO**, on the Bahian riverbank, where there are a cluster of reasonable **hotels** near the bus station; the *Belvedere* and the *Palace* on Rua André Falcão are more upmarket but good value.

The **waterfall** is some way out of town and not yet served by a local bus, although there are plans for one. You'll be approached by taxi drivers offering return trips for around $15, a little expensive, but they do know the best spots. Otherwise, traffic down the signposted road is light but accommodating to hitchers; once you get there the best view is from the **cable car**, if it's working.

If you feel like really getting off the beaten track, take the bus from Paulo Afonso to **PIRANHAS**, a picturesque small riverside town 80km south, where there are beaches on the river, a small *pousada*, friendly inhabitants, and little to disturb the rural quiet.

Penedo and around

A couple of hours **south of Maceió** is the livelier colonial town of **PENEDO**, served by four buses daily from Maceió's *Rodoviária*. For once they leave you in the centre of the town. There are several colonial **churches** here which are all marked on a useful map of the town, obtainable at the **tourist office** in the main central square, the Praça Barão de Penedo. Penedo is strategically placed at the mouth of the São Francisco river, and while the trading prosperity it might have expected as a result never quite materialised, it's still a busy little place, much of whose life revolves around the river and the waterfront. It is well supplied with good **places to stay**: try *Pousada Colonial*, Praça 12 de Abril (good views), or *São Francisco*, on Avenida Floriano Peixoto, both in the heart of town; nearer the *Rodoviária*, on Rua Siqueira Campos, are the *Turista*, the *Majestic* and *Hotel Vitória* – all are about the same price, with rooms starting at $5. A good **restaurant** is *Forte da Rocheira* on Rua da Rocheira.

The waterfront park, with shaded paths and kiosks selling drinks, is a good place to watch the toing and froing of the boats. You can negotiate with boat-owners to go on **cruises** to various places, for around $3 an hour irrespective of numbers. The main destinations are **PIASSABUSSÚ**, a sleepy and little-visited fishing village right on the mouth of the river; and the village of **NEÓPOLIS**, opposite Penedo, where there's nothing to do except have a drink and catch the ferry back – but it's a nice trip.

If you feel adventurous, have a lot of time and enough Portuguese to make people understand where you want to go, it is possible to go **up the river by boat** as far as Piranhas, and from there get a bus to Paulo Afonso and the falls. Most of the river boats work particular stretches of river, and unless you're very lucky you'll need to take several, over several days, to get as far as Piranhas. Starting from Penedo, the river towns you pass through before Piranhas are PORTO REAL DO COLÉGIO, SÃO BRÁS, TRAIPÚ, GARARÚ, and PÃO DE AÇÚCAR.

Sergipe: Aracajú and around

From Maceió seven buses a day run to the neighbouring state of **Sergipe** and to **ARACAJÚ**, its capital, a little-visited and rather anonymous place. Built on the flat southern bank of the Sergipe river, its American-style grid layout, unusual in Brazil, is the clue to its lack of character. Although the Portuguese founded a colony here in 1592, the capital of the infant state was moved to nearby São Cristóvão. Then, in the mid-nineteenth century, there was a sudden vogue for purpose-built administrative centres (similar to the urge that led to the construction of Brasília a century later), and the core of modern Aracajú was thrown up overnight, becoming the state capital again in 1855. Like the other state capitals planned and built in the last century, Aracajú is – to put it mildly – something of an architectural desert. Oil wealth has stimulated a lot of recent building and given the city council enough money to keep everything clean and tidy, but there is a very un-Brazilian dullness about the place. The main redeeming features are the excellent beach at Atalaia, and the town's proximity to the small colonial towns of Laranjeiras and São Cristóvão; for all of which, see below.

The spanking new **Rodoviária** is miles out of town, linked to the centre by frequent local buses. The cheaper **hotels** are around the old bus station in the centre, concentrated on Rua General Carú and the Rua Santa Rosa: the *Brasília*, at Rua Laranjeiras 580, is more upmarket but still good value. Your first stop, though, should be the **tourist office**, either at the *Rodoviária* or at Avenida Barão de Moroim 593, off the central Praça Fausto Cardoso – free town maps, not just of Aracajú but Laranjeiras and São Cristóvão as well. In town, there's a pleasant boulevard overlooking the Sergipe river, with cafés and restaurants; and an *artes-anato* centre in a restored nineteenth-century building on Praça Olímpio Campos – a square easily recognised by its hideous cathedral.

The fine **beaches** of **ATALAIA** and **ATALAIA NOVA** are 16km south of town, with a frequent bus service taking around an hour. Atalaia's beachside bars, restaurants and hotels are all a good bit livelier than the city itself. The offshore oil rigs upon which the local economy depends can be seen in the distance, but don't seem to have polluted the sea. The less crowded beach at Atalaia Nova is on an island, Barra dos Coqueiros, a fifteen-minute boat trip from the ferry landing at Atalaia. There's a **campsite** on Atalaia beach, but if you don't mind fewer facilities

Atalaia Nova is the better bet, more scenic and quiet than Atalaia itself. If you don't fancy sleeping on the beach, ask the bar owners for room to sling a hammock.

Laranjeiras and São Cristóvão

Sergipe's main attractions are two attractive colonial towns that come as a welcome relief from Aracajú's anonymity, reminders of the time when sugar made the *sergipano* coast one of the most strategically valuable parts of Brazil. Innumerable skirmishes were fought around them during the Dutch wars, but no trace of their turbulent past survives into their tranquil present, as they slide from important market centres into rural backwaters.

The pleasantly decrepit village of **LARANJEIRAS** is forty minutes away from Aracajú, buses leaving from the old bus station in town. Dominated by a hill crowned with the ruins of an old *engenho* chapel, Laranjeiras boasts a couple of small museums as well as the inevitable churches. The **Museu Afro-Brasileiro** (Tues–Fri 9am–1pm & 3–5pm) concentrates on slave life and popular religion, while the **Centro de Cultura João Ribeiro** is mostly given over to *artesanato* and relics of plantation life. But the main attraction is simply wandering around the winding streets, with quiet squares, pastel-painted houses and small bars where locals sit around and watch the world go by. There are a couple of **pensões**, but no hotels as yet, and with any luck it will stay that way.

The other colonial town worth visiting is the old state capital of **SÃO CRISTÓVÃO**, also reached by local bus from Aracajú's old bus station. It was founded in 1590 and much of it hasn't changed since, as the shifting of the capital to Aracajú preserved it from the developers. Packed into its small area is the full panoply of a colonial administrative centre, including an old governor's palace, a parliament building and half a dozen period churches, together with the small **Museu de Arte Sacra e Histórico**, reputedly pretty good but undergoing restoration at the time of writing.

São Cristóvão is the only place worth stopping on the route south to Bahia, which runs inland from Aracajú through parched hill country before emerging (on the bus) some six hours later at Salvador, capital of Bahia state.

BAHIA

The oldest and most historic city in Brazil, **Salvador** was the capital of Brazil for over two centuries, before relinquishing the title to Rio in 1763. The bay on which the city was built afforded a superb natural anchorage, while the surrounding lands of **Bahia state** were ideal country for sugar cane and tobacco plantations. Salvador became the centre of the **Recôncavo**, the richest plantation zone in Brazil before the coming of coffee, and there's a string of colonial towns – like **Santo Amaro** and **Cachoeira** – within striking distance of the city.

The countryside changes to the south, with mangrove swamps and islands surrounding the town of **Valença**, before reverting to a spectacular coastline typical of the Northeast. **Ilhéus** is a thriving beach resort, as is **Porto Seguro** – oldest town in Brazil and site of the first Portuguese landings in 1500. **Inland**, the Bahian **sertão** is massive, a desert-like land which supports some fascinating frontier towns – the mining bases of **Jacobina** and **Lençóis**, and the river terminus of **Ibotirama** are just three.

Salvador

SALVADOR is one of that select band of cities which has an electricity you feel from the moment you arrive, and the confident sense of identity you find in a place that knows it's somewhere special. Second only to Rio in the magnificence of its natural setting, on the mouth of the enormous bay of Todos os Santos, there is no better description of Salvador than that by William Scully, who wrote the first guidebook to Brazil in 1866:

"Here, sheltered from every wind and surrounded by a country exuberantly rich, fleets may ride at anchor in a gulf which seems as if formed by nature to be the emporium of the world and receive its shipping, while the town itself, seen picturesquely crowning the high bluff that circles round the eastern side of the bay, appears a fitting mistress of the lovely scene."

Salvador's foundation in 1549 marked the beginning of the permanent occupation of the country by **the Portuguese**.

It wasn't an easy occupation: the Caeté Indians killed and ate both the first governor and the first bishop before succumbing, and Salvador was later the scene of a great battle in 1624, when the Dutch destroyed the Portuguese fleet in the bay and took the town by storm, only to be forced out again within a year by a joint Spanish and Portuguese fleet. In a climactic second naval battle in front of the city, legend has it that the Dutch admiral Adrian Patryd, his fleet outgunned and defeated, threw himself into the sea with the words "the ocean is the only tomb worthy of a Batavian admiral".

Much of the plantation wealth of the Recôncavo was used to adorn the city with imposing public buildings, ornate squares, and, above all, churches. Today, Salvador is a large, modern city, but significant chunks of it are still recognisably colonial. Taken as a whole it doesn't have the unsullied calm of, say, Olinda but many of its individual churches, monasteries and convents are magnificent, the finest colonial buildings anywhere in Brazil.

The other factor that marks Salvador out among Brazil's great cities is immediately obvious – most of the population is black. Salvador was Brazil's main slave port, and the survivors of the brutal journey from the Portuguese Gold Coast and Angola were immediately packed off to city construction gangs or the plantations of the Recôncavo: their descendants make up the bulk of the modern population. **African influences** are everywhere. Salvador is the cradle of *candomblé*, *macumba* and *umbanda*, Afro-Brazilian religious cults that have millions of devotees across Brazil. The city has a marvellous local **cuisine**, much imitated in other parts of the country, based on African ingredients like palm oil, peanuts and coconut milk. And Salvador has possibly the richest **artistic tradition** of any Brazilian city; only Rio can rival it.

A disproportionate number of Brazil's leading writers and poets were either born or lived in Salvador, including Jorge Amado, the most widely translated Brazilian novelist, and Vinícius de Morães, Brazil's best-known modern poet. The majority of the great names who made Brazilian **music** famous hail from the city – João Gilberto, co-inventor with Tom Jobim of *bossa-nova*; Astrud Gilberto, whose quavering version of "The Girl From Ipanema" was a global hit; Dorival Caymmi, the patriarch of Brazilian popular music; Caetano Veloso, the founder of *tropicalismo*, Brazil's declaration of musical independence in the 1960s; Maria

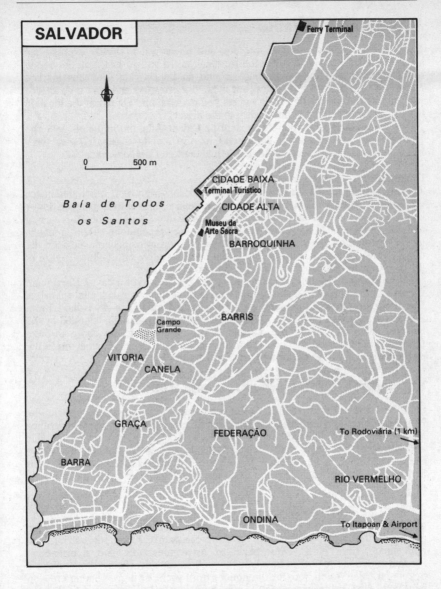

Bethânia, a fine singer and sister of Caetano; Gal Costa, the loveliest voice in Brazilian music; and Gilberto Gil, who when not touring Europe or America is Secretary of Culture in the city government. The city's music is still as rich and innovative as ever, and bursts out every year in a **Carnaval** that many think is the best in Brazil.

Arriving and orientation

The **airport** is 20km north of the city, and on arrival a shuttle express bus service, from directly in front of the terminal, takes you to Praça da Sé via the beach districts and Campo Grande, around an hour's ride. The bus marked *Politeama* also runs to the centre, but gets very crowded and isn't a good idea with luggage. A taxi to the centre will set you back around $8; pay at the kiosk in the arrivals area and hand the voucher to the driver.

The **Rodoviária** is 5km out. To reach the Cidade Alta and its hotels, take the *Barroquinha* bus (direct but infrequent), or the one to *Campo Grande* (very frequent) and change there to the shuttle bus marked *Campo Grande-Sé*.

Orientation

The city is built around the craggy, two-hundred-foot-high bluff which dominates the eastern side of the bay, and splits the central area into upper and lower sections. The heart of the old city, **Cidade Alta** (or simply Centro), is strung along its top, linked to the **Cidade Baixa**, below, by precipitous streets, a funicular railway and the towering Art Deco liftshaft of the Carlos Lacerda elevator, the city's largest landmark. Cidade Alta is the administrative and cultural centre of the city; Cidade Baixa the financial and commercial district.

In the last century the city expanded into the still elegant areas of **Barris** and **Canela**, to the north of Cidade Alta, and up to the exclusive residential suburb of **Barra**, the headland at the mouth of the bay around which the city is built. From Barra, a broken coastline of coves and beaches, large and small, is linked by the twisting **Avenida Presidente Vargas**, which runs along the shore through **Ondina**, **Rio Vermelho** and **Pituba**, the main beach areas. Further on is the one-time fishing village of **Itapoan**, after which the city peters out.

Information, getting around . . . and trouble

Salvador's **tourist information** is higher quality than anywhere else in the Northeast. The state tourist agency, *Bahiatursa*, is used to foreigners, every office has English and French speakers, and there's well-produced material on Salvador and the rest of the state as well: stock up if you plan to travel in Bahia, as elsewhere the service is nothing like as good. There's a free fortnightly *Calendário de Eventos* and a useful listings leaflet, *Eventos e Servicos*, but you'll have to buy a **city map** – more than worth the $1, excellent quality with places of interest clearly marked.

There are **information posts** on arrival at the airport (daily 9am–11pm) and the *Rodoviária* (daily 8am–9pm). The **main office** is on the ground floor of the governor's palace, the Palácio do Rio Branco, on Rua do Chile in Cidade Alta, almost on the corner of Praça da Sé (Mon–Sat 8am–6.30pm; ☎241-4333). The noticeboard here is a useful place to leave messages and information/ recommendations for other travellers, as well as for advertising things like air tickets for sale. Watch, too, for the notices from yacht owners, seeking crew on trips up to the Caribbean and the US, even occasionally to Europe and Africa.

Other information posts in the city are inside the Jorge Amado museum (Mon–Fri 9am–noon & 2–5pm), at Largo do Pelourinho, in Cidade Alta; downstairs in the Mercado Modelo (Mon–Sat 9am–6pm), the old market building on the waterfront in Cidade Baixa; and at the São Francisco church near the *Hotel Colón* (Mon–Fri 9am–noon & 2–5pm).

PERSONAL SAFETY: A WARNING

A warning about **personal safety** in Salvador is in order. There's no need to let fear interfere with your enjoyment of the city, but you should be aware that Salvador has more of a problem with robberies and muggings than anywhere else in the Northeast, and visitors are an obvious target. The usual **precautions** apply emphatically to Salvador: don't carry cameras around your neck or wear expensive watches, and don't take passports with you; only take as much money as you need for the day; and avoid ill-lit sidestreets at night. In addition, there are a few specific **danger spots** to avoid. Don't use the Lacerda elevator after the early evening: if you want to get from Cidade Baixa to Cidade Alta, or vice-versa, take a bus or a taxi. The sidestreets around Praça da Sé and Largo do Pelourinho, in Cidade Alta, are areas to avoid after dark and treat with caution even during the day; and give the Avenida do Contorno a miss too, the seafront road that runs north from the harbour past the *Solar do Unhão* restaurant. It's a shame to put it out of bounds, as it's a very scenic walk, but it's dangerous even in daylight, as gangs lie in wait for tourists who don't know any better: if you go to the restaurant, or the Museu de Arte Moderna near it, go and return by taxi – take this advice from somebody who didn't.

Getting around

Handily, many of the museums, churches and historic buildings are concentrated within **walking** distance of each other in Cidade Alta. Failing that, **taxis** are cheap and plentiful, although all the beach areas except Barra are a long ride from the centre.

There are three **local bus terminals**, and the bus system is efficient and easy to use. From **Praça da Sé**, there are local services to Barra and to **Campo Grande**, another central terminus with self-explanatory connections to *Aeroporto*, *Rodoviária* and *Itapoan* (also spelt *Itapoã*). On the pavement just up from Praça da Sé (towards the cathedral) are more stops, where fifty cents gets you a seat on a *frescão*, a comfortable express coach service, well worth using instead of the crowded city buses. There are only two routes on this service: buses marked *Iguatemí* run through the city to Barra, head down the coast to Rio Vermelho, and stop at the glossy shopping centre at Iguatemí, from where a short walkway leads to the *Rodoviária* – the fastest way to reach it by public transport, though still count on 45 minutes, minimum; the *Aeroporto* service, meanwhile, follows the same route until Rio Vermelho, before continuing along past Pituba to Itapoan, and on to the airport – cutting journey times to any of the beach areas to at least half that of a regular city bus. The other city bus terminal is **Estação da Lapa**, in Barris, which has connections to everywhere in the city: it's remarkably well laid out, with destinations clearly labelled, and you catch the *Bonfim* bus here, out to the southern headland of the city bay and the church of Nosso Senhor do Bonfim. To reach the centre, any bus with *Sé*, *C. Grande* or *Lapa* on the route card will do.

Salvador also has **ferry** services to islands in the bay and points on the mainland, and there are two ferry terminals. The **Terminal Turístico**, behind the Mercado Modelo, clearly visible from Cidade Alta, is for launch services – *lanchas* – and excursion boats to the island of Itaparica, across the bay, and ferries to the town of Maragojipe; the **Terminal da Estação Marítima**, past the docks to the right, handles the full-size car ferries to Itaparica.

The quickest way to get to the ferry terminals – and Cidade Baixa in general – is to take the **Lacerda elevator** or the **funicular railway**, both of which connect Praça da Sé in Cidade Alta with the heart of Cidade Baixa. They run every few minutes from early morning to late at night, and cost only a few cents a ride.

Finding a place to stay

Salvador is the second most popular tourist destination in Brazil and correspondingly full of hotels. Unless you want to stay on a beach, the best area to head for is Cidade Alta, not least because of the spectacular view across the island-studded bay.

Cidade Alta

There are several reasonable places along the main artery of **Avenida Sete de Setembro**, which runs into Cidade Alta: the *Imperial* and the *Anglo Americano* are both good value, with rooms starting at $8. But the largest concentration is in Cidade Alta itself, which begins past the Praça Castro Alves; immediately on the right here, **Rua Rui Barbosa** has the *Pousada da Praça* and the *Hotel Paris*. Along the main street, at Rua do Chile 7, the *Hotel Chile* has an imposing facade which the interior doesn't quite live up to, but if you can manage to get a room at the back, facing out across the bay, it's a good choice. You will find the very cheapest places ($3–5) are further along, in the decidedly seamy sidestreets around the Praça da Sé, but are none too secure. Much better, for only a couple of dollars more, is **around Terreiro de Jesus**, just along from Praça da Sé, where at the far end the *Hotel Colón* and the *Solar São Francisco* look out onto the São Francisco church – their disadvantage being that they're so popular with gringos, you only have to stick your nose out the door for someone to try and sell you something.

Perhaps the best area of all in Cidade Alta is **Pelourinho**, the heart of the colonial district, further along the crest of the bluff from Terreiro de Jesus; *Hotel Solara*, on the cobbled Largo do Pelourinho, is recommended (singles for $10). Even better is the inconspicuous *Hotel do Pelourinho*, Rua Alfredo de Brito 20 (☎243-9144), just before the square – medium range rather than cheap, around $15 for a double, but still a real bargain for the price, an old mansion house with courtyard, parrots, banana and palm trees, a good restaurant, and a fantastic view.

Staying at the beach

Barra is the closest of the beaches to the centre and the favoured haunt of the city's upper classes, attracted to the most scenic stretch of coast. Despite this, it's one of the more reasonably priced beach areas and has some good medium-priced hotels in the $15–20 range. On the sea are the *Hotel Solar da Barra*, Avenida Sete de Setembro 2998, and the *San Marino Hotel*, Avenida Presidente Vargas 889; a couple of blocks inland try the *Vila Romana* at Rua Professor Lemos de Brito 14. **Ondina** and **Rio Vermelho** are where most of the luxury hotels are, good areas to visit but expensive to stay.

Cheapest of all the beach areas – but not quite as scenic – is **Pituba**. Although handily close to the airport and *Rodoviária*, it's a little far from the centre, and buses late at night can be a problem. Good medium range hotels here are the *Amaralina Hotel*, Avenida Amaralina 790, and the *Hotel Universo* on Avenida Otávio Mangabeira. Cheaper options include the friendly *Hotel Pituba* at Avenida Manoel Dias de Silva 1614, or the *Pituba Praia Hotel*, at no. 2581.

Around the city

Most of Salvador's 25 museums and 34 colonial churches are concentrated within a short distance of each other in Cidade Alta, which makes sightseeing fairly straightforward. However, the sheer profusion of places worth visiting is a real problem; it's difficult to know where to start in a place so steeped in history. But there's no need to rush. A single meandering walk from the Praça da Sé, taking in all the highlights, but not stopping at any of them, would take no more than an hour; more realistically, you'll need at least two days, and possibly three, if you want to explore the city's history in depth.

From Praça da Sé to Terreiro de Jesus

The best spot to begin a walking tour is at the **Praça da Sé**, the square dominated by the impressive **Palácio do Rio Branco**, the old governor's palace. It was burnt down and rebuilt during the Dutch wars, and the regal plaster eagles were added by nineteenth-century restorers, who turned a plain, colonial mansion into an imposing palace. The interior is fine, a blend of Rococo plasterwork, painted walls and ceilings, and polished wooden floors, but only the beautifully restored reception area is open to the public (Mon–Sat 2–5pm). Also facing the square is the **Câmara Municipal**, the seventeenth-century city hall, graced by a series of elegant but solid arches.

Following the Rua do Chile up from the square takes you to Praça Quinze de Novembro, which everyone knows as **Terreiro de Jesus**. On the left is the plain **Catedral Basílica**, once the chapel of the largest Jesuit seminary outside Rome. Its interior is one of the most beautiful in the city, particularly the stunning panelled ceiling of carved and gilded wood, which gives the church a light, airy feel that's an effective antidote to the overwrought Rococo altar and side chapels. To the left of the altar is the tomb of **Mem de Sá**, third viceroy of Brazil from 1556 to 1570, and the most energetic and effective of all Brazil's colonial governors. It was he who supervised the first phase of the building of Salvador, and destroyed the Caeté Indians. Look in on the recently restored sacristy, too, while you're here – portraits of Jesuit luminaries, set into the walls and ceiling, gaze down intimidatingly on intruders.

The Museu Afro-Brasileiro

Next to the cathedral stands one of the best museums in the city, the **Museu Afro-Brasileiro** (Tues–Sat 9–11.30am & 2–5.30pm), contained within a large nineteenth-century building that used to be the university medical faculty; in the shady yard behind is the derelict, circular lecture theatre, now roofless and with trees growing inside. The main building, however, has been excellently restored, and houses three different collections, one on each storey.

Largest and best is on the **ground floor**, recording and celebrating the considerable black contribution to Brazilian culture. Four rooms are dedicated to different aspects of black culture – popular religion, *capoeira*, weaving, music and Carnaval – and everything, for once, is very well laid out. The section on *capoeira*, the balletic martial art the slaves developed, is fascinating, supported by photos and old newspaper clippings. But there are other highlights, too, like the gallery of large photographs of *candomblé* leaders, some dating from the last century, most in full regalia and exuding pride, strength and authority; and the famous carved panels by Carybé, in the exhibition room, past the photo gallery. Carybé, Bahia's

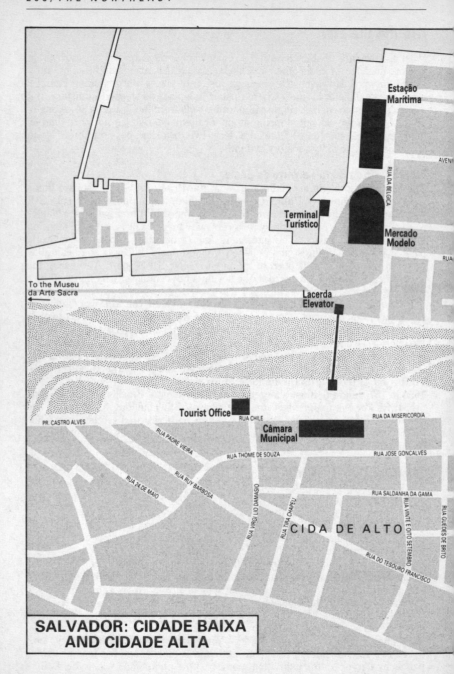

Estação
Marítima

AVENI

RUA DA BELGICA

Terminal
Turístico

Mercado
Modelo

RUA

To the Museu
da Arte Sacra

Lacerda
Elevator

Tourist Office

RUA CHILE

Câmara
Municipal

RUA DA MISERICORDIA

PR. CASTRO ALVES

RUA PADRE VIEIRA

RUA THOME DE SOUZA

RUA JOSE GONCALVES

RUA RUY BARBOSA

RUA 24 DE MAIO

RUA SALDANHA DA GAMA

RUA VIRGILIO DAMASIO

RUA TIRA CHAPEU

CIDA DE ALTO

RUA VINTE E OITO SETEMBRO

RUA GUEDES DE BRITO

RUA DO TESOURO FRANCISCO

SALVADOR: CIDADE BAIXA
AND CIDADE ALTA

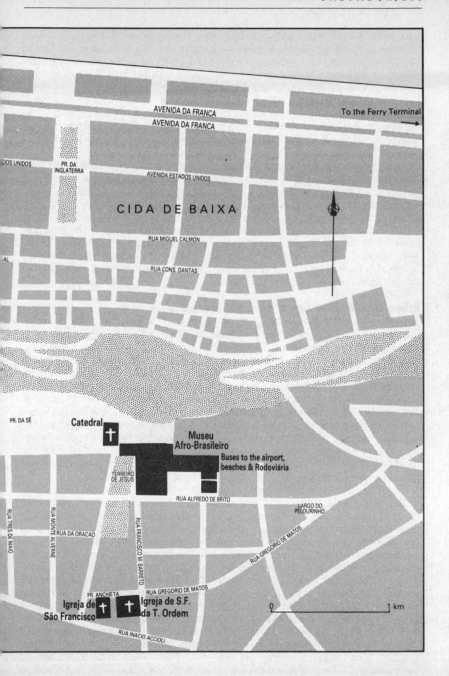

To the Ferry Terminal

AVENIDA DA FRANCA
AVENIDA DA FRANCA

DOS UNIDOS

PR. DA
INGLATERRA

AVENIDA ESTADOS UNIDOS

CIDA DE BAIXA

RUA MIGUEL CALMON

AL

RUA CONS. DANTAS

PR. DA SÉ

Catedral

Museu
Afro-Brasileiro

Buses to the airport,
beaches & Rodoviária

TERREIRO
DE JESUS

RUA ALFREDO DE BRITO

LARGO DO
PELOURINHO

RUA TRES DE MAIO

RUA MONTE ALVERNE

RUA DA ORACAO

RUA FRANCISCO M. BARRETO

RUA GREGORIO DE MATOS

PR. ANCHIETA

RUA GREGORIO DE MATOS

Igreja de
São Francisco

Igreja de S.F.
da T. Ordem

RUA INACIO ACCIOLI

0   1 km

most famous artist, was Argentinian by birth but came to Salvador thirty years ago to find inspiration and themes for his work in the city and its culture. The carved panels in the museum represent the gods and goddesses of *candomblé*, figures named for African gods but associated with Catholic saints as well. They are very beautiful, subtly carved and imaginatively decorated with scrap metal.

The **first floor** houses a rather dull Museum of the Faculty of Medicine, dominated by busts and dusty bookcases. Better is to look in the **basement**, at the **Museu Arqueológio e Etnológico** (Tues–Fri 9–11.30am & 2–5.30pm). Largely given over to fossils and artefacts from ancient burial sites, it also incorporates the only surviving part of the old Jesuit college, a section of the cellars, in the arched brickwork at the far end. A diagram at the entrance to the museum shows how enormous the college was, extending all the way from what is now the Praça da Sé to Largo do Pelourinho. It was from here that the conversion of the Brazilian Indians was organised, and one of the many Jesuit priests who passed through its gates was Antônio Vieira, whose impassioned sermons defending Indian rights against the demands of the Portuguese slavers are generally regarded as the finest early prose in the Portuguese language. After the Jesuits were expelled in 1759, the vultures moved in. Most of the college was demolished by the rich for building material for their mansions, part of the site was used to found a university, and the rest parcelled out and sold for redevelopment.

Praça Anchieta: the Churches of São Francisco

Terreiro de Jesus has more than its fair share of churches; there are two more fine sixteenth-century examples on the square itself. But outshining them both, on nearby **Praça Anchieta** (an extension of Terreiro de Jesus) are the superb, carved stone façades of the two buildings in a single, large complex dedicated to Saint Francis. Both the **Igreja de São Francisco** and the **Igreja da Terceira Ordem de São Francisco** are covered with a wild profusion of saints, virgins, angels and abstract patterns, but of the two the smaller facade of the Igreja da Terceira Ordem has the edge. Remarkably, the facade was hidden for 150 years, until in 1936 a painter knocked off a chunk of plaster by mistake and revealed the original frontage. It took nine years of careful chipping before the facade was returned to its original glory. The whole church is a strong contender for the most beautiful single building in the city, but continuing restoration work means that at present it's only open in the afternoon, from 2pm until 5.30pm.

The reliquary, or *ossuário*, here is extraordinary, the entire room redecorated in the 1940s in Art Deco style, one of the most unusual examples you're ever likely to come across. On the wall leading to the sacristy, there's an interesting early-eighteenth-century painting, which looks ordinary but isn't: look at it from one side and then the other, and see how the eyes follow you and the expression on the face changes. The sacristy leads into the centre of the complex, a small cloister, decorated with possibly the finest single piece of *azulejo* work in Brazil. Running the entire length of the cloister, this **tiled wall** tells the story of the marriage of the son of the King of Portugal to an Austrian princess; beginning with the panel to the right of the church entrance, which shows the princess being ferried ashore to the reception committee; and continuing with the procession of the happy couple in carriages through Lisbon, passing under a series of commemorative arches set up by the city guilds, whose names you can still just read – "The Royal Company of Bakers", "The Worshipful Company of Sweetmakers". The vigour and realism of the incidental detail in the street scenes is remarkable: beggars and cripples display their wounds, dogs skulk, children play in the gutter; while the panoramic view of Lisbon it displays is an important historical record of how Lisbon looked before the calamitous earthquake of 1755.

After this, the Igreja de São Francisco itself is a comedown, though upstairs there is a collection of religious art: not very high quality, but the best vantage point from which to see the interior.

Around Largo do Pelourinho

Continue down the narrow Rua Alfredo de Brito, next to the Museu Afro-Brasileiro, and you reach the beautiful, cobbled **Largo do Pelourinho**, still much as it was during the eighteenth century. Lined with solid colonial mansions, it's topped by the oriental-looking towers of the **Igreja da Nossa Senhora dos Pretos**, built by and for slaves and still with a largely black congregation. Across from here is the **Casa Jorge Amado** (Mon–Fri 9–11am & 2–5pm), a museum given over to the life and work of the hugely popular novelist, who doesn't number modesty among his virtues; you can have fun spotting his rich and famous friends in the collection of photographs.

Around the corner, in Rua Gregório de Matos, the cramped **Museu da Cidade** (Mon–Fri 8am–noon & 2–6pm, Sat 8am–noon) is jammed into a narrow four-storey tenement, with very rickety stairs made dangerous by a frayed carpet, so watch your step. The lower levels are given over to paintings and sculpture by young city artists, some startlingly good and some pretty dire, while luxuriously dressed dummies show off Carnaval costumes from years gone by. There are models of *candomblé* deities, and at the very top is a room containing the personal belongings of the greatest Bahian poet, Castro Alves, with some fascinating photographs from the turn of the century. Completing the constellation of museums around Pelourinho is the **Museu Abelardo Rodrigues** (daily 2–5.30pm) at Rua Gregório de Matos 45, a good collection of Catholic art from the sixteenth century onwards, well displayed in a restored seventeenth-century mansion.

From Largo do Pelourinho, a steep climb up Rua Luiz Vianna Filho rewards you with two more exceptional monuments of colonial architecture, the **Igreja do Carmo** (daily 8am–noon & 2–6pm) and the **Convento da Ordem Terceira do Carmo** (daily 9am–noon & 2–4pm), part of the latter now unfortunately a luxury hotel. Both are built around large and beautiful cloisters, with a fine view across the old city at the back, and have chaotic but interesting museums attached. The church museum is very eclectic, mostly religious but including collections of coins and furniture, with hundreds of unlabelled exhibits jumbled together in gloomy rooms. The highlight is a superbly expressive statue of Christ at the whipping post by Salvador's greatest colonial artist, the half-Indian slave **Franciso Manuel das Chagas**, whose powerful religious sculpture broke the formalistic bonds of the period – most of Chagas' work was completed in the 1720s. Unfortunately, Chagas died young of tuberculosis, leaving only a small body of work; this statue is appallingly displayed, jumbled together with much inferior work in a glass case in a corner of the rear gallery. In the convent museum next door is another Chagas statue, a lifesize body of Christ, this time sensibly displayed alone and, if anything, even more powerful. If you look closely at both statues, you'll find that the drops of blood are small rubies inlaid in the wood.

The rest of Cidade Alta is still largely colonial, and fascinating to wander around – although do it in daylight if you want to get off the main streets, and try to stick to where there are people around. Good streets to try are **Rua Gregório**

de Matos and the road on from the Carmo museums, **Rua Joaquim Távora**, which leads away from the heavier concentrations of tourists to the quiet Largo Cruz Pascoa and the lovely **Igreja do Pilar**; and eventually ends up at the fort of **Santo Antônio Além do Carmo**, which has a spectacular view across the bay. The only difficulty is finding a **bar** perched on the edge of the bluff with a view across the bay, to rest your legs and watch the spectacular sunsets. The best spots are the bar of the *Hotel do Pelourinho*, open to non-residents, an unnamed bar on the left just after Largo Cruz Pascoa, and the simple places on Largo Santo Antônio, in front of the fort.

The Museu da Arte Sacra

Despite the concentration of riches in Cidade Alta, you have to leave the old city to find one of the finest museums of Catholic art in Brazil: the **Museu da Arte Sacra** (Mon–Fri 1–5.30pm), off the Avenida Sete de Setembro down the steep Ladeira de Santa Teresa, near Praça Castro Alves. It's housed in a seventeenth-century convent, a magnificent building with much of its original furniture and fittings still intact, and with galleries on three floors surrounding a cloister. The chapel on the ground floor is lavishly decorated with elaborate, gilded carvings, and it leads into a maze of small galleries stuffed with a remarkably rich collection of colonial art, dating from the sixteenth century. The hundreds of statues, icons, paintings and religious artefacts are enough to occupy you for hours, the only real gap in the collection being the absence of anything by Chagas or by Aleijadinho (see the *Minas Gerais and Espírito Santo* chapter). There's still some high quality work, though: small soapstone carvings on the top floor, marvellous tiling in the sacristy behind the chapel, and a display of ornately carved religious accessories in solid gold and silver, in the *Galeria de Ouro*.

Cidade Baixa

Cidade Baixa, the part of the city at the foot of the bluff, takes in the docks, the old harbour dominated by the circular sixteenth-century **Forte do Mar**, the ferry terminals and the main city markets. For the most part it's ugly modern urban sprawl, but for once the developers can't be blamed: the area was always the ugliest part of the city because its low-lying situation deprived it of the sea breezes and cooler air of the higher ground above – William Scully found it "close, swampy, filthy and dilapidated". Since the sixteenth century, the city's inhabitants have only ventured down into the Cidade Baixa to work, choosing to live in the much pleasanter areas above and around.

All the same, it's not completely without interest. You are likely to at least pass through to get to the **ferry terminals**, the municipal one at the far end of the docks for services to towns on the other side of the bay, and the **Terminal Turístico**, in the old harbour, for excursions to Itaparica (see "Around Salvador" below). And there is one essential stop: the old covered market called **Mercado Modelo**. This is the large building set on its own by the old harbour, across the road from the foot of the Lacerda elevator. It houses a huge and very enjoyable arts and crafts market, always crowded with Bahians as well as tourists, with the best selection of *artesanato* in the city – bargaining is expected, but everything is very cheap even if you don't have the nerve. Some of the nicest souvenirs are the painted statues of *candomblé* deities – look for signs saying *artigos religiosos* – and if nothing here takes your fancy, there is also a shop on Praça de Sé. Even if you don't buy anything the building is a joy, a spacious nineteenth-century cathedral to commerce. There is always something going on in and around the market; displays of *capoeira* are common, and there is a good **information post** to the left of the front entrance. Upstairs you will find a couple of good **restaurants**, *Maria de São Pedro* and *Camafeu de Oxóssi*, looking out across the harbour; see under "Restaurants", below.

The Igreja do Bonfim . . . and the popular festivals

If the Museu da Arte Sacra is the finest expression of high Catholic devotion, then the Igreja do Bonfim, as everyone calls the **Igreja do Nosso Senhor do Bonfim**, in the western suburbs, is the centre of popular worship, focal point of colourful religious festivals which attract thousands of devotees from all over Brazil. To get there, take the *Bonfim* bus from the Estação da Lapa, or pick it up from the bottom of the Lacerda elevator.

The church is not, by any means, the oldest or most beautiful in the city – completed in 1745 with a plain, white exterior and simple interior – but it's easily the most interesting. The force of popular devotion is obvious from the moment you leave the bus. The large square in front of the church is lined with stalls catering for the hundreds of pilgrims who arrive every day, and you'll be besieged by small children selling *fitas*, ribbons in white and blue, the church colours, to tie around your wrist for luck and to hang in the church when you make your requests; it's ungracious to enter the church without a few. It's always at least half-full of people worshipping, often with almost hypnotic fervour: middle-class matrons and uniformed military officers rub shoulders with peasants from the *sertão* and women from the *favelas*.

For a clearer idea of what this place means to the people of Bahia, go to the right of the nave where a wide corridor leads to the **Museu dos Ex-Votos do Senhor do Bonfim** (Tues–Sat 8am–noon & 2.30–4pm, Sun 8am–noon). *Ex votos* are offerings from people to remind saints – or Jesus himself in this case – of who they are and what they want Him to do for them; and equally, people leave *ex votos* as a gesture of thanks and a commemoration of His power, something called *pagando a promessa*, paying the promise. (So if you ever hear your taxi driver exclaim "Salve-me Nosso Senhor do Bonfim" you know you're in deep trouble, although you can also rest assured that Nosso Senhor do Bonfim is widely acknowledged to be the most powerful divine help you can enlist.) An incredibly crowded antechamber gives you an idea of what to expect: lined to the roof with thousands of small photographs of supplicants, with notes pinned to the wall requesting intervention or giving thanks for benefits received; some of the photos date from the turn of the century. Every spare inch is covered with a forest of ribbons, one for each request, some almost rotted away with age, and many of the written pleas are heart-rending: for the life of a dying child, for news from a husband who emigrated south, for the safe return of sailors and fishermen, for success in an exam, for money to pay for a college education, for a favourite football team to win a championship – in short, a snapshot of popular worries and hopes. Hanging from the roof are dozens of body parts – limbs, heads, even organs like hearts and lungs – made of wood or plastic for anxious patients asking for protection before an operation, silver for relieved patients giving thanks after successful surgery. Some people blessed by a particularly spectacular escape pay tribute by leaving a pictorial record of the miracle: photos of smashed cars which the driver walked away from, or crude but vivid paintings of fires, sinkings and electrocutions.

Upstairs in the museum proper is the oldest material and recent offerings judged worthy of special display. It's not only the poor who come asking for help: there are several university classbooks deposited here, and military insignia commemorating promotion up to the rank of general. The more valuable *ex votos* are displayed here in ranks of cases, classified according to part of the body: silver heads and limbs you might expect, even silver hearts, lungs, ears, eyes and noses, but the serried ranks of silver kidneys, spleens, livers and intestines are novel. There are football shirts – the city's two big teams always make a visit at the start of the season – models of the church, and dozens of paintings, especially of fires and shipwrecks. Other paintings are vivid to the point of gruesomeness: people fall from horses, lie sweating with cholera, or display bullet wounds in the shoulder or limbs.

The two main **popular festivals** of the year, besides Carnaval, take place either in or near the Igreja do Bonfim. On New Year's Day is the **Procissão no Mar**, the "Sea Procession", when the statues of the seafarers' protectors, *Nosso Senhor dos Navegantes* and *Nossa Senhora da Conceição*, are carried in a decorated nineteenth-century boat across the bay from the old harbour to the church of Boa Viagem, on the shore down from Bonfim. The boat leaves at around 9am from Praça Cairú, next to the Mercado Modelo in Cidade Baixa, and hundreds of schooners and fishing boats wait to join the procession as the saints' boat passes: you can buy a place on the phalanx of boats that leaves with the saints, but the crowds are thick and if you want to go by sea you should get there early. On the shores of Boa Viagem, thousands wait to greet the holy images, there's a packed Mass in the church, and then *Nossa Senhora da Conçeicão* is taken back by land in another procession to her church near the foot of the Lacerda elevator. The celebrations around both churches go on long into the night, with thousands drinking and dancing the night away. The spectacle, with the bay as an enormous backdrop, is impressive enough: participating in it is exhilarating.

Soon afterwards, on the second Thursday of January, comes the **Lavagem do Bonfim**, second only to Carnaval in scale; it means "the washing of Bonfim". Hundreds of *baianas*, women in the traditional all-white costume of turban, lace blouse and billowing long skirts, gather in front of the Igreja de Nossa Senhora da Conceição, and a procession follows them the 12km along the seafront to the Igreja do Bonfim, with tens of thousands more lining the route: the pace is slow, and there is no shortage of beer and music while you wait. At the church, everyone sets to scrubbing the square spotless, cleaning the church and decorating the exterior with flowers and strings of coloured lights, and that evening, and every evening until Sunday, raucous celebrations go on into the small hours, the square crowded with people. If you have the stamina, the focus switches on Monday to Ribeira, the headland beyond Bonfim, for a completely secular preview of Carnaval. Here you can freshen up after dancing in the hot sun by swimming at the excellent beaches.

Eating

Eating out is one of the major pleasures Salvador has to offer, and the local cuisine (*comida baiana*) is deservedly famous. Restaurants away from the beaches look a lot more expensive than they actually are, and very high quality meals can be had for well under $10; you should treat yourself to at least one slap-up feed before leaving the city.

COMIDA BAIANA: DISHES AND INGREDIENTS

The secret of Bahian cooking is twofold: a rich seafood base, and the abundance of traditional West African **ingredients** like palm oil, nuts, coconut and ferociously strong peppers. Many ingredients and **dishes** have African names: most famous of all is *vatapá*, a bright yellow porridge of palm oil, coconut, shrimp and garlic, which looks vaguely unappetising but is delicious. Other dishes to look out for are *moqueca*, seafood cooked in the inevitable palm-oil based sauce; *carurú*, with many of the same ingredients as *vatapá* but with the vital addition of loads of okra; and *acarajé*, available on many street corners from the *baianas*, women in traditional white dress. Bahian cuisine also has good **desserts**, less stickily sweet than elsewhere: *quindim* is a delicious small cake of coconut flavoured with vanilla, which often comes with a prune in the middle.

Some of the best food is also the cheapest, and even gourmets could do a lot worse than start with the *baianas* on street corners, thick on the ground near bus stops and office buildings. Be careful of the *pimenta*, the very hot pepper sauce, which newcomers should treat with respect, taking only a few drops. The *baianas* also serve *quindim*, *vatapá*, slabs of maize pudding wrapped in banana leaves, fried bananas dusted with icing sugar, and fried sticks of sweet batter covered with sugar and cinnamon; all absolutely wonderful.

Restaurants

As a rule, the best areas for a sit-down meal are around the **Praça da Sé** and **Cidade Baixa**: the only problem is that restaurants here tend to open only for lunch or close early in the evening. Otherwise, there's no shortage of good restaurants in the seafront districts of Barra, Ondina and Rio Vermelho, but they are generally more expensive.

The best place for **beginners** is undoubtedly the *Restaurante do SENAC*, a municipal restaurant school in a finely restored colonial mansion on Largo do Pelourinho, opposite the Casa Jorge Amado. It looks very expensive from the outside, but it isn't: you pay a set charge – around $5 for lunch, $7 for dinner – and take as much as you want from a quality buffet of around fifty dishes, all helpfully labelled so that you know what you're eating. Off-season it can be a strange place to eat, as the large numbers of waiters stand lining the walls of the enormous dining rooms, outnumbering customers five or ten to one. If you go for dinner, try to finish before 10pm, when there's a rather touristy folklore show.

Once you've identified and sampled the dishes at *SENAC*, you can tackle the menus at other restaurants with more confidence. Best of all – with the most delicious *moqueca* I have ever come across – is the *Mini Cacique* (open lunchtime only Mon–Fri), Rua Rui Barbosa 29, the first street on the left between Praça Castro Alves and Praça da Sé. Small, inconspicuous, and constantly crowded, it's worth waiting for a table as the food is cheap for the quality. There are two more good Bahian restaurants next to each other, on the first floor of the **Mercado Modelo** in Cidade Baixa, the *Maria de São Pedro* and the *Camafeu de Oxóssi*, little to choose between them and both with great views across the bay if you can get a table on the terrace. Further along the coast, on the **seafront** Avenida do Contorno that heads left from the harbour, is the *Solar do Unhão*, which has a marvellous setting in the old slave quarters of a seventeenth-century mansion but doles out overpriced and mediocre food; go and return by taxi, as the area is dangerous even by day. The *Hotel do Pelourinho* (See "Finding a place to stay") has a good restaurant open to non-residents. Finally, another excellent Bahian restaurant, the *Bahia Antiga* (closed Sun) at Rua Moacir Leão 4 in Barris, near Cidade Alta, is a good option if you want to eat away from the beach areas in the evenings; it's tucked away but isn't far from the centre, so a taxi is the best option to get there.

Cheaper food in Cidade Alta is available from a host of eating houses and snack bars around Praça da Sé catering for office workers. The *Café Cuba* on the square itself does excellent ice cream and chilled fruit water-ices.

The other main area for eating out is at **the beaches** to the north. Especially at Barra and Rio Vermelho, the seafront promenade is lined with bars, cafés and restaurants, and the best option is to take a bus and hop off wherever you fancy. The non-Brazilian cuisines tend to be concentrated in **Barra**, where Salvador's upper middle class lives: there are two good Chinese restaurants on Rua Marquês de Leão, *Liu Fu* at no. 173 and *Yan Ping* at no. 253; and an Arabic one, the *Matbah*, on Rua Barão de Sergy 14 – getting a taxi from the Barra seafront is the easiest way to get there, as the road is a little obscure. Further down, the area around the *Teatro Maria Bethânia* in **Rio Vermelho** is good for bar food; the square, a popular meeting place for the young, has lots of cafés that are very lively at night. In **Pituba**, two good seafront restaurants specialise in Bahian food – the best, *Xeiro Verde*, at Avenida Otávio Mangabeira 929, is unfortunately open only for lunch. *Iemanjá*, just further up, is a better bet than the large, overpriced restaurants at the far end of Pituba, *Sabor da Terra* and *Roda Viva*. These last two, though, do have good **folklore shows** (despite the tacky way they are advertised) and are worth visiting on that account alone.

Nightlife and other action

Nightlife in Salvador is concentrated in the beach districts, although the **centre** – Terreiro de Jesus, Largo do Pelourinho and the area around Campo Grande – can be lively during the weekends as well. There's a good café, the *Cantina da Lua*, on the corner of Terreiro de Jesus and Rua Alfredo Brito, which often has live music on weekend nights; while the *Banzo Bar*, on Largo do Pelourinho, has cheap food and is popular with gringos. There is also a lively **gay scene** in the centre, with two good nightspots: the *Tropical Night Club*, on Rua Pau da Bandeira, one of the steep streets downhill from the Rua do Chile (go and return by taxi, it's not an area of town you should walk around at night); and the intriguingly named *Holmes 24th*, on Rua Gamboa de Cima, opposite the Rua Banco dos Ingleses, near Campo Grande (also safer by taxi).

The **beach districts**, though, are where the best bars, cafés and *dancetarias* are, lining the sea promenade from Barra northwards: again, take a bus and see what you like the look of. For **dancing** into the small hours, Amaralina and Pituba are probably the liveliest areas to head for, and Friday and Saturday nights are best. There are two rather upmarket places close to each other on Avenida Amarelina, *Mon Amour* at no. 863 and *Rive Gauche* at no. 829, and the *Carinhoso* on Avenida Otávio Mangabeira also has a good reputation. Bars, too, often have **live music** and at weekends the local papers have listings; try the Sunday edition of *A Tarde*. As far as specific places go, *Travessia* at Avenida Otávio Mangabeira 168 in Pituba (open 24hr Fri–Sun only) gets crowded and lively; and *Diolino*, at Largo da Mariquita in Rio Vermelho, has a remarkable selection of *batidas*, rum cocktails mixed with fruit juice and much more potent than they taste. There's often good music, too, at *Canteiros*, Rua Minas Gerais in Pituba, starting after 9pm on Friday and Saturday.

Music and Carnaval

Musically, Salvador marches to a different beat from the rest of Brazil. Instead of being connected to a single style, as Rio is to *samba* and Recife is to *frevo*, Salvador has spawned several and in recent years it has overtaken Rio to become the most creative centre of Brazilian music. A good example of this was the way the city absorbed and transformed reggae during the 1980s, so that by the end of the decade a new Bahian sound, exemplified by groups like *Reflexús*, dominated Carnaval processions throughout Brazil.

Some of the best music in the city comes from organised **cultural groups**, who work in the communities that spawned them, have clubhouses and a *bloco* or two for Carnaval. They are overwhelmingly black and a lot of their music is political. Two of the best are the *Grupo Cultural Olodum*, who have a house on Largo do Pelourinho, and *Ara Ketú*, who have the first floor of a house on Praça da Sé. At night, especially in the weeks before Carnaval, their *blocos* have public rehearsals around the clubhouses, and the music is superb. For the rest of the year, the clubhouses are used as bars and meeting places, often with music at weekends: black gringos can walk in and be sure of a warm welcome, while it would be sensitive for white gringos not to go unless invited or accompanied.

Having steadfastly resisted commercialisation, **Carnaval in Salvador** has remained a street event of mass participation: rather than having people crammed into grandstands, separate from the parading *blocos* below, the throbbing heart of Carnaval in Salvador is Cidade Alta, especially the area around Praça Castro Alves, which turns into a seething mass of people that once joined is almost impossible to get out of – not for the claustrophobic, but hugely enjoyable. You're more or less stuck with whatever you get swept up behind, which might be a sound system, a *trio elétrico* on a specially built lorry with banks of speakers on all sides, or an *afoxé*, Salvador's Africanised version of a *bloco*, hundreds strong.

From December onwards Carnaval groups hold public rehearsals and dances all over the city. Good spots are the Igreja da Nossa Senhora da Conceição, near the foot of the Lacerda elevator, Terreiro de Jesus, Largo do Pelourinho, and the area around the fort of Santo Antônio Além do Carmo. One of the oldest and best loved of the *afoxés* is *Filhos de Gandhi*, the "Sons of Gandhi", founded in the 1940s, who have a clubhouse in Rua Gregório de Matos, near Largo do Pelourinho, easily recognised by the large papier-mâché white elephant in the hall. Their rehearsals attract the whole Pelourinho area to join in. The other focal point of Carnaval is the northern beaches, especially around the hotels in Rio Vermelho and Ondina, but here it's more touristy and lacks the energy of the centre.

Information about Carnaval is published in special supplements in the local papers on Thursday and Saturday, and *Bahiatursa* offices also have schedules, route maps, and sell tickets for the Campo Grande grandstands. One point worth bearing in mind is that all-black *blocos* may be black culture groups who won't appreciate being joined by non-black Brazilians, let alone gringos, so look to see who's dancing before leaping in amongst them.

Local culture: *capoeira* and *candomblé*

Music and food are areas where the African influence in Salvador is very clear, but less well-known to visitors are **capoeira**, which began among slaves as a martial art and evolved into a graceful semi-balletic art form somewhere between fighting and dancing; and **candomblé**, the Afro-Brazilian religious cult that permeates the city.

Capoeira

Capoeira is not difficult to find in Salvador. It's usually accompanied by the characteristic rhythmic twang of the *berimbau*, and takes the form of a pair of dancers/fighters leaping and whirling in stylised "combat" – which, with younger *capoeiristas*, occasionally slips into a genuine fight when blows land by accident and the participants lose their temper. There are regular displays, largely for the benefit of tourists but interesting nevertheless, on Terreiro de Jesus and near the entrances to the Mercado Modelo in Cidade Baixa, where contributions from onlookers are expected. But the best *capoeira* is in the **academias de capoeira**, organised schools which have classes that anyone can watch free of charge. All ages take part, many of the children astonishingly nimble: although most *capoeiristas* are male, some girls and women take it up as well. The first and most famous *academia* is still the best, the *Associação de Capoeira Mestre Bimba*, named after the man who popularised *capoeira* in the city from the 1920s: it's on the first floor of Rua Francisco Muniz Barreto 1, Terreiro de Jesus, and has classes from 9am to 11am and 4pm to 7pm, Monday to Saturday (closed Wed). Other schools are at the other end of Cidade Alta, at the Forte de Santo Antônio Além do Carmo: the *Grupo de Capoeira Pelourinho*, with classes on Tuesday, Thursday and Saturday from 7pm to 10.30pm; and the *Centro Esportivo de Capoeira Angola*, open all day to 10.30pm on weekdays, though you have to turn up to find out when the next class is – late afternoon is a good time, as afternoon and evening sessions are generally better attended.

Candomblé

Candomblé is a little more difficult to track down. Many travel agencies offer tours of the city that include a visit to a *terreiro*, or cult house, but no self-respecting *terreiro* would allow itself to be used in this way – those which do are to be avoided. The best alternative is to go to the main *Bahiatursa* office, in the Palácio do Rio Branco, which has a list of less commercialised *terreiros*, all fairly far out in the suburbs and best got to by taxi. Make sure that the *terreiro* is open first: they only have ceremonies on certain days sacred to one of the pantheon of gods and goddesses, and you just have to hope you strike lucky – though fortunately there's no shortage of deities.

Each *terreiro* is headed by a *mãe do santo* (woman) or *pai do santo* (man), who directs the operations of dozens of novices and initiates. The usual object is to persuade the spirits to descend into the bodies of worshippers, which is done by sacrifices (animals are killed outside public view and usually during the day), offerings of food and drink, and above all by drumming, dancing, and the invocations of the *mãe* or *pai do santo*. There's a central dance area, which may be decorated, where devotees dance for hours to induce the trance that allows the spirits to enter them. A possession can be quite frightening: sometimes people whoop and shudder, their eyes roll up, and they whirl around the floor, bouncing off the walls while other cult members try to make sure they come to no harm. The *mãe* or *pai do santo* then calms them, blows tobacco smoke over them, identifies the spirit, gives them the insignia of the deity – a pipe or a candle, for example – and lets them dance on. Each deity has its own songs, animals, colours, qualities, powers and holy day; and there are different types of *candomblé*, as well as other related Afro-Brazilian religions like *umbanda* and *macumba*.

If you go to a *terreiro*, there are certain **rules** you must observe. A *terreiro* should be respected and treated for the church it is. Clothes should be smart and modest: long trousers and a clean shirt for men, non-revealing blouse and trousers or long skirt for women. The dancing area is sacred space and no matter how infectious you find the rhythms you should do no more than stand or sit around its edges. And *don't* take photographs without asking permission from the *mãe* or *pai do santo* first, or you will give offence. You may find people coming round offering drinks from jars, or items of food: it's impolite to refuse, but watch what everyone else does first – sometimes food is not for eating but for throwing over dancers, and the story of the gringos who ate their popcorn is guaranteed to bring a smile to any Brazilian face.

The area code for Salvador is ☎071

Listings

Airlines *Transbrasil*, Rua Carlos Gomes 616, Centro (☎241-1044) and Rua Portugal 3, Cidade Baixa (☎242-3344); *Varig/Cruzeiro*, Rua Carlos Gomes 6, Centro (☎243-1244) and c/o *Hotel da Bahia*, Campo Grande (☎237-3690); *VASP*, Rua do Chile 27, Cidade Alta (☎243-7277/7044) and Rua Almirante Marquês de Leão 455, Barra (☎243-7044). Weekly flights to Miami, Paris and Rome, as well as to all points on the domestic network.

Airport Taxis take around 45min from Cidade Alta and it's best to agree a flat-rate rather than go by the meter; should be around $10. The quickest bus is the *frescão* marked *Aeroporto*, from the stop between Praça da Sé and Terreiro de Jesus; about an hour's journey, more if the traffic's heavy.

Banks and Exchange For turismo rates, the *Banco do Brasil* has branches at the airport; at Avenida Sete de Setembro 733; and at Avenida Estados Unidos 561 in Cidade Baixa. Most of the other international banks with *câmbio* departments are also in Cidade Baixa, like *Lloyds* at Rua Miguel Calmon 22, near the Mercado Modelo. You'll get lower, but still reasonable, rates for dollars cash and travellers' cheques at the smarter beach hotels in Ondina and Pituba. On no account change on the street, especially around the Lacerda elevator: your wad will be snatched as soon as you get it out.

Consulates *France*, Travessa Francisco Gonçalves 1, Room 805, Cidade Baixa (Mon, Wed & Fri 9am–noon & 1–5pm, Tues & Thurs 9–11am & 1–5pm; ☎241-0168); *UK*, Avenida Estados Unidos 4, Room 1109, Cidade Baixa (Mon–Fri 8–11.30am & 1.30–5pm; ☎241-3222); *USA*, Avenida Antônio Carlos Magalhães, Ed. Cidadella Center, Room 410 (Mon–Fri 8.30–11.30am; ☎244-9166); *West Germany*, Rua Lucaia 281, Ed. WM, 2nd floor, Rio Vermelho (Mon–Fri 9am–noon; ☎247-7106).

Ferry Services Ferries from Terminal Marítimo in Cidade Baixa (any bus from foot of Lacerda elevator) leave every 30min to Itaparica island; a half-hour ride costing around twenty cents. Last boat back from Itaparica is at around 5.30pm; there are no night services.

Football Salvador has a couple of good teams. The most popular, *Bahia*, have a tradition of playing open, attacking football in the best Brazilian tradition. The biggest matches take place on Sunday afternoons in the Estádio Octávio Mangabeira, close to the centre; take the bus marked *Nazaré* from Campo Grande, or it's a short taxi ride. Seats (*arquibancada* or *cadeira*) start at $1.50, standing terraces are called *geral* or *comercial*.

Hospital English spoken at the private clinic at Rua Barão de Loretto 21, Graça *bairro*; where a consultation will set you back around $20.

Post Office Central post offices are found in the Mercado Modelo, Cidade Baixa, and at Rua Rui Barbosa 19–21, Cidade Alta, as well as at the airport and *Rodoviária*.

Shopping Main place for *artesanato* is the Mercado Modelo in Cidade Baixa, interesting enough to wander around but rather more commercialised and expensive than its equivalents in other Northeastern cities. Good, cheap leatherwork from the street stalls of Barroquinha, the steep street leading downhill just before Praça Castro Alves; and clothes and shoes in the commercial area further down, too.

Telephones Make international phone calls from offices in the airport and the Mercado Modelo; interstate calls from the *Rodoviária*, the Iguatemi shopping centre, and at Avenida Sete de Setembro 533, in Barra.

Theatres Big names in Brazilian music play the *Teatro Castro Alves* on Campo Grande, and the *Teatro Maria Bethânia*, on the coastal road in Rio Vermelho. The *SENAC* building on Largo do Pelourinho has an outdoor arena and basement theatre, used for plays, concerts and displays. Also scan posters, local papers (under *Lazer*), or ask at the tourist office.

Around Salvador: the north coast and Itaparica

Salvador looks onto a bay, the **Bahia de Todos Santos**, ringed with beaches and dotted with tropical **islands**. To the **north** of the city a string of fishing villages lie along a beautiful coastline – in short, no lack of places to explore.

North to Arembepe

The beaches of the **northern coast** are excellent and the villages in between small and friendly, all connected by buses which run along the coastal road. Hitching is fairly easy, too; traffic is light during the week, but what there is will often stop. **Buses** run from Salvador's *Rodoviária* to **AREMBEPE**, 50km away, a former hippy hangout now gone up in the world, though still peaceful and very pretty. The journey there takes you through some fine beaches and villages, and you can get off wherever takes your fancy. **Accommodation** is easy everywhere along this route, from chic *pousadas* to simple *pensões*, as you're heading along a well-beaten tourist track. Don't be put off, though – it's a beautiful coastline and the beaches are long enough to swallow the crowds.

The bay: Itaparica island

Itaparica is always visible from Salvador, looking as if it forms the other side of the bay, but in reality a narrow island, 35-km-long, that acts as a natural breakwater for the bay. After the local Indians were driven out, it was taken over by the Jesuits in 1560, making it one of the earliest places to be settled by the Portuguese. Its main town, also called **ITAPARICA**, was briefly the capital of Bahia before the Portuguese were expelled from Salvador, though little evidence remains here of these times, apart from a couple of small seventeenth-century chapels. The lovely island is now very much seen as an appendage of the city, whose inhabitants flock to its beaches at weekends, building villas by the score as they go. It's quiet enough during the week, though, and big enough to find calmer spots even at the busiest times. Apart from the beaches, Itaparica is famous for its fruit trees, especially its mangoes, which are prized throughout Bahia.

Most **ferries** leave you at the Bom Despacho terminal in Itaparica town, although some also go to the smaller anchorage at **MAR GRANDE**, a couple of kilometres away. For **getting around** once you're there, use the Kombis and buses which ply the coastline, or hire **bicycles** ($8 a day, the places easily spotted by the bikes piled up on the pavement). If you want to stay on the island, there are some reasonable **hotels**, but most are on the expensive side – rooms starting at $10 – thanks to Itaparica's popularity as a resort for Salvador's middle classes. Cheaper ones are often full from December to Carnaval; if you're on a budget, try the **campsite** and **youth hostel** in Itaparica town.

To see anything of the **other islands** scattered across the bay, all 31 of them and most either uninhabited or home to a few simple fishing villages, travel agents in Salvador offer day-long cruises in private schooners for about $10 a head: the kiosks in the the city's Terminal Turístico are the easiest places to buy tickets. It's less busy during the week, but crowded schooners have their advantages. If you manage to get on one full of Brazilian trippers you're likely to have a very lively time indeed, and drinks are often included in the price.

The Recôncavo

The **Recôncavo** proper, the early Portuguese plantation zone named after the concave shape of the bay, arcs out from Salvador along 150km of coastline, before petering out in the mangrove swamps around the town of Valença. It's one of the most lush tropical coastlines in Brazil, with palm-covered hills breaking up the green and fertile coastal plains. And it's still one of the most important agricultural areas in Bahia, supplying the state with much of its fruit and spices. Only the sugar plantations around Recife could match the wealth of the Recôncavo, but, unlike Pernambuco, the Recôncavo survived the decline of the sugar trade by diversifying into tobacco and spices – especially peppers and cloves. It was the agricultural wealth of the Recôncavo which paid for most of the fine buildings of Salvador and. until the cocoa boom in southern Bahia in the 1920s, Cachoeira was by some way the second city of the state. The beauty of the area, and the richness of its colonial heritage, makes it one of the more rewarding parts of the Northeast to explore.

Access is good as there's a main highway, the BR-324, which approximately follows the curve of the bay, with good local roads branching off to the towns in the heart of the Recôncavo. Thirty kilometres out of Salvador, a turn-off leads to Candéias, continuing on to Santo Amaro and the twin towns of Cachoeira and São Félix. Regular **buses** go to all these places from the *Rodoviária* in Salvador.

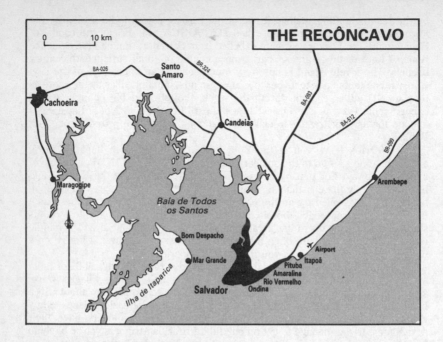

Candéias and Santo Amaro

CANDÉIAS is nowhere special, a modern market town 30km from Salvador, but 7km outside there's a good introduction to the history of the area in the **Museu do Recôncavo** (Tues–Fri 9am–noon & 2–5pm), situated in a restored plantation called the *Engenho da Freguesia*. It's much like the plantation museums in Pernambuco and elsewhere, with pictures and artefacts from three centuries illustrating the economic and social dimensions of plantation life. But here, the owners' mansion and the slave quarters have been impressively restored, juxtaposing the horrors of slave life – there's a fearsome array of manacles, whips and iron collars – with the elegant period furniture and fittings of the mansion. The only problem is that no bus service passes the museum: if you don't go by car you have to take a taxi from Candéias, around $10, or hitch.

SANTO AMARO, 73km from Salvador, is a lovely colonial town straddling the banks of a small river. It was the birthplace and is still the home of **Caetano Veloso**, one of Bahia's most famous singers and poets, who sings Santo Amaro's praises on many of his records. There's no tourist office, but you can get a free pamphlet with a street map from *Bahiatursa* offices in Salvador, and the best thing to do is simply to wander around the quiet streets and squares, absorbing the atmosphere. There are several buildings worth seeing, especially the tranquil **Convento dos Humildes** in Rua Arlindo Costa. Santo Amaro has seen better days, as several overgrown, ruined mansions, which once belonged to the sugar and tobacco barons, attest. The most atmospheric is the **Solar Araújo Pinto**, at Rua Imperador 1, part of which is being restored so that you can take a look inside.

If you feel like **staying**, there are several *pensões* in the centre of town, basic but adequate.

Cachoeira and environs

The twin towns of Cachoeira and São Félix are only a few kilometres away, separated by the Paraguaçú river. The river is spanned by an iron box-girder bridge built by British engineers in 1885 and opened by the Emperor Dom Pedro himself. **CACHOEIRA** is easily the more impressive of the two, one of the most beautiful colonial towns of the Northeast, with a profusion of fine old buildings as evidence that, in the eighteenth century, this was an important city. The rich sugar plantations of the Paraguaçú valley supported a trading centre that rivalled Salvador in size and wealth until the beginning of the last century. And it was the site of a short but vicious war in 1822 to expel the Portuguese from Bahia, when a docked Portuguese warship was stormed by the inhabitants, the city becoming the first in Brazil to declare allegiance to Dom Pedro I. The Portuguese general, Madeira de Melo, bombarded the town in retaliation, but this only provoked the countryside into general revolt, and troops from Cachoeira led a victorious assault on Salvador. After that began the long decline that turned it into the beautifully preserved small town it is today.

Cachoeira: the sights

One block up past the market, along the same street as the bus station, is the fine Praça Doutor Milton, with its Baroque public fountain. The square is dominated by the early-eighteenth-century bulk of the **Santa Casa da Misericordia**, which has a beautiful small garden. Down from the square, towards the river, turn left along Rua Treze de Maio and, a few yards on the left, is a cobbled street which leads to the **Capela da Nossa Senhora da Ajuda**, the city's oldest church. Begun in 1595 and completed eleven years later, it just about qualifies as sixteenth-century, which makes it a rarity. Sadly, the simple but well proportioned interior is often closed to visitors for fear of thieves, but if you bang on the door there should be someone around to let you in.

A few yards further along Rua Treze de Maio, again on the left, is Rua Ana Neri, with its small **Museu Hansen Bahia**, dedicated to the work of two Danish engravers who settled in the town. Further up, the impressive **Igreja Matriz de Nossa Senhora do Rosário** has two huge (five-metre-high) *azulejo* panels dating from the 1750s, while there's a good collection of religious art in the **Museu das Alfaias** (Tues–Fri 9am–noon & 2–4pm, Sat 9am–noon). **Praça da Aclamação**, to the right, is the finest square in the town, lined with civil buildings from the golden age of Cachoeira in the early eighteenth century. They include the Prefeitura Municipal, the town hall, and the old city chambers which now house a collection of colonial furniture and paintings. The other side of the square is dominated by the huge bulk of the **Conjunto do Carmo**, made up of two churches, a monastery and chapter house, all built in the eighteenth century. Part of this now lies in ruins, and the rest has been turned into a luxury hotel.

There's a lively local tradition of **woodcarving** in town and several sculptors have studios open to the public: get the tourist office (see below) to show you the two most famous, the studios of Louco and Doidão, on the map. Or check out the *artesanato* in the **Mercado Municipal**, near the bus station.

On the stretch of waterfront nearest the old centre is Praça Teixeira de Freitas, where for $1 a head canoeists take you out to the Ilha do Farol in the river, and over to SÃO FÉLIX. The main reason for going is the great view back across the river, with the colonial façades reflected in the water.

Candomblé in Cachoeira

The other thing Cachoeira is known for is **candomblé**, with some *terreiros* still conducting rituals in African dialects that nobody now speaks, recognisable as variants of West African and Angolan languages. One of the best known *candomblé* events is Cachoeira's fiesta of **Nossa Senhora da Boa Morte**, but its date varies (it always begins on the first Friday before August 15) so ask *Bahiatursa* in Salvador if in doubt. It's staged by a sisterhood, the *Irmandade da Boa Morte*, founded by freed women slaves in the mid-nineteenth century, partly as a religious group and partly to work for the emancipation of slaves, by acting as an early co-operative bank to buy people their liberty. All the local *candomblé* groups turn out with drummers and singers, and although the name of the fiesta is Catholic, it's a celebration of *candomblé*, with centre stage held by the dignified matriarchs of the sisterhood. The other great day in the *candomblé* year is the **festa de Santa Barbara**, on December 4 in São Félix, dedicated not to the saint but to the goddess Iansã. There are several other fiestas worth catching, like the **São João** celebrations, from June 22 to 24; while five saints' days are crammed into the last three months of the year; check with *Bahiatursa* for exact dates.

Some practicalities

The **Rodoviária** is near the centre, two blocks up from the river, and very close to all the main sights. There's a **tourist information post** in the Museu Hansen Bahia, on Rua Ana Neri (see above). If you want to **stay** in Cachoeira, there are several *pensões* near the bus station, as well as a few good medium-range **hotels**; try the *Hotel Colombo*, on the waterfront at Praça Teixeira de Freitas 19, the *Hotel Santo Antônio*, Praça Manuel 1, or the *Pousada do Guerreiro*, Rua Treze de Maio 14. There's no shortage of **restaurants** in the centre either. The local speciality is *maniçoba*, a stew of manioc leaves, okra and various kinds of dried and salted meat – which looks vile but tastes delicious, even when bought from the street vendors.

Valença and around

After Cachoeira, the coast becomes swampy and by the time you get to **VALENÇA**, five hours by bus from Salvador, you're in mangrove country. Fortunately, though, instead of alligators, the swamps are dominated by shellfish of all kinds, most of them edible. Valença lies on the banks of the river Una, about 10km from the sea, at the point where the river widens into a delta made up of dozens of small islands, most of which support at least a couple of fishing villages. At one time it was an industrial centre – the first cotton factory in Brazil was built here – but has long since reverted to fishing and boatbuilding. It's increasingly popular for trippers from Salvador, but is not (yet) over-commercialised.

The Town

Valença's **Rodoviária** is right in the centre of town: cross the bridge opposite and you're in the heart of things. There are a couple of colonial churches – the most interesting is the Igreja de Nossa Senhora do Amparo near the market – but

Valença is a place for walks, boat trips and lazing on beaches rather than sightseeing. By far the most interesting thing the town has to offer is the **boatyards**, the *estaleiros*, along the waterfront to the left of the bridge as you cross it from the bus station. They build a whole series of wooden boats here, largely by hand, ranging from small fishing smacks to large schooners, and local boatbuilders are renowned throughout the Northeast for their skill. You can easily appreciate their work: boats in various stages of completion, some just a ribbed keel, others ready to be painted, lie under palm or tile shelters with no sides. Provided you don't get in the way – try going around midday, when work stops for a couple of hours – and ask permission, people are pleased to let you take a closer look and often take pride in showing off their work. The plain wooden schooner hulls, with hand-fitted overlapping planks, have beautiful curves that even landlubbers can admire.

Around Valença by boat and on foot: Tinharé island

The town is a good base from which to explore the countryside around, a project best undertaken by **boat**. From the jetty to the left of the bridge, a boat leaves daily at 8am for an all-day cruise that's excellent value at $10, especially as it has an onboard bar selling cold beer, indispensable for an outing in hot weather. The exact itinerary is decided by popular demand, but will always centre on the island of **TINHARÉ** and its famous beaches at **Morro de São Paulo**. These provided an anchorage for the British admiral Lord Cochrane in 1822: as head of the Brazilian navy, he was instrumental in driving the Portuguese out of Brazil, as he had driven the Spanish a few years before from Peru and Chile, working together with Simón Bolívar. The **beaches** are superb, and the views from the hill, crowned with a simple nineteenth-century church, are breathtaking.

On the opposite side of the small island, in a hamlet called **PRAINHA**, is the **Casa da Sogra**, which looks like a bar but is the home of a local poet and sculptor, who has papered the walls with his poems and with decorative painted maps of the region and the road to Rio. There are no hotels here, but if you want to stay for a few days of idyllic tranquillity, the locals – mainly fishing families – rent out hammock space: there is little except grilled fish and shellfish to eat, but it's a lifestyle you could easily get used to. At least one boat calls every day if you want to get back to Valença.

The best beaches elsewhere are at **GUAIBIM**, 15km north of Valença, and it seems that half the population of the town pile onto buses heading this way at weekends: the last one back is at 5pm, but hitching is easy in daylight.

Otherwise, the best **walks**, apart from on Tinharé, are just before Valença, where there's a dirt road to the left as you arrive. Three kilometres down you'll find a series of gentle rapids on the river Una, the **Cachoeira de Candengo**, where you can cool off by plunging into the natural pools and lying on the rocks with the water flowing around you. There are paths along the river bank, too, which allow you to explore further.

Valença practicalities

Accommodation is easy to find. There are several hotels and *pensões*: the *Hotel Tourist*, Rua Marechal Floriano 167, the *Guaibim* on Praça da Independência, and the *Universal*, on Rua Marquês do Herval, are all friendly and good value. If you're on a tighter budget, the rented hammock space on Tinharé island costs next to nothing. A good way of getting around is by **bicycle**. They can be hired cheaply all over the place: look out for signs saying *Aluga-se bicicleta*.

The **restaurants** in the town are simple and reasonably priced, and the food is excellent; the combination of fresh seafood and palm oil – Valença is famous for its *dendê* – is definitely special. Try the seafood *rodízio* (where you pay a flat fee and have all you can eat from a succession of dishes) at the *Akuarius*, on Praça da Independência, or the mouthwatering *moqueca* at the *Makulelê*, on Rua Governador Gonçalves, which has the added attraction of live music.

From Valença there are five daily **buses** back to Salvador, or you can continue south to Ilhéus and Porto Seguro; for which see below.

Inland: the Bahian sertão

The **Bahian sertão** is immense: an area considerably larger than any European country and comprising about a third of the total land area of the Northeast. Much of it is semi-desert, endless expanses of rock and cactus broiling in the sun. But it can be spectacular, with ranges of hills to the north and broken highlands to the west, rearing up into the tableland of the great **Planalto Central**, the plateau that extends over most of the state of Goiás and parts of Minas Gerais. No part of the Bahian *sertão* is thickly populated, and most of it is positively hostile to human habitation: in places, no rain falls for years at a stretch. Its inhabitants suffer more from drought than anywhere else in the Northeast, and in parts of the *sertão* there's still desperate poverty.

The Bahian *sertão* provided the backdrop to one of the most remarkable events in Brazilian history, the **rebellion** of the messianic religious leader, **Antônio Conselheiro**, who gathered thousands of followers, built a city called Canudos, and declared war on the young Republic in 1895 for imposing new taxes on an already starving population. The rebels held out for two years. The forces sent confidently north from Salvador were terribly mauled by the *sertanistas*, who proved to be great guerrilla fighters, with an intimate knowledge of the harsh country, which the city troops found as intimidating as their human enemies. Twice military columns were beaten, and then a third force of over a thousand troops commanded by a national hero, a general in the Paraguayan war, was sent against the rebels. In the worst shock the young Republic had suffered up to that point, it was completely annihilated: the next expedition discovered the bleached skulls of the general and his staff laid out in a neat row in front of a thorn tree. Not until 1897, when a fourth expedition was sent against it, did Canudos fall, and almost all of its defenders were killed: Antônio Conselheiro himself had died of fever a few weeks before the end. One member of the force, **Euclides da Cunha**, immortalised the war in his book, *Os Sertões*, generally recognised as the greatest Portuguese prose ever written by a Brazilian – it was translated into English as "Rebellion in the Backlands". To this day there's no finer introduction to the Bahian *sertão*: far more than a diary of a campaign, gripping though it is in this respect, it went beyond the conflict to explain how the history, culture and very landscape of the *sertão* had given birth to such a war.

Despite its reputation, not all the *sertão* is desert. Winding through it, like an enormous snake, is the **São Francisco river**, sprawling out into the huge hydro-electric lake of **Sobradinho**, which entombs the site of Canudos. River and lake support a string of towns, notably Paulo Afonso and Juazeiro, dealt with earlier for convenience; see "Alagoas and Sergipe" and "Inland from Recife" respectively. Another possible destination to the north is **Jacobina**, in the midst of spectacular hill country, where gold and emeralds have been mined for nearly three centuries. The other main route into the *sertão* is westwards, along the BR-242, which eventually hits the Belém–Brasília highway in Goiás: possible stop-off points on this route are the old mining town of **Lençois** and the river town of **Ibotirama**.

Feira de Santana

Whether you choose the route north or west, you're likely to pass through **FEIRA DE SANTANA**, 112km from Salvador, which if it weren't for the different landscape would bear a striking resemblance to Caruarú in Pernambuco. Like Caruarú, it styles itself "The Gateway to the *Sertão*" – with some justification – and it, too, supports an enormous market, the *Feira do Couro*, literally "leather market". Leatherwork is the main form of *artesanato* in the *sertão*, as you'd expect from cattle country. The market happens every Monday, taking over the centre of town with thousands of stalls and tens of thousands of customers, and you can find virtually anything. It's the best place to buy leatherwork in the Northeast, with cheap and very high quality wallets, handbags, satchels, cases and bags of every shape and size, many of them beautifully tooled. You should get there early, as the market starts to wind down after lunchtime, although it does go on all day. Buses leave every fifteen minutes from Salvador on market day, every half-hour the rest of the week: the journey takes about two hours.

If you can't make it there on a Monday the permanent **Mercado de Artesanato** in the centre has a wide range of leather goods every day of the week. Apart from the market, though, there's little reason to come, or to stay. The town itself is rather ugly and the countryside around is nothing special; it's best to make a day trip from Salvador.

North: to Jacobina

After Feira de Santana, the BR-324 strikes into the interior proper. The scenery is dull for the first couple of hours, but then the road climbs into the highlands of the **Chapada Diamantina**, with rock massifs rising out of the scrub, vaguely reminiscent of the American southwest. At the small town of CAPIM GROSSO the BR-407 branches off on a 300km journey north to Juazeiro, but sticking with the BR-324 for another hour brings you to the old mining town of **JACOBINA**. It nestles on the slopes of several hills with panoramic views over the **Serra da Jacobina**, one of the first parts of the *sertão* to be settled in strength by the Portuguese. The clue to what attracted them is the name of one of the two fast-flowing rivers that bisect the town, the Rio de Ouro, "Gold River". **Gold** was first found here in the early seventeenth century, and several *bandeirante* expeditions made the trip north from São Paulo to settle here. Although cattle and farming are now more important, mining still continues: there are emerald mines at nearby Pindobaçú, two large gold mines, and the diamonds which gave the Chapada Diamantina its name. The last big rush was in 1948, but miners still come down from the hills every now and then to sell gold and precious stones to traders in the town – you'll notice that many of them have precision scales on their counters.

The **town** itself is notably friendly – they don't see many tourists and people are curious – while the altitude takes the edge off the temperature most days, which makes it a good place to walk. It's a typical example of an interior town, quiet at night save for the squares and the riverbank walks, where the young congregate, especially around the *Zululândia* bar in the centre; while their parents pull chairs into the streets and gossip until the TV soaps start. In all directions, **paths** lead out of the town into the surrounding hills, with spectacular views, but it still gets hot during the day and some of the slopes are steep, so it's best to take some liquid along. The *Hotel Serra do Ouro* runs trips out to the **emerald mines** of Pindobaçú, around 60km to the north, and to the **gold mines** of Canavieiras and Itapicurú, though these are a bit disappointing in some respects: to the untrained eye uncut emeralds look like bits of gravel.

Some practical details

It's about a six-hour ride to Jacobina on the two daily **buses** from Salvador. There's no tourist office, although you might be able to get hold of a pamphlet with a street map from *Bahiatursa* in Salvador. Still, it's small enough to get by without one. The bus leaves you near the centre, where there are several cheap **hotels** and *pensões*. The best hotel, the *Hotel Serra do Ouro*, is on the outskirts, built on a hillside with a magnificent view of the town, but with single rooms starting at $20 it's a little expensive.

Jacobina is a good place for getting acquainted with the **food** of the interior: *carne do sol com pirão de leite* is rehydrated dried meat with a delicious milk-based sauce; *bode assada* is roast goat, surprisingly tender when done well; and *buchada*, a spicy kind of haggis made from intestines, is much nicer than it sounds but not for delicate stomachs. Good **restaurants** are *Carlito's*, on the banks of the Rio Ouro, and the *Cheguei Primeiro*, which only serves *caça* (game): the best dish is *tatú*, armadillo, which has a tender white flesh that tastes vaguely like pork. You should also try *doce de burití*, a tangy, acidic-tasting paste made from the fruit of the burití palm; it's sold in neat boxes made from the wood of the palm, which keep it fresh almost indefinitely.

There is even a **nightspot** called *Status* on the slopes of the Serra da Caixa above the town, only accessible by taxi – it calls itself a nightclub, but is more of a *dancetaria*, worth checking out on Friday and Saturday nights.

West: Lençóis and Ibotirama

The route **west** into the *sertão* is along the BR-242, which skirts Feira de Santana and swings south, where a turn-off signposted to Brasília heads inland, into the heart of the *sertão*. The scenery is remarkably similar to that along the Jacobina road a couple of hundred kilometres to the north: you're still in the tablelands of the Chapada Diamantina, with its rock spurs and mesas forming an enormous chain of foothills to the Planalto Central.

Lençóis . . .

Five hours' ride down the BR-242, **LENÇÓIS** is another mining town. It's a funny name for a town – it means "sheets" – and it derives from the camp that grew up around a diamond strike in 1844. The miners, too poor to afford tents, made do with sheets draped over branches. Lençóis is a pretty little town, in the midst of walking country that, if anything, is even more spectacular than the Serra da Jacobina. Most of its fine old buildings were built in the second half of the last century, when the town was a prosperous mining community, attracting diamond buyers from as far afield as Europe. The **Mercado Municipal**, next to the bridge over the river Lençóis that runs through the centre, is where most of the diamonds were sold – it has Italian and French style trimmings tacked on to make the buyers feel at home. The centre of the town, stretching between two lovely squares, Praça Otaviano Alves and Praça Horácio de Matos, is made up of cobbled streets, lined with well-proportioned two-storey nineteenth-century houses with high, arched windows. On Praça Horácio, the **Subconsulado Francês**, once the French consulate, was built with the money of the European diamond buyers, who wanted an office to take care of export certificates. On Praça Otaviano Alves there's a municipal **tourist information post**, often closed, but several people will offer themselves as guides to the town: at a dollar or two for an extensive tour they're not expensive, and as life is not easy around here hiring one might help someone out.

There are only two direct **buses** a week to Lençóis from Salvador, run by *Viação Auto-Paraíso* – the departure days change regularly. Several of the company's buses to Brasília stop at Lençóis as well, though. The best, and most expensive, **place to stay** in town is the *Pousada de Lençóis*. Cheaper, but still good, are the *Hospedaria São José* on Praça Aureliano Sá, and the *Pensão Diamantina* on Rua Miguel Calmon. There's a **campsite** in the centre, *Lumiar Camping*, on Rua Abelardo André.

Local **artesanato** is very good, particularly the bottles filled with coloured sand and arranged into intricate patterns: get a guide to take you to the **Salão das Areias** on the outskirts of town, where you can see the sand being gathered and put into bottles by local artisans – even children do it. You can buy the finished product at *Gilmar Nunes*, Rua Almirante Barroso, or at *Manoel Reis*, Rua São Felix.

... and the surrounding area

The countryside around Lençóis is promising walking territory. Some places you could probably manage yourself, like the **Gruta do Lapão**, a remarkable grotto over a kilometre long, with a cathedral-like entrance of layered rock and stalactites. It's a short drive or a long walk from the centre (though it's best to have someone take you there). The only other place within easy reach is the **Cascatas do Serrano**, where the river flows over a rock plate forming a series of small waterfalls and pools that are good for swimming – very popular with the town's children.

Anywhere more distant and you'll need a proper **guide**, as the countryside can be difficult to negotiate: at the *Pousada de Lençóis*, a short way up the hill from Praça Otaviano Alves, there's a resident American guide, Ray Funck, who also runs an *artesanato* shop; he may not be able to guide you himself, but can certainly recommend someone and suggest places to head for. Standard rates for a guide are between $8 and $12 a day and you may need to go the first part of the journey by car or taxi, as some places are up to 30km away. You can usually negotiate this with the guide, who will know somebody – and you'll have to arrange a place and time for them to pick you up if you don't feel like walking all the way back. Sunglasses, a hat and protective cream are all essential, as well as taking along liquids: it can get very hot and several of the walks are strenuous.

Places you're likely to have suggested to you as possible destinations are **Morro do Pai Inácio**, a 300-metre-high mesa formation 27km from Lençóis: don't be deceived about how near it looks. It is, though, much more easily climbed than seems possible from a distance, and you're rewarded with quite stunning views across the tablelands and the town once you get to the top, which is covered in highland cacti, trees and shrubs. Thirty kilometres away, but with much easier road access, is **Rio Mucugezinho**, another series of small waterfalls and pools that are fun to swim in; a closer river beach is the **Praia do Rio São José**, also called **Zaidã**. Finally, and most spectacular of all, is highest waterfall in Brazil, the **Cachoeira Glass**, a small stream that tumbles four hundred metres down over a mesa, becoming little more than a fine mist by the time it reaches the bottom. It's closer to town than most of the other places, and if you only feel up to one day's walking it's the best choice.

Ibotirama and the São Francisco river

Another couple of hundred kilometres down the road is the small river town of **IBOTIRAMA**, where the São Francisco is almost a kilometre wide and all highway traffic – including the buses – is ferried over to the other side on huge rafts. The **waterfront**, where there's a market and a crowd of riverboats with flat tops and open sides, is by far the most interesting part of the town. Fishing is important here, and the enormous river fish can be seen piled up all over the riverbank, ready for salting. There are several **hotels** and *dormitórios*, the best the *Hotel Velho Chico*, *Hotel Santo Antônio* or the *Hotel de N. Senhora de Fátima*. Unless there are empty spaces on a bus passing through from Brasília you'll have to get up early to catch the Salvador bus, which leaves at 4am (Tues & Sat only).

Apart from the waterfront, the town's not much, but it is an important river trading centre and a good starting point for **boat** travelling. You can go as far as Juazeiro, 800km downriver, along the Sobradinho lake: there is a direct service once a month, run by the *Companhia de Navegação do São Francisco*; and another boat makes a monthly journey downriver to Pirapora in Minas Gerais, from where there are bus connections to Belo Horizonte. Either route can take up to a week and it's best to buy tickets in Salvador, where *Bahiatursa* can give you the dates of sailings and make arrangements. Hammock space costs around $20 either way, and is much more comfortable than a cabin, a *camarote*.

Smaller launches make runs to **other river towns** in both directions, while canoes from Ibotirama will ferry you to two islands, **Gado Bravo** and **Ilha Grande**, half an hour's paddling away. Both have fine sandy beaches during the dry season, approximately March to October.

South from Salvador

The BR-101 highway is the main route to the **southern Bahian coast**, a region immortalised in the much-translated and filmed novels of Jorge Amado (see below). From the bus window you'll see the familiar fields of sugar replaced by huge plantations of *cacau*, cocoa, the raw material of chocolate and cocoa. Southern Bahia produces two-thirds of Brazil's cocoa, almost all of which goes for export, making this part of Bahia the richest agricultural area of the state. The *zona de cacau* seems quiet and respectable enough today, with its pleasant towns and prosperous countryside, but in the last decades of the nineteenth century, and the first decades of this, it was one of the most turbulent parts of Brazil. Entrepreneurs and adventurers from all over the country carved out estates here, often violently – a process chronicled by Amado in his novel *The Violent Lands*.

Ilhéus

In literary terms **ILHÉUS**, Amado's birthplace, is the best known town in Brazil, scene of his most famous novel, *Gabriela, Cravo e Canela*, translated into English as "Gabriela, Clove and Cinnamon" – by far the best known Brazilian novel internationally. If you haven't heard of it before visiting Ilhéus, you soon will; it seems that every other bar, hotel and restaurant is either named after the novel or one of its characters.

The town is on the coast 400km south of Salvador, where the local coastline is broken up by five rivers and a series of lagoons, bays and waterways. Much of it is modern but it's still an attractive place, with the heart of Ilhéus perched on a small hill that overlooks one of the largest and best beaches in Bahia. The **Rodoviária** is some way from the centre, but buses outside marked *Centro* or *Olivença* take you into town. There's a **tourist information** post at the *Rodoviária*, with good town maps, and also one in the centre on Avenida Soares Lopes, near the large 1930s cathedral, whose extravagant Gothic towers and pinnacles make a useful landmark. Before you head for the beaches, take the time to look around the town. Near the modern cathedral, the oldest church in the city, the **Igreja Matriz de São Jorge**, finished in 1556, has a religious art museum (Tues–Fri 9am–noon & 2.30–4.30pm, Sat 9am–noon); while the domed roof and towers of the **Igreja de Nossa Senhora de Lourdes** dominate the shoreline nearest to the centre. Domes are rare in church architecture in Brazil, and this combination of dome and towers is unique.

Bars and beaches: Olivença

The main leisure options in Ilhéus have changed little from Amado's time: hanging around in the **bars** and squares, and heading for the beaches. The *Vezúvio* on Praça Dom Eduardo, the cathedral square, is the most famous bar in Brazil; in the book it's owned by the hero Nacib, and is a watering hole of the cocoa planters. You pay a little extra on the drinks – no doubt Jorge Amado gets a cut – but it's a good bar, with famous Arab food. Apart from the centre, the main concentration of bars is along the fine beach promenade of the Avenida Atlântica, the beach itself called simply Avenida. There are other **beaches** to the north, past the port; the first is called **Isidro Ramos** (bus from the centre or Avenida), followed by **Praia do Marciano** and **Praia do Norte**.

Most locals prefer the coastline to the **south**, including the village of **OLIVENÇA**, served by local buses from the centre. Half an hour out of town is the beautiful beach at **CURURUPE**, where governor Mem de Sá trapped the Tupiniquim Indians in 1567 between his troops and the sea. It was called the "Battle of the Swimmers", after the Indians' desperate attempts to escape by water, but it was more of a massacre than a battle, and the tribe was almost wiped out. Today there are a series of bars and some holiday homes, peaceful groves of palm trees, and no hint of the place's dark past. In Olivença itself the main attraction is the **Balneário**, public swimming baths built around supposedly healthy mineral water from the river Tororomba, which flows through the place. The healing powers of the water are exaggerated, but the baths complex is very pleasant, with an artificial waterfall, and bar and restaurant attached. The coast between Ilhéus and Olivença is very beautiful: you can **camp** virtually anywhere along the way.

Ilhéus practicalities

Your best bet for **accommodation** in Ilhéus is probably on one of the beaches, although there's no shortage of places in the centre if you prefer. There are several reasonable hotels on Malhado beach, near the port; try the hotel and motel *Barravento*, next door to each other, on Rua Nossa Senhora de Graças. In the centre the *Lucas* on Rua Sete de Setembro, and the *Central* on Rua Araújo Pinto are alright; the *Ilhéus Praia* on the cathedral square rather more upmarket. Or go for one of several places along the Ilhéus–Olivença road: there are frequent buses back into town.

Buses to Ilhéus from Salvador take around six hours and are run by *Expresso São Jorge*: the only one you can catch if you want to see the pleasant countryside en route is at 10.30am, for which you have to book at least a day in advance; otherwise take one of the three night departures. There are **direct buses** from Ilhéus, once a week, to Rio and São Paulo, but book at least two days ahead for these.

Porto Seguro

The other main destination in southern Bahia is the resort area around the town of **PORTO SEGURO**, where Cabral "discovered" Brazil in 1500, a couple of thousand years after the first Indians populated the country. Founded in 1526, it has some claim to being the oldest town in Brazil, and some buildings still survive from that period. The story goes that in 1500 **Pedro Alvares Cabral** and his men, alerted to the presence of land by the changing colour of the sea and the appearance of land birds, finally saw a mountain on the horizon, which must have been Monte Páscoal, to the south of today's Porto Seguro. First landfall was made on Good Friday, on a beach to the north of Porto Seguro, and the anchorage Cabral used was probably the cove where today stands the village of Santa Cruz de Cabrália. The Indians were friendly at first – they might have been better advised to massacre everyone, since Cabral claimed the land for the King of Portugal, and thus began over three centuries of Portuguese rule.

The town . . . and Arraial da Ajuda

Porto Seguro has been developed as a holiday town – there are direct flights from Rio now – and between December and Carnaval it gets very crowded, with prices rather high as a result. The colonial area, **Cidade Alta**, is built on a bluff overlooking the town, with fine views out to sea and across the river Buranhén. The **Igreja da Misericórdia** here, begun in 1526, is one of the two oldest churches in Brazil. The **Igreja de Nossa Senhora da Pena**, nearby, dates from 1535 and has the oldest religious icon in Brazil, a Saint Francis of Assisi, brought over in the first serious expedition to Brazil in 1503. There are the ruins of a Jesuit church and chapel (dating from the 1540s) and a small, early fort: the squat and thick-walled style of the churches shows their early function as fortified strongpoints, in the days when Indian attacks were common. Near the ruins of the Jesuit college is the **Marca do Descobrimento**, the two-metre-high column sunk to mark Portuguese sovereignty in 1503; on one side is a crude face of Christ, almost unrecognisable now, and on the other the arms of the Portuguese crown.

Cidade Baixa, below, is where the modern action is. The riverside Avenida 22 de Abril is a mass of bars, restaurants and hotels, with less crowded beaches as it leads away from the town. After the road curves around the headland you come to the ferry crossing point for **ARRAIAL DA AJUDA** over the river; on the other side, the village is some forty minutes' walk from where the ferry leaves you. It's still partly a fishing village but is now very much taken over by the tourist trade, with a couple of luxury hotels and dozens of *pensões*. The beaches are still beautiful, though, better for camping than the ones around Porto Seguro itself. The best time to go is in the first half of August, when there is a pilgrimage centred around the supposedly miraculous freshwater spring near the village church – an event which serves as an excuse for a mini-carnival, blending into celebrations of Porto Seguro's fiesta, centred around the Igreja da Pena. **Carnaval** itself in Porto Seguro and Arraial da Ajuda is one of the largest in Bahia outside Salvador; good, crowded fun, with its fine beaches and reliable weather.

Practical information: accommodation and moving on

Most of the visitors in Porto Seguro are on the chic side, so unless you camp out, **accommodation** can be expensive. Finding somewhere to stay will be the least of your worries, though; there must be more hotels and *pensões* per head of population than anywhere else in Brazil, with everything from luxury hotels to flophouses. The best equipped **campsite** is *Camping da Gringa*, at the edge of town, or there's another on Mundaí beach, which starts in front of Cidade Alta.

There are two **buses to Porto Seguro** daily from Salvador, run by *Expresso São Jorge*, and direct buses (and flights) to Rio. **Tourist information posts** are at the *Rodoviária* and the airport.

PARAÍBA

Most people travelling north from Recife head directly for Ceará and Rio Grande do Norte's beaches, missing out **Paraíba state** and its capital of **João Pessoa** altogether. This is a mistake, as it is the most attractive of the smaller Northeastern cities, with everything you could reasonably ask for: fine beaches, a beautiful setting on the mouth of the river Sanhauá, and colonial remains, including one of Brazil's most striking churches. In addition, not enough foreign travellers make it to the city for the Pessoenses to have become blasé about them, and you're likely to be approached by smiling kids anxious to practise their hard-learned English.

Out of the city, there are fine beaches to the north and south, while the highway inland leads to **Campina Grande**, a market town strategically placed at the entrance to the *sertão*. The main target of the interior, though, is actually in neighbouring Ceará state, but dealt with here since it's most easily accessible from Paraíba – the fascinating pilgrim town of **Juazeiro do Norte**.

João Pessoa

JOÃO PESSOA is one of the oldest and one of the poorest cities in Brazil, and has the air of dilapidated elegance you find in Brazilian cities that have been left behind by modern development. Walking around, it feels as if you have slipped back to the Thirties, as of all the Northeastern cities this is the one least scarred by modern developers. As a result, **Cabo Branco** and **Tandaú** are two of the region's finest urban beaches, though it's not the beaches themselves that are unique, but the ageing style of the seafront: three storeys is the maximum height here and the absence of skyscrapers on the shoreline comes as a pleasant surprise.

Arriving and getting your bearings

The **Rodoviária** in João Pessoa is conveniently near the city centre. Any bus
from the **local bus station**, opposite the *Rodoviária*'s entrance, takes you to the
city's one unmistakable, central landmark: the circular lake, the Parque Solon de
Lucena, which everybody simply calls **Lagoa**, spectacularly bordered by tall
palms imported from Portugal. All **bus routes** converge on the circular Anel
Viário skirting the lake, and it's from here that you can catch buses for the beach
districts, as well as buses further afield – to the northern beaches, the neighbouring town of Cabedelo, and the village of Penha to the south of the city.

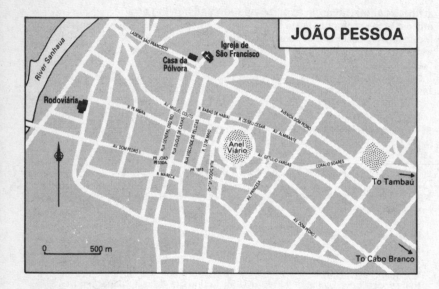

Some orientation

João Pessoa's centre is just up from the Lagoa, at the opposite end from **Avenida
Getúlio Vargas**, which leads to the beachside *bairros* of Cabo Branco and
Tambaú. At the city's core you'll find two small squares, **Praça João Pessoa** and
Praça 1817, with most of the central hotels clustered around the latter. The
oldest part of the city is just to the north of Praça João Pessoa, where **Rua
Duque de Caxias** ends in the Baroque splendour of the **Igreja de São
Francisco**. The steep **Ladeira de São Francisco**, leading down from here to
the lower city and the bus and railway stations, offers a marvellous view of the
rest of the city spread out on the banks of the river Sanhauá, framed by trees.

The two sweeping bays of **Cabo Branco** and **Tambaú** are separated by the
futuristic, circular, luxury *Hotel Tambaú*, where the highest concentration of
nightspots is found. The southern boundary of the city is the lighthouse on Ponta
de Seixas, the cape at the far end of Cabo Branco. Locals claim it as the most easterly point of Brazil, a title disputed with the city of Natal to the north – though the
Pessoenses have geography on their side.

Getting around: the local buses

Using the Anel Viário is the key to João Pessoa's **bus system**: you can change here for wherever you want to go, but the close positioning of half a dozen stops at the end of the Lagoa nearest the centre makes the whole business confusing at first. To make sense of it, a useful itinerary of all the city bus routes is printed in the yellow pages in the centre of the local telephone directory. You're likely to use buses marked *Cabo Branco* and *Tambaú* to go to the **beaches**, where many of the hotels and most of João Pessoa's nightlife are concentrated.

Information and some practical details

Official **tourist information** is not one of João Pessoa's strong points: the booth at the *Rodoviária*, run by the state tourist board, *PB-Tur*, theoretically opens office hours but in practice sometimes closes because of staff shortages. At the inconveniently sited central office at Avenida Getúlio Vargas 301, a ten-minute walk from the centre, you can get a free city map but little else.

The **main post office** is on Praça Pedro Américo, two blocks downhill from Praça 1817 in the direction of the bus stations. Domestic and international **telephone calls** are cheapest from the *TELEPAR* building, off Rua Visconde de Pelotas in the centre, open until 10pm daily.

Finding a place to stay

Hotels follow the same pattern as elsewhere in the Northeast: the very cheapest are the *dormitórios* opposite the bus station, the *Hotel São Pedro* at Rua Irineu Pinto 231 being the best bet. In the medium range are the hotels in the centre, which is only ten minutes by bus from the beaches, where the most expensive hotels are concentrated.

The centre

The comfiest place downtown is the *Tropicana*, at Rua Alice Azevedo 126, but at $20 for a double room it's overpriced. Much better value is the *Hotel Aurora*, Praça João Pessoa 51, which is clean and comfortable, with a range of rooms at different prices; get one with a fan (*ventilador*) rather than airconditioning, which is too noisy to leave on while you sleep.

Cheaper and more downmarket hotels include the *Hotel Recife*, Rua Alice Azevedo 200, near the *Tropicana*, and a couple of choices on Avenida Rodrigues de Aquino, which leads south from Praça João Pessoa: the *Hotel Kennedy*, at no. 17, and the *Hotel Franklin*, at no. 293 – the latter named after Franklin Roosevelt, who visited the city in 1943 to hold a summit with Getúlio Vargas and sign a deal to build an airbase nearby. Best of all of the cheapies is the *Pedro Américo* on the small, bustling square of the same name: rooms above the square are noisy during the day but the view more than compensates for the traffic.

The beach districts, and camping

At the **beach**, the *Hotel Tambaú* is worth seeing for its architecture but is luxury class and correspondingly expensive: anyone catching a taxi from here stands of good chance of being classed as a rich sucker and being taken for a ride (literally). You could, however, splurge on the slightly less exorbitant *Manaíra Praia Hotel*, Avenida Flávio Ribeira 115, or the medium-priced *Sol-Mar Hotel* at Avenida

Rui Carneiro 500. Best value, though, is the *Hotel Gameleira* at Avenida João Maurício 157: with only eighteen rooms it fills quickly. To reach any of the above places, take the *Tambaú* bus from the *Rodoviária* or the Anel Viário.

The beautiful **campsite**, on a promontory past the Ponta de Seixas, can be reached by taking the *Cabo Branco* bus to its terminal and then walking (for about 45min) past the lighthouse and along the road down the other side until the signposted fork to the left. Easier on the legs is taking the *Penha* bus from the Anel Viário or the local bus station: it passes near the campsite but only runs every couple of hours. Clean and well run, on a fine beach with a spectacular view of the city, the campsite is often full, especially from January to March, so it's advisable to book beforehand in the centre at Sala 18, Rua Almeida Barreto 159 (☎08-221-4863) – or you can book a place by phone, if your Portuguese is up to it.

Around the city

The centre of João Pessoa is dotted with **colonial churches, monasteries and convents**, some of which are extremely beautiful. Until a couple of years ago they were all being allowed to fall into almost complete ruin but, not a moment too soon, the state government and the Ministry of Culture mounted a crash restoration programme, for once using historians and archaeologists to return the buildings to their original glory, rather than gutting them. Access to the best buildings can be difficult while work continues: they are meant to have been completed by the end of 1990, but such projects tend to take longer than scheduled.

São Francisco

Unfortunately, this is especially true of João Pessoa's most spectacular church, the **Igreja de São Francisco**, which sits in splendid isolation atop the hill that bears its name, at the end of Rua Duque de Caxias. The best time to try and see it while work continues is in the morning: tip the workmen to get in.

The exterior alone is impressive enough. A huge courtyard is flanked by high walls beautifully decorated with *azulejo* tiling, with pastoral scenes in a series of alcoves. These funnel you towards a large early-eighteenth-century church that would do credit to Lisbon or Coimbra: its most remarkable feature is the tower topped with an oriental dome, a form the Portuguese encountered in Goa and appropriated for their own purposes. Older than the church by a few decades is the stone cross opposite the courtyard, at the foot of which is a group of finely carved pelicans, symbolising Christ. Pelicans were once believed to tear flesh from their own chests to feed their young, and were often used to represent selfless love.

The church itself is only half of the complex, but it's the only part that remains open while restoration work goes on. Beside and behind it stands the **Convento de Santo Antônio**, which you reach through the marvellously carved wooden panels and doors on the right. If you can get in, it's the architectural highlight here. Beyond the carvings in the entrance, there's a small but exquisite cloister, with arches surrounding a shady green garden centred upon an elaborately carved stone fountain. There are plans to install a museum here and, going by the work completed so far, it looks like being a sensitive restoration worthy of the original builders.

From São Francisco to São Pedro

The other places worth seeing in the centre are all within a short walk of São Francisco. Down the steep Ladeira de São Francisco, to the left of the church, is the oldest building in town, the **Casa de Pólvora**, a relic of the times when the Dutch and the Portuguese fought for control over this stretch of sugar-rich coastline. It's a squat, functional building that was once the city arsenal and is now the local museum (Tues–Fri 9am–noon & 2–4pm), mostly given over to a collection of enlarged photographs of the city in the early decades of this century. Much of it is still recognisable, and were it not for the absence of charabancs and men wearing hats you could step outside and imagine yourself walking around the photographs. Back up the hill and round to the right takes you onto Rua General Ossório and to a seventeenth-century monastery, the **Mosteiro de São Bento**, whose tall, airy chapel was, until restoration started, home to a colony of bats. The cathedral, the **Igreja da Misericórdia**, a block further down on the left, has a well-proportioned interior that for once forgoes the Rococo excesses of many colonial cathedrals. Other colonial churches are cheek by jowl on Rua Visconde de Pelotas, down from the cathedral: the Igreja de Santa Tereza and the Igreja de Nossa Senhora do Carmo are very much working churches, taking over the strain while the restoration programme proceeds, and look rather more lived-in as a result. But the most agreeably battered church is the **Igreja de São Pedro**, at the bottom end of the Ladeira de São Francisco, worth seeing for the faded but still elegant little square on which it's built. You may have to knock at the orphanage next door to be let into the church and the children will show you around. There is a macabre mausoleum, which is falling to pieces – the kids like to shock by pulling bones out from the drawers; the best way to get them to stop is by threatening to tell the priest.

Beaches and markets

The beach areas of Tambaú and Cabo Branco are linked to the centre by frequent buses from the Anel Viário and the local bus station.

The **Cabo Branco** seafront is especially stylish, with a mosaic pavement and thousands of well-tended palm trees to complement the sweep of the bay. This is best viewed from the **Ponta de Seixas lighthouse**, where there is a plaque and a monument to mark Brazil's easternmost point: to get there, take the *Cabo Branco* bus to its terminal on the promontory at the end of the bay, and walk up the hill. There is a park at the top and a couple of tacky souvenir shops, but the main thing is the **view**, which is glorious – Cabo Branco beach stretches out before you in an enormous arc (6km long, if you were wondering), which the absence of tall buildings makes all the more impressive. Cabo Branco itself is the city's exclusive upper-class suburb, where the rich stay hidden in their large detached houses, whose high walls shut out both the people and the view. This leaves the fine beach indecently bereft of the usual string of bars and hotels, and only the rustle of wind in the palm trees disturbs the calm elegance of the mansions, a universe away from the poverty of the rest of Paraíba.

Far livelier is **Tambaú**, dominated by its eponymous hotel, which forms one end of a small square. By day, this hosts the stalls of the **mercado de artesanato**, small beer by Bahian or Pernambucan standards, and difficult for foreigners to make headway when bargaining, because everyone assumes you must be staying in the hotel and charges accordingly. (You'll find a wider range at more reasonable prices at the state-run *Casa do Artesão Paraibano*, Rua Maciel Pinheiro 670, near the *Rodoviária*.) Still, Paraíba has distinctive artesanato that's worth checking out: painted plates and bowls, and striking figurines made out of sacking and wood.

From the market onwards you do begin to encounter the familiar clusters of beachside bars and restaurants, and at weekends they and the beach get crowded. The **beach** itself (confusingly called Praia de Manaíra as well as Tambaú) is dirtier than Cabo Branco but more fun: there are the usual simple cafés and vendors selling fruit and fish, and *jangadas* aplenty. Anywhere here is a good place for a *caipirinha* and a view of an invariably spectacular sunset.

Eating and drinking

As usual in a coastal capital, the centre tends to get deserted after dark, as people looking for a night out head for the beaches, particularly Tambaú. However, there are several places in the centre worth looking at.

Restaurants and bars in the centre

The *Casino da Lagoa* is a bar/restaurant in a small park looking out across the Anel Viário, on the right coming down from the centre: the food is no more than average but the view is excellent, especially at night. Also worth checking out is the *Cordon Bleu*, a restaurant combined with an art gallery dedicated entirely to local talent; very central at Rua Duque de Caxias 63. Again, the food is middling and overpriced, but the art is vivid and good and the place itself is a pleasure to be in, very 1930s, with a piano bar attached; you almost expect Bob Hope and Dorothy Lamour to come waltzing through the door. The best **sertão food** in the city is served at *Recanto do Picuí*, a restaurant on the Avenida Beira-Rio, which runs parallel to the river behind the *Rodoviária*. The *carne do sol* here is excellent, best accompanied by green beans and *batata doce assado*, roast sweet potatoes.

Finally, stop by the *Bar do Pólvora*, behind the Casa de Pólvora, down the hill from the Igreja de São Francisco. No more than a bar with tables set out on the patio behind the old arsenal, serving only beer, *caipirinhas* and soft drinks, it has two major advantages: one is the view out across the river, which is stunning; the other is the clientele – young, student-dominated and very Bohemian. Best time to go is Thursday evening, when a small fee is charged for a table and there's a show, whose basic format is a few groups/poets/singers doing spots, plus whoever else in the audience feels like doing a turn. As you might expect, some of the acts are appalling, notably the local poets reading interminable extracts from their work, but the music is sometimes superb, as is the setting – beneath the ancient walls of the arsenal, the mango trees rustling under a starry, tropical sky.

Stubborn **vegetarians** can try the *Natural*, Rua Rodrigues de Aquino 177, down from Praça João Pessoa – unfortunately only open for lunch.

Beach eating

If you want a more sedate evening, or you happen to be in town midweek, there is no shortage of restaurants in the **beach areas**. The more expensive ones ($10–25 range) are in Cabo Branco: *Búzios*, on the seafront at Avenida Cabo Branco 4924, is a good seafood restaurant. Nearby, at no. 5100, is *Marina's*, one of the few seafront bars in Cabo Branco, which also does seafood. A local speciality is *polvo ao leite de coco*, octopus in coconut milk, particularly succulent at the *Peixada da Praia*, Avenida Olinda 64, the road running inland opposite the *Hotel Tambaú*.

Nightlife: live music, dancing and clubs

João Pessoa has a suprisingly rich **music scene** for a city of its size: the only nights it is difficult to catch something are Sunday and Monday. There are two good **forró dance halls**: *Bardan*, towards the bottom end of the Avenida Epitácio Pessoa in Tambaú, and *Deboche*, on Avenida Júlia Freire in the *bairro* of Torre – the latter easiest got to by taxi. Both are open Friday and Saturday nights, and don't really get going until after midnight, continuing right through until dawn.

The bar *Travessia*, near the *Hotel Tambaú* on Rua General Edson Ramalho, one block in from the beach, has live music (Tues–Sat), with the main show (usually) on Tuesday nights: generally local musicians doing a variety of Northeastern styles, with the occasional *choro* thrown in. More upmarket is the stylish *Raízes*, something between a bar and a nightclub, on Avenida Nossa Senhora dos Navegantes, again near the *Hotel Tambaú*: its shows are on Wednesday, Friday and Saturday nights, often featuring stints by nationally known Northeastern musicians like Elba Ramalho (a native of the state), Fagner and Alceu Valença. Also, *Gambrinu's* restaurant, at Rua Coração de Jesus 18, in Tambaú, has live music on Wednesday evenings, but you have to have a meal as well.

If you want somewhere less formal to do your drinking and listening, head for the square in front of the *Hotel Tambaú*. It's surrounded by restaurants and bars, and on Friday and Saturday nights tables and chairs are put out in the square, drink starts flowing, and after about 9pm things start getting very lively. Every other bar has a *forró* trio, and guitarists and accordion players stroll through the crowds. There's no shortage of good, cheap food sizzling on the charcoal grills of the street vendors if your budget doesn't stretch to a restaurant. In the streets behind there are any number of small **bars and clubs**, which close down and re-open too quickly to keep track of them, so just wander around and stop by anywhere you see lights and music. These smaller bars tend not to get going until 11pm at the earliest, as they rely on people moving on from the seafront places.

Finally, note that there are a couple of **gay bars** in the streets behind Avenida Nossa Senhora dos Navegantes, but it's not an exclusively gay area.

Along the coast

Just to the **south** of João Pessoa is the fishing village of **PENHA**, served by local buses from outside the *Rodoviária* or from the Anel Viário. Strung out along a fine beach set in the midst of dense palm forest, Penha is distinguished from other fishing villages roundabout by a nineteenth-century church, the **Igreja de Nossa Senhora da Penha**, that is a pilgrimage centre and focus of much popular devotion. The beach near the church is also used by followers of *candomblé*, who identify the Virgin with Iemanjá, the goddess of the sea. The legend is that over a century ago an image of the Virgin was dredged up by fishermen in their nets, and worked so many miracles that the community adopted her as their patron saint and built the simple chapel to house her icon. Along the beach there are several rustic **bars** where you can eat and also string a hammock for a nominal fee. Discreet camping on the beach is also possible.

North: the route to Cabedelo

Penha apart, most of the readily accessible **beaches** are to the **north**, off the road that leads to Cabedelo, 18km or 45 minutes by frequent local buses from the Anel Viário in João Pessoa – they get very crowded at weekends. The road runs a little inland and there are turn-offs leading to the beaches on the way: it seems to depend more on the drivers' whim than a timetable as to whether the bus takes you right to the beach, but hop on the *Cabedelo* bus anyway, and get off at the relevant turn-off if need be; it'll only be a short walk to the sea.

There are two places before Cabedelo itself where you might want to get off. The first, **BESSA**, is the generic name for the stretch of coastline north of Tambaú. Six kilometres out of town is a turn-off that leads to the yacht club and a cluster of bars, which have a rather more upmarket clientele than the next village along, **POÇO**, where there is a chapel, some weekend homes, a fine palm-fringed beach with the obligatory bars, and several good fish restaurants. Of these, *Badionaldo* serves delicious crab stew (*ensopado de carangueijo*), a local speciality. Heading back, you could walk the 10km along the beach to Cabedelo. Or hourly buses there, or back to João Pessoa, leave from the bus stop near the church – there are no buses back to town after dark.

Cabedelo

CABEDELO itself is older than it looks. It was much fought over in the Dutch wars, and the star-shaped fort of **Santa Caterina** (Tues–Sat 2–4pm), dating from 1621, is the main sight in the village. Unfortunately, *Petrobrás* have built a series of oil storage tanks right up to its ramparts, and it's difficult to get a sense of its strategic position, commanding the only deep water anchorage on this stretch of coast. It's an anchorage that served as João Pessoa's port for three centuries and was the sole reason for Cabedelo's existence until *Petrobrás* decided it would make a good site for an oil terminal. As a result, the town beach (Praia de Camboinha) looks beautiful, but is regularly polluted by spillages from oil tanks and docked ships, and a vaguely petrochemical smell hangs over it in humid weather.

Believe it or not, Cabedelo is the starting point for the famous **Transamazon highway** – the *Transamazônica* – and there's a sign proving it over the João Pessoa road. It has a certain logic. The Transamazon was always as much a grand symbolic gesture as a physical thing in the minds of its creators, so it had to stretch from the extreme west of Brazil to the extreme east. On top of that, it was also seen as the conduit along which would flow the "people without land" to the "land without people", as poor Northeasterners were funnelled towards Amazonia; a political signal to the large landowners of the Northeast that the government had no intention of tackling the region's problems by implementing agrarian reform. So the only thing the poor of Paraíba got was a convenient escape route.

Inland to Campina Grande

The BR-230 highway, a good quality asphalt road, bisects Paraíba and leads directly into the *sertão*. The green coastal strip is quickly left behind as the road climbs into the hills: two hours driving and you arrive in the second city of Paraíba, **CAMPINA GRANDE**, linked to João Pessoa by hourly bus. It's a large town, similar in many ways to Caruarú in Pernambuco: even the slogan you see at the city limits – "Welcome to the Gateway of the *Sertão*" – is identical. Like Caruarú, Campina Grande owes its existence to a strategic position between the *agreste* and the *sertão* proper. It's a market town and centre of light industry, where the products of the *sertão* are stockpiled and sent down to the coast, and where the people of the *sertão* come to buy what they can't make. There's a large Wednesday and Saturday **market** where you can see this process unfolding before your eyes. You may also see evidence of the fierce competition between Campina Grande and João Pessoa. Campinenses proudly contrast their industries and commercial ability with the decadence and stagnation of João Pessoa, and perhaps they have a point. To the traveller, though, João Pessoa's elegance is something of a contrast with Campina Grande, which even locals admit is rather ugly. Still, it's a good place to sample the distinctive culture of the *sertão*, without having to suffer its discomforts.

The market operates all year round, but in June there is a month-long **festival** that uses the São João holiday – the **festas juninas** – as an excuse for a general knees-up, and is the best time to visit. The wonderfully named **forrodrómo** in the centre of town, an enormous cross between a concert hall and a *dancetaria*, is where it all happens.

The **climate** in Campina Grande is always pleasant, as its height takes the edge off the coastal heat without making it cold, though you may need a sweater at night during the rainy season.

Practicalities

The **Rodoviária** is on the outskirts of town; local buses marked *Centro* take you downtown. The cheaper *dormitórios* are clustered around the old railway station in the centre, now turned into a **tourist centre** with an information post, which gives out a useful city map. A good **restaurant** with regional food, the *Panorâmico*, which forms part of the centre, is an added motive for a visit.

The nearest the city comes to a luxury **hotel** is the *Ouro Branco*, right in the centre at Rua Coronel João Lourenço 20, but you'll get better value and a good view to boot at the *Rique Palace*, which occupies the top floors of the city's tallest building, at Rua Venâncio Neiva 287. There are several other reasonable mid-range hotels close to each other around the city centre: try the *Hotel Serrano*, just out of the centre at Rua Tavares Cavalcanti 27, the *Majestic* at Rua Maciel Pinheiro 216, and the *Belfran*, Avenida Marechal Floriano Peixoto 258.

Although the city sprawls out into anonymous industrial suburbs, the **central layout** is compact and easy to get the hang of. The city's heart, and most useful landmark, is the obelisk of the **Parque do Açude Novo**, straddling the **Avenida Floriano Peixoto**, which bisects Campina Grande from west to east. The stretch of the avenue from the obelisk to the cathedral is the centre proper, where most of the things to do and see are concentrated.

The market and the city

Every Wednesday and Saturday the **market** takes over the area around the cathedral and the municipal market behind it, and although not quite on the scale of Caruarú or Feira da Santana in Bahia, it is the largest in the northern half of the Northeast. Saturday is busiest, but to catch it at its peak you either need to arrive on the Friday or make an early start from João Pessoa, as it starts to wind down from around noon. A highlight are the cries, improvised verses, chants and patters of the scores of streetsellers: you may be lucky enough to come across hawkers going head to head, when two vendors set up shop next to each other and try to outdo the other in extravagant claims and original turns of phrase. Sometimes sellers of *cordel* (see "Recife") recite chunks of the ballads to whet the public's appetite, and clusters of people gather around to shout comments and enjoy the story. If you miss the market, but still fancy trying to get hold of **artesanato and cordel**, good places are the co-operative *Casa do Artesão*, Rua Venâncio Neiva 85, near the Rique Palace, and *Kaboclinha*, nearby at Rua Vidal de Negreiros 36.

There are two **museums** in Campina Grande. By some way the best is the **Museu de Arte Assis Chateaubriand**, part of the complex of buildings in the Parque do Açude Novo (Tues–Fri 10am–1pm & 2–5pm, Sat 10am–1pm). It's a source of justifiable civic pride, boasting a good gallery of modern art, devoted entirely to Brazilian artists, with a special emphasis on work from the Northeast. Some of Brazil's greatest modern painters are represented, notably Cândido Portinari, whose large canvases fuse social realism with modernist technique in their depiction of workers and workplaces. The most intriguing part of the museum is the *atelier livre*, a kind of gallery of work in progress by local artists, where there are temporary exhibitions: local painters, carvers and sculptors bring things to exhibit or sell. They are not very cheap, but for the quality and originality the price is often more than reasonable.

A total contrast, the **Museu do Algodão** (same hours as above) is in the tourist centre in the old railway station. It concentrates on the history of the cotton plantations of the area, including some fearsome chains, stocks, iron collars and whips used against the slaves.

Lagoa Seca

The village of **LAGOA SECA** is just a short bus or taxi ride away from Campina Grande: buses leave from Avenida Floriano Peixoto. Like Alto do Moura outside Caruarú it's a village of craft workers that has turned out *artesanato* for two generations. The people are friendly, and you can see many of the artists at work carving religious figures in their yards and in front of their houses. It was in Lagoa Seca that the sacking and wood figurines that you find throughout Paraíba originated.

Into the *Sertão*

The BR-232 continues threading its way though the *sertão* to the town of **PATOS**; hot, flyblown, and looking like a spaghetti western set with pick-ups instead of horses. If you need to stop, use the *Hotel JK*, Praça Getúlio Vargas. Then it's on to **SOUSA**, an otherwise unremarkable *sertão* town five hours west of Campina Grande, with two hotels and one of the Northeast's more unusual sights, the **Vale dos Dinosauras**, "Dinosaur Valley", formed by the sedimentary basin of the Peixe river. At one time, difficult though it is to imagine in this searing semi-arid landscape, all was swamp and jungle. Various prehistoric reptiles left their footprints, preserved in stone, at several sites in the area around the town. The only way to get to them is by battered taxi over the dusty road. The nearest site is called *A Ilha*, about 5km out of town, and it'll cost you around $5. Here the prehistoric tracks are striking. The beast clearly lumbered along the river bed for a while and then turned off, and you can see a regular series of footprints the size of dinner plates, some with two claws visible at the front.

The pilgrim route: Juazeiro do Norte

The main centre of the deep *sertão* is 160km west, in the south of Ceará state, where a series of hill ranges, higher ground blessed with regular rainfall, provides a welcome respite. Food crops can be grown here, and every available inch of land is used to grow fruit and vegetables, or graze cattle. Here there are two towns within a few kilometres of each other, CRATO and **JUAZEIRO DO NORTE**, and it was in this area that one of the most famous episodes in the history of the Northeast took place.

Miracle At Juazeiro

In 1889 Juazeiro was no more than a tiny hamlet. There was nothing unusual about its young priest, **Padre Cícero Romão Batista**, until women in Juazeiro claimed the wine he gave them at communion had turned to blood in their mouths. At first it was only people from Crato who came, and they were convinced by the women's sanctity and the evidence of their own eyes that Padre Cícero had indeed worked a miracle. As his fame grew, the deeply religious inhabitants of the *sertão* came to hear his sermons and have him bless them. Despite himself, Padre Cícero came to be seen as a living saint: miraculous cures were attributed to him, things he had touched and worn were treated as relics. The Catholic church began a formal investigation of the alleged "miracle", sent him to Rome to testify to commissions of enquiry, rejected it, sent him back to Brazil and suspended him from the priesthood – but nothing could shake the conviction of the local people that he was a saint. Juazeiro mushroomed into a large town by *sertão* standards, as people flocked to make the pilgrimage, including legendary figures like the bandit chief Lampião.

By the end of his long life, Padre Cícero had become one of the most powerful figures in the Northeast. In 1913 his heavily-armed followers caught the train to the state capital, Fortaleza, and forcibly deposed the governor, replacing him with somebody more to Padre Cícero's liking. But Padre Cícero was a deeply conservative man, who restrained his followers more often than not, deferred to the Church, and remained seemingly more preoccupied with the next world than with this. When his more revolutionary followers tried to set up a religious community nearby at Caldeirão, he didn't deter the authorities from using the airforce against them, in one of the first recorded uses of bombs on civilians. When he finally died, in 1934, his body had to be displayed strapped to a door from the first floor of his house, before the thousands thronging the streets would believe he was dead. Ever since, pilgrims have come to Juazeiro to pay homage, especially for the anniversary of his death on July 20. The **pilgrims** are called *romeiros*, after Padre Cícero's middle name, and an enormous white statue of the priest looks out from a hillside over the town he created.

Arriving in Juazeiro

When booking a ticket to Juazeiro make sure you specify Juazeiro *do Norte*, or you run the risk of ending up in Juazeiro in Bahia, several hundred kilometres south! The **Rodoviária** is a couple of kilometres out of the town, which is smaller than its fame suggests. There is one central square where you'll find the best **hotel**, the *Panorama*, but finding somewhere to stay is the least of your worries in a town geared to putting up pilgrims: there are small hotels and *dormitórios* everywhere.

Leaving town, seats fill up fast on the daily buses to João Pessoa, Recife and Fortaleza, so if you're staying overnight book a ticket when you arrive. Alternatively, it is usually possible to get a seat on one of the **pilgrim coaches** parked around town, whose drivers sell seats for the same price as the bus – you don't get to choose the destination, but as coachloads come from all the major cities that shouldn't be a problem.

Making the pilgrimage

If you want to do what the pilgrims do, the first stop is Padre Cícero's **tomb** in the church of **Nossa Senhora do Perpétuo Socorro**, to the left of the square. There is a small monument outside, always decorated with *ex votos*, the tokens brought by those praying for help: you will offend if you pick up or handle them. Inside the plain church there is a constant stream of *romeiros* praying intensely and queueing to kiss the marble slab by the altar, which you might think is the grave but isn't: that is outside to the left, an unpretentious tomb covered in flowers and ribbons. The church is surrounded by souvenir shops, which specialise in the figurines of Padre Cícero with hat and walking stick that you can find all over the Northeast.

The next destination is the **statue** of Padre Cícero on the peak of the **Serra do Horto**, the hill that looks down on the town. There are two ways of getting there and the soft option is to take a taxi for 3km along a road that winds up the hill – a route which can be walked if you want to see the fine views of the **valley of Cariri** unfold, with the town of Crato visible to the west. The other way is to follow the **pilgrim route**, a track from the town directly up the hill: it isn't signposted but people will willingly direct you to it if you ask for *a picada dos romeiros* or *a Via Sacra*. It's a brisk hour to the top, and at several points the pilgrims have cut steps to help you up. Thousands walk the trail on July 20, "paying the promise", performing penances for help received: a few hardy souls make the journey on their knees.

Once on top, the main attractions are not so much the statue – 25m high but hardly a masterpiece – as the panoramic views and the **chapel** and **museum of ex-votos** next to it. Room after room is piled high with stacks of offerings from the grateful thousands for whom Padre Cícero interceded over the decades: countless artificial limbs, wooden models of bits of body, photos of disasters escaped and crashes survived, even football jerseys from victorious players, including one from Brazil's winning 1970 World Cup team. As a demonstration of the hold popular religion has on the daily lives of millions of *nordestinos*, only the *ex votos* at the church of Bonfim in Salvador rival it.

You finish up with Padre Cícero's **house**, signposted from the church where he is buried, and now a cross between a museum and shrine. It's a simple dwelling, with large rooms, a garden, and glass cases displaying everything anybody could find that was even remotely connected to the great man: his glasses, underwear, hats, typewriter, bed linen, even the bed he died in. Just for good measure, there are bundles of Indian arrows, fossils and a coin collection thrown in.

The last act of pilgrimage is to be **photographed** to prove to the folks back home that you've made the trip. This ensures a steady flow of work for the many photographers clustered around the last church on the way to the hill, the Igreja Matriz de Nossa Senhora das Dores. They all have a series of props to help you pose: lifesize statues of Padre Cícero, dozens of hats, toy elephants and so forth, and although the snap takes two or three hours to develop it comes ready mounted in a mini-viewer, far more durable than a photo proper – the ideal souvenir.

RIO GRANDE DO NORTE

Arriving in **Natal**, capital of the small state of **Rio Grande do Norte**, the new hotels and office blocks lend an illusory air of modernity to what is one of the oldest and most conservative states in Brazil. It is also one of the smallest and most thinly populated, the only two places of any size being the capital and the interior town of **Mossoró**. For as long as anyone can remember more of the state's inhabitants have lived beyond its borders than within it, driven to emigration by the grinding poverty that is the norm in the interior. The reasons are simple: unequal land distribution, and an accident of geography. Rio Grande do Norte is where the Northeastern sugar belt that begins far to the south finally peters out, drastically changing both history and landscape.

North of Natal, the *sertão* drives down practically to the coast, and the idyllic palm-fringed beaches give way to something wilder as the coastline changes character, massive sand dunes replacing the flat beaches and palm trees. There is practically no *agreste* to provide insurance against hard times in the form of rich soil and market towns. Instead, the coast is dotted, more and more sparsely, with small fishing villages, rather than the prosperous old sugar towns further to the south; the *sertão* is flatter and less flinty, and given over almost completely to cattle, mostly scrawny, scratching a living along with the people. The black Brazilian population shrinks with the sugar zone, and in Rio Grande do Norte dwindles to almost nothing.

Natal

NATAL is a small city of about 400,000 people, built on the banks of the Potengí river, and founded sixty years later than planned, after the Potiguar Indians stifled the first Portuguese landing on the coast in 1538. They continued to hold the invaders off until 1598, when the Portuguese built the star-shaped fort at the mouth of the river that is the city's most enduring landmark. Natal is at the heart of one of the most spectacular strings of beaches in the Northeast: in fact, given that you could hire a beach buggy in Genipabú, just north of Natal, and drive along 250km of dunes uninterrupted until Areia Branca, practically on the border with Ceará, Natal is at one end of what amounts to a single enormous beach.

Stranded at the eastern tip of the Northeast, away from the main international tourist routes, and with little industry to provide employment, Natal has lately been developing tourist facilities with the desperation of a place with few other economic options. It's become a popular destination for Brazilian holidaymakers, lured by the sun and sand rather than the city itself, which is mostly modern and has a sloppily developed seafront: you will look in vain for the colonial elegance of João Pessoa or Olinda. But the beaches, among the best in Brazil, do compensate, and amid the development and hotels there are still good nightspots and *dancetarias*, as well as the best Northeastern restaurant you could hope to stumble upon.

Arriving, orientation and getting around

Natal's **airport**, Augusto Severo, is about 15km south of the centre on the BR-101 highway: you'll almost certainly have to take a taxi if you arrive here. The **Rodoviária** is also a long way out from the centre, on Rua Capitão Mor Gouveia in the suburb of Cidade de Esperança (☎231-1170) but you can get a local bus into town at the bus stop on the other side of the road, opposite the Rodoviária entrance; the stops immediately outside are a setting down point for buses to the outer suburbs only, and will take you in the wrong direction. Most buses from across the road pass through the centre: those marked *Av. Rio Branco, Cidade Alta* and *Ribeira* are the most common. Or **taxis** from the *Rodoviária* into the centre are also plentiful and cheap.

After quarter of an hour you turn into Natal's main thoroughfare, **Avenida Rio Branco**, which runs past the oldest part of the city, **Cidade Alta** (where precious little that's old remains) and terminates in a scruffy square, Praça Augusto Severo, site of the useful **local bus station**. From here, steep descents lead to the **city beaches**, and the coastal road to the **southern beaches**, now being rapidly developed; though the beaches to the north are less crowded and more beautiful.

Just out of the centre are the quiet and pleasant grid-pattern suburbs of **Petrópolis** and the incongruously named **Tirol**, after the birthplace of the Austrian planner who laid them out in the 1930s.

Getting around the city

Natal's **bus system** is easy to master, and in a hot city with hills and scattered beaches it's worth spending a little time getting used to it. At the **local bus station** (see above), and from **Avenida Rio Branco**, you can get buses to most of the places you might want to go to, including the out of town beaches: all the buses to the southern beaches, like Areia Preta and Ponta Negra, can be caught from here or the seafront, the one marked *Mãe Luiza* is one of the most frequent; while buses marked *Via Costeira* head along the southern coastal road out to Ponta Negra. Several bus routes run from the centre to the *Rodoviária*, taking at least half an hour and often longer because of their circuitous routes: *Via Tirol, Rodoviária*, and *Cidade da Esperança* will you get you there eventually, but it's more direct (and not expensive) to take a taxi.

Information

There are **tourist information posts** at the *Rodoviária* and airport, with good free maps of the city but little else. The main **tourist centre** is in the old prison, perched on top of a hill, on Rua Aderbal de Figueiredo in Petrópolis, where there are various overpriced stalls selling *artesanato* and beautiful views of the beaches and city.

Finding a place to stay

Hotels are plentiful and, as ever, rather more expensive in the beach areas. In the **centre** the easiest options are along Avenida Rio Branco, which has a string of good, cheap hotels: the *Fenícia* at no. 586, *Bom Jesus* at no. 374, *Natal* at no. 740, and *São Paulo* at no. 697. In the same area is the *Casa Grande*, Rua Princesa Isabel 663, which is very good value for money. More upmarket central hotels are the *Reis Magos* on the beach at Avenida Café Filho 822, the *Sol* on Rua Heitor Carrilho 107, and the *Samburá* at Rua Professor Zuza 262.

Petrópolis is also a good bet, quieter, easier to find your way around and close to the centre. There is a crowded and friendly *pensão* popular with both young

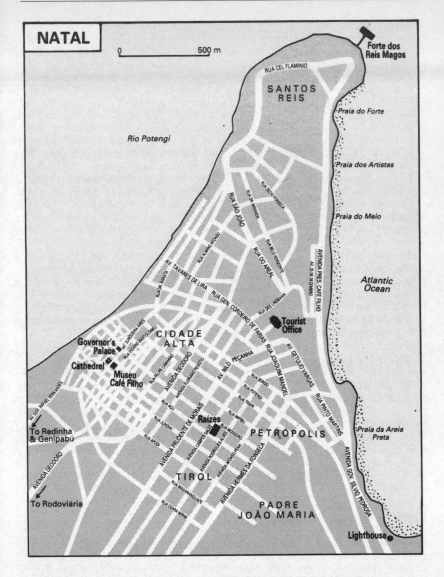

gringos and Brazilians called the *Pousada Meu Canto*, at Rua Manoel Dantas 424, which has a lovely garden but an overbearing hostess. More expensive, more comfortable and with excellent regional food is the *Pousada O Caipira* at Rua Manoel Machado 354 (☎222-7497).

Another option would be staying at one of the **beaches outside the city**, like Ponta Negra and Pirangí to the south or Redinha and Genipabú to the north.

The City

For a city that was founded nearly four centuries ago there is surprisingly little of historical interest in Natal itself, apart from the distinctive, whitewashed star of the **Forte dos Reis Magos** (Tues–Sun 8am–noon & 2–5pm), dominating the river entrance. Like most of Brazil's colonial forts it looks very vulnerable, directly overlooked by the hill behind it and with thick, surprisingly short walls – both qualities which must have been necessary in its defenders. Although there is not much to see apart from a token museum of local culture, it's interesting to wander around.

The oldest part of the city is formed by the closely packed streets and small squares of **Cidade Alta**, running north of Avenida Rio Branco to the river – but the street plan itself is one of the only things that remains from colonial times. Instead, the architecture that has survived the thrust for development is clustered around the administrative heart of the city, **Praça João Maria**, dominated by the governor's palace, built in tropical Victorian style in 1873, the town hall, and the **Cathedral**, built in 1768 but unexceptional for all that. Smaller, and rather more interesting, is the **Igreja de Santo Antônio** behind the cathedral, also known as the Igreja do Galo, after the eighteenth-century bronze cock crowing on top of its Moorish tower. A block from the cathedral is the most interesting museum in a city largely bereft of them: the **Museu Café Filho** (Tues–Fri office hours only), dedicated to the only Rio Grandense to become president of Brazil – a corrupt and incompetent paternalist, despite the attempts by the museum to present him as a statesman. But he had the good taste to live in a fine two-storey mansion, at Rua da Conceição 630, which is worth seeing – more than can be said for the yellowing papers and heavy furniture of the long dead president.

The city beaches

What Natal lacks in attractions for the culturally minded, it makes up for in facilities for the beach bum. There are fine **beaches** right inside the city, beginning at the fort where arcs of sand sweep along the bay up to the headland and **Mãe Luiza lighthouse**, a useful point to take bearings from. Buses marked *Mãe Luiza* take you from the seafront to the foot of the hill crowned by the lighthouse, which you can walk up. From the top there is a magnificent view of the **Praia do Meio***, the beach that stretches from the fort to the headland of the Ladeira do Sol, and the **Praia da Areia Preta**, curving between the headland and the lighthouse. All the beaches are lined with stalls serving the usual array of cold drinks and food, and numerous **hotels** and **bars** are strung along the inland side of the seafront, which gets lively on weekend evenings.

On the other side of the lighthouse is another enormous beach, **Mãe Luiza**, accessible along the tourist development highway known as the *Via Costeira*, which takes you to the out-of-town beaches of Ponta Negra, 10km away (see "South of Natal", below). None of the city beaches are protected by reefs, and the beaches near the centre of town especially ought to be treated with respect: the combination of a shelving beach and rollers roaring in from the Atlantic often makes the surf dangerous, and tourists are drowned every year.

---

*Technically it's three beaches, the small **Praia do Forte** next to the fort, and then the **Praia dos Artistas** before the **Praia do Meio** proper, although people use "Praia do Meio" to refer to them all.

Eating

Beaches apart, **restaurants** are one of Natal's strongest points. The strong regional cuisine has, if anything, been strengthened by the influx of Brazilian tourists, as many see Northeastern food as part of their holiday.

Undoubtedly the best of a high-quality field, well worth the $15–20 you will spend, is *Raízes* ("Roots"), at Avenida Campos Sales 609, the corner with Rua Mossoró, in Petrópolis – the **best restaurant in the Northeast** outside Salvador, and certainly the best anywhere for the food of the *sertão*. The time to go is in the evening, when you should order the truly magnificent *ceia nordestina*; a succession of dozens of dishes in small helpings that enable you to eat yourself stupid. There are about forty different things to try: some, like *carne do sol*, you will probably recognise; others, like *paçoca* (dried meat pounded in a mortar with beans and manioc flour) and the squash-like vegetables of the interior, *inhame* and *jerimum*, you probably won't. The highlights of the feast are the unexpectedly good things – the delicious hard cheeses, and the delicate home-baked biscuits. Even the drinks that come with the meal are regional: a stone tumbler of *cachaça da terra*, the home-produced sugar cane rum, smooth, viscous and with little relation to the factory-produced firewater; delicious *batidas*, and excellent liqueurs made from interior fruit – try the *genipapo* or the *goiaba*.

If you want to take your acquaintance with *cachaça da terra* a stage further, there is a good place to do so near *Raízes*: *Olho d'Agua*, Avenida Campos Sales 525, which specialises in the stuff, straight or flavoured with herbs and fruits, especially *cajú*. They sell bottles of your preferred rum with your name printed on the label as a souvenir.

Other good places are the *Bar do Cação* on the seafront near the fort, which does good oyster and shellfish dishes, and *Casa da Mãe* at Rua Pedro Afonso 230 in Petrópolis, which specialises in *galinha cabidela*, chicken stewed in a sauce enriched by its own blood and giblets. The giblets are sieved out before serving, and it's delicious.

Homesick Brits could try *Chaplin*, on the seafront at Praia dos Artistas, which as well as serving food has an area it advertises as "o pub inglé", which bears about as much relation to the real thing as you'd expect – but where you can play darts if you ask for the *dardos*.

Entertainment

Most of Natal's nocturnal action takes place on or around the beaches rather than in the centre. One good spot to head for is **Praia dos Artistas**, the stretch of beach about halfway between the fort and the headland, where Avenida 25 de Dezembro runs parallel to the seafront. By day you can relax on the beach, while on weekend nights you can dance to live regional music – *forró* a speciality – at the *Casa da Música Popular Brasileira*, a good *dancetaria* on Avenida 25 de Dezembro. It's much patronised by young couples and on Friday and Saturday it runs very late: tempting though it is to take the most direct route back to the centre afterwards, up the hill, it's dangerous late at night – take a taxi instead.

As most of the tourists are Brazilian, Natal is a good place for **music**, and several places along the seafront have live music and/or **dancing**. Try *Carinhoso* at Praia da Areia Branca, at the seafront Avenida Sílvio Pedrosa 95 (live music every night except Mon). There are also two good places next to each other on

Rua Dr. José Augusto at Praia dos Artistas: both *Calamar* at no. 2 (music Thurs–Sun) and *Asfarn* at no. 8 (music Wed–Sun) do good food and have fine sea views, but *Asfarn* just edges its rival. Either will do as a place to sip a *caipirinha* and watch the sunset, but even better is the *Canto do Mangue* on the banks of the river Potengi: it's a taxi-ride away near the municipal fish market in the *bairro* of Ribeira, where Rua Coronel Flaminio runs into Rua São João. It's also one of the best places to eat fish in the city and a speciality is fresh fish fried and served in tapioca with coconut sauce (*peixe ao molho de tapioca*).

South of Natal

Talking of things to do and places to go around Natal boils down to talking about **beaches**. The easiest southern beach to get to from Natal, and also the liveliest in either direction, is **PONTA NEGRA**, 10km out of town along the Via Costeira, with regular buses from the local bus station that you can catch from the seafront. It's a popular destination for people from the city, especially at weekends; there are bars with live music on Friday and Saturday nights and Sunday afternoons, and several **hotels** and *pousadas* if you feel like staying. The beach, incidentally, running along a sweeping bay, is magnificent.

After Ponta Negra, the sands get less crowded. The only problem is getting to them without a car, as there are usually only one or two buses a day to most of the villages from Natal's bus station: check the times with the tourist office, but they usually leave early in the morning and you may not be able to get back to Natal the same day. This is not a problem, though, since the coastline is beginning to be developed. The villages normally have a *pousada* or two, and it is easy to come to an arrangement about stringing up hammocks in bars and houses. An alternative way of reaching the beaches is to take a **bus** along the main BR-101 highway to Recife from the *Rodoviária*, and get off at NÍZIA FLORESTA, from where there are pick-ups, lorries and a local bus service along the dirt road to the coastal fishing villages and beaches of **BARRA DE TABATINGA** and **BÚZIOS**.

More direct is to take the bus from the Natal *Rodoviária* to **PIRANGÍ DO NORTE**, 30km out of town. (Another route to the same stretch of coast, but entering it from the north rather than the south, is to take a bus from either the *Rodoviária* or the local bus station, depending on which line you choose, to COTOVELO, from where you can walk or hop local buses south to Pirangí.) Apart from the beach, the village's other famous attraction is the biggest **cajú tree** in the world. Although Brazilians know *cajú* as a fruit the taste and colour of custard, its seeds, once roasted, become the familiar cashew nut. It's difficult to believe this enormous (over 7000 square metres) expanse of green leaves and boughs could be a single tree; it looks more like a forest. But it is, centuries old and with branches that have spread and put down new roots. It still bears over a ton of fruit annually, so it's not surprising that Pirangí is known for its *cajú*-flavoured rum.

North of Natal

Most of the recent hotel-building and development has been funnelled south of Natal by the building of the Via Costeira, which makes the **northern beaches** an attractive option. The two main places to head for are Redinha and Genipabú.

REDINHA, a small fishing village facing the city on the northern mouth of the Potengí river, marks the southern end of the enormous beach that effectively makes up the state's northern coastline. The beaches are notable for their huge shifting **sand dunes**, many metres high, which cluster especially thickly to tower over Genipabú. Redinha itself (hourly buses from the local bus station in Natal) is surprisingly underdeveloped for somewhere so close to the city, retaining the air of a simple fishing village, with a small chapel and beachside stalls that fry the freshly caught fish and chill the beer to wash it down with.

There are three ways to get to **GENIPABÚ**: by direct but infrequent bus from Natal's local bus station; by taking the Redinha bus until you reach the turn-off leading to the northern beaches, marked "Algimar", five minutes before Redinha itself; or, making a day of it, by taking the bus to Redinha and then walking the 8km along the huge and largely deserted beach.

Genipabú is still a fishing village, but these days depends more on tourism for its income. There's no need to look down your nose at it, though, as the beach is large enough for you to get away from the crowds. The massive dunes are spectacular and great fun to run down: the sand is so fine it often looks like it came from an egg-timer. A favourite local pastime is to roar up and down them in **beach buggies**, exhilarating but not for those who get travel sick easily. There are innumerable outfits and individuals offering rides by *bugre*, or you can hire them out (about $7 an hour). Good excursions along the dunes are to the mineral water spring at PITANGUI, and the lovely beach of JACUMÃ.

West to Ceará

The highway **west** to Fortaleza, capital of Ceará state (see below), would be one of the most dramatic in the region if it followed the coast: sadly, though, the BR-304, a good quality tarmac road, takes a more direct inland route and is pretty dull as a result. The **interior** of Rio Grande do Norte is flatter than the *sertão* of the states to the south, plains of scrubby *caatinga* and cacti only rarely broken up by hills or rocky escarpments. Even on a moving bus you can feel the heat, and you get some idea of why this is one of the poorest and most unforgiving areas in the Northeast. From Natal three daily **buses** make the 500-kilometre run to Fortaleza, taking around nine hours. It's a good stretch of road to do overnight: about the right length to get some sleep, and no spectacular scenery for you to regret missing.

Mossoró

The one place you might think of stopping off at before crossing into Ceará state is **MOSSORÓ**, in many ways an archetype of the *sertão* town in which so many of the inhabitants of the Northeastern interior live. Mossoró has a population of about 100,000 and is growing fast, although you wouldn't guess it from the centre, very much that of a small market town – market, square, and a couple of ornate, 1930s public buildings, with white plasterwork set off against walls of bright pink, looking for all the world like wedding cakes.

All the practical details
Mossoró is 276km from Natal, about four hours' drive, and served by several coaches a day. **Arriving**, the *Rodoviária* is on the edge of town and there are

regular **local buses** into the centre; or it's about ten minutes by taxi. It is easy to **get your bearings**, despite the lack of town maps and tourist information. The main street is **Avenida Augusto Severo**, which runs down past the municipal market and local bus station to the two linked squares which are the hub of the city, **Praça Vigário Antônio Joaquim**, where the cathedral is, and **Praça da Independência**. To the left is the road leading to the old jail and town museum; straight on takes you to the river Apodí, where – over the bridge – is a small **artesanato market** and a pleasant **bar**, *O Sujeito*, built on the riverbank. The best (but expensive – $20 minimum) **hotel**, the *Hotel Termas,* is a couple of kilometres out of town, built around some thermal pools. The others are simple and all in the centre of town: try the *Hotel Charlott*, Avenida Augusto Severo 143, which is clean and serves good regional food.

Leaving, you can get a bus to the *Rodoviária* from the small local bus station on the fringes of the municipal market.

The market and the battle of Mossoró

The quickest way to get a flavour of Mossoró is by wandering around the **municipal market**. It gives you an instant handle on the social and economic fabric of the *sertão*, both from the goods on sale – dried meat, medicinal herbs and barks, slabs of salt – and the wiry, straw-hatted peasants and townspeople milling around. The brightly painted lorries and buses, most of which you wouldn't see outside a museum in the developed world, are the more remote villages' only link with Mossoró and, through it, to the outside world. On the fringes of the market simple stalls sell food and rum and iced *caldo de cana* (sugar cane juice) to the shoppers, and small vendors spread their wares out on the pavement. Look for the *funilaria*, kerosene lamps and other simple household items made with great ingenuity from old tins.

However, the main places of interest in the city have to do with Mossoró's enduring claim to fame, a glorious moment in 1924 when the townspeople fought off a full-scale attack by the legendary bandit leader **Lampião** and his band. It's an event that's still celebrated every June 13 with Masses and re-enactments. To follow the Lampião trail, first stop is the **Igreja de Santo Antônio**, near the centre. In accordance with Northeastern form there was no question of a surprise assault when Lampião mounted his attack. He had announced his intention to hold the town to ransom well in advance and had taken landowners in the surrounding countryside hostage to show he meant business: an audacious thing to do, since even then Mossoró was the second city of Rio Grande do Norte. He sent two notes to the mayor demanding money, but the townspeople decided to resist him, digging trenches in the main streets and fortifying public buildings. On June 13, 1924, Lampião attacked with a band of about fifty outlaws, or *cangaçeiros*, and there was fierce fighting, concentrating on the church, where the mayor, his family and retainers had barricaded themselves in. By late afternoon the bandits were driven off with several wounded, one dead, and one famous black outlaw, Jararaca (see below), wounded and captured. Despite being a humiliating defeat for him, the battle of Mossoró became one of the most famous events in Lampião's much celebrated life. On the church there's a plaque commemorating the event, and you can still see the walls and tower pockmarked with bullet holes, carefully preserved.

The next step is to make your way to the **Museu Histórico Municipal**, housed in the oldest building in town, a solid early-nineteenth-century building that was once a jail and is now a combined museum and council chamber: it's signposted to the left from Praça Vigário Antônio Joaquim. It contains a remarkable collection of photographs and newspaper articles of the attack and its aftermath, together with things like guns used, clothing taken from the bandits, and maps of how the action developed. The most fascinating pieces are the powerful and eloquent photographs of the wounded **Jararaca**, kept in a cell in the very building which houses the museum. Jararaca was in jail for a day, treated by the town doctor, interviewed by the local paper, visited by town luminaries, constantly photographed by the town photographer, and then was taken out at dawn to the municipal cemetery, stabbed, thrown into an already open grave, and shot. Reading what he said that day, it's clear he knew his fate, but he expressed no fear or regret, only his determination to die like a man, which by all accounts he did. The final stop on the tour is a visit to his grave, in the **cemitério municipal** near the church. The grave isn't signposted but anyone, except a priest, will point you in its direction, left of the single path as you enter: just say *Jararaca* and look quizzical. The final twist is that the outlaw got his own back in death, becoming a mythical figure and saint for the poor of the region, despite attempts by the church and the municipal authorities to put a stop to it – hence the lack of a signpost and the fact there is no path to his grave. His grave is covered with flowers, candle stumps, *ex votos* and prayers written on scraps of paper, and regularly visited by supplicants. The best time to see this popular devotion in action is on December 13, when thousands flock to Mossoró from all over the interior of Rio Grande do Norte to celebrate the holy day of Santa Luzia, the city's patron saint.

CEARÁ

Ceará, about half the size of Britain but with only seven million inhabitants, has long borne the brunt of the vagaries of the Northeastern climate. Droughts were recorded here as early as the seventeenth century. Also, compared to the states to the south and east, the Portuguese arrived late, and colonisation didn't seriously begin until the eighteenth century. In the 1870s, as many as two million people may have died in a famine provoked by drought, and as recently as the early 1980s people were reduced to eating rats, while the populaton of Fortaleza grew by about a third as people fled drought in the interior.

Yet for all its problems Ceará has kept a strong sense of identity, making it a distinctive and rewarding state to visit. Its capital, **Fortaleza**, is the largest and most cosmopolitan city in the Northeast after Recife and Salvador. The **sertão** is unforgiving to those who have to live in it, but in Ceará it rewards the traveller with some spectacular landscapes: as you travel west the flat and rather dull plains of Rio Grande do Norte gradually give way to ranges of hills, culminating in the extreme west of the state in the highlands and lush cloud forest of the **Serra da Ibiapaba**, the only place in Brazil where you can stand in jungle and look down on desert. To the south there are the hills and fertile valleys of **Cariri**, with the pilgrim city of **Juazeiro do Norte** (covered under "Paraíba", above). And the coastline boasts some of the wildest, most remote and beautiful **beaches** in Brazil.

Save for a few sheltered valleys with relatively reliable rainfall, sugar cane does not grow in Ceará and it never developed into the plantation economy of other Northeastern states. Ceará was and remains **cattle** country, with the main roads and centres of population in the state following the route of the old cattle trails.

As settlement by the Portuguese, and serious economic development, began over a century later than in the sugar zone states, and only really got going in the last century, there are very few buildings that date back to colonial times – nothing colonial remains in Fortaleza, for example.

Fortaleza

FORTALEZA is a sprawling city of around 1.5 million inhabitants, and for well over a century it has been the major commercial centre of the northern half of the Northeast. More recently it has poured resources into expanding its tourist trade, lining the fine city beaches with gleaming luxury hotels. Taken together, this means that no trace remains of the city's eventful **early history**, the clue to which is in its name: Fortaleza means "fortress". The first Portuguese settlers arrived in 1603 and were defeated initially by the Indians, who killed and ate the first bishop (a distinction the city shares with Belém), and then by the Dutch, who drove the Portuguese out of the area in 1637 and built a fort of their own. In fact the Portuguese were restricted to precarious coastal settlements until well into the eighteenth century, when the Indians were finally overwhelmed by the determined blazing of cattle trails into the interior.

It was from Fortaleza that the independence movement from Portugal in northern Brazil was organised, and it was one of the few places where the Portuguese actually made a fight of it, massacring the local patriots in 1824 before being massacred themselves a few months later. The city did well in the **nineteenth century**, prospering as the port city of a hinterland where ranching was expanding rapidly. For decades, though, one of the city's most important exports was the people of the state. Coastal shipping lines transported *flagelados* wholesale from Fortaleza during drought years to the rubber zones of the Amazon and the cities of southern Brazil. And today, the city still acts as a staging post for migrants arriving from the interior looking to get out of the state. The welfare office for migrants, the *Posto de Apoio ao Migrante* at the *Rodoviária*, is one of the first things you see if you'll arrive by bus.

Orientation and arrival

The only visible legacy of this crowded history in modern Fortaleza is the city's name, and a gridded street pattern laid out in the nineteenth century by a French architect, Adolphe Herbster. He was contracted by the ambitious city fathers to turn Fortaleza into "the Paris of the North": you can only hope they got their money back.

The **layout of the city** is easy to grasp, despite its size. The **centre** is laid out in blocks and forms the commercial, administrative and religious heart, with markets, shops, public buildings, squares, and a forbiddingly ugly concrete cathedral. To the west of the centre undistinguished urban sprawl finally gives way to the beaches of **Barra do Ceará**, but most of the action is to the **east**, where the main city beaches and the chic middle-class *bairros* of **Praia de Iracema** and **Meireles** are to be found, linked by the main seafront road, **Avenida Presidente Kennedy**. These give way to the *favelas* and docks of the port area, **Mucuripe**, the gateway to the eastern beaches, notably **Praia do Futuro**, beyond which the city peters out.

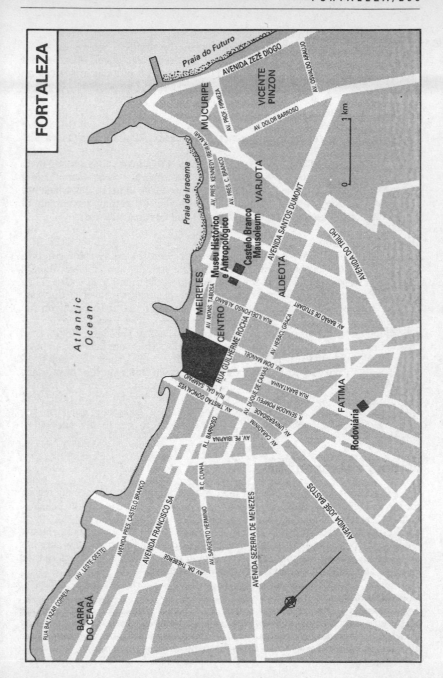

FORTALEZA

Atlantic Ocean

Praia do Futuro

Praia de Iracema

AVENIDA ZEZÉ DIOGO

AV. OSVALDO ARAUJO

VICENTE PINZON

AV. PROF. FIRMEZA

MUCURIPE

AV. DOLOR BARROSO

AV. KENNEDY (BEIRA MAR)

AV. PRES. C. BRANCO

VARJOTA

AVENIDA SANTOS DUMONT

AVENIDA DO TRILHO

Museu Histórico e Antropológico

Castelo Branco Mausoleum

MEIRELES

RUA ILDEFONSO ALBANO

ALDEOTA

AV. BARÃO DE STUDART

AV. MONS. TABOSA

CENTRO

RUA GUILHERME ROCHA

AV. HERACLY GRACA

AV. DOM MANOEL

RUA GAL. SAMPAIO

AV. TRISTÃO GONÇALVES

RUA DUQUE DE CAIXAS

RUA BARATANHA

R. SENADOR POMPEU

AV. UNIVERSIDADE

FATIMA

Rodoviária

AV. CARAÇONHA

R.L BARROSO

R.C. CUNHA

AV. PE. IBIAPINA

AVENIDA PRES. CASTELO BRANCO

AVENIDA FRANCISCO SA

AV. DR. THEBERGE

AV. SARGENTO HERMINIO

AVENIDA SEZERRA DE MENEZES

AVENIDA JOSÉ BASTOS

RUA BALTIZAR CORREIA

(AV. LESTE-OESTE)

BARRA DO CEARÁ

0   1 km

Arriving and getting around

The **Rodoviária** is some way from the centre in the southern suburb of Fátima. Numerous buses run into town – those marked *Aguanambí*, *Alencar* and *Ferroviária* are the most direct. The number and variety of **local buses** can be bewildering at first, especially as there are several **local bus stations**. The ones you are likeliest to use are in front of the railway station, on Praça Castro Carreiro, for routes heading east to the main city beaches; and on Praça Capistrano de Abreu, for buses to the western half of the city and the fishing villages and beaches of the western coast, like Caucaia, Paracuru, São Gonçalo do Amarante and Trairi.

For **getting around the city**, useful **bus routes** that take you out to the main beach areas and back to the city centre are those marked *Leste–Oeste*, *Caça e Pesca*, *Meireles*, *Mucuripe* and *P. Futuro*. There are loads of **taxis**, too, which are cheap even by Northeastern standards and essential for getting around late at night, when buses stop running to the beaches and far-flung suburbs.

Tourist information

Fortaleza is geared towards catering for visitors and the **tourist information posts** of the local tourist board, *EMCETUR*, are friendly and efficient, though there's relatively little in English save for sections of the monthly *Itinerário*. They give out excellent free city maps, and if you're planning to travel in the state outside Fortaleza you should stock up on the relevant literature here. If you can make a stab at reading Portuguese, the thick booklet *Roteiro Turístico do Ceará* is a thorough and invaluable guide to the main attractions of Fortaleza, the principal coastal beaches, and the larger towns of the interior. There are information posts open until 11pm in the airport and at the *Rodoviária* – the airport will book hotel rooms for you but the *Rodoviária* won't. The **main information post** (daily 8am–noon & 2–6pm) is in the old municipal city prison in the centre, on Rua Dr. João Moreira, and should be your first port of call: the staff know their stuff, speak all the major European languages, and are especially good on the complicated bus journeys that are often necessary to get to the out-of-town beaches.

Finding a place to stay

The cheapest hotels are, as ever, in the centre, which hums with activity during the day but empties at night, and the more expensive ones are out by the beaches, notably Praia de Iracema and Meireles. But this is not a hard and fast rule; there are literally hundreds of hotels of all shapes and sizes in the city, including luxury hotels in the centre and cheap ones in the beach areas, although very few bargains are to be had on the seafront itself. You should remember that Fortaleza can get very hot, and either air conditioning or a fan is essential.

Central hotels

The **cheapest hotels** are near the main *EMCETUR* post in the centre, and are clustered especially thickly along Rua Senador Pompeu: there is little to choose between the *Fortaleza Hotel* at no. 706, the *Savoy* at no. 492, the *Primavera* at no. 1012 and the *Maranhense* at no. 716. In the same area and price range, but with the advantages of looking onto the pleasant tree-shaded Passeio Público, is the *Passeio*

Hotel, Rua Dr. João Moreira 221. For a little more money – about $10 a night – you can stay at a number of very good value central hotels, the best of which is probably the *Hotel Caxambú*, near the cathedral at Rua General Bezerril 22, where the price includes air conditioning, private shower and a sumptuous breakfast. For location, it's pipped by the *Lord*, on the centre's largest square, Praça José de Alencar. Other good central options are the *Blumenau Hotel*, at Rua 25 de Março 705, and the *Chevalier*, just south of the centre at Avenida Duque de Caxias 465.

Beach hotels

The best bet if you want a beach hotel is to head for the eastern beach *bairros* of **Praia de Iracema** and **Meireles**. Although most of them are on the expensive side, moving only a block or two inland will save you considerable amounts of money. If you can't bear to be away from the sea, the best value of the luxury hotels is the *Samburá Praia*, Avenida Beira Mar 4530; or try the group of more modestly priced hotels at the very beginning of the beach, cheaper because you have to walk up a couple of hundred metres before the beach is clean enough to swim from – the *Iracema Plaza Hotel*, Avenida Presidente Kennedy 746, and the cheaper but dirtier *Brisa da Praia* at no. 982. In the same area is a cluster of reasonable hotels on Avenida Aquidabã: the *Marazul* at no. 412, the *Praia de Iracema* at no. 430 and the *Apart-Hotel Aquidabã* at no. 630. Remarkably, there is one genuinely **cheap** hotel, the *Hotel da Praia* at Avenida Presidente Kennedy 1696, right on the seafront sandwiched between far more expensive choices: it's almost certain to be bought out by developers in the not too distant future, but if it's still there it's easily the cheapest hotel on a prime seafront site.

Inland, there are any number of hotels a short distance from the sea. A popular option for younger Brazilian and foreign travellers is one of the many **pousadas**, smaller family-run hotels that come in all price ranges: popular and modestly priced are *Nossa Pousada* at Rua Ana Bilhar 123 in Meireles, and *Pousada da Praia*, Avenida Monsenhor Tabosa 1315. There are also scores of hotels in the blocks immediately inland from the seafront: recommended, in the order which you come across them heading out from the centre, are *Marina Praia Hotel*, Rua Paula Barros 44, Meireles; *Zen Praia Hotel*, Avenida Antônio Justa 1898; and the *Aldeota Praia Hotel*, Rua José Lourenço 459 – Aldeota is the transitional *bairro* between chic Meireles and the more downmarket Mucuripe.

Exploring the city

While not the most visually attractive of Brazilian city centres, there is enough going on in the heart of Fortaleza to merit more attention than it usually gets from visitors. It certainly can't be faulted for being boring: the streets are very crowded, with shops and hawkers colonising large areas of pavement and squares, so that much of the centre often seems like a single large market. Fortaleza is an excellent place for **shopping**, and you should stock up here if you're heading west, as you won't get comparable choice until you hit Belém, 1500km away. Clothes are plentiful and cheap, and Fortaleza is the largest centre for the manufacture and sale of **hammocks** in Brazil (see below). As ever, there is also good *artesanato* to be had, notably lace and leather. Tourists tend to do their shopping in a couple of obvious places, like around the *EMCETUR* tourist centre in the old prison, and in front of the seafront hotels in Praia de Iracema – you'll be able to bargain but the prices are, by Brazilian standards, relatively high.

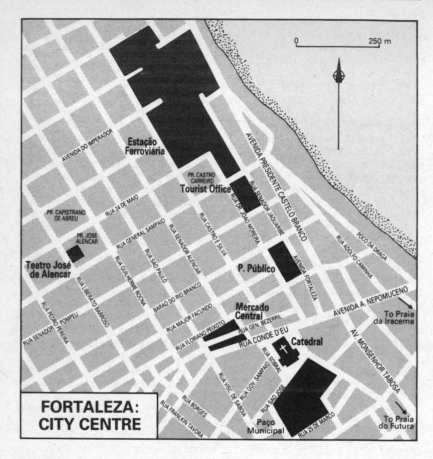

**FORTALEZA:
CITY CENTRE**

The Mercado Central: buying a hammock

Much better and more interesting, if you can take the dirt, the potholes, the smells and the crowds, is the **Mercado Central**, a huge commercial complex where hundreds of small stores and shops are jammed into a series of narrow streets and alleys. It's next to the cathedral, and if you can't see it you will probably be able to smell it, as it includes a large fish and meat market. This is the best place to **buy a hammock** in the city: if you're going to use one on your travels, purchase it with care. Cloth ones are the most comfortable, but are heavier, bulkier, and take longer to dry out if they get wet. Less comfy in the heat, but more convenient, much lighter and more durable are nylon hammocks. Aesthetically, however, nylon hammocks are no match for cloth ones, which come in all colours and patterns. You ought to be able to get a perfectly adequate cloth hammock, which will stand up to a few weeks travelling, for around $10 for a single and $15 for a double: for a nylon hammock, add $5 to the price. If you want a more elaborate one, and some handwoven hammocks are very fine, you will pay more. Easing the path to slinging hammocks once you get home are metal *armadores*, which many hammock and most hardware shops sell: these are hooks mounted on hinges and a plate with bolts for sinking into walls. When buying a hammock you are going to use, make sure it takes your body lying horizontally across it: sleeping along the curve is uncomfortably bad for your back.

The old prison: Museu de Arte e Cultura Popular

When you've finished shopping, drop in on the *EMCETUR* tourist centre in the **old prison** overlooking the sea at the bottom of Rua Senador Pompeu. This is not just to visit the tourist information post here, but to sit having a beer in a bar in the one-time exercise yard, shaded by mango trees, and to see the best museum in the city, the **Museu de Arte e Cultura Popular** (Mon–Sat 7am–6pm, Sun 7am–noon). Well laid out in a single huge gallery, this is a comprehensive collection of Cearense *artesanato* of all kinds, together with a sample of the painting and sculpture produced by the best of the state's modern artists. The imaginative juxtaposition of more traditional popular art with modernism is what distinguishes it, and the two collections dovetail neatly. Both are of very high quality: the modern art is often startlingly original, as in the sculptures of bolts, nuts and scrap metal of Zé Pinto, but in style and subject matter you can see how profoundly it is rooted in the tradition of popular art all around it. There is work in all Ceará's considerable range of materials and styles: leather, ceramics, wood carvings, lace, cloth, prints, *ex votos*, saints, *cordel*, and much more – all beautifully displayed. Wandering around is made easier by the design of the building, whose thick walls keep the heat out, leaving the interior pleasantly cool.

The Passeio Público and the Paço Municipal

Next to the prison is another survivor of nineteenth-century Fortaleza: the old municipal boulevard, the **Passeio Público**, now a pleasant shady square popular with children, families, and courting couples. It looks out over the waterfront, and stallholders set up chairs and tables under the trees, from where they sell cold drinks and simple food. It's a good place to go in the late afternoon or early evening, when the workers stroll around after they get out of their offices watching the variety of street entertainers and hawkers. The municipality often lays something on: small fairs, dances – the ubiquitous *forró* pumped out by Tannoy or thumped out by trios – or concerts. Even without entertainment, it has a relaxing feel, and is certainly the best place, away from the beaches, to watch the sunset.

Another refuge from the heat and the bustle is the **Paço Municipal**, behind the cathedral and within easy smelling distance of the Mercado Central. This was the site of the original nucleus of the city, the Dutch fort built in 1637, of which no trace remains. Now it houses the city council's office, a small **gallery** of modern art and, out the back, a small park with shady trees, a stall selling soft drinks, and a stream: don't drink the water.

Praça José de Alencar

The nerve centre of this part of the city, however, is its largest square, **Praça José de Alencar**, four blocks inland from the railway station at the heart of the commercial district. In the late afternoon and early evening, the crowds here attract *capoeira* groups, streetsellers of all kinds, and especially *repentistas*. Fortaleza seems to specialise in these street poets, who with great skill and wit gather an audience by improvising a verse or two about those standing around watching, passing around a hat for you to show your appreciation. If you refuse, or give what they consider too little, the stream of innuendo and insults, in a variety of complicated metres, is unmistakable, even if you don't understand a word.

On the square you'll also find the one truly impressive building in the city, the beautiful **Teatro José de Alencar**, named after the great nineteenth-century novelist and poet, a native of the city. Built in the first decade of this century, the fine tropical Edwardian exterior is in fact only an elegant facade, which leads into an open courtyard and the main body of the theatre. It was built in ornate and beautifully worked cast-iron sections, bolted together, which were brought over complete from Scotland and reassembled in 1910. Surprisingly, for a building made out of iron, it is extremely cool and pleasant to be in, even when the sun is at its height: the ironwork is open and lets in the air without trapping heat, a masterly example of Scottish design in the least Scottish setting imaginable. The theatre is very much a functioning building, though it's not open to the public during the day, unless it is hosting an exhibition or a recital. The best time to see it is at night, when it opens for business, a favourite venue for Cearense music of all varieties and exhibitions in the courtyard. Friday and Saturday are the likeliest nights to find something on: the *EMCETUR* staff can let you know what's happening, or try looking under the heading *Lazer* in the local papers.

If it's nightlife you want, however, the centre is not the place to find it: soon after dark it empties, and the focus of city life shifts towards the beach areas.

The city beaches

The main city beach is the **Praia de Iracema**, whose scores of apartment blocks and hotels laid out on a grid pattern are a resort by day and the main focus for Fortaleza's nightlife. The water is not as clean as it could be, due to the proximity of docks both east and west: the further away from the centre, the better for swimming. That said, Iracema is the best bet for sunset watching: the seafront boulevard is well laid out, punctuated by clumps of palm trees, and there is no shortage of watering holes.

If you're a beach devotee, cleaner water, higher rollers and better seafood is to be had further out past Mucuripe at **Praia do Futuro**: take buses marked *Caça e Pesca* or *P. Futuro* from Rua Castro e Silva in the centre, or *Mucuripe* to its terminal and make a connection. The beach *barracas* here are very good: the fried fish is fresh and comes in enormous portions. The only disadvantage is the irregularity of buses back to town, none at all running after dark, which makes watching the sunset here difficult unless you are prepared to pay $8 for a taxi.

A couple of museums

If you get bored with the beaches, there are two places worth seeing a few blocks inland from Iracema on Avenida Barão Studart. There's the shambolic but fascinating museum of the history of the state, the **Museu Histórico e Antropológico** at no. 410 and, right opposite, the unmistakable modernist rectangle of the **Mausoléu do Presidente Castelo Branco**, last resting place of the state's most famous son, the military president of Brazil from 1964 to 1966. The monument is a recent construction but already the concrete has streaked and the wood started to rot. This shabbiness seems thoroughly appropriate: it radiates embarrassment rather than pride and for good reason – Castelo Branco, who organised the coup of 1964 and became the military's first president, was the hinge of the door that slammed shut on Brazilian democracy in 1964. He stepped down in 1966 and was killed in an air crash near Fortaleza the following year. His role in the coup was never forgiven by most Brazilians and his premature death was seen as poetic justice. Not many people visit the deserted sarcophagus these days.

Much more fun is the **museum** (Tues–Fri 7.30am–12.30pm & 2.30–5.30pm, Sat & Sun 8am–noon & 2–6pm) directly across the road. In a macabre touch, in the garden facing the mausoleum is the prize exhibit: the crumpled wreck of the small plane in which Castelo Branco met his end! The museum itself has an eclectic collection of artefacts, photos and pictures jumbled together in no particular order, and little labelling, but it's interesting for all that. It is the only place outside the centre that you can get an idea of the history of the city, and there is a fascinating room that concentrates on the religious traditions of the state, with personal relics of Padre Cícero of Juazeiro do Norte (see p.243), and of the lesser known but equally interesting **Beato Lourenço**, a full-blown millenarian leader who split from Padre Cícero in the 1930s and founded the community of Caldeirão, near Juazeiro, in which food and the proceeds of work were shared equally. The landowners of the region denounced them as communists, and they were bombed out of existence by the Brazilian air force, in its first combat action, in 1937. It was one of the first bombings of civilians anywhere in the world, but the museum chooses not to tell you about that aspect of it: don't be deceived into thinking you're only dealing with folklore.

All the action: eating and dancing

You'll be alright in the centre during the day if you want something to eat as there are countless places to grab a snack. However, most central restaurants close at night and, anyway, you're much better off dining out around **Iracema beach**, which has the usual mix of bars, restaurants, tourists and cruising locals. Or try the fish restaurants at **Praia do Futuro** (see "The city beaches", above).

Forró: dancing and clubs

Although there's not the same interest in food as there is in, say, Natal, the city's redeeming feature is **forró**, for which Fortaleza is justly famous. Nowhere is it so popular and there is no better way to see what Cearenses do when they want to enjoy themselves than to spend the night in a *dancetaria* in Fortaleza. And spending the night is literally what you need to do: although most *dancetarias* open at 10pm, people don't really start arriving until around midnight, and peak time is in the early hours of the morning. Every night there will always be a *forró* on somewhere – check in local papers, or ask at *EMCETUR* – but Friday and Saturday nights are best.

The largest and most popular venue is also the most inaccessible; the *Clube do Vaqueiro*, way out on the periphery of the city along the BR-116 highway leading east to Natal. Given that *forró* there starts at 10pm, buses are impossible and a taxi is the only alternative: a round trip from the centre will set you back about $15, so make very sure there is actually something on before you go – usually there is *forró* every Wednesday and on two or three other evenings as well (☎229-2799 for details). As its name implies, the club has everything for the cowboy: the huge complex periodically hosts rodeos during the day, and at night the cavernous interior throbs with *forró* rhythms and hundreds of dancing couples. **Entrance** costs $2, and there is food and drink available, but the **dancing** is the thing – the local couples are a joy to watch.

Levanta Poeira, at the Mucuripe end of the seafront, is smaller but much easier to reach, with a fabulous seafront location at Avenida Presidente Kennedy 3988. It's strange to see this bare, unpretentious dance hall sandwiched between the luxury hotels and expensive restaurants of the most upmarket area of the entire city, but it's the highlight of the seafront in the smaller hours of the weekend: again, $2 to get in, simple food, booze, and the usual virtuoso dancing.

Around Fortaleza: the beaches

The **beaches** of Ceará are what attract most visitors and both east and west of Fortaleza they stretch unbroken for hundreds of kilometres. They are invariably superb, a mixture of mountainous sand dunes, palm trees and Atlantic breakers, wilder than the sheltered reef beaches of the southern states of the Northeast. Even some of the most remote beaches have been "discovered" by tourists, but there is no need to scorn them on that account: the coastline is more than big enough to swallow large numbers of property developers and visitors without getting crowded. It's easy to bewail the passing of the simple life in the fishing villages, but talk to their inhabitants and you'll find they are still functioning communities, making money from tourists on the side. What travellers see as an idyllic, rustic existence seems more like poverty to those who live it.

Any description of the beaches becomes repetitive: they are all stunning. Travelling along the coast, while often leisurely, is not difficult. To reach the beaches, as a rule, you will need to get off at a town and catch a connection to the nearby coast, and the local bus network covers most places: at the better known beaches, shoals of pick-ups and beach buggies meet the buses from Fortaleza.

Heading east: Aracati, Canoa Quebrada and around

East of Fortaleza there are two basic routes. The first heads along a coastal road that branches off the BR-116 just south of the city to Beberibe: at the *Rodoviária* the bus companies that run this route are *Empresa São Benedito* at kiosk 15 (2 daily as far as Iguape), or *Viação Aracati*, kiosk 5 (3 daily; can also be picked up in the centre from Praça Escola Normal).

The first coastal village is **AQUIRAZ**, where there are the beaches of **Iguape** and **Prainha**. From here the road continues for 30km to CASCAVEL, 12km inland but a starting point for two more beaches: **Caponga**, and, less crowded, **Aguas Belas**. Twenty kilometres further on is **BEBERIBE** itself, the drive there a lovely one on a country road through palm forests and dunes. The irregularly shaped dunes of Beberibe's beach, **Morro Branco**, are fifteen minutes away by local bus or an hour's walk. Five kilometres from here is the small fishing village and mineral water spring of **PRAIA DAS FONTES**.

Viação Aracati also run a more direct service to **ARACATI**, two hours from Fortaleza, a once-properous small textile town with half a dozen derelict, and a couple of functioning, eighteenth-century churches. It is also the jumping off point for one of Ceará's better known and most fashionable beaches, **Canoa Quebrada**, half an hour along a dirt road from Aracati: pick-ups meet every bus from the city so access is no problem. Canoa Quebrada is popular with foreigners and young Brazilians alike, the atmosphere is relaxed, and it's even fairly lively at night. Certainly, if you want company and *movimento* it's the beach to head for. Curiously, the beach served directly by asphalted road from Aracati,

Majorlândia, is less crowded and a lot quieter, which only goes to show how fickle tourists are. It's certainly as good as Canoa Quebrada, there are *jangadas* lined on the beach and surf here as well, and it's just as easy to stay.

West

The choice of strands **west of Fortaleza** is equally rich. Only 8km from Fortaleza is the fine beach of **Caucaia**, a favourite day trip for the city's inhabitants and crowded at weekends. To get there, take the *Empresa Vitória* bus from Praça da Lagoinha or Avenida Tristão Gonçalves, the broad road running up from the railway station in the centre of Fortaleza. From Caucaia, local buses head out to the beach villages of **ICARAÍ**, where even by Cearense standards the coastline is really something, with dunes, lagoons, palm forests and enormous expanses of sand: the road ends up in the fishing village of CUMBUCO.

Frequent buses from the Fortaleza *Rodoviária* (tickets from *Brasileiro Transporte*; kiosk 6) go to **SÃO GONÇALO DO AMARANTE**, only an hour from Fortaleza. From there, you can head on to the beaches of **Pecém**, 5km away, and the glorious palm-forest beach of **Taíba**, 6km on. Not all the buses to São Gonçalo continue to the beaches, but if not there are pick-ups and local buses and, as a last resort, it isn't too far to walk. The beach of **Paracurú** (frequent buses from the *Rodoviária*; also with *Brasileiro Transporte*) is being rapidly developed and gets crowded during weekends, but is less frenetic during the week.

After Paracurú, you head out of Fortaleza's influence and the further west you go, the less crowded the beaches become. A good place to head for, reasonably remote but not impossible to get to, is **TRAIRI**, served by direct buses from the *Rodoviária* in Fortaleza, which take around three hours. From here it's a few kilometres to the beautiful and usually deserted beaches of **Mundaú** and **Freicheiras**. When the tide is out, you can walk for an hour along the beach to the fishing hamlet of **GUAJIRU**. There is no electricity or running water, but the people are friendly and the scenery marvellous.

The increasingly popular beach of **Jericoacoara** is rapidly becoming the western counterpart to Canoa Quebrada, "discovered" and fashionable, but a lot more remote than Canoa Quebrada and unlikely to become as crowded: during the rains you can only get there by boat. For the rest of the year, take a bus from Fortaleza *Rodoviária* to GIJOCA, about an eight-hour journey, where pick-ups ($5 a head) meet the bus and take you over the dunes for an hour to Jericoacoara. The dunes here are huge, like hills, and there are a few bars where you can string hammocks.

On to Piauí: the Serra da Ibiapaba

Apart from the beaches, there is little to detain you as you head west from Fortaleza, though it's a fine drive, with rocky hills and escarpments rising out of the *sertão* and the road snaking through occasional ranges of hills. You pass through the state's second largest town, **SOBRAL**, an ugly industrial centre nestling in the middle of a spectacular landscape very typical of the interior of the Northeast: fiercely hot, cobalt blue skies, flinty hills and *caatinga*. It would be very easy to sit back, enjoy the scenery, and head directly west for Piauí and Maranhão in one go, but if you did you'd miss one of the finest sights Ceará state has to offer: the beautiful cloudforest and hills of the highlands that run down the border between Ceará and Piauí – the **Serra da Ibiapaba** – and the caves of **Ubajara**.

Serra da Ibiapaba

You reach the Serra on buses arriving from either east or west, along the BR-222 highway that links Fortaleza with Teresina, capital of the neighbouring state of Piauí. Get off at **TIANGUÁ**, on the Cearense side of the border: from here there are frequent local connections to the small village of Ubajara (see below), also served by direct buses from Fortaleza (*Ipu Brasília* line; kiosk 12).

Whether you approach from Teresina or Fortaleza the effect is the same. The buses drive across a bakingly hot plain, which begins to break up the nearer you get to the state border, rearing up into scattered hills and mesas covered with scrub and enormous cacti. Then on the horizon, in view hours before you actually start to climb it, all the hills seem suddenly to merge into a solid wall that rears up 900m from the parched plain below, its slopes carpeted with thick forest: the **Serra da Ibiapaba**.

Ironically, the abundance of the highland forest is part of the explanation for the parched landscape below. The sheer slopes of the serras are well watered because they relieve any clouds of their surplus water before they drift over the plains below. As the bus begins to climb, winding its way through gorges choked with forest, the broiling heat of the plain is left behind and the air gets fresher and more comfortable. When you reach the tableland on top, it seems another world. Everything is green and fertile: the temperature, warm but fresh with cool breezes, is an immense relief, and the contrast with the conditions only half an hour's drive away below couldn't be more marked.

In Tianguá, a pleasant, sleepy town, there is a good **hotel**, the *Serra Grande*, but it's best to press on to Ubajara, 15km away.

Ubajara: walks and views

En route you'll see how *nordestinos* treasure those few parts of the interior blessed with fertile soil and regular rainfall: the highlands are intensively farmed by smallholders and supply fruit, vegetables, sugar and manioc for the whole region. **UBAJARA** itself is a small, friendly village nestling in beautiful hills. There are a couple of simple but perfectly adequate **hotels** near the single church and quiet square, together with a couple of **bars** and **restaurants**. It's a pleasant, non-touristy place to stay, but probably the best option is to head the couple of kilometres out of town, along the road leading away from Tianguá, to the *Pousada da Neblina*. This is a comfortable place, standing in splendid isolation at the foot of a hill covered with palm forest, one of the finest locations for a hotel in the state. It has a restaurant and swimming pool and is remarkable value at $6 single, $8 double. The village taxi meets buses and there is a very occasional local bus, but it's also a very enjoyable walk. At night, staying in the *pousada*, you get an idea of why the forest here is so luxuriant: much of it is above cloud level, and the mists that envelop the jungle most evenings, a hauntingly beautiful effect, keep the forest constantly moist.

A twenty-minute walk along the road from the *pousada* leads to the gatehouse of the **Parque Nacional de Ubajara**, which ensures that the magnificent forest remains untouched. Continue past the gatehouse and you come to the *mirante*, a viewing platform with a small café built onto the rim of an escarpment. North and south the serra breaks into ridges covered with forest and tumbles down into the plain, which stretches as far as the eye can see. The view is broken up by jagged hills, towns and villages connected by vein-like roads, and the whole panorama is laid out as if seen from the cockpit of an aeroplane.

From here a **cable car** swoops down 400m to the cave complex of the **Grota de Ubajara**. It's been waiting to be repaired since it broke down in 1987, but if the cable car is working again it's an unforgettable ride, plunging down and skimming the top of the forest before arriving at the caves. If it's not, or you feel more adventurous, there is a **path** down which can be negotiated with a guide: on no account try it on your own; though it's not dangerous, you need somebody to make sure you don't stray off the path. The forest wardens, one of whom is always on duty at the gatehouse, will take you down if you make arrangements the day before. You'll be met at the gatehouse early in the morning, so you do the bulk of the walk before the heat gets up: take liquids, and wear trainers or decent walking shoes. Going down takes a couple of hours, returning twice that, but there are streams and a small waterfall to cool off in along the way. You should also take batteries for the wardens' torches if you want to **explore the caves**; huge caverns with grotesque formations of stalactites and stalagmites. Technically the wardens are meant to guide you as part of their job, but as they're extremely badly paid they appreciate some recompense for spending several hours of their time making sure you come to no harm.

PIAUÍ

Piauí is, as its inhabitants say, shaped like a ham, with a narrow neck of coastline 27km long that broadens out inland to cover an area roughly the size of Britain. It's a very distinctive state, but unfortunately most of the reasons for this are depressing. Despite its size it has less than two million inhabitants and by far the lowest population density in the Northeast. With virtually no natural resources except the *carnaúba* palm, and subject to drought, it is also Brazil's poorest state.

Few travellers spend much time in Piauí. The capital, **Teresina**, is strategically placed for breaking the long bus journey between Fortaleza and São Luis, but it's a modern, rather ugly city where the heat can be oppressive. The southern half of the state merges into the remoter regions of Bahia and forms the harshest part of the Northeast. Much of it is uninhabited, largely trackless, arid badlands, in the midst of which lies, ironically, the oldest inhabited prehistoric site yet found in Brazil. Cave paintings show that this desert was once jungle. Other than the capital, there are two places worth making for: the pleasant coastal town of **Parnaíba**, which has excellent beaches, and the **Parque Nacional de Sete Cidades**, good walking country with weird and striking rock formations. For some reason, this poorest of states has an excellent **highway** system and the main roads between Teresina and Parnaíba and towards Ceará are very good: as the country is largely flat, the buses really fly.

Piauí was sparsely settled by cattle drovers moving westwards from Ceará in the second half of the eighteenth century, and has a violent history. The few Indians were never really conquered and were assimilated with the newcomers rather than being defeated by them, leaving their imprint in the high cheekbones and copper skin of a strikingly handsome people. Apart from cattle, the only significant industry revolves around the **carnaúba palm**, a graceful tree with fan-shaped leaves that grows in river valleys across the northern half of the state. The palm yields a wax that was an important ingredient of shellac, from which the first gramophone records were made, and for which there is still a small export market. It's also a source of cooking oil, wood, soap, charcoal and nuts, and many livelihoods depend on it.

The Parque Nacional de Sete Cidades

The **Parque Nacional de Sete Cidades** comprises thirty square kilometres of nature reserve which could hardly be more different from the forest reserve of Ubajara a couple of hundred kilometres west. Here it's the spiky, semi-arid vegetation of the high *sertão* that is preserved – gothic cacti and stubby trees. The really special feature of the reserve is its eroded **rock formations**, many streaked with prehistoric rock carvings. From the air they look like the ruins of seven towns, hence the name of the area, and their striking shapes have given rise to all sorts of ridiculous theories about the area having been a Phoenician outpost in the New World. In fact the rock sculpting is the entirely natural result of erosion by wind and rain.

There are two ways of **getting to the park**, depending on whether you approach from Ceará state or elsewhere in Piauí. Coming **from Ceará**, get off the bus at the town of PIRIPIRI, from where a free bus or transit van leaves at 6am (Tues–Fri) and takes you to the national park hostel run by the *IBDF*, the Brazilian forestry service. If you arrive too late, or on a day when the bus isn't running, take a local bus from Piripiri to the turn-off to the park 15km north, and either walk (3hr) or hitch from there. Thumbing a ride around here is easy, since foreigners are such a rarity that the first car to pass invariably stops. Coming **from Teresina or Parnaíba**, get a bus to PIRACURUCA and from there hitch a lift or take a taxi to the park – the taxi ride costs about $10. If you need to stay to catch a bus, there are perfectly adequate, cheap and clean **hotels** near the bus stations in both Piripiri and Piracuruca; and there's accommodation in the park itself, see below.

Despite such good facilities and its position near the main Teresina–Fortaleza highway, not as many people visit the park as you might expect. Consequently, it's the ideal place to get off the beaten track without actually venturing far from civilisation.

Into the park

There are two **places to stay** in the park, both of them more than acceptable. At the entrance is the moderately priced *Fazenda Sete Cidades*, with a restaurant, pool, and regular pick-up shuttle into the park itself, which you can use whether you stay there or not. More convenient for walking, and just as comfortable, is the cheaper *IBDF* **hostel** in the centre of the park, again with a restaurant and bathing nearby in a natural spring.

Walking in Sete Cidades is not difficult, There are a series of **trails** and several **campsites**, and the staff at both the *Fazenda* and the hostel are good at suggesting routes; there are very cursory sketch maps on sale, but don't rely on their accuracy. The walks are not especially strenuous, but take care all the same. It gets extremely hot and a stout pair of shoes, plenty of liquids and a broad-brimmed hat are essential. Start out as near sunrise as you can manage, when the park is at its most beautiful. And when you approach the rocks make some noise: rattlesnakes sometimes sun themselves on them, but they are very shy and slither away if they can hear you coming. The **rock formations** themselves make very good landmarks and their different shapes have lent them their names: the "Map of Brazil", the "Tortoise", the "Roman Soldier", the "Three Kings", the "Elephant" and so on.

Carnaúba country: Parnaíba

Heading **west** from Ceará or from Sete Cidades towards Amazonia, there are two routes you can follow. The fastest and most direct is simply to take the highway through Teresina and on to São Luis, or, a day from Teresina, to Belém and Amazonia proper. But if you have the time, there is a much more interesting and scenic route **north** up the BR-343 highway, a fine drive through a plain studded with *carnaúba* palm plantations to Parnaíba and the coast. From Parnaíba there is a direct bus service, over country dirt roads that get seriously difficult to travel in the rainy season, to São Luis, capital of neighbouring Maranhão state, where the Amazon region begins.

Parnaíba

PARNAÍBA, with its attractive natural anchorage on the river Igaraçu, was founded over fifty years before Teresina. For the Portuguese, it was the obvious harbour from which to ship out the dried meat and *carnaúba* of the interior and, in the nineteenth century, it was a thriving little town: you can still see the chimneys of the cotton factories put up by British entrepreneurs a century ago. Then the river silted up, the port moved to Luiz Correia at the mouth of the river, and the town slipped into decline. Today, Parnaíba has a lazy feel, but is still the second largest city in the state with around 60,000 inhabitants. Located anywhere else it would be a thriving resort town; the **beaches** nearby are excellent.

The modern **Rodoviária** is on the edge of town and buses for the short ride to the centre leave from outside. The centre is small and contains all Parnaíba's **hotels**, the best of which is the *Cívico*, Avenida Chagas Rodrigues 474. There's also cheap but clean accommodation at the *Marimbá*, on Avenida Capitão Claro, and other modest hotels near the main square, Praça da Graça. Or stay out at the coastal village of Luiz Correia (see below) and its beaches Atalaia and Coqueiro: hourly buses to Luiz Correia and Atalaia leave from the local bus station next to Praça Santo Antônio, three blocks along the pedestrianised shopping street that leads down from Praça da Graça.

There is not too much to do in Parnaíba except waste time pleasantly. The commercial area in the centre is busy, and **Praça da Graça**, with its palms and cafés, is an enjoyable place to hang about. The liveliest place in town, though, is the riverfront **Avenida Nações Unidas**, a grandiose name for a small promenade lined with cafés and restaurants, and the only place you can stay out reasonably late.

Around Parnaíba

You might as well follow the locals and head off to the **beaches** if you want to relax. Not served by bus, but only a short taxi ride away, is the **Lagoa do Portinho**, a freshwater lake with palms and simple chalets to stay in, and a good restaurant.

There are simple hotels and *dormitórios* if you want to stay in **LUIZ CORREIA**, basically a fishing village 8km north of Parnaíba, with a small modern port attached. From here you can either walk or get the bus to the huge and popular **Praia de Atalaia**. At weekends practically the entire population of Parnaíba decamps here and the crowded bars reverberate to *forró* trios.

A less crowded beach, **Coqueiro**, is 12km from here, but there are only a couple of buses a day. Hitching is easier and quicker, but there's little traffic there on weekdays – ask around in Luiz Correia.

Local buses to Luiz Correia and Praia de Atalaia leave from the terminus next to Praça Santo Antônio in Parnaíba; they take about twenty minutes to arrive in Luiz Correia, and another five to hit the beach – stay on till the end of the line to be dropped at the liveliest stretch.

Teresina

People from **TERESINA** tell a joke about their city: "Why do vultures fly in circles over Teresina? Because they glide with one wing and have to fan themselves with the other!" Brazil's hottest state capital, Teresina sits far inland on the east bank of the river Parnaíba, where it bakes year round in an *average* temperature of 40°C (which means it regularly gets hotter than that). The rains, meant to arrive in February and last for three or four months, are not to be relied upon. Ironically, twice in the last five years, they have actually flooded Teresina – you can't win against the weather in this part of Brazil. Unless you're used to such heat, you'll find it tiring to move around; rooms with at least a fan, and preferably air conditioning, are a necessity.

There's not a great deal to do or see in Teresina, but there's enough to occupy yourself for a day if you feel like breaking the long bus journey from Ceará. Besides having some comfortable hotels, it's the only place between Fortaleza and São Luis where you can do things like have money cabled out to you and cash travellers' cheques.

Arriving and finding a place to stay

The **Rodoviária** is on the outskirts of the city and has a **tourist information post** run by the state tourist organisation *PIEMTUR*: pick up free booklets with a centrefold city map. Frequent buses run into the centre from outside, and there are cheap taxis, too.

All **hotels** are in the central district, nearest the river. Overlooking the river itself is the luxury *Luxor Hotel do Piauí*, while cheaper places nearby are around Praça Saraiva: the *Fortaleza* on the square itself; the *Vitória* at Rua Senador Pacheco 1199; and the *Central*, at Rua Treze de Maio 85 – all are cheap ($5–10) but adequate places. Reasonable middle-range hotels are the *Royal Palace*, Rua Treze de Maio 233, the *Sambaíba*, Rua Gabriel Ferreira 230, and the *Teresina Palace*, Rua Paissandú 1219.

Around the centre: markets and museums

Thankfully, in such a hot place, most of the things worth seeing and doing are reasonably close to each other. The best place to start is the **market** that occupies most of the main square of the city, technically called Praça da Bandeira, but universally known by its old name, **Marechal Deodoro**. It's a smaller, more urbanised version of the Northeastern market, with packed stalls forming narrow streets, determined shoppers, energetic sellers, noise, loud music and plenty of *caldo de cana* kiosks, where you can slurp freshly crushed sugar cane and watch the city at work. There is *artesanato* scattered around, and the hammocks from the interior are high quality: both are cheaper here than in the craft shops run by *PIEMTUR*.

Overlooking the market, in one of the very few fine old buildings in the city, the **Museu do Piauí** at Marechal Deodoro 900 (Tues–Sat 8am–5.30pm, Sun 8–11am) is definitely worth seeing. A governor's palace in the nineteenth century, it has been beautifully restored, with the exhibits well displayed in simple but elegant rooms, many with high arched windows and balconies perched just above the crowded market stalls. The collection is the usual eclectic mix, and pride of place must go to a collection of early radios, televisions and stereograms, a must for lovers of 1950s and 1960s kitsch; and to the collection of art and *artesanato* in the Sala de Arte Popular and the Sala dos Artistas Piauienses. There are fine examples of the two things that distinguish *artesanato* in Piauí, sculpture in straw and beautifully tooled leather. The art is vivid, simple and varies from the strikingly good to the awful.

You might also want to investigate the crafts and culture complex run by *PIEMTUR*, the **Centro de Comercialização Artesanal**, in the old military barracks at Rua Paissandú 1276, overlooking Praça Dom Pedro Segundo. It's small, but a pleasant place to wander around: the *artesanato* is laid out in booths and is good quality, although a little expensive; the leatherwork is especially good. Upstairs is a nice café with restaurant attached, where the *carne do sol* is good.

Restaurants and nightlife

The city's **nightlife** lacks the focus of the coastal capitals, but there is life after dark. The bank of the river Parnaíba is the best place from which to enjoy the sunset. A kilometre or so south of the centre, along the riverfront road, is **Prainha**, a series of bars and restaurants built along the riverbank, shaded by planted trees: buses (*Prainha*) run there, but are very infrequent by late afternoon – use the taxis in Teresina, which are cheap.

There are good **restaurants** in the city and the air-conditioned ones have one very obvious thing in their favour. Although the food is good the prices are medium to expensive, rather than cheap – the ritziest is the restaurant of the *Luxor Hotel*, called *Forno e Fogão*, where it's worth paying a little more for good **regional food**, given the comfort and level of service. Otherwise, good seafood is to be had at *Camarão de Elías*, Avenida Pedro Almeida 457, in the *bairro* of São Cristóvão, near the centre. Piauienses excel at meat: try the *cabrito*, young goat, deliciously tender and served either roasted over charcoal, or *ao leite de coco*, stewed in coconut milk. Good places are *Asa Branca*, Avenida Frei Serafim 2037, in the centre, with live music (Thurs–Sat); and *Celso's Drinks*, Rua Angélica 1059, a short taxi-ride away in the *bairro* of Fátima.

MARANHÃO

Maranhão is where the separate but interlinked worlds of the Northeast and Amazonia collide. Although classed as a Northeastern state by Brazilians, its climate, landscape, history, and capital of **São Luis** are all *amazônico* rather than *nordestino*. Maranhão is the only state in the Northeast which more people migrate to than emigrate from. Drought is not a problem here; the **climate** is equatorial – humid, hot and very wet indeed. The rainy season peaks from January to April, but most months it rains at least a little, and usually a lot – although only in concentrated, refreshing bouts for most of the year. Maranhão has more fertile, well-watered land than the rest of the Northeast put together. Much of it is flat, the east and north covered with palm forest, and the centre and west riddled, in typical Amazonian fashion, with large rivers and fertile riverine plains – one of the main rice-producing areas of Brazil.

Further west begins the tropical forest and savanna of Amazonia proper, as you hit the eastern boundary of the largest river basin in the world. The **coast** also changes character: the enormous beaches give way, from São Luis westwards, to a bewildering jumble of creeks, river estuaries, mangrove swamps and small islands, interspersed with some of the most remote beaches in Brazil – three hundred miles of largely roadless coastline with towns and villages accessible only from the sea.

Like most zones of geographical transition, Maranhão also marks a historical and cultural divide. The **people** are a striking contrast to the ethnic uniformity of the states immediately to the east: here blacks, Indians and Europeans form one of the richest cultural stews to be found in Brazil. Catch the great popular festival of **Bumba Meu Boi** in June and you'll get some idea of how different from the rest of the Northeast Maranhão really is.

The main centres of population in the state are on and around the island of São Luis, and deep in the interior along the banks of the river **Tocantins**, a tributary of the Amazon but a mighty river in its own right. The contrast between the two regions could hardly be more stark. Only thirty years ago the Tocantins river was the boundary between Brazil and largely unknown Indian country. Today, as people flood into eastern Amazonia, **Imperatriz**, with nearly 250,000 inhabitants, is the second city of the state, and even dozy, historic São Luis, founded in 1612, is being transformed by docks and factories linked to the huge development projects of eastern Amazonia – the subject of much international controversy.

Routes into Maranhão: from the east

There are two **routes** into Maranhão from the east; scooting along the good asphalted highway that links Teresina to São Luis, an eight-hour coach ride; or lurching along country roads from Parnaíba, which is more interesting but not to be attempted in the rainy season, when the non-asphalted roads in Maranhão become quagmires. Either way, there's little to detain you before you get to São Luis and you can watch the land transform itself into the tropics along the way. The *carnaúba* palm of Piauí gives way to the taller trunk and straight fronds of the most common tree in Maranhão, the **babaçú palm**, on which even more livelihoods depend than on *carnaúba*: it provides nuts, cooking oil, soap, charcoal, rope fibre, timber and thatch.

Some time before you reach the arched bridge that connects the island of São Luis to the mainland, you are already driving through **palm forests** that are themselves only a preliminary to the rainforest proper further west. São Luis, a city built across the junction of two rivers and the sea, on an island within the larger delta formed by the **Pindaré** and **Itapicurú** rivers, has the umbilical connection with rivers that marks an Amazon city, but is also a seaport with ocean beaches.

São Luis

SÃO LUIS is a poor city, the most emphatically Third World of all the state capitals of the Northeast.

It smells, the streets are grimy and potholed, there are power cuts, things don't work, the historic city centre is literally falling to pieces, and the infant mortality rate is 136 per thousand live births, putting São Luis up there with poor African countries. Sometimes it even looks like an African city as it has a huge black population, a legacy of plantation development during the eighteenth and nineteenth centuries. It is also far larger than it seems from the compact city centre; about 700,000 people live here, most of them in sprawling *favelas*, with the middle classes concentrated in the beach areas of Ponta da Areia, São Francisco and Olho d'Agua, linked to the rest of the city by a ring road and the bridge built out from the centre across the river Anil.

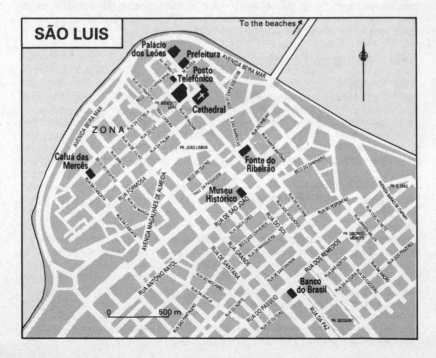

But, for all its problems, São Luis is still a fascinating place, undeservedly neglected by travellers. Even in its decayed state, the historic centre is one of the largest and most impressive complexes of **colonial architecture** in Brazil. In a way, its dilapidation lends it a unique atmosphere: there are people packed cheek by jowl, workshops, stalls, brothels, *dormitórios* – in short, a living and breathing heart of a city, not something lifelessly preserved for consumption by outsiders. The **beaches**, too, are magnificent, and for the most part have been spared the intrusive urban development of some city beaches in Brazil. Above all, try to visit in June, when you can enjoy the festival for which the city is famous – **Bumba Meu Boi**; here, it counts for more than Carnaval.

Arriving and orientation

The squalid **Rodoviária** is near the centre; any of the local buses from the stop to the left of the entrance will get you to the heart of town in about fifteen minutes. **Taxis** from the bus station operate on a coupon system; tell the man handing out chits where you're going ("Centro", or "Calhau" or "São Francisco" if you want to stay on a beach) and get a coupon with the fare you should pay printed on it.

The **city's central layout** is easily grasped. Built on a headland that slopes down to rivers on two sides, the largest square is **Praça Deodoro**, from where the narrow but crowded Rua da Paz and Rua do Sol, each only with room for one lane of traffic and perilously tight pavements, lead down to **Praça João Lisboa**, which marks the edge of the **Zona** – the nickname for the colonial core of the city. From here steep streets lead down to the river waterfront. It's on the buildings fronting Praça João Lisboa that you will first see the lovely, glazed tile frontages, the *azulejos*, that are the city's signature*.

Information and getting around

São Luis doesn't make life easy for its visitors. *MARATUR*, the local tourist board, has an **information office** near the cathedral, on Avenida Dom Pedro Segundo, but in the unlikely event of it being open the only thing it has on offer is a brochure with a rough sketch map of the city centre – actually worse than useless, because it doesn't name even the most important streets and squares.

Local buses, essential for getting around the urban sprawl, have no central-ised station: you have to mill with the crowds at the few strategically placed central **bus stops** – most of which aren't marked. The most useful is at the bottom of Rua da Paz, for buses to the *Rodoviária* (*Alemanha*), the beach and residential suburb of Olho D'Agua, and the out-of-town fishing villages of Raposa and Ribamar; all of these buses can also be caught opposite the *Banco do Brasil* building on Praça Deodoro. For the beaches nearer the centre, and the hotels scattered around the beach areas, take buses marked *P. Areia*, *São Francisco* or *Calhau* from the stop on Rua dos Remédios, the street that goes down past the *Banespa* building on the corner with Deodoro.

---

*Salvador has finer individual examples of *azulejo*, but taken as a whole the *azulejos* of colonial São Luis are unmatched for the scale of their use and their abstract, almost Arabic beauty. Most are early-nineteenth-century; some, with characteristic mustard-coloured shapes in the glazing, date back to the 1750s. Remarkably, many of the oldest tiles arrived in São Luis by accident, as ballast in cargo ships.

Finding a place to stay

Places to stay are divided between the beaches and the centre: there are a few medium-range beach places but no cheap ones. Although São Luis has relatively few hotels, finding somewhere is rarely a problem.

The best **central** hotel is the luxury-class *Vila Rica* on the imposing Avenida Dom Pedro Segundo. There is an equally sumptuous *Quatro Rodas* out on Calhau beach, nicknamed "Paraíso dos Gringos" by the locals. Medium range hotels in the centre are the *Hotel Central*, overlooking the small but lovely Praça Benedito Leite, the *Lord* at Rua Joaquim de Távora 258, and the *Solar do Carmo* nearby. **Cheaper**, but on the squalid side, are the *Atenas Palace* at Rua Antônio Raiol 431, and the many *dormitórios* in the **Zona**: best bets here are the *Estrela*, Rua da Estrela 370, in a crumbling but still impressive colonial building, and the *Solar do Imperador*, next door to the *Hotel Central*. Best option of all, though you'll need an *IYHF* card, is the **youth hostel**, in a restored colonial mansion at Rua 14 de Julho 93: very central, a beautiful place to stay and dirt cheap.

Beach hotels cluster thickest in São Francisco, next to the beach at Ponta da Areia, but even this close to the city centre there are very few of them. The nearest to the beach is the *Ponta da Areia*, Avenida dos Franceses 13, and there's also the *São Francisco* and the *Panorama Palace* a few blocks inland – you'll pay at least $20 single at any of them. There is a cheaper *pousada*, *Tia Maria*, at Quadra 1, Lote 12 in Ponta da Areia, but the best option if you just want a beach is the *Chalé da Lagoa*, on the island's finest beach of **Araçagí**, 15km out of town; see under "Beaches", below, for details on getting there.

The Zona

The **Zona** covers a small headland overlooking the confluence of the river Anil and the Atlantic Ocean, and though it may not look like much, a defensible harbour on this flat coastline was of some strategic importance. Now the waterfront is no more than a landing place for fishing boats and ferries, but slave ships once rode at anchor here, bringing in workers for the cotton and sugar plantations upriver. Then, the harbour was crowded with cargo boats, mostly from Liverpool, shipping out the exports of what – from about 1780 to 1840 – was a prosperous trading centre, for the first and last time in its history.

But the Zona predates even that colonial boom. São Luis shares with Rio the distinction of having been founded by the French, and is the only city in Brazil to have been ruled by three European countries. The French, decimated by a lethal combination of malaria and Indians, were soon dislodged by the Portuguese in 1615; then the Dutch sacked the city and held the area for three years from 1641, building the small fort that now lies in ruins on a headland between Calhau and Ponta da Areia. Over the next hundred years, the original shacks were replaced by some of the finest colonial buildings in northern Brazil. Many have fallen into decay, but you can get a taste of the period on the imposing **Avenida Dom Pedro Segundo**, the eastern boundary of the colonial zone, where the governor's palace and the *prefeitura* dominate the brow of the hill that looks out across the river.

A walking tour

The only way to **explore the Zona** is on foot. A good place to begin is Praça Benedito Leite, in front of the *Hotel Central*; the café next door to the hotel is a

favourite place for people to meet. The cathedral is ugly, but the complex of official buildings that stretch out before it on Avenida Dom Pedro Segundo are splendidly proportioned survivors of the pre-Baroque colonial era.

The oldest is the municipal hall, on the corner next to the *Panorama* café,
which dates from 1688: it still houses the *prefeitura* and is called the **Palácio La
Ravardiere**, after the French buccaneer who founded São Luis and is commemo-
rated by a piratical bust on the pavement outside. In November 1985 the building
was torched by an angry crowd, with the newly elected mayor inside, after an
election acrimonious even by Maranhense standards. While it was encouraging
to see the people participating so directly in the political process, it's a pity this
historic building was the one to be damaged: restoration work has closed it for
the time being. Next door, barring another outburst of popular discontent, is the
tropical Georgian elegance of the state governor's residence, the **Palácio dos
Leões** (Mon, Wed & Fri 3–6pm), built between 1761 and 1776. A lovely building
with magnificent views across the bay, it's worth taking the trouble to be there for
its limited opening hours, if only to walk on the beautiful hardwood floors, over
two centuries old. The palace should be open at the times given; official visits,
elections and political crises permitting.

Opposite the Palácio dos Leões, steps lead down to the steep colonial street,
Beco Catarina Mina, that takes you to the heart of the Zona, block after block of
buildings, some restored but mostly crumbling. With its cobbled streets, *azulejos*
and the vultures on the tile roofs, the Zona remains physically much as it was 150
years ago, although the colonial merchants and plantation owners who built it
would have turned up their noses at its modern inhabitants. As economic decline
bit deep, they sold up and moved on: their town houses were split into tenements,
a red-light district grew up from the waterfront, and much of the Zona is now like
an eighteenth-century *favela*. It's not dangerous to wander around, however,
except late at night.

Beco Catarina Mina runs into the finest array of *azulejos* in the city, the tiled
facades of the **Praça de Portugal**, with the **Mercado da Praia Grande**'s
gorgeous arches perfectly set off by the piercing blue tiles, symmetrical windows
and balconies of Rua do Trapiche. The market is hidden, with the entrances sunk
into arcades: it smells of fish, fruit and spices, and the *lanchonetes* here serve the
best cheap food in town. The streets around here, the heart of the Zona, are the
most interesting in the city. At siesta time, when there are no cars, you don't have
to close your eyes to slip back a couple of centuries.

The **churches** have exteriors that date for the most part from the seventeenth
century. The most beautiful are the Byzantine domes of the **Igreja do Desterro**
at the southern end of the Zona, but none of the church interiors has survived
successive restorations. It was in these churches that the Jesuit **Padre Antônio
Vieira** preached his sermons 300 years ago, berating the plantation owners for
enslaving Indians before the Jesuits had a chance to do so; sermons which are
often taken to be the finest early Portuguese prose ever written.

Three good museums

Nearest to the Praia Grande market, the **Centro Cultural Domingos Vieira**, Rua
28 de Julho 221 (Mon–Fri 8am–6pm), is a high quality collection of *artesanato*
housed in one of the few colonial mansions in the Zona to have been restored to its
former glory. Out back there is a shaded courtyard and a stall selling soft drinks,
while the highlight of the collection is the display of decorated *bois* upstairs, the

centrepiece of the *bumba-meu-boi* troupes that swirl through the city streets on June nights. If you can't be here then, these fantastically decorated dancing bulls, dripping sequins, velvet and ribbons, give you an idea of what you've missed.

Further up is the **old slave market**, a small, sinister-looking whitewashed building on Rua da Cascata, behind the military police barracks. Its old name was **Cafuá das Mercés** and it now houses, fittingly, the **Museu do Negro** (Tues–Fri 2–5.30pm). Slaves who survived the journey across from West Africa were marched up here from the harbour and kept in the holding cells until they could be auctioned off in the small square outside. Many people died of disease and cruelty, and the place still has an eerie, sombre atmosphere, with little light or air filtering in through the thick walls and barred windows. It's a small but excellent museum. Downstairs there are panels explaining the slave trade and the history of the building, with a horrifying display of whips, stocks, manacles, and even a muzzle. Upstairs, there is heartening proof of how black culture survives and prospers in modern Maranhão, with photographs of *mães e pais de santo*, the leaders of the many Afro-Brazilian religions that flourish in São Luis, some dating back to the 1920s and all in splendid regalia. It's worth remembering that some of the patriarchs and matriarchs you see here would have lived through slavery, Brazil being one of the last countries to abolish it, in 1888. The attendants at the museum are good people to ask about seeing *Tambor de Minas*, the variety of *candomblé* most popular in the city: if they like the look of you, they'll tell you where to go and when.

Completing an exceptionally good trio of museums is the **Museu Histórico e Artístico** (Tues–Fri 2–6.30pm, Sat & Sun 3–6pm), in a splendidly restored early-nineteenth-century town house at Rua do Sol 302, just outside the Zona. A more traditional museum than the other two, concentrating on high art and artefacts rather than popular culture, it is still very good. The seventeenth- and eighteenth-century religious art of Maranhão rivals any in the Northeast, but only what little survived wars and the plundering of corrupt politicians is displayed here.

One more place worth seeing is just outside the Zona proper: the **Fonte do Ribeirão**, the old public fountain. Built in 1796, it's one block north from the bottom of Rua do Sol. Sunk into a cobbled square, surrounded by the unspoilt colonial houses of the Largo do Ribeirão and crowned by two young imperial palms with their characteristically bulbous trunks, it's a pleasant place to end your tour of the Zona with a cold beer.

Bumba-meu-boi

Bumba-meu-boi, which dominates every June in São Luis, is worth making some effort to catch: there's no more atmospheric popular festival in Brazil. A dance with distinctive music, performed by a costumed troupe of characters backed by drummers and brass instruments, it blends the Portuguese, African and Indian influences of both the state and Brazil. It originated on the plantations, and the troupes the Maranhenses rate highest still come from the old plantation towns of the interior – Axixá, Pinheiro and Pindaré. To mark the day of São João on **June 24**, the interior towns send their bands to São Luis, where at night they sing and dance outside churches and in squares in the centre. Seeing the spectacular dances and costumes, and hearing the spellbindingly powerful music echoing down the colonial streets, is a magical experience.

The action

Although the climax comes over the weekend nearest to June 24, *bumba* takes over the city centre at night for the whole month. Dozens of stalls spring up in the areas where the troupes rehearse before setting off to the two churches in the centre around which everything revolves: the **Igreja de São João Batista**, on Rua do Paz, and the **Igreja de Santo Antônio**, four blocks north. Along the waterfront, stalls go up selling simple food and drinks, including lethal *batidas* with firewater rum – try the *genipapo*. Many choose to follow the **bois**, as the troupes are called, through the streets: if you feel less energetic, the best place to see everything is Praça de Santo Antônio, the square in front of the church where all the *bois* converge, where you can sit and drink between troupes.

Bumba-meu-boi has a stock of characters and re-enacts the story of a plantation owner leaving a bull in the care of a slave, which dies and then magically revives. The bull, black velvet decorated with sequins and a cascade of ribbons, with someone inside whirling it around the heads of dancers and musicians, is at the centre of a circle of musicians. The songs are belted out, with lyrics declaimed first by a lead caller, backed up only by a mandolin, and then joyously roared out by everyone when the drums and brass come in. You couldn't wish for a clearer symbol of the cultural influences that make Brazil what it is: the brass sounds Mediterranean, the dancers dressed as Indians, and the drumming like nothing you'll have ever heard. *Bumba* drums are unique: hollow, and played by strumming a metal spring inside, they give out a deep, haunting, hypnotically powerful backbeat.

The troupe is surrounded by people singing along and doing the athletic dance that goes with the rhythm. There are certain old favourites which are the climax of every performance, especially "São Luis", the unofficial city anthem: *São Luis, cidade de azulejos, juro que nunca te deixo longe do meu coracão . . .* – "São Luis, city of *azulejos*, I swear I'll never keep you far from my heart . . .", it begins, and when it comes up there is a roar of recognition and hundreds of voices join in. The sound of the people of the city shouting out their song radiates from Praça de Santo Antônio across the centre, turning the narrow streets and alleys into an echo chamber.

Bumba-meu-boi starts late, the troupes not hitting the centre until 11pm at the earliest, but people start congregating, either at the waterfront or in the square, soon after dark. *Bois* don't appear every night, except during the last few days before the 24th: ask at the place you're staying, as everyone knows when a good *boi* is on. *Bumba-meu-boi* troupes are organised like samba schools; towns and city *bairros* have their own, but thankfully the festival hasn't been ruined by making them formally compete against each other. Informal rivalries are intense, all the same, and Maranhenses love comparing their merits: most would agree that *Boi de Madre de Deus* is the best in the city, but they are eclipsed by the troupes from the interior, *Boi de Axixá* and *Boi de Pinheiro*.

Beaches: Ponta da Areia, Calhau, Olho d'Agua and Aracagí

São Luis is blessed with a chain of excellent **beaches**, still largely unspoilt by development, although that may not last if an absurd and unnecessary seafront road is driven along the coast: preliminary work has already messed up the nearest city beach, **Ponta da Areia**, but the real damage will be done if it carries on north to Calhau and Olho d'Agua. Fortunately, there's a good chance they'll run out of money and for the time being you can still enjoy the simple pleasures of chairs and tables plonked on the sand, unpretentious bars and restaurants, and a delightful coastline of palm-forest hills and headlands. One word of **warning**: although they don't shelve steeply, these are ocean beaches and the surf can be dangerous. People drown every month, so take care.

Calhau, almost as easy to get to by local bus as Ponta da Areia, is larger and more scenic: when the tide is out there is a lovely walk along the sands to Ponta da Areia, two hours' leisurely stroll west. After Calhau comes **Olho d'Agua** (local buses from Rua da Paz), equally fine, and finally **Aracagí**, 15km out of town, the loveliest beach of all. Hourly buses leave for here in the morning from Rua da Paz, but unless you hitch or hire a car you won't make it back the same day; there is a small hotel, though, the *Chalê da Lagoa*.

Eating and drinking

At weekends virtually the entire city moves out to the beaches, which are large enough to swallow up the masses without getting too crowded. You will quickly discover one of the delights of this coast: the **seafood**. The seas and rivers around here teem with life, most of it edible. The beach stalls do fried fish, the prawns are the size of large fingers, and whatever they don't cook you can buy fresh from a stream of vendors – juicily tender crabs, battered open with bits of wood, or freshly gathered oysters, dirt cheap, sold by the bagful, helpfully opened for you and sprinkled with lime juice.

Except during *Bumba-meu-boi* and Carnaval, São Luis is quieter than most Brazilian cities of its size. The largest concentration of nightspots is just over the bridge, in **São Francisco**, a little on the tacky side for the most part, although there is a good Japanese restaurant, the *Samurai*, at Avenida Castelo Branco 21. **Bars** in the centre open and close with bewildering rapidity: good places to look for them are around Largo do Ribeirão and Praça João Lisboa. On Avenida Dom Pedro Segundo, the *Café Panorama* serves moderate pizzas and wicked *caipirinhas* on a terrace with a fine view out across the bay, where you can watch the ochre sails of fishing smacks sliding by.

Eating out in the centre is rewarding, thanks to the abundant seafood. The best in town is the *caldeirada de camarão* (shrimp stew) at the *Base do Edilson* restaurant, served with *pirão*, a savoury manioc porridge that's the perfect accompaniment. The restaurant is buried deep in the *bairro* of Vila Bessa, at Rua Paulo Kruger de Oliveira 32; it's only a short ride from the centre, so take a taxi rather than attempt to find it – it's worth the effort. Good *caldeirada* is also to be had at the *Base do Germano*, also a short taxi ride from the centre on Avenida Venceslau Brás, in the *bairro* of Camboa: its founder was killed in a brawl over a parking space in 1986, but his family carries on the tradition. The Largo do Ribeirão, a lovely setting for a meal, is well supplied with restaurants: the *Solar do Ribeirão* is cheaper than it looks, and there are many others. The *MARTUR Itinerário* includes a good listings section – concentrate on the ones which say *Cozinha típica*. One thing which you won't find outside Maranhão is *cuxá* – a delicious dish made of crushed dried shrimp, garlic, and the stewed leaves of two native plants.

Boat rides: along the coast

Travel in Maranhão outside São Luis is made difficult by a road system that is limited and – given the rains – often precarious. If you want to travel **along the coast** the most practical way is by boat, an option, however, that is not to be taken lightly as it's hard going: no schedules or creature comforts, and no-one who speaks English. Don't do it unless you're healthy, a good sailor, not fussy about what you eat, have at least basic Portuguese and aren't too worried about time. But if you want to get completely off the beaten track, there's nothing to rival a sea journey.

The place to start is the **Estação Marítima** in São Luis, on the waterfront at the end of Avenida Dom Pedro Segundo. This is the local bus station that São Luis lacks, except it's for boats, which supply the nearby coastal villages and towns, take on passengers and cargo, and wait for the tides. Brightly painted, many with masts, rigging and sails that make seadogs growl with approval, these boats are built by artisans along the coast who still know how to put an oceangoing vessel together from timber.

There are sailings to the main coastal towns to the **west** about once a week. Pick a destination and ask at the booth in the *Marítima* station for the day and time: you either buy your passage there and then, or negotiate with the captain. The main coastal towns, as you head west, are GUIMARÃES (half a day away), TURIAÇÚ (two days), and LUIS DOMINGUES and CARUTAPERA (three days). Take plenty of food and drink; Maranhenses scratch limes and smell them to guard against seasickness, and it does seem to help.

Nearby destinations: São José do Ribamar

Fortunately, not all the interesting places are that difficult to get to. Easiest of all are the fishing towns of the island of São Luis: RAPOSA, a simple village on a beach, an hour away by local bus from Deodoro or Rua da Paz; and **SÃO JOSÉ DO RIBAMAR**, which you can reach on the bus marked *Ribamar* from the same stops.

It's 32km to São José, about an hour's drive; a lovely route through thick palm forest and small hills. The bus deposits you in the small town centre, where straggling houses on a headland have sweeping views of a fine bay: it's easy to stay over, as there are several **pensões** in the centre. São José is an important fishing town, as well as being a centre of skilled boatbuilding by traditional methods – you can see the yards, with the half-finished ribs of surprisingly large boats, behind the houses running inland from the small landing quay and large beach. There's a very relaxing feel to the town. The people are friendly, the scenery splendid, and it's not difficult to while away a few days doing nothing in particular. There are some good **restaurants**, too: the *Ribamar* has a terrace looking out to the bay, and the rustic *barracas* on the waterfront are ideal spots to chat and watch the sunset from.

A lot of the **boats** that ply the coast both east and west drop in at São José, and it's a convenient place to begin a boat trip. Easiest places to head for, and with a fair degree of certainty that there'll be a boat back within a day or two, are ICATÚ, the mainland village on the other side of the bay, and PRIMEIRA CRUZ on the east coast. From the latter, it's a short hop to the interior town of HUMBERTO DE CAMPOS, where you can catch a bus back to São Luis.

Across the bay: Alcântara

ALCÂNTARA is set in a wonderful tropical landscape on the other side of the bay of São Marcos from São Luis: one-time capital of the state, now no more than a poor village built around the ruins of what was once the richest town in northern Brazil. São Luis had already eclipsed it by the end of the eighteenth century, and for the last 200 years it has been left to moulder quietly away. The measure of its decline is that there are now no roads worthy of the name that go there: the only way is by sea, taking the **ferry** that leaves daily (around 8am) from the *Estação Marítima* in São Luis – check the exact times the day before, as they depend on the tides.

Alcântara is a ninety-minute chug across the bay, which can still sometimes get choppy enough to make you thankful you've arrived. There's a fine view of ruins and the houses of the town as you arrive, strung out along a headland looking back across the bay, the skyline dominated by imperial palms; you face a short walk uphill after you disembark. Most of the **ruins** you see are seventeenth-century: Alcântara, founded in 1648, was the first capital of Maranhão and the main centre of the first stretch of coastline that the Portuguese converted to sugar plantations.

The main square, **Praça da Matriz**, gives you an idea of how grand it must have been in its heyday, surrounded on three sides by colonial mansions. The best **restaurant** in town is here, at the clean and comfortable *Hotel Pelourinho* – home-brewed fruit liqueurs a speciality; try the guava (*goiaba*). In the centre of the square is a curious corroded stone post, erected in 1647, on which you can still see the carved arms of the Portuguese crown: this is the *pelourinho*, a whipping post, set up to mark the King of Portugal's claim to the coast.

If you thought the buildings in the colonial zone of São Luis were in bad repair, Alcântara proves how much worse things can get. Very few of the oldest buildings survive; for the most part only the facade and walls are standing, many with coats of arms still discernible. The roofs went generations ago and most have large trees growing out of them. On the main square is a small **museum**, in a restored mansion with a fine *azulejo* frontage, which has a good collection of artefacts and prints to give you an idea of what the place was once like. It doesn't keep regular opening hours, but they will open it up for you if you ask nicely: they'll know where the key is at the hotel.

The ruins, the views, the beaches and the friendliness of the people combine to make Alcântara a very atmospheric place. Short **walks** or **canoe rides** in either direction take you to deserted **beaches** where there are rustic cafés and bars with chilled beer and, provided you don't mind eating fish, you won't starve.

Some practical details

Boats back to São Luis leave daily between 1pm and 2pm, so if you want to stay for more than a couple of hours you'll have to spend the night. It's worth doing, as the moonlight shows the ruins to best effect, and the two **hotels** on Praça da Matriz are both good and moderately priced. Even cheaper is to string your **hammock** in a house: groups of children meet incoming boats looking for tourists for exactly that purpose, so finding somewhere is easy. The kids are surprisingly good guides, too. The deal will include an evening meal and breakfast, simple but wholesome: just don't drink the water. Just off the main square there's a *TELMA* post, from where you can make **telephone calls**.

The Interior

Travel in the **interior** of Maranhão is limited by the road system: there is only one highway out of São Luis, which forks east to Teresina and west to Belém. Although asphalted now, chunks of it often get washed away during the rainy season. You'll usually get through eventually – even if you have to push with the rest of the passengers – but things like timetables cease to have any meaning.

The **road to Belém** is now a lot better than it was, although the link south to Imperatriz can still be a bit dodgy. There's little to keep you in central Maranhão, although the journey is interesting: travel by day if you can. The area you pass through was first populated on a large scale thirty years ago and the towns, the largest en route being BACABAL and SANTA INÊS, are young but growing rapidly. By the time you get to Santa Inês you're in Amazonia, but don't expect to see any forest en route to Belém: most was cut down for cattle ranching twenty years ago.

Although there's nowhere worth getting off the bus, this final western stretch of Maranhão is fascinating. Inland, a **gold rush** has been going on since 1982. Watch the people who get on and off at the roadside villages past Santa Inês, especially at the town of MARACASSUMÉ – many are *garimpeiros*, gold miners. Just over the border with Pará you even get to see a gold camp, called CACHOEIRA, where a village has developed around a gold strike: you can just about see the diggings from the road, but it's not advisable to get off for a closer look.

South to Imperatriz

At Santa Inês a fork heads south to **IMPERATRIZ**, a mushrooming city on the Belém–Brasília highway; 250,000 people or more where as recently as twenty years ago there was only a small town of about 10,000. You can also get there by **train**, along the railway to the **Carajás** iron and bauxite deposits: the line was built by the Brazilian *CVRD* mining company, which runs the train. It leaves weekly from the port of ITAQUÍ, just outside São Luis, where the ores are loaded onto the massive supertankers you see lumbering out to sea every day or two from the city. You'll need to check with *MARTUR* about the day and time of departure, and ticket arrangements – the passenger service along the railway is a recent innovation, and in this part of the world it's easier and quicker to travel if you're a lump of bauxite than a human being.

Unless you have a good reason, though, like wanting to catch a bus south to Brasília or north to see the huge dam at TUCURUÍ, just over the border in Pará (and one of the most controversial of the large Amazon development projects), there's little reason to go to Imperatriz. The town is teeming with people on the move, and even basic facilities have been swamped. The atmosphere here is made worse by the violent **land conflicts** in the region, and Imperatriz is where the gunmen hang out between contracts.

Most of the people in the towns of southern Maranhão live in appalling squalor: AÇAILÂNDIA, the town before Imperatriz, is a prime example, with 80,000 people living almost entirely in shacks that get washed away every year. Imperatriz is little better. If you must **stay**, the best places are the *Hotel Posseidon*, Rua Paraíba 740, and the *Hotel Presidente*, Rua Coronel Manoel Bandeira 1774. But Imperatriz is a rough city; don't go unless you have to, stick to the few well-lit streets after dark, and keep an eye on your bags at all times.

travel details

Buses

From Recife to Goiana (6 daily; 2hr); Amarelo (every 30min; 1hr); Itamaracá (every 30min; 1hr); Igarassú (every 30min; 40min); Porto de Galinhas (every 30min; 1hr); São Jose da Coroa Grande (hourly; 1hr 30min); Caruarú (at least hourly; 2hr); Petrolina (3 daily; 8hr); Maceió (20 daily; 4hr); Natal (20 daily; 3hr); Aracajú (11 daily; 6hr); João Pessoa (10 daily; 2hr); Salvador (7 daily; 14hr); Fortaleza (7 daily; 12hr); Belém (2 daily; 35hr); Belo Horizonte/Brasília (4 daily; 35hr–48hr); Rio (4 daily; 36hr); São Paulo (4 daily; 40hr).

From Maceió to Paulo Afonso (2 daily; 4hr); Penedo (4 daily; 2hr); Aracajú (7 daily; 5hr).

From Salvador to Cachoeira (every 30min; 2hr); Santo Amaro (every 30min; 2hr); São Felix (every 30min; 2hr 30min); Ilhéus (4 daily; 10hr); Porto Seguro (2 daily; 12hr); Feira de Santana (every 15min; 2hr); Valença (3–4 daily; 5hr); Jacobina (2 daily; 6hr); Lençóis (2 weekly; 12–15hr); Rio (6 daily; 48hr); São Paulo (4 daily; 48hr); Recife (4 daily; 15hr); Brasília (3 daily; 36hr); Belém (1 daily; 48-60hr).

From João Pessoa to Penha (every 2hr; 45min); Cabedelo (every 30min; 45min); Campina Grande (hourly; 2hr); Juazeiro do Norte (2 daily; 10hr); Fortaleza (3 daily; 9hr); Mossoró (several daily; 4hr).

From Teresina to São Luis (several daily; 10hr); Belém (1–2 daily; 24hr); Fortaleza (at least 1-2 daily; 15hr).

Ferries

From Salvador to Itaparicá (every 30min; 30min); Maragojipe (1 daily at 3pm; 1–2hr).

CHAPTER FOUR

THE AMAZON

Although the rest of the world knows that the river Amazon extends from the Peruvian Andes all the way to the Atlantic coast of Brazil, in Brazil only the stretch between Manaus and Belém is actually known as the **Rio Amazonas**: above Manaus the river is called the **Rio Solimões** until it crosses into Peru, where it once again becomes the Amazonas. The daily flow of the river is said to be enough to supply a city the size of New York with water for nearly ten years, and its power is such that the muddy Amazon waters stain the Atlantic a silty brown for over 200 kilometres out to sea. This was how its existence was first identified by a Spanish sailor, Vicente Yanez Pinon, sailing the Atlantic in search of El Dorado. He was drawn to the mouth of the Amazon by the sweet freshness of the ocean or, as he called it, the *Mar Dulce*.

To many Indian tribes, the Amazon is a gigantic mythical anaconda, a source of life and death. In its upper reaches, the Rio Solimões from Peru to Manaus, it is a muddy yellow, but at Manaus it meets the darker flow of the Rio Negro and the two mingle together at the famous "meeting of the waters" to form the Rio Amazonas. There are something like 80,000 square kilometres of **navigable river** in the Amazon system, and the Amazon itself can take ocean-going vessels virtually clean across South America, from the Atlantic coast to Iquitos in Peru. Even at the Óbidos narrows, the only topographical obstruction between the Andes and the Atlantic, the river is almost 2km wide and for most of its length it is far broader: by the time it reaches the ocean the river's gaping mouth stretches further apart than London and Paris.

Ecology and development

The Amazon is far more than just a river. Its catchment basin contains, at any one moment, over one-fifth of all the world's fresh water and the **rainforest** it sustains covers an area of over 2,500,000 square miles. The Amazon forest is a vitally important cog in the planet's biosphere controls. There are over 1000 tributaries (several larger than the Mississippi), whose combined energy potential is estimated at over 100,000 megawatts daily (an endlessly renewable supply equivalent to five million barrels of oil a day). *Eletronorte*, the region's electricity supply company, aims to be providing 22,000 megawatts from Amazonian hydroelectric power by the end of this decade.

Although in 1639 Pedro Teixeira travelled 2000 miles up the Amazon and claimed all the land east of Ecuador for Portugal, the Portuguese really gained control of the Brazilian Amazon, in a political sense, through the Treaty of Madrid in 1750. Four years later, Governor Mendonça Furtado was appointed Boundary Commissioner and began his tour of inspection in the Amazon. He saw the prosperity of the Carmelite missions on the Rio Negro and initiated the Directorate System of controlling "official" Indian villages which were essentially labour camps. Having seen how effective the Carmelite missionaries had been in manipulating native workers, the Governor was determined to do the same. Some Indians, remaining free in the regions upstream on major tributaries, tended to gather in villages at portage points like difficult rapids where they acted as guides and muscle-power for traders. Others retreated deeper into the forest.

The region was only integrated fully into the Brazilian political scene after Independence in 1822. And even then it remained safer and quicker to sail from Rio de Janeiro to Lisbon than to Belém, let alone Manaus. Within a few years of Independence the region was almost lost to Brazil altogether when the bloody **Cabanagem Rebellion** (see "Belém") overthrew white rule and attempted to establish an independent state. When things had quietened down a little, in the mid-nineteenth century, US Navy engineers were sent to the Amazon to check out its potential resources. They reported that it was wealthy in forest gums, fruits, nuts and excellent timber, and provided with a ready-made transport network in the form of rivers which gave direct contact with the Atlantic. Within a few years one of those forest gums – **rubber** – was to transform the future of the Amazon.

Until Charles Goodyear invented the rubber tyre, the Amazonian economy had ticked over at a bare subsistence level, sustained by the slave trade and lumber. But the new demand for rubber coincided handily with the introduction of steam-ship navigation on the Amazon in 1858, beginning an economic boom as spectac-ular as any the world has seen. By 1900 both Manaus and Belém were extraordinarily rich cities, and out in the forest were some of the most wealthy and powerful men in the world at that time, beyond the reach of the newspapers, conscience and worries of the nineteenth-century European scene. Men like Nicolas Suárez, who earned a reputation as an autocratic ruler of a rubber-tapping region larger than most European countries. Controlling the whole of the region around the upper Madeira river – even into modern day Peru – he was a legen-darily harsh employer even by the standards of the day.

When the rubber boom ended, almost as suddenly as it had begun, following the success of rubber plantations established in the Far East (with smuggled Brazilian seeds), development of the region once again came to an almost complete halt, relying on the export of the traditional products of the forest to keep the economy going at all. There was a brief resurgence during World War II, when the rubber plantations in the Far East were controlled by the Japanese, but it is only in the last twenty years or so that large-scale **exploitation – and destruction – of the forest** has really taken off, along with a massive influx of people from other parts of Brazil, the Northeast in particular, in search of land.

There are three main **types of Amazon forest**: the *várzea* or floodplain zones, regularly flooded by the rivers; the *igapós*, which are occasionally flooded; and the *terra firma*, generally unflooded land which forms the majority of the surface area. Each forest type differs in the nature of its vegetation and the potential of its land use. Much of the *terra firma* is high forest where life exists as much in the upper canopies as it does on the ground. In the extreme northern and southern limits of the Amazon Basin, and to some extent taking over where mankind has caused most devastation, there are extensive coverings of wooded and scrubby savannas. When the forest is destroyed it generally remains productive for only a few years before turning to scrub. Added to this there's the contribution to the greenhouse effect from burning the cleared forest and the fact that, from a global perspective, the forest can be seen as the kidneys and lungs of the planet – clean-ing toxic substances from the atmosphere and putting oxygen back through photosynthesis.

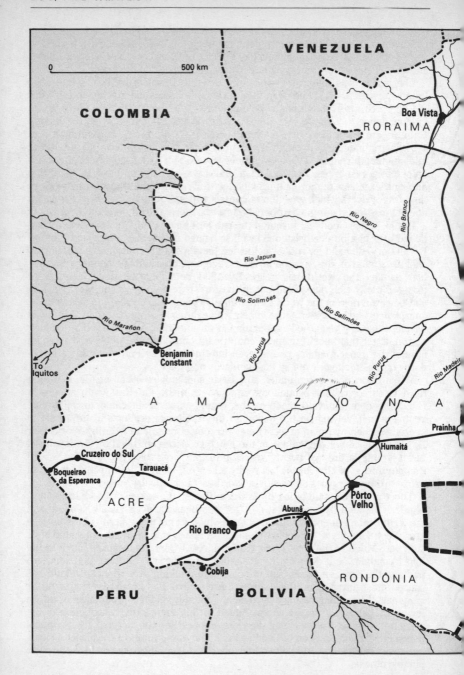

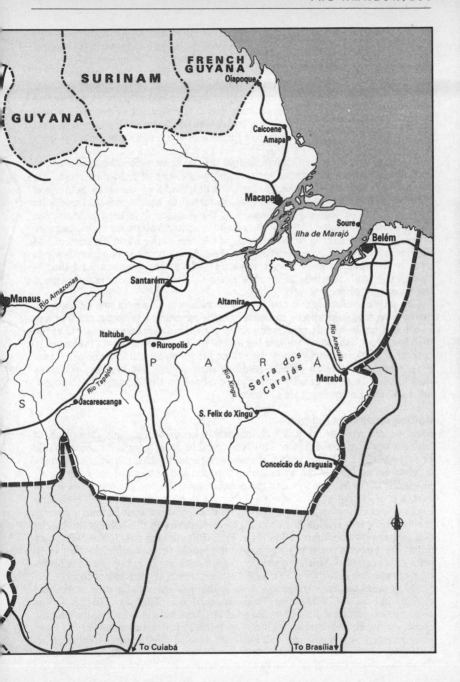

The destruction of the Amazon forest also takes a severe toll on the area's unique **flora and fauna**. There are believed to be as many as 15,000 animal species in the Amazon – thousands of which have still to be identified – and untold numbers of so far unclassified plants. Since they remain unknown, it is impossible to say quite what damage the destruction of the rainforest is doing; but there can be no doubt that many animal species and plant types will be lost before anyone has had a chance to study them. The loss of this gene-pool – with its potential use for medicines, foods, and others unknown – is really serious: but perhaps only the indigenous people of the forests will really know what has been lost – if they survive.

The Brazilian riposte, of course, is that the western nations have no right to occupy any moral high ground, or to stand in the way of what they see as the essential economic development of their country. And they generally further add that the area being lost is insignificant compared to what survives. For all the damage to the ecology and the peoples of the Amazon, it is hard to argue that Brazil should be denied the right to exploit the mineral and natural resources by people who have already raped so much of the rest of the world. Settlement and development are still being actively encouraged, and many multinationals are at work in the Amazon basin – Volkswagen, Goodyear and Nestlé among them – investing in cattle ranches, paper mills, rice plantations, timber mills, mining and sugar cane for *álcool* (for fuel).

The one **hopeful sign** is that these companies and others are increasingly discovering that cultivation – particularly cattle ranching – is not an efficient way to use the jungle, and that the productivity of the land decreases rapidly after the first few years. Scientists are just beginning to demonstrate (and developers to accept) that the virgin forests – with their fruits, roots, nuts, medicinal plants, dyes, game etc – are an endless resource that can actually be more profitable than cleared land if managed properly. For more on the Amazon environment, see also "The Environment" in *Contexts*.

Getting around the Amazon

Most people who visit Brazil will, at some time or other, have dreamt about taking **a boat up the Amazon**. This is not hard to do, but nor is it as comfortable or easy-going – or for that matter as interesting – as daydreams might have made it seem. Going upriver can be tough on the stomach and, given the unchanging monotony of the forest scene and the distance from the bank at which you travel, even a little boring at times. On the other hand, it's a great deal more exciting than the bus. The classic journey is the four or five days from **Belém**, a friendly coastal city worth visiting in its own right, to **Manaus** in the heart of the jungle; and perhaps on from there to Iquitos in Peru. But sticking only to the main channel of the Amazon is not the way to see the jungle or its wildlife: for that you'll want to take trips on smaller boats up smaller streams, an option which is particularly rewarding in the west. For details of river travel, see the box opposite.

Thirty years ago river travel was virtually the only means of getting around the region, but in the 1960s the **Transamazonica** – Highway BR-230 – was constructed, cutting right across the south of Amazonia and linking the Atlantic coast (via the Belém–Brasília highway) with the Peruvian border at Brazil's western extremity. It remains an extraordinary feat of engineering – although an incredibly dull road to travel – and is still being improved. Access to the *Transamazonica* from Belém or Brasília is via ESTREITO, the settlement at the

RIVER JOURNEYS

Any journey up the Rio Amazonas is a serious affair. The river is big and powerful and the boats, in general, are relatively small, top-heavy-looking wooden vessels on two or three levels. As far as **spotting wildlife** goes there's very little chance of seeing much more than a small range of tropical forest birds – mostly buzzards around the refuse tips of the ports en route. The river is nevertheless a beautiful sight and many of the settlements you pass are fascinating to the traveller's eye. Going upriver from Belém or Santarém, the smaller boats tend to hug the river banks, bringing the spectacle much closer. Going downstream, however, large and small boats alike tend to cruise with the mid-stream currents, taking advantage of the added power they provide.

It's important to **prepare** properly for an Amazon river trip if you want to ensure your comfort and health. The most essential item is a **hammock** which can be bought cheaply (from about $8) in the stores and markets of Manaus, Santarém or Belém. Loose **clothing** is OK during daylight hours but at night you'll need some warmer garments and long sleeves against the chill and the insects. A **blanket** and some **insect repellent** are also recommended. Enough **drink** (large containers of mineral water are the best option, available in the bigger towns) and extra **food** – biscuits, fruit and the odd tin – to keep you happy for the duration of the voyage are also a good idea. Most people complain about the food and it's certainly true that a lot of people get literally sick of the rice and beans served on board which is, of course, cooked in river water. There are toilets on all boats, though even on the best they get filthy within a few hours of leaving port. It is essential to take your own roll of **toilet paper**. From a medical point of view, it is important to have had a **yellow fever** inoculation and have started a course of **anti-malaria** pills well before entering the Amazon.

There are a few things to bear in mind when you're choosing **which boat** to travel with. Whether starting the voyage at Manaus, Belém or Santarém, the basic options are the same. A regular *ENASA* service on a three-storey ship connects the three ports at least once a week; this is the most consistently reliable operator, though there are no fixed schedules in the Amazon. These boats are reasonably comfortable and good value at around $75 for first class shared cabins (Belém to Manaus), but they stick to the middle of the river – so you don't see much – and their service has gone a little downhill over the last few years.

Better value still, and usually more interesting in the degree of contact it affords between tourists, Brazilians and the crew, is the option of choosing a **smaller boat**. There are plenty of these along the waterfront in all the main ports, and it's simply a matter of going down there and establishing which ones are getting ready to go to wherever you are heading. Going all the way between Manaus and Belém you might find the smaller boats stopping at Santarém, Óbidos or other ports along the way. This is fine if you don't mind spending a day or two waiting for your next connection to load up. The Belém to Manaus trip usually costs a little under $50 for first class hammock space on the smaller boats. This means sharing a deck with scores of other travellers, which will almost certainly ensure that the journey never becomes too monotonous. The smaller vessels also tend to let passengers stay aboard a night or two before departure and after arrival, which can help save a few pennies.

First class hammock space is in any case almost always a better bet than a **cabin** (*camarote*). Most cabins are unbearably hot and stuffy, and at least on the deck you get fresh air. The boats get extremely crowded, so arrive early and establish your position: the best spots are near the front on the side that will be closest to the bank as you sail.

junction where the BR-230 turns west off the old north–south highway, the BR-153/BR-010.

One thing to bear in mind while travelling is that there are three **time zones** in the Amazon region. Belém and eastern Pará are on the same time as the rest of the coast; halfway across Pará (at the Rio Xingú) the clocks go back an hour; and the extreme west and the state of Acre is a further hour behind. Remember, too, that local people only observe these rules about half the time.

EASTERN AMAZONIA

Politically divided between the state of Pará and the 47-year-old territory of Amapá, the Eastern Amazon is essentially a vast area of forest and savanna plains centred around the final seven hundred miles or so of the giant river's course. **Belém**, an Atlantic port near the mouth of the estuary, is the elegant capital of Pará and a worthwhile place to spend some time. It overlooks the river and the vast **Ilha de Marajó**, a marshy island in the estuary given over mainly to cattle farming, but with a couple of good beaches.

Pará has always been a relatively productive region. In the late eighteenth century it was an important source of rice (allowing Portugal to be "self-sufficient" in the commodity), and it also exported cacao and, later, rubber. Very little of the wealth, however, ever reached beyond a small elite, and falling prices of local commodities on the world markets have periodically produced severe hardship. In the 1830s resentment exploded in the Cabanagem Rebellion, ruthlessly fought and equally harshly suppressed.

Today, the state is booming once again, largely thanks to vast mineral extraction projects in the south. The *campo* of southern Pará, below **Marabá** and the Tocantins-Araguaia rivers, is essentially a scrubby savanna known locally as *caatinga*: traditionally the home of the *Gê*-speaking Indians, it forms the major part of the central Brazilian plateau or shield. Over the last twenty years some of the most controversial developments in the Amazon have been taking place here: particularly the vast **Grande Carajás** industrial scheme, based around a huge deposit of iron and other ores, and the associated hydroelectric operation at **Tucuruí**, whose dam has flooded an enormous area of forest and Indian land. Not far away are the famous **Serra Pelada** gold mines.

The territory of **Amapá**, in the northeastern corner of the Brazilian Amazon, is a fascinating place in its own right. A poor and little-visited area, with access made difficult by awful roads, it nevertheless offers the possibility of an adventurous overland route to French Guiana and on into Surinam, Guyana and Venezuela. It's possible to do much of this journey by ocean-going boat.

Connections in the region are pretty straightforward, in that you have very few choices. The main throughway is still the Amazon, with stops at **Santarém** – a city entirely dominated by the river but again in the throes of rapid development – and **Óbidos**, far less enticing. As far as **roads** go there are good highways south from Belém towards Brasília (the BR-010) and east into the state of Maranhão (the BR-316). In the north there's just one poor road from **Macapá**, the capital of Amapá, up towards the border. The BR-010 crosses the powerful Rio Tocantins near Estreito (in Maranhão) close to the start of the **Transamazonica**. If you're coming from the south, connections with westbound buses and other traffic are best made at ARAGUAINA˙ (in Goiás) where there's a small *Rodoviária* and several hotels (*Hotel do Norte*; *Hotel Esplanada*). The first stop on the *Transamazonica* within Pará is **Marabá**, some 460km (12hr) by bus from Belém. Continuing from here, the *Transamazonica* passes through **Altamira** on the navigable Rio Xingu, a small new city over 300km west of Marabá where there's another massive hydroelectric dam scheme. With a population that's grown from 15,000 in 1970 to over 100,000 today, it's at the centre of an area of rapidly vanishing jungle.

From Altamira there's another long 500km haul to **São Luis do Tapajós**, for connections to Santarém, a major Amazon port at the mouth of the Tapajós river, and for buses to the nearby town of **Itaituba** (via Rurópolis). A further 350km to the southwest, the *Transamazonica* reaches **Jacareacanga** and the state border between Pará and Amazonas. Situated well over an hour's walk from the main road itself, Jacareacanga has only a couple of basic hotels to choose from, though there is room for slinging hammocks at the **Rodoviária**. The new road now carries on to **Humaitá** on the Rio Madeira in Amazonas, **Porto Velho**, the capital of Rondônia, and via **Rio Branco** into Acre and the western border town of **Cruzeiro do Sul**.

Belém

Strategically placed on the Amazon river estuary close to the mouth of the mighty Rio Tocantins, **BELÉM** was founded by the Portuguese in 1616 as the City of Our Lady of Bethlehem (Belém). Its original role was to protect the river mouth and establish the Portuguese claim to the region, but it rapidly became established as an Indian slaving port and a source of cacao and spices from the Amazon. Such was the devastation of the local population, however, that by the mid-eighteenth century a royal decree was issued in Portugal to encourage its growth: every white man who married an Indian woman would receive "one axe, two scissors, some cloth, clothes, two cows and two bushels of seed".

Despite the decree, a declining labour force and in the 1780s the threat of attack by a large contingent of Mundurukú Indians meant that Belém was in decline by the end of the eighteenth century: in the nineteenth it was to sink still further, as the centre of the nation's bloodiest rebellion, before an extraordinary revival as the most prosperous beneficiary of the Amazon rubber boom. It is this last event that shaped the modern city, whose elegant central avenues lead from the luxuriant Praça da República down to the port, past a historical sector which is still replete with Portuguese colonial architecture. And Belém remains the economic centre of the north, and the chief port for the Amazon.

The Cabanagem Rebellion

The **Cabanagem Rebellion** ravaged the region around Belém for sixteen months between January 1835 and May 1836, in the uncertain years following independence and the abdication of Pedro I. Starting with political division among Brazil's new rulers, it rapidly became a revolt of the poor against racial injustice: the *cabanas* (huts) were mostly black and Indian or mixed-blood settlers who lived in relative poverty in cabana huts on the floodplains and riverbanks around Belém and the lower Amazon riverbanks. After years of unrest the pent-up hatred of generations burst into Belém in August 1835. After days of bloody fighting, the survivors of the Belém authorities fled, leaving the *cabanos* in control. In the area around the city many sugar mills and *fazendas* were destroyed, their white owners being put to death. Bands of rebels roamed throughout the region, and in most settlements their arrival was greeted by the non-white population spontaneously joining their ranks, looting and killing. The authorities described the rebellion as "a ghastly revolution in which barbarism seemed about to devour all existing civilisation in one single gulp".

The rebellion was doomed almost from the start, however. Although the leaders declared independence from Brazil and attempted to form some kind of revolutionary government, they never had any real programme, and nor did they succeed in controlling their own followers. An English ship became embroiled in the rebellion in October 1835, when it arrived unwittingly at Belém port with a cargo of arms which had been ordered by the authorities before their hasty departure a couple of months previously. The crew were killed and their cargo confiscated. Five months later, the following March, an English naval force arrived demanding compensation from the rebels for the killings and the lost cargo. The leader of the *cabanos*, Eduardo Angelim, met the English captain and refused any sort of compromise: British trade was threatened too, and the fleet commenced a blockade of the fledgeling revolutionary state. Meanwhile, troops from the south prepared to fight back, and in May 1836 the rebels were driven from Belém by a force of 2500 soldiers under the command of Francisco d'Andrea. Mopping-up operations continued for years, and by the time the Cabanagem Rebellion was completely over and all isolated pockets of armed resistance had been eradicated, some 30,000 people are estimated to have died – almost a third of the region's population at that time.

Expansion and Boom

Since the mid-eighteenth century, Belém had attracted many forest and savanna Indians, who settled on the floodplains and islands roundabout. They were neither slaves nor employees of the colonists, but survived on a mixture of subsistence and cash-crop agriculture, and by supplying the forest produce – from wild game to rubber, fruits, medicines, skins and feathers – that was consumed in or exported from the city. Some moved into the city itself (even after a government order in 1815, demanding that all Indians were to leave Belém and return to their place of birth within two weeks) and those who survived the rebellion were to form the basis of a new class that emerged in the late nineteenth century – families that managed to make a decent living from the encroaching western industrial civilisation by supplying it with important drugs, turtle oil, and tobacco. Some also entered the lower artesan ranks as carpenters, blacksmiths and leather workers.

By the end of the nineteenth century, thanks to the rubber boom, Belém was a very rich town, accounting for close to half of all Brazil's rubber exports. At this time rubber was being collected from every corner of the Amazon. As a result of the boom, thousands of poor people moved into Belém from the Northeast, bringing with them new cultural inputs such as music and dance, plus, of course the *candomblé* and *macumba* Afro-Brazilian religions. After the crash of 1914, the city suffered another disastrous decline – but it kept afloat, just about, on the back of Brazil nuts and the lumber industry. In World War II, Belém was an important strategic base for the American fleet.

Today it's a friendly city with a Parisian feel and a suprisingly modern skyline. Belém still has its fair proportion of disenfranchised, disempowered peoples like the beggars, rastas and hippies who operate along Avenida Presidente Vargas, but the general atmosphere is one of warmth and fun loving. Always warm and often hot (and often wet too), the **climate** is generally very pleasant with an average temperature of around 25°C.

Arrival

Belém's **Rodoviária** is some 2km from the centre on Av. Governador José Malcher, near the Almirante Barroso ring-road: the *Aeroclube* #20 bus will take you downtown via avenidas Nazaré and Magalhães Barata. There are excellent facilities and services at the *Rodoviária*, including a Parátur information office (not always open, even when it's meant to be). If you arrive by scheduled airline, Belém **airport** is 15km out – there's the usual system of co-op taxis, for which you buy a ticket at the kiosk. **Boats** dock on the river near the town centre, from where you can walk or take a local bus up Avenida Presidente Vargas.

Presidente Vargas is the modern town's main axis, running from the Praça da República and the landmark Teatro da Paz right down to the riverfront. Most of the hotels, restaurants, shops and businesses are along the Avenida, or just off it. At the top end, opposite the Teatro, there's a cinema and the swish *Belém Hilton Hotel*. Slightly further down, on block 7, you'll find the *FUNAI* office and shop, the *Varig* offices and the *Hotel Excelsior*. On block 6 there's the *Cafe Express* – very lively in the evenings (good juices) – the *Vasp* office and, on the corner, the **telephone** place. The central **post office**, one of the most impressive in South America, is on block 4; while the *Hotel Central* on block 3 is closer to the river and the *ENASA* riverboat company building at the Avenida's beginning.

Tourist information is available at Parátur offices at the *Rodoviária* and airport, or downtown at the *Feira de Artesenato do Estado* on Praça Kennedy; there's also a helpful municipal information office at Avenida Nazaré 231. **Maps** and town guides can be bought cheaply from the newspaper stands in Avenida Presidente Vargas.

Accommodation

There are plenty of expensive **hotels** in Belém; the best being the highly central *Hotel Excelsior Grão Pará*, Av. Presidente Vargas 718 (☎222-3255), and the *Equatorial Palace*, Av. Braz de Aguiar 612 (☎224-8855). Another upmarket place, the *Novotel*, Av. Bernado Sayão 4804 (☎229-8011), has swimming pools on an attractive terrace overlooking the Guamá river just ten minutes from the city centre. Much more affordable at around $8 single or $12 double, the completely unstylish *Hotel Lis* is on the corner of Rua João Diego with Travessa Padre Entiquio, out towards the old part of town from the Praça da República.

For the best value in town, and almost as well placed as the Excelsior, the *Hotel Central*, Av. Presidente Vargas 290 (☎222-3011), is a splendid old building with elegant rooms from around $5 per person, though most are without private toilet facilities: excellent rooftop breakfasts. Other downtown hotels in a similar low to middle range include the *Hotel Novo Avenida*, Av. Presidente Vargas 404 (☎223-8893), and *Hotel Sete Sete*, Rua 1 de Março 77 (☎222-7742). Cheaper still are the *Hotel Grajaú* and *Pensão Canto do Rio*, with the usual shabby charm of accommodation nearer to the port. If you arrive late at night and just want to sleep, the *Hotel Sagres*, Av. Gov. Malcher 2927 (☎228-3999), is right by the *Rodoviária*. There's **camping** in a pleasant environment over 15km out of town at Benfica.

The City

The **Praça da República**, as well as being an attractive central park with a surplus of trees affording valuable shade, is a perfect place from which to get your bearings and start a walking tour of Belém's downtown and riverfront attractions. The praça itself is sumptuously endowed with fine statues and columns focusing on its fountain centrepiece. Overlooking all this is the most obvious sign of Belém's rubber fortunes – the nineteenth-century Rococo **Teatro da Paz** (free but rarely open), an opera house where Anna Pavlova once danced. Beside it, modern reality is reflected in the young men cleaning other people's big cars on the sidewalk, using the roots of the old trees as cupboards for their buckets and sponges.

Heading down Presidente Vargas towards the river, the old part of town – the **Cidade Velha** – lies off to the left, full of crumbling Portuguese colonial mansions and churches. The oldest church of all is the **Igreja das Mercês** (Trav. Frutuoso Guimarães 31), near the *Hotel São Geraldo*. Architecturally it's nothing special, but as a living, working relic it's totally fascinating, full of quaint little touches. The holy water, for example, is dispensed from an upside-down rum bottle with the label half torn off.

This is a pleasant area to wander, and it's not much further to the river docks, overlooked closely by the old fort. **Ver O Peso market** is not quite the colourful spectacle it once was, but it remains the liveliest spot in town early in the morning (apart from one or two of the more energetic nightclubs) and one of the best traditional markets in Brazil. Ver O Peso ("see the weight") was originally a slave market, but these days its main commodities are fish, fruit and vegetables, manioc flour, nuts and other jungle produce. There's not much that is aimed at tourists but there are interesting sections devoted to medicinal plants and herbs, and a growing sector selling locally produced craft goods. Incidentally it's not a good idea to go to the market area at any time other than the morning: it's a dangerous place. The nearby square offers views across to the old Portuguese **Fort** which, in typically Brazilian style, is now predominantly a bar and restaurant.

Opposite the fort are two more important churches – the **Cathedral** of Nossa Senhora da Graça, in Praça Frei Caetano Brandão (built in 1748 and hung with some fine paintings), and the **Igreja Santo Alexandre**. The latter, also an eighteenth-century construction, now houses a small religious art museum.

Avenida Nazaré: the Basílica and Museu Goeldi

Two of the most important and worthwhile sights in Belém lie inland from the Praça da República along Avenida Nazaré. The first of them is the **Basilica de Nossa Senhora de Nazaré** on Praça Justo Chermont. Created in 1908, and supposedly modelled on St Pauls in Rome, it rates – internally at least – with the most beautiful temples in South America. It somehow manages to be both ornate and simple at the same time, a cruciform structure with a fine wooden ceiling and attractive Moorish designs decorating the sixteen main arches. Most importantly, however, this is home to one of the most revered images in Brazil, **Nossa Senhora de Nazaré**. The story of the image is littered with miracles: it is said to have been originally sculpted in Nazareth in the early years of Christianity, from where it found it had found its way to Spain by the eighth century. Here it had to be hidden from the Moors, and somehow survived to end up in Portugal, where the first important miracle occurred in the twelfth century, when the mayor of Porto de Mós, Fuas Roupinho, was saved from certain death (plunging off the

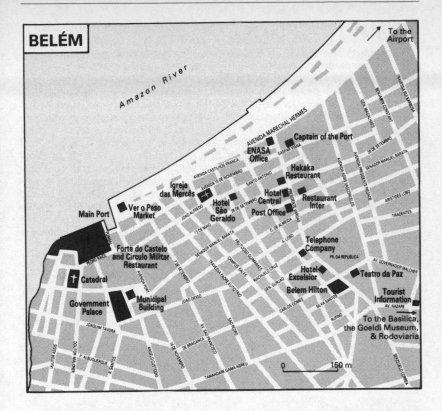

BELÉM

To the Airport

Amazon River

Captain of the Port

AVENIDA MARECHAL HERMES

ENASA Office

Hakaka Restaurant

Igreja das Mercês

Hotel Central

Hotel São Geraldo

Post Office

Restaurant Inter

Ver o Peso Market

Main Port

Telephone Company

Forte do Castelo and Circulo Militar Restaurant

Hotel Excelsior

Belem Hilton

Teatro da Paz

Catedral

Tourist Information

Government Palace

Municipal Building

To the Basilica, the Goeldi Museum, & Rodoviaria

0   150 m

edge of a cliff on horseback) by the intervention of the Virgin. He built a chapel in celebration (in Nazaré), and from here the Jesuits brought the image to Brazil in the seventeenth century. On the first attempt to bring it to Belém, the image was lost in the jungle, where it was rediscovered in 1700 by a rancher. He built a rough shrine to house the Virgin, and word of its miraculous properties rapidly spread; today that shrine has grown to an impressive church, and the cult of Nossa Senhora de Nazaré is stronger than ever.

The most obvious sign of the thriving cult is the annual **Cirio de Nazaré**, a religious festival for which something approaching a million people flock to Belém on the second Sunday in October. A copy of the image is carried in a vast parade from the Cathedral to the Basilica, and two weeks later it returns: in between are all the usual secular festivities of a Brazilian celebration. If you hope to stay at this time of year, you'll need to book a room well in advance.

Two long blocks up Avenida Magalhães Barata (the continuation of Nazaré) from the Basilica, you'll find the excellent **Museu Paraense Emílio Goeldi** at no. 376 (Tues–Sun 9am–noon & 2–6pm; museum buildings – but not the zoological gardens – closed after midday on Friday and Saturday; hour-long guided tours at 9.30am and 2.30pm most days). The gardens alone are worth a visit, and quite apart from the collections of plants, birds, animals and Indian artefacts, any money you spend here (entrance to the zoological gardens is free, but there's a small charge for the museum) goes not only to the upkeep of the museum and its grounds but also to a wide programme of research in everything from anthropology to zoology. Founded in 1866, this is one of only two Brazilian research institutes in the Amazon, and plays a vital role in developing local expertise*.

Inside, set in a compact but beautifully laid out botanical garden, is a small **zoo**. Tapirs, manatees, big cats, huge alligators, terrapins, electric eels and an incredible selection of birds make this place an important site for anyone interested in the forest. By Brazilian standards the animals are reasonably kept, too – although the jaguars barely have room to turn round, and the larger birds seem horribly cramped. The **museum**, particularly the geology, ecology, archaeology and anthropology sections, is equally fascinating and well laid out. There is an excellent description of the region from its pre-ceramic hunter-gatherer stage (10,000–1000 BC) through the period of early ceramics and incipient agriculture (3000–200 BC) until the emergence of forest agriculture as encountered by the Portuguese in the sixteenth and seventeenth centuries. Some of the early Marajó island ceramics are particularly impressive: marvellous pots and bowls which are virtually the only reminder of a culture that had already vanished when the Portuguese arrived. Finally, the museum's **souvenir shop** has probably the best selection of t-shirts and the like in the city – it's not the cheapest place in town, but quality is high and the money goes to a good cause.

Further out: the Bosque

Rather further from the centre there's one final site worth a short trip, the **Bosque**. About half an hour by yellow bus from Ver O Peso market, these public **botanical "gardens"** (daily 9am–noon & 3–4.30pm) are actually a small reserve of relatively virgin plantlife – or as virgin as is possible within the confines of a large modern city. There are also some archaeological exhibits from the region, and all in all it's a worthwhile outing for a breath of fresh air. Alternatively, of course, you could head for the beach: see "Around Belém".

Food and drink

Belém is a great place to eat out, and an opportunity to get acquainted with the distinctive cuisine of the Amazon region. As you might expect, a good deal of it is based on fish: the best are two large river fish, *filhote* and *pirarucú*, which yield succulent steaks delicious either charcoal-grilled or served with a variety of sauces. Other **local specialities** include *maniçoba*, where sausages and a variety of fatty smoked meats are stewed with manioc leaves into a dark green mush (better than it sounds); *tacacá*, a shrimp dish whch is an Amazon version of *vatapá*; *açaí*, a deep purple liquid pulp made from the fruit of a palm tree, and sold on street corners everywhere in the city, which makes a refreshing drink when mixed with sugar, or when mixed with *farinha* is a staple food of the poor; and most famous of all, *pato no tucupí* – duck stewed in a fermented manioc and chicory sauce. This can be delicious, and it's an essential accompaniment to any local festival.

---

*If you want to help out financially on a regular basis – and the government is cutting research spending in Brazil to the bone – write to: O Senhor Director, Museu Paraense Emilio Goeldi, Caixa Postal 399, 66040 Belém.

Amazonian fruit, the basis of an amazing variety of exotic ice creams, desserts and *sucos*, is also exceptional. It is impossible to give English translations, as none of them are to be found outside the Amazon. Most exotic of all is the remarkable *cupuaçú*, which floods your palate with a taste unlike anything you'll have had before; also worth trying are *bacurí*, *graviola* (*cherimoya* in Spanish), *ata* (also called *fruta do conde*), *burití* and *acerola*.

There are dozens of good **restaurants** in Belém, but four are particularly worth splashing out on. *Avenida* has a great setting overlooking the Basilica at Avenida Nazaré 1086 (☎223-4015), excellent food and air conditioning – though it's a bit short on atmosphere. The city's large Japanese population supports a Japanese restaurant, *Miako*, behind the *Hilton* at Travessia 1 de Março 766: great Japanese food (though avoid the sushi) and a wide selection of *sucos* made from Amazonian fruit. The *Círculo Militar* restaurant, Praça Frei Caetano Brandão (☎223-4374), beside the old fort, not only serves delicious food – try the lobster or *filhote na brasa*, and *pudim de cupuaçú* for dessert – but also offers panoramic views over a busy part of the Amazon from within the grounds of the city's historic fort. You can sip cool drinks and fill your belly while vultures circle in the sky above the river and small children from the port swim during the hot afternoons. At *Lá Em Casa*, Avenida José Malcher 982 (☎223-1212), the food is if anything even better – *pirarucú na brasa*, roasted fish served with onion and coconut sauce, and the sweet tray, laden with fruit desserts, are particularly wonderful.

In addition, there are plenty of more **ordinary places** where you can sample the local specialities. *Restaurant Inter*, 28 de Setembro 304 near the *Hotel Central*, is a good example: superb value and large delicious helpings, frequented mostly by Belém's office workers at lunchtimes. The very central *Restaurant Hakata*, with tables out on the pavement at Rua Dr. Morris 294 (again near the *Hotel Central*), is a lively meeting place in the evenings – among its wide selection it prepares good oriental dishes. Just off block 4 of Avenida Presidente Vargas, the *Restaurant Gostosão*, Rua Aristides Lobo 388, serves good, inexpensive evening meals – and very good fish salads. *Na Brasa*, Avenida Nazaré 124 (☎223-4394), not far from the *Avenida*, is also reasonable value.

For Brazilian **snacks** and a lively local ambience there are a few places such as the *Café Milano* on Avenida Presidente Vargas and the *Bar do Parque* (see below) at Praça da República. **Ice creams** can be had at the *Casa dos Sucos* on Presidente Vargas, in a wide variety of local fruit flavours, or at *Tribon*, Rua Municipalidade 1643.

Bars and Nightlife

Belém can be a very lively place, especially at weekends, but one of the best **bars** is also the quietest, the *Bar do Forte* on the battlements of the old Portuguese fort overlooking Ver O Peso market: the entrance is just past the *Circulo Militar* restaurant. Here you sit outside, among eighteenth-century cannon pointing out to sea, and enjoy a fine view. The other outdoor bar in the centre is a famous meeting spot right in the heart of the Praça da República, in front of the theatre: the *Bar do Parque*. It's open all day and there's always something going on, including, very often, a *batucada* on weekend nights. Other **downtown bars**, **restaurants** and **cinemas** cluster in two spots: Praça da República and Praça Justo Chermont, by the Basilica. These are where everyone congregates in the early evening.

Belém's real **nightlife** rarely begins much before 10 or 11pm, when the focus switches to the western *bairro* of Condor, on the banks of the river Guamá. (The area is named after the German Kondor flying-boat that established the first regular air service in the Amazon, between Belém and Manaus, in the 1920s.) There are numerous clubs to choose from, particularly lively on Thursday, Friday and Saturday, and you'll need to take a taxi there and back. *Lapinha*, Travessia Padre Eutiquio 3901 (☎229-3188; no entry charge), is the best known and most enjoyable, though it rarely gets going much before midnight. It's not too glitzy, there's usually good food and a live band at weekends (again, after midnight), and it may be the only club in the world which has three toilets – "Men", "Women" and "Gay". Other places to try are the *Palácio dos Bares* in Condor and, much more upmarket but a place which often has good samba bands, the *Bar Teatro Maracaibo*, Alcindocacela 1299 (☎222-4797).

> The phone code for Belém is ☎091

Listings

Air Services from Belém airport (15km; ☎231-6022) to all major Brazilian cities almost every day. Twice weekly flights to Miami; occasional charters to Orlando. Daily flights to Macapá. Taxis cost $5–8, depending on which part of town you're connecting with – at the airport, kiosks sell tickets for co-op taxis. Light planes and air taxi services mostly use a different airport, Aeroporto Julio César. *Aerotur* (☎233-3786) are one of the bigger air taxi operators.

Airlines *Varig*, Av. Presidente Vargas 768 (☎224-2344 or airport ☎233-3541); *VASP*, Av. Presidente Vargas 620 (☎222-9617 or ☎233-0941); *Transbrasil*, Av. Presidente Vargas 780 (☎224-3677 or ☎233-3941); *TABA*, Av. Governador José Malcher 883 (☎2333235 or ☎233-0034).

Art Galleries *Galeria Teodoro Braga* (Av. Gentil Bittencourt 650); *Galeria Angelus* (Praça da República, in an annexe of the Teatro da Paz); *Galeria Ismael Nery* (Av. Presidente Vargas 645); *Galeria Portinari* (Trav. Quintino Bocaiuva 1205).

Boats leave Belém frequently for upstream Amazon river destinations – Santarém, Manaus and even as far as Porto Velho – and also for coastal cities such as Salvador and Rio. *ENASA* (Av. Presidente Vargas 41; ☎223-3011) have large boats heading upstream four or more times a month – $35 for food and first class hammock space for a five-day journey. Other boats are generally faster, smaller and more expensive ($50 to Manaus) – speak to the captains on the docks. These smaller boats also move upstream closer to the river banks, and offer more wildlife and sightseeing potential than *ENASA*'s vessels. A ferry to Macapá leaves about twice a week (26hr; tickets around $9, inclusive of hammock space and food, from *RGTM*, Avenida Castillo Franca 234, by Ver O Peso market. There are boats every day to the port of Souré on the Ilha de Marajó (4hr).

Buses as usual from the *Rodoviária*, on Av. Governador José Malcher (☎228-0500) almost 5km from Avenida Presidente Vargas (up Av. Nazaré and Av. Magalhães Barata to where it meets the Almirante Barroso ring road). The best way to get there from downtown districts is the *Aeroclube* #20 bus. The *Rodoviária* has all the usual services, as well as buses to most major destinations within Brazil.

Car Hire from *Tagide* (☎224-2741).

Consulates *Belgium*, Av. Nazaré 1054 (☎223-5624); *Bolivia*, Av. Magalhães Barata 661, Casa 5 (☎224-3007); *Colombia*, Trav. Benjamin Constant 1303; (☎223-5888); *West Germany*, Trav. Campos Sales 63 (☎222-5634); *Italy*, Av. Presidente Vargas 197 (☎223-4672); *Spain*, Rua Jeronimo Pimentel 61 (☎222-0197); *UK*, Rua Gaspar Viana 490 (☎223-4353); *USA*, Rua Oswaldo Cruz 165 (☎223-0800).

Crafts and local perfumes are among the best buys for visitors to Belém. Local quartz and other crystals and haematite jewellery (made from a highly polished, black-grey, metallic-looking stone) are all popular. Generally speaking the best places to look are in Ver O Peso market or along Avenida Presidente Vargas. Failing that you can shop at the *Feira de Artesanato da Parátur* on Praça Kennedy; the *Perfumaria Phebo* (Trav. Quintino Bocaiuva 687); *Perfumaria Orion* (Trav. Frutuoso Guimarães 270/272); or at the more expensive airport shop.

Festivals The main event is the *Cirio de Nazaré* or Festival of Candles (see above), for two weeks from the second Sunday in October. Also, as usual, Carnaval.

Money Exchange The *Banco do Brasil* (Presidente Vargas 248) and many of the larger shops, travel agents and hotels will change both travellers' cheques and dollars cash. The *Hotel Central* generally offers reasonable rates, though not as "up-to-date" as in Rio and the southern cities.

Post Office The central post office is an impressive building on Avenida Presidente Vargas.

Shopping Belém is one of the best places in the world to buy hammocks (essential tackle if you are about to go upriver) – look in the street markets between Avenida Presidente Vargas and Ver O Peso, starting in Rua Santo Antônio, one-and-a-half blocks down from the *Hotel Central*. This is a lively street market where you can buy anything from digital watches to unusual rubber-crafted knives and keyrings.

Tourist Information available from the city municipal information office, Av. Nazaré 231, or from Parátur at the *Rodoviária*, airport and Praça Kennedy. Cheap maps and town guides from newspaper stands in Presidente Vargas.

Travel Agents *Mundial Turismo*, Av. Presidente Vargas 780 (☎223-1981), runs river and city tours, trips to Marajó and other excursions, as well as selling air tickets to most destinations; *Sourétur*, Av. Alcindo Cacela 2378, 2nd Floor (☎229-6302), specialises in tours to the Ilha do Marajó; *Ciatur*, Av. Presidente Vargas 645 (☎228-0011), offers most of the same packages at roughly the same prices.

Around Belém

Although Belém is over a hundred kilometres from the ocean, there are some good **river beaches** nearby, all of them popular with city crowds at weekends and holidays. An even shorter trip is to the village of **ICOARAÇÍ** – only 18km or about half an hour by bus from the *Rodoviária* – which is the best place to visit local **ceramic workshops** and the cheapest place to buy the very fine pottery. Still very much based on the ancient designs of the local Indians, the skill involved in shaping, engraving, painting and firing these pots is remarkable. Some of the ceramics are very large and, except to the expert eye, barely distinguishable from the relics in the Goeldi museum.

The closest and most popular of the beaches are Outeiro and Mosqueiro, both easy day trips. **OUTEIRO**, a picturesque and often busy little town, can be reached in under an hour by bus and ferry. **MOSQUEIRO**, some 20km north of Belém, is actually an island, though it's well connected by road and bridge. The beaches are beautiful and relatively unspoilt, though they can get very crowded at holiday times, and there are all the usual beach facilities – stalls selling chilled coconut milk, bars and good restaurants. **Praia Murubira**, with safe swimming and sailing, is probably the best of those close to Mosqueiro town: the *Hotel Murubira* (☎771-1256) here is relatively expensive at about $15 a double – cheaper places in town include the *Ilha Belha*, Av. 16 de Noviembre 409 (☎771-1448; about $7) and the similarly priced *Farol*, less comfortable but right on the beach (☎771-1219). Mosqueiro is also a good place to **camp**. Buses run frequently from Belém's *Rodoviária*, a journey of around two hours. At Carnaval and during the July Festival de Verão, Mosqueiro is particularly lively, with *blocos* on the beach.

Salinópolis

If you're determined to have ocean beaches, then the place to head is **SALINÓPOLIS**, Pará's main coastal resort, on the southeastern lip of the Amazon. A fast 230km by bus from Belém (several buses daily from the *Rodoviária*), it's a relaxed place with plenty of good Atlantic strands: though none that can really compare with the great beaches further south. The *Hotel Salinas* overlooking the beach is friendly and good value at under $4 a night for singles.

Ilha do Marajó

The **Ilha do Marajó**, the vast island in the estuary opposite Belém, is bigger than Belgium or Denmark. Created by the accretion of silt and sand over millions of years, it's a wet and marshy area, the western half covered in thick jungle, the east flat savanna, swampy in the wet season (January to June), brown and dry the rest of the time. On this savanna are *fazendas* where huge water buffalo are ranched – some 60,000 of them roam the island – and supplying meat and hides to the markets in Belém is still Marajó's main trade. The island is also famous for its giant *piraracú* fish which, at over 400lb, is the biggest freshwater breed in the world. Other bird and animal life abounds, including numerous snakes and venomous insects, so be careful where you walk.

In history, although it was settled by Jesuits at an early stage, the island has something of a reputation for lawlessness. Its earliest inhabitants have left behind burial mounds, 1000 years old and more, in which many examples of the distinctive Marajó pottery were found. Large pieces, decorated with geometric engravings and painted designs, these are virtually the only reminder of a vanished people – the best examples are in the Goeldi museum in Belém. When the Jesuits arrived and established the first cattle ranches, the island was inhabited by Nhemgaiba Indians; later its vast expanses offered haven to runaway slaves and to free Indians who wanted to trade with Belém without too much direct interference from the white man's culture. The water buffalo, ideally suited to the marshy local conditions, were imported from India around the turn of the century – or, if you believe local legend, were part of a French cargo bound for Guiana, and escaped when the ship sank. River navigation around Marajó is still a tricky business, the course of the channels constantly altered by the ebb and flow of the ocean tides. Nonetheless the main port of **SOURÉ** (hotels *Souré* and *Marajó*) is a growing resort offering pleasant beaches where it's difficult not to relax under the shade of ancient mango trees (watch out in March and April though, when the ripe mangos begin to fall!). Other magnificent empty **beaches** can be found all around the island – the **Praia do Pesqueiro**, about 13km from Souré, is one of the more accessible and well served in terms of transport and eating and sleeping facilities .

If you want to see the interior of the island – or much of the wildlife – you have to be prepared to camp or pay for a room at one of the *fazendas*: book with travel agents in Belém or take your chance on arrival. **Organised trips** can be booked at most travel agencies in the city (see "Listings"). It is also easy enough to get to Marajó yourself. By river – a four-hour trip each way – **boats** leave in the mornings on weekdays (be at the port before 8am to be sure of finding an early one if you don't want to stay overnight). There are also evening boats, usually leaving Wednesday and Saturday around 8pm. And there are **air taxis**, charging around $50 for a thirty-minute flight; if you can get a group of people together to charter a whole plane (the smallest are five-seaters) you may get a better deal.

Southern Pará: Marabá

The southern half of Pará, south and west of Belém, is real frontier territory. Nowhere else can you witness as clearly the opening up of virgin territory – in the notorious Serra Pelada gold mines or the Grande Carajás project – or the conflict between settlers and Indians, between established interests and new arrivals. Fascinating though this might be, it does not constitute a tourist attraction, and nor do locals on the whole welcome overcurious outsiders: wherever you go, take care of yourself.

MARABÁ, on the banks of the Rio Tocantins almost 500km south of Belém, is often described as the worst of all Amazon towns. It's the market centre for the region, and also the place where the ranchers, construction workers, truckers and goldminers come for entertainment: it has a bad reputation for theft and violent crime, and it's not a place you should (or would want to) hang around any longer than you have to. It is a city of three parts, all of them easily reached by bus from Araguaiana, on the road south, or from Belém. The earliest part of town was founded on the south side of the river on ground which was liable to flooding; later settlers created the New City on the north side, hoping to escape the waters. Then in the 1970s the completion of the *Transamazonica* led to the foundation of New Marabá, back on the south side. Although each has its own church, the rapid growth of the town is eroding the physical distinctions – all three are linked by bridges across the river. All around the town, development is reflected in rising land values, as the *Transamazonica* and Grande Carajás projects continue to bring new settlers – and with them further conflict between *fazendeiros* and landless new arrivals.

Buses will drop you at the **Rodoviária** at km4 on the *Transamazonica* in New Marabá: small local buses or taxis run from here to just about every part of town. The **airport** (☎324-1243) is just 3km out of town near the New City. The *Hotel São Felix* and *Hilda Palace* are relatively cheap and basic downtown places. In New Marabá there's the *Hotel Plaza*, Folha 32 (☎321-1661); while in the New City the choice is essentially between the *Hotel Vitória*, Av. Esp. Santo 130 (☎528-1175), and the *Hotel Keyla*, *Transamazonica* 2427 (☎324-1175). Nearer the *Rodoviária* there's the basic *Pensão Nossa Senhora do Nazaré*, cheaper but somewhat noisy.

Money can usually be changed (dollars cash only) in the larger hotels and shops, but generally at poor rates: you'd do better to change it before you arrive.

Serra Pelada gold mines

About 100km to the southwest of Marabá, in the **Serra Pelada**, a number of huge gold nuggets were discovered in 1980. The discovery sparked off the biggest gold rush of the century, and within a couple of years there were as many as 100,000 *garimpeiros* hacking away at the landscape. The scene here – the mountainside stripped of all vegetation, the landscape pock-marked with vast craters scraped out by the most basic of methods, is surely familiar from dozens of colour magazine spreads: a vision of hell unseen outside the imaginings of Hieronymus Bosch, as thousands of prospectors scraped away at the mud, barely distinguishable from it. One or two made their fortunes – above all the famous José Maria who struck a patch with over 1000 kilos of gold and became one of the richest men in Brazil overnight. But far more barely made a living, and many lost their lives. Now the mines are in terminal decline, the gold all but played out, though as many as 20,000 *garimpeiros* still toil away in hope.

The mines can be reached quite easily by taking a bus to the settlement of KILO SEIS, then another three-hour bus journey to Serra Pelada itself. Along the way there's a strict police control which confiscates alcohol and other contraband. But Serra Pelada is not a tourist attraction, though it has been visited by a lot of newsmen in recent years. There have been frequent violent disturbances at the workings: in 1988, for instance, ten gold prospectors were shot dead by military police while protesting for improved safety precautions. Around 5000 miners blockaded the road and railway bridges over the Tocantins river until fired on indiscriminately by charging policemen.

If you do visit, the settlement of **SERRA PELADA** has a main square surrounded by bars and eating places: the *Hotel Serra de Ouro* is probably the safest bet if you want somewhere to stay, though nowhere here feels exactly comfortable.

Carajás

The **Serra dos Carajás** is a range of steep hills about 160km west of Marabá. Even today, much of it is heavily forested and astonishingly beautiful, fed with moisture by the clouds and mists that are a feature of the local climate. But it is also the heart of the most extensive and ambitious development project in the Amazon. Its story starts in the 1960s, when the military authorities were making determined efforts to discover whether the Amazon's rumoured mineral deposits really existed. In 1968 a geological survey helicopter, off course, developed engine trouble and landed on one of the hills in the Carajás range. While it was being repaired the geologists on board discovered, to their astonishment, that they were standing on a hill composed almost entirely of high grade iron ore. Further exploration established rich deposits of many other minerals too.

Today Carajás has good roads, a modern airport and neatly planned towns where miners and technicians live. The open-cast mining operation is highly sophisticated. In one valley, for example, a stepped series of bauxite and iron ore processors has been built: at the top enormous bulldozers and excavators empty ore into dumper trucks the size of a house. These in turn offload onto a giant conveyor belt, which carries the mineral down the hillside and through preliminary processing to the valley floor, where it is loaded into railway wagons and transported 900km east to the port of Itaquí, outside São Luis. From there it is either exported directly, or taken to the vast new aluminium factory in São Luis.

The bizarre thing about Carajás, if you visit, is its order. There are no villages strung out along the roads, there are no farmers tilling by the road, no roadside vendors, no bars and cheap hotels, no prostitutes, no bus stations, no protest. There are no poor people. It is entirely unlike the rest of Amazonia. The explanation is that no-one without a permit may enter: along the roads are police checkpoints, and outside them huddle the familiar shanty towns filled with people hoping for work within the officially declared **Mineral Province of Carajás**.

Carajás itself is effectively a no-go zone: supplied by air, sealed off by road, with a permanent cheap labour pool to be admitted as needed and then expelled. Within the region, the CVRD (*Companhia do Vale do Rio Doce*, the state-owned mining company) is in complete control: although it is a civil body, it can and does call upon military and police support when it needs it.

Even when you are here, the scale of it all is hard to comprehend: apart from the mining itself, a completely new network of power generation, transport and processing plants has been created, with a railway to the coast connecting with new port facilities and aluminium factories, and an enormous hydroelectric scheme at Tucuruí (see below). The original plan was for a total investment of 62 billion dollars – a substantial proportion of Brazil's current foreign debt. Under military rule construction targets were met, but at an enormous **environmental and political cost**.

Communities living in the path of the development were simply moved (usually without compensation) or ignored. The railway, for example, cuts through the Gaviões Indian reserve, a problem which was solved by simply getting dispensation from FUNAI to build there. Tucuruí was the setting of one of the most celebrated corruption cases of the military years (see below), while the construction of the *Alcoa* aluminium plant at São Luis is a good example of the way environmental issues and the needs of local people were simply ignored. Some 22,000 people were moved from their homes, without compensation, to allow the plant to be built and environmental guarantees, though given, appear to have been ignored. Resentment in São Luis is fuelled by the plant's thirst for water and electricity. Power to the plant comes from new lines direct from Tucuruí: they stop at the factory, keeping it brightly lit even when the city is suffering one of its frequent power cuts. Many locals believe that the plant has priority when it comes to water, too.

Meanwhile in the serra itself the lands of several thousand Indians, and a huge chunk of rainforest, are being transformed into a giant industrial park. Hundreds of Indians have already died, others are now suffering as a result of disease, pollution, deforestation, and land invasions on the fringe of the project. Twelve fully loaded trains, each over 2km long, run daily through the territory of the Guajajara and Gavioes Indians, while landless settlers moving up from Marabá are also laying claim to their lands and destroying brazil nut groves vital to the local economy. In the Xikrin Indian reserve, which lies close to the central mines, *garimpeiros* who have managed to penetrate the cordon have polluted local rivers with mercury, used to separate out gold after panning.

Tucuruí

TUCURUÍ town, some 225km to the north of Marabá, was until 1977 no more than a pin on a surveyor's map. Today over 60,000 people live here amid air-conditioned office blocks, supermarkets, a modern hospital and even green tennis courts; it has a dusty red main street and a tendency to noise, with construction by day and construction workers by night. The entire city was built by *Eletronorte* to house the workers building Brazil's largest dam – over 12km long and with a flooded reservoir covering 4000 square kilometres of rainforest, the fourth largest artificial lake in the world. Now on stream, the Tucuruí dam is projected to supply eight million kilowatts a year throughout the 1990s.

The new city of Tucuruí is served by an older settlement about 9km distant. Today this old town is the site of brothels and other entertainment for the region's workers. Many of the people working and living in the old town are refugees from the flooded area.

The cost of building the dam is unknown, but it's estimated that at one stage three million dollars was being spent every day. Corruption was almost inevitable, and the **"Capemi case"** was one of the most public scandals of the years of military rule. Rather than simply drowning the vast tracts of forest in the area of the reservoir, *Electronorte* invited tenders for the timber to be cleared and sold by 1983. There were plenty of companies with all too much experience of clearing rainforest, but the contract was won, in 1979, by a company called *Capemi* – a company which dealt mainly with investing military pensions and had no experience of the lumber industry. The decision caused outrage, millions of dollars went missing, and clearance started two years late, succeeding in removing less than a quarter of the high quality hardwood available. It was a textbook example of the widespread corruption that marked the final years of military rule, and has never been properly investigated: part of the deal by which the military relinquished power was that there should be no investigation of human rights or financial abuses involving military personnel.

In human terms the cost was high too. The lake flooded a section of the Parakanan Indian Reserve and necessitated the re-routing of the *Transamazonica* through another part of it. It also destroyed the homeland of the Trocara, a group of Indians who had been "discovered" by FUNAI only in 1970.

If you want to **stay in Tucuruí** there are a number of possibilities. The *Hotel Transamerica*, Rua Brasil (☎787-1161), and the *Hotel Rio Doce*, Rua Lauro Sodre 663 (☎787-1146), are reasonable value starting at around $4 a head: next door to the latter, the *Hotel Marajoara*, Rua Lauro Sodre (☎787-1489), is another central possibility. The **Rodoviária** is close by on Rua Lauro Sodre: the **airport** (☎787-1489) is a six-kilometre taxi ride away.

Amapá

The territory of **Amapá**, north of the Amazon, is one of Brazil's poorest regions, with a reputation for being highly malarial. Traditionally it was dependent primarily on rubber exports, but manganese was discovered in the 1950s and this, together with timber and other minerals, is now the main source of income. A standard gauge railway links the mining camps, northwest of the capital at Macapá, to the Amazon port of Porto Santana, crossing en route the dry, semi-forested plains of the region.

The main reason to come here is to get to **French Guiana**: the key road in Amapá connects Macapá with the town of **OIAPOQUE**, on the river of the same name which delineates the frontier. Even this road is paved only as far as the town of CALÇOENE, beyond which it degenerates to little more than a dirt track. An irregular **bus service** costing around $5 attempts the journey from Calcoene to Oiapoque about three times a week, taking between 12 and 24 hours depending on the state of the rains. Macapá to Calcoene costs $8 and takes around eight hours. If you are not a citizen of a European Community country, the US or Canada, you will need a visa to enter French Guiana: there are French consulates in Belém, Manaus, Brasília, Rio and São Paulo, but try to arrange this before you leave home.

A more leisurely option is to go by **boat** from Macapá to Oiapoque, a journey of two days (one night): boats depart once a week or so, but there's no regular schedule. If you're interested in this possibility, you simply have to go to the docks and ask around: if a boat is leaving, seek out its captain and negotiate for hammock space, which should cost around $12 in either direction. The best hammock spaces are those with open sides, preferably on the middle deck. Most travellers, however, cross the border the easy way – by **flying** from Macapá to the capital at Cayenne (around $150). Once you're across the border you'll probably want to fly from the border settlement of St. George to Cayenne in any case, since overland transport is atrocious.

If you are going to travel overland, then buy **French francs** in Belém or Macapá. You can get them in Oiapoque but the rates are worse, and you can't depend on changing either Brazilian currency or US dollars for francs in St. George. Dug-out taxis are the usual means of transport between Oiapoque and St. George, about ten minutes downriver. Brazilian **exit stamps** can be obtained from the *Polícia Federal* at the southern road entrance into Oiapoque; on the other side you have to check in with the *Gendarmes* in St. George. The border along the Oiapoque river is still a sensitive one, although the last time there were actual hostilities was in 1808–17, when a Brazilian force crossed the border and occupied Cayenne. It was during this period that Brazil obtained the lucrative Cayenne pepper seeds for its own export market.

Macapá

MACAPÁ, on the north bank of the Amazon and right on the equator, is the gateway to the territory of Amapá and home to three-quarters of its population. Surrounded by uninhabited forests and hills, it dominates the northern section of the Amazon estuary. If you're coming from Belém you'll actually arrive at PORTO SANTANA, just twenty minutes by bus from Macapá though it lies on the other side of the equator (Macapá is in the northern hemisphere, Porto Santana in the southern): there are regular ferries from Belém docks, taking about 26 hours.

The countryside around Macapá is, like the Ilha do Marajó in the estuary, roamed by large herds of water buffalo. In town there's not a great deal to do: the **São José Fort**, overlooking the river, was built in 1764, constructed almost entirely of material used as ballast in Portuguese ships. Nearby, on the Praça Veiga Cabral, you could fill some more time checking out the eighteenth-century **Igreja São Jose de Macapá** and the **Museum of Science and History** (Mon–Fri 8am–noon & 2–5.30pm, Sat & Sun 8am–5pm).

For **accommodation** the *Hotel Tropical*, Av. Antônio Coelho de Carvalho 1399 (☎231-3759), is excellent value from around $7 double. The *Hotel São Antônio* is better placed on the main praça, and even cheaper, but not quite as good; or there's the clean and friendly *Hotel Mara* in Rua São Jose (☎222-0859). As for **food**, Macapá's position as a river and sea port means that there's plenty of excellent fish. The *Lennon Restaurant* downtown is a popular eating place, but greater variety can usually be found at the *Restaurant Boscão*, Rua Hamilton Silva 997 (☎222-0859), or *Peitans* on the first block of Avenida Mãe Luzia. For unrestrained night-time entertainment, try the *Marco Zero* **nightclub**.

For boats to the north or back to Belém, the **Captain of the Port** (Avenida FAB 427; ☎222-0415) can be contacted at his offices most weekdays between 8am and 5pm. Most **buses** leave from Praça Veiga Cabral, while the **railway** for the interior starts at Porto Santana, some 28km beyond Macapá.

Up the Amazon: Santarém and around

Around 700km west of Belém – but closer to 800 if you're following the river –
SANTARÉM is the first stop of any significance on the journey up the Amazon.
Only in recent years has it also become possible to reach Santarém overland by
bus: a new dimension in transport that has opened up a couple of arduous but
rewarding routes. A rough road runs south from Santarém to join the
Transamazonica, and from here you can continue south to Cuiabá or take the
Transamazonica itself. If you are heading up from Cuiabá, or even from Brasília,
the new road can cut travel time considerably – you can go straight to Santarém
and get a boat to Manaus from there, saving a detour of several days via Belém.

Although it's the third largest city on the Amazon – and economically swollen
by the recent gold rush in the hinterland – Santarém is not a large place, and it
has an amazingly sleepy atmosphere. There are attractive narrow streets in the
old centre, but the character of the city is defined by the two mammoth rivers
that meet here, the Amazon and the Rio Tapajós. When the Amazonian tides turn,
as they regularly do, the crystalline blue waters of the Tapajós become a muddy
Amazon brown for a few hours. Once you get down to it there's not a great deal to
do in Santarém – and it's a relatively expensive place to stay – but its position

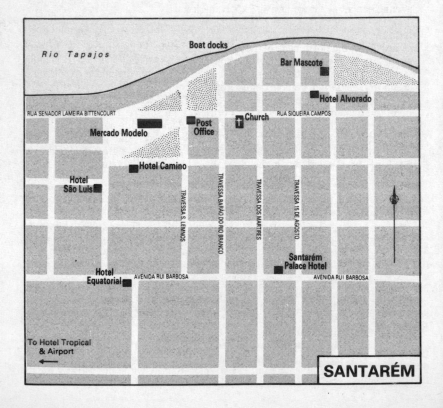

makes it a natural pit-stop on any Amazon trip, and for that purpose it serves pleasantly enough. It's also a staging post for visiting **Fordlândia** or **Itaituba**, or for continuing overland into the rest of Brazil.

Santarém started life in the seventeenth century as a Jesuit mission to the Tapuiçu Indians. It was one of the earliest settlements in the Amazon, and its relative isolation made it a refuge for runaway slaves and for Indians who, as at Belém, could trade with the Portuguese without becoming too closely involved with them. There was always, then, a substantial black population and in the early nineteenth century the **Cabanagem Rebellion** had widespread support here – and was put down with typical ferocity. In the aftermath of the American Civil War, Santarém was chosen as a base for **Confederate refugees**. They came in the hope of establishing a new slaving state here, and as with similar attempts elsewhere they failed dismally. Few stayed long, but they've left their mark in family and trade names – Higgins or MacDonald – that still crop up locally. Several dozen *confederado* descendants remain in Santarém and meet monthly to play bingo and raise money for their annual Christmas party. If you're interested you can contact them through Irene or Maria Julieta Wanghon (☎229-6075): though none of them speak any English or appear significantly different from their neighbours.

Meanwhile, in 1874 an Englishman named Henry Wickham settled at Santarém with his wife. He was to be almost single-handedly responsible for the collapse of the Amazon rubber boom, smuggling quantities of valuable rubber seed from the heart of the Amazon (at a price of £10 for every 1000 seeds). The seeds he collected were transported to Kew Gardens, in London, for germination, before being sent on to British-owned plantations in Asia which were already prepared and waiting. It took over twenty years for the first crop to mature to anywhere near peak production, but when it did the bottom fell out of the Brazilian rubber market. British plantations produced 4 tons of rubber in 1900, but 71,000 tons by 1914. This was not only more than Brazil was producing, but also a great deal cheaper, since the plantations were far more efficient than the labour-intensive wild rubber-tree tapping practiced in the Amazon. Rubber was to feature again in local history through the development of Fordlandia (see below).

Rooms and food

There are no mid-range **hotels** in Santarém, but there are two expensive ones and a number of adequate cheapies. Flashiest of them is the *Hotel Tropical*, Av. Mendonça Furtado 4120 (☎522-1533), built by *Varig* for the opening of the Santarém–Cuiabá highway, and way overpriced. The two-storey *Hotel Santarém Palace*, Av. Rui Barbosa 726 (☎522-5285), is a much better choice at this end of the range, with excellent views over the city. Of the cheaper places, the best are the *Hotel Equatorial*, Avenida Rui Barbosa (about $3 a night), with spacious rooms, some with bathrooms, or the young and friendly *Hotel Alvorado*, with lively music in the lobby and excellent value singles from $3.50 (hammock space on the patio available for $1 a night). Less promising, but still perfectly alright, are the *Hotel São Luis* on the Praça do Pescador and the *Hotel Camino* in Praça Rodrigues dos Santos.

Decent **places to eat** are surprisingly scarce. The patio of the *Mascote Bar* is popular, and a great place to look out over the activity in the port, but its food is expensive. The fancy hotels also have pricey restaurants. For cheaper food you're mainly reliant on stalls – either in the market (though you need a strong constitution) or in the downtown streets towards the main pier where the ocean liners dock. These serve delicious skewered chicken or **fish**, but you are strongly advised not to eat fish in Santarém, as mercury pollution is a real and growing danger.

Transport

Santarém is a busy port, serving river communities for over 300km around as well as the long-distance services to Manaus and Belém. **Boats to Manaus and Belém** leave most days: the journey time is two to three days in either direction and the cost varies from $10 to around $30, so it's worth shopping around. Head for the docks nearer the large concrete wharves, where you can ask the various captains when they're leaving and how much they'll charge. The *Rio Nilo* line to Manaus has a good reputation, though like most boats it gets crowded at times (as usual, first class hammock space is the best option; cabins are almost twice as expensive and feel three times as hot during the day). *ENASA*'s offices can be found at Rua Senador Lameira Bittencourt 459 (☎522-1138).

Milk boats operating between Santarém and the interior are an effective and inexpensive way to check out the surrounding rivers. The tiny *Costa Sima*, for example, is often prepared to carry passengers on its trips out to the small island communities where *mestizo* families live in houses on stilts, suspended over the water when the river is high. The *Costa Sima* moors along with the others on the beachfront before reaching the main pier. Make arrangements directly with the captain on the boat. Sometimes trips are overnight so it's worth taking a hammock, food, drink and insect repellent. For more **local tours** of the port and surrounding districts, ask at the *Hotel Tropical*.

Buses to Marabá, Belém, Cuiabá and São Luis leave from the *Rodoviária* on Avenida Cuiabá (☎522-1342). The **airport** (☎522-4838) is about 13km from the centre: there's no bus and taxis are relatively expensive (from $7), but it's sometimes possible to hitch a lift with *Varig* employees in their bus which leaves around 8am most mornings from the *Varig* offices by the *Hotel Equatorial*. The best **travel agent** in town, also a useful place for general information, is *Santarém Turismo*, Av. Adriano Pimentel 6 (☎522-4823).

Around Santarém

Although most travellers continue up or down the Amazon from Santarém, it's also possible to head south, up the Rio Tapajós. One popular outing is to the **meeting of the waters**, where the blue Tapajós merges with the brown Amazon, and then on to **ALTER DO CHÃO**, site of the original settlement and now a local weekend resort. There's a beautiful sandy river beach here, curving round to almost enclose the tranquil waters of the Lago Verde, a turquoise lagoon where the fishing is reputedly excellent (though again mercury pollution is a danger).

You can get to Alter do Chão by bus or by finding a boat at the docks in Santarém, or you can take a tour: check at the *Hotel Tropical* or *Santarém Turismo*. These agents can also arrange more substantial trips to take in the places below.

Fordlandia and Belterra

Fordlandia and Belterra are the fruits of an attempt by Henry Ford to revive the Amazon rubber trade in the first half of this century. Ford's intention was to establish an Amazon plantation to challenge the growing power of the British and Dutch controlled rubber cartels, based in the Far East. He was sold a vast concession on the banks of the lower Tapajós river by a local man named Villares. What no-one seemed to notice at the time was that Villares also organised the Amazon survey, which ended up visiting only his piece of land. Though it was vast – almost 2,500,000 hectares in all – the tract of land he sold had marginal potential for a plantation of any kind. It depended on seasonal rather than regular rains, it was hilly and therefore awkward to mechanise, the soil was sandy and overleached, and it was beyond the reach of ocean-going vessels for several months every year.

Nevertheless, Henry Ford went ahead with a massive investment, and the construction of **FORDLANDIA** (200km south of Santarém) began in 1928. Cinemas, hospitals and shops were built to complement the processing plants, docks and neat rows of American staff homes: there was even an independent power supply, designed in Detroit. Nothing like it existed within a thousand kilometres in any direction. Unfortunately the rubber planting proceeded at a much slower rate. Difficulties were encountered in trying to clear the valuable timbers which covered the land, and even when it was cleared there was a shortage of rubber tree seeds. After five years only about 1000 hectares a year were being cleared and planted, at which rate the process would still have been only half completed in the year 3000.

In the 1930s a new site for the plantation was established at **BELTERRA**, and high-yield rubber seeds were imported back from Asia. Belterra is a plain, around 150m above sea level, about 50km from Santarém on the east bank of the Tapajós, in a position navigable all year round. Even here, though, Ford never looked likely to recover his money, and poor labour relations combined with poor growth to ensure that he didn't. Although the plantations are still operative, they have always suffered from loss of topsoil and from South American Leaf Blight (the fungus *microcycous uli*), and have never made a significant contribution to the world's rubber supply. By the late 1930s Ford himself had lost interest and in 1945 he sold out to the Brazilian government for $250,000: having already invested well in excess of $20 million. The Belterra Hospital still has the best medical service in the Santarém region.

If you do visit, these are pretty bizarre places – American towns transplanted to the jungle, white picket fences and all.

Itaituba

Since finding itself in the path of the *Transamazonica* highway, **ITAITUBA** has become a classic example of Brazilian rapid growth. Situated on the Tapajós river not far from SÃO LUIS DO TAPAJÓS, the town is caught up in the throes of a gold rush based around the rivers of the interior (and the chief source of the mercury polluting these waters). The airstrip is always busy and, if the consequences of the boom are combined with the *Transamazonica*, the effects have been far more evident than that of the rubber boom earlier this century.

A quiet rural town in the 1960s, today Itaituba has a population of around 30,000 and rising. First Street, parallel to the river, is permanently busy. Where recently cattle grazed by the riverside, you'll nowadays find taxi ranks, shops, gold-buying agencies and a pleasant colonial-style frontage opposite a fine row of mango trees. There are a few **hotels** in town but they're usually full: if you've the choice there's little reason for stopping here long.

Óbidos

Around forty million years ago, when the Andes began to form themselves by pushing up from the earth, a vast inland sea burst through from what we now know as the main Amazon basin. The natural bursting point was more or less the site of modern day **ÓBIDOS**. The huge sea squeezed itself through where the Guianan shield to the north meets the Brazilian shield from the south, and cut an enormous channel through alluvial soils in its virgin route to the Atlantic. The river is some seven kilometres wide at Santarém, while at Óbidos, about 100km upstream, it has narrowed to less than two kilometres. Physically then, Óbidos is the gateway to the Amazon; there's an old fort to protect the passage, and most boats going upstream or down will stop here for an hour or two at least.

In the Cabanagem Rebellion, most of the town's leading white figures were assassinated by rebels and the town was looted and left ungoverned for years. Describing this period, the English botanist Richard Spruce remarked that anti-white feeling ran so strong in Óbidos that the mob considered that to have a beard was a crime punishable by death. Thankfully, this is no longer the case. On the other hand, there are few positive reasons to stop. There's really very little of interest in the town, and hardly any facilities for visitors. The *Bras Bela* is a reasonable mid-range hotel if you do find yourself stuck here for a night.

WESTERN AMAZONIA

An arbitrary border, a line on paper through the forest, divides the state of Pará from the western Amazon. Encompassing the states of Amazonas, Rondônia and Acre and the Territory of Roraima, the western Amazon is dominated even more than the east by the Amazon and Solimões rivers and their tributaries. In the north, the forest revolves around the rios Negro and Branco, before phasing into the wooded savannas of Roraima. In the northeast, the **Casiquare Canal** is a natural waterway forming an incredibly remote link between the Amazonian and Orinoco river systems. To the south, the rios Madeira, Purús and Juruá meander through the forests on their way to the sea from the prime rubber region of Acre and the recently colonised state of Rondônia. It is as real a jungle region as exists on the planet.

The hub of this area is, of course, **Manaus**, more or less at the junction of three great rivers – the Solimões/Amazonas, the Negro and the Madeira – which between them support the world's greatest surviving forest. There are few other settlements of any real size. In the north, **Boa Vista**, capital of Roraima, lies on an overland route to Venezuela by bus. South of the Rio Amazonas there's **Porto Velho**, capital of the newly colonised state of Rondônia, and, further west, **Rio Branco**, the main town in the relatively wild and unexplored rubber growing state of Acre – where the now famous Chico Mendes lived and died, fighting for a sustainable future for the forest.

Travel is never easy or particularly comfortable in the western Amazon. The main routes passable by road emanate from Manaus, from Pará in the east or Mato Grosso in the south. From Manaus it's possible to go by bus to Boa Vista and Venezuela; a minimum of 24 hours to Boa Vista on the unpaved BR-174 through the stunning tropical forest zone of the Waimiris tribe, with over fifty bridges en route. You can also head east to the Amazon river settlement of **Itacoatiara**; or south to join the *Transamazonica* at **Humaitá** for connection to **Porto Velho** (over 860km, mostly paved). From Porto Velho the *Transamazonica* continues unpaved into Acre, for **Rio Branco** and routes on to Peru: alternatively the newly paved BR-364 offers quick access south to Cuiabá, Mato Grosso, Brasília and the rest of Brazil.

Yet again, the rivers are an equally important means of communication. Entering from the east, the first places beyond Óbidos are the small ports of **Paratins** and Itacoatiara (with bus connection for Manaus if you're really fed up with the boat) before you reach the mouth of the Madeira. From here it's a matter of hours till Manaus appears at the confluence of the rivers Negro and Amazonas. It takes another five to eight days by boat to reach the Peruvian frontier. Even here the river is several kilometres wide, and still big enough for ocean-going ships.

It rains a lot in the western Amazon – up to 150 inches a year in the extreme west and about 70 inches around Manaus. The humidity rarely falls much below eighty percent, and the temperature in the month of December can reach well into the 40s Celsius. This takes a few days to get used to, until you do it's like being stuck in a sauna with only air conditioning or cool drinks to help you escape. The heavy rains fall between February and September most years, with a relatively dry season from October to January.

Manaus

Most visitors are surprised to learn that **MANAUS** – the capital of Amazonas and the hub of the whole Amazon region – isn't actually on the Amazon at all. Rather it lies on the Rio Negro, six kilometres from the point where that river meets the Solimões to form (as far as Brazilians are concerned) the Rio Amazonas. Just a few hundred metres away from the tranquil life on the rivers, the centre of Manaus perpetually buzzes with energy; always noisy, crowded and confused. Everywhere you turn, shops and stalls are selling everything from imported Persian rugs to Taiwanese toys and plastic sunglasses. There's a ready market for them among Brazilians; but above all, since its establishment as a Free Port, Manaus has specialised as a centre for electronic commodities.

Escaping from the frenzy is not easy, but there is the occasional quiet corner, and the sites of the port, markets, Opera House and some of the museums make up for the hectic pace in the downtown area. In the port and market areas, where the infamous *Porto do Manaus* smell is inescapable, pigs and chickens line the streets and there's an atmosphere which seems unchanged in centuries.

For the Amazon hinterland, Manaus has long symbolised "civilisation". Traditionally, this meant simply that it was the trading centre, where the hardships of life in the forest could be temporarily escaped and where manufactured commodities to make that life easier could be purchased – metal pots, steel knives, machetes and the like. Virgin jungle seems further from the city these days – just how far really depends on what you want "virgin forest" to mean – but there are still waterways and channels within a day's river journey of Manaus where you can find dolphins, alligators, kingfishers and the impression, at least, that man has barely penetrated.

Manaus in history

The name Manaus came originally from the Manau tribe which was encountered in this region by São Luis do Maranhão, exploring the area in 1616. He called the spot São Luis del Rio. But it was Francisco do Motta Falco who really founded Manaus by building up the settlement and encouraging others to remain there with him.

The city you see today is primarily a product of the rubber boom and in particular the child of visionary state governor **Eduardo Ribeiro**, who from 1892 transformed Manaus into a really important city. Since the middle of the century steam navigation, which began in 1858, had opened up the jungle, spurring the rubber boom and mass immigration. It was Ribeiro who ordered the building of the Opera House and, through the French Koch brothers, oversaw the design of its strange baroque interior. Whole streets were wiped out in the process of laying down broad Parisian avenues and boulevards interspersed with Italian piazzas centred on splendid fountains. In 1899 Manaus was the first Brazilian city to have trolley buses and only the second to have electric lights in the streets. By the turn of the century it was an opulent metropolis run by elegant people who dressed and housed themselves as fashionably as their counterparts in any large European city.

Manaus was a boom town and, as such, could do whatever it liked. An English company built Manaus's drainage system and the yellow bricks used in the building of the Customs House arrived in Manaus on a Scottish ship as prefabricated blocks, to be erected in 1906 around the peak of the Amazonian rubber boom.

For the rich it was a place of luxury – palaces and grandiose mansions were erected; time was passed at elaborate entertainments, dances and concerts. But this heyday lasted barely thirty years, and by 1914 the rubber market was collapsing fast. Ribeiro himself had meanwhile committed suicide in 1900. There was a second brief boost for Brazilian rubber during World War II, when plantations in the Far East fell under Japanese control, but today's prosperity is largely due to the creation of a **Free Trade Zone** in 1966. Over the next ten years the population doubled, from 250,000 to half a million, and many new industries moved in, especially electronics companies. An impressive new international airport was opened in 1976 and the floating port, supported on huge metal cylinders to cope with variations of as much as 14m in the level of the river, was modernised to cope with the new business.

Today, Manaus is still an aggressive commercial and industrial centre for an enormous region – the Hong Kong of the Amazon. Over half of Brazil's televisions are made here and electronic goods like this are around a third cheaper here than in the south. All of this helps encourage domestic tourism – Manaus airport is crowded with queues of Brazilians going home with their arms laden with TVs, hi-fis, computers and telephones.

Another good reason for the rush of people into Manaus is the lack of attraction of anywhere around. The smaller towns up and down the rivers have barely any facilities at all. Where there's no road or mine the area is more or less abandoned by the rest of Brazil – no urban facilities or entertainment, no football teams, and very little chance of making enough money to pay for the expensive import by river of any luxury commodities. The air-conditioned suburbs of Manaus, then, are home to a growing and increasingly competent workforce and to multinational companies keen to take advantage.

Arrival

If you arrive in Manaus by river, your **boat** will dock right in the heart of the city, by the Mercado Municipal. This really is the best way to come. If you're arriving from Peru or Colombia, don't forget to have your passport stamped at the Customs House. The **Rodoviária** is some 4km from the centre: buses run down Avenida Constantino Nery (#507 is the most direct) from just outside to the heart of town. The **airport** is 9km from town in the same direction: bus #608 will take you in, or there are taxis for between $8 and $10.

The main *Emamtur* **tourist information office** is some way out at Rua Taruma 379 (☎234-2252/5514/5983; Mon–Fri 7am–7pm, Sat 7am–1pm) on Praça 24 de Outubro. You can pick up **maps** and some of the more useful brochures at the big downtown hotels: try the *Lord* or *Amazonas*.

It's not hard to get used to the **layout** of the town, and most things of interest huddle close to the water. From the floating port where the big ships dock, riverboat wharves extend round past the market, from one end of Rua Dos Andradas to the other. The busiest commercial streets are immediately behind, extending up to the Avenida Sete de Septembro, with the cathedral marking one end of the downtown district, the Praça da Polícia the other. Beyond Sete de Setembro, towards the Opera House, it's a bit calmer, with more offices and fewer shops. The busy streets between the *Hotel Amazonas* and the cathedral are the main hub of city communications, with **buses** to local points around the city and suburbs: another good connection point for city buses and taxis is the slightly less hectic Praça da Polícia.

Finding a place to stay

Plenty of travellers end up in Manaus, so there's a wide range of **places to stay**, with a number of perfectly reasonable **cheap hotels**, especially in the area around Avenida Joaquim Nabuco. One of the very cheapest places, the *Hotel Lars* at Rua Dos Andradas 196 (☎234-9864), is slightly closer to the dock area: very basic but reasonably clean and good value for a downtown location from around $3 a night (make sure that there is a working fan in the room and try to get one which is well ventilated but safe). Most rooms are shared and you can choose a bed or to use the hammock hooks. The *Hotel São Francisco* on block 5 of Bocaiúva, going towards the new bridge, is cheap, clean and friendly – it also has a laundry. An old port mansion coverted with thin wooden partitions, the *Hotel Bela Vista*, on the corner of Dos Andradas and Joaquim Nabuco, offers basic accommodation with shared toilets and showers from $2 a night. Also on the same block of the Avenida Joaquim Nabuco, the *Hotel Pensão Sulista* (☎234-5814) is an interesting building though its rooms are small at the price of $5.

Slightly more **upmarket** alternatives include the *Hotel Doral* (☎232-4102), further down Joaquim Nabuco and easily spotted by the bright jungle murals painted all over the front; air-conditioned single rooms here start at $12. More expensive again, though in the same area as the *Lars* and *Bela Vista*, the *Hotel Janelas Verdes* is very pleasant, handy for both the port and downtown districts, and fairly good value at $25 for all mod cons. If you want to be closer to the city's main commercial districts, rooms at the *Hotel Nacional* at Rua Dr. Moreira 59 (☎233-7533) start at $15.

In the **luxury** class, the downtown choices are the four-star *Hotel Amazonas* on Praça Adelberto Valle (☎232-2957), near the docks, and the three-star *Hotel Lord*, a couple of blocks inland on Rua Marcílio Dias at the corner of Quintano Morais. If it's luxury you're after, though, the popular *Tropical Hotel* (☎234-1165/1164), some 15km out of town on the Estrada da Ponta Negra (8km from the airport) might be the better choice. Built in 1978 out by the chic city beach known as the Praia Ponta Negra, the *Tropical* has a swimming pool, tennis courts, good night-life, fine river beaches and even offers water-skiing on the Rio Negro. The *Tropical* has its own buses from downtown (outside the *Banco do Brasil*, near the Cathedral) and the airport.

If you want to **camp**, the World Wildlife Fund will allow you to do so inside their small reserve for $4 a day.

The City

Manaus is above all a river port, and it's this reality that you'll come back to time and time again as you wander the streets. Only in the main shopping districts in the middle of the day, or in clubs at night, can you forget the location, but in one way or another virtually everything in Manaus seems related to either the river or the forest – from the fish on your plate to the powerful tropical rainstorms that catch every visitor to Manaus by surprise at some time or another.

Around the docks

Since it's the docks that have created Manaus, it seems logical to start your exploration here – and it's certainly the most atmospheric part of town. The **port** itself is an unforgettable spectacle. A constant throng of activity stretches along the riverfront while the ships tied up at the docks bob serenely up and down. Boats are getting ready to leave, or having just arrived are busy unloading. People are cooking fish at stalls to sell to the hungry sailors and their passengers, or the workers once they've finished their shift of carrying cargo from the boats to the distribution market. There's produce of every kind: manufactured goods, sacks of rice and beans and cement, and bunches of bananas by the thousand. Hectic and impossibly complex and anarchic as it appears to the unaccustomed eye, the port of Manaus is in fact very well organised, if organically so. During the day there's no problem wandering around, and it's easy enough to find out which boats are going where just by asking around. At night, however, this can be a dangerous area and is best avoided: many of the rivermen carry guns.

For a better general view of the area, cross over the main roads to the front of the *Hotel Amazonas*. Looking to the right, the impressive **Customs House** stands between you and the floating docks. Erected in 1906, the Customs House was shipped over from Britain in prefabricated blocks. The floating docks, too, were built by a British company, at the beginning of the century. To cope with the river rising over a 14m range, the concrete pier is supported on pontoons which rise and fall to allow even the largest ships to dock here all year round. The highest recorded level of the river so far was in 1953, when it rose some 30m above sea level. In front of the Customs House, nearer to the hotel, are the offices of the **Captain of the Port**, where you can check details of riverboat departures.

More or less directly ahead, the city's relationship to the surrounding environment is also visually obvious in the covered **Mercado Municipal** (whose elegant Art Nouveau roof was designed by Eiffel) where tropical fruit and vegetables,

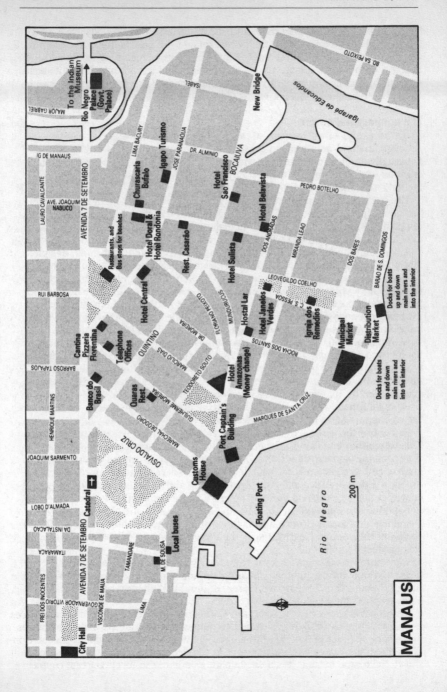

jungle herbs, scores of different fresh fishes, and Indian craft goods are jumbled together on sale. Between this public market and the port is the wholesale **port distribution market**, whose traders buy goods from incoming boats and sell them on wholesale to shops, market stall-holders and restaurants. It's at its busiest first thing in the morning: by the afternoon most of the merchants are swinging in their hammocks by their empty plots.

The commercial centre

Things are almost as busy in Manaus's downtown **commercial centre**, but although it starts only a few metres inland, the atmosphere is totally different. Essentially an electronics market which has evolved out of the Free Trade Zone era, this is the hub of the modern city. Everything from shoes to hi-fis can be bought – reasonably priced by any country's standards.

The city's most famous symbol, the **Teatro Amazonas** or Opera House (Mon–Sat noon–5pm), seems even more extraordinary coming in the midst of this rampant commercialism. Until you actually see it, it's hard to believe that after the Opera's completion in 1896 the Russian Ballet were to dance here in Manaus and Jenny Lind once sang. The whole incongruous, magnificent thing, designed by Domenico de Angelis in a pastiche of Italian Renaissance style, took seventeen years to build and cost in the region of $3 million. The wrought-iron skeleton of the building was brought from Scotland and the stone from Italy: the domed roof tiles were shipped in from Alsace Lorraine, over 60,000 of them glazed in the Brazilian national colours. On the inside the dome is supported by an entirely metal framework set on heavy cast-iron columns which rise from the foundations.

As you enter you can see these vast columns, covered in plaster, rising through the lobby. The Verona marble doorways are topped by busts of popular Brazilian artists. From here an iron stairwell leads up to the **Noble Room**, on the left, decorated with panels painted by Domenico de Angelis. In the main **auditorium** the stage is 30m by 15m and there's a huge backdrop – the *pano de boca* – painted by Crispim do Amaral with a representation of the meeting of the waters. The orchestra pit, operating on a hydraulic system, can be raised or lowered by 3m.

In front of the Teatro, the wavy black-and-white mosaic designs of the **Praça São Sebastião** are again said to represent the meeting of the waters. In the centre of the square stands the "Monument to the Opening of the Ports", a marble and granite creation with four ships that represent four continents – America, Europe, Africa and Asia/Australasia – and children who symbolise the people of those continents. Across the praça is the beautiful little **Igreja de São Sebastião**. Inaugurated in 1888, it predates the Teatro by several years: Domenico de Angelis is once again responsible for the painting on the ceiling as you enter the church. Nearby, too, is the **Palácio da Justiça**, which was supposedly modelled on Versailles.

Some three blocks further away from the river, up Rua Tapajós, you'll find the **Central Post Office**, another imposing reminder of the glorious years of the rubber boom. On the pavement around the back there's an ornate, much-photographed antique post box, dated 1889.

Heading back towards the river, the **Cathedral** on Avenida Sete de Setembro is a relatively plain building, surprisingly untouched by the orgy of adornment that struck the rest of the city. But judging by the number of people who use it, the cathedral plays a more active role in the life of the city than many more showy buildings. Around it is a shady park, popular with local courting couples, with views across to the buildings and ships of the floating harbour. On the right-hand side of the cathedral there's a pleasant garden café – *O Sabor da Terra* – open in the daytime only.

Museums

Manaus has a couple of excellent museums and a number of lesser ones, where you could easily fill a couple of rainy days in the city. The **Instituto Geográfico e Histórico do Amazonas** (Mon–Fri 9–11am) is west of the cathedral, past the City Hall and the Praça Dom Pedro II (where a crowd of street women work round the clock) at Rua Bernardo Ramos 117. Housed in the Casa de Bernardo Ramos, the Institute's small museum includes a collection of ceramics from various tribes, a range of insect displays and indigenous tools like stone axes and hunting equipment.

The **Museu Salesiano do Índio** (Mon–Sat 8–11am & 2–5pm) lies in the opposite direction, east along Avenida Sete de Setembro to its junction with Rua Duque de Caxias. The museum is run by the Salesian Sisters, who have long-established missions along the Rio Negro, especially with the Tukano tribe. There are excellent, carefully presented displays of Indian material culture, with exhibits ranging from sacred ritual masks and inter-village communication drums to fine ceramics, superb palm-frond weavings and even replicas of Indian dwellings.

Other museums worth a visit include the **Museu Tiradentes** on Praça Heliodoro Balbi (Mon 2–6pm, Tues–Fri 8am–noon & 2–6pm). Run by the Amazonian Military Police, this is a collection of local history where the best exhibits are probably the historical photos. The **Museu do Homen do Norte** (Museum of Northern Man; Mon 8.30am–12.30pm, Tues–Fri 8am–noon & 2–6pm) at Avenida Sete de Setembro 1385, near Avenida Joaquim Nabuco, offers a quick overview of human life and ecology in the Amazon region. Not far away at Avenida Joaquim Nabuco 1074, the **Espaço Cultural** (Tues–Sat 3–8pm, Sun 5–8pm) is probably the best art gallery in Manaus, which is not saying a great deal. Finally, the **Museu de Minerais e Rochas**, Estrada do Aleixo 215 (Mon–Fri 8am–noon & 2–6pm), has an extraordinary range of minerals, rocks and fantastic crystals.

Eating out and other entertainment

There are very few places in Manaus where you can sit down and enjoy any peace: in the parks you're certain to be interrupted by someone hassling you or wanting to practise their English, while on the streets every square centimetre seems to be used by someone – usually as a sales pitch. Even the cafés and bars are too full to give you much elbow room. One advantage of the crowds is that there's **street food** everywhere: especially around the docks and in busy downtown locations like the Praça do Congresso. One traditional dish you should definitely try here is *tacacá* – a working man's snack that consists essentially of yellow manioc root juice in a hot spicy dried-shrimp sauce. It's often presented in traditional gourd bowls, *cuias*.

One of the best places for a brief respite from the chaos **near the docks** – though it's not cheap – is the *Hotel Amazonas*, whose air-conditioned lounge is probably the coolest spot west of Belém. There's a very plastic café next to the lobby and the rather exclusive *Mandy's Bar* next door. Another surprisingly quiet spot, across the extremely busy and dangerous main road from here at the bottom of Dos Andradas, is a *Lanchonete/Bar* just below the *Hotel Lars*, which serves drinks, snacks and full meals quite cheaply, with tables effectively cooled by large fans.

On the other side of the commercial district, straight down the main pedestrian drag Rua Guilherme Moreira, the pleasant **Praça da Polícia** is home to several modern eating and drinking places, like the excellent Italian restaurant *Cantina Pizzeria Fiorentina*.

The area of budget hotels around **Avenida Joaquim Nambuco** is also a good place to eat, with a selection of bars and restaurants, most of which are quieter and offer better service than the downtown places. The *Quaras Restaurant* and *Restaurant Casarão* are popular with gringos and locals alike, or if you want to eat huge chunks of jungle beef, try the *Churrascaría Búfalo*, all on the Avenida Joaquim Nambuco.

One of the most **atmospheric** places to eat in Manaus is the *Bar Galo Carijo*, which serves delicious fish from 5.30pm every evening. They generally offer a range, fresh from the nearby port market, including *jaraqui* (a smallish fish), *pacú*, *tucunaré* and *acará* (another small one) – all of these names come from the original Guarani Indian language. You'll find the bar on the corner going down Leão towards the port; it also serves drinks all day. The *Bar and Restaurant Central* (on Rua Barrosso, block 2) serves reasonable food and beer in a typical open-air local scene just one block from Sete de Setembro, towards the Opera House. Or there's the *Canto da Peixada*, Rua Emilio Moreira 1677, whose quality is attested by the crowds that always eat here. *Xiko's* pizzeria is one of the liveliest places to eat in the evening: or if you get a hankering for **Chinese** food there's a fair selection at the *Restaurante China*, Getúlio Vargas 1127.

A little **further out**, in a suburban setting overlooking the Rio Negro, the *Restaurant São Francisco* has an excellent reputation for fish dishes. It's a twenty-minute walk from the centre, following Bocaiúva down from the *Hotel São Francisco* and across the new bridge, then straight on to the first major bend in the road where the restaurant commands views over the river. The restaurant and bar *La Barca*, Rua Recife 684 (☎236-8544), has good service and live music at weekends.

Nightlife

Even when they're going to work most people in Manaus, or at least those that can afford it, seem to dress as if they were going to a nightclub. When they do go out at night, they simply take most of these clothes off. The city's **nightlife** is, as ever, remarkably good: it doesn't get going until well after 10pm and continues through much of the night. The best downtown **club** by some way is *Catedral* (☎232-7793), at Saldanha Marinho 609 near the cathedral; expect to spend at least $10. *Jet Set*, Rua 10 de Julho 439 (☎234-9309), can also be good, though you should check what's on: they have live music. Good **discos** include a popular Saturday night spot out at the *Hotel Tropical*, and *Faces in the Groove* on Avenida Djalma Batista. Lively night-time **bars** include the *Club de los Ingleses*, Viraldo Lima 27 (after 10.30pm Thurs–Sat), and *Poney Club*, Avenida 7 de Setembro, both in the centre; or *Lobos*, Av. Getúlio Vargas, at the corner with Dr. Machado. There are also a couple of piano bars, Brazilian style, on Avenida Djalma Batista – *Classe A*, at no. 705, and *Clave de Sol*, at no. 1018. If you simply want a drink in the centre of town, try the *Opção Bar* at Rua Dr. Almino 272.

> The phone code for Manaus is ☎092

Listings

Airlines *Varig/Cruzeiro* have offices at 284 Rua Marcílio Dias (☎234-1116), between the *Hotel Amazonas* and the Praça da Polícia. Note that if you're flying to Iquitos in Peru, it works out up to $70 cheaper to buy two tickets (Manaus–Tabatinga and Tabatinga–Iquitos) rather than a direct Manaus–Iquitos one – you might have to get off and check in again at Tabatinga: this isn't always necessary so speak with the air hostess/steward on board first. Other airlines with offices in Manaus include: *Vasp*, Rua Dr. Moreira 179 (☎234-1266); *Transbrasil*, Rua Dr. Moreira 150 (☎212-1356); *TABA*, Av. Eduardo Ribeiro 664 (☎232-0806); *Lloyd Aereo Boliviano*, Av. Eduardo Ribeiro 620 (☎212-1188); *Air France*, Rua Dos Andrades 387, first floor (☎234-2798); *KLM*, Av. Japura 335 (☎234-6060); and *British Airways*, Av. Eduardo Ribeiro 355 (☎234-8986).

Airport The airport is 9km from downtown Manaus on Avenida Santos Dumont; ☎212-1210 for information. Bus #608 connects with the centre (Av. Constantino Nery, Praça 15 de Novembro and the end of the line in the first block of Rua da Instalação), but it's easier to take a taxi for around $8–10.

Buses The *Rodoviária* is at Rua Recife 2800 (☎236-2732). Daily departures to Boa Vista with *União Cascavel* (very busy route so book well in advance); to Porto Velho and Campo Grande most days (also *União Cascavel*); to Humaitá and Manicore (several daily) with *Expresso Transamazonica*; and to Itacoatiara (4 daily) with *Marlin*. Local buses to the *Rodoviária* leave from Avenida Constantino Nery (the most direct is the #507 – you get off at the *Petróleo Sabba*, a Shell garage surrounded by clouds of coffee smoke from a nearby factory, at the major intersection).

Car Hire *Internacional Locadora*, Av. Duque de Caixas (☎233-5288); *Belauto*, Av. Constantino Nery 520 (☎233-2566); *Hertz*, airport and Rua São Luis (☎232-8155).

Cinemas *Chaplin*, Av. Joaquim Nabuco 1094 (☎232-7531); *Cinema Novo*, Av. Joaquim Nabuco 1447 (☎233-0476); *Cantinflas*, Rua José Clemente 500; *Grande Otelo*, Av. Getúlio Vargas 114/118; *Oscarito*, Rua Ramos Ferreira 1195a; *Studio Centre*, Av. Eduardo Ribeiro 520 (☎234-6624); *Cine Qua Non*, Av. Joaquim Nabuco 1074; and *Carmen Miranda*, Rua 24 de Maio at the corner with Joaquim Sarmento.

Consulates *Belgium*, Q-D House 13 Murici (☎236-1452); *Bolivia*, Rua Fortaleza 80, Adrianópolis (☎232-0077); *Colombia*, Rua D.Libania 62 (☎234-6777); *Denmark*, Rua Miranda Leão 45 (☎233-6094); *West Germany*, Rua Barroso 355, No 4 (☎232-0890); *Netherlands*, Rua Dr. Moreira 129 (☎232-5380); *Italy*, Rua Belo Horizonte 240, Adrianópolis (☎234-8059); *Japan*, Rua Lima Bacuri 255 (☎232-2000); *Peru*, Av. Tapajós 536 (☎234-7900); *UK*, Avenida Eduardo Ribeiro 520 (☎234-1424); *USA*, Rua Maceió 62 (☎234-4546); *Venezuela*, Rua Marcal 116 (☎233-2531).

Emergency Medical Help *Hospital dos Acidentados*, Av. Joaqim Bambuco 1771 (☎234-1683). For private emergency ambulance call ☎234-4266.

Environmental Information Up-to-date eco-info from the German backed INPA (*Instituto Nacional de Pesquisas de Amazónia*). Try also the Amazon Natural Science Museum, Colonia Cachoeira Grande, Rua Estrada de Belém, Parque 10 (Tues–Sun 9am–5.30pm; $1), where there are fish, insects and a 37,000-gallon aquarium.

Maps from *Casa dos Mapas*, Rua J. Clemente, on the first block up the hill from Av. Getúlio Vargas (☎231-1700).

Money Exchange The *Banco do Brasil* is at 111 Praça 15 de Novembro, and the *Banco de Londres* at Rua Dr. Moreira 147. There's a Casa de Câmbio at Avenida Sete de Setembro 711.

Photographic Shop on Rua Enrique Martins, a walkway off the Avenida Eduardo Ribeiro, between blocks 3 and 4.

Post Office The main one is in the centre of the electronics market on Rua Marechal Deodoro at the corner with Theodoreto (Mon–Fri 8am–6pm, Sat 8am–noon). The best post office for sending international packages is at Rua Dr. Moreira 340.

River Transport The main *ENASA* ticket office is at Rua Marechal Deodoro 61 (☎232-4280) also at Rua Monsenhor Coutinho 233 (☎234-3151/3478); *Lloyds Brasileño* and *Ibarra* tickets from *Agencia Selvatur* in the *Hotel Amazonas*, (☎232-3151).

Shopping Good *artesanato* can be bought from the covered market area and there's one reasonable stall in the street market behind the *Hotel Amazonas*. There are also two very good shops selling quality Indian crafts: *Souvenir Vitória Regia*, near the Opera House on Avenida Eduardo Ribeiro; and the *Casa do Beija-Flor* (House of the Hummingbird), Rua Quintino Bocaiúva 224. Most everyday commodities – shoes, radios, Walkmans, razors, cosmetics, digital watches etc – can be found in the street market. Interesting *macumba* and *umbanda* magico-religious shops selling incense, candles, figurines and bongos, can be found on the first block of Rua da Instalação, parallel to blocks 3 and 4 of the Avenida Eduardo Ribeiro. Duty free electronic and all kinds of other luxury items can be bought from the *Duty Free Commercial Centre*, Avenida 7 de Setembro 826, a modern shopping complex built in 1980. There's also the *Manaus Shopping Centre*, Avenida Eduardo Ribeiro 520.

Tourist Information *Emamtur*, Rua Taruma 379 on Praça 24 de Octubro (☎234-2252/5514/5983; Mon–Fri 7am–7pm, Sat 7am–1pm).

Travel Agencies For tours and boat tickets try *Hoagem Turismo*, Rua Joaquim Nabuco 854 (☎232-5686); *Selvatur*, Praça Adalberto Valle – ground floor of *Hotel Amazonas* (☎234-8639), *Safari Turismo*, Avenida Eduardo Ribeiro 520 (☎234-8651); *Amazon Explorers*, Quintino Bocaiúva 189 (☎232-3052), and *Cristovão Amazonas Turismo*, Rua Marechal Deodoro 98 (☎233-3231); all offer a variety of city tours and river trips.

Around Manaus

Most visitors to Manaus rightly regard a river trip as an essential part of their stay: the various options are listed in the box below. Even if you can't afford the time to disappear up the Amazon for days at a stretch, however, there are a number of sites in the immediate vicinity of Manaus that make worthwhile day excursions.

Meeting of the Waters and the Parque Ecólogico Janauary

The most popular and most widely touted of the short trips is to the **meeting of the waters**, where the Rio Negro and the Rio Solimões meet to form the Rio Amazonas some 10km from Manaus. For several kilometres beyond the point where they join, the waters of the two rivers continue to flow separately: the muddy yellow of the Solimões contrasting sharply with the black of the Rio Negro. It's a strange sight, and one well worth seeing.

Most of the tours (for operators, see the travel agents under "Listings", above) leave the docks at Manaus and pass by the shanty town of EDUCANDOS and the Rio Negro riverside industries before heading out into the main river course. Almost all will also stop in at the **Parque Ecólogico Janauary**, an ecological park some 7km from Manaus on one of the main local tributaries of the Rio Negro. Usually you'll be transferred to smaller motorised canoes to explore its creeks (*igarapés*), flooded forest lands (*igapós*) and abundant vegetation.

One of the highlights of the area is the abundance of *Vitória Regia* – the extraordinary giant floating lily for which Manaus is famous. Found mostly in shallow lakes, it flourishes above all in the rainy months. The plant, named after Queen Victoria by an English naturalist in the nineteenth century, has huge leaves – some over a metre across – with a covering of thorns on their underside, as protection from the teeth of plant-eating fish. The flowers are white on the first day of their life, rose-coloured on the second, and on the third they begin to wilt: at night the blooms close, imprisoning any insects that have wandered in, and releasing them again as they open with the morning sun. In the rainy season you'll explore the creeks and floodlands by boat; during the dry season – between September and January – it's possible to walk around.

Praia Ponta Negra and the Zoo

The river beach at **Praia Ponta Negra**, about 15km out of Manaus near the *Hotel Tropical*, is another very popular local excursion, and at weekends is packed with locals. It's an enjoyable place to go for a swim, with plenty of bars and restaurants serving freshly cooked river fish. The beach is at its best between September and March, when the river is low and exposes a wide expanse of sand, but even when the rains bring higher waters and the beach almost entirely disappears, plenty of people come to eat and drink. *Soltur*'s Ponta Negra bus leaves every half hour: catch it by the cathedral on Rua Tamandaré, or at the bus stop in Avenida Epaminondas.

The nearby **military zoo** (Tues–Sun 9am–noon & 1.30–5.30pm) is also an army jungle training centre, and many of the animals in it were captured, so they say, on military training exercises out in the forest. There's a wide variety of jungle wildlife including what is claimed to be the largest number of jaguars bred in captivity anywhere. To get there take the *Compensa* or *São Jorge* bus from the military college on Avenida Epaminondas.

Cachoeira do Tarumã

The waterfalls of **Cachoeira do Tarumã** are the last of the local beauty spots within easy reach of Manaus city. They don't offer unspoiled beauty any more, thanks to commercialisation and weekend crowds, but the place is fun, there's good swimming, and on busy weekends you'll often find live music in the bars. The cascades themselves, supplied by the Rio Negro, are relatively small whitewater affairs which more or less disappear in the rainy season (April to August). *Soltur* buses run approximately every twenty minutes from a stop by the cathedral, taking about half an hour; a taxi will charge around $15 return.

River trips from Manaus

Standard tours on the rivers around Manaus generally cost from $30 to $40 per person per day (minimum of four or five people), inclusive of transport (mostly by boat and canoe), food and some kind of roof over your head at night. Anything more luxurious than this and you start having to pay a lot more. Most people prefer to pay less and take along any luxury items – sleeping bags, drinks, chocolate or the like. Insect repellent, toilet paper, swimming things, sun protection, a torch and some means of keeping your possessions dry are essential, as is ensuring that you'll have plenty of drinking water and food that you can eat.

The amount and nature of the **wildlife** you get to see depends mainly on how far away from Manaus you go and how long you can devote to the trip. At $30–40 a day or more, you have to be pretty keen to be very successful. Birds like macaws, jabarus and toucans can generally be spotted; and you might see alligators, snakes and a few species of monkey on a three-day trip (though you can see

JUNGLE BOATS AND OPERATORS

Any of the **travel agents** mentioned in the Manaus "Listings" will offer some kind of tour into the jungle: *Selvatur* and *Amazon Explorers* tend to have the widest range, but also large groups and relatively high prices. *Green Life Lodge Expeditions*, PO Box 1230, 69-000, Manaus (☎234-3759), operate a wide selection of tours – there's a full-day river tour lasting about ten hours from $20; they also have a floating lodge outside of Manaus which ties in with their 2/3-day trips (including meeting of the waters, Rio Negro for regina lilies and a few alligators); and they do deeper expeditions of up to nine days into the forest. *Safari Turismo*, Av. Eduardo Ribeiro 520 (☎234-8651), offer reasonable three-day trips (two nights) including the usual attractions – meeting of the waters, *igarapés*, alligators, rubber plantations and piranha fishing – from about $125 per person. A recommended jungle **guide**, Luiz Motta (Rua Carla Topinamba Morre, quadra 22, casa 30; take the *Vista Bella* bus) does three-day (two night) trips into the forest from about $35 per person inclusive of food and transport (minimum of four people).

Milk boats are a very inexpensive way of getting about on the rivers around Manaus. These smaller vessels, rarely more than 20m long, spend their weeks serving the local riverine communities by delivering and transporting their produce. You can spend a whole day on one of these boats for as little as $2 or $3, depending on what arrangement you make with the captain. The best place to look for milk boats is down on Flutuante Tres Estrelas, one of the wooden wharves behind the distribution market. Approach the ones that are obviously loading early in the morning of the day you want to go, or late in the afternoon of the day before. Generally speaking, boats for the interior – some of them preparing for trips up to a month long – can be found at the Escadaria dos Remédios docks.

The main operator of boats on **regular river journeys** is *ENASA*, Rua Marechal Deodoro 61 (☎234-3478). They operate a four-day **Manaus to Belém** service with stops at Paratins, Oriximiná, Óbidos, Santarém, and Breves. Carrying cargo and passengers, the *ENASA* boats generally have at least 25 cabins ($150, or over $200 for a private bath and decent air conditioning) and room for around 300 hammocks on the middle deck (from $40). Rigid timetables soon break down in the Amazon, so there are no fixed departure dates even for *ENASA* boats. Until recently *ENASA* were also running an amazing four-star catamaran cruiser, with air-conditioned cabins, restaurant, video lounge, bar, sun-deck, swimming pool etc, between Manaus and Belém. The prohibitive cost of tickets meant that there was never sufficient demand, and the service has been suspended till further notice, but it's worth checking to see if it has been reinstated at more affordable rates.

Boats from **Manaus to Porto Velho** (a five-day upstream trip on the Rio Madeira) or up the Solimões to **Peru** (5–8 days) leave frequently but to no regular schedule from the main docks and some of the smaller wharves around the Escadaria dos Remédios. They will usually display signs with their destinations marked up.

many of these anyway at the Parque Janauary). For even a remote chance of glimpsing wild deer, tapirs, armadillos or wild cats then a week-long trip is the minimum, preferably more. On any trip, make sure that you'll get some time in the smaller channels in a canoe, as the sound of a motor is a sure way of scaring every living thing out of sight.

There are a few Brazilian **jungle terms** every visitor should be familiar with: a *regatão* is a travelling boat-cum-general-store, which can provide a fascinating introduction to the interior if you can strike up an agreeable arrangement with one of their captains; an *igarapé* is a narrow river or creek flowing from the forest into one of the larger rivers (though by narrow around Manaus they mean less than 1km wide); an *igapó* is a patch of forest which is seasonally flooded; a *furo* is a channel joining two rivers and therefore a short cut for canoes; a *paraná*, on the other hand, is a branch of the river which leaves the main channel and returns further downstream, creating a river island.

It's worth checking on exactly how many days you get in the forest when booking a trip upriver with one of the agencies. Some of the "three-day" tours involve little more than half a day actually exploring the forest, the majority of the time spent on the big river getting there; yet it is this bit – in canoes up smaller tributaries – that most people are prepared to spend $35 a day or more for.

The Rio Solimões: to Peru

The stretch of river upstream from Manaus, as far as the pivotal frontier with Peru and Colombia at Tabatinga, is known to Brazilians as the **Rio Solimões**. Once into Peru it again becomes the Rio Amazonas. Although many Brazilian maps show it as the Rio Marañon once it enters Peru, Peruvians don't call it this until the river forks into the Marañon and Ucayali headwaters, quite some distance beyond Iquitos.

From Manaus to Iquitos in Peru, the river remains navigable by large ocean-going boats, though few travel this way any more. Since the collapse of the rubber market and the emergence of air travel, the river is left to smaller, more locally oriented river boats. Many travellers do come this way, however; and, although most complain about the food and many get upset stomachs, it can be a really pleasant way of moving around – lying in a hammock, reading and relaxing, maybe chatting to your neighbours. Against this, there are all the inherent dangers of travelling by boat on a large river. Boats have been known to sink (though this is rare) but they do frequently break down, causing long delays, and many captains seem to take great pleasure in overloading boats with both cargo and passengers. In spite of the discomforts, however, the river journey remains popular; and it's unarguably an experience that will stick in the memory.

The river journey is also, of course, by far the cheapest way of travelling between Brazil and Peru. There are reasonable facilities for visitors in the border town of Tabatinga, where you'll almost certainly have to stop: most boats will terminate at the border whichever direction they've come from. If you're on a tight budget it's worth asking the captain of your boat if you can sling your hammock on board for a couple of nights before leaving and after arriving – many people do this and there's usually no problem.

The boat trip from Manaus to Tabatinga – five to six days upstream, about four days down – costs $35 to $40 inclusive of food (though it is wise to take some of your own to supplement the poor fare on board). If you want to break the journey between Manaus and Tabatinga you can do so at TEFE, around halfway; but there's no reason to stop here unless you really can't face the boat any longer. Of the boats, the *Almirante Monteiro* and *Capitan Pinheiro* both have a good reputation, but this kind of thing can change overnight. On the other side of the border, the boat trip to Iquitos from Tabatinga costs around $15 and takes four or five

days; sometimes more, rarely less. Coming downstream from Iquitos to
Tabatinga gives you two or three days on the river. Again, it's advisable to take
your own food and water: all normal supplies can be bought in Tabatinga.

The Three-Way Frontier

The point where Brazil meets Peru and Colombia is known as the **three-way
frontier**, and it's somewhere you may end up staying for a few days sorting out
red tape or waiting for a boat. Most Brazilian boats will leave you at BENJAMIN
CONSTANT, across the river from Tabatinga, but if you do have to hang around
then Tabatinga, or the Colombian town of Leticia, are the only places with any
real facilities. A fleet of motorboat taxis connect these places, and Islandia in
Peru: Benjamin to Tabatinga takes half an hour and costs around $2; Tabatinga to
Islandia fifteen minutes and $1. When you're making plans, bear in mind that the
three countries have differing time zones: make sure you know which you are
operating on.

TABATINGA is the place to complete Brazilian exit (or entry) formalities with
the Polícia Federal, and it also has an airport with regular flights to Manaus and
Iquitos. Many of the boats into Peru leave from here, too, though if you're coming
the other way you'll almost certainly have to cross to Benjamin Constant for
services towards Manaus. Accommodation is not particularly easy here; another

THREE-WAY FRONTIER

good reason to stay on the boat if you can. The *Hotel Paje* is basic and clean; the *Hotel Miraflores* slightly more expensive and comfortable. It is possible to change dollars at the *Banco do Brasil* here, but you'll often get a better deal by crossing over to Leticia, buying pesos in the Colombian bank, and then changing these into cruzados at the Casa de Câmbio in Leticia (Leticia is also a good place to buy hammocks).

If you are staying around for a few days then **LETICIA** – little over ten minutes' walk away – is in any case a more interesting place. With an economy based on tourism and contraband (mostly cocaine) it has more than a touch of the Wild West about it: there are no entry formalities at all, though you should carry your passport with you. A couple of good, basic hotels are the *Residencial Leticia* and the *Residencial Monserrate*. Late in the afternoons there's a ritualised ceremony at the frontier, as the Colombian and Brazilian flags are lowered, a ritual which seems hopelessly out of place in the middle of the jungle. From Leticia it's possible to make trips out to Monkey Island or visit local Indian communities (ask at the *Residencial Leticia*). If you want to go further **into Colombia** you'll need to have picked up a tourist card from the Colombian consulate in Manaus (or Iquitos): canoes to PUERTO ASIS connect with the Colombian road and bus system.

Heading **into Peru** many of the boats actually leave from Tabatinga, although Peruvian authorities and passport control are in PUERTO ALEGRE or RAMON CASTILLA. The large *Huallaga* is one of the best **boats** – it was used by Werner Herzog in the filming of the epic *Fitzcarraldo* – charging around $12 for the four-day trip to Iquitos.

Up the Rio Negro

The **Rio Negro** flows into Manaus from northwestern Amazonas, one of the least explored regions of South America. There's virtually nothing in the way of tourist facilities in this direction, but it is possible to make your way up the Rio Negro boat by boat from Manaus to Barcelos, from Barcelos to São Gabriel, and from there on to the virtually uncharted borders with Colombia and Venezuela. The going is hard and to leave Brazil via these routes requires expedition-level planning. But it's an exciting trip. One piece of good news is that the black colour of the Rio Negro is caused by vegetable acidity leached from the surrounding forested basins and the Columbian foothills where the river's source lies: this acidity helps keep down the number of insects (particularly mosquitoes) along the river, making it much more comfortable to sleep on the river beaches than on those of most major Amazonian tributaries.

The first part of the journey, from Manaus to **BARCELOS**, is relatively easy. There are *TABA* flights three times a week ($50) and boats at least twice a week ($8) – the river journey takes about thirty hours, and the *Nosso Motor* is particularly recommended, with good, fresh river food aboard. Other boats leave fairly frequently but with no predictable regularity from the Escadaria dos Remedios docks behind the central market: look for the destination signs. In Barcelos the *Hotel Oasis* ($3–4 a night) is run by a German family, serves good food and can organise excellent jungle tours lasting up to five nights and really getting deep into the forest where there's a better chance of spotting wildlife than there is closer to Manaus.

At least two days further upriver, the town of **SÃO GABRIEL DA CACHOEIRA** is the next settlement of any size. Boats from Barcelos leave at irregular intervals, but generally several times a week. Expect to pay between $10 and $15. It's a beautiful place where the jungle is punctuated by volcanic cones, one with a Christ figure standing high on its flank. Superb views can be had across the valley from the slopes around the town, and there's a good *pensão* and several restaurants.

A little further upriver you reach the **Rio Negro Forest Reserve** – local guides will take you camping there from around $20 a day. At present this park zone – a massive triangle between the headwaters of the Rio Negro and its important tributary the Rio Uaupés, both of which rise in Colombia – is crawling with military personnel. It's a sensitive zone, partly because of fears of narcotics smuggling, but also in terms of the national frontier: Venezuela, Brazil and Colombia meet here, and the Rio Negro itself forms the border between Venezuela and Colombia for some way. There are also plans to put a highway through the park – the projected BR-210 or *Perimetral Norte* – which is destined to run from Macapá on the Atlantic coast to São Gabriel on the Rio Branco, passing south of Boa Vista on the way. From São Gabriel it should eventually make its way, if the plans go ahead, across the Amazon via Tabatinga to Cruzeiro do Sul, where it would link up with the westerly point of the *Transamazonica*, making it feasible to do an enormous circle by road around the Brazilian Amazon. Exactly when this will happen is anybody's guess, but recent history has shown – in Brasília and the construction of the *Transamazonica* – that this is a determined nation and that things have a tendency to happen quickly. On the other hand, some of the regions they are talking about putting this road through are incredibly remote.

You may also be able to get a guide to take you into the **Parque Nacional do Pico da Neblina**. The Pico da Neblina itself, Brazil's highest peak at 3014m, is on the far side of the park, hard against the Venezuelan border.

To proceed **beyond São Gabriel** by river is more difficult, particularly in the dry season from May till October. The river divides a few hours beyond São Gabriel. To the right, heading more or less north, the Rio Negro continues (another day by boat) to the community of CUCUI on the Venezuelan border – there's also a very rough road from São Gabriel. It is just about possible to travel on from here **into Venezuela** and the Orinoco river system, through the territory of Yanomami Indians. But this involves a major expedition requiring boats, guides and considerable expense: cost aside it is also potentially dangerous, and you should get a thorough update on the local situation before attempting this route. The left fork is the **Rio Uaupés** where the **Araripirá waterfalls** lie a day or two upstream, just before the border settlement of IAURETE. The Uaupés continues, another day's journey, along the border to the Colombian town of MITU. Again, this is a potentially hazardous area, home to Maku Indians and, more worryingly, to coca-growing areas and members of the Colombian underworld.

Roraima

The **Territory of Roraima**, in the far north of Brazil butting against Guyana and Venezuela, is an active frontier zone – pushing forward the boundaries of "development", indigenous "acculturation" and, in some regions, perhaps even international borders. It's one of the youngest parts of Brazil in a very literal sense:

when the grasslands here were discovered in the mid-eighteenth century they were thought to be ideal cattle country, and it was the Portuguese who first moved in on them. But the current national borders weren't finally settled until the early part of this century. Over the last couple of years there has been a massive gold rush here, with an influx of as many as 50,000 *garimpeiros* (compared to a total population of around 200,000 previously). This is centred above all in the northwest, up against the Venezuelan border in the Serra Pacaraima, formerly the territory of the Yanomami Indians.

In 1989 the plight of the **Yanomami**, a relatively recently "discovered" people living on both sides of the border whose lands were being invaded by prospectors and their numbers decimated by new diseases, brought about an international outcry which forced the Brazilian government to announce that they would evacuate all settlers from Yanomami lands. But the project was abandoned almost as soon as it began: protection of the region's valuable mineral reserves was deemed to necessitate the strengthening of the country's borders and the settlement of the area as protection (the military have a strong vested interest in its development); and the plan was simply unrealistic – any attempt to move the *garimpeiros* would have led to a bloodbath. Meanwhile the Yanomami continue to see their land and their people dwindle. The environmental effects remain to be seen, but the widespread use of mercury is already polluting many of the rivers in the region: a further threat to the Yanomami. The next few years are likely to be make or break for these people – for more on them see "The Environment" in *Contexts*.

The Rio Branco

It's relatively easy to get from **Manaus to Boa Vista** by road, though in the rainy season you may find yourself getting bogged down constantly along the way, but it's also possible to take a boat all the way from Manaus up the Rio Negro and Rio Branco as far as CARACARAÍ, from where there's a regular bus service to Boa Vista (some boats also go from Caracaraí to Boa Vista, but they're few and far between). This isn't an easy trip and it has been known to take over two weeks, with lots of stopping and starting and depending on local riverside people for hospitality and food. If you can get a boat which is going direct, all the better. Expect to pay at least $50 for the trip, more if you're boat hopping. It's sometimes easier to travel first to Barcelos from where there are occasional boats bound up the Rio Branco, but it's all very much hit and miss once you're on the rivers.

Those who do make it up the Rio Branco are generally rewarded for their steadfastness by the sight of river dolphins, alligators, plenty of birdlife and even the odd snake. At Caracaraí there are virtually no facilities, but the police station has been known to offer free hammock space to travellers.

Boa Vista

BOA VISTA must be one of the largest small towns on earth. Unrelentingly hot, modern and concrete, its planners laid it out on a grand scale, with broad tree-lined boulevards divided by traffic islands and a vast Plaza do Centro Cívico, swirling with traffic, from which streets radiate just unevenly enough to confuse the otherwise perpendicular grid. Clearly this is meant to be a fitting capital for the development of Roraima – and there are large stores full of ranching and mining equipment which reflect that growth. Busy as it is, though, Boa Vista has far to go to fill its ambitious designs. The huge streets seem half empty;

distances, in this heat at least, seem vast. Nor, though it's a reasonably pleasant place to while away a day or so, is there anything at all of interest.

On the edge of town, where nothing else has yet been built, stands the large, modern **Rodoviária**, with several shops, a *lanchonete* and a local **tourist office** which never seems to be open. Taxis, which are relatively expensive here, line up outside; on the main road beyond them (from the same side as the terminal) you can catch a local bus towards the centre. This takes something of a detour, round past an army base and some outlying areas, before heading back to near the bus station where it turns down past the prison and heads down the broad Avenida Benjamin Constant towards the central praça. Coming from the **airport**, some 3km outside town, you'll have to take a taxi. Arrival in Boa Vista can be awkward, since thanks to the gold rush and international interest in the plight of the Yanomami Indians there are lots of military personnel about who are very suspicious of foreigners: you're likely to have your luggage taken apart and be questioned about your motives. The best bet is probably to play the dumb tourist, and say you're heading for Venezuela.

About three blocks before the praça you'll pass a couple of the cheaper **places to stay**, the *Hotel Roraima* at no. 321 (☎224-3721) and the *Hotel Brasil*, next to each other on the right-hand side – most easily recognised by the petrol station and *Restaurant/Bar Marisa* opposite. The *Brasil* is a bit of a hole, but the *Roraima* is not bad; the better rooms are upstairs. If it's full, try one block down and one to the right: here there's a line of merchants offering to buy gold and diamonds from the *garimpeiros* (they'll also change **dollars** and travellers' cheques at fair rates), and at the end the *Hotel Paraíso* on the upper floor of a modern building at Rua Araújo Filho 228 (☎224-2022). The *Hotel Tres Nações*, opposite the *Rodoviária*, is also cheap and reasonably clean, but it's a long way out. Back on Benjamin Constant just before the praça, the *Hotel Brasa* is slightly better than the *Brasil* if you're stuck for a room. If you're prepared to pay a little more, then the two-star *Hotel Euzébio*, Rua Cecília Brasil 1107 (☎224-4618), is better value, especially for two: air conditioning, a pool and breakfast included. It's about five blocks from the *Roraima* along the street opposite (past the petrol station), or two blocks up a broad boulevard from the back of the Palácio Municipal and just down to the left – from the *Rodoviária* it's easier to get a taxi. Finally there are two more expensive hotels in Boa Vista; the three-star *Tropical* on the main square (☎224-4800), and the *Praia* down by the river.

The **post office** and a couple of **banks** can be found on the main praça, and the *telefónico* on the street behind the Palácio Municipal leading towards the *Hotel Euzebio*. *Lanchonetes* are everywhere, though more substantial **restaurants** are surprisingly scarce: there's the *Marisa* opposite the *Hotel Roraima*; the *Gondola*, where you can sit outside at the corner of Benjamin Constant and the praça; and a couple of good fish places down on the river near the Casa do Artesanato. **Avenida Jaime Brasil**, which leads from the praça down to the river, is where you'll find most of the shops in Boa Vista, and it's busy pretty much all day: it's worth taking a walk down here to see what's happening and to take a stroll along the bank of the Rio Negro. The **Casa do Artesanato**, on the riverbank, is also worth a visit: its selection of handicrafts is not wide but there's some interesting stuff and it's all very cheap.

The **Venezuelan Consulate**, one of the main reasons to spend time in Boa Vista, is three blocks along the continuation of Benjamin Constant on the far side of the praça. If you hope to get a visa in a single day then arrive early: hours are

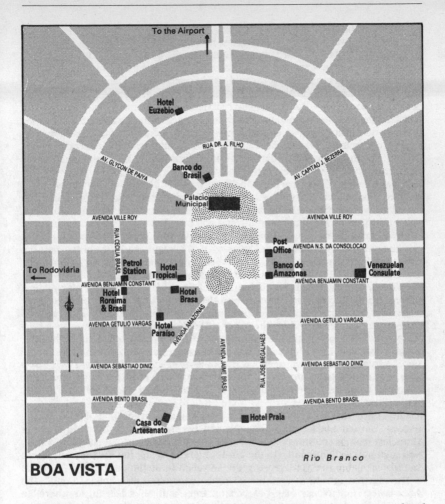

To the Airport

Hotel
Euzebio

RUA DR. A. FILHO

AV. GLYCON DE PAIVA

Banco do
Brasil

AV. CAPITÃO J. BEZERRA

Palacio
Municipal

AVENIDA VILLE ROY

AVENIDA VILLE ROY

RUA CECILIA BRASIL

Post
Office

AVENIDA N.S. DA CONSOLOCAO

To Rodoviária

Petrol
Station

Hotel
Tropical

Banco do
Amazonas

Venezuelan
Consulate

AVENIDA BENJAMIN CONSTANT

AVENIDA BENJAMIN CONSTANT

Hotel
Roraima
& Brasil

Hotel
Brasa

AVENIDA GETULIO VARGAS

Hotel
Paraíso

AVENIDA AMAZONAS

AVENIDA GETULIO VARGAS

AVENIDA JAIME BRASIL

RUA JOSE MEGALHAES

AVENIDA SEBASTIAO DINIZ

AVENIDA SEBASTIAO DINIZ

AVENIDA BENTO BRASIL

AVENIDA BENTO BRASIL

Casa do
Artesanato

Hotel Praia

Rio Branco

BOA VISTA

officially 8–11.45am but they may open in the afternoon to give your completed visa back. You'll need to show a passport and have a photo and an onward ticket – though you may be able to get round the latter by having plenty of money and a good excuse. From the Consulate they'll send you to a doctor for a cursory medical examination ($6 for this privilege) and from there you go to a clinic for a blood test (free) which they claim is for malaria. Having passed these you can go back in the afternoon, clutching the certificates, to pick up your passport and visa.

When it comes to **leaving**, you should book as far in advance as possible for all forms of transport. Buses – to Manaus, Bonfim on the Guyanan border or Santa Elena in Venezuela – all seem to be booked at least a day in advance, and sometimes two or three. Planes are little better, though you might get lucky with the waiting list: *Varig* have an office at Rua Araújo Filho 91 (☎242-2226), and there are several air taxi companies based at the airport.

On to Venezuela and Guyana

It's relatively straightforward to go from Boa Vista to Santa Elena in Venezuela, with a daily *União Cascavel* bus leaving at 8am. The road is dirt, but in the dry season at least it's not too bad: on a good day you might make it to the border in six hours, but on a bad one you could easily double that. The journey, across a vast flat savanna that is dusty in the dry season, boggy in the wet, offers very little in the way of scenery. But there is a great deal of wildlife, especially birds: white egrets, storks and all sorts of waders in the rainy season, flycatchers and hawks; and also the chance of some fairly large animals, including giant ant-eaters. As the border approaches the land begins to rise slightly: to the northeast lies **Monte Roraima**, the fourth highest peak in Brazil at 2875m, at the point where Brazil, Guyana and Venezuela meet.

Allow a couple of hours to cross the border itself (the bus waits while everyone queues to have their passports stamped and luggage checked); **SANTA ELENA** is barely twenty minutes further. You will have to spend at least one night here, since transport leaves in the morning and you have to get an entry stamp in town. A tiny place with the real feel of a border town – low, corrugated-roofed houses and dusty streets – Santa Elena enjoys a great climate, dry and not too hot, but offers absolutely nothing to do. You can see the whole place in an hour's walk, and decide that there's nothing to see in twenty minutes. The Brazil bus stops by the *Hotel Macking* (about $5 double), which is as good a place to stay as any: others include the similarly priced *Auyantepuy*, round the corner, and the more expensive but more comfortable *Fronteras* (good value doubles). There's good food at the *Restaurante Itália* (the spaghetti is the cheapest thing to eat in a relatively expensive town) and the *Auyantepuy*. The *Aeropostal* office, for flights out, is just down from the *Auyantepuy*: you have to pay cash. Money is hard to change here: various traders will accept cash dollars or cruzados – try *Las Quatro Esquinas*, opposite the *Macking* – but there's nowhere at all to change travellers' cheques. **Leaving**, there's a 5am bus to Ciudad Bolívar (14hr; $9) and a daily flight (2hr; $20).

Guyana is less straightforward. It's easy enough to get to BONFIM on the border (two daily buses with *Taguatur* and *Eucatur*), though the road is pretty grim, less easy to continue beyond there. Get your Brazilian exit stamp in Bonfim and then walk – about 5km – to the border marked by the Rio Tucurú, where you can hire a boat to row you across to the Guyanan settlement of LETHEM. This is a friendly enough town but there's only one expensive hotel (though the *Government Rest House* may put you up free) and no roads to anywhere: to continue on to Georgetown you have to fly. One further problem is that Guyanan entry regulations are very strict, and they're worried about people moving in from Brazil – you may simply be refused entry. All in all, if you want to go to Guyana, it's easier to fly; there are flights from Boa Vista to Georgetown.

Rondônia and Porto Velho

A large, partially deforested region in the southwest corner of the Brazilian Amazon, the **state of Rondônia** has already undergone the first phase of its environmental destruction. Roads and tracks, radiating like fine bones from the spinal highway BR-364, have already dissected almost the entire state as scores of thousands of settlers and many large companies move in on the land. Poor landless groups, the surviving representatives of once proud Indian tribes, are a common sight huddled together under plastic sheets at the side of the road.

The state was created only in 1981, having evolved from an unknown and almost entirely unsettled zone (then the Territory of Guaporé) over the previous thirty years. The new, fast-changing Rondônia was named after the famous explorer, Indian "pacifier" and telegraph network pioneer Marechal Cândido Rondon. It's not exactly one of Brazil's major tourist attractions, but it is an interesting area in its own right and also offers a few stopping-off places between more obvious destinations. **Porto Velho**, the main city of the region, is an important pit-stop between Cuiabá and either Manaus or the frontier state of Acre. Rondônia also offers border crossings to Bolivia and access to overland routes into Peru.

Given that it is such a recently settled region, the system of road **transport** is surprisingly good, and combines well with the major rivers – Madeira, Mamoré and Guaporé. The main focus of human movement these days is the fast BR-364, which caused another surge of development after its completion in the 1980s; but Porto Velho is astride a major meeting of the ways – the *Transamazonica* meets the BR-319 from Manaus just to the north, while the BR-364 provides communication with the centre-west of Brazil, via Cuiabá, and west to the Peruvian border through Rio Branco.

Porto Velho

The capital of Rondônia State, **PORTO VELHO** overlooks the Amazon's longest tributary, the mighty Rio Madeira. With over 350,000 inhabitants these days, Porto Velho has evolved from a relatively small town in just twenty years. Settlers have arrived in enormous numbers in search of land, jobs and, more specifically, the mineral wealth of the region: gold and casserite (a form of tin) are found all over Rondônia.

Seen from a distance across the river, Porto Velho looks rather more impressive than it does at close quarters. The two bell towers and Moorish dome of the cathedral stand out strikingly above the roof tops, while alongside the river three phallic, black water towers sit like waiting rockets beside a complex of military buildings. A little further downstream the modern port and the shiny cylindrical tanks of a petrochemical complex dominate the riverbank.

In the town itself, the main street – Avenida Sete de Setembro – has an almost festival atmosphere about it. Noise is used as much as visual display to attract shoppers and *garimpeiros* in town to sell their gold. Music shops blare out their sounds; the *Compro Ouro* shops shout out their gold buying prices; and market stall-holders chatter on about their predominantly cheap plastic wares. Every other lamp post seems to have a loudspeaker attached to it.

Food and a bed
There are some excellent places **eat and drink** in Porto Velho, though beer here is three times as expensive as it is on the coast. Food, on the other hand, tends to be a little cheaper. One of the most pleasant spots is the *Lanchonete Madeira-Mamoré*, overlooking the river on the port side of the railway sheds; here you can get drinks, snacks and fish meals in a basic but trendy atmosphere – very pleasant in the afternoons, very popular in the early evenings. Not exactly cheap, but thoroughly recommended as a unique treat for sublime fresh fish, the *Flutuante*

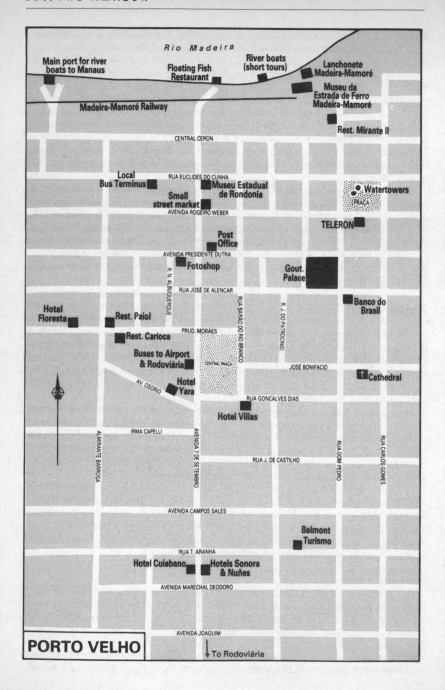

Rio Madeira

Main port for river boats to Manaus

Floating Fish Restaurant

River boats (short tours)

Lanchonete Madeira-Mamoré

Museu da Estrada de Ferro Madeira-Mamoré

Madeira-Mamoré Railway

Rest. Mirante II

CENTRAL CERON

Local Bus Terminus

RUA EUCLIDES DO CUNHA

Museu Estadual de Rondonia

Small street market

Watertowers

PRAÇA

AVENIDA ROGEIRO WEBER

TELERON

Post Office

AVENIDA PRESIDENTE DUTRA

Fotoshop

Gout. Palace

R. N. ALBUQUERQUE

RUA JOSÉ DE ALENCAR

RUA BARÃO DO RIO BRANCO

R. J. DO PATROCINIO

Banco do Brasil

Hotel Floresta

Rest. Paiol

Rest. Carioca

PRUD. MORÃES

Buses to Airport & Rodoviária

CENTRAL PRAÇA

JOSÉ BONIFACIO

Cathedral

AV. OSORIO

Hotel Yara

RUA GONCALVES DIAS

Hotel Villas

ALMIRANTE BARROSA

IRMA CAPELLI

AVENIDA 7 DE SETEMBRO

RUA J. DE CASTILHO

RUA DOM PEDRO

RUA CARLOS GOMES

AVENIDA CAMPOS SALES

Belmont Turismo

RUA T. ARANHA

Hotel Cuiabano

Hotels Sonora & Nuñes

AVENIDA MARECHAL DEODORO

AVENIDA JOAQUIM

PORTO VELHO

↓ To Rodoviária

Rio Madeira Beira-Rio (daily 11am–2.30pm & 7pm–midnight) is a flashy restaurant floating on the Rio Madeira close to the railway yard. The food is fantastic, and there's usually live music at weekends.

Nearer the heart of town, the *Restaurante Pizzeria Roma*, on Rua Albuquerque between Morães and José de Alencar, serves good Italian food at reasonable prices. For more traditional fare try the *Restaurante Paiol*, more or less next to the *Hotel Floresta* on the corner of Almirante Barroso and Morães. Good Brazilian staple meals can be found just over the road at the *Restaurante Carioca* – excellent value as the meals (from around $2) are big enough to feed two or three people; the set menu can include dishes of beans, rice, spaghetti, tomato and onion salad, farinha and a meat dish! Close to the military complex on the other side of the town centre, the *Restaurant Mirante II* has a good view over the river and live music on Friday evenings. Later in the evening the bar *Wau Wau*, Avenida Carlos Gomes 1616, in the *Hotel Vila Rica*, generally offers good entertainment.

Looking for **somewhere to stay** you've again got plenty to choose from. Near the top of the range, the *Hotel Floresta*, Rua Almirante Barroso 502 (☎221-5669), has a swimming pool and restaurant, as well as air conditioning, TV, fridge and shower in almost every room from around $20. At half this cost, there's the very pleasant *Hotel Cuiabano* on Sete de Setembro just up from T. Aranha, with rooms set around a courtyard. The *Hotel Nunes*, opposite the *Cuiabano*, is clean, cool and good value from $5 a night. Both of these tend to be a bit noisy during the day, since they're located on the main commercial drag, but at least they're convenient. The dingy *Hotel Sonora*, next door to the *Nunes*, charges $6 a night, and is only worth checking out if there's no room elswhere. Better alternatives include the clean, modern *Hotel Yara* on Avenida Osorio ($7), and the cheaper, friendly but rather basic *Hotel Villas* just off Sete de Setembro, on Gonzales Dias.

The town and its museums

Although it is a lively town and an enjoyable place to spend some time, Porto Velho doesn't have much in the way of a developed tourist scene. The main attraction is undoubtedly the wonderful **Madeira-Mamoré Railway Museum** (Mon–Fri 8am–6pm; free). Inside the large workshop there are hundreds of museum pieces and railway relics; unmissable for railway buffs and pretty interesting for even the least sympathetic visitor. It looks like a vast auction shed: everything here was shipped across the Atlantic and on up the Amazon and Madeira rivers. Much of it dates from the great years of British railway engineering: the station masters' clocks (from Liverpool – John Bruce and Sons, "makers to the Admiralty"); clock faces from Cardiff and Barry; *Kempe's Engineers' Yearbook* for 1926 ("a compendium of the modern practice of civil, mechanical, electrical, gas, marine, mine and metallurgical engineering . . . 33rd edition"). Outside the museum shed there's an assortment of old engines and carriages, some of them looking ready to go tomorrow, others in a poor state of repair. Sitting in the railway yard, they are a sad reminder of the life, blood and sweat that went into the building of the railway.

Sadly, the Madeira-Mamoré (or Mad Maria) Railway was closed in 1960. It was built to provide a route for Bolivian rubber to the Atlantic and the markets of Europe and the eastern USA and was completed, in 1912, just in time to see the price of rubber plummet and the market dry up. Some estimates say that as many as 50,000 men died – mostly of malaria – building the railway, though in truth the figure was probably a tenth of that. Nevertheless, it took a terrible toll. The project was first attempted by British engineers in 1872; by 1874, two British companies had already been forced to admit defeat with most of their labour force – mainly Irish workers – having died on the job. In 1878 a North American company, P.T. Collins, took nearly a year to lay six kilometres of track before again being stopped by epidemics. In 1883 Brazilian engineers started a sixteen-month scheme which also ended in tragedy. By 1903, with the price of rubber still rising, Brazil agreed to attempt the railway link with Bolivia once again, in part as compensation for having annexed the Bolivian territory of Acre. But it wasn't until Jekyll and Randolf – the US company who had helped build the Panama Canal – appeared on the scene in 1907 that the railway really began to make headway. By this time advances in engineering technology and medical practice gave them a better chance, but it was still five more years before the first train ran.

The line was nationalised in 1931, and in 1972 many of the tracks were ripped up to help build a road along the same difficult route. Recently, though, about 25km of track has been put back to work to provide trains from Porto Velho to the nearby resort of Teotónio (see below).

The other museum in town, the **Museu Estadual de Rondônia** on Sete de Setembro, has an interesting collection of ethnographic artefacts gathered from indigenous tribes of the region. There's little else to see: the **Government Palace** is not a very inspiring building, and the **Cathedral** is better appreciated from the far side of the river.

Excursions from Porto Velho

There are a few **local trips** worth attempting if you have the time. Most obvious is a short trip on one of the **floating bars** – *Fluvetur* or *Baretur* (☎221-6642) – competitive outfits which both offer much the same deal. They set out at intervals during the day – there's almost always a 5pm sundowner tour, and more frequent sailings at weekends – and for a few dollars and the price of a beer or two you can spend a pleasant couple of hours travelling up and down the Madeira, sharing the two-storey floating bar with predominantly local groups. The atmosphere is almost invariably good, and there's often impromptu music. You can find the bars down at the port, directly behind the railway museum.

Another weekend river excursion is to SANTO ANTÔNIO, only some 7km away by boat, a favourite local resort where there are waterfalls and you can swim. The revamped **steam train** (details and current timetables available at the Railway Museum) now runs the 28km to TEOTÓNIO – an attractive fishing settlement, site of the annual fishing competitions and also accessible either by river (around one and a half hours) or by road – access via the BR-364 for 18km, then almost 30km more by minor road. Much closer to town, the peaceful **Parque Circuito** is a very pleasant woodland within half an hour's walk of downtown Porto Velho.

Listings

Airport Belmont Airport (☎221-3935) is just 7km out of town – regular flights from here to most major Brazilian destinations. Take a taxi between here and the city; you can find them downtown at the plaza in Sete de Setembro.

Buses Local buses to the *Rodoviária* and the airport leave from the small market zone in the Rua Euclides da Cunha, just off Sete de Setembro at the port end.

Film can be bought from the shop on Avenida Presidente Dutra, on the other side of Sete de Setembro from the post office.

Money Exchange Available from the *Banco do Brasil* at the corner of José Alencar and Dom Pedro II (câmbio upstairs). Cash can also be changed at the *Hotel Floresta*.

Post Office The main post office is in Avenida Presidente Dutra, just off Sete de Setembro (Mon–Fri 9am–5pm).

Riverboats The main commercial port is easily located about 1km upstream from the railway yards; you'll have to go there to check out all the possibilities. For Manaus there are frequent boats offering first and second class passages (first class tickets from about $35 for the four-day downstream trip). You can also take the short trip to Humaitá and get on the bus there, which normally shortens the journey by at least 24 hours, but unless you're in a hurry the boat trip is more comfortable. Even in first class you'll need a hammock for sleeping and some extra food and drink to make the trip more enjoyable and easy on the stomach. The boats at the port generally display their destinations; otherwise it's a matter of asking the crew of each vessel and making a deal with the captain whose itinerary suits you best. Boats often leave on Thursdays, arriving Manaus on Monday. Less frequently there is passage available on boats going upstream to Guajará-Mirim: to go much further than this by river requires a lot of time and patience – it can easily take two weeks or more to reach Madre de Dios in Peru.

Rodoviária on Avenida Kennedy, just a couple of blocks from Sete de Setembro, but about twenty blocks along that from the centre. Buses leave regularly for Guajará-Mirim, Abuna, Cuiabá, Manaus and Rio Branco.

Telefónica The *Teleron* office, for international calls, is at the corner of Avenida Rogeiro Weber and Dom Pedro II, uphill slightly from the centre, just behind the main government building.

Travel Agencies in Porto Velho tend to do little more than sell air tickets to other parts of Brazil and make expensive hotel bookings. Nevertheless, they can sometimes offer useful contacts for some local sightseeing – try *Belmont Turismo*, T. Aranha 2385 (☎221-0091/ 6150), or *Iamatur Turismo*, 7 de Setembro 684 (☎221-2701).

Around Porto Velho

The backbone of modern Rondônia, the **BR-364** highway links the state more or less from north to south, connecting Porto Velho with Cuiabá, Brasília and the wealthy south coast markets. The state's main towns are strung out along the BR-364, almost all of them – including Porto Velho itself, JI-PARANÁ and VILHENA at the border with Mato Grosso – marking the points where the road crosses major waterways. It's a fast road, and in the final analysis there's little to stop for anywhere in this direction: you're better off heading straight through to Cuiabá.

Heading **west from Porto Velho** is a very different matter, and soon begins to feel like real pioneering. The further you go, the smaller and wilder the roads, rivers and towns become. The main attractions for the traveller are Rio Branco and the border crossings into Peru, in the state of Acre; and Guajará-Mirim, where you can cross into Bolivia or undertake an adventurous visit to the Forte Príncipe da Beira. The BR-364 in this direction is essentially a red dirt track, or at least it was at the time of writing – in this corner of the Amazon things are changing very fast indeed, and the first things to be improved are generally road surfaces.

Most of the land beside the road between Porto Velho and Abunā has already been bought up by big companies. They haven't yet done much in the way of development, but signs have been erected to mark the plots and much of the forest has suffered initial clearing and burning. Meanwhile many of the smaller *fazendas* have started actively producing beef cattle and other tropical cash crops.

Water birds like the *Garça Real* (an amazing white Royal Heron) can frequently be spotted from the bus, fishing in the roadside streams and ditches, but the general picture is one of an alarming rate of destruction with columns of wood-smoke rising wherever you look (for further details of the Amazonian environmental crisis, see *Contexts*).

At **ABUNÃ** – some five hours out of Porto Velho – there are often queues at the ferry which takes vehicles over the wide Madeira river into Acre. It's not a particularly pleasant town – caught in the middle of a gold rush, it has expanded too fast for its own good, and the river itself is awash with gold-mining machinery floating on large balsawood rafts. Following the road towards Rio Branco, Bolivia lies across the Rio Abunã to your left: if you want to cross the border, the closest place to do so is **Guajará-Mirim** to the south. The road there turns off before the ferry crossing, following the Rio Mamoré via the small settlement of TAQUARAS.

Guajará-Mirim: Bolivia and the Rio Guaporé

GUAJARÁ-MIRIM is easy enough to reach on the daily bus from Porto Velho, and once you get there it's a surprisingly sophisticated place with several hotels, the best of which is probably the *Hotel Mini-Estrela*, Avenida 15 de Novembro 460. There are, however, only two reasons you might come here – to get to Bolivia or to head up the Mamoré and Guaporé rivers on an trip probably destined for the Forte Príncipe da Beira.

The valley of the **Rio Guaporé**, around 800km in length, is an obvious destination for an adventurous break from routine town to town travelling. Endowed with relatively accessible rainforest, a slow-flowing river and crystal-clear creeks, it is a favourite fishing region with townspeople from Porto Velho. Likely catches include the huge *dourado*, the *tambaqui*, the *pirapitanga* and *tucunaré*. Heading towards the Guaporé, there are amazing rapids on the Rio Mamoré river just south of Guajará-Mirim, close to the place where the Rio Pacaás Novas flows in.

If you want a purpose to your river trip, the star-shaped **Forte Príncipe da Beira** is the place to head for. Built in 1773 by the pioneering Portuguese colonists, this was an advanced border post designed to mark out Portuguese territory from the Spanish lands across the river in the Bolivian jungle. Underground tunnels and passages lead directly down to the river by the small settlement of Costa Marques. By river, it will take at least three days to reach the fort from Porto Velho: the first day by bus to Guajará-Mirim, then two or three more by boat to the fort itself or 20km further to the town of Costa Marques where there is a hotel, restaurants and even a small airstrip. If you go by bus from Porto Velho you can get there rather quicker: along the BR-364 to PRESIDENTE MÉDICI where you have to change buses and roads for the BR-429 to Costa Marques.

As for **Bolivia**, if all you want to do is see it then you can join a sightseeing tour by motor barge from Guajará-Mirim. These leave frequently, visiting the main sights on the river, and often stopping at the islands between Guajará-Mirim and Guayaramerin, on the Bolivian side. If you actually want to cross the border it's equally easy to get a boat over the Rio Mamoré to **GUAYARAMERIN**. This is something of a contrast to the Brazilian town – far more of a border outpost – and there are no roads, but there is a good air taxi service to La Paz, Cochabamba and Santa Cruz with *TAM* and *LAB*. If you intend travelling into Bolivia, get your passport stamped by the Bolivian Consul in Guajará-Mirim (Avenida 15 de Novembro, block 7) and an exit stamp from the Polícia Federal before crossing the river. If you want to stay in Guayaramerin, try the *Hotel Plaza*, four blocks from the port.

Acre and Rio Branco

Crossing from Rondônia into the state of Acre, territory annexed from Bolivia during the rubber boom days in the first years of this century, there's nowhere to stop before you reach the capital at Rio Branco. The state is a vast frontier forest zone, where it comes as a real surprise to find that **RIO BRANCO** is one of Brazil's funkiest cities. It's a small place with little of specific interest to point at, but it's exceptionally lively, with a strong student influence that means plenty of music and events to fill a stay of a few days. Arriving at night (as you usually do) after a fifteen-hour bus journey through the desolation of what's left of the jungle between here and Porto Velho, the brightly coloured lights and animated streets can make you wonder if you've really arrived at all, or simply drifted off to sleep. By the light of day Rio Branco doesn't have quite so much obvious charm, but it remains an interesting place full of interesting people.

Much of the reason for all this life is that Rio Branco is a federal **university** town, second only to Belém (and before Manaus) on the student research pecking order for social and biological studies associated with the rainforest and development. Consequently the place has more than its fair share of young people, and of Brazilian intellectuals. On top of this, the region's burgeoning development means that Rio Branco is also a thriving and very busy market town, pivotally sited on the new road and with an active, if tiny, river port.

Arrival and other practicalities

Rio Branco is divided in two by the Rio Acre. You'll probably arrive in the south, where both the *Rodoviária* and airport are situated, but you'll want to spend any time here across the river where you'll find the commercial zone and most of the hotels. In the dry season, there is a good river **beach** on the curve in the river – just upstream from the bridges and on the *Rodoviária* side of town.

Arriving and leaving

The **Rodoviária** (AC-040, 1018, Cidade Nova; ☎224-1182/6179; just about walking distance from the centre, or take a taxi) is served basically by two companies: *Viação Rondônia*, Rua Sertaneja 512, operate several buses daily to Porto Velho; *Empresa de Transporte Acreana*, B.A. Monteiro 655, have several daily services south to Xapurí and the frontier at Brasiléia. Tickets for both companies can be bought at the offices in the *Rodoviária* between 9am and 5pm (Mon–Sat only). If you're heading on to **Cruzeiro do Sul** at the western extremity of the *Transamazonica*, there are still no regular buses. The road is improved each dry season, so this may change, but for now the only overland route is by hitching with one of the many trucks that travel this route every day. Most people who can afford it fly, and if you ask a local how to get to Cruzeiro they will say that it is impossible to go by road because there isn't one. This is certainly true between the months of November and May when the rains carry away the unsurfaced track, making it virtually impassable even for four-wheel drive vehicles.

The **airport** (*Internacional Presidente Médici*; ☎224-6692) is not far beyond the *Rodoviária*, though from here you definitely will want a taxi into town. There are regular fights to Belém, Campo Grande, Manaus, Porto Velho, Cruzeiro do Sul, Rio and São Paulo. The main airlines operating these routes are *Taba*, Rua

Quintino Bocaiúva 94 (☎224-6883); *Varig/Cruzeiro*, Rua Marechal Deodoro 115 (☎224-2226); and *Vasp*, Rua Marechal Deodoro 89 (☎224-6585).

Accommodation

There is no shortage of **hotels** in Rio Branco, though the better ones aren't cheap. The *Hotel Rio Branco*, Rua Barbosa 193 on the corner of the Avenida Getulias Vargas (☎224-1785), is modern, with excellent service and TVs in all rooms, from $16 per person. Nearby, but not such good value, the *Pinheiro Palace Hotel* charges around $25 a night. Lower down the road, the *Hotel Inácio Palace*, Rua Barbosa 82 (☎224-6397), has rooms starting at about $10. The *Hotel Loureiro*, Marechal Deodoro 196, is central, modern and starts at about $7 a night. On the other side of town, over the river towards the *Rodoviária*, the *Hotel Sucessor*, Rua 17 de Novembro 1149, costs only $2.50, which is good for what you get. Very close to the *Rodoviária*, the *Hotel Uirapurú* is also good value; clean, with fans in most rooms and its own pool table.

Eating and drinking

For **eating out** it is hard to beat the *Restaurant Casarão*, on Avenida Brazil by the bottom end of the Praça Plácido de Castro, near the *Teleacre* office. The food here is good, particularly the fish dishes; and, at weekends, there is live music and the atmosphere can be quite vital. On just about any evening it's also a good place to meet people – a hang-out of students, musicians and poets. The *Pizza Palace*, Rua Barbosa 62, is a relatively quiet spot, next to the *Hotel Inácio Palace*. There are a couple of typical wooden verandah **bars** overlooking the river and port area, down the alley leading into the main commercial market zone, by the Praça da Bandeira. And for street food there are some good, extremely cheap stalls by the outdoor market, near the old bridge at the bottom of Avenida Getúlio Vargas.

Other practical details

The **post office** is on Epaminondas Jácome, and the *Teleacre* **telephone** office is at Avenida Brasil 378, near the bottom of Praça Plácido de Castro, on the corner with Rua Barbosa. Set back from the little park off Avenida Getúlio Vargas, the *Banco do Brasil* (Mon–Fri 9am–5pm) will change US dollars and travellers' cheques; you can also change dollars at the airport restaurant. The **street market** along Avenida Getúlio Vargas is the best place to shop for almost anything you might need. As well as the usual fruit and vegetables there's an indoor section for eveything from machetes, fishing nets and medicinal herbs to umbrellas and Michael Jackson tapes. There are a couple of **travel agencies** in town – *Occidental Travel*, on the corner of Avenida Getúlio Vargas and Rua Barbosa, and *Acretur*, next to the *Hotel Rio Branco* – offering organised trips to Brazil nut forest ranges and *seringuales* (rubber tapping zones), starting at about $15 a day.

The city

If you set out to explore Rio Branco, you'll soon find that there's not a great deal to see. The main square – the large **Praça Plácido de Castro** – has little to recommend it in terms of design, its main feature being the Lion's Club plaque dated 1984. But it is a lively and popular social centre for the town, with concerts, mime, and all kinds of live activities happening throughout the year. It's events like these, the life of the bars and restaurants, and simply wandering around the

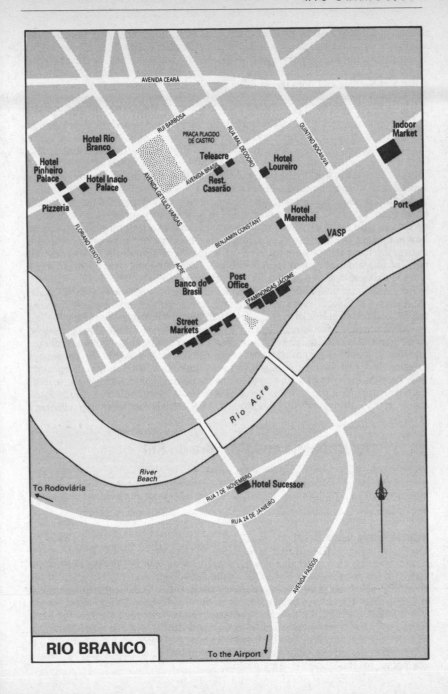

AVENIDA CEARÁ

RUI BARBOSA

PRAÇA PLACIDO
DE CASTRO

RUA MAL DEODORO

QUINTINO BOCAIUVA

Indoor
Market

Hotel Rio
Branco

Teleacre

Hotel
Loureiro

Hotel
Pinheiro
Palace

AVENIDA BRASIL

AVENIDA GETULIO VARGAS

Hotel Inacio
Palace

Rest.
Casarão

Pizzeria

FLORIANO PEIXOTO

Hotel
Marechal

Port

BENJAMIN CONSTANT

VASP

ACRE

Banco do
Brasil

Post
Office

EPAMINONDAS JÁCOME

Street
Markets

Rio Acre

River
Beach

To Rodoviária

RUA 7 DE NOVEMBRO

Hotel Sucessor

RUA 24 DE JANEIRO

AVENIDA PASSOS

N

RIO BRANCO

To the Airport

streets and markets that constitute the real attraction here. The **port** is also worth seeing; small and shabby, but still an interesting spectacle in its own right. There are no regular organised **boat trips**, but it's often possible to travel on the rivers with traders and in *fazendeiros'* riverboats: ask in the *Bar dos Linguarudos*, down Rua Sergipe and onto the wooden steps behind the covered market on Rua Benjamin Constant.

The relaxed air of Rio Branco masks many tensions, above all to do with population movement – people are still arriving here from the east – and the development of the jungle by small ranchers and multinational companies. When the leader of the rubber tappers' union – Chico Mendes – was shot dead by hired gunmen working for the cattle ranchers in 1988, the plight of the forest peoples of Acre came to the attention of the world. The political situation in Acre remains uneasy, with the second- and third-generation tappers and gatherers joining forces with the native population in resisting the enormous economic and armed might of the advancing cattle-based companies. The basic conflict in Acre is fairly simple to understand – on the one side there are people who have lived here for a long time and who know how to manage the forests in a sustainable way; on the other, newcomers who aim to turn the trees into pasture for beef cattle and short-term profit, destroying not only the forest but also many local livelihoods. The battle still goes on at a number of local, national and even international boardroom levels.

Acre, and in particular Rio Branco, is also a strong base for some of Brazil's fastest growing **religious cults**. A number of similar cult groups are based in the region, connected essentially by the fact that they use forest "power plants" – like the hallucinogenic vine *banisteriopsis* – to induce visionary states. Having evolved directly out of native Indian religious practice and belief, these cults are deeply involved in a kind of green nature worship which relates easily to the concept of sustainable forest management. The groups operate in a vaguely underground way, keeping their sanctuaries secret to non-participants. Interestingly, these cults have now spread to the fashionable coastal areas of Brazil where, behind closed doors in São Paulo and Rio de Janeiro, intellectuals participate in visionary ceremonies.

On to Peru: Brasiléia and Cruzeiro do Sul

There are really only two onward routes from Rio Branco, and both of them end up in Peru. You can either head south to Brasiléia (which is actually on the border with Bolivia) and from there continue to Assis Brasil for the border crossing, or head west to Cruzeiro do Sul and Brazil's westernmost extremity.

Brasiléia and Assis Brasil

The small town of **BRASILÉIA** is six hours ($4) by bus from Rio Branco and if you're crossing the border this is where you have to visit the Polícia Federal for your exit (or entry) stamp. The office (daily 8am–5pm) is just to the right of the church as you head from the international border with Bolivia, the bus terminal just to the left. If you have to stay the night, the *Hotel Major*, Salinas 326, charges less than $1.50 a night for a single room, and you can change money at the *Casa Castro*, over the river on the road towards Assis Brasil. You can cross to Bolivia here but there seems little point. The small town of COBIJA on the other side has a few expensive hotels and no onward land transport: though you can fly out, or attempt an adventurous river trip onwards.

ASSIS BRASIL itself is a further 90km beyond Brasiléia, though the rough road can be slow going by bus, and from here it's just a two-kilometre walk across the border to INAPARI in Peru (*Hotel Aquino*, basic and very cheap; or camping by the football pitches over the road from hotel). Trucks leave Inapari most days for Puerto Maldonado, a journey that can take several days in the rainy season (November to March). From Puerto Maldonado there are decent road and regular air links with Cuzco and the rest of Peru. In Assis Brazil you can camp near the river and it's safe to leave your bags at the police station. If you set off early enough from Rio Branco, and the buses connect, it's just about possible to get across the border the same day.

Cruzeiro do Sul

Totally isolated on the western edge of the Brazilian Amazon, Cruzeiro do Sul is a town of some 15,000 inhabitants, many of whom, as in Rio Branco, are social science or biology students. The only dependable links with the outside world are by air to either Rio Branco (and from there the rest of Brazil) or Pucallpa (a jungle city in the Peruvian Amazon). The road to Rio Branco is generally only passable between June and October and even then there is no bus service: travellers must depend on hitching lifts with trucks. Even if you can find a truck going all the way to Rio Branco, you could easily spend anything from three days to over a week on the road even in the dry season.

There is little obvious attraction to Cruzeiro, though it's possible to make river trips to extraordinarily isolated *seringais*: they can be booked through most hotels from around $15 to $20 a day. The *Hotel Novo Acre* is very good value, and the *Hotel Flor de Maio*, overlooking the Rio Ituí, is also cheap (from around $2 a night). But the only reason people come here is to cross from Brazil to Peru or vice versa – and even then this is one of the more obscure border crossings. The quickest way to Peru once you're here is to **fly** direct to Pucallpa – about one hour in a small plane which generally leaves on Tuesdays ($40 minimum per person – check details with *SASA*, Boulevard Taumaturgo 25; or with *TASA*, Peoreira 84, ☎322-3086). The rougher option, only possible in the rainy season between November and March, is to go **by boat**, which takes anything between one and two weeks and involves at least two or three days walking between the Ucayali and Juruá watersheds. Brazilian border formalities are in Cruzeiro at the Federal Police offices. Peruvian formalities are in Pucallpa. There is no bus link between the airport and Cruzeiro town centre some 7km away: taxis cost $6.

For up-to-date information about the **road situation** and trucks heading towards Rio Branco, check with the land transport group *Organizacão Geral Transportes*, Avenida Celestino M. Lima 62 (☎322-2093). Airlines that operate flights within Brazil from Cruzeiro include: *Taxi Aéreo Vale Jurua*, Rua Barbosa 132 (☎322-2587); *Taba*, Travesa Pedreira 84 (☎322-2279); and *Varig-Cruzeiro*, Avenida Celestino M. Lima 48 (☎322-2359).

Buses

From Belém to Marabá (1 daily; 14hr); Brasília (1 daily; 36hr); Santarém via Marabá (several weekly; 50hr plus); Salvador (1 daily; 32hr).

From Manaus to Boa Vista (1 daily; 24hr); Porto Velho (1 daily; 25hr plus).

From Porto Velho to Manaus (1 daily; 25hr plus); Cuiabá (1 daily; 22hr); Rio Branco (1 daily; 15hr).

From Marabá to Tucurui (several weekly; 6hr); Santarém (several weekly; 36hr); Belém (several weekly; 14hr); Araguaina (several weekly; 13hr); Itaituba (several weekly; 34hr); Huamaita and Porto Velho/Manaus (infrequent and irregular; 2–4 days).

From Rio Branco to Porto Velho (1 daily; 15hr); Cruzeiro do Sul (trucks only; 30hr plus); Brasília (1 daily; 6hr).

Boats

From Belém to Santarém (several weekly; 2–3 days); Manaus (several weekly; 4–5 days); Macapá (several weekly; 26hr).

From Santarém to Manaus (1 daily; 2–3 days); Belém (several weekly; 2–3 days).

From Manaus to Santarém (1 daily; 2 days); Belém (several weekly; 4 days); Porto Velho (1 weekly; 5 days); Tabatinga (several weekly; 5 days plus).

From Tabatinga to Manaus (several weekly; 4–5 days); Iquitos (several weekly; 3 days).

From Porto Velho to Manaus (1 weekly; 3–4 days).

Planes

From Belém to Manaus (1 daily; 2hr); Porto Velho (1 daily; 5hr); Brasília (1 daily; 2hr); Boa Vista (1 daily; 4hr); and daily to all other main Brazilian cities.

From Manaus to Belém (1 daily; 2hr); Porto Velho (1 daily; 2hr); Boa Vista (1 daily; 2hr 30min); Rio Branco (several weekly; 2hr 30min); and daily to all other main Brazilian cities.

From Porto Velho, Rio Branco and Marabá there are daily services to all major Brazilian cities.

CHAPTER FIVE

BRASILIA AND GOIAS

Almost 1000km from Rio and located in the barren *sertão* of the Goiás highlands – very much in rural, peasant Brazil – **Brasília** is the largest and most interesting of the world's "planned cities". Declared the national capital in 1960, the futuristic city is located in a federal zone of its own – Brasília D.F.– right in the centre of Goiás state. But until the city's construction this was one of the world's largest isolated regions, and the opening up of communications, coupled with a concerted drive to exploit the hinterland, has led to a process of rapid transformation.

Much of the finance for Brasília, and for the transamazonian road network which has appeared over the last three or four decades, was borrowed by the Brazilian authorities on a more or less conditional basis – the condition being that they agreed to a massive "development" campaign for the region. Funds and tax incentives were made available to persuade some of the largest national and international companies to take part, and by the late 1960s it suddenly became feasible (because of the new roads) and economically viable (because of the favourable bureaucratic assistance from Brasília) to drop bulldozers by helicopter into the interior. The bulldozers felled trees around the edge of a clearing until the perimeter met the path of another incoming bulldozer. In this way, **forest clearance** on a gigantic scale led, in a matter of years, to the creation of enormous pasturelands for beef cattle, mostly for the European and American fast-food markets. One of the worst aspects of this kind of development was that – technically – the tax relief was only available to companies who were utilising at least half of the land they had claimed. Which sounds reasonable until you realise that all that the companies were expected to do was to clear half the land by felling the trees and burning off the stubble. For many of the largest companies, forest involvement was little more than a financial game, the cost of which was the extermination of huge tracts of the world's remaining virgin forest. Although **cattle ranching** is still one of the leading industries in the region, there are signs that this particular type of "development" is slowing down: the tax advantages are now much less and, on top of that, most of the best and easily accessible land has already been claimed and at least partly cleared.

Brasília's only real attraction – but reason enough to stop – is its unique **city architecture**. The futuristic forms of the National Theatre, Cathedral and Congress buildings are a sight you'll never forget: cold, concrete and utterly compelling. There are parks and the large man-made **Lake Paranoá** close to the city and, within day-trip distance, there's the small rural town of **Cristalina** where crystals and semi-precious stones are more common than bread. When it's time to move on, Brasília is surrounded by rivers, hills and well-farmed countryside. It's also well connected by long, but good quality, **roads** to the rest of the country – to the Mato Grosso to the west, to Rio, the Northeast, and São Paulo and the South; and to Belém and, more recently, Rondônia and Acre in the Western Amazon.

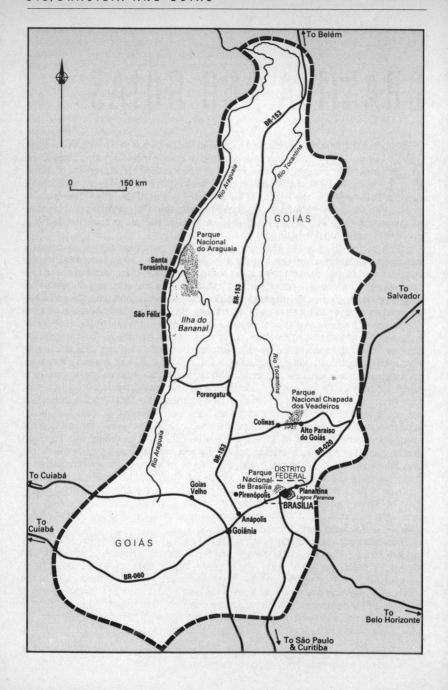

The **state of Goiás** itself remained largely unexplored until this century. Much of the northern half was composed of relatively virgin forest, a haven for previously unknown Indian tribes. Today, long bus rides take you into the scenic **Chapada dos Veadeiros** national park and, more arduously, to the world's largest river island, the **Ilha do Bananal**. In the south, **Goiânia** is the state – as opposed to the national – capital. This area was more heavily populated, based around old gold-mining settlements, an overspill from Minas Gerais. Some of the established towns here are remarkably beautiful, such as **Anápolis**, **Pirenópolis** and the original state capital, **Goiás Velho**, but on the whole there's very little for the average sightseer outside Brasília and Goiânia.

BRASÍLIA

The idea of a **Brazilian inland capital** was first mooted in 1789, and a century later (in 1891) the concept was written into Article 3 of the Republic's constitution, which stated ". . . from now on an area of 14,400 square kilometers will belong to the government for the creation of a new capital". Many sites were considered; indeed, in 1913 President Roosevelt visited the western edge of the *planalto* and remarked that "any sound northern race could live here; and in such a land, with such a climate, there would be much joy of living". But the idea had to wait for fulfilment until 1956 when **Juscelino Kubitschek** became president, on the promise that he would build the city if he won the election. He had to get it finished by the end of his term of office, so work soon began in earnest.

The site was quickly selected by aerial surveys of over 50,000 square kilometres of land. In less than four years a capital city had to be planned, financed and built in the face of apparently insurmountable odds: the building site was 125km from the nearest railway, 190km from the nearest airport, over 600km from the nearest paved road; the closest timber supply was 1200km distant, the nearest source of good steel even further. Still, in **Oscar Niemeyer**, the city's architect, Brasília had South America's most able student of Le Corbusier, founder of the modern planned city and a brilliant designer of buildings. Alongside Niemeyer, who was contracted to design the buildings, **Lúcio Costa** – now in his late-eighties – was hired for the awesome task of Brasília's urban planning.

The design and construction

Costa produced a **city plan** described variously as in the shape of a bow and arrow, a bird in flight or an aeroplane. Certainly, on maps or from the air, Brasília appears to be soaring, wings outstretched, toward the eastern Atlantic coast. The main public buildings, government ministries, Palace of Justice and Presidential Palace, line the "fuselage", a five-mile-long dusty and windswept grass mall known as the **Eixo Monumental** (Monumental Axis). The main residential districts wing out to the north and south, in the arc of the bow while the commercial areas are clustered where the wings join the fuselage (or the bow and arrow meet).

Money for the **construction** came from all over the world in the form of grants and loans, and from the printing of more paper *cruzeiros*, a move which didn't do the Brazilian inflation rate much good. The whole operation was incredibly expensive, not least because everything – workers, food, cement etc – had to be flown in, since work started long before the first access roads appeared. At the time of construction, and even after inauguration, many considered the whole scheme to be a complete waste of time and money: even Rio's *Correio da Manhã* newspaper coined the phrase "The Limit of Insanity!"

Nevertheless, exactly three years, one month and five days after the master plan was unveiled, 150,000 people arrived in Brasília for the official **inauguration**, in April 1960. It must have been a hectic time. There were only 150 first-class hotel rooms completed (for 5000 visiting dignitaries), but the celebrations went ahead, topped by a spectacular 38-ton firework display.

When the smoke cleared in the morning it was clear to everyone that, despite the finished government complexes, 94 apartment blocks, 500-odd one- and two-storey houses plus their local schools and shops, there was still years of work left to do. Road junctions were expected to be eliminated, pedestrians and apartments still had to be separated from traffic, and the block accommodation was to be surrounded by trees – the flats supposedly close enough to the ground for a mother to call her child. Indeed, thirty years on, user-friendly touches such as these have yet to emerge.

The costs: financial and environmental

On the face of it at least, Kubitschek had lived up to his electoral campaign promise of fifty years' progress in five. What he hadn't made clear before, though, was just how much it would cost Brazil. When Kubitschek stood down in 1960, his successor, **Janio Quadros**, broadcast an important message to the nation, saying "All this money, spent with so much publicity, we must now raise – bitterly, patiently, dollar by dollar, *cruzeiro* by *cruzeiro*". With outstanding foreign loans of two billion dollars, to many the city seemed an antisocial waste of resources, while for most economists, it was responsible for Brazil's hyper-inflationary spiral.

The costs were obviously very high, but they did also include the construction of two new **major highways** – one connecting Brasília with Belém, on the mouth of the Amazon, the other connecting the city (and therefore the Atlantic coast) with the first ever **transcontinental** road. This might not have been particularly well constructed at its western edges, but – in good weather – it now became more or less possible to drive from Brasília across the southern Amazon and on to the Pacific Ocean, via Peru and the Andes. Ever since the 1960s, these roads have been quietly revolutionising the interior, though their success – like Brasília's – has been patently double-edged: with the burgeoning of the new "Green" consciousness, the roads' contribution to the disappearance of huge chunks of tropical rainforest can no longer be seen as development. These days even Andreazza (Minister of Transport in the early 1970s) admits that the large cattle ranches in the forest were a "serious mistake".

The City

Imagine what it would be like touching down on another planet, and you'll have some idea of what confronts you when you first arrive in **BRASÍLIA**: there is a clinical, science-fiction aspect at work in the city. Other visitors have had less kind things to say about the city. Simone de Beauvoir, visiting in 1963 with Jean-Paul Sartre in tow, described the place as "elegant monotony"; while the Royal Institute of British Architects poked fun by renaming Brasília "The Moon's Backside".

The city was intended for a population of half a million by the year 2000. However, there are already two million people living in and around Brasília and within ten years this could easily double again. Most of the people who live here do so for economic reasons. A large service sector followed the bureaucrats and businessmen into the new city and, behind that, a whole trail of retailers and smaller merchants arrived to compete for the new markets. It's the kind of place where it's easy to imagine ingenious traders working their way up from a street stall outside the shopping sector to a plush office in the finance sector.

Brasília's good points are all fairly obvious **architectural** ones, but there are other attractions, too. Magnificent sunsets send a golden glow over the twin concrete towers of the National Congress building*; pleasant parks, popular for weekend picnics, encircle the entire city; and in the downtown zone, by the central bus station, the lively atmosphere revolves around a busy mess of people and trade. Yet Brasília can also be as alienating as any city and, unlike most other Brazilian cities, people here seldom stop or smile to acknowledge a fellow human being. Moreover, on some very basic points, Brasília has certainly failed as a planned city. Thirty years on, few people have got anything good to say about it as a real live city – no-one would dream of comparing it to Paris, London or Rio for nightlife and entertainment. Many officials arrive for work on Monday and leave for home on Thursday because they find the city either too oppressive or just plain boring at the weekend. At the most basic level, there's a devastating lack of street corner bars and ad hoc market places, things which provide a major social hub elsewhere in Brazil.

Part of the problem is that the city plans were too simplistic and out of date. Based on Le Corbusier's original theories, which equated urban progress with geometrical order, rectilineal planning and a mechanised, bureaucratic organisation, Costa failed to make long-term provision for future growth of the entire Federal District. The most fundamental short-sightedness of the city plan is Brasília's total domination by the **road traffic** system, and to the traveller walking the footways, this is the obvious gripe against the city. To be fair though, at the very centre of the city, Costa had imagined an area resembling the streets and squares of Venice – smaller in scale but giving colour to the centre of the Eixo Monumental. The political reality for Kubitschek, however, was to deal with the large, costly parts of the plan first – so the area soon became dissected and taken over by large roads, in direct contradiction to the master plan.

In a similar way, the area to the south of Lake Paranoá has developed in a haphazard manner. The north side, originally planned as a series of parks and public places, is occupied by private clubs belonging to the elite, which effectively cuts the rest of the city off from the lake. Temples of a fast developing nation, the two ultra modern banks – *Banco Central* and *Banco do Brasil* – dominate the downtown landscape with their huge dark glass presence. Meanwhile, in spite of incipient crime, growing slums, water shortages, transportation problems and lack of entertainment, the city continues to grow faster than anyone ever imagined.

---

*Sometimes called the "Capital of the Third Millennium", Brasília's design has a mystic side. On Brazilian Republic Day – April 21 – the sun rises through the concrete "H" shape of the parallel twin towers which poke out of the National Congress building, provoking images of a futuristic Stonehenge. Other curious theories associate modern Brasília with Ancient Egypt's pyramids and temples. The aerial view of the city, the winged bird shape, is vaguely reminiscent of the mystical Egyptian Ibis bird, and the National Research Council's building is similar in form to Rameses II's temple. The cemetery, too, is laid out in the shape of a spiral – life's symbol and essential pattern .

Arriving, getting around and orientation

Although initially quite confusing, Brasília is laid out with geometric precision. Unlike most cities, it has no true heart or centre. Instead, it is neatly divided into sectors: there are residential sectors – each with their own shopping and other facilities – hotel sectors, embassy sectors and banking and commercial sectors. Roads are numbered, rather than named, with digits representing their position and distance north or south of the **Eixo Monumental**, and east or west of the other main axis, the **Eixo Rodoviária**. The different sectors are given acronyms, most fairly easy to work out if you're wondering where in the city the name refers to: the Setor Hoteleiro Sul (Southern Hotel Sector) is more often represented as SHS, the Setor Hoteleiro Norte as SHN.

ADDRESSES

Most people in Brasília live in *Superquadras* – massive apartment blocks, some of which you can see coming in along the Eixo Rodoviária from the airport. Finding out where someone lives or works can seem impossible from the **address**, but there is an almost perfect internal logic to the system. For example, the address

SQN 208

Bloco H – 304

70000 Brasília DF

means Superquadra north no. 208, block H, apartment 304. Unfortunately, addresses are rarely written out in full: you'll have to watch out for Q (quadra; and often used for Superquadra, too) and bl. (bloco).

A little city orientation

The downtown *Rodoviária*, the city's central bus station, is the main hub of movement within Brasília, with the Eixo Monumental passing around it and the Eixo Rodoviária crossing over the top of it. Up above the *Rodoviária*, on a level with the Eixo Rodoviária and the main commercial blocks, at a glance you can see the main areas of interest to the visitor. Looking east, towards the main government buildings, you can see the unmistakable Aztec form of the Teatro Nacional and the conical crown of the Cathedral a little further away to the right: both are within easy walking distance. Slightly further away, but still within a half-hour's stroll, are the strange bowls and towers of the National Congress buildings. Immediately on either side of the *Rodoviária* there are two separate shopping centres, one to the north, another to the south, and these vast concrete boxes are overshadowed only by the TV Tower and the nearby *Hotel Nacional*.

Points of arrival

The **airport** (☎248-5131/5588) is 12km south of the centre and bus #102 runs every hour from there into Brasília, dropping you at the downtown *Rodoviária* (see below). Inter-city and long distance **buses**, as well as **trains**, all use the new **Rodoferroviária** (☎233-7200/7800), the bus/railway station west of the centre at the Parque Rodoferroviária, in Setor Noroeste; the entrance is on the Eixo Monumental. From here, the #131 bus leaves regularly for the downtown *Rodoviária*, the bus route taking in most of the Eixo Monumental, including the

BRASÍLIA

famous statue of Juscelino Kubitschek. Once at the **downtown Rodoviária** go up the escalators to the second level for the shopping centres and upper roads, from where you can see most of central Brasília.

Getting around the city

By dividing the city into a few geographically distinct zones – essentially the head, heart and tail of the design – it is not difficult to see most of Brasília's sights **on foot** in one or two days – though it can't be stressed too highly that it gets extremely tiring wandering around the open city in the heat of the day. There are two or three **city bus routes**, instead, which can save you a lot of shoeleather. Details of these are given in the text, but there's a **circular bus route** which is very handy for a cheap overview of the city: bus #106 leaves from and returns to the downtown *Rodoviária* after a long outer city tour – just try to avoid this route between 4pm and 6pm on weekdays when the buses are particularly crowded. It's also a good idea to keep a watchful eye out for pickpockets in the queues for the buses, though, once on the bus, you should be alright.

The city has a good **taxi** service, which costs a minimum of $2 even for the shortest ride: flag a taxi down when you want one, or pick one up at at the many ranks throughout the city. Most people, if they can, drive their own cars, and if you want to join them, see "Listings" for addresses of **car hire** firms; it'll cost you from $25 a day.

For some people, one day is enough in Brasília, and if you want someone else to take care of things then expensive but reliable **city tours** leave from the *Hotel Nacional* (see below for address) most days. There are two different three-hour tours (with the option of combining them into an all-day session), starting at 8.45am and 1.45pm; and there's a night tour which starts at around 7.30pm.

Information

Although there are **information desks** at both the airport and the *Rodoferroviária*, they're not equipped to do much more than book tourists into the flashier hotels. For more help than this – though still very limited – the main **tourist information office** in the *Centro de Convenções*, beyond the TV Tower and near the Burití Palace, has photocopied maps and general brochures available. Much the same information is generally available, too, from either the *Hotel Nacional*, which is much easier to find, or from one of the many travel agents in the shops around the base of the hotel.

Finding a place to stay

Cheap accommodation is very difficult to find in Brasília. The central sectors cater only to the credit card brigade looking for middle- to top-of-the-range hotels which go for $20–100 a night. Instead, most budget travellers take a bus out to one of the satellite settlements which have sprung up around the city, such as NÚCLEO BANDEIRANTE (bus #160 from the downtown *Rodoviária*) and TAGUATINGA (bus #702 from the downtown *Rodoviária*). Or you can camp, not a bad option, as there are several sites in and out of the city.

The central sectors

In the **Setor Hoteleiro Sul** (SHS), most of the hotels are high-class affairs. The five-star *Hotel Nacional* (Lote 1; ☎226-8180) is superb, but its prices are much as you would expect – over $70 per person. Lower down the scale, but still plush, modern and with a roof garden and pool, the *Hotel Bristol* (Q4, bl. F; ☎225-6170) costs from about $50 a night. The *Hotel Nações* (Q4, bl. 1; ☎225-8050) in the same sector starts at $36, but doesn't have a pool, and the *Byblos* (Q3, bl. E; ☎223-1570) is cheaper, too.

Slightly less expensive hotels – like *El Pillar* (SHN, Q3, bl. A; ☎224-5915) – are found in the **Setor Hoteleiro Norte** (SHN). Cheaper still, but far from being central, there are a few very reasonable hotels at the **Saída Sul** junction. Here, the *Hotel Paranoa* (from about $10) is as clean and well serviced as any of the others: it's reached by taking the airport bus from the downtown *Rodoviária* and getting off at the Saída junction.

The outer settlements

Outside the city centre itself, the hotels are cheaper, often in the $5–10 bracket, and the environment less oppressive. In **Núcleo Bandeirante** ("Pioneer's Settlement") for example, you get real value for money and a friendly welcome at both the *Hotel Jurema*, Avenida Central 1390, and *Hotel Buriti*, 2nd Avenue 1415. Núcleo Bandeirante was originally called *Cidade Livre* or "Free City" because it wasn't split up into sectors; unlike in central Brasília, you could build where you liked. In **Taguatinga**, the *Hotel São Paulo*, near the supermarket, has a good reputation: cheap (around $7 a night) and friendly.

Camping

Camping is possible in several places. The most central, *Camping de Brasília*, is in Setor Áreas Isoladas Norte, behind the Buriti Palace and Kubitschek Monument. It's the cheapest place in the city, at under $1 a day, but keep your valuables in a locker: take the #109 bus from the downtown *Rodoviária*. Further out, there are some pleasant woods where camping is allowed free of charge, about 10km out of the city on the BR-041. And the *Bela Vista* campsite (☎226-2663) more or less lives up to its name – 46km out of town on Estrada da Ponte Alta/Estrada da Marila.

Around the sights

Brasília's overriding attraction is the bizarre environment produced by its stunning **architecture**. The blue sky which normally hangs over the city contrasts well with the modern buildings and the deep red, dusty earth of the *planalto*. And the bold, clean lines of the architecture seem symbolic of a fresh start. There are no exceptional museums or historical sites; it's the city itself that's on show, which – in many ways – is less than satisfying since, unlike other Brazilian cities, there is little human contact to be made.

It's a very strange place to tour around. To some, it appeals as a futuristic metropolis, to others it seems like an open-air prison: perhaps the most apt comparison is with a gigantic *Rodoviária*, a great concrete complex dominated by road systems. Class and race barriers do exist here, though the most obvious dividing line in Brasília is the question of **car** ownership, which confers status and power. If you haven't got a car, you're part of the underclass. Traditionally, no-one walks if they can help it, but although the open spaces are vast and daunting, on foot you can get a closer, more intimate look at the city. In any case, if you're going to rely on the buses, there are usually queues in the downtown *Rodoviária*.

Below, the main sights in Brasília are divided into three basic sections, following the head, body and tail concept of the bird or aeroplane that the city resembles; the outlying areas of the city are dealt with afterwards.

The Power Complex

Separated from the commercial centres and the downtown *Rodoviária* by the esplanade of ministry buildings, the area known as the **Power Complex** comprises the National Congress, Palace of Justice, Itamaratí Palace, Planalto Palace, History Museum and the Supreme Court. All of these places are within a few minutes' walk of each other and can be seen in half a day, though you can easily spend more time than this exploring if you get sidetracked.

At the centre of the complex is the **Praça dos Tres Poderes** (Square of Three Powers), representing the forces emanating from the Congress, the Judiciary and the Foreign Office. The **Congresso Nacional** (Mon–Fri 8am–noon & 2–5pm, Sat & Sun 9am–noon & 2–5.30pm) is the heart of legislative power and one of the most obvious landmarks in Brasília – in a way, everything else flows from here. If you accept the analogy of the city built as a bird, then the National Congress is the beak of the beast, something it clearly resembles with its twin 28-storey towers. The two hemispheres, one on either side of the towers, house the Senate Chamber (the smaller, inverted one) and the House of Deputies, and it's interesting to note that these were designed so that the public could climb and play on them. This egalitarian principle extends further, too: the Congresso Nacional permits visitors to attend debates when in session, something you might want to enquire about.

The **Palácio da Justiça** (Mon–Fri 8am–noon & 2–6pm) is beside the Congress building, on the northern side of the Esplanada dos Ministerios. Created in 1960 with a concrete facade by the socialist architect Niemeyer (who eventually won the Lenin Peace Prize for his overall work), the building was covered with fancy – and, to many, elitist – marble tiles by the military government during the 21 years of dictatorship. Now that democracy rules once again, the tiles have been removed, laying bare the common, symbolic, concrete, artificial waterfalls flowing between the pillars. On the southern side of the Congress building, the **Palácio Itamaratí** (open Mon–Fri; ring ☎211-6640 for permission to visit) is the vast Foreign Office structure, combining modern and classical styles, and again quite striking in appearance. Sitting over the water, outside the building, the *Meteor* statue by Bruno Giorgi is a stunning piece of work, its five parts representing the five continents, the water symbolic of the divinity. There are also some fascinating water gardens here and, inside, a good art collection of Brazilian and other works.

Behind the National Congress, on the northern side, the **Palácio do Planalto** (Mon–Fri 9–10.30am & 3–5pm) houses the president's office. This has been closed to visitors recently but if you can't get in there's usually a changing of the guard out front at 8.30am and 5.30pm daily. Also here, stuck between the Planalto Palace and the Supreme Court, the **Museu Histórico de Brasília** in Praça dos Tres Poderes (daily 9am–5pm) is of limited interest to most, telling the tale of the

CENTRAL BRASÍLIA

transfer of the capital from the coast to the central *planalto*. The **Supremo Tribunal Federal** (Mon–Fri noon–6pm) itself – or the Supreme Court – is open to the public, although entrance is with formal dress only (ie no shorts and t-shirts); outside there's a concrete monument to Justice.

From here, you can take a **bus** to the downtown *Rodoviária*, or it's a twenty-minute walk west through the esplanade of ministry buildings to the Cathedral and downtown commercial centre.

The Cathedral and the commercial sectors

Between the Power Complex and the downtown *Rodoviária*, and within walking distance of either, lies the **Catedral Nacional** (daily 8–11am & 1–7pm; Mass at 6.15am Mon–Fri, 5.30 on Sat, 8.30am & 10.30am on Sun) – one of Brasília's most striking edifices. It marks the spot where the city of Brasília was inaugurated in 1960 and is built in the form of an inverted chalice and crown of thorns: its sunken nave means that most of the interior floor is below ground level. Outside, on ground level, a moat surrounds the incredible stained-glass domed roof. Some of the glass roof panels in the interior reflect rippling water from outside, adding to the sense of airiness in the Cathedral, while the statues of Saint Peter and the angels, suspended from the ceiling, help to highlight the feeling of elevation. Nevertheless, although some forty metres in height and with a capacity of 4000, the Cathedral is surprisingly small inside. Incidentally, a sign on the way in reads "Please don't wear shorts or bermudas inside the Cathedral".

Around ten minutes' walk away, closer towards the shopping centres and *Rodoviária*, on the northern side of the Eixo Monumental, the **Teatro Nacional**, built in the form of an Aztec temple, is a marvellous looking building. The theatre lobby often mounts good art exhibitions – with futuristic and environmental themes – and there are three completed halls inside: the *Martins Pena*, the *Villa-Lobos* (the largest, seating 1200) and the much smaller *Alberto Nepomuceno*. Unfortunately, the theatre can only be of limited interest to foreigners, since most productions are in Portuguese.

Following the walkways, just over (and under) the main road (Eixo Rodoviária Norte), the **commercial sectors**, or *Conjuntos*, provide proof that human life does exist in Brasília. There are two basic shopping sectors, one on either side of the downtown *Rodoviária*, the closest Brasília gets to having a heart. Both stand three storeys high, crammed with all kinds of shops and eating places. The **northern sector** is much more upmarket than its neighbour across the way, essentially a modern indoor shopping centre, always very busy and generally entertaining. The flashy jewellery and furniture shops combine with restaurants and fast food outlets, and unlike the modern shopping centres in other Latin American cities, Brasília's are not just a playground for the rich; everyone seems to frequent the place. Outside, the huge rectangular concrete block which contains this hive of activity is covered with massive product advertisements. The **southern sector**, reached by following the pavement over the top of the *Rodoviária*, is rather down at heel in appearance, but boasts an excellent vegetarian restaurant and New Age shop – *Cheiro Verde* – with brilliant views from its terrace, overlooking the Cathedral. The restaurant is easy to find; it's on the eastern side below the large *El Dorado* sign. Stuck underground between the two giant shopping blocks, the downtown **Rodoviária** is also on three levels, and here you'll find more shops, toilets, snack bars and an information office.

The tail end: TV tower and Kubitschek memorial

The tail end of Brasília's layout provides less gripping an attraction, though there are several places you'll want to visit on any extended stay in the city. The **TV Tower** lookout platform (daily 10am–5pm) is an obvious city landmark and easily reached on foot or by bus (the #131 from the *Rodoviária*): it's at Eixo Monumental, Setor Oeste. The 218-metre-high tower is a good place from which to get Brasília into perspective, and inside there's a reasonable restaurant and *churrascaria* with magnificent views, a bar and a gift shop. At the weekend, it's also popular for its **craft market**, held around the base.

If you're so inclined, the **Planetário**, or planetarium, on Eixo Monumental (on the side of the *Centro de Convenções*; Sat & Sun at 4pm for children and 5.30pm for adults) is a relatively short walk from the TV Tower. Next to this, still on the Eixo Monumental, is the **Centro de Convenções** itself, Brasília's Convention Centre, an unusual and futuristic building, and home of the city's main tourist office.

Close to here, a little further to the west, is the famous **Juscelino Kubitschek (JK) Memorial** (daily 8am–6pm; small entrance fee), the statue standing motionless inside an enormous question mark – though you can also get here on bus #131 from the *Rodoviária* or from near the TV Tower. More interesting than the monument is the **museum** below, covering both the history of Brasília and Kubitschek's life, with some fascinating photographs and documentary records. Finally, a little stroll to the north of Eixo Monumental from the JK Monument brings you to the **Palácio do Buriti**, administrative seat of the Federal District, set in its own little square with pretty illuminated fountains.

The rest of the city

Beyond the central sights, there's little to Brasília that warrants a longer stay, though there are some low-key city destinations that can fill in the time. All are fairly close to each other and they're best tackled in the order given.

A couple of decent museums lie within a short distance of the downtown *Rodoviária*: the **Museu de Arte de Brasília** (Tues–Sun 2–7pm) is near the *Hotel Brasília Palace* and is worth an hour or so; while the **Museu Etnográfico** (Av. L-2 Norte, 609, bl. D; Mon–Fri 8am–noon & 2–6pm) contains some excellent archaeological, prehistorical and ethnographical exhibits. The interesting **Fátima** chapel lies between the superquadras 307 and 308, in front of the commercial sector 107 and 108 – this was the very first building inaugurated in Brasília, built by Oscar Niemeyer and looking like a cross between a nun's wimple and a marquee.

Fifteen minutes from here, **Dom Bosco's Sanctuary** (Av. W-3 Sul, Q702; daily 8am–6.30pm) was named after Dom Bosco – an Italian priest who, in 1833, had a dream that "between the 15th and 20th parallels, where a lake had formed, a great civilisation will be born". It would be churlish not to accept that Brasília fulfils the prophecy and the Sanctuary is suitably modern, a blue-tinted glass-based building.

Also quite central, there's a pleasant park, **Parque Rogério Pithon Farias**, with a heated public swimming pool, a boating lake, snack bar and woods. You can get there on bus #114 from the *Rodoviária*, or from the JK Memorial by walking back towards the *Rodoviária* – it's signposted on the right 300–400m to the east. From the entrance it's a good two-kilometre walk through a relatively barren section of the park to the main recreation zone.

On the southern side of the city, over a limb of Lake Paranoá in the sprawling new residential district (see below), you'll find the lively **Centro Comércio Gilberto Salomão**. Particularly active in the evenings, this offers a range of nightclubs, beer gardens and restaurants – and the world's first three-in-one (270-degree panorama) screen cinema. Near the bridge over this southern lake channel, which separates the southern residential sector from the main city, the **Jardim Zoologico** feature many species of wildlife and a botanical reserve. There's also an open-air theatre which stages animal-based events most Sunday afternoons. Lastly, the **Palácio da Alvorada** – the presidential residence – on the edge of Lake Paranoá, is a beautiful building, though, since you can't get to see inside, probably isn't worth the taxi ride you'll have to take to get there ($5 return from the *Rodoviária*).

Eating, drinking and other entertainment

The wide range of varied **restaurants** is one of the best things about Brasília, though prices are comparatively expensive for Brazil. There's a fair number of **bars**, too, and though Brasília isn't exactly the towering cultural capital you're led to believe, there's always something on at one of the **galleries and theatres** that's diverting enough.

Restaurants

Brasília gives you more opportunity than most Brazilian cities to find unusual ethnic food, and vegetarians, too, are well catered for with at least a couple of specialist restaurants. Good, quick snacks and juices are generally available in *lanchonetes* and bars in either of the *Conjunto* shopping centres, but for excellent Brazilian and ethnic food, try one of the places listed below. Most of these are more expensive than usual: if you want to keep the price down, stick to meat dishes – the fish has to come a long way and, not surprisingly, is very expensive.

Le Chaumiere, Comércio Local Sul, Q404, bl. A, lj. 13 (☎242-7599). Excellent, expensive French food; you won't get away for less than $20 a head, the pricey imported wine is extra.

Comida Brasileira, Comércio Local Sul Q302, bl. B, lj. 37 (☎226-0560). Brazilian food served daily noon–4pm & 6pm–midnight; Sunday lunch only.

Cuba-Libre, Comércio Local Sul, Q202, bl. A, lj. 26/28 (☎244-2579). A Cuban eating-house with spicy food.

Feijao Verde, Comércio Local Sul, Q201, bl. B, lj. 25 (☎224-6362). Good Brazilian food served daily 11am–3pm & 6pm–midnight.

Le Français, Comércio Local Sul, Q203, bl. B, lj. 27 (☎225-4583). Superior French food served Mon–Sat noon–3pm & 7–11pm. Expensive.

Ken's Kitchen, Comércio Local Norte, Q302, bl. B, lj. 7 (☎226-6733). A vegetarian restaurant; lunches only at weekends.

Komatsu, Setor Habitaçöes Sul, C.C. Gilberto Salomão, bl. C, lj. 38/39 (☎248-3020). A busy Japanese restaurant. Reasonably priced by Brazilian standards.

Korea House, Comércio Local Sul, 212, bl. A, lj. 26/28 (☎244-2579). Very fine Korean food, a rare speciality in Brazil.

Mâe Natureza, Av. W-2, Sul, Q505, bl. A, lj. 54 (☎244-8025). A well recommended vegetarian restaurant.

Tabu, Setor Hoteleiro Sul (*Hotel Nacional*). A lively *churrascaria*, with live music at the weekend.

Trapiche, Comércio Local Sul, Q104, bl. D, lj. 1 (☎225-8883). Excellent fish dishes, with live music most Thurs, Fri & Sat evenings. Not one for broke travellers.

Trattoria Palace, Comércio Local Sul, Q404, bl. C, lj. 27 (☎226-9900). Good Italian food and live music towards the end of the week.

Bars and discos

Even discounting the hotel bars – and there are plenty of those – there's still quite a selection of **places to drink**. But it has to be said again, that realistically, you're not going to have the time of your life at night in Brasília: save your money for when you get to Rio. That said, among the most popular bars are *Degrau's* (CLN 304, bl. B; ☎226-1319) and *Piantella* (CLS 202, bl. B, lj. 34; ☎226-4162), both worth a fling. Also recommended for a visit is the *Gang Executive Bar* in the *Hotel Torre Palace* (SHN, Q4, bl. A; ☎226-3360) and the *London Tavern* (Q409 Sul).

For **dancing**, your greatest choice is in the *Conjunto Venâncio* shopping centre – notably *Le Bateau* and the **gay club**, *Aquarius*. Another good disco is *Zoom* (Centreo Comercial Gilberto Salomao, bl. A; ☎248-5153). The *Gates Pub* (Q403 Sul) is got up to look like an English pub, but sometimes has music and dancing.

Exhibitions, galleries and theatre

Good international photography and art **exhibitions** are often held in the lobby of the *Teatro Nacional*, Setor Comércial Norte, Eixo Monumental (☎223-5620), though for a wider range of – generally fairly mediocre – **art galleries** you have to be prepared to travel further afield. The *Aliança Francesa* building (Av. W-4 Sul, between blocks 708 and 907; ☎242-7500) is usually worth a browse. Also of some repute are the *Espaco Cultural* (CLS, Q405, bl.B, cj. 16; ☎224-4827); *Oscar Seraphico* (SCS, bl. M, lj. 1; in the Gilberto Salomão building; ☎225-7713); and *Performance* (CLS, Q116, bl. A. lj. 7; ☎245-5131).

One of the best new **theatres** is the *Teatro Galpão* (between Q308 Sul and Av. W-3 Sul). Also in the city are *Teatro Alvorada* (SGAN 916, Conjunto D; ☎274-3030); *Teatro Dulcina* (SDS ed. FBT, bl.C, lj. 30; ☎226-0188); and *Teatro Escola Parque* (W-3, Q508).

Listings

Airlines Mostly found around the *Hotel Nacional* in the various agents' shops. The main Brazilian companies are *TAM* (SHS *Galeria Hotel Nacional*, lj. 61; ☎223-5168); *Transbrasil* (CLN, Q102, A 2; ☎223-4568); *Varig/Cruzeiro* (CLS, Q306, B 20; ☎242-4111); *VASP* (SHS, *Galeria Hotel Nacional*, lj. 53/54; ☎225-8300). Also represented are *KLM* (SHS, *Galeria Hotel Nacional*, lj. 74; ☎224-5397/225-5513); *Iberia* (Ed. Venancio 2000 bl. B, lj. 40-A Terreo; ☎226-1908/226-0456); *Air France* (SHS, *Galeria Hotel Nacional*, lj. 39/40; ☎223-4299/223-4152); *Lufthansa* (SHS, *Galeria Hotel Nacional*, lj. 01; ☎223-2050/223-5002).

Banks Easily spotted in the Setor Bancario Sul (SBS), including the *Banco do Brasil* and the *Banco Regional*. *American Express* has an office in *Kontik-Transtur*, Setor Comercial Sul, Edificio Central.

Bookshops English novels can be found on the ground level of the northern shopping centre; enter from opposite the *Teatro Nacional*.

Car Hire *Kontik-Transtur SA* (SCS Ed. Central S1001/1008; ☎224-9636) offer a good service. There's the usual *Hertz* operation based in the Setor Hoteis Norte (*Hotel Eron Brasilia*; ☎226-2125) and at the airport (Stand 20; ☎248-4466). *Unidas* work from the gallery below the *Hotel Nacional* (lj. 60; ☎225-5191) and the airport (Stand 24; ☎248-6227).

Crystals Great value gems and jewels are available from the shop *Pedras Nativas*, Venâncio 2000, Terreo.

Embassies *Australia* (SHIS, Ql 9, cj. 16, casa 1; ☎248-5569); *Canada* (SES, Av. das Nações, Q803, lote 16, sl. 130; ☎223-7515); *Denmark* (SES, Av. das Nações, lote 26; ☎242-8188); *UK* (SES, Av. das Nações, Q801, cj.K, lote 8; ☎225-2710); *USA* (SES, Av. das Nacões, lote 3; ☎223-0120).

Emergencies Medical ☎192; Police ☎190; Fire Brigade ☎193.

Festivals Festa da Cidade on April 21 (Inauguration anniversary); Feira dos Estados in last week of June; Dom Bosco's Day, a procession on Lake Paranoá on Aug 31; Grande Prêmio Automobilistico (motor racing over 1000km) on Sept 7; Festival of Brazilian Cinema in Oct.

Hospitals *De Base* (SMHS, Q101; ☎225-0070); *Santa Lucia* (SHLS, Q716, cj. C; ☎245-3344); and *UNIMED* (SHLS, Q716, cj. A; ☎245-1155).

Money Exchange At the *Banco do Brasil* (SBS, Ed. Sede I, terreo; ☎212-2215); *Banco Sudameris Brasil* (W/3 Sul Q513, bl. B, lj. 15/19; ☎244-5055).

Post Office The small, white building (Mon–Sat 9am–6pm) in the open grassy space behind the *Hotel Nacional*. Collect your poste restante from here, too.

Saunas *Basian Kara* (SDS, ed. Venancio IV, lj. 0505; ☎225-3621); and *Caribe* (SCLN 205, bl. B, lj. 19; ☎274-5993).

Shopping You can buy almost anything in the two downtown shopping centres. The northern centre seems to offer a wider range of slightly more expensive products. For *artesanato* and other craft goods, there's a good market underneath the TV Tower on Sat, Sun and most public holidays. A smaller market next to the Cathedral sells an incredible range of dried and dyed flowers. For regional craft specialities try the *Galeria dos Estados*, in the subway connecting the Southern Banking Sector (Setor Báncário Sul) with the Southern Commercial Sector (Setor Comércial Sul).

Trains Regular services from the *Rodoferroviária* for Araguari, Campinas, Ribeirão Preto, São Paulo, Uberaba and Uberlândia. The São Paulo train leaves on weekdays at 8.50pm (arriving 23hr later); $9 first class, $14 for the more comfortable sleeper.

Travel Agents For local tours and air tickets try *Andre Safari and Tours Ltda* (SHIS, QI. 07, bl.B, sala 201; ☎248-3953); *Buriti* (SCS 402, bl. A, lj. 27; ☎225-2686); *Kontil* (SCS, Edificio Central, lj. 1001/1008; ☎224-9783); *Presmic* (SHS, *Galeria Hotel Nacional*, lj. 33/34; ☎225-5515); and *Valetur* (SHS, *Galeria Hotel Nacional*, lj. 30/31; ☎224-7166).

Around Brasília: some ideas

The main attraction beyond the city limits is **Catetinho** (daily 8am–5.30pm), the very first building built in Brasília and once the residence of Kubitschek. Built on stilts, it was originally constructed in 1956 for the financiers, planners and designers to work from. Luciano Pereira, the present curator, actually helped to build the place. A quaint, mostly timber, construction, it still retains some of the president's furniture and other objects. To reach it, you'll have to take the bus to Belo Horizonte from the *Rodoferroviária* and get off after 27km at Catetinho.

A little closer, but in the opposite direction (along the road towards Formosa and Salvador), the **Parque Nacional de Brasília** is a popular place for picnics amongst the woodlands, and there are also natural springs, swimming pools and baths – take the Estrada to Sobradinho, along the BR-020. Only about 8km from the downtown area, residents of the city flock here in their thousands at weekends. There are designated areas set aside for the protection of local flora and fauna, and an orchid house contains some rare species.

Lake Paranoá

Further afield, but well worth the effort, are the attractions of **Lake Paranoá**. Buses from the downtown *Rodoviária* go right around the lake in a couple of hours: bus #100 covers the southern half, finishing up in a shanty settlement after crossing the main dam; you then change to bus #101 which continues back to Brasília, taking a route which gives some superb views of the city. A man-made recreation area, created by the diversion of three rivers to humidify the dry climate, the forty-square-kilometre lake is already suffering from an algae problem, but its waters are the scene of water sports, clubhouses and the **Ermida**

Dom Bosco. This – providing the second namecheck in the city for the priest (see above) – is a small conical hermitage, sitting alone on the edge of the lake, around 30km from the *Rodoviária*. It offers fine views over the lake towards the Alvorada Palace, while below the nearby Paranoá dam you can see amazing waterfalls during the heavy summer rains.

Planaltina and Cristalina

An historic but sleepy town, **PLANALTINA** is a possible day trip from Brasília. It's around 40km east of the city, beyond the Saída Norte, and three-quarters of the way there the road crosses the divide between the Amazon and Plate watersheds. The town itself is a typical example of a traditional Goiás town: like many communities on the Planalto Central it was founded by *bandeirantes* and evolved into a small market town. Nowadays, there are a few unremarkable colonial buildings left in the centre, a museum and some good restaurants. But there is a distinct air of small-town tedium here. As soon as it gets dark, the streets empty as the locals settle down to watch the TV soaps behind their shutters.

More distant, more rustic and of greater interest is the settlement of **CRISTALINA**, around 100km south of Brasília, on the BR-040 towards Belo Horizonte. It's a small, attractive place, based around the mining and marketing of semi-precious stones and, if you're in the market, quartz crystals and Brazilian amethyst can be bought here at very reasonable prices. The journey itself, though, is one of the main reasons to come: a good place to make for to see the distinctive, savanna scenery of the Planalto.

GOIÁS STATE

Out of Brasília, the main attractions in the **State of Goiás** comprise a few interesting small cities, of which **Goiânia** is the largest, and the natural beauty of both the **Chapada dos Veadeiros** national park and the river island, **Ilha do Bananal**. The region is fairly well served by bus, particularly on the Brasília–Belém route. Nevertheless, this is not a region which attracts many visitors. Most people travel straight through en route to more exotic destinations, like the Amazon and Mato Grosso, or are stopping off on their way to the coast. Still, if you have the time and inclination, there are basic hotels and good food in most of Goiás' smaller towns.

Goiânia

The other modern, planned city in central Brazil, **GOIÂNIA** was founded in October 1933, becoming the state capital four years later. A million strong, cheaper than Brasília, with some good hotels and only 209km from the federal capital, you might well find yourself stopping over here, too: handy, since Goiânia is very well connected by road to most other Brazilian cities.

Goiânia hit the international headlines in 1987 when a salvaged X-ray machine was broken open by a scrap merchant's family and the radioactive crystals inside were unwittingly spread around the town. The purple, glowing crystals caused serious illness and sections of the city were sealed off for weeks. Now life seems to have returned to normal, Goiânia back to earning its living as a market centre for the surrounding agricultural region, which specialises in rice and soya growing.

Although its clean, modern main streets and buildings are handsome enough, laid out in concentric circles right in the centre, there's none of Brasília's striking architecture, and Goiânia has very little to delay you for more than a night. The **Parque Mutirama**, in the eastern sector of the city, is a recreation centre with woods and a planetarium (Sat at 8pm, Sun at 3.30pm & 4.30pm); while on the other side of town there's a zoo and an ethnographical museum, at Avenida Anhanguera. The city has more value as a base for exploring the region, though again, it's quite difficult to get excited by the possibilities. The unusual geological formations around PARAUNA are reputed to be worth seeing, and there are around thirty thermal springs at the resort town of CALDAS NOVAS, 185km from the city.

All the practicalities

The **airport**, *Santa Genoveva* (☎264-1600/1611), is 6km out of town, from where there are flights to some major cities (like Belém), though Brasília is a better bet for most destinations. Buses connect with the centre of town. **Buses** from out of town stop at the *Rodoviária* (Rua 44, setor Norte Ferroviário; ☎224-7078), a few kilometres out of the centre and, again, there are services into town (as well as to Brasília, Campo Grande, Cuiabá, Goiás Velho, Rio de Janeiro and São Paulo).

Goiânia has several reasonable **hotels**, including the *Hotel Itaipú* (☎223-5655), near the old *Rodoviária* in the airport sector. Several places, too, along and around Avenida Anhanguera in the centre: the *Hotel Antônio*, Avenida Anhanguera 6296F; the *Umuarama*, Rua 4, 492, on Praça João (☎224-1555); the *Samambia*, Avenida Anhanguera 1157, Setor Universitario (☎261-1444); and the *Hotel Presidente*, Avenida Anhanguera 3692, in the central sector (☎224-0500). You can **camp** at both *Itanhanga*, Avenida Princ. Carolina, Setor Mansoes do Campus (☎224-2700), 13km out of town, and *Tangara*, Jardim Rosa do Sul (☎225-7214), 18km away.

Eating out in Goiânia means the usual range of *churrascarias*: *Restaurant Serradourada*, Rua 84, 497, southern sector; *Vera Cruz*, Avenida Araguaia 453, central sector; and the *Restaurant do Gaucho* on Praça Tamandaré, in the western sector. For good local dishes try the *Restaurant O Boladeiro*, Rua 10, 704, western sector, which is particularly good on Sunday. The *Restuarant Don Quixote*, Rua 5, 710, also on Praça Tamandaré, features the delicious speciality of *peixe ao molho de camarão* at quite a reasonable price. **Vegetarian food** is available at *Arroz Integral*, Rua 93, 326, setor Sul, and you'll find excellent **ice cream** at the *sorvetaria Casa Verde* on Praça Tamandare (western sector).

In terms of **nightlife**, there isn't much. The *Zoom* disco, Avenida República do Libano 2533, western sector, is busy at weekends and there are a few **bars**, like *Beb's*, Avenida República do Libano 2353, western sector; *Jota's*, Avenida República do Libano 2526, western sector; and *Hippopotamus*, Avenida Assis Chateaubriand, 1188, western sector.

Some listings

Airlines *Varig*, Av. Goiás 285, Centro (☎224-5049); *VASP*, Rua 3, 569, Centro (☎223- 4266).

Authorisation to enter the Ilha do Bananal can be obtained from the Park Director, Rua 229, 95, Setor Universitario 74000.

Car Hire *Unidas*, Rua 6, 450, Centro (☎224-1180); *Belauto*, Av. República do Libano, 1713, western sector (☎225-7519).

Hospital *Hospital do Inamps*, Av. Anhanguera 4379, western sector (☎223-5601).

Travel Agencies *Transworld*, Rua 3, 560, Galeria Central, Centro (☎224-4340); *Incatur*, Av. Goiás 151, Centro (☎225-2622); and *Valetur*, Rua Tocantins, 310, Centro (☎224-9400).

Anápolis and Pirenópolis

A couple of small towns lie within easy reach of Goiânia, with enough accommodation choices and local interest that you might want to base a couple of days'
side-trip around them.

Anápolis

Directly between Goiânia and Brasília (only 57km from the state capital), on the
BR-060, **ANÁPOLIS** is a large and modern town, centre of a rich agricultural area.
Indeed, arriving from the north, the skyscrapers and new ring-road tell you that
you've crossed the line separating the poor Northeast and Amazon regions from
more developed parts of the country. But unless you're interested in tractor show-
rooms and cattle feed wholesalers there's little here to tempt you, though there's a
history museum at Rua Celestino Batista 323 (Mon–Fri 7am–5pm), in the town
centre; and on Avenida Brasil there's a commercial art gallery of some interest,
called *Antônio Sibasolly*. If you're going to stay here, the best **hotel** choices are the
Hotel Calcara, Rua 14 de Julho 905 (☎324-3740); *Hotel Gaucho*, Rua D'Abandia 88
(☎324-4707); *Hotel Itamaraty*, Rua Manoel D'Abandia 209 (☎324-4812); and, close
to the *Rodoviária*, on Avenida Brasil, the *Hotel Serra Dourada* (☎324-0051).

Pirenópolis

It's probably better to press on to **PIRENÓPOLIS**, a mountain town 66km to the
north of Anápolis, and located in classic *cerrado* countryside. The surrounding
area is renowned for sightings of UFOs and the colonial settlement itself is the
best base from which to explore the local **Serra dos Pirineus** hills, which rise
up to over 1300m above sea level. The town was originally a gold-mining settlement and the **mines** of Abade, 17km out of town, are of some interest if you can
get to them. Otherwise, it's worth trying to coincide with the colourful *Festa do
Divino Espírito Santo*, which takes place in Pirenópolis six weeks after Easter: a
costumed religious festival, it consists of dances, mock battles between Moors
and Christians and other lively entertainments.

For **accommodation** in Pirenópolis, try the *Hotel Rex* at Praça Emanoa Jaime
Lopes 15 (☎331-1121); *Pousada das Caralhadas*, Praça Matriz 1 (☎331-1313); and
the rundown, *Hotel Central*, right in the centre. For a bite **to eat**, the *Restaurant
As Frio*, Rua Pref. Sizenando Jayme 16, serves excellent food.

Goiás Velho

Established in 1727, **GOIÁS VELHO** was a gold-mining settlement of some
standing, founded originally by *bandeirantes* on the trail of precious loot. As the
name hints, it was once the state capital, a role it retained until 1937 when
Goiânia, 144km away, took over. For all that, it's neglected these days, and is on
no-one's tourist itinerary, but it's by far the most interesting place to head for
while in Goiás. It's the only place in the state where a significant sense of the colonial past is to be felt, and the narrow cobbled streets, solid traditional stone
houses and occasional clopping sound of mules combine to produce a tranquil,
timeless atmosphere – not that there's anything much to do except to savour it. If
you want to trace the story of the gold-seekers, the **Museu Bandeirantes** is at
Praça Brasil (Tues–Sat 7.30–11am & 1–5pm, Sun 7.30am–noon), while also of

some interest is the **Museu de Arte Sacra** on Praça Castelo Blanco (Tues–Sat 7.30–11am & 1–5pm, Sun 7.30am–noon). To cool off, around 7km beyond the town it's possible to swim at the **Cachoeira Grande**.

There are some reasonable **hotels** in town if you decide to stay – and Goiás Velho is pleasant enough for a night at least. Try one of *Hotel Serrano*, Avenida Dr. Deusdete Ferreira da Moura (☎371-1981), *Hotel Municipal*, Rua Dr. Americano do Brasil, or *Hotel Vila Boa* (with a swimming pool), Morro do Chapeu do Padre (☎371-1000). **Camping** is possible in a couple of places, at *Chafariz da Carioca*, near the town centre, and on the banks of the Rio Bacalhau, 3km towards Goiânia. There's good **food** at the restaurant *Pito Acesso*.

Chapada dos Veadeiros

A picturesque national park, the **Chapada dos Veadeiros** is just over 200km (or around three hours by bus) north of Brasília. It's well worth taking your own tent and **camping** equipment as that way it's possible to explore further afield.

The national park is located more or less between the settlements of CAVALCANTE and **ALTO PARAISO DE GOIAS**, to the south, where there is a small, very basic hotel (by the *Rodoviária*). The buses from Brasília stop here and from Alto Paraiso, a trail heads west towards COLINAS; it's a two-hour walk to the main area of the park (or local buses most days from Alto Paraiso), which you enter just prior to reaching the settlement of SÃO JORGE. There are several sets of stunning waterfalls within a day's walk of here, on the headwaters of the Rio Negro, and basic accommodation in São Jorge, though it's more fun to stay in the area if you've brought your own tent.

Ilha do Bananal

In the very northwest of Goiás State, the **Ilha do Bananal** is the world's largest river island, over 300km long from head to tail. Although created as a national park, it has since lost over fifty percent of its area to settlers and development. Nevertheless, it remains beautiful and wild in places, home to the remnants of the **Carajás Indians**. In 1958, the British explorer, Hanbury-Tenison, visited the island and witnessed two shamans performing ritual dances. Yet just thirteen years later, there were only 800 Indians left on the island, and today the few hundred survivors are far outnumbered by the many thousands of non-Indian Brazilian settlers – and the only obvious Indian dances are those performed on the command of government officials. This apart, it's an easy place to immerse yourself in the wonders of the forest. Wildlife is varied and plentiful, and it's even possible to spot a maned wolf or otters if you've the time to spend searching during the rainy season. The Ilha do Bananal is, however, quite remote and requires some serious bus journeys to get there. Moreover, **permission to visit** should be obtained in advance from the Park Director in Goiânia; Rua 229, 95, Setor Universitario, 74000 – though you may be allowed entry without this permission.

The **usual approach** to Bananal is from Brasília or Goiânia via the BR-153 road to Belém. You have to change buses at **PORANGATÚ**, eight hours north of Brasília, and as the buses to the next staging point, São Felix do Araguaia (see below), are not that frequent, if you arrive after about 4pm you'll have to make an overnight stop. Porangatú's *Rodoviária* is on Avenida Adelino Americo; on the same street try the *Hotel Lord* or the *Hotel Mariti*.

From Porangatú it's another five hours to **SÃO FELIX DO ARAGUAIA**, where there are some limited services, including a pizzeria and the *Mini Hotel Araguaia*, Avenida Araguaia 344. Whether you go further by road from here, or decide to head straight into the park, it is advisable to buy a good stock of food and drink to take with you: such luxuries are very hard to come by deeper in. Although it's possible to enter the National Park of Bananal by boat from São Felix (you'll need advance permission from the *FUNAI* office in town), having made it this far, most visitors opt to make the three-hour journey north to **SANTA TERESINHA**, a tiny settlement but the best base for exploring the Ilha do Bananal. Here, there is a good, but very small, **hotel** and access to local **boats**, which is the only means of travel onto the island.

Tocantins

In 1989 the new state of **Tocantins** was created by the simple expedient of drawing a line through the state of Goiás. It was created not so much because it is a geographical or cultural unit, but to create jobs for local politicians: President Sarney was desperately in need of support at the time and came up with the idea of the state to satisfy regional leaders. So don't expect Tocantins to have any sense of identity or history; it's merely a bureaucratic invention, and may well soon vanish from the maps as suddenly as it appeared.

It has no capital – there are plans to build one at the obscure village of MIRACEMA DO NORTE – and no maps or tourist information set-up. The most contact you are likely to have with the state, unless you head for the Ilha do Bananal (see above), is passing through on your way to Belém, on the Belém–Brasília highway which bisects Tocantins. The scenery en route is very representative of the rest of the state: flat, largely deforested plains, with the odd clump of palm trees or bedraggled remnants of forest. The towns on the way are flyblown and hot – all emphatically places to pass through rather than visit.

travel details

Buses

From Brasília to Rio (daily; 20hr); São Paulo (daily; 16hr); Belém (daily; 36hr); Goiânia (hourly; 2hr 30min); Cuiabá (daily; 20hr); Campo Grande (daily; 24hr); Porangatú (daily; 8hr); Chapada dos Veadeiros (several weekly; 3hr).

From Goiânia to Rio (daily; 18hr); São Paulo (daily; 14hr); Brasília (daily; 2hr 30min); Campo Grande (daily; 18hr); Goiás Velho (daily; 3–4hr); Porangatú (daily; 9hr).

Trains

From Brasília to São Paulo, via Araguari, Campinas and Ribeirão Preto (weekdays only; 23hr).

Planes

From Brasíia and Goiânia to Rio, São Paulo, Belém and Manaus there are several flights every day. Regular flights several times a week to Belo Horizonte, Cuiabá, Fortaleza, Foz de Iguaçu, Santarém and Salvador; and less frequent flights to São Felix de Araguaia and Teresina.

CHAPTER SIX

THE MATO GROSSO

V ery Brazilian, both in its vastness and its frontier culture, the **Mato Grosso** is essentially an enormous plain rippled by a handful of small mountain ranges. The northern half of the region – the state of Mato Grosso – is sparsely populated and has no major settlements. Most of the rest of the Mato Grosso – the state of Mato Grosso do Sul – is either seasonal flood plain or open scrubland: Bolivian swamps and forest border it to the west; the mighty **Araguaia** and **Paraná** rivers (one flowing north, the other south) form a natural rim to the east; while the **Paraguay** river and the country named after it complete the picture to the south. The name Mato Grosso, which means "thick wood", is more appropriate to the northernmost state, where thorny scrubland passes into tropical rain forest and the land begins its incline towards the Amazon.

The simple road network and the limited sprinkling of settlements make **getting about** within the Mato Grosso fairly hard work. Distances are enormous, and although most of the buses and trunk roads are good, any journey is inevitably a long one. But the variety of ecological formations alone makes the trip a unique one and, for the adventurous traveller, there's any one of a wide range of fascinating locations – from swamps and forests to endless cattle ranches, riverine villages or jungle Indian reservations. The Mato Grosso, however, was too much for one adventurer: Colonel Fawcett, a British explorer, disappeared into its interior in 1925, never to be seen again.

The cities of Mato Grosso are particularly deceptive, since although surprisingly modern and developed they've only recently received the full trappings of civilisation. Portuguese colonists began to settle in the region fairly late, at the time of the great **Cuiabá** goldrush of the early eighteenth century, though Cuiabá town itself remained almost completely isolated from the rest of Brazil until its first telegraph link was installed in the 1890s. Masterminded and built by a local boy made good – a down-to-earth army officer called Rondon – the telegraph lines were Mato Grosso's first real attempt to join the outside world. These days, with the completion of Highway BR-364, Cuiabá has again become a staging post for pioneers; this time for countless thousands of Brazilian peasants in search of land or work in the freshly opened Western Amazon states of Rondônia and Acre. Cuiabá can't exactly claim to be a resort town, but it is a natural stepping stone for exploring either the southern Mato Grosso, or the more local scenery of **Chapada dos Guimarães**.

Until a few years ago Cuiabá was capital of the entire Mato Grosso. **Campo Grande** in the south, however, was also growing rapidly and playing an increasingly important financial and administrative role within Brazil, and in the late 1970s the old state was sliced very roughly in half – Campo Grande becoming capital of the brand new state of **Mato Grosso do Sul**. This tightening of political control over the various Mato Grosso regions reflects their rapid development and relative wealth; a complete contrast to the poorer, even more expansive and much more remote wilderness of the Amazon basin.

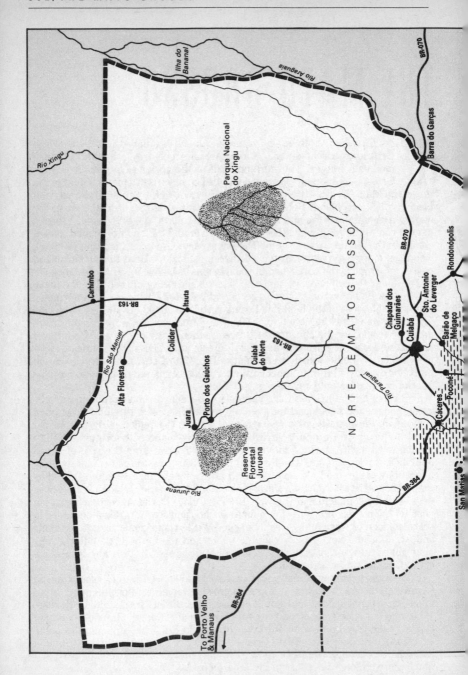

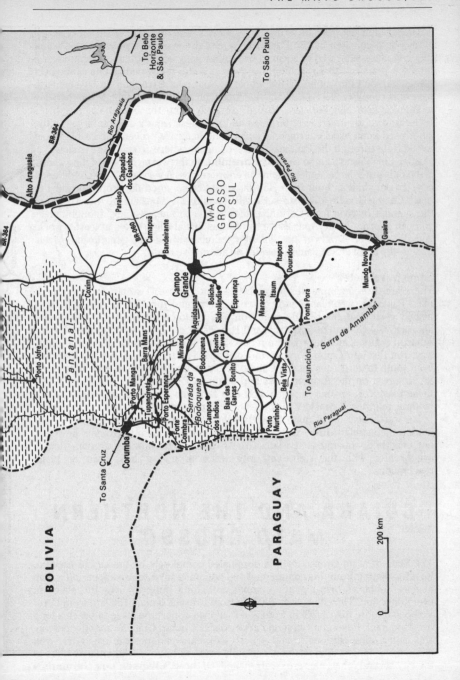

Topographically, and in terms of its tourist potential, the Mato Grosso will always be dominated by the **Pantanal**, one of the world's largest swamps – and the only place where cows seem to live in harmony with jaguars. Despite over a hundred years of cattle ranching, the swamp is still renowned as one of the best places for spotting wildlife in the whole of South America, and so far seems to have absorbed Brazil's typically bovine attack on the environment. More than five million cayman alligators are "culled" annually from the Pantanal, though it's better known for its array of birdlife and its endless supply of piranha fish – the latter used in an excellent regional soup dish. So far it's proved impossible to put a road right through the Pantanal, so travelling anywhere around here is slow.

After Cuiabá and Campo Grande, **Corumbá**, on the western edge of the swamp, is the only other large settlement in the entire region. A very small, air-conditioned city, it's only half an hour from Bolivia, yet it takes a good day from Corumbá to reach Campo Grande, the nearest Brazilian outpost. It is possible to travel through the Pantanal by river from Corumbá, directly to a port near Cuiabá, though unless you can afford a luxury tour this adventurous fluvial route takes at least a week, and often longer. A railway line, linking Corumbá with Campo Grande and – eventually – the coast at São Paulo, provides an alternative route.

Some travel notes

There are three main **routes** through the Mato Grosso. Two fan out around the main Pantanal swamplands in tweezer-like form and run east to west: the most heavily used road, the BR-364, runs from São Paulo on the coast to Cuiabá, passing relatively close to both Goiânia and Brasília before heading on to the Western Amazon regions; another road from São Paulo, the BR-374/163/262, and the railway, run through Campo Grande to Corumbá. The third road, the BR-163, runs from south to north, connecting Campo Grande with Cuiabá, and extending north to Santarém on the Amazon river and south to Paraguay and Asunción. Given these distances, anyone in possession of a Brazilian **air pass**, or simply limited by time, might well consider the occasional plane hop.

It's worth bearing in mind, too, that the Mato Grosso is officially one hour behind the standard **time** of Brasília and the coast. In Campo Grande, however, not everybody operates on Mato Grosso time so it's always a good idea to synchronise with the right authority when arranging bus, train or plane reservations.

CUIABÁ AND THE NORTHERN MATO GROSSO

The State of Mato Grosso itself is dominated completely by the city of **Cuiabá**. Roads radiating from this commercial and administrative centre appear on a map like the tentacles of a gigantic octopus extending hungrily over the plains in every direction. The city is over 1000km from Brasília, almost 1500km from Porto Velho and more than 1700km from São Paulo: an opportune place to break a long overland haul. Beyond its strategic importance, though, Cuiabá's friendly personality, interesting city centre and superb ice-cream parlours can easily trap you into staying longer than planned, certainly since within a 100-kilometre radius of the city several other sites are easily visited. Of these, **Chapada dos Guimarães** offers the most spectacular natural attractions, closely rivalled by the hot baths at **Aguas Quentes**.

Cuiabá is the best springboard for a trip into or through the Pantanal (see below), but as far as other long expeditions go, the **Northern Mato Grosso** (Norte de Mato Grosso) has disappointingly little to offer. No longer a true frontier zone, it's an established cattle-ranching region where cows are much bigger business than tourism. With almost no tourist development outside Cuiabá and the Pantanal, the reality for most travellers will be an intrepid journey by bus (and perhaps river) to some other distant city. The most arduous of the options is the awful **Highway BR-163** from Cuiabá to Santarém via Cachimbo. Otherwise, the fastest road is **Highway BR-364**, crossing the Mato Grosso and passing through Cuiabá on its route between São Paulo and Porto Velho.

Cuiabá

The southern gateway into the Amazon, **CUIABÁ** has always been firmly on the edge of Brazil's wilderness. Following the discovery of a gold field here in 1719, the town mushroomed as an administrative and service centre in the middle of Indian territory, thousands of very slow, overland miles from any other Portuguese settlement. To the south lay the Pantanal and the dreaded Paiaguá people who frequently ambushed convoys of boats transporting Cuiabá gold by river to São Paulo. The fierce Bororo tribe, who dominated the Mato Grosso east of Cuiabá, also regularly attacked many of the mining settlements. Northwest along a high hilly ridge – the *Chapada dos Parecis*, which now carries Highway BR364 to Porto Velho – lived the peaceful Parecis tribe, farmers in the watershed between the Amazon and the Pantanal. By the 1780s, however, most Indians within these groups had either been eliminated or transformed into allies: the Parecis were needed as slave labour for the mines, the Bororo either retreated into the forest or joined the Portuguese as mercenaries and Indian hunters; while the Paiaguá fared worst of all, almost completely wiped out by cannon and musket during a succession of punitive expeditions from Cuiabá.

The most important development came during the 1890s, when a young Brazilian army officer, Lieutenant **Cândido Rondon**, built a telegraph system from Goiás to Cuiabá through treacherous Bororo territory – assisted no doubt by the fact that he had some Bororo blood in his veins. By 1903 he had extended the telegraph from Cuiabá south to Corumbá, and in 1907 he began work to reach the Madeira river, to the northwest in the Amazon Basin. The latter expedition earned Rondon a reputation as an important explorer and brought him into contact with the fascinating Nambikwara Indians. Since then, Cuiabá has been pushing forward the frontier of development and the city is still a stepping stone and crossroads for pioneers. Every year, thousands of hopeful settlers stream through Cuiabá on their way to a new life in the western Amazon.

The established farmlands around the city now produce excellent crops – maize, fruits, rice and soya. But the city itself thrives on the much larger surrounding **cattle ranching region**, which contains almost a quarter of a million inhabitants. Future prosperity is assured, too: a large lead ore deposit is being worked close to the town, and some oil has been discovered at Várzea Grande; but it is more sustainable industries, like rubber and palmnut gathering, that will provide exports in years to come.

Arriving and finding a place to stay

The **Rodoviária** on Avenida Marechal Rondon is an ultra-modern complex, 3km from the city centre: it's a fifteen-minute ride into Cuiabá on bus #117. The **airport** (buses and taxis connecting with Cuiabá city centre) is 12km out, on the opposite side of Cuiabá to the *Rodoviária*.

For details of leaving Cuiabá by bus and air, see "Listings", at the end of the city account.

Information

You'll be able to get **tourist information** on arrival at both the airport (☎381-2211) and *Rodoviária* (☎321-0102); the offices at both open daily between 8am and 6pm. The local tourist board, *TURIMAT*, also has an office in the city centre, on Praça da República (Mon–Fri 8am–5.30pm; ☎322-5363).

In addition, there are quite a few **tour agencies** based in Cuiabá. All of them run trips into the Pantanal or to the closer sites, like Chapada dos Guimarães, although their real work is selling flights within Brazil to businessmen and local well-to-do families. As far as tours within the region go, they all seem to work with the same operators, and charge around $50 a day per person (though it's often worth bargaining). Among the most reliable are the agency in the foyer of the *Mato Grosso Palace Hotel*; *Transpan Travel Agency*, 13 de Junho 270; *Confiança*, Rua Cândido Mariano 434 (☎321-4142); *Cuiabá Tour*, Rua Barão de Melgacão 3508 (☎322-0513); and, specialists in arranging Pantanal hotel bookings, *Selva Turismo*, Rua Barão de Melgacão 3594 (☎322-0153).

Accommodation

With the *Rodoviária* so close, most people prefer to stay in or near the busy city centre. That said, the real **budget hotels** and **dormitórios**, like the *Hotel Santa Luiza* and *Cesars Dormitório*, are mostly found around the old bus station, four or five blocks south of the centre along Rua Baltazar Navarro: the *Santa Luiza* is probably best.

Closer in, of the **middle range** places, the *Avenida Hotel* (☎321-6162) is as good as any: just two blocks from Praça da República, in an old building on the corner of Barão de Melgacão and Getúlio Vargas, it's clean, has air conditioning and a rooftop breakfast bar for less than $4.50 single. Cheaper and more intimate, the *Hotel Samara*, at Joaquim Murtinho 150, is equally central – rooms have showers and a fan. At the *Hotel Mato Grosso*, Rua Comandante Costa 2522 (☎321-9121), within three blocks of the Praça, a single room will cost you around $10.

Most of the other places are rather **expensive**. Behind the Cultural Foundation, for instance, the *Mato Grosso Palace Hotel* starts at around $30; while the *Santa Rosa Palace Hotel*, Avenida Getulio Vargas 600 (☎322-9044), offers more or less the same plush and modern facilities at slightly better prices.

Nearer the Rodoviária there's very little choice and, unless you're leaving by bus early the next day, it's much better to head into the city. If you have no other option, though, the possibilities are: the *Colorado Palace Hotel*, on the main road opposite the *Rodoviária*, noisy and not particularly good value; and the *Hotel Cascavel*, cheaper and with a view over platform 15 of the *Rodoviária*. If you need to stay out by the **airport**, there's always the upmarket *Hotel Aeroporto*, Avenida Governador Ponce de Arruda 780 (☎381-1930).

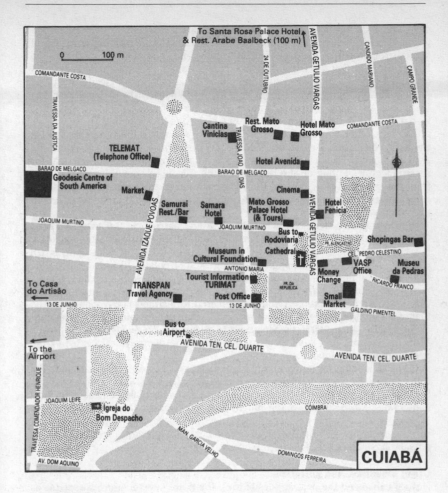

Around the city

Perhaps because of its busy feel, Cuiabá is an exciting place to spend a few days. There's certainly more to see and do here, in the city's relatively self-contained centre, than in the cities of Mato Grosso do Sul and even the buildings reflect more history than the shiny new skyscrapers of Campo Grande are ever likely to see.

The central **Praça da República** is a hive of activity from daybreak onwards. It's the city's main meeting spot, and cathedral, post office, the cultural foundation and university all face onto the square, while under the shade of its large trees, hippies from the Brazilian coast sell crafted jewellery and leather work. The most interesting old mansion in town, now the **Fundação Cultural de Mato Grosso**, is on the square at no. 151. It houses three excellent **museums** (Mon–Fri 7am– 6pm, Sat & Sun 2–6pm; small charge) of history, natural history and anthropology, with exhibits ranging from prehistoric times through to colonial period pieces. There are some fascinating old photos of Cuiabá, along with rooms full of stuffed creatures from the once forested region; and, best of all, a superb array of Indian artefacts. The **Catedral do Bom Jesus**, next to the cultural foundation, is fashioned out of a pinkish stone with a very square Moorish facade. Vast and rectangular on the inside, its main altar is overshadowed by a mural reaching from floor to ceiling. Original, if not a great work of art, it depicts a sparkling Christ, floating in the air above the city of Cuiabá and the cathedral.

The only other church of any real interest in Cuiabá is the **Igreja de Nossa Senhora do Bom Despacho** (Mon–Fri 7am–6pm, Sat & Sun 2–6pm), on Avenida General Mello: worth seeing as much for its religious art collection as for its architecture. Sitting on the hill, across the Avenida Tenente Coronel Duarte from the cathedral side of town, Bom Despacho used to dominate the cityscape before office blocks and towering hotels sprang up to dwarf it in the latter half of this century.

Just to the east of Praça da República, a few narrow central lanes – Pedro Celestino, Galdino Pimentel and Ricardo Franco – form a crowded shopping area. It's here that you find the **Museu das Pedras** (Mon–Fri 9am–5pm; small charge), difficult to spot amongst the congested streets at Ricardo Franco 195. Packed tightly into just two rooms, the museum specialises in gemstones, crystals, fossils, Stone Age artefacts, stuffed animals, birds and snakes. In one display case there's a large fossilised bone, discovered locally and boldly claimed to be that of a *Tyrannosaurus rex*. A more authentic claim can be found five blocks west of the square, along Barão de Melgacão from the *Hotel Avenida*: here, in **Praça Moreira Cabral**, is a small post marking the true geographical centre of the South American continent.

If you're looking for **souvenirs**, Cuiabá isn't a bad place to poke around. Try *Casa do Artesão*, Praça da Major João Bueno 315 (Tues–Fri 9am–3pm & 6–10pm, Sat 9am–2pm) or *FUNAI*'s *Artindia* shop, Rua Barão de Melgacão 3900, for local handicrafts. More curious is the *Magic Shop* on Avenida Tenente Duarte, near the corner with Avenida G. Ponce – its shelves are stacked with coloured candles, ceremonial swords, North American Indian ceramic figurines, incenses, diabolic pots, strings of jungle beads and seed pods.

Other museums and galleries

Having exhausted the central possibilities, there are several other **museums** in Cuiabá in which you could spend some profitable time. The **ethnographic collection** at the office of the *Foundation for Indian Affairs* (*FUNAI*), Rua São Joaquim 1047, is quite extensive, and the **Museu Marechal Rondon**, Avenida Fernando Correia da Costa (Mon–Fri 7.30–11.30am & 1.30–5.30pm) also focuses on local Indian culture: it's out of town, off Highway BR-364's exit to Rondonópolis, in the sector known as Cidade Universitária. Both museums are worth an hour of your time if you have any interest at all in the local indigenous culture. And next to the university theatre, also in Cidade Universitaria, you can visit the less interesting **Museu de Arte e Cultura Popular** (Mon–Fri noon–6pm) and the small **zoological garden**, run by the army, near the university.

Finally, focusing mainly on work by early Repúblican and modern Brazilian artists, there are two **art galleries** in Cuiabá – one in the *Casa da Cultura* (Rua Barão de Melgacão), the other, *Laila Zharan*, at Avenida Marechal Deodoro 504.

Eating, drinking and nightlife

Cuiabá has a surprising range of cuisine and some excellent restaurants. Here, as in most of Brazil, eating out is very much part of the way of life and is often combined with live musical entertainment.

Restaurants

The best-known restaurant in Cuiabá is the *Peixaria Flotante* (daily 11am–11.30pm), a floating eating-house by the Ponte Nova, 6km out of town, which specialises in fresh river fish: to get there, take the bus from the *Hotel Avenida*, following Rua Barão de Melgacão nineteen blocks towards the suburb of Varzea Grande, turn left at the end and the restaurant is by the bridge.

Excellent **regional dishes** can be found at *O Regionalíssimo*, on Rua 13 de Junho (11.30am–2.30pm & 7–11pm; closed Mon), where there's sometimes live music at the weekends. On Wednesday they serve a speciality dish of beef with green bananas. The *Restaurante Mato Grosso* (by the hotel of the same name, on Rua Comandante Costa) is a cheaper alternative for treating yourself to local fish or beef. Just around the corner on Travessa Dias, the very popular and trendy *Cantina Vinicias* serves food with a wide range of drinks (good *pinga*). Or there are several **churrascarías**, including the very good and central *Recanto do Bosque* on Candido Mariano (11am–3pm & 7pm–1.30am; Mon lunch only).

Away from the regional restaurants, there's plenty of choice, too. *Árabe Baalbech*, next to the *Santa Rosa Palace Hotel* on Avenida Getulio Vargas, is an expensive Brazilian-Arabian restaurant. And at the *Gourmet*, Candido Mariano 1092 (11am–2.30pm & 6pm–midnight; closed Tues), you're likely to get Portuguese dishes and, more often than not, local fish in coconut milk – all to the sound of live Brazilian music. *Mama Aurora*, a **pizzeria** at Avenida Don Aquino 391 (daily 6pm–midnight), also has live music most Friday nights. *Karlitus Pizzeria* has the added attraction of a riverside panorama: it's by the Ponte Julio Muller on Praça Porto, ten blocks west of Praça da República along 13 de Julho and a couple of blocks south; about twenty minutes' walk.

For **cheaper eating** and *lanches* there are plenty of places in the area around Praça Alencastro, and in the shopping zone between Pedro Celestino and Galdino Pimentel. The best spot for a drink, inexpensive food, and live Brazilian music is *Shopingas Bar* on Rua Pedro Celestino – a modest but friendly evening focus for young Cuiabanos, and as good a place as any to meet the local people.

Bars, nightlife and ice cream

Although beer is twice as expensive here as it is on the coast, you'll find that **nightlife** in Cuiabá revolves mainly around the bars and restaurants in the town centre. Some places with a good atmosphere have already been mentioned, like *Shopingas Bar* and *Cantina Vinicias* – see above. Beyond the downtown area, along the large Avenida C.P.A. (the easterly continuation of Avenida Tenente Celestino Duarte), there are several more places, bars and clubs – *Pino's Bowling Alley*, *Bilisko's Bar*, *Disco Kedo d'Agua* and the trendy *Millionaires' Discoteca* are all recommended, provided you have plenty of cash.

Ice-cream parlours are an essential ingredient of any city with temperatures often over 40°C. The best in Cuiabá, judging by their popularity, are *Alaska*, Rua Pedro Celestino 215, and *Patotinha*, Avenida Isaac Provoas 761.

Listings

Airlines and air travel *Varig* and *VASP* fly to most major cities daily (Brasília $56; Manaus $120; Rio $110; Campo Grande $40); tickets from the airport or, in advance, from *VASP*, Rua Pedro Celestino 32 (☎321-4122), or *Varig*, Rua Antônio João 258 (☎321-7333). *FAB* occasionally have seats available on cheap flights to Porto Velho and Manaus (☎381-2211). For international flight bookings and confirmations, consult the city's travel agents; see "Information", above.

Air taxis For the few that can afford it, or if you're travelling in a big group, an air taxi service is a useful way of getting to some of the more remote places. The companies are all based at the main airport: *Guara* (☎381-2971); *Protaxi* (☎381-2241); *Scala* (☎381-2491); *Tanobras* (☎381-3791); and *Tanomat* (☎381-2288).

Banks and Exchange Travellers' cheques and notes can be exchanged in the *Banco do Brasil* on Praça Alencastro; dollars can be cashed at some of the jewellers' shops along Ricardo Franco, in the *Abudi Palace Hotel*, Coronel Escolastico 259, or in some of the larger hotels nearer the centre. Cuiabá is the only place in the region where you're likley to be able to change travellers' cheques.

Buses For information phone ☎321-4703. Several buses daily to Goiania, Porto Velho and Campo Grande, on the main tarmacked routes in and out of the Mato Grosso; they're all long journeys (24hr to Porto Velho; $16 – about half this for the others). To or from Manuas, the road beyond Porto Velho is very bad, slowed by endless river crossings; and there's a track north through the forests to Santarém, but it's only viable in very dry spells and you'll be lucky to find a bus which will take you all the way. Both of these trips take from three days to a week. Buses heading for Porto Velho are frequently overloaded with personal luggage, agricultural tools and household effects.

Festivals There are no truly spectacular festivals in or around Cuiabá, but June and July is the most eventful period. At São Antônio do Leverger, the dry and relatively cool month of July is designated a beach festival; and at the same time of year there's a summer festival in the Chapada dos Guimarães; see below for details of both places.

Photo equipment There's a decent photographic shop, *Cuiabá Color*, at Rua Joaquim Murtinho 789 (☎321-5031), with a colour laboratory and the usual gadgets and materials.

Telephones National and international telephone facilities at *Telemat*, Rua Manoel dos Coimbra 258 (Mon–Sat 9am–6pm; ☎321-4353).

Yellow fever Heading out of Cuiabá, there's a yellow fever outpost on the roads to Porto Velho and Santarem where everyone gets a jab unless they can present an up-to-date certificate of inoculation.

Around Cuiabá

There isn't a lot in terms of organised tourism in the region **around Cuiabá**, and what there is is mostly aimed at local people. Nevertheless, the scenery around **Chapada dos Guimarães** makes a fascinating side-trip from the city, and travellers are always welcome, too, at both the hot springs of **Aguas Quentes** and the beach at **São Antônio do Leverger**.

Chapada dos Guimarães

A paved road winds its way up to the scenic mountain village of **CHAPADA DOS GUIMARÃES**, less than 70km from Cuiabá. There are several daily **buses** from the *Rodoviária*, a two- to three-hour ride costing around $1; or you could hitch from the signposted exit by the *Rodoviária* in Cuiabá.

Chapada is an interesting settlement in its own right, containing Mato Grosso's oldest church – the **Igreja de Nossa Senhora de Santana**, a fairly plain colonial temple built in 1779. But these days it also has something of a reputation as a centre for the Brazilian "New Age" movement, and health food stores and hippy communities have sprung up here in the last ten years. If this doesn't grab you, Chapada dos Guimarães' other attraction is its public **swimming pool**, supplied by a natural spring, that provides welcome relief from the heat all year round.

It's not the village itself, however, which brings most people out to Chapada. The stunning countryside, a grassy plateau scattered with low trees, provides a marvellous backdrop for photographing the local flora and birdlife. Within walking distance, there are waterfalls, weird rock formations and precipitous canyons. And the area is of great archaeological interest, too, with some partially excavated sites in the vicinity. The most spectacular of all the sites around the village is the **Véu de Noiva** waterfall, which drops over a sheer rock face for over sixty metres, pounding into the forested basin below. You get there by walking or, if you're lucky, hitching from the village of BURUTI, on the road from Cuiabá, about 12km before Chapada dos Guimarães. Alternatively the falls can be found within a couple of kilometres of the road if you jump off the bus some 6km beyond SALGADEIRA (ask the driver to show you the track).

If you're thinking of **staying**, both food and accommodation are available in Chapada dos Guimarães. But if you've got a tent or a hammock this is as good a place to use it as any.

Aquas Quentes and São Antônio

The hot baths of **AGUAS QUENTES** function as a local weekend and honeymoon resort, 90km west of Cuiabá, just off Highway BR-364 towards Rondonopolis. Apart from the baths, though, there is little of interest to the traveller. The water, said to be mildly radioactive, comes in four different pools, the hottest at around 42°C, and is apparently a cure for rheumatism, liver complaints and even conjunctivitis – but don't let that put you off. There are daily buses from the *Rodoviária* in Cuiabá and the resort has **hotels**, bars and restaurants.

Closest **beach** to Cuiabá is at **SÃO ANTONIO DO LEVERGER**, 35km south of the city on the Rio Cuiabá. It's as much fun as most of the beaches on the coast, even if it seems a little incongruous given the jungle backdrop. Again, there are **buses** every day from the *Rodoviária* in Cuiabá.

Out from Cuiabá: routes, destinations and practical details

Cuiabá is a central point for all sorts of long-distance trips within Brazil, and a launching pad for continued travelling into neighbouring countries. The two main regional highways, the BR-163 and the BR-364 are accessible from the city: the **BR-364** is particularly important as a link between the Amazon and almost all other regions, and whether you're coming from São Paulo, Rio, Brasília or the Northeast, this is the route to take if you want to travel overland into the Western Amazon. What follows is a brief rundown of the onward possibilities from Cuiabá, taking in some of the more important stopovers and pointing out the problems and pitfalls of travelling in this largely undeveloped region. Some of the places mentioned are covered elsewhere in the text; page and section references will tell you where you to find the relevant accounts.

To the Pantanal

It's little more than 200km by road from Cuiabá to the two main northern ports of the Pantanal: Porto Jofre and Cáceres. And while Corumbá, being in the swamp itself, has much more Pantanal character than Cuiabá, the city is still a potential starting point for either a few days exploration or a river trip. For a start, if you decide to make the trip to Corumbá, it's downriver from Cáceres, so it takes only two to three days, rather than the six to ten required to complete the upstream journey. There are a number of tourist agencies in Cuiabá running organised tours; see p.366. Also, unless you're travelling to or from Bolivia via Corumbá, Cuiabá may well be on your planned itinerary anyway, and could be included as a Pantanal pit-stop. All round – in terms of communications, buses and planes – it's worth considering Cuiabá as a first stop for travel into the Pantanal.

A detailed description of the Pantanal, information about independent travel within the region, and contacts for joining organised tours are all found under the section on "The Pantanal", p.390.

West on the BR-364: Cáceres, Rondônia and on to Porto Vehlo

Heading **west from Cuiabá**, Porto Velho and Rio Branco are both possible desti-nations, as well as serving as relaxing stops on the way to Manaus, Peru or Bolivia. Following Rondon's telegraph link to Manaus in the early twentieth century, **Highway BR-364** was the next development to open up the Northern Mato Grosso and southwestern Amazon. Paving the BR-364 cost around US$600,000,000, and was partly financed by the World Bank. Construction was held up for a while when anthropologists realised that it was planned to cut straight through **Nambikwara** tribal lands, and the road was eventually completed by making a large detour around these Indians, who still live in small, widely scattered groups which have very little contact with each other. Each domestic Nambikwara group is essentially an extended family, usually around twenty individuals, living in touch with little more than three or four related, and similar, settlements.

Leaving the industrial fringes of Cuiabá behind, the road soon enters the well established pastoral farmlands to the west. At Cáceres (see "The Pantanal"), three hours out of Cuiabá, the highway starts to leave the Pantanal watershed and climbs gradually towards the inhospitable but beautiful ridges of the **Chapada dos Parecis** and the state frontier with Rondônia. Here everyone has to pass through the **yellow fever checkpoint**: busloads of people spend half an hour either getting inoculated or showing their vaccination certificates. The Nambikwara Indians live to the south of the Chapada escarpment, while to the north the Parecis and various groups still get by. The process of occupation in this region is so recent and intense that the Indians have suffered greatly; most of their demarcated lands have been invaded already and the situation is worsening all the time. The Indians don't generally come out to the highway, though sometimes you'll see a family or two selling crafted goods – bows and arrows, beads or carvings – beside the road at small pit-stops.

The second half of the 23-hour trip passes through the remains of tropical rainforest. There's the occasional tall tree left standing, but more usually it's acres of burnt out fields and small frontier settlements, crowded with people busy in mechanics' workshops or passing the time playing pool. This is **Rondônia** (see p.328), a relatively recently established jungle state. Seen from the air, Rondônia looks like a fish skeleton, with parallel feeder roads running at right angles in both directions for a hundred kilometres or more into the forest, on either side of the highway. These bureaucratically designed roads, little more than 30km apart, carved up the region for rapid "development" and, by amassing the plots of disillusioned or intimidated peasants, some people were able to establish vast, though officially illegal, claims. Without government support and ill-adapted to the forest environment, convoys of landless peasants can be seen camping beside the road on their way to find a new life in the West. However, these thousands of colonists, mostly from Brazil's poor Northeast, are now being pushed on out of Rondônia as the official programme has already been overrun by a spontaneous influx of settlers far larger than anyone dreamed of. The official attitude is that the opening up of western Amazonas is a great opportunity for a generation of the landless poor, but even if you ignore the plight of the indigenous Indians, the reality is very different. And it will become disastrous if the warnings now emanating from ecologists and other scientists are based on fact: if the region turns to desert by the twenty-first century, as some currently predict, then the same generation who initially benefited will lose everything, and future generations will face real suffering.

JI PARANÁ is the only town of any real size along the BR-364, growing – in the ten years from 1970 to 1980 – from a town of 9000 people to one of over 120,000. Its main drag is dominated by a massive Ford showroom, while thousands of gigantic tree trunks sit in enormous piles. Even from the bus you can hear the electronic grating noise of circular saws, slicing the forest into manageable and marketable chunks. And on the outskirts of town, hundreds of small, new wooden huts are springing up every month. It's another five hours, through decimated jungle scenery, before you reach the jungle frontier town of Porto Velho (see p.329), capital of Rondônia state.

Southeast on the BR-364: to Rondonopolis and São Paulo

For those who arrived in Cuiabá from the Amazon, the city acts as a gateway to the rest of Brazil. From the earliest times, São Paulo was the main source of settlers arriving in the Mato Grosso, though until this century the route followed the river systems. These days, the BR-364 runs all the way (over 1700km) from Cuiabá to São Paulo, with several daily buses taking around 24 hours minimum. On the headwaters of the Pantanal's São Lourenço river, two to three hours from Cuiabá, **RONDONOPOLIS** acts as a base for visiting the local **Bororo Indians**. In the present political climate, visits to Indian reservations are not always permitted – and you might consider the ethics of such visits before you decide to go. In any case, permission must be obtained first from *FUNAI*, in Brasília, and they'll decide if, when and where you can go. Meanwhile, if you decide to stay here, there's a range of **hotels** in Rondonopolis, the cheaper ones, as usual, near the bus station; those beside the main square are more upmarket.

JATAI is almost halfway to São Paulo, about ten hours from Cuiabá in the state of Goias. This is where many passengers will be getting off and on the bus, changing to one of the other routes which emanate from here – to Brasília, Goiânia, Belo Horizonte, Rio de Janeiro, the Northeast and Belém.

Along the BR-163: north to Santarém

Crossing the hills to the **north** of Cuiabá, the road into the Amazon – almost 2000km of it – is a bold attempt to cross what is still essentially a vast wilderness. As the plain begins to dip down towards the Amazon basin, the areas around the road have been opened up for cattle, this transitional zone one of the best areas south of Boa Vista for large scale ranching in Brazil. There are plenty of open grasslands and it's dry enough in the dry season to burn off the old pastures to make way for fresh shoots with the first rains. Interspersed among the grasses and tangled bamboo and creeper thickets there are large expanses of cane, grown as fodder for the cows after the pasture has been burnt.

Colonel P.H. Fawcett, the famous British explorer, vanished somewhere in this region in 1925, on what turned out to be his last attempt to locate a lost jungle city and civilisation. He'd been searching for it, on and off, for twenty years, the story entertainingly told in his edited diaries and letters, *Exploration Fawcett*. This last expedition was in the company of his eldest son, Jack, and following their disappearance various theories were put forward as to their fate: existing as prisoners of a remote tribe or, more fancifully, adopted chiefs. More likely, they were murdered out in the wilds, as were dozens of other explorers over the years, although Fawcett had already survived a couple of decades of travel among the Indian tribes of the Mato Grosso without harm. This brutal end to Fawcett's explorations was confirmed in 1985, when the same team who had identified the body of the Nazi Josef Mengele, identified bones found in a shallow grave to be that of the colonel, who had finally run out of luck.

In Colonel Fawcett's day there was only river transport, where possible, and one's own steam most of the time, and even now this route is a major adventure, taking between four days and four weeks depending on the rains (which are worst between November and March). Probably the most remote and underused of the Transamazonica Highway's offshoots, the BR-163 has a bad reputation in terms of both the actual road surface and the outlaw mentality which you'll find in many of the villages along the route. Much of the highway within the Mato Grosso has been partially paved, but once into Pará State and beyond CACHIMBO, the road is worse and traffic is often held up trying to cross the numerous large rivers. From here on, it's tropical rainforest, or what's left of it, along the roadsides.

Buses leave irregularly from Cuiabá for Santarém, so it's as well to make enquiries at the *Rodoviária* well in advance to be sure of a seat. It is possible, though neither easy nor recommended, to **hitch** with trucks: this could take a very long time; on the other hand, you might get on a truck going all the way. Most vehicles travelling this route will be going via SÃO LUIS DE TAPAJÓS, a new road settlement close to the fascinating town of Itaituba in the Eastern Amazon (see p.289). From here, the Tapajos river is navigable down to the Amazon proper at Santarém, though it's usually faster to stay on the bus or stick with a trucker's lift if you've got one.

MATO GROSSO DO SUL

A fairly new state, **Mato Grosso do Sul** is nevertheless considered to be one of Brazil's better-established economic regions. It has a distinct Wild West flavour: close to the border with Paraguay and just a bit further from Argentinian *gaucho* territory, it's not uncommon to end up dancing Spanish polkas through the night in some of the region's bars. Until the eighteenth century the whole region was Indian territory and was considered an inhospitable corner of the New World. A hundred and fifty years and numerous bloody battles later, the Mato Grosso do Sul might now be developed and "civilised" but – thankfully – it's still a place where you can forget about industrial ravages and enjoy nature's riches.

The region's wealth comes predominantly from cattle ranching, something you don't even escape in the state capital, **Campo Grande**, which sports cowboy supply shops along its modern city streets. It's a useful base from which to delve deeper into the Mato Grosso. The city is connected to Corumbá by railway and road, so reaching the **Pantanal** is fairly easy. But the swamp is vast, stretching right across the state from north to southwest, so you can also get a good look at the wildlife from a variety of road-linked places closer to Campo Grande – like **Coxim**, north of the city, or **Aquidauana**, to the west.

The train line from Corumbá runs **east** through Campo Grande to Bauru, a twenty-hour ride across the plains of Mato Grosso do Sul: this is the route to take if you're heading on to São Paulo, another six hours beyond Bauru. The **south** of the state is favoured by the beautiful hills of the **Serra da Bodoquena** and **Serra da Maracajú** and, deep in the Bodoquena hills, you can visit the spectacular **Bonito caves**. A railway line heads south from Campo Grande, too, to **Ponta Porã** on the Paraguayan border, from where there's a two-day overland route to Asunción. And a connecting, but geographically direct, bus route exists from Campo Grande via **Dourados** and **Mundo Novo** to Guaira and the amazing falls of Foz do Iguaçú in the neighbouring state of Paraná.

Campo Grande

Nicknamed the "brunette city" because of its chestnut-coloured earth, **CAMPO GRANDE** has in less than forty years been transformed from an insignificant settlement into a buzzing metropolis, with a population approaching half a million. Founded in 1889, the city was only made the capital of the new state of Mato Grosso do Sul in the late 1970s, and its downtown area combines sky-scraping banks with rancher's general stores. Unnervingly reminiscent of Dallas, it's a relatively salubrious market centre for an enormous cattle-ranching region.

An obvious place to break one of the long journeys between either Cuiabá or Corumbá and the coast, Campo Grande tries hard to shake off the feeling that it's a city stuck in the middle of nowhere. Apart from the *gaucho* influence on some of the shops, the town centre is much like that of any other medium-sized city; the people are friendly and there's little manifest poverty. The generally warm evenings inspire the locals to turn out on the streets in force. Chatting over a meal or sipping ice-cold beers at one of the restaurants or bars, between Avenida Afonso Pena and Rua Maracajú, the guitars, maracas and congas are often brought out for an impromptu music session.

Arriving and finding a place to stay

The **Rodoviária** is a ten-minute walk from the centre, four blocks down Avenida Afonso Pena: coming from the main downtown square, turn right at block 14 by the funfair and it's just a block away. A surprisingly large bus terminal for a city of this size, it also houses six hairdressers, a cinema, bookshops and several bars. **Tickets** out of the city should be bought in advance from one of the kiosks on the first floor; see "Listings" for destinations and details.

Arriving by train from São Paulo, Corumbá or Ponta Porã, the **railway station**, within easy walking distance of the main square, is on Avenida Calógeras, just five or six blocks from the downtown area and close to both the *Hotel União* and the *Grande Hotel Caspar* (see below). The other point of arrival is the Internacional Antônio João **airport** (info on ☎624-7950), 7km out of town, on the road towards Aquidauana. Buses to the *Rodoviária* cost around $1–2; or take a taxi into the centre for around $10.

Accommodation

The **cheapest** hotel in town is the *Plaza Hotel*, at Rua Maracujá 140 – quaint, very friendly and relatively near to all the important bits of Campo Grande. Otherwise, there are a couple of very reasonable hotels **near the railway station**: the *Grande Hotel Caspar*, Avenida Mato Grosso 2 (☎383-5121), on the corner within sight of the station, is quite large and charges $5 single; while the *Hotel União*, half a block further down Avenida Calogeras, is friendly, clean and safe – rooms go for just under $4 single. Slightly nearer the centre, just beyond the all-night clatter from the railway yards, the *Hotel Paulista* is a bit cheaper and has a good reputation with travellers. And there are a couple more, smaller, hotels along Avenida Calogeras, towards the *Casa do Artesanato*: the pleasant *Hotel Prata* (on block 21) charges less than $5 for a double room; *Hotel Fenícia*, Avenida Calogeras 2262 (☎383-2001), is slightly more expensive, small and domestic.

Generally speaking, the hotels **near the Rodoviária** are less welcoming than others in town, and even slightly seedy at times. Right beside the bus terminal you'll find the modern, air-conditioned *Caranda Hotel*, at Rua Joaquim Nabuco 62 (☎382-8384); $12 single and $15 double. Around the corner, on Avenida Afonso Pena, heading towards the centre, there's the very basic *Santa Inês Hotel*, with single rooms from $3 a night.

Top of the range downtown is the four-star *Jandaia*, Rua Barão de Rio Branco 1271 (☎382-4081), catering primarily for expense-account cowboys and other visiting business people: it's plush and plastic. The *Palace Hotel*, Rua Dom Aquino 1501 (☎384-4741), is less impersonal and somewhat nearer most people's pockets, at around $8.50 for a single and $10 a double.

The City: sights, food and nightlife

Tourism is almost non-existent in Campo Grande, and there are really only two significant attractions. The **Museu do Bosco** (daily 7–11am & 1–5pm) is in the university building, facing the Praça da República, at Rua Rio Branco 1811–43. A fascinating place, it's crammed full of exhibits, ranging from superb forest Indian artefacts to over 10,000 terrifying dead insects. Most impressive of all, though, is the vast collection of stuffed birds and animals, including giant rheas (the South American version of an ostrich), life-like anacondas and examples of the Brazilian

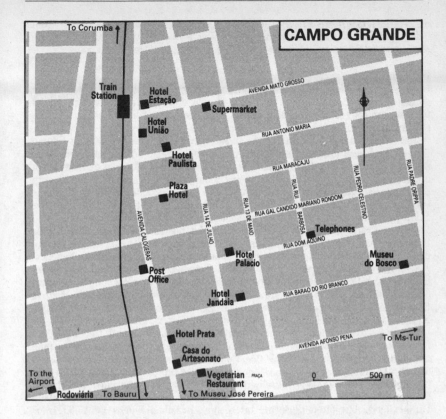

marsupials – the gamba and the quica. If you have to spend the night in Campo Grande, then make the effort to visit this museum. Closer to the city centre, the **Casa do Artesanato**, on the corner of Avenida Calogeras and Avenida Afonso Pena, is slightly disappointing considering the huge region it is supposed to represent. A small hall selling mostly local craft works, the best pieces are without a doubt the wood carvings, often depicting mythical symbols like fish-women and totemic figures.

If you're desperate for culture, there is another museum, the small **Museu José A. Pereira** (8–11am & 1–4.30pm), which deals with local history, out at Cidade Universitaria, several kilometres from the city centre: to get there, take a taxi which will cost $5–6, or it's a forty-minute walk following the street signs east along Avenida Calogeras. Nearer in are two galleries specialising in local, contemporary art: *Art Com*, Rua Manoel Inacio de Souza 905, and the *Centro Cultural de Mato Grosso*, Rua 26 de Agosto 463.

Perhaps a better insight into contemporary Mato Grosso culture are the **cowboy shops** along Rua 14 de Julho, selling gunbelts, holsters, saddles and boots. The busiest shopping streets are mostly congregated in the square formed by avenidas Calogeras and Afonso Pena, with ruas Gal. Candido Mariano Rondon and Pedro Celestino. You can pursue the matter further by going **horseracing**, out at the *Hipódromo*, run by the *Jóquei Clube de Campo Grande*. Apart from being quite good fun, it's another interesting aspect of the local culture; the *Hipódromo* is 5km along Highway BR-167, beyond the exit for Dourados.

Food and drink

During the hot afternoons, the good **juice bars** are popular, like the one on the corner opposite Praça da República. And there are scores of *lanchonetes* – one of the best and biggest is around the corner from the *Grande Hotel Caspar*, near the railway station.

As a cattle-ranching market centre, a lot of cows get roasted daily in Campo Grande, so if you like **beef steaks**, you're in for a treat. *Vittorio's Churrascaria*, Avenida Afonso Pena 1907, and *Cabana Gaúcho*, next door, are lively steak houses, less than a block down from the main square. A statement by its very presence, the **vegetarian restaurant** on the opposite side of the road serves excellent food and is generally crowded at lunchtimes. Just down from here, the smaller *Pingo de Ouro* restaurant is cheap and quiet, with good set menus.

Other food is good, too. The best **Chinese** places are *China*, Rua XV de Novembro 318 (11am–2pm & 7–11pm), where the fried duck (*pato frito*) is recommended; and the *Hong Kong Restaurant*, Rua Maracajú 131, specialising in delicacies including local tofu and regional curries. For **pizza** there's a good place (open late) on block 17 of Barão do Rio Branco, near the Museo do Bosco; but for greater comfort and as authentic an atmosphere as you could hope for, the *Pizzaria Scarolla*, Avenida Afonso Pena 216 (5–11.30pm), and the *Cantina Romana*, Rua da Paz 237 (11am–2pm & 7pm–midnight), prepare delicious Italian dishes.

A broader range of food and some **nightlife** can be found in both the *Radio Club Restaurant*, Rua João Cripa 1280, which features live music (Mon–Sat 7pm–midnight), and *Miglos*, Avenida Afonso Pena 2386 – more music and excellent fish dishes (Thurs–Sat 7pm–1am). Otherwise, at weekends, the *churrascarias* and other large restaurants generally serve food to the energetic sounds of Paraguayan polkas. The *Glauber Rocha* **theatre** is out of town, in Cidade Universitaria, but often performs interesting Brazilian works (☎387-3311 for details, or see the local press).

Listings

Air taxis A useful means of communication within the state: the *Mato Grosso do Sul* service is one of the more reliable set-ups; Avenida Eduardo E. Zahran 2683 (☎626-3111 or ☎384-6416).

Buses Several daily to São Paulo (14hr; $11); Cuiabá (11hr; $7.65); and Corumbá (7hr; $6.50). There's a 9am bus to Brasília (24hr; $15) and a 7pm service to Belo Horizonte (23hr; $15); while several daily buses run to Ponta Porã on the Paraguayan frontier and along a relatively well-worn trail to Asunción. Daily buses, too, to Dourados and Aquidauana, with less frequent connections to Bonito and Porto Murtinho. See "Travel Details", too.

Consulates If you're heading into either Paraguay or Bolivia from Campo Grande, you should check on border procedures and visa requirements. The Paraguayan consul is at Rua 14 de Julho 1845, the Bolivian consul at Rua Dom Aquino 1354 – both are open Mon–Fri 9am–5pm.

Exchange In the *Banco do Brazil*, just off the main square at Avenida Afonso Pena 1336; or, if you're persuasive, in one of the larger hotels.

Post office Very central, between the railway staion and the main square, on the corner of Avenida Calogeras and Dom Aquino (Mon–Sat 9am–5.30pm).

Saunas As if the everyday heat wasn't enough, there are two saunas in Campo Grande: *Rádio Clube*, Rua Barão de Rio Branco 1968, and *Sereima*, Rua Joaquim Murtinho 1990.

Trains The main rail routes are to either Bauru/São Paulo or to Corumbá: two trains go in each direction every day. For Bauru/São Paulo, the first leaves at 2.50am (21/28hr; first class $6.50/$8), the slightly faster night train at 7pm (19/25hr; same price); trains for Corumbá leave at 8.57am (11hr; first class $6.50) and 8.10pm (9hr; first class $3.50). Expect delays. The other track runs south to Ponta Porã and the Paraguayan frontier; one daily at 10am (8hr; first class $3). Second class tickets are generally fifty to seventy percent cheaper on all routes; and bear in mind that most locals take the bus to São Paulo and Corumbá, rather than the train, since it's almost twice as quick.

Travel agencies *Dallas*, Barão de Rio Branco 1484 (☎384-2030) and *Vox Tour*, Rua Gal. Candido M. Rondon 1777 (☎383-7322), are best for flights, or for help in sorting out an organised tour to one of the local sites, like the Pantanal or Caves of Bonito (see below), though there are no bargains – allow for at least $25 per day per person.

North to Coxim

Easily reached by bus from Campo Grande, in around three to four hours (or from Cuiabá in six or seven hours), **COXIM** is a small town with some basic **accommodation** possibilities. Few non-Brazilians ever get off the bus here, but those who do generally have good reports. On the eastern edges of the Pantanal, Coxim is a fantastic **fishing** centre and there's one fisherman, Pirambero, who runs excellent trips into the swamp, down the Taquari River, to catch piranhas – ask for him at the port. Apart from fishing, **swimming** in the Taquari river, around Campo Falls, is a popular pastime, too, in spite of the razor-teethed fish. Also, nearby on the Coxim River, the **Palmeiras Falls** is a good place for a picnic or to camp a while. From November through to January, Coxim is *the* place to see the incredible *piracema* spectacle – thousands of fish, leaping clear of the river, on their way upstream to the river's source to lay their eggs.

The history of the area around Coxim is that of the Indians, and there were constant clashes here between resident tribes and early settlers. The area of scrub forest to the east of Coxim and Campo Grande used to be the territory of the **Caiapó** Indian nation, who ambushed miners along the routes to Goias and Cuiabá from São Paulo, posing a serious threat to Portuguese expansion and development in the mid-eighteenth century. In reaction to the successful use of Bororo Indian mercenaries against their main villages in the Camapua area, the Caiapó took their revenge on the growing numbers of Portuguese settlers and their farm slaves. In 1751 – the same year that the governor of Brazil declared an official war campaign against them – the Caiapó went as far as attacking the town of Goias, beyond the northern limits of their usual territory.

South: Dourados, Mundo Novo, Ponta Porã and the Paraguayan border

There's no great draw – in fact, no draw at all – in the towns south of Campo Grande en route to the Paraguayan border. The only place of any size is **DOURADOS**, 224km from the state capital. Its name is a reminder of the fact that the spot was first settled by travellers en route to the Cuiabá gold mines. These days, it's the region's most important agricultural centre, but there's little of interest to the tourist except bus connections to points further south and west.

MUNDO NOVO, about eleven hours by bus from Campo Grande (or buses from Dourados), is another transport terminus, if anything even less attractive. From here, buses run to Porto Frajelli and Iguaçú, and to the crossing point for ferries to Guaira; while many of the Campo Grande–Ponta Porã buses also come this way. If you get stuck overnight, the *Hotel Novo* is close to the *Rodoviária* and very reasonable.

Travelling by **train to Ponta Porã** is a more interesting possibility, a route worth considering even if you don't intend crossing into Paraguay. A diverting five- or six-hour trip, the train leaves Campo Grande daily (except Sun) at 6.30am, passing the small towns of BELICHE, SIDROLÂNDIA, MARACAJÚ and ITAUM before reaching Ponta Porã – not a particularly spectacular ride, though there are occasional glimpses of the **Serra da Maracajú** away to the west as you go.

Ponta Porã and the Paraguayan border

Despite the distinctly unthrilling towns that have gone before, **PONTA PORÃ** itself is an attractive little settlement, right on the Paraguayan border up in the Maracajú hills. The Avenida Internacional divides the settlement in two – on one side of the street you're in Brazil, on the other in the Paraguayan town of PEDRO JUAN CABALLERO. On the Paraguayan side you can polka the night away, gamble your money till dawn or, like most people there, just buy a load of imported goods at the duty free shops. There's a strange blend of language and character, and even a unique *mestizo* cuisine, making it an interesting place to spend a day or two. Ponta Porã also has a tradition as an old established distribution centre for *maté* herb – made into a tea-like drink containing caffeine.

There are plenty of **hotels** to choose from, though most budget travellers tend to go for the *Alvorada* or *Dos Viajantes* (over the road from the railway station), both of which are cheap and friendly. The *Internacional*, Rua Internacional 1267, is a middle-range hotel, with regular hot water, while for a plusher stay just outside of Ponta Porã, on the Avenida Presidente Vargas, it's hard to beat the *Pousada do Bosque* and its welcoming swimming pool.

Crossing the border is a simple procedure for most non-Brazilians. An exit stamp must be obtained from the *Polícia Federal* (Rua Mal. Floriano 1483; ☎431-1428) on the Brazilian side, then it's a matter of walking four or five blocks down Rua Guia Lopes to the Paraguayan customs and control. If you need a visa for Paraguay you can get this from the Consulate on Avenida Internacional on the Brazilian side. Once in Paraguay, there's a reasonably good road direct to CONCEPCIÓN, a major source of imports and contraband for Brazilians: daily buses make the five- or six-hour trip in good weather; it's another five hours further to Asunción. Otherwise, the **return train to Campo Grande** leaves Ponta Porã daily at 8.45am (except Sun).

Bela Vista and Porto Murtinho

The two other, more interesting, destinations on the Paraguayan border are Bela Vista and Porto Murtinho. Both are to the west of Ponta Porã and though they're harder to reach, they do have hotels and restaurants once you're there. Although it's not technically legal to cross the frontier into Paraguay at these places, they are worth visiting for their natural splendour alone. The way to get to either of them is by **bus** or truck from Dourados (a good day's journey); again, many of these buses run via, or from, Mundo Novo. It's sometimes possible to **hitch** with trucks taking the roads and dirt tracks from Bonito or Aquidauana (see below), but it will almost certainly take longer, and will probably involve night-time driving or camping beside the road – though there are a handful of small settlements en route.

Bela Vista

In **BELA VISTA** you can explore the natural delights of the Piripucu and Caracol rivers, behind which are the unspoilt peaks of the Tres Cerros and Cerro Margarida. There's also the extraordinary **Nhandejara bridge**, with a natural underground passage over thirty metres long. Most Brazilians, however, come here for the opportunity to buy imported goods: over the border is the Paraguayan town of Bela Vista, which has a road connection (a day's travel) to Concepción.

Porto Murtinho

Remote and tranquil, **PORTO MURTINHO** sits on the banks of the Paraguay River, over 400km southwest of Campo Grande, and near where the river finally leaves Brazilian territory. Well blessed with abundant wildlife and luxuriant vegetation, the town marks the very southern limits of the Pantanal swamplands. It's quite a cheap place from which to make excursions in river boats, though you might be expected to haggle over the price a little, since there are often several boatsmen to choose from at the river front. The exclusive *Hotel dos Caminantes* can also arrange trips for you.

Porto Murtinho is also accessible by bus or air from Campo Grande but the road system in this part of Mato Grosso do Sul is extremely complex and not all that well established. Thousands of tracks cover the region, and even official road maps make it look like a maze.

East: the train to Bauru and São Paulo

Campo Grande sits on the long train line which connects Corumbá with São Paulo, via the rail junction of Bauru. The whole journey can't be done in much under 38 hours, even assuming precision timing with connections, and the section from Campo Grande to Bauru takes around twenty hours (another six hours onto São Paulo). This long route is only part of an even longer **railway system** that links the Mato Grosso do Sul with Bolivia and even Paraguay: originating in São Paulo, it connects with the Bolivian *Tren de los Mortes* to Santa Cruz from where it's possible to continue by train into Chile or via La Paz into Peru, over Lake Titicaca (by boat or around it on a bus) and on to Cuzco. The side track from Campo Grande south to the Paraguayan frontier at Ponta Porã (see above) also offers an interesting route to Asunción.

Details of the Campo Grande–Bauru route follow; the westward section, from Campo Grande to Corumbá, is covered later in this chapter.

Sadly, the journey **from Campo Grande east to Bauru** isn't usually as exciting as it is long. For nearly 1000km the way lies across gently undulating savanna plain, though the train – winding its way slowly over pasture land and past sugar cane fields – is infinitely more relaxing and comfortable than the comparable bus trip. The most common sights as you go are the white beef cattle and enormous termite mounds, contrasting sharply with the deep-red earth. For most of the journey the train passes through a thin carpeting of small, horse-and-buggy type

---

CORUMBÁ TO SÃO PAULO BY TRAIN: ALL THE FACTS

For all its external scruffiness, the train is quite comfortable and remarkably clean, especially if you can afford to travel first class.

●**Tickets** cost around $13 for the 31-hour journey from Corumbá to Baurú ($7 second class), and there's one train daily all the way, two from Corumbá to Campo Grande and from Campo Grande to Baurú; and four daily from Baurú to São Paulo. See "Travel Details" at the end of the chapter, too.

●**First class seats** are reclining armchairs, plastic-covered and well padded. In second class you'll find wooden benches – and most of the passengers. Metal shutters can be pulled down over the windows to give invaluable shade against the sun and, occasionally, protection against over-enthusiastic gangs of stone-throwing children. The train is rarely crowded, even in second class, except when army garrisons are transferring between Corumbá and São Paulo.

●It's a long, dusty journey whichever train you take. **Food and drink** are available, either in the relatively expensive restaurant car (over $3 for a meal, though drinks and beer are better priced) or from the wandering waiter who brings coffee, brandy, cold drinks and sandwiches round at regular intervals.

●If you're making the full journey eastwards, from Bolivia, it's useful to know that Bolivians, Brazilians and the Federal Police see this train as an integral section of the **cocaine** trail, so be very careful whose baggage you agree to look after.

---

homesteads with the odd *fazenda* dotted among them, stopping only at the rare settlements large enough to merit a railway station. The halfway mark is roughly at TRES LAGOAS and further on, near ANDRADINA, the train crosses the impressive Paraná river, just downstream from the enormous Jupia dam. At Bauru (covered on p.430) there's a six-hour link through to São Paulo, which is theoretically designed to connect with the Corumbá/Campo Grande train: it frequently fails to do so, leaving hundreds of people spending the night in or around the station square.

West: to Aquidauana and Corumbá

There are two trains daily on the section of the route **west to Corumbá** (at 8.15am or 8pm), and the journey only takes eleven hours, but many people still prefer to take the night train (the *expresso*) which is marginally faster and has sleeping compartments ($18 for a double). Take the day train, though, if you want to catch the scenery, which becomes increasingly swamp-like the further west you travel.

A few hours west of Campo Grande, the savanna becomes forested as the train approaches the first real range of hills since leaving the Atlantic coast. Sticking up like a gigantic iceberg into the vast southern Mato Grosso, the **Serra de Maracajú** forces the train to follow a rocky river through a breathtaking wooded gorge. In the 1860s these hills provided sanctuary for local Terena Indians during a period of Paraguayan military occupation. Under their somewhat crazy and highly ambitious dictator, Lopez, the Paraguayans invaded the southern Mato Grosso in 1864, a colonial adventure that resulted in the death of over half the invasion force, mostly composed of native (Paraguyan) Guarani Indians. It was one period in Brazilian history when Whites and Indians fought for the same cause, and it was in the magnificent Serra de Maracajú hills that most of the guerrilla-style resistance took place. Beyond the gorge, interesting geological formations dominate the horizon: vast towering tors, known as *torrelones*, rise magnificently out of the scrubby savanna.

The attractive station of **CAMISÃO** serves the *fazendas* of a relatively lush valley supporting tropical fruits, sugar cane and, of course, beef cattle. A magical spot in the shade of water-eroded *torrelones*, the platform is generally crowded with women selling juicy mangoes which provide excellent refreshment for the rest of the trip.

Aquidauana and the Bonito caves

The next town – **AQUIDAUANA**, 130km from Campo Grande – is a larger settlement, a lazy-looking place, and very hot, sitting under the beating sun of the Piraputanga uplands. One of the several "entrances" into the Pantanal, it's better known as a base for visiting the Bonito cave systems (see below). Above all else, though, Aquidauana offers plenty of scope for climbing or hill walking, and there are some superb views across the swamp. The **river** running through the town boasts some pleasant sandy beaches, which are quite clean and safe for swimming: **fishing** championships are an integral part of the annual São João festival here. There's a reasonable choice of **hotels** in the town, including the very popular *Hotel Fluminense*, near the railway station; and a few decent restaurants within walking distance of the station, too.

The nearby village of **ANÁSTACIO** – connected by several small buses every day – has some nice beaches of its own, but is best known for the large *jaú* fish (often weighing over 75 kilos) that live in its river. And 50km from Aquidauana, the *Cabana do Pescador* luxury fishing lodge, on the Miranda River, is another relaxing destination and possible base from which to take a tour to the Bonito caves; there are frequent buses from the *Cabana* to both Aquidauana and Bonito.

Close to both the Formoso and Formosinho rivers, **BONITO** feels somewhat isolated, yet it's only three hours south of Aquidauana by bus, or four or five from Campo Grande. It's the main base for visiting the largest known cave system in western Brazil; anyone visiting the caves is expected to report to the *Prefeitura* in Bonito first. If you need to sort out **accommodation**, then the *Hotel Bonanza* and *Hotel Florestal* are both basic but clean and friendly; and it's possible to camp near the town at **Ilha do Padre**.

The **caves** themselves, 26km beyond the town, can be reached by truck or jeep; guides and transport can be hired in Bonito from around $20 for the day (ask at the *Prefeitura*). Of the two main systems, the best known is **Lago Azul**, whose showpiece is an amazingly clear blue lake 30m deep and over 150m long. The other caves are known as **Nossa Senhora Aparecida**. Unless you've got all the right underground clobber, you'll only be able to see quite limited sections of the caves, but it's a worthwhile trip nevertheless.

There are other attractions in the Bonito vicinity, most notably the crystalline water of its rivers and the opportunity they give for underwater swimming or just relaxing amidst the natural surroundings. Fresh water dolphin (*boto*) are quite a common sight here, while along the rivers near Bonito there are a number of small **waterfalls**, the largest just over fifteen metres high.

On to Corumbá: the Terena tribe and Miranda

From Aquidauana the train enters the traditional territory of the **Terena tribe**, for whom there was little peace even after the Paraguayans had gone home. The late nineteenth century saw an influx of Brazilian colonists into the Aquidauana and Miranda valleys as the authorities attempted to "populate" the regions between Campo Grande and Paraguay – the war had only made them aware of how fertile these valleys were. Pushed off the best of the land and forced, in the main, to work for new, white landowners, the Terena tribe remained vulnerable until the appearance of **Lieutenant Rondon** (after whom the Amazonian state of Rondônia was named). Essentially an engineer, he came across the Terena in 1903 after constructing a telegraph connection – poles, lines and all – through virtually impassable swamps and jungle between Cuiabá and Corumbá. With his help, the Terena managed to establish a legal claim to some of their traditional land rights. Considered by *FUNAI* (the Federal Agency for Indian Affairs) to be one of the most successfully "integrated" Indian groups in modern Brazil, the Terena have earned the reputation of possessing the necessary drive and ability to compete successfully in the market system – a double-edged compliment, which could be used by the authorities to undermine their rights to land as a tribal group. Living mostly between Aquidauana and Miranda, the actual focus of their territory is the town and railway station of **TAUNAY** – an interesting little settlement with mule-drawn taxi wagons and a peaceful atmosphere.

MIRANDA, a small town on the southeastern edge of the Pantanal swamp, is the largest community between Aquidauana and Corumbá. Once the scene of historic battles, these days Miranda has a reputation for excellent fishing and the town is certainly a pleasant enough place to try your hand. The morning train from Campo Grande normally offers a sunset over another range of hills – the **Serra da Bodoquena** (home of the Bonito caves) – while, crossing the Paraguay River at around 8pm or 9pm, it's another few hours before the lights of Corumbá illuminate the horizon.

CORUMBÁ AND THE PANTANAL

An open swampland larger than France, the **Pantanal** is a slightly daunting region to visit – one of the rare places in Brazil where you're more likely to find wildlife than nightlife. No road or railway track crosses the swamp, making it a tricky place to travel: the easiest, and probably the best, way to experience the Pantanal is by taking an organised tour or staying at a recommended *fazenda*-lodge. At least one night in the middle of the swamp is essential if you want to see or do anything other than sit in a bus or jeep the whole time; three- or four-day excursions will give you a couple of full days in the swamp. Without an organised trip, travellers are dependent upon hitching lifts in trucks and local cargo boats, which inevitably takes much longer than expected. Organised tours are also more likely to go out of their way to show you the wildlife, than will a captain whose boat is brimming over with live cattle. The *fazenda*-lodges are generally reached by jeep and the deeper into the swamp the lodge, the better your chances of spotting the more elusive wildlife. Alligators, jaguars, anacondas and *tuiuiú* (giant red-necked storks) are all quite common sights in the Pantanal. Having said that, it's only fair to mention that you'll still see more cows than any other creature in the swamps.

Most organised tours enter the Pantanal by road and spend a couple of days exploring in canoes or on horseback from a land base. The most obvious initial target is **Corumbá**, the third city of the Mato Grosso. There's some decent accommodation here and no end of agencies and operators running trips into the swamp. Other routes into the swamp are from Cuiabá, to the north, through settlements like **Porto Jofre** and **Cáceres**.

Corumbá

Far removed from mainstream Brazil, hard by the Bolivian border and 400km west of Campo Grande, the city of **Corumbá** provides a welcome stop after the long train ride from either Santa Cruz (in Bolivia) or Campo Grande. As an entrance to the Pantanal, Corumbá has the edge over Cuiabá in that it is already there, stuck in the middle of a gigantic swamp, only 119m above sea level. Not surprisingly, Corumbá didn't start out as a great source of attraction to travellers. As early as 1543, it proved an inhospitable place to an expedition of 120 large canoes on a punitive campaign against the Guaicuru tribe. Sent by the Spanish governor of Paraguay, it encountered vampire bats, stingrays, biting ants and plagues of mosquitos. And while it doesn't seem quite so bad today, it's easy to understand why air conditioning is such a big business here.

It's Corumbá's unique location on the railway link between the Andes and the Atlantic which brings most travellers to the town. Ironically, the same swamp which deterred European invaders for so long has rapidly become an attraction. Teeming with wild animals, and particularly rich in birdlife, the Pantanal is taking on an increasingly special role as one of the world's last relatively unspoilt regions.

The City

Commanding a fine view over the Paraguay River and across the swamp, the city is small and is really only busy in the mornings – indeed it's one of Brazil's most laid-back towns south of the Amazon. Even at the port, nothing seems to disturb the slow-moving pool games taking place in the bars. The reason for this quite enjoyable lethargy is the heat: just sitting in the shade of a tree in the main square is like taking a sauna. Because of the heat, there's a very open-plan feel to the city and the people of Corumbá seem to be equally at home sitting at tables by bars and restaurants, or eating their dinners outside in front of their houses. In every street, there's at least one television blaring away on the pavement, and it's not unusual to be invited into someone's house for food, drinks or – at weekends – for a party.

Corumbá revolves around two main axes – the **port** and the railway – more or less at opposite ends of the city. If you're intending to stay more than one night, the port end is probably your best bet. Within a few blocks of the river front you'll find the **Praça da Independênca**, where most of the shops and reasonable hotels are located. A large, shaded, park-like area, the Praça has an unusual collection of steamrollers, antique waterwheels, ponds and a children's playground: it's alive with tropical birds early in the day, and by evening it's crowded with couples, family groups and gangs of children relaxing as the temperature begins to drop. The large but otherwise unimpressive church on this square is useful as a prominent landmark to help get your bearings in this very flat, rectangular grid-patterned city.

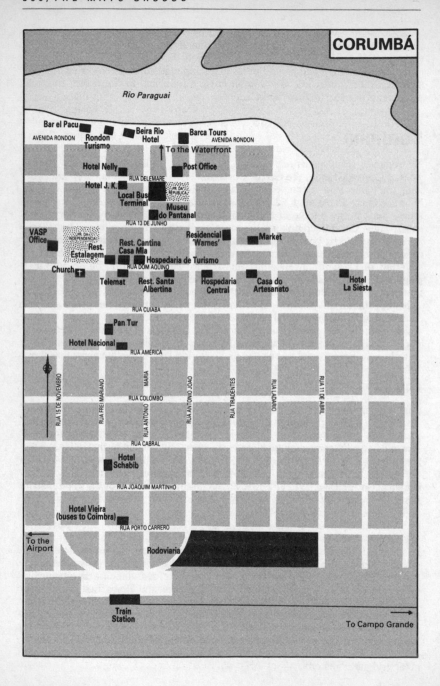

CORUMBÁ

Rio Paraguai

Bar el Pacu
AVENIDA RONDON
Rondon
Turismo
Beira Rio
Hotel
Barca Tours
AVENIDA RONDON

To the Waterfront

Hotel Nelly
Post Office

Hotel J. K.
RUA DELEMARE

Local Bus
Terminal
PR. DA
REPUBLICA
Museu
do Pantanal

RUA 13 DE JUNHO

VASP
Office
PR. DA
INDEPENDENCIA
Rest.
Estalagem
Rest. Cantina
Casa Mia
Residencial
'Warnes'
Market

Church
Hospedaria de Turismo
RUA DOM AQUINO

Telemat
Rest. Santa
Albertina
Hospedaria
Central
Casa do
Artesanato
Hotel
La Siesta

RUA CUIABA

Pan Tur

Hotel Nacional
RUA AMÉRICA

RUA 15 DE NOVEMBRO

RUA FREI MARIANO

MARIA

RUA ANTONIO

RUA COLOMBO

RUA ANTONIO JOAO

RUA TIRADENTES

RUA LADARIO

RUA 11 DE ABRIL

RUA CABRAL

Hotel
Schabib

RUA JOAQUIM MARTINHO

Hotel Vieira
(buses to Coimbra)
RUA PORTO CARRERO

To the
Airport
Rodoviaria

Train
Station
To Campo Grande

A stone's throw away you'll find the fascinating **Museu do Pantanal** (Tues–Fri 8–11am & 2–5pm, Sat 8am–noon; nominal charge), at Rua Delamare 939. It faces onto the smaller Praça da República, just to the side of the local bus terminal. The old, remarkably cool museum building is home to some fine natural history exhibits: if you need advice or information about the local flora or fauna, contact the museum office. Apart from the museum, the only other thing to see is the **Casa do Artesanato** (Mon–Fri 8–11.30am & 2–5.30pm, Sat 8am–noon) at Rua Dom Aquino Correa 405, four blocks from Praça da Independencia. It's housed in Corumbá's most historic edifice – the old prison – and is a good place to track down some local craft work.

All the practical details

The **Rodoviária** (☎231-3783) is close to the railway station (see below) and several daily buses leave from here to Campo Grande, São Paulo and even further afield; much quicker than the train, but slightly more expensive (to Campo Grande is $6 for a seat, $12 a *leito*). The *Andorvinha* bus company (☎231-3783) also has services leaving from its office at the corner of Rua Antônio Maria 815 and Rua América for Miranda, Aquidauana, Puerto Suárez (for the Bolivian frontier) and the main destinations eastwards.

Dominating Rua Porto Carrero, on the outskirts of Corumbá, the **railway station** (☎231-2876) is a hive of activity, with people queueing at every available hatch or doorway. It's a good idea to buy your tickets at least an hour in advance of the train, if not the day before; the ticket office usually opens an hour or so before departure times – to Bauru and São Paulo at 8.55pm (30/36hr; $8.50/$10); and Campo Grande at 7.15am (11hr; $3). See "Listings" for the service to Santa Cruz.

The **airport** (☎231-1456) is within half an hour's walk (or a $5 taxi ride) of the city centre and the railway station. If you've got a Brazilian airpass it's worth checking beforehand whether you can use it at Corumbá airport – some people have found that they had to buy regular tickets on flights from here. Only *VASP*, Rua XV de Novembro 392 (☎231-4441), fly regularly from Corumbá; tickets from the office on Praça da Independencia or, easier still, at the airport after 9.30am. Boeing 737s fly from here to Campo Grande/São Paulo at midday and Cuiabá/Brasília at 2pm. There's also an **air taxi service**, run by *Etapa* (check at their airport desk or ring ☎231-2203); while for **flights to Santa Cruz**, *TAM* offers a reasonable alternative to the train, flying twice a day from Corumbá ($30 one-way).

Finding a place to stay

Hotels in Corumbá vary considerably. At the top of the range is the flashy *Hotel Nacional*, Rua America 936 (☎231-6868), near the corner with Frei Mariano – around $16 single, and smack between the river and the railway station, it's convenient but overpriced. In a similar vein, the *Hotel La Siesta*, Rua Dom Aquino 47 (☎231-1575/2023), costs around $14 single, but has the added luxury of a swimming pool. Also in Rua Dom Aquino are the *Hospedaria de Turismo*, quite a cheap, new one-star place, and the *Hospedaria Central* – even cheaper and very popular with gringos. Slightly more central, for the shops and the port, are the *Hotel Nelly*, Rua Delamare 902 (☎231-3185), and *Hotel J.K.*, Rua Delamare 903 (☎231-47530), both with a range of clean rooms at under $3 single.

Nearer the railway station, the *Hotel Shabib*, Rua Frei Mariano 1153, and the *Hotel Vieira*, opposite the station building on Rua Porto Carrero, are relatively inexpensive. Of the two, the *Shabib* is the friendlier and some of the staff speak English, a rare trait in Corumbá. Perhaps the only hotel with any real character in Corumbá, though, is the *Beira-Rio Hotel*, Rua Manoel Cavassa 109 (☎231-2554), which has rooms overlooking the river and the Pantanal for less than $7 single; as well as its own boats for guests' use – entrance is from the waterfront.

Eating and drinking

Most of the decent **restaurants and bars** are to be found either on or within a block of Rua Frei Mariano, which connects Praça da Independencia with the railway station. And there are plenty of snack bars around the main square, too.

The *Restaurant Estalagem*, on the corner of Rua Frei Mariano and Dom Aquino, specialises in pizzas, beer and (occasionally) live music. For upmarket local cuisine try *Peixaria do Lulu*, Rua Antônio João 410 (11am–2pm & 6–11pm), or the smart *Cantina Casa Mia*, opposite the telephone office on Rua Dom Aquino. Just down the road (on the next block of Dom Aquino), the *Restaurant Santa Albertina* offers Pantanal dishes – including piranha soup at very reasonable prices – and an almost domestic environment. Round the corner, opposite the covered market, a favourite place – and by far the cheapest – is the garden of *Residencial Warnes*, a cheap pension run by a Bolivian family. This is open only at lunchtime and has just a few tables; but the people are friendly, the food is good Andean cooking, and it's hard to beat sitting in the shade of their honeysuckle plants on a sultry afternoon.

There are several more places to eat and drink down on the **river front**. Among these, *El Pacu Bar* serves excellent food in a pleasant, fan-cooled, atmosphere. The others are slightly rougher looking, but they offer more scope if you want a game of pool with your drink.

Listings

Boats from Corumbá A new luxury cruiser, the *Sabrina*, sails south into Paraguay, through Argentina and via the Atlantic up to Rio de Janeiro; unfortunately it's well beyond the pocket of anyone travelling on a tight budget: details and prices from Rua Cabral 1498 (☎231-3022). Significantly cheaper, though rather hit and miss, is the opportunity of joining a cargo boat bound for Asunción. If you do find a Paraguayan trading boat, you should check with the *Polícia Federal* (at the railway station) and the Paraguayan Consulate (see below) before leaving town.

Cameras and film A choice of three shops: *Foto Studio Carlos*, Rua 13 de Junho 795; *Foto Mauignier*, Rua 13 de Junho 787; and *Fotocor*, Rua Delamare 871.

Cinema At block 12 of Rua Delamare; rarely the latest films.

Consulates *Paraguay*, Avenida Antônio João 226 (☎231-4803); *Bolivia*, Rua Antônio Maria Coelho 852 (☎231-5606).

Exchange Not easy, except at the desk in the *Hotel Nacional*, Rua America 936 (☎231-6868). It takes a little longer at the *Banco do Brasil*, Rua 13 de Junho 914. For dollars cash, it's worth trying the taxi ranks on the main square, or at the railway station.

Post office Opposite the museum on the Praça da República (Mon–Fri 9am–5pm).

Shopping As well as the *Casa do Artesanato*, Rua Dom Aquino Correa 405 (see above), two of the shops on Praça da Independencia are devoted entirely to hunting, fishing and cowboy paraphernalia, like saddles and guns.

Tourist information What little there is can be obtained from the *Pantur* travel agency, Rua Frei Mariano 1254, or in the *Casa do Artesanato*, Rua Dom Aquino Correa 405. And try the Secretary of Culture's office, Rua Delamare 1557.

Train to Bolivia The service to Santa Cruz in Bolivia starts at *La Brasilena* station in Quijarró (see "Around Corumbá"), 10km by bus from Corumbá (hourly buses from Praça da República). There are two main types of train: the slow one, or *omnibus*, leaving at 6.15pm daily (except Thurs & Sat; 24hr; first class $12); and the *ferrobus*, departing at around 7.30am on Friday & Sunday (12hr; first class $10, second class $6). Timetables vary considerably, so check at the station in Corumbá or Quijarro at least a couple of days in advance if possible.

Travel and tour agencies *Corumbátur*, Rua 13 de Junho 785 (☎231-1532); *Pantanal Express*, Avenida Rondon 1355 (☎231-5353); *Turismo Pantanal*, Rua Manoel Cavassa 219. All have the same kind of trips, and work with the same boat, jeep or *fazenda* operators, so it's worth shopping around to get the best deal. And see the boxed list of operators under "The Pantanal", below.

Around Corumbá: Quijarro, Forte de Coimbra and Porto Manga

Apart from the Pantanal itself, there isn't a great deal to visit around Corumbá. Probably the most interesting places are the lively little Bolivian border town of **QUIJARRO**, half an hour away (frequent buses from Corumbá's Praça da República), and the Forte de Coimbra, 80km to the south. Theoretically, the fort can only be visited with previous permission from the *Brigada Mista* in Corumbá (Avenida Rondon 1735; ☎231-2861), although visitors unaware of this fact are sometimes allowed in. On the other hand, the *Brigada Mista* is as good a place as any to find out about transport to the fort.

The fort is accessible only by water, and is most easily reached via **PORTO ESPERANÇA**, an hour by bus (one leaves from outside *Hotel Vieira* several times a day) or train from Corumbá. The journey there is an interesting one along the edge of the swamp, and once in Porto Esperança you should have little difficulty hiring a boat, or finding a guide, to take you a couple more hours downriver to the fort. It's also possible to approach the fort in traditional fashion, by following the Paraguay river all the way from Corumbá in a boat, but this takes around seven hours and involves going through a tour agency in town.

The **Forte de Coimbra** (8.30–11.30am & 1.30–4pm) was built in 1775 to defend this western corner of Brazilian territory and, more specifically, to protect the border against invasion from Paraguay. In 1864 it was attacked by the invading Paraguayan army, which had slipped upriver into the southern Mato Grosso. Coimbra provided the first resistance to the invaders, but it didn't last for long as the Brazilian soldiers escaped from the fort under cover of darkness, leaving the fort to the aggressors. Nearly three thousand Paraguayans continued upstream in a huge convoy of ships and, forging its way north beyond Corumbá, the armada crossed the swamps almost as far as the city of Cuiabá, which was saved only by the shallowness of its river. Nowadays the fort is a pretty dull ruin (except perhaps for military enthusiasts), but it's a fine trip there.

If you have enough time, guides can be hired at the fort for the three-hour boat trip to the little visited **Gruta Buraco do Inferno** (about $10) – caves which are sculpted with huge finger-like stalactites and stalagmites. Like the fort, the caves are in a military area, so it's not advisable to try and go there alone. If you're especially interested, another military outpost, the **Forte Junqueira**, built in the eighteenth century, can also be visited in a day from Corumbá. It's only three or four hours away by boat, and trips can be arranged through local travel agencies or ring ☎231-3016 for information.

You may also be able to visit one of the planet's largest **manganese** deposits, currently being mined in the Urucum hills, just south of the city. The hills rise more than 800m above the level of the swamp, and although much of the area is technically out of bounds for the moment, organised visits to the mines of *Urucum Mineração SIA* at MINERADORA, 24km south of Corumbá, can still be arranged through most tour agencies in Corumbá – or contact the company office at Avenida Rondon 1351 (☎231-1661).

Finally, if you're not going to have the time to get any further into the Pantanal, then small **PORTO MANGA** is an ideal place to taste the swamp life without spending a lot of money. Situated where the Campo Grande road crosses the Paraguay river – about an hour by bus from Corumbá – it's renowned as a centre for wildlife and fishing, particularly in September. There are a couple of **hotels** and various potential **camping** locations in and around the settlement.

CROSSING THE BOLIVIAN BORDER

Crossing into or out of Bolivia from Corumbá is a slightly disjointed procedure. **Leaving Brazil**, you should get an exit stamp from the *Polícia Federal* at Corumbá's railway station (easiest before 11am or between 7pm and 9pm) before picking up a **Bolivian visa** (if you need one) from the Consulate at Rua Antônio Maria Coelho 852 (☎231-5606). After that, it's a matter of taking the bus (every hour from Praça da República) the 10km to the border, checking through Bolivian immigration and receiving your passport entry stamp. **Train tickets for Santa Cruz** should be bought at *La Brasilena* railway station in Quijarro, a few minutes by *colectivo* or bus from the immigration offices.

Entering Brazil from Bolivia is essentially the same procedure in reverse, although US citizens should remember to pick up visas in the Brazilian Consulate in Santa Cruz before leaving.

The Pantanal

Taking off into **the Pantanal** is what most people have in mind when they arrive in Corumbá, and though there are various ways to do this, the basic point to bear in mind is that the deeper you go into the swamp, the better your chances of seeing the wildlife. Short boat or jeep trips are relatively cheap, but offer little more than the flavour of the swamp. Instead, you should plan to stay at one of the **fazenda-lodges**, well away from the town or main roads, which cost from around $20 per person per night. Probably the most economical alternative is to buy a passage (around $15 for a six- to ten-day trip; hammock essential) on one of the few **boats** still crossing the Pantanal, between Corumbá and Cáceres or Porto Jofre (both connected by road to Cuiabá). All the details are given below, as well as descriptions of the various routes into the swamp: you've a head start if you're already in Corumbá, since lots of lodges and swamp settlements are easily accessible from there; but it's simple to see the Pantanal **from Cuiabá**, too. Apart from the text, the boxed sections below contain more specific information about what to take and where to go and stay.

The swamp: some facts and history

The Pantanal floods twenty thousand square kilometres of land on an annual basis. Much like an immense sponge, the swamp seasonally absorbs the swollen waters of three large rivers – the Paraguay, the Taquari and the Cuiabá. Separated from the Amazon watershed by a fifteen-kilometre portage near Cuiabá, this isolated corner of Brazil occupies a unique ecological niche within the continent, and is home for a magnificent diversity of wildlife. During the **rainy season** (Jan–April), it's a vast flooded plain with islands of scrubby forest amidst oceans of floating vegetation. At other times of the year, when it looks more like a rolling savanna, the Pantanal is still very boggy, and transport is necessarily dominated by the rivers, natural water channels and hundreds of well-hidden lagoons.

The **dry season**, with its peak normally around September, transforms the Pantanal into South America's most exciting natural wildlife reserve. Its infamous piranha and alligator populations crowd into relatively small pools and streams, while the astonishing array of aquatic birds follow suit, forming very dense colonies. Treeless bush savanna alternates with wet swamp, while along the major river banks grow belts of rainforest populated with colonies of monkeys (including spider monkeys and black gibbons). During the rains, small islands of vegetated land crawl with wild animals – jaguars, tapirs, cabybaras (the world's largest rodents) and wild boar living side by side with domesticated cattle. The cows in the swamp tend not to eat or need additional salt, since there's so much of the mineral in the ground and plants; a vestige of the Pantanal's early geological position below the ocean.

The Pantanal in the past

Very little is known about the Pantanal's **history** . At the time of early Portuguese explorations, and the first unsuccessful attempts at populating the region by the Spanish in the sixteenth century, the region was dominated by three main tribes. In the south lived the horse-riding **Guaicuru**, who adopted stray or stolen horses and cattle from the advancing white settlers, making the tribe an elite group amongst Indians. Wearing only jaguar skins as they rode into battle, they were feared by the neighbouring **Terena** (Guana) tribe, who lived much of their lives as servants to Guaicuru families. In many ways, the nature and degree of their economic and social interaction suggests that the two might once have been different castes within the same tribe. Another powerful tribe lived to the north – the **Paiaguá**, masters of the main rivers, lagoons and canals of the central Pantanal. Much to the chagrin of both Spanish and Portuguese expeditions into the swamps, the Paiaguá were superbly skilled with both their canoes and the bow and arrow.

It wasn't until the **discovery of gold** in the northern Pantanal and around Cuiabá during the early eighteenth century that any genuine settlement schemes were undertaken. A rapid influx of colonists, miners and soldiers led to several bloody battles. In June 1730 hundreds of Paiaguá warriors in 83 canoes ambushed the annual flotilla carrying some nine hundred kilos of gold south through the Pantanal from Cuiabá. They spared only some of the women and a few of the stronger black rowers from the flotilla: all of the gold and most of the white men were lost. Much of the gold eventually found its way out of Brazil and into Spanish Paraguay where Cautiguacu, the Paiaguá chief, lived a wealthy life in Asunción until his death 55 years later.

The decline of the gold mines during the nineteenth century brought development in the Pantanal to a standstill and the population began to decline. This century has seen the establishment of unrestricted cattle grazing ranches – *fazendas* – and by 1970 there were over twenty million cows roaming the swamp. The BR-364 skirts around the Pantanal and Ministry of Transport plans for a *transpantaneira* road have been shelved for the sake of the region's ecological balance. For all that, tourism remains the likely next stage for "development" in the region.

Into the swamp: routes from Cuiabá and Corumbá

If you speak with the locals about visiting the Pantanal they will almost certainly recommend going in by road. This is usually cheaper and quicker than hiring a boat or going on one of the cruises. The main problem, though, is knowing where to go and which company or *fazenda*-lodge to choose. We've listed a series of possible **routes** and starting places, below, and have included some lodges: although many of them are located near the main Corumbá–Campo Grande road, and can be easily reached by jeep or bus, they nevertheless offer access deeper into the swamp, on horseback or by canoe.

Cuiabá is probably the easiest place from which to make a swamp trip under your own steam, with three main routes into the Pantanal; **Corumbá**, bang in the swamp, is the main centre for bus or jeep excursions.

Barão de Melgaço

One of the simplest ways into the swamp is to take the bus from Cuiabá to **BARÃO DE MELGAÇO**, a small and quiet swamp village, some 65km south down the BR-364, and then west along a rougher road for another 70km. Here,

---

GETTING IN AND OUT OF THE SWAMP: PRELIMINARY HINTS

●The Pantanal is a difficult and dangerous place to travel. There are few roads, and although hundreds of tracks sneak their way into the swamp, they are only used by *fazenda* workers who know them inside out. An inexperienced driver or hiker could easily get lost – or worse. That said, there's no better way to see the wildlife than to camp deep in the swamp, away from roads, tracks or *fazenda*-lodges, but to do this you'll need a local **guide**, generally available only at lodges or in end-of-the-track settlements like Porto Jofre. Also, it's important to take all the **equipment** you need with you if you're going to go-it-alone like this in the Pantanal – food, camping gear, a first aid kit, etc.

●Most people go on **organised tours** (see the list of operators below), entering the swamp in jeeps or trucks and following one of the few rough roads that now connect Corumbá, Aquidauana, Coxim and Cuiabá (via Pocone or Cáceres) with some of the larger *fazenda* settlements of the interior. It's also still possible to **bus** and **hitch** from Cuiabá, though there's too little traffic on most other Pantanal entry roads to make this a viable plan elsewhere.

●Arriving alone at somewhere like Cáceres, Porto Jofre, Coxim or Aquidauana, it's then a matter of finding a boat going your way or paying a local guide or *fazendeiro* to take you on a trip into the swamp. This will **cost** from around $20 per person per day, including canoe or vehicle transport and a guide/boatman/driver. Local guides and *fazendeiros* usually prefer to use the road networks to reach *fazenda*-lodges within the swamp, and explore in canoes or on horseback from there.

there's a reasonable **hotel** by the river, while the *Pousada de Barão* lodge (from around $25 a day) is just one hour away by boat. Barão isn't quite in the true swamp, and the relative ease of access means that there isn't as much wildlife as you can see from some of the interior *fazendas*, or even around Porto Jofre. But if you're short on time and just want a taste of the Pantanal, Barão will do.

FAZENDA-LODGES, TOURS AND OPERATORS

You should spend at least two nights in the swamp to get anything out of the trip, though with *fazenda*-lodges charging from $20 to $50 a night, this can prove a little expensive. Ultimately, the price depends on who you book through – $50 through agents in Cuiabá or Corumbá; $20 if you deal direct with a *fazenda*-lodge owner in Porto Jofre, Cáceres, Aquidauana and even Corumbá.

Rancho Kue (Aquidauana; ☎241-1875). From around $30 per person per night, this is one of the best located *fazendas*, right in the centre of the swamp, close to the confluence of the Paraguay and São Lourenço rivers.

Fazendola Leque (office in Corumbá at Rua America 262; ☎231-1598). Much cheaper and more easily accessible from Corumbá, this offers a more basic Pantanal welcome. Recommended for bird and wildlife spotting; four days for around $75, including road transport to and from Corumbá. Horses and canoes for use by guests.

Pantur (Rua Frei Mariano 685, Corumbá; ☎231-4343). Day and half-day trips in and around Corumbá, from around $20 per person. Among their most interesting tours, the *Passeio Rodo Fluvial* goes south through the iron-ore and manganese rich scenery of the Urucum hills, before canoeing into the swamp near Porto Esperança (see "Around Corumbá", above).

Transtur/La Barca Tur (office on the right, at the bottom of the road leading to the waterfront from Praça da República, in Corumbá; ☎231-3016/2871/5222). This company has a fleet of barges, imaginatively converted into floating bars and hotels, down at the waterfront in Corumbá. The large floating hotels cost over $400 a day for eight people (ie $50 per person including food but not drink) – add another $40 a day for any additional passengers.

Rondon Turismo (near *El Pacu*, see below, on Corumbá waterfront). A friendly company run by local people who know the swamp and rivers well; boat hire for around $7 an hour, boats for up to four people at $35 a day; or haggle over a price for a more extended Pantanal excursion.

El Pacu Bar (on the waterfront, Corumbá). The owner, Herman, is a good person to talk to about organising a three- or four-day trip for 4–5 people by road into the Pantanal; from around $35 per person.

Expediturs (Rua Visconde de Pirajá 414, Grs. 1005/6, 22410, Ipanema, Rio de Janeiro; ☎287-9697/9048). A converted eight double-cabin tour boat, the *Cidade Barão de Melgaço* (*CBM*) leaves Corumbá on the tenth day of every month, arriving in Barão de Melgaco one swamp and seven days later. It's expensive (around $500 including food, airport transfers etc) and, being organised from an office in Rio, it's not exactly easy to get your money back if things don't work out. However, it might just turn out to be the relaxing holiday of a lifetime. No fixed schedule of dates, but up-to-date details from *Pantur*'s office in Corumbá (see above).

From Britain. If you want to book ahead, there are one or two British companies who offer South American tour itineraries which include a couple of days in the Pantanal with an English-speaking tour leader: try *Journey Latin America* (16 Devonshire Road, London W4 2HD; ☎081-747 3108); and *EXPLORE* (7 High Street, Aldershot, Hampshire GU11 1BH; ☎0252-319448).

Incidentally, you should also be able to reach Barão by **boat** from Corumbá, if *Expediturs*, based in Rio de Janeiro, live up to their promises, but it will be an expensive ride: see the boxed list of operators, above, for more details.

Pocone and Porto Jofre

The most exploited option from Cuiabá is to follow the route south to Pocone and Porto Jofre.

There are daily buses from Cuiabá's *Rodoviária* and, as far as **POCONE** itself (about 100km from Cuiabá), the road is paved and the ride fairly smooth. Like Barão de Melgaço, Pocone is not real Pantanal country, but it's a start and there's plenty of **accommodation** if you need to stay over. On the main square, Praça Roncon, the *Hotel Skala* and a couple of restaurants take most of the trade; the *Pousada Pantaneira*, on the Porto Jofre road, offers more accommodation, as well as swamp trips of a fairly traditional nature; while slightly cheaper, and nearer the bus station, you can also sleep or eat at the *Hotel Santa Cruz*.

The swamp proper begins as you leave the town, following the bumpy track. You'll start to see wildlife from the road (though only along the second half of the journey), and after 120km, having crossed some 89 wooden bridges in varying stages of dilapidation, the track eventually arrives at **PORTO JOFRE**. After Cuiabá, Porto Jofre appears as little more than a small fishing hamlet, literally the end of the road. This is as far as the *transpantaneira* route has got, or ever looks like getting, thanks to technical problems and the sound advice of ecological pressure groups. As far as **accommodation** goes, the *Santa Rosa Pantanal Hotel*, an annex of the *Santa Rosa* in Cuiabá, has an exceptional location on the banks of the Cuiabá River near Porto Jofre, but it's expensive (from $35 full board). If you have a hammock or a tent, it's usually alright to sleep outside somewhere, but check with someone in authority first (ask at the port) and don't leave any valuables unattended.

From Porto Jofre, there are **boats to Corumbá** at least twice a month, normally on their way downstream from PORTO CERCADO, and the journey takes two to four days. The boat is actually a cement barge; more details under "Routes from Corumbá", below. It's also possible to arrange a day or two's excursion up the sandy **Itiquira** River from Porto Jofre.

Cáceres

Although less used than the Porto Jofre route, **CÁCERES** is another good target from Cuiabá, 233km west of the city. It's a three- to four-hour journey by bus, several daily leaving from the *Rodoviária* in Cuiabá. On the upper reaches of the Paraguay river, which is still quite broad even this far upstream, Cáceres is a relatively new town, apparently made up of wooden shacks, bars and pool rooms. Of the **hotels**, the *Santa Terezinha* is the best value, clean and hospitable; *Hotel Fenix* is more expensive and has little extra to offer.

The touristy *Hotel/Fazenda Barranquinho*, which can be reached by track or boat in around three hours from Cáceres, is 60km away on the confluence of the Paraguay and Jauru rivers. It's a beautiful spot, but is still not far enough into the swamp for the best chance of spotting **wildlife**. Best bet for this is to take one of the **boats to Corumbá** from Cáceres: either a cattle-boat, run by the *Serviço de Navegação da Bacia da Prata*, or cement barge, operated by *Portobras* (office on Cáceres waterfront; ☎222-1728); each usually runs twice a month. Again, there's more information under "Routes from Corumbá", below.

The only road to go further into the Pantanal is the track that leads on to the **Bolivian border** settlement of SAN MATIAS; from here you can fly to Santa Cruz, or hitch the bad road to ROBORE (in Bolivia) which is on the Corumbá–Santa Cruz railway line. If you take this route, you'll need to get a Brazilian exit stamp from the Polícia Federal in Cáceres first.

Routes from Corumbá: Pantanal boat journeys

Corumbá is ideally placed for getting right into the Pantanal by bus or jeep. The main road between Corumbá and Miranda, on the route to Campo Grande, crosses through a large section of the swamp, including Porto Manga (see "Around Corumbá"), LONTRA and LEQUE at the Paraguay ferry crossing. And the box above details **fazenda-lodges** near Corumbá offering accommodation and Pantanal trips.

At present, two basic types of **boat** cross the Pantanal on a regular basis – cement barges and cattle-boats – both operating out of Corumbá. Neither have fixed itineraries, so it's a matter of checking on departure dates when you arrive at Corumbá.

A **cement barge** has been ferrying dust to Cáceres and Porto Jofre for years and, leaving twice a month, it usually takes about a week to go upstream, with plenty of time for relaxing and looking out for wildlife. The barge, though, does tend to keep to the main channel of the Paraguay river, which obviously doesn't give you a very good chance of spotting anything particularly shy or rare. The only other problem is that travelling on the cement barge hasn't been strictly legal since 1985, when the son of a Naval Minister accidentally died while on board one of them; passengers have consequently been "smuggled" aboard the barge in dinghies, under cover of darkness, although you might find it's still possible to buy a ride simply by asking the *commandante* of the barge company, *Portobras* – the office is at Corumbá's waterfront. If you manage to get a ride, as well as bedding and a hammock, take some extra food (tins, biscuits, bottled drinks etc), insect repellent and a few good books.

A **cattle-boat** (run by *Servico de Navegacão da Bacia da Prata*) also runs between Corumbá and Cáceres, leaving twice a month and often picking up passengers from the ports at either end. Other cattle-boats leaving Corumbá are willing to take passengers on round-trips within the swamp, delivering and picking up cows from various *fazendas*. If you can find space on one of these boats, then it's a very inexpensive way of seeing some of the Pantanal: take your own hammock and food and drink and it'll cost around around $10 for three or four days.

travel details

Trains

From Campo Grande to Corumbá (2 daily; 11hr); Bauru (2 daily; 20hr); Ponta Porã (1 daily; 6hr).
From Corumbá to Campo Grande (2 daily; 11hr); Bauru (1 daily; 32hr); Santa Cruz (daily from Quijarro; *ferrobus/rapido* 12hr, *omnibus/*slow train 18hr).
From Ponta Porã to Campo Grande (1 daily Mon–Sat; 6hr).

Buses

There are scores of different bus companies, competing for the same routes as well as opening up new ones. Each company advertises destinations and departure times at their ticket office windows, making it relatively easy to choose a route and buy a ticket.
From Cuiabá to Porto Velho (4 daily; 23hr); Manaus (2 daily; 3–4 days); Campo Grande (6

daily; 10hr); Rondonopolis (10 daily; 3hr); Coxim (6 daily; 6hr); Santarém (irregular; 3–6 days depending on the rainfall); Goiania (6 daily; 14hr); Brasília (6 daily; 20hr).

From Campo Grande to Corumbá (4 daily; 7hr); Dourados (6 daily; 4hr); Aquidauana (8 daily; 2hr); Bonito (1 daily; 5hr); Ponta Porã (4 daily; 5–6hr); Cuiabá (6 daily; 10hr); São Paulo (8 daily; 16hr); Brasília (2 daily; 23hr); Rio de Janeiro (4 daily; 22hr).

From Corumbá to Campo Grande (4 daily; 7hr; and change here for most onward destinations); Rio de Janeiro (4 daily; 32hr); São Paulo (4 daily; 26hr).

Planes
From Cuiabá and Campo Grande Several daily flights (*VASP* and *Varig*) to Brazil's main cities.
From Corumbá Daily flights (*VASP* only) to Rio de Janeiro, São Paulo, Campo Grande, Cuiabá, Manuas; and to Santa Cruz in Bolivia (*TAM* or air taxi service).

Boats
From Corumbá to Cáceres or Porto Jofre Irregular cement barges taking up to 10 days to travel through the Pantanal; see the text.
From Cuiabá (via Porto Jofre or Cáceres) to Corumbá Irregular boats and cement barge (3–6 days).

CHAPTER SEVEN

SAO PAULO

Paulistas, the citizens of the **State of São Paulo**, never tire of saying that their state is Brazil's economic powerhouse, and they produce a mountain of statistics to sustain the boast. The state's 35 million inhabitants represent about a quarter of Brazil's total population, yet the state contributes 40 percent of the federal tax revenues, and consumes 60 percent of the country's industrial energy to produce two-thirds of its industrial output. A highly capitalised agricultural sector produces 80 percent of Brazil's oranges, half of its sugar, 40 percent of its chickens and eggs, and 22 percent of its coffee. Yet while *Paulistas* crow that without their muscle, Brazil's economy would collapse, other Brazilians feel that São Paulo has developed at their expense. The state, it's argued, attracts capital away from the other regions, which are basically seen as sources of cheap labour and as guaranteed markets for São Paulo's products.

This economic pre-eminence is a relatively recent phenomenon. In 1507, São Vicente was founded on the coast near present-day **Santos**, the second oldest Portuguese settlement in Brazil, but for over three hundred years the area comprising today's state of São Paulo remained a backwater. The inhabitants were a hardy people, of mixed Portuguese and Indian origin, from whom – in the seventeenth and eighteenth centuries – emerged the **bandeirantes**; frontiersmen who roamed far into the South American interior to secure the borders of the Portuguese Empire against Spanish encroachment, capturing Indian slaves and seeking out precious metals and gems as they went.

Not until the mid-nineteenth century did São Paulo become rich. Cotton production received a boost with the arrival of Confederate refugees in the late 1860s, who settled between **Americana** and **Santa Bárbara d'Oeste**, about 140km from the then small town of **São Paulo** itself. But after disappointing results with cotton, most plantation owners switched their attentions to coffee and, by the end of the century, the state had become the world's foremost producer of the crop. During the same period, Brazil abolished slavery and the plantation owners recruited European and Japanese immigrants to expand production. Riding the wave of the coffee boom, British and other foreign companies took the opportunity to invest in port facilities, railways, power and water supplies, while textile and other new industries emerged, too. Within a few decades, the town of São Paulo became one of South America's greatest commercial and cultural centres, sliding from a small town into a vast metropolitan sprawl.

Even if the thought of staying in the city of São Paulo is repellent, the state does have other attractions. The beaches north of Santos, especially on the **Ilha de São Sebastião** and around **Ubatuba**, rival Rio's best, while those to the south – near **Iguape** and **Cananéia** – remain relatively unspoiled. **Inland,** the state is dominated by agribusiness, with seemingly endless fields of sugar cane, oranges and soya interspersed by anonymous towns where the agricultural produce is processed. But for the novelty in tropical Brazil of a winter chill, or to escape scorching summer temperatures, make for **Campos do Jordão**, São Paulo's enticing mountain resort.

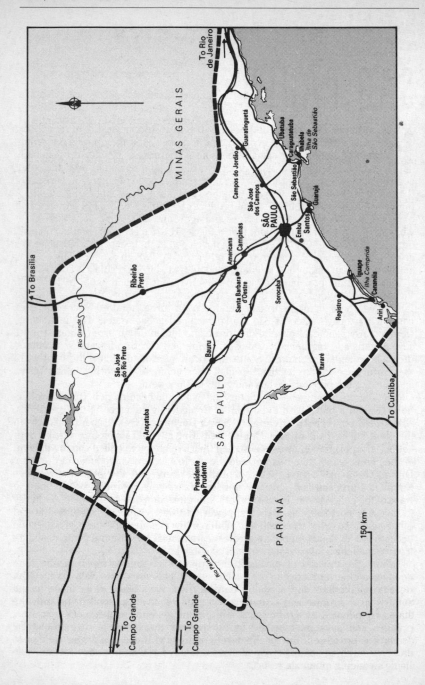

SÃO PAULO CITY

Rio is a beauty. But São Paulo – São Paulo is a city.

Marlene Dietrich.

In 1554, the Jesuit priests José de Anchieta and Manuel da Nóbrega established a mission station on the banks of the Rio Tietê in an attempt to bring Christianity to the Tupi-Guarani Indians. Called **São Paulo dos Campos de Piratininga**, it was 70km inland and 730m up, in the sheer, forest-covered inclines of the Serra do Mar, above the port of São Vicente. The gently undulating plateau and the proximity to the Paraná and Plata rivers facilitated traffic into the interior and, with São Paulo as their base, roaming gangs of *bandeirantes* set out in search of loot. Around the mission school, a few adobe huts were erected and the settlement soon developed into a trading post and a base from which to secure mineral wealth. In 1681, **São Paulo** – as the town became known – became a seat of regional government and, in 1711, it was constituted as a municipality by the king of Portugal, the cool, healthy climate helping to attract settlers from the coast.

With the expansion of **coffee** plantations westwards from Rio de Janeiro, along the Paraibá Valley, in the mid-nineteenth century, São Paulo's fortunes looked up. The region's rich soil – *terra roxa* – was ideally suited to the growth of coffee, and from about 1870, plantation owners took up residence in the city, which was undergoing a rapid transformation into a bustling, regional centre. British, French and German merchants and hoteliers opened local operations, British-owned railways radiated in all directions from São Paulo, and foreign water, gas, telephone and electricity companies moved in to service the city. In the 1890s, enterprising "coffee barons" began to place some of their profits into local industry, hedging their bets against a possible fall in the price of coffee, with textile factories being a favourite area for investment.

As the local population could not meet the ever increasing demands of plantation owners, factories looked to **immigrants** to meet their labour requirements. As a result, São Paulo's **population** soared, almost tripling to 69,000 by 1890 – and, by the end of the next decade, increasing to 239,000. By 1950 it had reached 2.2m and São Paulo had clearly established its dominant role in Brazil's urbanisation.

As industry, trade and population developed at such a terrific pace, buildings were erected with little time to consider their aesthetics: in any case, they often became cramped as soon as they were built, or had to be demolished to make way for a new avenue. However, some grand **public buildings** were built in the late nineteenth and early twentieth century, and a few still remain. None, though, are as splendid as those found in Buenos Aires, a city that developed at much the same time. In São Paulo, beauty counted for little and when, occasionally, graceful buildings raised their heads, they were almost always immediately overshadowed by some new monstrous edifice, or simply knocked down. Even now, conservation is seen as not being profitable, and São Paulo's concerns are more to do with rising population, rising production and rising consumption – factors that today are paralleled by rising levels of homelessness, pollution and violence.

Paulistanos talk smugly of their work ethic, supposedly superior to that which dominates the rest of Brazil, and speak contemptuously of the idleness of *cariocas* (in reply, *cariocas* joke sourly that *Paulistanos* are simply incapable of enjoying anything, sex in particular). But work and profit aside, São Paulo does have its attractions: the city lays claim to have long surpassed Rio as Brazil's **cultural** centre, and São Paulo is home to a lively music and arts world. The city's **food**, too, is excellent, thanks to immigrants from so many parts of the world.

Arriving and orientation

The prospect of arriving in a city of sixteen million inhabitants, spread over an area of 30,000 square kilometres, is likely to frighten you to bits. However, while it's true that urban development has been carried out with an almost complete lack of planning, **SÃO PAULO** is far more manageable than you might imagine. Greater São Paulo is enormous, but the main shopping, entertainment and hotel districts are easy to move between, and the areas of historic interest are extremely limited. Even so, São Paulo's streets form something of a maze and even for the briefest of visits it's well worth buying a **map**, like the *Guia Quatro Rodas*, available at any newspaper kiosk.

Some orientation

São Paulo's traditional centre is seen as the areas around **Praça da Sé** and **Praça da República**, the two sections of the city bisected by a broad avenue, the **Vale do Anhangabaú**, which in turn is bridged by a pedestrian crossing, the **Viaduto do Chá**. The area around Praça da Sé is where you'll find the Pátio do Colégio, which dates back to the early years of the Jesuit mission settlement, and the commercial district of banks, offices and shops, known as the **Triângulo** – originally comprising Rua Direita, Quinze de Novembro, São Bento, and Praça Antônio Prado. The area around Praça da República now forms an extension of the main commercial district, but there are also many hotels and apartment buildings here, too.

The *bairros* to the **west** of the centre contained some of the city's first industrial suburbs and were home for many immigrants, but with the exception of the Museu da Hospedaria do Imigrante there's hardly anything of interest here. **North** of the city is the neighbourhood of **Bom Retiro**, in the past the centre of the Jewish community in São Paulo, and due north of here, across the Rio Tietê, is the **Rodoviária Tietê**.

Just **south** of the commercial district is **Bela Vista**, usually referred to as "Bixiga", São Paulo's "Little Italy", centred on **Rua 13 de Maio**. And immediately to the south of Praça da Sé is **Liberdade**, the Japanese neighbourhood, with its centre around Praça da Liberdade and Rua Galvão Bueno.

To the southwest of the centre is **Avenida Paulista**, an avenue of high-rise office blocks which effectively divides the traditional centre from the **Jardims**, the middle- and upper-class garden suburbs. Rua Augusta, which begins in the centre at Praça Franklin Roosevelt, crosses Avenida Paulista passing through the Jardims, changing its name as it goes, becoming **Rua Colômbia**, **Avenida Europa** and finally **Avenida Cidade Jardim** – this interconnecting road, and those running off it, being where most of São Paulo's best restaurants and shopping streets are located. **West of the Jardims**, just across the Rio Pinheiros, is the **Universidade de São Paulo** and the Instituto Butantã, while to the southeast is the **Parque Ibiapuera**, one of the city's few parks and the location of more museums and exhibition centres.

AVOIDING TROUBLE IN SÃO PAULO

Use a little common sense and you're unlikely to encounter any real problems in the city. With such a mixture of people in São Paulo, you're far less likely to be assumed to be a foreigner than in most parts of Brazil, and therefore won't make such an obvious target for pickpockets and other **petty thieves**.

At night, though, pay particular attention if you're staying in a hotel around **Luz** and, though not as bad, around **Praça da República** – and take special care late at night in **Bixiga** and **Praça Roosevelt**. Always carry at least some money in an immediately accessible place so that, if you are accosted by a **mugger**, you can quickly hand something over before he starts getting angry or panicky. If in any doubt at all about visiting an area you don't know, don't hesitate to take a taxi.

Greater São Paulo includes huge, sprawling, industrial suburbs where people are housed in a mixture of grim-looking high-rise tenements, small houses and, on just about every patch of wasteland, *favelas* – the slum homes for some two million of the city's inhabitants. The most important **industrial areas** are the so-called "A B C D" *municípios* of Santo André, São Bernardo, São Caetano and Diadema, the centre of Brazil's motor vehicle industry and of the city's militantly left-wing political tradition. In the 1940s, Santo André elected Brazil's first Communist Party mayor, while out of the Metal Workers' Union and the auto workers strikes of the late 1970s, which heralded the end of the country's supposed economic "miracle", emerged Lula, the leader of the PT, the Workers Party.

Points of arrival

You'll probably **arrive** in São Paulo by plane or bus, though there are a few inter-city train services. Watch your belongings at all times, as thieves thrive in the confusion of airports and stations.

Airports

São Paulo is served by two airports, *Congonhas* and *Garulhos*, which are connected to each other by air-conditioned *executivo* buses leaving at roughly half-hourly intervals (or 45min at night), stopping off on the way at the Tietê *Rodoviária*. At similar intervals, buses link the airports with Praça da República (at the intersection of Rua do Arouche), from where you can take a taxi, bus or Metro to elsewhere in the city. *Paulistur* maintains very helpful tourist information desks at both airports.

Nearest to the centre, **Congonhas** airport (☎531-7444) handles services within the State of São Paulo and the shuttle services (the *Ponte Aérea*) to Rio, Curitiba and Belo Horizonte.

Other domestic, and all **international** flights use **Garulhos** airport (☎945-2111), 30km from the city. When entering the country, after having your passport stamped be sure to retain the immigration form if you don't want any problems when leaving. The *Banco do Brasil* has a branch at the airport where you can change money at the official rate, but by discreetly asking around in the gift shops you can usually find someone willing to give you a better deal (though not as good as you'll get in the city itself). When **leaving Brazil**, you'll have to pay a $9 departure tax (payable in *cruzados* or dollars). Note that bad weather frequently leads to the diversion of planes from Garulhos to Congonhas.

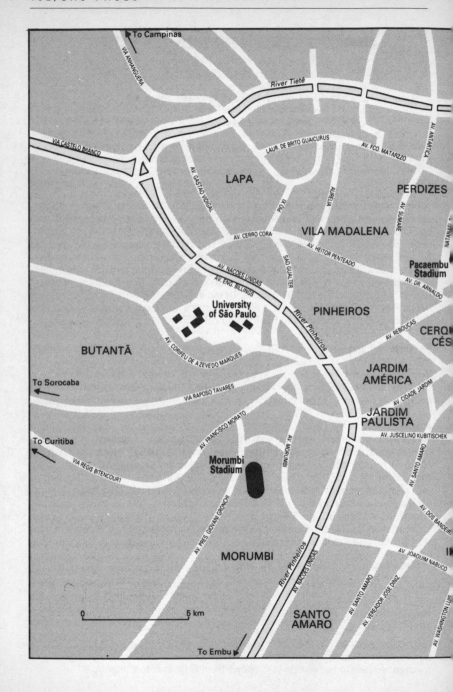

To Campinas

VIA ANHANGUERA

River Tietê

VIA CASTELO BRANCO

LAUR. DE BRITO GUAICURUS

AV. FCO. MATARZZO

AV. ANTÁRTICA

AV. GASTÃO VIDIGAL

LAPA

PERDIZES

PIO IX

AURELIA

AV. SUMARE

NATANAEL

AV. CERRO CORA

VILA MADALENA

AV. HEITOR PENTEADO

SÃO GUALTER

Pacaembu Stadium

AV. NAÇOES UNIDAS

AV. ENG. BILLINGS

AV. DR. ARNALDO

University of São Paulo

River Pinheiros

PINHEIROS

AV. REBOUÇAS

CERQ CÉS

BUTANTÃ

AV. CORIFEU DE AZEVEDO MARQUES

JARDIM AMÉRICA

To Sorocaba

VIA RAPOSO TAVARES

AV. CIDADE JARDIM

JARDIM PAULISTA

AV. FRANCISCO MORATO

AV. JUSCELINO KUBITISCHEK

To Curitiba

AV. MORUMBI

AV. SANTO AMARO

VIA REGIS BITENCOURT

AV. DOS BANDEIR

Morumbi Stadium

AV. JOAQUIM NABUCO

AV. PRES. GIOVANI GRONCHI

River Pinheiros

AV. NAÇOES UNIDAS

MORUMBI

AV. SANTO AMARO

AV. VEREADOR JOSE DINIZ

AV. WASHINGTON LUIS

0   5 km

SANTO AMARO

To Embu

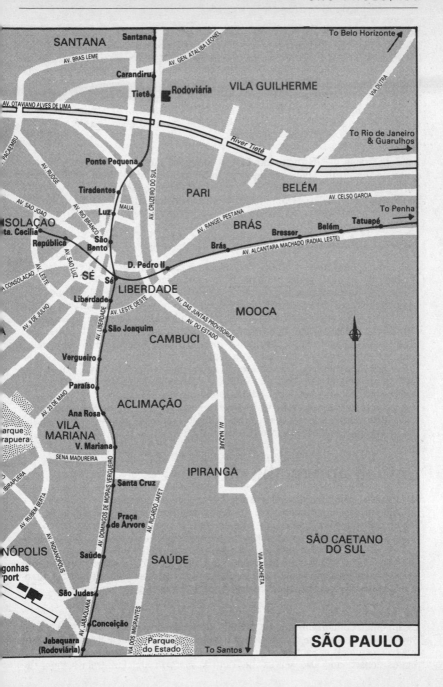

Bus stations
Inter-city **bus services** arrive at one of two *Rodoviárias*. **Jabaquara** (☎235-0322)
is for buses to and from the Santos region and São Paulo's south coast as far as
Peruíbe. All other bus services to and from destinations within Brazil and neighbouring countries use the **Tietê** (☎235-0322) terminal. Both *Rodoviárias* are on the
Metro system (see below) and a night bus (#510M) runs between the *Rodoviárias*,
passing through the centre at Praça da Sé. To save a trip out to either *Rodoviária*,
bus tickets to most destinations can be bought at travel agents in the city.

Trains
Inter-city trains use **Estação da Luz** at Praça da Luz, at the edge of the city
centre to the north. There are services to the interior of the State of São Paulo
(for Campo Grande and Corumbá, change in Bauru), to Brasília, Belo Horizonte
and Rio de Janeiro. To or from the city centre itself, take the Metro (from the Luz
station) or a taxi, which will cost about \$2.

Tourist information

There are several **tourist offices** and booths scattered about the city (and at the
airports) that provide information on the city and State of São Paulo.
   The city's **information booths** are especially helpful for general directions, or
for local bus and Metro details, and a very good map of the downtown area is
given away free. There are booths along Avenida Ipiranga, on Praça da República
(Mon–Fri 9am–6pm, Sat noon–4pm, Sun 9am–1pm); at Praça da Liberdade
(Mon–Fri 9am–6pm, Sat & Sun noon–4pm); Teatro Municipal (Mon–Fri 9am–
6pm, Sat 9am–1pm); Avenida São Luís, on the corner of Praça Dom José Gaspar
(Mon–Fri 9am–6pm); at the Sé Metro station (Mon–Fri 9am–6pm, Sat & Sun
9am–1pm); and at the shopping centres, *Morumbi* (Mon–Fri 9am–6pm) and
Ibirapuera (Mon–Fri 9am–6pm, Sat noon–4pm).
   A good map, but otherwise very limited information on the State of São Paulo,
is available from tourist offices at Praça Antônio Prado 347 (Mon–Fri 10am–5pm)
and at Avenida São Luís 115 (Mon–Fri 9am–6pm).

Getting around the city

São Paulo's **public transport** network is excellent and, despite the traffic congestion and an almost perpetual rush hour, you can move around the city by Metro,
bus or taxi with remarkable ease. The one time *not* to attempt to travel is when it
rains: São Paulo's drainage system is hopelessly inadequate to cope with the tropical storms and, as roads are transformed into rivers, the city grinds to a halt –
just take cover in a bar or *lanchonete* and sit it out. As a **safety precaution**,
always make sure you have some small notes at hand, so as not to attract attention to yourself when fumbling through your wallet or bag for change.

The Metro
Clean, quiet, comfortable and fast, São Paulo's **Metro** would be by far the easiest
way to move around the city were it not limited to just two lines: the **north–south**
line has terminals at Santana and Jabaquara (the *Rodoviária* from where buses to
Santos depart) and also serves the Tietê *Rodoviária* and Luz train station; the

east–west line has terminals at Carrão and Marechal Deodoro, and intersects with the north–south line at Praça da Sé.

The Metro operates every day from 5am until midnight. **Tickets** cost a few cents and are bought either as singles (*ida*), doubles (*dople*), or valid for ten journeys. You can also buy integrated bus/Metro tickets, the buses stopping at the Metro stations, with the names of their destinations well-marked.

Buses

Traffic congestion rarely allows São Paulo's **buses** to be driven at the same terrifying speeds as in Rio. The network is efficient and, apart from the ordinary buses, it also includes trolley buses and a few double-decker buses – painted red and introduced in the 1980s by Jânio Quadros, São Paulo's Anglophile ex-mayor.

But **bus routes** often snake confusingly through the city and working out which bus to take can be difficult. The number of the bus is clearly marked at the front, and there are cards at the front and the entrance (towards the back) which indicate the route. At **bus stops** (usually wooden posts) you'll have to flag down the buses you want: be attentive or they'll speed by. Buses run between 4am and midnight, but avoid travelling during the evening rush hour (5–7pm) when the buses are overflowing with passengers.

SOME USEFUL BUS ROUTES

The *Guia Quatro Rodas* for São Paulo gives the numbers and routes taken by all the city's buses. Below are listed a few buses to some likely destinations.

From Praça da República along Avenida Paulista (via Liberdade): #595P.

From Praça da República to Avenida Brigadeiro Faria Lima (via Rua Augusta): #702P.

From Praça da República to Butantã (via Rua Augusta and Avenida Brigadeiro Faria Lima): #7181.

From Avenida Ipiranga to Butantã and Universidade de São Paulo: #702U.

From Metro Ana Rosa along Avenida Paulista: #875P.

From *Rodoviária* Tietê to *Rodoviária* Jabaquara via Largo de São Bento and Avenida Liberdade: #501M (midnight–5am only).

Taxis

Taxis in São Paulo are abundant and cheap. With irregular – or no – bus services at night, taxis are really the only means of transport after midnight. There are two main types: the yellow *comuns* and the *radiotáxis*.

The **comuns**, generally small cars that carry two passengers, are the cheapest and are found at taxis ranks or hailed from the street. **Radiotáxis** are larger and more expensive, and are ordered by phone: try *Coopertax* (☎941-2555) or *Ligue Táxi* (☎272-9960). Both types of taxi have meters, but the price is adjusted for inflation from a price sheet that should always be displayed on the taxi's window. Both types also have two fare rates, and a flag, or *bandeira*, is displayed on the meter to indicate which fare is in operation: fare "1" is charged from 6am to 10pm, but after 10pm and on Sunday and public holidays fare "2" is charged, costing twenty percent more. Just in case the driver is tempted to take a longer than necessary route to your destination, it's a good idea to keep an eye on your map as you go.

Finding a place to stay

Hotels in São Paulo tend to be busiest during the week when people visit the city for work. Nevertheless, finding somewhere to stay is rarely a problem and, as there are several areas where hotels are concentrated, you should be settled in quite quickly.

Most of the cheap and medium-priced places are in rather seedy parts of the city where walking alone at night may feel uncomfortable. However, the dangers are often more imaginary than real and, by simply being alert and taking taxis late at night, you should have no problems.

With almost weekly inflation adjustments, the real **price** of hotels remains pretty much the same throughout the year, but in the quieter summer months (December and January) prices may be lower. Weekend **discounts** are often given, especially at the better hotels that otherwise cater largely to business executives.

Luz

The area around Estação da Luz, the main train station, is mainly one of small downmarket clothes shops, street hawkers and offices – and contains São Paulo's cheapest hotels. At night the area is known as a particularly grim red-light district and, in fact, many of the more obviously disreputable hotels only rent out rooms by the hour. Still, use your head, and finding somewhere to stay around here is easy, with most of the hotels located in the direction of Avenida Ipiranga and Avenida Rio Branco.

Rua das Andradas: *Ofir* (☎223-8822) at no. 258 has good, clean rooms with bathrooms; about $7 for a double.

Rua Aurora: *Santa Teresinha* at no. 205 offers very basic accommodation for about $2 single; the *Copacabana* (☎222-0511) at no. 26 is $7 for a double and an extra $1.50 for a bathroom; *Istria* (☎222-7522), no. 519, is reasonably comfortable, about $7 for a double with bathroom.

Rua do Timbiras: the *Pauliceía* (☎220-9433) has good double rooms for $4, or $6 with a shower; *Plaza Apolo* (☎222-9333) at no. 483 is a large, good value hotel – doubles with bathroom start at about $8.

Rua Santa Ifigénia: *Hotel Luanda* at no. 348 and *Hotel Braga* at no. 493 both have simple, but adequate, double rooms for $3–4 without a shower.

Praça da República

In the traditional centre of São Paulo, there are lots of medium-priced hotels in the streets around Praça da República. Bus and Metro services are excellent from here to all parts of the city. At night the area has a more comfortable feel than around Luz, but there are still a lot of seedy-looking individuals milling around the Praça.

Avenida Ipiranga: *Plaza Marabá* at no. 757 and *Alfa* at no. 1152 are both very comfortable and efficient hotels, charging $15–20 for double rooms; several other hotels of a similar category along this street, too.

Rua Sete de Abril: *São Sebastião* at no. 364 is around $6 for a clean and quiet single room with shower, just moments from the entrance to the Metro.

Rua Dom José de Barros: *Joamar* (☎221-33611), at no. 187, is just a block from República Metro station and is clean and friendly (about $7 for a single with a bathroom); others, too, along here are in the same mould.

Avenida Vieira de Carvalho: *Amazonas* (☎220-4111) at no. 32, virtually on Praça da República itself, is right next to where the buses to both airports stop; very comfortable doubles, with a bathroom, go for about $15.

Rua Augusta

Rua Augusta is best known for the *Cá d'Oro* (at no. 129; ☎256-8011) and *Caesar Park* (at no. 1508; ☎285-6622), two of São Paulo's finest hotels where you won't get a double room for less than $150 a night. However, along and just off this same road are some far more affordable options worth seeking out. The hotels on Rua Augusta are ideally located, midway between the city centre and Avenida Paulista; it's the northern boundary of the more fashionable Jardims, and the area is very safe at night.

Rua Augusta: *Estela* at no. 1047 has basic rooms for around $5 per person; *Augusta Plaza* (☎284-0866) at no. 1255 has dark, but otherwise very comfortable rooms for about $15 double with bathroom. Other hotels along this road are similarly priced.

Rua Peixoto Gomide: the *Alteza* at no. 41, just around the corner from the *Augusta Plaza*, has simple rooms which go for around $7.

Liberdade

As well as great food, Liberdade – São Paulo's Japanese *bairro* – also has a few medium-priced hotels whose guests are mainly Brazilian-Japanese and visiting Japanese businessmen, who are seeking Japanese-style food, baths and cleanliness. Even if you can't afford to stay here, have a Japanese buffet breakfast ($5), at the luxury *Nikkey Palace Hotel* (Rua Galvão Bueno 425).

Rua Galvão Bueno: *Banri* at no. 209 (☎270-8877); a very popular and comfortable hotel with double rooms with a Japanese bath tub for about $16.

Rua dos de Gloria: *Isei* (☎278-6677) at no. 290 provides comfortable, but unrecognisably Japanese, double rooms for $11.

Around the City

For visitors and locals alike, the fact that São Paulo's history extends back for over four centuries, well beyond the late-nineteenth-century coffee boom, usually goes completely unnoticed. Catapulted virtually overnight from being a sleepy, provincial market town into one of the western hemisphere's great cities, there are few places in the world that have totally turned their backs on the past as São Paulo has done. In the nineteenth century, colonial São Paulo was all but levelled and replaced by a disorganised patchwork of wide avenues and large buildings, the process constantly repeating itself since – today, not only has the city's colonial architectual heritage all but vanished, but there's little physical evidence of the coffee boom decades either.

Nevertheless, a few relics have, somehow, escaped demolition and offer hints of São Paulo's bygone eras. But what remains is hidden away discreetly in corners, scattered throughout the city, often difficult to find and less than thrilling when you do. An easy and cheap introduction to São Paulo is to join a **guided tour**, organised by the city's tourist authorities. Travelling by foot, or by bus and Metro, there are ten different routes to choose from, visiting a wide range of sites. They each cost about 50¢, and tours depart on weekends at 9am and 2pm from the Praça da Sé Metro station – full details from the city's various tourist information booths.

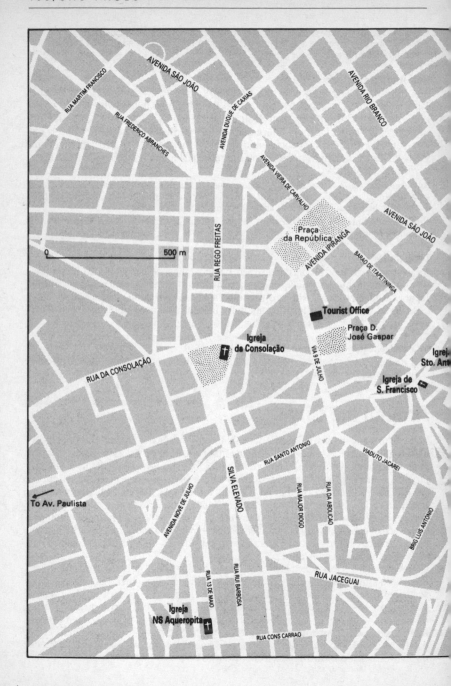

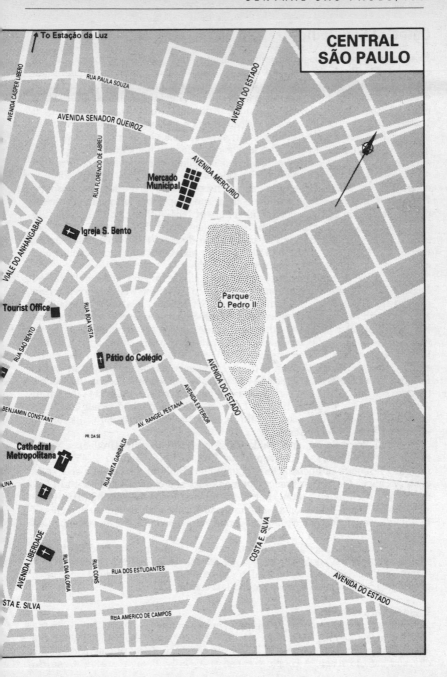

CENTRAL SÃO PAULO

To Estação da Luz

AVENIDA CASPER LIBERO

RUA PAULA SOUZA

AVENIDA SENADOR QUEIROZ

AVENIDA DO ESTADO

RUA FLORENCIO DE ABREU

AVENIDA MERCURIO

Mercado Municipal

VIALE DO ANHANGABAU

Igreja S. Bento

Parque D. Pedro II

Tourist Office

RUA BOA VISTA

RUA SAO BENTO

Pátio do Colégio

AVENIDA DO ESTADO

AVENIDA EXTERIOR

BENJAMIN CONSTANT

AV. RANGEL PESTANA

PR. DA SE

RUA ANITA GARIBALDI

Cathedral Metropolitana

LINA

COSTA E. SILVA

AVENIDA LIBERDADE

RUA DA GLORIA

RUA CONS

RUA DOS ESTUDANTES

AVENIDA DO ESTADO

STA E. SILVA

RUA AMERICO DE CAMPOS

Colonial São Paulo

Praça da Sé is the most convenient starting point for the very brief hunt for **colonial São Paulo**. The square itself is a large expanse of concrete and fountains, dominated by the **Catedral Metropolitana**, a huge neo-Gothic structure with a capacity of 8000 but otherwise unremarkable. Completed in 1954, it replaced São Paulo's eighteenth-century cathedral, which was demolished in 1920. During the day the square outside bustles with activity, always crowded with hawkers and people heading towards the commercial district on its western fringes. At night it's transformed into a campsite for homeless children, who survive as best they can by shining shoes, selling chewing gum or begging. Along Rua Boa Vista, on the opposite side of the square from the cathedral, is where the city of São Paulo originated. The whitewashed Portuguese Baroque **Pátio do Colégio** is a replica of the college and chapel that formed the centre of the Jesuit mission that was first founded here in 1554. Although built in 1896 (the other buildings forming the Pátio were constructed later this century), the chapel is an accurate reproduction, but it's in the **Casa de Anchieta** (Tues–Sun 1–5pm), part of the Pátio, where the most interesting sixteenth- and early-seventeenth-century relics – mostly old documents – are held.

Just a couple of hundred metres from the Pátio do Colégio, at Avenida Rangel Pestana 230, near the intersection with the Praça da Sé, the well-preserved **Igreja do Carmo** (Tues–Fri 7.30–11am & 1–4pm, Sat & Sun 7.30–10am) was built in 1632 and still retains many of its seventeenth-century features, including a fine Baroque high altar. Over the other side of the square, a two-minute walk down Rua Senado Feijó is the **Igreja de São Francisco** (daily 8am–6pm), a typical Portuguese colonial church with some interior wood carvings from the eighteenth century – though the rest of the decoration is of much more recent origin. Before leaving this area, at Praça do Patriarca, by the Viaduto do Chá (the pedestrian bridge linking the two parts of the commercial centre), the **Igreja de Santo Antônio** is worth a glance. Built in 1717, its yellow and white facade has been beautifully restored, but – again – the interior has been stripped of its former eighteenth-century accoutrements.

North of Praça da Sé, at Avenida Tiradentes 676 (by the Tiradentes Metro station), is the **Igreja e Convento da Luz** (daily 8–11am & 2–4.30pm), a rambling structure of uncharacteristic grandeur. Built on the site of a sixteenth-century chapel, the former Franciscan monastery and church dates back to 1774, though it's been much altered over the years and today houses the **Museu de Arte Sacre** (Tues–Sun 1–5pm). The museum's collection includes examples of Brazilian seventeenth- and eighteenth-century wooden and terracotta religious art and liturgical pieces.

A block and a half south of here, on Avenida Tiradentes, the **Jardim da Luz** was São Paulo's first public garden, whose intricate wrought-iron fencing and rich foliage provides evidence of the garden's former grace. Sadly, it's long since been overcome by the general squalor around Luz station.

Bandeirante remains

No houses from the colonial era remain standing in the city centre, but out in the suburbs a few simple, whitewashed adobe **homesteads** from the time of the *bandeirantes* have been preserved. However, they're in fairly remote parts of the city and hard to reach. A couple you can visit easily, though, are the **Casa do**

Bandeirante, Praça Monteiro Lobato, in Butantã (Tues–Fri 10.30am–5pm, Sat & Sun 9am–5pm), a small, typical *Paulista* dwelling containing eighteenth-century farm implements; and the **Casa do Seranista**, Praça Dr. Ênio Barbato 21, in Caxingui (Tues–Sun 10.30am–5pm), a well-preserved eighteenth-century *bandeirante* house with an interesting collection of Indian artefacts.

The rest of the city centre: the coffee era and beyond

The coffee boom that led to the dismantling of São Paulo's colonial buildings provided little in terms of lasting replacements. In the city's first industrial suburbs, towering brick chimneys are still to be seen, but generally the areas are now dominated by small workshops and low-income housing.

Even in the city centre, there are very few buildings of note, most of the area given over to unremarkable shops and offices. To the north of Praça da Sé, at Rua da Cantareira 306, you'll find the **Mercado Municipal** (see under "Shopping"), an imposing, vaguely German neo-Gothic hall, built in 1933. Just across the Viaduto do Chá, in the direction of Praça da República, is the **Teatro Municipal**, São Paulo's most distinguished public building, an eclectic mixture of Art Nouveau and Italian Renaissance styles. Work began on the building in 1903, when the coffee boom was at its peak and São Paulo at its most confident, and the interior reflects that confidence – covered in marble, onyx and bronze and recently renovated. It's still the city's main venue for classical music.

Improved communications and, in particular, the British-owned railway network, did much to stimulate São Paulo's explosive growth in the late nineteenth century. Built in 1901, on the site that had been occupied since 1864 by a much smaller terminal, the **Estação da Luz** was – and remains – the city's main train station. Everything was imported from Britain for its construction, from the design of the project to the smallest of screws, and although the refined decoration of its chambers was destroyed by fire in 1946, interior details – iron balconies, passageways and grilles – bear witness to the majestic structure's original elegance.

When the coffee plantation owners began to take up residence in the city, from about 1870, they built their lavish **mansions** from British iron, Italian marble, Latvian pine, Portuguese tiles and Belgian stained glass. However, no sooner than they were built, the central mansions were abandoned, as the city centre took on a brash and commercial character, and the coffee barons moved to new homes in the Higienópolis district, a short distance west of Praça da República. The central mansions were all knocked down, but a few remain in Higienópolis, the Art Nouveau influenced **Vila Penteado**, on Rua Maranhão, a fine example and one of the last to be built in the area.

Avenida Paulista and the Triángulo

By 1900, the coffee barons had moved on again, flaunting their wealth from their new mansions, set in spacious gardens stretching along the three-kilometre-long **Avenida Paulista** – then a tree-lined avenue set along a ridge three kilometres southwest of the city centre. In the late 1960s, and throughout the 1970s, Avenida Paulista resembled a giant building site, with banks and other companies competing to build ever taller buildings. There was little time for creativity, and along the entire length of the avenue it would be difficult to single out one example of decent modern architecture. There are, however, about a dozen Art Nouveau or

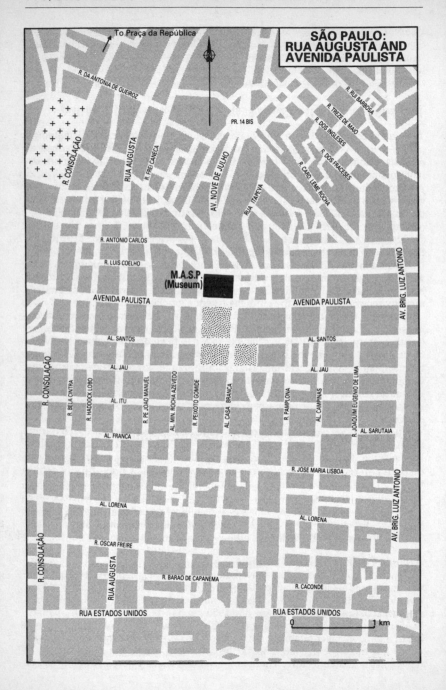

To Praça da República

**SÃO PAULO:
RUA AUGUSTA AND
AVENIDA PAULISTA**

R. DA ANTONIA DE QUEIROZ

R. RUI BARBOSA

R. TREZE DE MAIO

R. DOS INGLESES

PR. 14 BIS

R. DOS FRACESES

R. CARD. LEME ROCHA

R. CONSOLAÇÃO

RUA AUGUSTA

R. FREI CANECA

AV. NOVE DE JULHO

RUA ITAPEVA

R. ANTONIO CARLOS

R. LUIS COELHO

M.A.S.P.
(Museum)

AVENIDA PAULISTA

AVENIDA PAULISTA

AV. BRIG. LUIZ ANTONIO

AL. SANTOS

AL. SANTOS

R. CONSOLAÇÃO

AL. JAU

AL. JAU

R. BELA CINTRA

R. HADDOCK LOBO

R. PE JOÃO MANUEL

AL. MIN. ROCHA AZEVEDO

R. PEIXOTO GOMIDE

AL. CASA BRANCA

R. PAMPLONA

AL. CAMPINAS

R. JOAQUIM EUGENIO DE LIMA

AL. ITU

AL. SARUTAIA

AL. FRANCA

R. JOSE MARIA LISBOA

AL. LORENA

AL. LORENA

AV. BRIG. LUIZ ANTONIO

R. CONSOLAÇÃO

R. OSCAR FREIRE

RUA AUGUSTA

R. BARAO DE CAPANEMA

R. CACONDE

RUA ESTADOS UNIDOS

RUA ESTADOS UNIDOS

0   1 km

Art Deco mansions along Avenida Paulista, afforded official protection from the developers' bulldozers. Some lie empty, the subjects of legal wrangles over inheritance rights, while others have been turned into branches of *McDonalds* or prestigious headquarters for banks.

At the northern edge of the **Triángulo**, the traditional banking district and a zone of concentrated vertical growth, there's the thirty-storey **Edifício Martinelli** (at Avenida São João), the city's first skyscraper. Modelled on the Empire State Building, Martinelli was inaugurated in 1929 and remains an important landmark, only dwarfed by Latin America's tallest office building, the 42-storey **Edifício Itália**, built in 1965 on Avenida São Luís. With little of the majesty of most skyscrapers in New York, the Itália towers above the city centre's newer commercial district and, on cloud- and smog-free days, the building is a good vantage point from which to view the city. In the 1940s and 1950s **Avenida São Luís** itself was São Paulo's version of Fifth Avenue, lined with high-class apartment blocks and offices and, though no longer fashionable, it still retains a certain degree of elegance.

Cerqueira César and the Jardims

Avenida Paulista marks the northeastern boundary of **Cerqueira César**, and beyond that are the **Jardims**, laid out in 1915 and styled after the British idea of the garden suburb. From the city centre, Rua Augusta crosses Avenida Paulista, and passes through the middle of Cerqueira César, joining with Rua Colômbia and – dividing Jardim América and Jardim Paulista – Avenida Europa and Avenida Cidade Jardim. Cerqueira César largely consists of apartment buildings for the city's upper middle class, while the Jardims themselves are dominated by luxury houses – protected from Third World realities by high walls, complex alarm systems, guards and fierce dogs. These exclusive residential neighbourhoods have long since taken over from the city centre as the location of most of the city's best restaurants and shopping streets, and many residents never stray from their luxurious ghettos.

Immigration and São Paulo: the outer bairros

São Paulo is a city built on **immigrants**: largely due to immigration, São Paulo's population grew one hundred fold in 75 years to become the country's second largest city by 1950. Besides sheer numbers, the mass influx of people had a tremendous impact on the character of the city, breaking up the existing social stratification and removing economic and political power from the traditionally elite groups at a much earlier stage than in other Brazilian cities. And with many *bairros* associated with particular ethnic groups, the city also has considerable life. There are several sights within the city associated with immigration, worth basing a short tour around, but best of all is simply to visit the *bairros* where the immigrants and their descendants have established communities: the food, as you'd expect, is just one reason to do this.

The Hospedaria dos Imigrantes

Although there had been attempts at introducing Prussian share-croppers in the 1840s, mass immigration didn't begin until the late 1870s. Initially, conditions were appalling for the immigrants, many of whom succumbed to malaria or yellow fever while waiting in Santos to be transferred inland to the plantations. In response to criticisms, the government opened the **Hospedaria dos Imigrantes** (Rua Visconde de Parnaíba 1316, near Brás Metro station) in 1887, a hostel in the eastern suburb of Brás. Now partly used as a museum (Tues–Sun 1–5pm), containing period furniture, documents and photographs, the building is an imposing structure – one which had its own railway siding and platform for unloading immigrants and their baggage. Originally, the ground floor was occupied by offices, a hospital, currency exchange, kitchens and dining halls, while the dormitories were on the upper floor. Near the entrance, a separate building contained the rooms where new arrivals met their prospective employers, the government providing interpreters to help the immigrants make sense of work contracts. Designed to hold 4000 people, the hostel housed as many as 10,000 at times, the immigrants treated little better than cattle. In its early years, it was a virtual prison: the exit ticket was securing a contract of employment. Control was considered necessary since few immigrants actually wanted to work in the plantations, and there was a large labour leakage to the city of São Paulo itself.

Bixiga and the Italians

Immigration to São Paulo is most closely associated with the **Italians**, who constituted 46 percent of all arrivals between 1887 and 1930. In general, soon after arrival in Brazil they would be transported to a plantation, but most slipped away within a year to seek employment in the city or move on south to Argentina. The rapidly expanding factories in the districts of Brás, Mooca and Belém, to the east of the city centre, were desperately short of labour, and well into the twentieth century the population of these *bairros* was largely Italian. But it is **Bixiga** (or, officially, Bela Vista) where the Italian influence has been most enduring. Originally home to freed slaves, by the early twentieth century Bixiga had established itself as São Paulo's "Little Italy". Calabrian stonemasons built their own homes with leftover materials from the building sites where they were employed, and the narrow streets are still lined with such houses. In an otherwise ordinary house at Rua dos Ingleses 18, the **Museu Memória do Bixiga** (Wed–Sun 3–6pm) enthusiastically documents the history of the *bairro*, and there's a small collection of photographs and household items. You'll find Italian **restaurants** throughout the city, but the area of greatest concentration is Bixiga. The central Rua 13 de Março, and the streets running off it, are lined with cantinas, pizzerias and bars, and at night this normally quiet neighbourhood springs to life (see "Eating" for restaurant listings).

As immigration from Italy began to slow in the late 1890s, arrivals from other countries increased. From 1901 to 1930 **Spaniards** (especially Galicians) made up 22 percent, and **Portuguese** 23 percent, of immigrants, but their language allowed them to assimilate extremely quickly. Only Tatuapé developed into a largely Portuguese *bairro*.

Liberdade: the Japanese

The first 830 **Japanese** immigrants arrived in Santos in 1908 from where they were sent on to the coffee plantations. By the mid-1950s a quarter of a million Japanese had emigrated to Brazil, most of them settling in the State of São Paulo, and unlike most other nationalities, the rate of return migration among them has always been small: many chose to remain in agriculture, often as market gardeners, at the end of their contract. The city's large Japanese community is centred on **Liberdade**, a *bairro* just south of the Praça da Sé. Rua Galvão Bueno and intersecting streets are largely devoted to Japanese restaurants and shops selling semi-precious stones, Japanese food and clothes. The **Museu Histórica da Imigração Japonesa** (Wed–Sun 2–6pm), at Rua São Joaquim 381, has excellent displays on the contribution of the Japanese community to Brazil since their first years on the coffee plantations.

The Arabs

São Paulo's **Arab** community is quite substantial. Commonly associated with petty commerce, Arabs started arriving in the early twentieth century from Syria and the Lebanon and, as they were then travelling on Turkish passports, they're still usually referred to as *turcos*. Family ties remain strong and, with the civil war in the Lebanon, the community has been considerably enlarged. Many of the boutiques in the city's wealthy *bairros* are Arab-owned, but it's in the streets **around Rua 25 de Março**, north of Praça da Sé, where the community is concentrated. At Rua Comandante Abdo Schahin 40, the *Empório Syrio* sells Arab delicacies, and on the same road there are some excellent Arab **restaurants**, always full with local merchants. The community is fairly evenly divided between Muslims and Christians, and hidden away at Rua Cavalheiro Basilio Jafet 15 there's a beautiful **Orthodox church**.

Bom Retiro: the Jews and Koreans

Like the Arabs, the **Jewish** community has prospered in São Paulo. Mainly of east European origin, many of the city's Jews started out as itinerant pedlars before concentrating in **Bom Retiro**, a *bairro* near Luz train station. As they became richer, they moved to the suburbs to the south of the city, but some of the shops in the streets around Rua Correia de Melo are still Jewish-owned: there are some good Jewish **restaurants**, a community centre and a synagogue. As the Jews move out, **Koreans** – São Paulo's latest immigrant arrivals – move in. Bom Retiro has become the main location for Korean-owned businesses, mainly shops selling cheap clothes.

São Paulo's other museums

São Paulo certainly has no shortage of museums. Some have already been covered in the text, but the rest – with only a few exceptions – are disappointing for a city of São Paulo's importance. Collections have frequently been allowed to deteriorate and exhibits are generally poorly displayed. Nevertheless, you might find something of interest somewhere in the city, and the list below picks out some of the best – and worst – choices.

Art

Museu de Arte de Contemporânia.
Parque do Ibirapuera, Pavilhão da Bienal and Rua da Reitaria 109 (Universidade de São Paulo); Tues–Sun noon–5pm.
Based on two sites, the museum regularly alters its displays, drawing upon its huge collection. Though it holds work by important European artists, such as Picasso, Modigliani, Léger and Chagall, and Brazilians that include Tarsila do Amaral, Di Cavalcanti and Portinari, the pieces that are selected for exhibition can be disappointing.

Museu de Arte de São Paulo (MASP).
Avenida Paulista 1578, Cerqueira César; Tues–Fri 1–5pm, Sat & Sun 2–6pm.
Museu de Arte de São Paulo is considered to be the most important museum of Western art in Latin America and is the great pride of São Paulo's art lovers. While there's a fine collection of work of great European artists from the last five hundred years, very little space is devoted to Brazilian and other Latin American artists. MASP is one of Brazil's few museums that regularly receives important visiting exhibitions; and the museum's excellent restaurant is open for lunch and afternoon tea.

Fundação Maria Luíza e Oscar Americano.
Avenida Morumbi 3700, Morumbi; Tues–Sun 10am–5pm.
Opposite the Palácio dos Bandeirantes (the seat of the State government), the museum features a collection of items that belonged to the Brazilian Royal Family, most important of which are the landscapes of Franz Post. There's also a small collection of twentieth-century Brazilian art that includes Segall, Di Cavalcanti and Portinari. Excellent afternoon teas are served here, too!

Museu de Arte Moderna.
Parque do Ibirapuera; Tues–Fri 1–7pm, Sat–Sun 11am–7pm.
A collection of third-rate modern Brazilian painting, sculpture and design.

Museu Lasar Segall.
Rua Afonso Celso 388, Vila Mariana; Tues–Thurs & Sun 2.30–6.30pm, Fri & Sat 2.30–8pm.
As most of Lasar Segall's work is contained in this museum, the Latvian-born naturalised-Brazilian painter is relatively little known outside Brazil. Having participated in the German expressionist movement at the beginning of the century, Segall's later work was influenced by the colours of his adopted homeland.

Pinacoteca do Estado.
Avenida Tiradentes 141, Luz; Tues–Sun 2–6pm.
The State of São Paulo gallery, containing an extensive and important collection of late-nineteenth- and twentieth-century Brazilian art.

History, anthropology and natural science
Museu da Casa Brasileira.
Avenida Brigadeiro Faria Lima 774, Jardim Paulistano; Tues–Sun 1–5pm.
The museum contains exhibits of Brazilian clothing and household decoration from the sixteenth century onwards.

Museu Militar.
Rua Jorge Miranda 308, Luz; Tues–Fri 7am–6pm.
The exhibits comprise arms, trophies, medals, photographs and other documents that relate to the Brazilian army's role in the Paraguayan War, World War II and the revolutions of 1924 and 1932. The military's often brutal record in government after the 1964 "revolution" is, hardly surprisingly, completely ignored.

Museu Paulista (Museu do Ipiranga).
Parque da Independência, Ipiranga; Tues–Sun 9.30am–5pm.
Articles relating to Brazil's nineteenth-century struggles for independence and Repúblicanism are the central exhibits of this particularly lifeless museum.

Museu de Folclore.
Parque do Ibirapuera; Tues–Sun 2–5pm.
An extremely cramped collection of musical instruments, household appliances, handicrafts and exhibits relating to such themes as traditional medicine.

Museu da Imagem e do Som.
Avenida Europa 158, Jardim Europa; Tues–Sun 2–10pm.
Purporting to "gauge the values of man and Brazilian society", the museum's largely temporary exhibitions use photographs, film and sound sources to illustrate the dynamics of social change.

Instituto Butantã.
Avenida Vital Brasil 1500, Butantã; Mon 1–5pm, Tues–Sun 9am–5pm.
Founded in 1901, the Institute is one of the world's foremost research centres for the study of venomous snakes and insects and the development of anti-venom serums. There's a museum that documents the history of the Institute's work, but most interesting are the huge snake pits, where dozens of species are visible, and the rooms containing spiders and scorpions.

Shopping

São Paulo's **shopping** possibilities are as varied as the city's restaurants and, for *Paulistanos* with the means, as important an activity. In the wealthy southwestern suburbs of Cerqueira César and the Jardims, shops are far more impressive than those in just about any other Brazilian city, and the quality way above par. Even if you can't afford to buy in them, the shopping centres and shops are worth a tour, if only to take in the opulent surroundings. And there's a fine selection of **markets**, too, where you can pick up a decently priced souvenir or two and some good food.

Shopping Centres
The rich victors of the Brazilian economic "miracle" wander São Paulo's shopping centres – air-conditioned temples to hedonism – able to feel utterly insulated from their less fortunate fellow citizens. Each centre tries to outdo the other, with mirrored walls, water fountains and ice-skating rinks, and you won't feel closer to North America than this during your stay in Brazil.

Eldorado, Avenida Rebouças 3970, Pinheiros; Mon–Fri 9am–10pm, Sat 9am–7.30pm (bus #702P from Praça da República).

Ibirapuera, Avenida Ibirapuera 3103, Moema; Mon–Sat 9am–10pm (bus #675C from Metro Ana Rosa, or #696A from Praça da República).

Iguatemi, Avenida Brigadeiro Faria Lima 1191, Jardim Europa; Mon–Fri 9am–10pm, Sat 9am–7pm (bus #702P from Avenida Ipiranga).

Morumbi, Avenida Roque Petroni Jr. 1089, Morumbi (bus #675C from Metro Ana Rosa).

Downtown shopping

The main shopping streets in the centre of the city are near **Praça da República**, especially the roads running off Avenida Ipiranga: Rua Barão de Itapetinga, Rua 24 de Maio, Rua Sete de Setembro and, between them, Rua Dom José de Barros. Most of the shops around here sell clothes, but you'll rarely find the latest fashions.

Cerqueira César and the Jardims

This is where the money is, and where all the best shops are. There are lots of trendy boutiques selling clothes and, compared to European or North American prices, they can be excellent value. Rua Augusta, Avenida Europa and Avenida Cidade Jardim, and the streets running parallel and off them, are where you'll find most of the shops. There are no obvious "souvenirs" of São Paulo, but the following places are worth checking out for unusual Brazilian items:

Ana (*Arte Nativa Aplicada*), Rua Mário Ferraz 339, Jardim Paulista. High quality cotton and wool fabrics, and scarfs printed with Indian motifs.

Arte-India (*Funai*), Rua Augusta 1371. Basketwork and feather handicrafts made by Indians.

Confraria dos Entusiastas do Vinho, Avenida Cidade Jardim 790, Cidade Jardim. A large stock of fine Brazilian wines, normally difficult to find in Brazil, let alone abroad.

O Bode, Rua Bela Cintra 2009, Cerqueira César. Carefully selected handicrafts from throughout Brazil, including items from the State of São Paulo.

Markets

Lots of choice here, from handicrafts to flowers, and one – the Mercado Municipal – that ranks as one of the best markets in Brazil.

Comunitária de Trocas do Bixiga, Praça Dom Orioni, Bixiga (Sun 10am–4pm). A flea market with little worth purchasing, but lots of atmosphere.

Mercado Municipal, Rua da Cantareira 306, Centro (Mon–Sat 5am–4pm). About the most fantastic array of fruit, vegetables and fish that you're likely to find anywhere in Brazil.

Feira de Arte e Artesanato, Praça da República, Centro (Sun 8am–1pm). Handicrafts from throughout Brazil, semi-precious gems and spicy food from the Northeast.

Feira Oriental, Praça da Liberdade, Liberdade (Sun 2–6pm). Japanese-Brazilian handicrafts and Japanese food.

Feira de Antiguidades, Museu de Arte de São Paulo (MASP), Avenida Paulista 1578 (Sun 10am–5.30pm). A fun place to browse, but don't expect much worth buying.

Mercado de Flores, Largo de Arouche, Centro. A dazzling, daily display of flowers.

Eating

Eating out is an important pastime for middle- and upper-class *Paulistanos*. The vast number of **restaurants** in the city is a source of great pride; people like to claim that São Paulo's range of restaurants is second only to New York's. Certainly, it would take years to exploit all of the city's eating options, but while dining out can be one of the great joys of São Paulo the experience can also be disappointing. Except for Arab and Japanese communities, overseas contacts are few, and the city's "ethnic" restaurants have moved further and further away from the original recipes that they model their dishes on. Nevertheless, by avoiding comparisons, even food in these places can be excellent.

As for the **cost** of a meal, you can get away with paying just a couple of dollars for a standard dish of rice, beans and meat at a small, side-street restaurant. Even at the most elegant of restaurants in the wealthiest neighbourhoods, you'll be very hard-pressed to pay more than $30 per person. All of São Paulo's restaurants are concentrated where the money is, in the city centre and in the middle- and upper-class suburbs of the city's southwest. The listings below are arranged alphabetically and, though it's impossible to be comprehensive, they do give an idea as to the range of available options.

Fast food, snacks, coffee and ice cream

Paulistanos are reputed to be always in a hurry and on just about every block there's somewhere serving **fast food**. *Lanchonetes* do snacks and cheap, light meals and – in direct competition – *McDonalds* are opening at a frightening rate. Claiming to have invented the traditional *Bauru* sandwich (made with roast beef, salad and melted cheese) is the *Ponto Chic* at Largo do Paissandu 27 (Centro), while **sandwich bars** popular with a younger crowd include the *Frevo*, Rua Oscar Freire 603 (Cerqueira César), and the *Companhia Paulista de Sanduíches* at Rua Prof. Arthur Ramos 395 (Jardim Europa). There are plenty of **pizzerias**, with the *Margherita*, at Alameda Tietê 255 (Cerqueira César), and the *Marco Polo*, Rua Franz Schubert 35 (Jardim Europa), both well-recommended.

Oddly, for a city built on immigrants and coffee, São Paulo has no **café** tradition. **Coffee**, though, is drunk endlessly in the form of *cafézinhos* (small cups of strong, black coffee). It's not usually lingered over, but if you want to take your time look out for somewhere with an *espresso* machine. One place where coffee is at its very best is *Café Floresta*, in the Edifício Copan shopping mall.

There are a few good **tearooms**; *Jasmin*, at Rua Haddock Lobo 932 (Cerqueira César), is especially inviting. At *As Noviças*, Avenida Cotovia 205 (Moema), waitresses dressed as nuns serve teas against a background of religious music.

La Basque at Alameda 1444 (Cerqueira César) sells excellent quality **ice cream**. Other places with a large choice of flavours, as well as other delicious desserts, include *Alaska*, at Rua Dr. Rafael de Barros 70 (Paraíso), and *Swenson's*, Rua Padre João Manoel 1249 (Cerqueira César).

Arab

In Brazil, "Arab" restaurants serve Lebanese or Syrian food, typically a large variety of small dishes of stuffed vegetables, salads, pastries, pulses, minced meat, spicy sausages and chicken. In general, Arab restaurants in São Paulo are extremely reliable and excellent value.

Al Kaukab, Rua Com. Abdo Schahin 130, Centro. A meeting point for the local Arab community, the food's excellent and cheap, the atmosphere always lively.

Almanara, Rua Oscar Freire 523, Cerqueira César. Medium-priced, the good fixed-priced lunch menu is worth investigating.

Arabe, Rua Com. Abdo Schahin 102, Centro. Crowded at lunchtime with Lebanese diners, for the rest of the day the restaurant is a focus for dawdling, elderly Arabs; fine, cheap food.

Au Liban, Rua Jerónimo da Veiga 30, Itaim Bibi. Near Jardim Paulista, this is quite an expensive choice, but the menu is more sophisticated and varied than is typical.

El Tarbuch, Rua Com. Abdo Schahin 144, Centro. Another restaurant and café serving the Lebanese community; good food, huge portions and lots of local colour.

Brazilian

Apart from *lanchonetes* and *churrascarias* (see below), Brazilian food is surprisingly hard to come by in São Paulo. This may be because of the immigrant origins of so many of the city's inhabitants, or simply because Brazilian food is for the home, not for occasions when you go out to eat. Still, the selection below should prove good enough for most tastes.

Bolinha, Avenida Cidade Jardim 53, Jardim Europa. Moderately priced Brazilian food; the restaurant is especially noted for its *feijoadas*.

O Profeta, Alameda dos Aicás 40, Indianópolis. Authentic dishes from Minas Gerais.

Tia Carly, Alameda Ribeirão Preto 492, Bela Vista (closed Sun dinner). Excellent, cheap "home cooking" with *feijoadas* served on Wednesday and Saturday.

Ver-o-Peso, Alameda Nhambiquaras 1360, Moema (closed Mon). Interesting and inexpensive Amazonian and Northeastern food and drinks.

Churrascos
Beef in a bewildering variety of cuts is the centre of any **churrasco**, or barbecue, but lamb, chicken and pork are also usually served.

Baby-Beef Rubaiyat, Avenida Viera de Carvalho 116, Centro. A popular *churrascaria* with businessmen, but the meat – especially the baby beef – is very good and not excessively priced.

Bar das Putas, Rua da Consolação (near the intersection with Rua Maceió), Consolação. Fantastic steaks at unbelievably low prices.

Bassi, Rua 13 de Maio 334, Bixiga. Expensive without being extortionate, you're unlikely to find better meat in São Paulo.

Costela de Ripa, Rua João Cachoeira 298, Itaim Bibi (lunch only on Sun). Beef ribs are the speciality of this unpretentious and reasonably priced *churrascaria*.

Dinho's Place, Alameda Santos 45, Paraíso. One of the city's oldest *churrascarias*, distinctive because of its Wednesday and Saturday *feijoada* buffets, where the ingredients are cooked and served separately; reasonably priced.

Galeto's, Alameda Santos 1112, Cerqueira César. Cheap – something that's reflected in the quality of the meat.

The Place, Rua Haddock Lobo 1550, Cerqueria César. Come here to mingle with the trendy, rich and famous at the bar rather than for the food.

Rodeio, Rua Haddock Lobo 1498, Cerqueira César. No longer as fashionable as it was, but still expensive and good.

French

There are several excellent, but expensive French restaurants in São Paulo. Expect to pay at least $20 a head, and possibly even double that amount.

L'Arnaque, Rua Oscar Freire 518, Cerqueira César. Interesting, but not always successful, French-Brazilian nouvelle cuisine. Pleasant surroundings attract a trendy clientele; the fixed-priced menu is good value, but still not for the budget conscious.

La Casserole, Largo do Arouche 346, Centro (closed Sat lunch and Mon). An old favourite for a romantic evening out and always reliable – though expensive – food.

Le Coq Hardy, Avenida Adolfo Pinheiro 2518, Alto da Boa Vista (closed Mon). Arguably São's Paulo's best traditional French restaurant, and almost certainly its most expensive.

Roanne, Rua Henrique Martins 631, Jardim Paulista (closed Sat lunch and Sun). Nouvelle cuisine of a high standard. The daily changing "menu confiance" helps to limit the damage to your wallet in this relaxed, yet sophisticated restaurant.

German

German restaurants in São Paulo – in fact throughout Brazil – are unimaginative in their range of dishes, with menus usually based on pork, potatoes and sauerkraut. But you'll eat heartily for $3–4 a meal.

Juca Alemão, Rua Min. José Galotti 134, Brooklin Paulista. "Typical" plain German food of the kind Brazilians go for. Cheap, with a following of mainly young people.

Miguel, Avenida Moema 684, Moema. Cheap but run-of-the-mill food, served with excellent *chopp*.

Alt Nürnberg, Avenida João Carlos da Silva Borges 543, Santo Amaro (closed Sat lunch and Sun). São Paulo's swankiest German restaurant, the menu's still pork based, but there's a wide range of accompanying dishes. Expect to pay up to about $10 per person.

International

Restaurants that claim to have "international" menus are often best avoided, since the dishes tend to be characterless and expensive. However, in São Paulo this is not completely true: there are some attempts at creativity, though most places are still pricey and rather formal.

Manhattan, Rua Bela Cintra 2238, Cerqueira César. A friendly atmosphere, superb Brazilian cocktails, fresh oysters, steak tartar and crêpes attract the trendy set, who can afford the (roughly) $10 a head price tag.

Os Monges, Rua Tuim 1041, Indianópolis (closed Sun). With a dark and gloomy atmosphere, this medium-priced restaurant is designed to look like a monastery: religious music and waiters dressed as monks! The dishes have names like "the seven capital sins", but don't expect too much.

Paddock Jardins, Avenida Brigadeiro Faria Lima 1541, Jardim Paulistano (closed Sun). An expensive and elegant place that combines Brazilian and foreign recipes – to good effect.

Italian

With so many immigrants from Italy, it's hardly surprising that the city has a huge number of Italian restaurants, ranging from family-run *cantinas* and pizzerias to elegant, expensive establishments. São Paulo's Italian restaurateurs are the children or grandchildren of immigrants, and have adapted recipes to suit Brazilian tastes and the availability of ingredients. For a fun night out, head for Bixiga, São Paulo's "Little Italy", where there are countless inexpensive restaurants.

Capuano, Rua Conselheiro Carrão 414, Bixiga (closed Sun night and Mon). One of the oldest trattorias in Bixiga, where simple Italian cooking is produced in a lively environment.

Famiglia Mancini, Rua Avanhandava 81, Centro. The food's not that great but the atmosphere is, especially late at night when it's crowded with young people.

Gigetto, Rua Avanhandava 63, Centro. Just off Rua Augusta on a road where there are several other Italian restaurants, this one is always crowded with lively Brazilian families. The food's excellent and very inexpensive.

Jardim de Napoli, Rua Dr. Martinico Prado 463, Higienópolis (closed Mon). A simple *cantina* where some of São Paulo's best Italian food is served at astonishingly low prices.

La Locandeira, Rua Dr Mário Ferraz 465, Itaim Bibi (lunch only). Fine pasta dishes in this modestly priced restaurant, sited in one of the city's most exclusive shopping districts.

L'Osteria do Piero, Alameda Franca 1509, Cerqueira César (evenings only; closed Sun). Huge portions of fairly authentic food at low prices.

Roperto, Rua 13 de Maio 634, Bixiga. A *cantina* serving northern Italian dishes.

Japanese

With the largest Japanese community outside Japan, São Paulo has many excellent Japanese restaurants that serve food as good as that in Japan itself. Where Brazilian-Japanese food does differ is in the emphasis placed on meat and fish; you get much more of both all round in Brazil. Make for Liberdade, São Paulo's "Japanese quarter", where restaurants and sushi bars (serving raw fish) are all about. The three restaurants listed below are recommended wholeheartedly.

Sushi-Yassu, Rua Tomás Gonzaga 110 A, Liberdade (closed Mon). Excellent sushi and other fish dishes, but not cheap (about $8 a person).

Tanji, Rua dos Estudantes 166, Liberdade (evenings only; closed Wed). Specialising in sushi, the quality of the food depends on the owner's general mood.

Yamaga, Rua Thomaz Gonzaga 66, Liberdade. Small and mainly attracting Japanese diners, an excellent meal here will cost around $4 a head.

Jewish

Few members of São Paulo's sizeable Jewish community have opened restaurants, and fewer still have opened Jewish restaurants. The ones that do exist, though, are very cheap and – with only one exception – all are in the Jewish district of Bom Retiro. Expect heavy eastern European dishes that are rather unsuited to the tropics. Recommended are:

Cecília, Rua Amazonas 63, Bom Retiro (lunch only; closed Mon). A small, neighbourhood restaurant.

Europa, Rua Correia de Mello 56, Bom Retiro. A simple restaurant with an extensive menu and extremely good food.

Sara, Rua da Graça 32, Bom Retiro (Mon–Fri 11am–7pm, Sat & Sun 11am–3pm). Busy café/snack bar.

Z-Deli, Alameda Lorena 1214, Cerqueira César (Mon–Fri 9am–7pm, Sat 9am–3pm). Trendy people who live or work in the neighbourhood come to this small restaurant, modelled on a New York gourmet deli.

Miscellaneous: Seafood, Eastern, Far Eastern and European

There's a mixed bunch of other restaurants in São Paulo, some of the best detailed below, including a couple that are something of a novelty for Brazil. Seafood is usually good, too, as – little more than an hour from the coast – São Paulo can always count on extremely fresh fish. All of the city's seafood restaurants are expensive, but worth trying if you're not on a tight budget.

Chamonix, Rua Pamplona 4146, Jardim Paulista (evenings only; closed Mon and last Sun of month). São Paulo's best fondue restaurant – don't expect genuine Swiss quality, but be prepared for genuine Swiss prices.

China Massas Caseiras, Rua Mourato Coelho 140, Pinheiros. Huge quantities of extremely cheap Chinese-style food, served in a lively atmosphere.

Genghis Khan, Avenida Rebouças 3241, Pinheiros. Medium priced but unexciting Chinese food.

Govinda, Rua Princesa Isabel 379, Brooklin Paulista (closed Sun). São Paulo's only Indian restaurant, dishes are tempered to suit unfamiliar Brazilian tastebuds. Very expensive, the restaurant isn't worth going to for the food but for the lavish decoration.

Hungaria, Alameda Joaquim Eugênio de Lima 766, Cerqueira César (closed Sat lunch and Sun). Expensive stews and Hungarian food at its least interesting.

Korea House, Rua Galvão Bueno 43, Liberdade. One of the very few Korean restaurants in the city despite the large Korean community. Many dishes are prepared at the table, and the often spicy meals are very different to Chinese or Japanese cooking. Around $4 per person.

La Trainera, Avenida Brigadeiro. Faria Lima 511, Jardim Paulistano. The best seafood in the city – and perhaps the most expensive.

Vivenda do Camarão, Rua Groenlândia 513, Ibim Bibi. Wonderful prawn dishes at moderate prices.

Portuguese

There are very few Portuguese restaurants in São Paulo, and you pay for what you get: if it's cheap, it tends not to be very good.

Abril em Portugal, Rua Caio Prado 47, Centro (evenings only; closed Sun). One of the better known of the city's Portuguese restaurants, but the food doesn't warrant its reputation. Live *fado* music, though, and moderate prices.

Marquês de Mariaval, Rua Haddock Lobo 1583, Cerqueira César (closed Mon). Excellent food, but uncomfortably formal and very expensive – around $25 per person.

O Rei do Bacalhau, Avenida Brigadeiro Faria Lima 2174, Pinheiros (closed Mon). Specialising in cod dishes, expect to pay about $10 per person.

Presidente, Rua Visconde de Parnaíba 2424, Brás (closes daily at 9.30pm and all day Sun; Sat lunch only). Very good food, reasonably priced and in an area which once had a large Portuguese community.

Vegetarian

There's nowhere easier in Brazil to be vegetarian than in São Paulo: barring *churrascarias*, most restaurants offer non-meat dishes. The following, specifically vegetarian restaurants are very inexpensive, and have unusually varied menus extending well beyond brown rice and beans.

Cheiro Verde, Rua Peixoto Gomide 1413, Cerqueira César.

Da Fiorella, Rua Bernardino de Campos 294, Brooklin Paulista (closed Sun evening and Mon).

Mel, Rua Araújo 75, Centro (Mon–Fri lunch only) and Avenida Brigadeiro Faria Lima 1138, Jardim Europa (Mon–Fri lunch only).

Bars, nightlife and entertainment

Whether you're after "high culture", live music, a disco or just a bar to hang out in, you won't have much of a problem in São Paulo. Some ideas are detailed below but for the full picture of **what's on** and where, consult the supplement in the São Paulo edition of the weekly magazine *Veja,* or the daily newspaper *Folha de São Paulo,* which lists cultural and sporting events.

Bars

The bars that you'll find scattered throughout the city depend largely upon the neighbourhoods that they're in for their character. Some of the liveliest, a few with live music, are found around Rua 13 de Maio in Bixiga (Bela Vista), and in the fashionable Jardims neighbourhood. The following bars are all recommended.

Bar Brahma, corner of Avenida São João and Avenida Ipiranga, Centro. Cheap beer in one of the city's oldest bars.

Café do Bixiga, Rua 13 de Maio 76, Bela Vista. Excellent *chopp* and a carefully nurtured Bohemian atmosphere.

Clydes, Rua da Mata 70, Itaim. Young, wealthy, beautiful people preen to the accompaniment of jazz and country music.

Ferros Bar, Avenida Radial Leste-Oeste, near Praça Franklin Roosevelt. Especially popular with gay women.

Finnegan's Pub, Alameda Itú 1541, Cerqueria César. Very friendly and busy late into the evening.

Ritz, Alameda Franca 1088, Cerqueira César. During the day a quiet restaurant serving hamburgers and sandwiches, at night as a bar it becomes a popular spot for young people, many of whom are gay.

Live music and dancing

São Paulo has quite an imaginative **jazz** tradition, with *Opus 2004* (closed Mon) at Rua Consolação 2004 (in Consolação) having a consistently good programme. Also in Consolação, the *Saint Germain* (closed Mon) at Rua Frei Caneca 304, has a well-earned reputation. In Bixiga, the *Café Piu-Piu* (closed Mon), at Rua 13 de Maio 134, is a lively venue for some very good jazz and *choro* – as well as the most appalling rock and Country & Western music.

If it's more obviously **Brazilian music** that you're seeking, check the newspaper entertainment listings for touring artists or, if feeling slightly adventurous, go to a **gafieira**, a dance hall that's the meeting place of working-class and Bohemian chic. A *gafieira* that's always packed to the rafters with migrants from the Northeast dancing to *forró* is *Pedro Sertanejo*, Rua Catumbi 183, Brás (Sat 9pm–4am, Sun 8pm–midnight). The *Som de Cristal* at Rua Rego Freitas 470 (Centro) is a good place to discover how the *lambada* should really be danced. Regular performances of Brazilian folk, popular and New Wave music are given at the *Centro Cultural de São Paulo*, at Rua Vergueiro 1000 (by the Vergueiro Metro station), and are either free or charge only a modest admission fee. If you're around, one of the most enjoyable outings is to the *Clube do Choro*, held on Saturday and Sunday nights in Jardim América (at Rua João Moura, between Rua Artur Azevedo and Rua Teodoro Sampaio): the street is closed off, a stage erected and tables and chairs put out so that you can sit and listen to some excellent music. There's a small cover charge and food and drink is available, too.

Discos

Many of São Paulo's **discos** cater exclusively to teenagers. However, if you feel comfortable among well-heeled yuppies try the *Roof* at Avenida Cidade Jardim 400 (Jardim Europa), vulgar but compensated for by its magnificent views across the city. At Rua Consolação 3247 (Cerqueira César), *Woodstock* offers live rock music and a very good dancefloor. The *Cais*, downtown at Praça Franklin Roosevelt 134, has a far broader mix of dancers participating in its well-cultivated Acid House image.

Cinema, theatre and classical music

Check the entertainment listings in *Veja* or the *Folha de São Paulo* to find out what's on and expect little but the cinema during the summer months from December to February. In general, **films** arrive in São Paulo immediately after release in North America and Europe, and are subtitled rather than dubbed. Charging less than $1 to get in, most cinemas are on Avenida Paulista, but there are also several downtown on Avenida São Luis. Keep a special watch out for what's on at *CineSesc*, Rua Augusta 2075 (Cerqueira César), *Bixiga*, Rua 13 de Maio (Bixiga), and the *Centro Cultural de São Paulo* Rua Vergueiro 1000, by the Vergueiro Metro station, which are devoted to Brazilian and foreign art films.

São Paulo is Brazil's theatrical centre and boasts a busy season of classical and avant-garde productions; a visit to the **theatre** is worthwhile even without a knowledge of Portuguese. Theatre tickets are extremely cheap and there are **ticket offices** which have details of all current productions: *Casa do Espectador*, Rua Sete de Abril 127, Centro (Mon–Fri 10am–6pm) and *Vá ao Teatro*, Shopping Ibirapuera, Moema (Mon–Fri 9am–9pm, Sat 9am–3pm). The *Brasileiro de Comédia,* Rua Major Diorgo 311, and the *Teatro Sérgio Cardoso*, Rua Rui Barbosa, both in Bixiga, have particularly good reputations.

The focal point for São Paulo's vibrant **opera** and **classical music** season is the *Teatro Municipal*, in Praça Ramos de Azevedo, in the city centre, where, in the 1920s, Vila Lobos himself performed. As an operatic and classical music centre, traditionally São Paulo was less important than Rio, but now Brazilian and foreign performers divide their time between the two cities. Many of São Paulo's churches have free **recitals**, most notably the beautiful Gregorian chants at the *Basílica de São Bento* (Largo de São Bento, Centro) every Sunday at 10am and 5pm.

> The area telephone code for São Paulo is ☎011.

Listings

Airlines *Aerolíneas Argentinas*, Praça. D. José Gaspar 16, Centro (☎255-6022); *Aeroperu*, Rua da Consolação 329, Centro (☎257-4866); *Alitalia*, Av. São Luis 123, Centro (☎257-1722); *Avianca*, Av. São Luis 50, Centro (5th floor; ☎259-8455); *British Airways*, Av. Ipiranga 331, Centro (☎259-6144); *Canadian*, Av. São Luis 50, Centro (cj. 71; ☎259-9066); *Iberia*, Av. Ipiranga 318, bl. B, Centro (12th floor; ☎258-5333); *KLM*, Av. São Luis 120, Centro (☎257-4011); *Lan Chile*, Av. São Luis 165, Centro (2nd floor; ☎259-2900); *Líneas Aéreas Paraguayas*, Av. São Luis 50, Centro (12th floor; ☎259-9833); *Lloyd Aéreo Boliviano*, Av. São Luis 72, Centro (☎258-8111); *Lufthansa*, Av. São Luis 59, Centro (☎256-9833); *Pan Am*, Av. São Luis 50, Centro (25th floor; ☎256-3933); *Pluna*, Av. São Luis 174, Centro (☎231-2822); *SAS*, Av. São Luis 50, Centro (28th floor; ☎259-4300); *Swissair*, Av. São Luis 187, Centro (☎258-6211); *TAP*, Av. São Luis 187, Centro (☎259-5155); *Transbrasil*, Av. São Luis 250, Centro (☎259-7066); *Varig-Cruzeiro*, Rua da Consolação 368, Centro (☎258-2233); *VASP*, Rua Libero Badaró 106, Centro (☎37-1161); *Viasa*, Av. Ipiranga 318, Centro (1st floor; ☎257-9122).

Bookshops The following shops stock English-language books: *Bestseller*, Av. Tietê 184, Cerqueira César; *Cultura*, Av. Paulista 2073, Cerqueira César; *Kosmos*, Av. São Luis 162, Centro. More English-language books, plus a wide selection of Portuguese works on Brazilian history and politics, from *Brasiliense*, Rua Barão de Ipateninga 99, *Seridó*, Edifício Copan shopping mall, and *Seibú*, Rua da Consolaçáo.

Car Rental The main difficulty in driving in São Paulo is finding a parking space. Otherwise, roads are well signposted and it's surprisingly easy to get out of the city. Car rental firms are: *Avis*, Rua da Consolação 347, Centro (☎256-4166); *Budget*, Rua da Consolação 328, Consolação (☎256-4355); *Hertz*, Rua da Consolação 439, Centro (☎256-9722); *Interlocadora*, Largo Sta. Cecília 140, Centro (☎222-2037); *Localiza*, Rua da Consolação 419, Centro (☎231-3055); *Nobre*, Rua Martins Fontes 205, Centro (☎255-8922).

Chemists A 24-hour service at *São Paulo*, Rua Teodoro Sampaio 2014, Pinheiros (☎815-8829); *Tabajara*, Rua Brig. Luís Antônio 1628, Bela Vista (☎288-3483); *Drogadec*, Av. 9 de Julho 3606, Jardim Paulista (☎853-5413).

Consulates *Argentina*, Rua Araújo 216, Centro (8th floor; ☎256-8555); *Austria*, Av. Lorena 1271, Cerqueira César (☎282-6223); *Belgium*, Av. Paulista 2073, Cerqueira César (13th floor; ☎287-7892); *Bolivia*, Rua Quirino de Andrade 219, Centro (3rd floor; ☎255-3555); *Canada*, Av. Paulista 854, Bela Vista (5th floor; ☎287-2122); *Colombia*, Rua Marconi 53, Centro (10th floor; ☎255-6863); *Denmark*, Av. Indianópolis 381, Indianópolis (☎571-6933); *Eire*, Av. Paulista 2006, Cerqueira César (5th floor; ☎287-6362); *Netherlands*, Av. Brig. Faria Lima 1698, Jardim Paulistano (3rd floor; ☎813-0522); *Norway*, Av. Senador Queiroz 605, Centro (4th floor; ☎229-2764); *Paraguay*, Avenida São Luis 112, Centro (10th floor; ☎259-3579); *Peru*, Rua Suécia 114, Jardim Europa (☎853-9372); *Sweden*, Rua Oscar Freire 379, Cerqueria César (3rd floor; ☎883-3322); *Switzerland*, Av. Paulista 1754, Bela Vista (4th floor; ☎289-1033); *USA*, Rua Pe. João Manoel 933, Jardim América (☎881-6511); *UK*, Av. Paulista 1938, Cerqueira César (17th floor; ☎287-7722); *Uruguay*, Av. Campinas 433, Cerqueira César (7th floor; ☎284-5998); *Venezuela*, Rua Jerônimo da Veiga 164, Jardim Europa (16th floor; ☎883-3000); *West Germany*, Av. Brig. Faria Lima 1383, Jardim Paulistano (12th floor; ☎814-6644).

Cultural Institutes *Alliance Française*, Rua Gen. Jardim 182, Vila Buarque (☎259-8211); *Cultura Inglesa*, Av. Ipiranga 877, Centro (☎222-3866); *Instituto Italiano de Cultura*, Rua Frei Caneca 1071, Bela Vista (☎285-6933); *Goethe Institut*, Rua Lisboa 974, Pinheiros (☎280-4288); *União Cultural Brasil-Estados Unidos*, Rua Cel. Oscar Porto 208, Paraiso (☎885-1022).

Dentists Expensive, but with good reputations, are *Dental Office Augusta*, Rua Augusta 878, Cerqueira César (☎256-3104) and *Dr. José Miotto Adura Neto*, Av. Pavão 224, Moema (☎531-2236).

Exchange Changing money on the black market is more low-key in São Paulo than in Rio. Try the travel agents around Praça da República and the adjoining Avenida São Luís or *Turist Câmbio* at Avenida Paulista 529 (at the intersection with Alameda Eugênio de Lima). If you need to change money at weekends, try the souvenir shops and jewellers in Liberdade, the Japanese *bairro*, and expect only slightly under the newspaper-quoted black market rate.

Football There are three First Division teams based in São Paulo: Corinthians, who play at Parque São Jorge (Rua São Jorge 777; Metro Bresser and bus #278A); São Paulo, at Murumbi Stadium (Metro Ana Rosa and bus #775P; or simply bus 775P from Av. Paulista); and Palmeiras, at Palestra Itália (Parque Antártica; bus #208A or #208C from Av. São João). Matches are generally on Wednesday and Saturday.

Health Matters The private *Albert Einstein Clinic* (Av. Albert Einstein 627, Morumbi; ☎845-1233) is considered to be the best hospital in Brazil, and one where strict precautions are taken against the spread of AIDS.

Newspapers Most newspaper kiosks downtown and in Jardims sell English-language newspapers. Apart from the *Brazil Herald* and the *Latin American Daily Post*, the most easily available are the *International Herald Tribune* and the *Miami Herald*. *Farah's* (Rua Haddock Lobo 1503, Cerqueira César; open until midnight) has a very good selection of European magazines and newspapers (including the *Sunday Times* and *Guardian Weekly*), as does *Jardim Europa* (Av. Europa and Groenlândia; open 24hr).

Police To extend your stay, visit the *Polícia Federal*, Avenida Prestes Maia 700, Centro (☎223-7177 ext. 231); Mon–Fri 10am–4pm.

Post Office The main post office is downtown at Praça Correio, at the corner of Av. São João, and is open 8am–10pm. There are postal kiosks scattered throughout the city, including several along Avenida Paulista.

Public Holidays Most things in São Paulo close on the following days: January 1; January 25 (Founding of the City); Carnaval; Ash Wednesday; Good Friday; April 21 (Remembrance of Tiradentes); May 1 (Labour Day); June 2 (Corpus Christi); September 7 (Independence Day); October 12 (Nossa Senhora Aparecida); November 2 (Finados); November 15 (Proclamation of the Rebublic); December 25.

Record Shops The widest selection of Brazilian records in the city is from *Música da República*, Praça da República, Centro (reductions negotiable if you pay in dollars); second-hand Brazilian records (good for rarities) from *Seibú do Disco*, Rua Lisboa 45, Jardim América.

Telephones For long distance calls, *Telesp* (the state telephone company) have an office on Rua Sete de Abril (just off Praça da República); open 24hr.

Women's Groups *Centro Informação Mulher*, Rua Leôncio Gurgel, casa 11, Luz (☎229-4818); *Coletivo de Mulheres Negras*, Rua Estado Unidos 346, Jardim América (☎852-1750; evenings only); *Grupo Ação Lésbico-Feminista*, Caixa Postal 62618, São Paulo 01214; *União de Mulheres de São Paulo*, Rua Sto. Antônio 1395, Bela Vista. There are several *Delegacias da Mulher* (women's police stations), with the main one at Praça Dom Pedro II, Brás (☎228-6101 & ☎254-3361).

Around São Paulo

What only a few years ago were clearly identifiable small towns or villages have become swallowed up by Greater São Paulo. But, despite the traffic, escaping from the city is surprisingly easy, and there are even points on the coast that can make good day trips (for which see below, "The Paulista Coast").

Embu

Founded in 1554, **EMBU** remained a mere village until São Paulo's explosive growth in the twentieth century. But, just 27km west of the city, Embu couldn't have expected to remain unaffected by its growth – what is surprising is that it somehow managed to retain its colonial feel. Despite having a population of over 100,000, simple colonial-style buildings predominate in the town's compact centre.

In the 1970s, Embu was a favourite retreat for writers and artists from São Paulo, and many set up home in what was then still little more than a village. Today, the Sunday **handicraft market** (7am–6pm) in the main square, Largo 21 de Abril, makes the town a favourite with *Paulistano* day-trippers, although during the week Embu is far quieter. The shops around the main square stock a more or less similar selection of ceramics, leather items, jewellery and home-made jams to that which is sold in the market. Nearby, on Largo dos Jesuitas, the basic structure of the eighteenth-century **Igreja Matriz Nossa Senhora do Rosário** is typical, colonial Baroque, but its interior retains almost no original features. Otherwise, you might as well sit down and eat: there are several **restaurants** on Largo 21 de Abril and along the adjoining streets, and the town is a very good place to sample traditional *Paulista* cooking.

It takes about an hour to get to Embu from São Paulo. Take bus #056 from Conceição Metro station, or #179S from the Tietê *Rodoviária*.

Paranapiacaba

For most of its history, communications from São Paulo to the outside world were slow and difficult. In 1856 the British-owned *São Paulo Railway Company* was awarded the concession to operate a railway between Santos and Jundaí, north of

São Paulo, and the 139-kilometre line was completed in 1867. Overcoming the near vertical incline of the Serra do Mar, the line was an engineering miracle and is slowly being restored today.

Every Sunday at 9.30am, **trains** leave from São Paulo's *Estação da Luz* for **PARANAPIACABA**, southeast of the city and the last station before the line plunges down the coastal escarpment; it's a two-hour ride. As there's nowhere to stay in Paranapiacaba, and only snacks in the way of food, it's necessary to return to São Paulo on the same day, the trains departing at 4pm.

Paranapiacaba was the administrative centre for the railway and at one time was home to 4000 of its workers. Neatly laid out in the 1890s, the village has remained largely unchanged over the years and the workers' cottages, train station and other railway buildings are in excellent order: some are open to the public. At the **Centro Preservação da História de Paranapiacaba** (Sat & Sun 9am–5pm), there's a display of old photographs of the railway's early years and the attendants are a mine of information. Serious railway buffs who want to find out more about the preservation work on this line, and plans for others in Brazil, should visit the *Associação Brasileira de Preservação Ferroviária* in São Paulo, at Rua Economizadora 10 (Luz): it's best to go on Thursday when there are meetings open to the public, held from 8.30pm. At weekends there are short steam-engine excursions from Paranapiacaba along the most amazing stretch of the line, a cog-wheel section leading to the coast, from which there are stunning views.

THE STATE OF SÃO PAULO

Away from the city, it's the state's coastline that has most to offer. **Santos**, Brazil's leading port, retains many links with the past, and lots of the **beaches** stretching north and south from the city are stunning, particularly around **Ubatuba**. The towns and cities of the state's **interior**, on the other hand, are not so great an attraction – the rolling countryside is largely devoted to vast orange groves and fields of soya and sugar. However, if you're in search of Confederate history, you can pass through **Americana** or **Santa Bárbara d'Oeste**, while further west you can break the long train journey to the Mato Grosso at the railway junction, and otherwise uninspiring town, of **Bauru**. To escape the summer heat, the resort of **Campos do Jordão**, northeast of São Paulo, offers some attractive hill scenery and plenty of walking possibilities.

Campinas

One hundred kilometres northwest of São Paulo is **CAMPINAS**, gone slightly downhill since the nineteenth century when it was by far the more important of the two cities. It started life as a sugar plantation centre, produced coffee from 1870 and, most recently, has made its money as an agricultural processing and hi-tech centre. An attractive city, with a reasonably small centre, there aren't too many reasons for visiting, though it's profitable enough to take a tour around Largo do Rosário, with its **Catedral**, inaugurated in 1883. A few blocks southwest of here – around the train station – is the **Vila Industrial**, rows of small houses built for the city's new working class in the late nineteenth century. Better known, in Brazil at least, is **Unicamp**, the *Universidade Estadual de São Paulo*, 13km from the city centre. It was founded in 1969 on land belonging to Colonel Zeferino Vaz and, during the worst years of military terror, thanks to the protection afforded by Vaz, the university became a refuge for left-wing teachers who would otherwise have been imprisoned or forced into exile. *Unicamp* rapidly acquired an international reputation and today is considered one of Brazil's two or three best universities.

With a student population of 100,000, Campinas has a reasonably lively cultural life, centred on the **Centro de Convivência Cultural**, at Praça Imprensa Fluminense in the centre. It has a theatre, art galleries and is home to the fine *Orquestra Sinfonia*. To the south of the Praça, the folklore, history, Indian and natural history **museums** (Tues–Sat 9–10.50am & 1–5pm, Sun 9am–noon & 1–5pm) in the **Bosque dos Jequitbás** contain little of any interest, though the park itself is a pleasant place to while away an hour or two.

Some practicalities

Campinas is a major transport hub and there are **buses** from the city to most places in the state and many beyond. The highway to São Paulo itself is one of Brazil's best, and the hourly buses take an hour and a quarter. The **Rodoviária** in Campinas is at Rua Barão de Itapura, a twenty-minute walk from the city centre down Rua Saldanha Marinho. There are also several daily **trains** to Campinas from São Paulo's *Estação da Luz*, though they take around twenty minutes longer to make the same journey.

With São Paulo so close you won't need to stay in Campinas, but you might want to grab something **to eat**. The three branches of *Giovanetti* in Praça Carlos Gomes and Largo do Rosário are popular student meeting points, selling drinks and excellent sandwiches. *Cenat*, at Rua Barão de Jaguara 1260, serves excellent **vegetarian food**; *Tevere* (owned by a *Unicamp* philosophy professor), Avenida Coronel Silva Teles 439, has good **Italian** dishes; the tiny *Cantina Alemã* at Rua Luzitana 981 offers reasonable **German** food; the *Santa Gertrudis* at Rua Olavo Bilac 54 is the city's best **churrascaria**; and the *Éden*, Rua Barão de Jaguara 1224, is just a large hall serving huge portions of cheap, plain, food.

Confederates: Americana and Santa Bárbara d'Oeste

In the face of humiliation, military defeat and economic devastation, thousands of former **Confederates** resolved to "reconstruct" themselves in often distant parts of the world, forcing a wave of emigration without precedent in the history of the United States. Brazil rapidly established itself as one of the main destinations, offering cheap land, a climate suited to familiar crops, political and economic stability, religious freedom and – more sinisterly – the possibility of continued slave ownership. Just how many Confederates came is unclear, suggested numbers varying between 2000 and 20,000, and they settled all over Brazil, though it was in São Paulo where they had the greatest impact. Although Iguape, on the state's southern stretch of coast, had a large Confederate population, the most concentrated area of settlement was the Santa Bárbara colony, in the area around present-day Americana and Santa Bárbara D'oeste.

The region's climate and soil was ideally suited to the growing of **cotton** and the Confederates' expertise soon made Santa Bárbara one of Brazil's biggest producers of the crop. As demand for Brazilian cotton gradually declined, many of the immigrants switched to **sugar cane**, which remains the area's staple crop, though others, unable to adapt, moved into São Paulo city or returned to the United States.

Americana

Although there are perhaps as many as 100,000 Brazilians of Confederate descent, there are few obvious signs of this in the two towns most associated with them. **AMERICANA** is a bustling city of about 150,000 people, but there are only twenty-five English-speaking families. If curiosity does bring you here, to reach the centre from the *Rodoviária*, walk across the bridge in front of the building and keep straight on for about ten minutes. On the main square, Praça Comendador Muller, there's the simple, but perfectly adequate *Hotel Cacique*; and for food there are plenty of *lanchonetes* and a very good *churrascaria*, the *Cristal*, at Avenida Fortunato Faraoni 613. But apart from the odd Confederate emblem, don't expect much to do with the South.

Santa Bárbara D'Oeste

Thirteen kilometres west of Americana, **SANTA BÁRBARA D'OESTE** has more Confederate ties. Much the smaller of the two, there are about thirty families of Confederate origin here, most of whom still speak English with more than a touch of Dixie in their voice. Near the main square, a short walk from the *Rodoviária*, the excellent **Museu da Imigração** (closed Sun) has displays relating to the history of the Confederates in the area, and to that of other nationalities, chiefly Italian. About 10km from town, the **Cemitério do Campo** is a cool and shaded cemetery on a hill overlooking endless fields of sugar cane. It dates back to 1910 and all the tombstones, as well as the monument commemorating the Confederate immigrants, bear English inscriptions. There's a small chapel here, too, and a picnic area where, four times a year (the second Sun of Jan, April, July and Oct) around 250 members of the *Fraternidade Descendência Americana* arrive from throughout Brazil to renew old ties. The cemetery is very isolated and can only be reached by car: a taxi will charge around $10 to take you there, and will wait for you while you look around. However, as not all taxi drivers know exactly where the cemetery is, ask the museum attendant to order a taxi for you and have them give your driver precise directions.

As for **accommodation** in Santa Bárbara, there's only one hotel, the very simple *Municipal*, right by the *Rodoviária*; and there's only one **restaurant**, too, the *Bela Mesa*, at Rua General Osório 576.

Both Americana and Santa Bárbara are easy to get to from São Paulo, with buses to the two towns running every couple of hours and taking about two hours to cover the 150km.

Further west: Bauru

Northwest, beyond the Confederate towns, it's difficult to imagine a reason for visiting **BAURU** unless you're travelling by train to or from the Mato Grosso. The city was once a fairly important spa, used by *Paulistanos* as a weekend resort, but of late it's developed into a major agricultural processing centre, serving the orange, pineapple and sugar producers of the area. Still, given the length of the rail journey involved to reach Campo Grande and Corumbá to the west (see p.382 for more details), you may well want to break the monotony by stretching your legs at Bauru.

There are several adequate **hotels** within short walking distance of Bauru's **railway station**; the closest are easily spotted on the other side of the square from the main station entrance, but as they're convenient for the railway and only around $7 for a double, they're often full. There are another three hotels, slightly cheaper, on the corner of the block directly behind those on the square: there's not much to choose between any of them, and, again, they are often full. You're actually much more likely to find a bed at either the *Hotel Mateus* or *Hotel Continental*, three blocks from the station on Rua Azarias Leito – turn left out of the station entrance, follow Rua 1 de Agosto two blocks to the corner of Rua A. Leito, and you can see them on the left. Next door to each other, both have around ten relatively inexpensive beds (from $3); the *Continental* is more unusual, with the atmosphere of a private house and a café opening out onto the street.

There's usually a lively crowd in and around the station square. Even in the early hours of the morning, people are hanging out in the **all-night bars**, drinking or munching on enormous pizzas. More appropriately, this is a good place to try one of the ubiquitous "bauru" sandwiches found on most Brazilian menus (essentially a toastie with cheese, ham, tomato and sometimes peppers). For more substantial **meals**, the *Bella Napoli*, also near the station on Rua 1 de Agosto, serves decent "international" dishes.

If you've had enough of trains by the time you reach Bauru, there are frequent **buses** to São Paulo from the *Rodoviária* at Praça João Paulo II, taking just four and a half hours.

Campos do Jordão

When temperatures plunge to 15°C, São Paulo's citizens generally shiver and reach for their mothballed woollens. But to experience something approaching genuine cold weather they have to head into the highlands. East of the city, in the direction of Rio, is the **Serra da Mantiqueira,** which boasts the lively winter resort of **CAMPOS DO JORDÃO**, 1628m high. The town lies in the floor of a valley, littered with countless Swiss chalet-style hotels and private houses, and divided into three sections: **Abernéssia**, the older commercial centre and location of the *Rodoviária*; and, a fifteen-minute bus ride away, **Juaguaribe** and **Capivari,** where most of the boutiques, restaurants and hotels are concentrated.

The novelty of donning sweaters and legwarmers draws the crowds, who spend their days filling in the time before nightfall when they can light their fires. In all directions from Capivari there are good walks, and **trails** are well signposted. Much of the land has been stripped of forest cover to make way for cattle pasture, but in the higher reaches you'll still come across remains of the graceful *araucária* (Paraná pine) trees that once dominated the natural vegetation hereabouts. For a good **view** over Campos do Jordão and the surrounding Paraíba valley, take the **ski lift** from near the small boating lake in the centre of Capivari: it whisks you up to the **Morro do Elefante**, from where you can hire horses to get you further about.

Rooms and food

With about sixty **hotels** to choose from, finding a room is easy. But finding an affordable one – in the winter at any rate – can be difficult. You're best off walking along the tree-lined Avenida Macedo Soares (Capivari), where many of the cheaper hotels are found. Expect to pay around $10 for a double room in places like the *Itália* (no. 306) or the *Casa São José* (no. 827), or about $15 in slightly more comfortable ones like the *Nevada* (no. 27) and *Monte Blanco* (no. 262). Before accepting a room, check that it has an electric fire as even on warm summer days it can get quite chilly at night. Also in Capivari there's a small **youth hostel**, at Avenida Diego de Carvalho 86, but at the weekend it's often fully booked.

Most people eat in their hotels, so the choice of **restaurants** is comparatively limited. But you won't go hungry since there are several pseudo-Swiss restaurants that you can take potluck in: try *Só Queijo*, Avenida Macedo Soares 642, or the *Matterhorn*, Rua Djalma Forjaz 10. **Nightlife** is very much hotel-oriented, but people also congregate around the splendidly kitsch "medieval" shopping arcade in Capivari, drinking hot mulled wine at the top of the arcade's tower or – for a really big evening out – watching the electronic thermometer.

The Paulista Coast

Until fairly recently – despite its proximity to the city – most of the four hundred kilometres of the **Paulista coast** was overlooked by sun and beach fiends in favour of more glamorous Rio. Now, though, the beaches northeast of the port of Santos are easily accessible on the new BR-101 coastal highway, and the area is becoming increasingly commercialised. This part of the coast offers great contrasts, ranging from long, wide stretches of sand at the edge of a coastal plain, to idyllic-looking coves beneath a mountainous backdrop. Having the use of a car would be an advantage as the beaches near places accessible by bus are generally quite developed: see São Paulo's "Listings" for car rental addresses. Southwest of Santos, however, tourism has still to take hold, in part because the roads aren't as good, but also because the beaches simply aren't as beautiful.

The route to Santos: Cubatão

About 75km south of São Paulo, Santos is Brazil's most important port: but until the construction of the railway, travel between the two cities was a major trek. Today, buses take less than an hour to make the journey, along a multi-lane highway that offers no sense of how formidable a barrier the escarpment behind Santos used to be. Roughly midway between the two cities, the SP-150 highway passes **CUBATÃO**, said to be one of the most polluted towns on the planet. Although control of the level of factory emissions is minimal, it's not this which makes Cubatão stand out from other Brazilian industrial centres. The main problem with Cubatão is that the town lies in a valley where the clouds of sheer poison are unable to disperse. The results are disastrous: the rich tropical vegetation is dying and only now is the long-term damage to human beings coming to light.

Santos

SANTOS was founded in 1535, a few kilometres east of São Vicente, one of Portugal's first New World settlements. The city stands on an island, its port facilities and old town facing landwards with ships approaching by a narrow, but deep, channel. In a dilapidated kind of a way, the compact centre retains a certain charm that has not yet been extinguished by the development of an enormous port complex.

Arriving in Santos and getting orientated couldn't be easier. The **Rodoviária**, at Praça dos Andradas, is within easy walking distance of everywhere in the city centre: from it, walk across the square to Rua XV de Novembro, one of the main commercial streets. One block on, turn left at Rua do Comércio, along which are the remains of some of Santos' most distinguished buildings. Sadly, only the

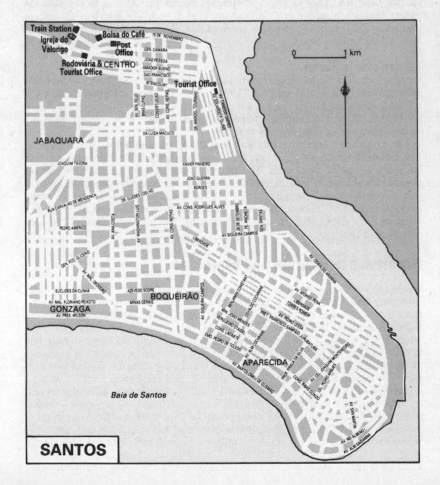

facades remain of most of the mid- and late-nineteenth-century former **merchants' houses** that line the street, but the elaborate tiling and wrought-iron balconies offer a hint of their lost grandeur. At the end of Rua do Comércio is the **railway station**, built between 1860 and 1867, and while the city's claim that the station is an exact replica of London's Victoria is a bit difficult to swallow, it is true that the building wouldn't look too out of place in a British town. Next to the station is the **Igreja de Santo Antônio do Valongo** (in Largo Marquês de Monte Alegre), built in 1641 in colonial Baroque style, but – as usual with its interior totally "restored" over the following centuries. Back on Rua XV de Novembro, at no. 95, is the **Bolsa de Café**, where coffee prices are fixed and the quality assessed. And at the end of the street is another Baroque building, the **Convento do Carmo**, again sixteenth-century in facade only.

Across town, twenty minutes by bus from Praça Maua in the centre, are Santos' **beaches**. They're huge, stretching around the Atlantic-facing Baía de Santos, and are attractive in a Copacabana kind of way. The problem, though, is that while the beaches themselves are kept tidy, the water is of doubtful cleanliness. I'd stick to the sands.

Staying over in Santos

Coming from São Paulo, be sure to remember that buses to Santos leave from the Jabaquara *Rodoviária* and not from Tietê. Once there, there are **tourist offices** at the *Rodoviária* and at Rua Jorge Tibiriçá 40 in Gonzaga, but their opening hours are very haphazard. **Changing money** in Santos is easy, with *câmbios* on Praça da República and on Rua XV de Novembro.

Except for the inexpensive *Potiguar*, near the *Rodoviária* at Rua Amador Bueno 116, **hotels** in Santos are in Gonzaga, a *bairro* of apartment buildings, restaurants and bars alongside the beach. The cheapest places here are the *Gonzaga*, at Avenida Presidente Wilson 36, and the *Ritz*, Avenida Marechal Deodoro 24, both very comfortable and charging aroud $12 for a double room. There are some reasonable seafood **restaurants** in the centre (try *Café Paulista* at Praça Rui Barbosa 8, or *Rocky* at Praça dos Andradas 5), but otherwise, again, they are almost all in Gonzaga.

Northeast: to Guarujá and Maresias

GUARUJÁ is São Paulo's most important beach resort, and getting there is easy. There are half-hourly buses from the city's Jabaquara *Rodoviária* that take little more than an hour to travel the 85km to the resort. From Santos, take a bus from Gonzaga along the beach avenue to Ponta da Praia, from where a ferry makes the ten-minute crossing across the Santos channel, and then it's a fifteen-minute bus ride on to Guarujá itself. The resort features a set of large apartment buildings alongside lengthy, rather monotonous beaches. In the summer, finding space on the main beach, **Pitangueiras**, can be difficult, and the beaches within walking distance, or a short bus ride, to the east are little better. In fact, without a car and considerable local knowledge Guarujá is best avoided and – in any case – finding a reasonably priced hotel in the summer can be almost impossible. Your best bet is to look around Praia das Pitangueiras (the *Hotel Rio* at Rua Rio de Janeiro 131 is just a block from the sea; small, friendly and popular at $12 for a double room); or at the adjoining Praia Guarujá (the *Guarujá Praia*, Praça Brigadeiro Franco Faria Lima 137, is one of several hotels here charging $10–15 for a double).

From Guarujá's *Rodoviária* there are buses east as far as Ubatuba (see below), stopping off at points along the way. For much of the first 90km the road passes inland, but approaching **MARESIAS**, the road again skirts the coastline and the landscape grows increasingly mountainous. Maresias is quiet resort, much more attractive than Guarujá, consisting of a few simple **hotels** (*Pousada da Barra* is highly recommended), a campsite and a couple of **restaurants** (*Le Bistrot* makes an attempt at French dishes). The beaches, especially those back in the direction of Guarujá, are small and extremely pretty, all within walking distance of the resort.

São Sebastião

Twenty-seven kilometres further east is **SÃO SEBASTIÃO**, a bustling little town on the mainland directly opposite the island of Ilhabela (see below). Founded in the first years of the seventeenth century, sugar cane and coffee farms were responsible for São Sebastião's growth until the eighteenth century, when the town entered a period of decline. Emerging from this stagnation only in the last few decades, the town has retained many of its colonial buildings. And, unlike in other similar towns, they've not been taken over by wealthy city dwellers, since the town's beaches, in both directions from the centre, are poor and completely cut off from the open sea by the much more beautiful Ilhabela, directly opposite.

Praça Major João Fernandes is the heart of São Sebastião and the location of the **Igreja Matriz**, built in 1636 (though its interior is twentieth-century plaster) and almost as old as the town. Along the waterfront near the square are innumerable **bars** and seafood **restaurants**, where excellent meals will cost you about $3. Because of the proximity to Ilhabela, there's a similarly large selection of **hotels**, the best of which – well worth the splurge – is the *Pôrto Grande*, a whitewashed colonial building with park-like gardens stretching down to its own beach. A double room goes for around $35, and the hotel is a ten-minute walk from the centre, on Avenida Guarda Mór Lobo Viana. Cheaper hotel options include: the *Roma*, Praça Major João Fernandes ($15 double and very comfortable); the *Beira Mar*, Rua Expedecionários Brasileiros 258 ($10 double; good value and with nice sea views); and plenty of other choices charging about $6 a room on Rua Três Bandeirantes, one street from the main square by the sea.

Ilhabela

Without a shadow of a doubt, **Ilhabela** is one of the most beautiful spots on the coast between Santos and Rio. Of volcanic origin, the island's startling mountainous scenery rises to 1370 metres and is covered in dense, tropical foliage. Its dozens of waterfalls, beautiful beaches and azure seas have contributed to its popularity; old or new, most of the buildings are in simple Portuguese colonial styles, as far removed from brash Guarujá as you can get. The hotels are generally expensive and are often fully booked, so many people choose to stay in São Sebastião instead – not a bad idea, since transport connections are good. **Ferries** (4.30–1.30am; 24hr in summer) depart from São Sebastião's waterfront every half an hour and the crossing takes about twenty minutes. The ferry is met by a bus, which goes to the village of **VILA ILHABELA** at the northeastern end of the island. A much more scenic route is to take the direct launch (every couple of hours; 7am–7pm) to Vila Ilhabela, a voyage that takes 45 minutes.

Ilhabela village

Almost all of the island's 6000 inhabitants live along the sheltered western shore, with the village of Ilhabela the only population centre. The small village has a few pretty colonial buildings, and is dominated by the Igreja Matriz, a little church built in 1662. Most of the **hotels** are within a short walk from the centre of the village and, if you do find a room, expect to pay a minimum of $20 for a double; to avoid disappointment it's wise to phone and reserve a bed. Next to the bus stop, and across the road from where the launch docks, at Rua Dr. Carvalho 46, you'll find the friendly *Hotel São Paulo* (☎0124/72-1158), the cheapest place to stay. If that's full, try the *Hotel Costa Azul* (☎0124/72-1365), five minutes away at Avenida Francisco Gomes da Silva Prado 71. There's unpretentious luxury at the *Pousada dos Hibiscos*, ten minutes' walk south along the coast at Avenida Pedro de Paula Morais 714 (☎0124/72-1375), but double rooms here go for about $35. Dotted along the western shore, there are several **campsites**, but these, too, are usually packed in the summer.

Around the rest of the island

Getting around the island can be a problem as the only bus route is along the island's western shore. However, hitching lifts is quite easy, or for about $10 a day you can rent a motorbike (look for signs outside the luxury hotels). There are beaches just minutes' walk from the village centre, and if you like calm waters you need go no further.

The **north coast** beaches, 5–9km from the village, have more surf, but for Atlantic rollers cross the island to the **Praia dos Castelhanos**. The walk along the unpaved road will take at least two hours, but 7km along the road stop at the *Jardim Tropical* (entrance fee $1) for a drink and a refreshing shower under a waterfall or a dip in a natural pool.

To Ubatuba

From São Sebastião, the highway continues along the coast passing frustratingly close to deserted beaches of dazzling beauty. Buses stop in CARAGUATATUBA, an ugly little town with a long, gently curving beach alongside the main road, but you're better off carrying on towards **UBATUBA**. The town is only slightly more attractive, but that's of little importance when you consider the local beaches, 72 in all, on islands and curling around inlets.

The town is centred on Praça 13 de Maio, a couple of blocks from the *Rodoviária* (at Rua Conceição). On the square there's a very helpful **tourist office** (daily 9am–6pm) which supplies maps of the coast and will make hotel reservations for you.

As far as **accommodation** goes, Ubatuba makes a good base if you plan to explore the outlying beaches. Hotels are concentrated in the area around Rua Conceição, towards the beach, and you'll be lucky to find a double room for less than $10. On Rua Conceição itself, comfortable and reasonably cheap are the *Atlântico* (no. 185) and the *São Nicolau* (no. 213), while the *Xaréu*, around the corner at Rua Jordão Homem da Costa 413, is slightly more expensive, charging about $15. Most **restaurants** are on Avenida Iperoig, which curves alongside the town's beach, the Praia de Iperoig, and you'll find a good variety of seafood, Italian and other types to choose from.

The beaches

Although there's nothing wrong with the town's Praia de Iperoig, Ubatuba is best used as a base from which to visit some of Ubatuba's 71 other beaches accessible by bus or private boat. The least developed are to the **northeast** of town, with the furthest, Camburi, 46km away on the border with the Rio state. To get to them, take the **local bus** marked "Promirim" from the *Rodoviária* and ask the driver to stop at whatever palm-fringed cove that takes your fancy.

To the south of town are the more commercial beaches, again easily reached by bus from the town centre. **Enseada**, 9km away, is lined with beach-front hotels, none of which have rooms for less than $20. In a bay protected from too lively a surf, the beach is popular with families, and in the summer it's always uncomfortably crowded.

Across the bay from Enseada are a series of beautiful isolated beaches that draw fewer people. Walk out of town on the main road for about 2km until you reach **RIBEIRA**, a yachting centre and colourful fishing port. From here, there are trips on sailing **boats** to the **Ilha Anchieta**, a nearby island where only a few fishermen live, or further afield along the coast: these will cost between $7 and $15, depending on the itinerary. Beyond Ribeira are sandy coves that you can reach by clambering down from the trail on the cliff above the sea.

Southwest of Santos

The coastal escarpment **southwest of Santos** begins its incline 20–30km inland from the sea. Lacking the immediate mountain backdrop, and with large stretches of the coast dominated by mangrove swamp, this region was for years left more or less untouched by tourism. However, holiday development companies have been moving in recently, aiming at *Paulistanos* who can't afford places further north.

Heading south from Santos, the road follows the coast as far as PERUÍBE, then moves inland onto higher, firmer terrain before heading back to the coast down the Serra do March. The road is slow, but passing through small fishing villages, banana and sugar plantations and cattle grazing land, you're reminded that there's more to Brazil than just beaches. Incidentally, from São Paulo, rather than travel via Santos it's much faster to take a direct bus to Iguape and Cananéia, avoiding the coastal road altogether.

Itanhaém

The coastline between Santos and **ITANHAÉM**, 61km south, is, in effect, one long beach which – were it not for the new holiday complexes that line the entire stretch – would be simply unremarkable rather than unattractive. Founded in the sixteenth century, there are a few remaining facades from Itanhaém's early years, most notably the **Covento de Nossa Senhora da Conceição**, a semi-ruined chapel and monastery.

If you do decide to stay over, in the summer you're likely to have problems in finding a **hotel** room. Most of the people coming on holiday here are lower-middle-class *Paulistanos* staying in holiday complexes owned by workers' associations, and there are only a few, small hotels. Your best bet is the *Hotel Atlântico* at Rua Cunha Moreira 68 or, failing that, the bigger and more expensive *Pollastrini* at Praça 22 de Abril.

Iguape and the Ilha Comprida

IGUAPE, roughly two and a half hours further south by bus, was founded in
1538 by the Portuguese to guard against the possibility of Spanish encroachment
on the southern fringes of the Empire. On the southern tip of the estuarine island
of Papagaio, Iguape was well placed as a base for exploring the southern *Paulista*
interior, up the Rio Ribeira do Iguape. Far from possible markets, it was slow to
develop and attempts to settle immigrants – most notably Confederate refugees –
were met with abject failure. But because Iguape remained a backwater for so
long, many of its colonial buildings survive today, albeit in extremely dilapidated
states.

During the summer, Iguape is popular with *Paulista* holidaymakers, seeking a
beach vacation away from the sophistication, crowds and expense of resorts
further north. Facing the town is a second island, the **Ilha Comprida**, 86km long
and 3km wide, whose interior is of light forest, while on the Atlantic-facing side
an uninterrupted beach stretches the entire length of the island. In the summer it
gets very crowded near the access road across the island, but if you want to be
alone just walk south for a few kilometres. Continual **ferries** make the five-minute
crossing to the northern part of the island and, until 7pm, **buses** take passengers
across the island to the beach.

A couple of kilometres south of the the access road crossing the island, there
are several **campsites**, bars and *lanchonetes* on the Ilha Comprida itself. There
are also several **hotels** on the island, with the *Alpha* and the *Vila das Palmeiras*
both charging about $12 for a double room. A much better choice of hotels,
though, is to be found in Iguape: the *Zé Juca* at Avenida Ademar de Barros 598,
the *Demartis* at Rua Rebello 258 and the *Rio Verde* at Rua Antônio José de Moraes
86 are amongst the cheapest.

Cananéia

Like Iguape, **CANANÉIA** is on an island, lying between the mainland to which
it's linked by a short bridge, and the Ilha Comprida. There's constant **ferry**
service between the town and the Ilha Comprida, from where you can either take
a bus (every hour) or walk the three kilometres to the beach. Where the road
hits the beach, there are a couple of simple hotels and bars. In the summer it gets
quite crowded here but, as in the north of the island (see above), you don't have
to wander far for a quiet piece of sand.

In the centre of Cananéia, especially along Ruas Tristão Lobo, Bandeirantes
and Dom João II, there are many simple ochre-coloured and whitewashed colonial and nineteenth-century buildings. Except for a few, such as the seventeenth-
century church, they're in very poor condition and for many only the facade
remains.

Cananéia's "best" **hotel** is the *Gloria*, across from the *Rodoviária*, but its rooms
are damp, the staff unfriendly and general atmosphere institutional – one to
avoid. Most other hotels are along or near the waterfront in the same vicinity:
good bets are the *Beira-Mar* at Avenida Beira Mar 219, the *Recanto do Sol* at Rua
Pedro Lobo 271 or, more expensive because of their swimming pools, the *Cabana
do Bugre* and the *Coqueiro*, both on Avenida Independência. You can **eat**
extremely well in Cananéia, with the menus of the mainly Japanese-owned restaurants including clams, mussels, conch, octopus and, Cananéia's speciality,
oysters; especially recommended are the *Teruko Oda* and the *Tía Ines*.

On from Iguape and Cananéia

Cars are permitted to drive along the beach between Iguape and Cananéia, and it's possible to hitch a lift for that 50km. Otherwise, **buses** have to take a circuitous route inland and the distance is lengthened to over 80km. There are several buses a day between the towns, or you can travel by **boat**; departures are from Iguapi on Monday and Thursday, and continue south to Ariri (see *The South* chapter; "Bay of Paranaguá"), returning the following day. If travelling south to Paraná, you'll have to change buses in **REGISTRO**, an hour from both Iguape and Cananéia. Registro is in the heart of a Japanese tea-growing region, and if you're unlucky with connections stay at the *Lito Palace* ($12 a double room), Avenida Jonas Banks Leite 615, or the cheaper *Regis*, at Rua São Francisco Vavier 83; and eat at the *Ebissuya*, Rua Getúlio Vargas 401.

travel details

Buses

From São Paulo to Bauru (7 daily; 4hr 30min); Campinas (hourly; 1hr 15min); Cananéia (4 daily; 4hr 30min); Iguape (4 daily; 3hr 30min); Santa Bárbara d'Oeste (8 daily; 2hr); Santos (every 15min; 1hr); Ubatuba (6 daily; 3hr 30min); Belo Horizonte (hourly; 12hr); Campo Grande (8 daily; 16hr); Corumbá (4 daily; 26hr); Curitiba (hourly; 6hr); Florianópolis (8 daily; 12hr); Recife (4 daily; 40hr); Rio (every 30min; 6hr); Salvador (4 daily; 30hr).

From Campinas to Curitiba (5 daily; 6hr).
From Santos to Cananéia (2 daily; 4hr 30min).
From Ubatuba to Paraty (3 daily; 1hr 30min); Rio (2 daily; 5hr).

Trains

From Bauru to Campo Grande (2 daily; 20hr); Corumbá (1 daily; 32hr).
From São Paulo to Bauru (3 daily; 6hr 35min); Campinas (10 daily; 1hr 35min); Brasília (1 daily Mon–Fri; 23hr); Rio (1 daily; 9hr).

CHAPTER EIGHT

THE SOUTH

The states forming the **south** of Brazil – **Paraná, Santa Catarina** and **Rio Grande do Sul** – are generally considered to be the most developed part of the country. The smallest of Brazil's regions, the south maintains an economic influence completely out of proportion to its size. This is largely the result of two factors: the first is an agrarian structure that, to a great extent, is based on highly efficient small and medium-sized units; and the second is the economically over-active population which produces a per capita output considerably higher than the national average. With little of the widespread poverty found elsewhere in the country, Brazilians tend to dismiss the south as being a region that has more in common with Europe or the United States than South America.

Superficially, at least, this view has much going for it. The inhabitants are largely of European origin anyway and live in well-ordered cities where there's little of the obvious squalor prevalent elsewhere. However, beneath the tranquil setting there are tensions: due to land shortages people are constantly forced to move vast distances – as far away as Acre in the western Amazon – to avoid being turned into mere day-labourers, and *favelas* are an increasingly common sight in Curitiba, Porto Alegre and the other large cities of the south. From time to time these tensions explode as landless peasants invade the huge, under-used *latifúndios* found in the west and south of the region, but little has been done to appease demands for genuine land reform.

For the tourist, though, the region offers much that's attractive. The **coast** has a subtropical climate that in the summer months (November to March) attracts Brazilians who want to avoid the oppressive heat of northern resorts. And the coast has a vegetation and atmosphere that feels more Mediterranean than South American. Much of the Paranaense coast is still unspoilt by the ravages of mass tourism, and building development is virtually forbidden on the beautiful islands of the **Bay of Paranaguá**. By way of contrast, tourists have encroached along Santa Catarina's coast, but only **Balneário Camburiú** has been allowed to develop into a concrete jungle. Otherwise, resorts such as those on the **Ilha do Santa Catarina** remain small, and do little to detract from the region's natural beauty.

The **interior** is even less visited. Much of it is mountainous and the home of people whose way of life seems to have altered little since the arrival of the European pioneers last century. Cities in the interior that were founded by Germans (such as **Blumenau** in Santa Catarina), Italians (**Caxias do Sul** in Rio Grande do Sul) and Ukrainians (**Prudentópolis** in Paraná) have lost most of their former ethnic character, but only short distances from them are villages and hamlets where time appears to have stood still. The highland areas between **Lages** and **Vacaria**, and the grasslands of Rio Grande do Sul, are largely given

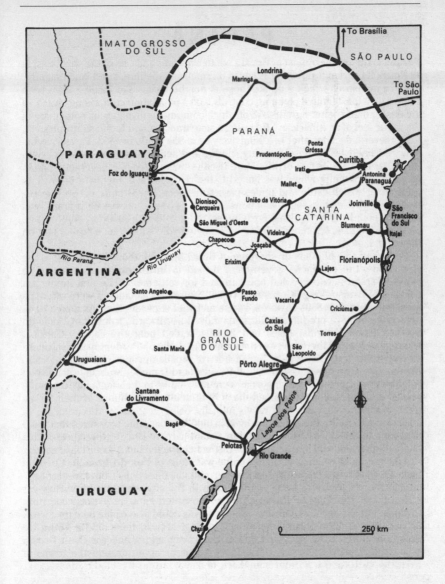

over to vast cattle ranches, where the modern *gaúchos* keep alive many of the skills of their forefathers.

Travelling around the south is generally easy, and there's a fine **road** network. Most north–south **buses** stick to the road running near the coast, but it's easy to devise routes passing through the interior, perhaps taking in the Jesuit ruins of **São Miguel** or the spectacular waterfalls of **Foz do Iguaçu.**

PARANÁ

Paraná is the northernmost of Brazil's southern states and one of the wealthiest in all Brazil. Its agricultural sector is based on small and medium-sized land holdings, modern industries which – unlike those of neighbouring São Paulo – have been subject to at least limited planning controls, and a population comprising largely of the descendants of immigrants. All of which combine to give Paraná something of the vague feel of an American Midwestern state transplanted to the subtropics.

For several decades after breaking away from São Paulo in 1853, Paraná's economy remained based on pig-raising, timber extraction and *erva mate* (a South American tree, the leaves of which are used to make a tea-like beverage), and in its early years the province was linked to the rest of Brazil only by a network of trails along which cattle and mules passed between Rio Grande do Sul's grasslands and the mines and plantations of the northern provinces. Paraná was sparsely populated by Indians, Portuguese and mixed-race *caboclos*, who worked on the *latifúndios*, scratched a living as semi-nomadic subsistence farmers or, on the coast, fished.

Then, because of a labour shortage in Brazil brought about by the end of the slave trade, the provincial government turned to **immigration** as a means to expand Paraná's economy and open up land for settlement. The first immigrant colonies of British, Volga-Germans, French, Swiss and Icelanders were utter failures, but, from the 1880s onwards, others met with some success. As mixed farmers, coffee or soya producers, Germans moved northwards from Rio Grande do Sul and Santa Catarina; Poles and Italians settled near the capital, Curitiba; Ukrainians centred themselves in the south, especially on Prudentópolis; Japanese spread south from São Paulo; and a host of smaller groups, including Dutch, Mennonites, Koreans, Russian "Old Believers" and Danube-Swabians established colonies elsewhere with varying success rates. Thanks to their isolation, the immigrants' descendants have retained many of the cultural traditions of their forefathers, traditions that are only now gradually being eroded by the influence of television and radio, the education system, and by economic pressures that force migration to the cities or to new land in distant parts of Brazil. Nevertheless, this multi-ethnic blend still lends Paraná its distinct character and a special fascination.

Unless you're heading straight for the waterfalls of **Foz do Iguaçu**, **Curitiba** makes a good base. Transport services fan out in all directions from the state capital and there's plenty to keep you occupied in the city while you're waiting for connections. The **Bay of Paranaguá** can be visited as a short excursion from Curitiba, but the bay's islands and colonial towns could also easily take up a week or more of your time. Inland, the strange geological formations of **Vila Velha** are usually visited as a day trip from Curitiba, but – by changing buses in Ponta Grossa – you can head west to the Ukrainian-dominated region around the towns of **Prudentópolis** and **Irati**; and from there, head yet further west to Foz do Iguaçu.

Curitiba

Founded in 1648 as a gold-mining camp, **CURITIBA** was of little importance until 1853 when it was made capital of Paraná. Since then, the city's population has steadily risen from a mere few thousand, reaching 140,000 in 1940 and some 1.8

million today. It's said that Curitiba is barely a Brazilian city at all, a view that has some basis. The inhabitants are overwhelmingly of European origin, descendants of Polish, German, Italian and other immigrants who settled in Curitiba and in surrounding villages that have since been engulfed by the expanding metropolis. On average, Curitibanos enjoy Brazil's highest standard of living: the city boasts health, education and public transport facilities that are the envy of other parts of the country. There are *favelas*, but they're well hidden and, because of the cool, damp winters, sturdier than those in cities to the north. The wooden houses of Curitiba's lower and middle classes often resemble those of frontier homesteads and frequently betray their inhabitants' central European origins, with half-hip roofs, carved window frames and elaborate trellis work. As elsewhere in Brazil, the rich live in mansions and luxury condominiums, but even these are a little less ostentatious, and need fewer security precautions, than usual.

Many late-nineteenth- and early-twentieth-century buildings have been saved from the developers who, since the 1960s, have ravaged most Brazilian cities, and there's a clearly defined **historic quarter** where colonial buildings have been preserved. Much of the centre is closed to traffic and, in a country where the car has become a symbol of development, planners from all over Brazil descend on Curitiba to discover how a city can function effectively when pedestrians and buses are given priority. Thanks in part to the lack of traffic, it's a pleasure just strolling around and, what's more, you can wander the city, day or night, in reasonable safety.

One result of its being so untypical of Brazil is that few visitors bother to remain in Curitiba longer than it takes to change buses or planes. At most, they stay for a night, prior to taking the early morning train to the coast. But it deserves more than this: although there's some truth in the image of northern European dullness, Curitiba's attractive buildings, interesting museums and variety of restaurants make a stay here pleasant – if not overly exciting.

Arriving and finding a place to stay

Curitiba is easy to reach from all parts of Brazil and, once here, you'll find yourself in a Brazilian city at its most efficient. Flights to most major Brazilian cities depart from *Alfonso Pena* **airport**, about thirty minutes from the city centre. Taxis to and from the airport charge about $5, or take a bus marked *Aeroporto*: in the centre, they leave from outside the *Hotel Presidente* on Rua Westphalen.

The main bus and train stations (the **Rodoferroviária**) are located adjacent to one another, about ten blocks from the city centre. Almost every hour, express **buses** depart for São Paulo, Rio, Florianópolis and Porto Alegre and, though less frequently, most other state capitals are also served as are most major towns in neighbouring states. Buses to towns in Paraná, and to Paraguay via Foz do Iguaçu, leave from the same station. The only remaining passenger **trains** from Curitiba are an occasional service to Lapa (see "Around Curitiba") and the line to Antonina and Paranaguá (see "Bay of Paranaguá", below), both of which have become major tourist attractions.

From the *Rodoferroviária*, it takes about twenty minutes to walk to the centre, or there's a minibus from almost in front of the station: catch it at the intersection of Avenida Afonso Camargo and Avenida Sete de Setembro, to the left of the entrance to the station's driveway.

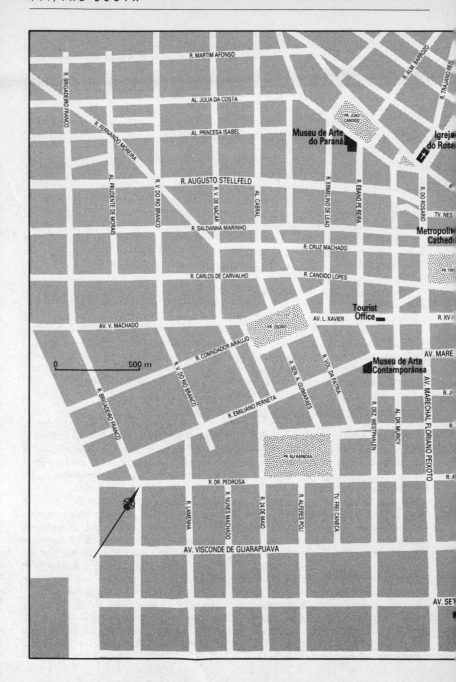

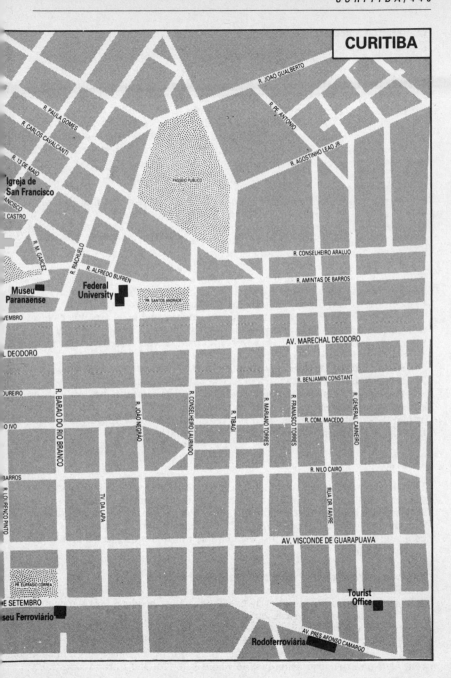

CURITIBA

R. JOAO GUALBERTO

R. PE. ANTONIO

R. AGOSTINHO LEAO JR.

R. PAULA GOMES

R. CARLOS CAVALCANTI

R. 13 DE MAIO

Igreja de San Francisco

ANCISCO

E CASTRO

R. M. GARCEZ

R. RIACHUELO

R. ALFREDO BUFREN

PASSEIO PUBLICO

R. CONSELHEIRO ARAUJO

R. AMINTAS DE BARROS

Museu Paranaense

Federal University

PR. SANTOS ANDRADE

VEMBRO

AV. MARECHAL DEODORO

L DEODORO

R. BENJAMIN CONSTANT

OUREIRO

R. BARAO DO RIO BRANCO

R. JOAO NEGRAO

R. CONSELHEIRO LAURINDO

R. TIBAGI

R. MARIANO TORRES

R. FRANASCO TORRES

R. GENERAL CARNEIRO

O IVO

R. COM. MACEDO

BARROS

R. NILO CAIRO

R. LOURENCO PINTO

TV. DA LAPA

RUA DR. FAIVRE

AV. VISCONDE DE GUARAPUAVA

Tourist Office

E SETEMBRO

seu Ferroviário

AV. PRES AFONSO CAMARGO

Rodoferroviária

Information and getting around

PARANATUR, the state **tourist information** organisation, has its headquarters near the *Rodoferroviária*, at Avenida Sete de Setembro 2077 (Mon–Fri 8am–noon & 2–6pm), and maintains a branch at the airport. The municipal tourist body, *SEITUR*, has offices in a disused tram on Rua das Flores (Mon–Fri 8am–noon & 2–6pm, Sat 8am–noon) and at the *Rodoferroviária*.

Curitiba is small enough to be able to **walk** to most places, but there's an extremely efficient municipal **bus** network. In the city centre, the two main bus terminals are at Praça Osório and Praça Rui Barbosa, from where buses head out into the suburbs. **Taxis** are easy to come by and, as distances are generally small, they're cheap, too.

Accommodation

If your sole reason for being in Curitiba is to catch the dawn train to the coast, stay at one of the numerous cheap and medium-priced **hotels** in front of the *Rodoferroviária* on Avenida Afonso Camargo: the *Jaraguá Curitiba* is $30 for a double; the *Império*, $8 a double. On the intersecting Avenida Sete de Setembro, at no. 1951, the *San Raphael* and, just across the road, the *Piratini*, both charge about $8 for a double room; while at no. 1866, the *Condor* charges about $14. Running off these two avenues, on Rua Mariano Torres there's the *Itamarati* ($8 double) and the *Doral Torres* ($14 double), while at no. 386 of the parallel Rua Francisco, the *Costa Brava* charges about $15 for a double room.

Places to stay **in the centre** are widely scattered, and most are either cheap and squalid or, especially those in the vicinity of Praça Osório and Rua das Flores, expensive and flash. However, a couple of very pleasant and central medium-priced hotels worth considering are the *Hotel O'Hara*, Rua XV de Novembro 770, on Praça Santos Andrade, and the *Grande Hotel Candeias*, Rua XV de Novembro 582. Both are about $25 for a double room.

Otherwise, there's an extremely friendly and secure **youth hostel**, with no curfew, at Rua Padre Agostinho 645, in Mercês, a suburb that's a safe (even late at night) twenty-minute walk from the centre, on the opposite side of the city from the *Rodoferroviária*: it's around $3 by taxi to the hostel.

The City

Being comparatively compact, Curitiba is best explored on foot and, apart from the museums – many of which are located in the central commercial district – most interest is concentrated in the historic centre. The main commercial district, with the Rua das Flores (part of Avenida XV de Novembro) at its heart, is only a couple of blocks south of the historic quarter, which is concentrated around the Lagoa da Ordem.

The commercial district: Rua das Flores and around

The **Rua das Flores** – a pedestrianised precinct lined with graceful, and carefully restored, pastel-coloured early twentieth-century buildings – is the centre's main late afternoon and early evening meeting point: its bars, tearooms and coffee shops crammed with customers. Few of the surrounding streets are especially attractive, but don't fail to visit the former city hall, at Praça Generoso Marques, across from the flower market. Built in 1916, the building is a magnificent Art Nouveau construction that now houses the **Museu Paranaense** (Mon–

Fri 10am–6pm, Sat & Sun 1–6pm). One of Curitiba's more interesting museums, it displays a limited but attractive collection of artefacts charting the history of Paraná from pre-colonial times into the twentieth century.

There are a number of **other museums** within the commercial centre (the tourist office has a complete list), but only two are really worth going out of your way for. Of obvious interest to railway buffs, the **Museu Ferroviário**, in Praça Eufrásio Correia (Tues–Fri 1–7pm, Sat & Sun 8am–1pm), contains relics from Paraná's railway era. The display relating to the history of the Curitiba–Paranagua line is particulary interesting (though, unfortunately, the explanatory text is only in Portuguese), and the building housing the museum was the original terminus of the line. The **Museu de Arte Contemporânea**, at Rua Westphalen 16 (Mon–Fri 9am–6pm, Sat 9.30am–6pm, Sun noon–6pm), concentrates on Paranaense artists in its permanent and temporary exhibits. A brief look round the museum's diminutive collection will be enough to recognise that Paraná is unlikely to establish itself as a trendsetter in the Brazilian contemporary art scene.

A couple of blocks north from Rua das Flores is Praça Tiradentes where the **Catedral Metropolitana** is located. Inaugurated in 1893, and supposedly inspired by Barcelona's cathedral, it's a totally unremarkable neo-Gothic construction.

The historic quarter

Near the cathedral, a pedestrian tunnel leads to Curitiba's **historic quarter**, an area of impeccably preserved eighteenth- and nineteenth-century buildings. With few exceptions, the whitewashed buildings of the old town are of a style that would not be out of place in a small village in Portugal. Today the buildings all have state preservation orders on them and do duty as bars, restaurants, art and craft galleries and cultural centres.

Two of Curitiba's oldest churches physically dominate the historic quarter. Dating from 1737, with the bell tower added in the late nineteenth century, the **Igreja da Ordem Terceira de São Francisco das Chagas** (on Rua São Francisco) is the city's oldest surviving building and one of the nicest examples of Portuguese ecclesiastical architecture in southern Brazil. Plain outside, the church is also simple within, its only decoration typically Portuguese blue and white tiling and late Baroque altars. The church contains the **Museu de Arte Sacra** (Tues–Sat 9am–noon & 2–7pm, Sun 9am–noon), with relics gathered from Curitiba's churches. Opposite the church is the mid-eighteenth-century **Casa Romário Martins**, Curitiba's oldest surviving house. A short distance uphill from here, on the same road, the church of **Nossa Senhora do Rosário** dates back to 1737, built by and for Curitiba's slave population. However, after falling into total disrepair, the church was completely reconstructed in the 1930s and remains colonial in style only.

Carrying on up the hill, the **Museu de Arte do Paraná**, on Praça João Cândido (Tues–Fri 10am–6pm, Sat 2–6pm, Sun 10am–2pm), contains work by mainly Paranaense artists of the nineteenth and early twentieth centuries, who were barely more talented than their present day successors.

Out of the centre: Parque João Paulo II

North of the old town, about 3km from the centre of Curitiba, the **Parque João Paulo II** was created to commemorate the Papal visit to Curitiba in 1980. In the heart of the park, the **Museu da Imigração Polonêsa** (Wed–Mon 9am–5pm) celebrates Polish immigration to Paraná. It's made up of several log cabins, built by Polish immigrants in the 1880s and relocated here from the Colônia Thomaz Coelho. The cabins contain displays of typical objects used by pioneer families, and one building has been turned into a shrine to the "Black Madonna of Czestochowa". There's a **snack bar** attached to the museum where homemade Polish (or, more accurately, Polish-Brazilian) cakes, snacks and superb locally produced vodkas are served, and a **shop** selling Polish handicrafts and wonderful postcards marking the Papal visit. The museum's staff are extremely helpful and are pleased to offer information about the museum and the history of Paraná's Polish community.

To get to the park, take the yellow #104 bus going to *Abranches* (a suburb with a high concentration of Poles) from Praça Tiradentes, or any bus that goes to the Palácio Iguaçu, a massive complex of state government buildings which borders the park.

Food, drink and entertainment

Given Curitiba's prosperity and its inhabitants' diverse ethnic origins, it's not surprising that there's a huge range of **restaurants**, far too many to list. What is strange, however, is that although Curitibanos take eating out very seriously, there are few genuinely good restaurants. Snacking on cakes in the excellent **cafés** is a good alternative. There's a fair amount of evening **entertainment**, too, based around the usual bars, cinemas and theatres.

Restaurants

Italian restaurants are mainly concentrated in Santa Felicidade (see "Around Curitiba", below), but downtown try the excellent *Bologna*, Rua Carlos de Carvalho 150 (closed Tues), or, across the road from the youth hostel, *A Landerna*, Rua Padre Agostinho 690 (Mon–Sat dinner only, Sun lunch only), a very good, though fairly expensive, pizzeria.

The *Warsóvia*, Avenida Batel 2059 (closed Mon; Sun lunch only), out from the centre in Batel, a northern suburb reached by bus from Praça Osório, serves heavy, vaguely **Polish** dishes. If that doesn't appeal, close by there's the *Maison du Crêpe*, Avenida Batel 1938, which – despite its name – has **Hungarian** pretensions and is best avoided; as are Curitiba's "Swiss" restaurants. More authentic is the *Hummel Hummel* in the historic centre, at Largo Coronel Eneas 40, which has hearty **German** food and boasts a menu extending well beyond the pork, sauerkraut and boiled potatoes typical of most German restaurants in Brazil.

There are some quite good **Portuguese** restaurants – *Alpendre*, in the centre at Avenida Visconde do Rio Branco 1046 (closed Mon; Sun lunch only), and, in Mercês, *A Camponesa do Minho*, Rua Padre Anchieta 978 – but all are very expensive (by Brazilian standards at least) as many of the dishes are based on imported dried cod (*bacalhau*). Also expensive is the *Ile de France*, downtown at Praça 19 de Dezembro 538 (dinner only; closed Sun), a reasonable attempt at **French** cuisine.

At the other end of the price spectrum are two **vegetarian** restaurants located downtown near one other: the imaginatively named *Vegetariano*, Rua Carlos de Carvalho 127 (lunch only; closed Sat), and the *Super Vegetariano*, Rua Cruz Machado 217 (closed Sat). Also central, cheap and offering large helpings of simple, but good, **Lebanese** food is the *Oriente Arabe*, Rua Ebano Pereira 26.

As far as **Brazilian** food's concerned, carnivores will have no problem stumbling upon a *churrascaria*, which are scattered throughout the city. Unusual soups are the speciality of the cheap and filling *Acrotona*, Rua Cruz Machado 408 (dinner only); close by, also downtown, the *Geraes*, Rua Visconde do Rio Branco 954 (closed Mon; Sun lunch only), offers very good Minas Gerais dishes. At Rua XV de Novembro 416, in an attractive turn-of-the-century building, also housing an arts cinema, are two restaurants serving good value, though somewhat dull, Brazilian and "international" meals, snacks and desserts. Being right in the city's commercial centre, this is a useful and pleasantly quiet spot to relax over lunch.

Cafés and tearooms
Modern Paraná was founded on coffee and European immigrants, and one result in Curitiba has been a profusion of "old world"-style cafés and tearooms, most concentrated on the Rua das Flores. Virtually unchanged in style and clientele since opening in the 1920s (elderly ladies and gentlemen in ill-fitting grey suits predominate) are the *Confeitaria Schaffer* (at no. 424), the *Confeitaria das Famílias* (no. 372) and the *Confeitaria Cometa* (no. 410), at all of which the coffee's good, the tea's bad and the cakes are sticky.

If it's merely the tea and cakes that you're after, and you're prepared to forego the bygone era atmosphere, try the *Petit Café*, Rua Cruz Machado 256, next to the *Caravelle Palace Hotel*, which is definitely Curitiba's best *confeitaria*.

Bars
During the late afternoon and early evening locals congregate in the pavement cafés at the Praça Osório end of Rua das Flores, but as the evening progresses the historic centre comes to life, its **bars** and restaurants attracting a mainly young and well-heeled crowd. On Praça Garibaldi, and the streets extending off it, there are numerous bars, many with **live music** (typically Brazilian rock music, jazz and what seem to be parodies of Country & Western), though finding somewhere decent is a bit hit-and-miss. In the past, the *Pub John Bull* (neither a pub nor recognisably English), near the corner of Praça Garibaldi and Alameida Dr. Muricy, attracted superior musicians and a fair mix of people, but things change fast.

Cinema and theatre
Films reach Curitiba fast and details of the latest releases are found in "Bom Programa", a weekly events leaflet distributed by the tourist office and most hotels. There's a good "arts" cinema in the *Galleria Schaffer*, Rua das Flores 424, showing non-Hollywood productions.

During the winter, the *Teatro Guaira* (Praça Santos Andrade, across from the Federal University) has a varied schedule of **theatre**, **ballet** and **classical music**. With three excellent auditoriums, the *Guaira* is justified in its claim of being one of the finest theatres in Latin America and is often host to companies from the rest of Brazil, and even international tours.

Listings

Airlines *Transbrasil*, Rua. Mal. Deodoro 410 (☎223-2614); *Varig/Cruzeiro*, Rua XV de Novembro 614 (☎222-2522); *VASP*, Rua XV de Novembro 537 (☎224-3303).

Car rental *Hertz*, Rua Emiliano Perneta 420 (☎223-0023); *Localiza*, Avenida Cândido de Abreu 336 (☎224-7764); *Nobre*, Rua Benjamin Constant 66 (☎222-9972).

Consulates *Austria*, Rua Mal. Floriano Peixoto 1237 (☎224-6795); *Denmark* and *Norway* are in Paranaguá at Rua Com. Correia Jr. 147 (☎422-2000); *France*, Av. Paraná 968 (☎253-4249); *Italy*, Rua Atilio Borio 680 (☎262-4042); *Netherlands*, Rua Mal. Floriano Peixoto 96, Sala 172 (☎222-0097); Switzerland, Av. Sete de Setembro 6780 (☎244-4363); *West Germany*, Av. Joâo Gualberto 1237 (☎252-4244).

Exchange At times, when there's a black market rate for the dollar, Curitiba is a good place to change money. Ask the travel agents on Rua XV de Novembro (try *Jade Turismo* at no. 477). Elsewhere in Paraná, except in Paranaguá and Foz do Iguaçu, don't count on being able to change dollars at a reasonable rate.

Feminism Contact the *Conselho Municipal da Condição Feminina*, Rua Claudino dos Santos 104, in the historic centre.

Handicrafts Several shops in the historic centre sell Paranaense crafts, especially African-influenced wood carvings from the coast. However, Polish and Ukrainian items are as "typical" a souvenir of Paraná as you're likely to find. For Ukrainian crafts, *Vecelko* (Rua Brigadeiro Franco 898; midway between the youth hostel and city centre) sells simple embroideries and intricately painted eggs. *Artesanato Típico Polonês* (in the Parque Joâo Paulo II) also sells Polish items, including painted eggs.

Hospitals In emergencies use the *Pronto-Socorro Municipal* at Avenida São José 738 (☎262-1121). Otherwise, go to *Nossa Senhora das Graça* at Rua Alcides Munhoz 433 (☎222-6422).

Market Every Sunday (9am–6pm), outside the university at Praça Santos Andrade, there's a handicraft market but you're unlikely to find anything terribly distinctive amongst the hippyish jewellery and leather items.

Post Office The main office is at Rua XV de Novembro 700, by Praça Santos Andrade.

Telephone Office Next to the main post office on Praça Santos Andrade.

Around Curitiba

Apart from heading down to the coast (see "Bay of Paranaguá") there are several places easily reachable by bus that are well worth seeing on day trips from Curitiba. On the city's outskirts, **Santa Felicidade** is near enough to visit for an evening, to eat at one of the many Italian restaurants there, while **Lapa**, a small colonial country town 80km southwest of the city is a pleasant place to go for a typical Paranaense Sunday lunch. Just under 100km west of Curitiba is **Vila Velha**, home of a strange rock formation that's the basis of a state park.

Santa Felicidade

Now almost an outer suburb of Curitiba, about 8km northwest of the city, **SANTA FELICIDADE** was founded as a farming colony in 1878 by Italians transferred from failed coastal settlements and by newly-arrived immigrants from northern Italy. Only the oldest inhabitants still speak their mother tongue and Santa Felicidade now has little Italian feel to it, the European legacy essentially that of grape and wine production. Across the road from the church there's an interesting **cemetery**, dating from 1886, but the only real reason to visit Santa Felicidade is for the **restaurants**, which line the main road, Avenida Manoel Ribas, alongside shops selling plants, wicker items, wine and other produce of the local smallholders.

The restaurants compete fiercely for the custom of Curitiba's nouveaux riches – each vying to surpass the next in vulgarity. It's easy to think you're entering the kind of lavish motel Brazilians surreptitiously check into. As far as the food goes, in theory most varieties of Italian regional cooking can be found, but it's best to avoid those claiming to specialise in Sicilian or Neopolitan dishes and instead try those with no particular regional claim. These places generally offer the northern Italian food in which the local cooking is rooted. Don't expect the same style of food (not to say wine, made from locally grown American grapes) that you may have tasted in Italy. Dishes have been adapted according to the availability of ingredients and the results are, at best, an interesting blend of local Brazilian and Italian influences – rustic dishes as eaten by the *colonos* themselves. At worst, they're simply poor imitations of Italian cooking. Whether in a restaurant decked out to look like a pseudo-Italian *palazzo*, a medieval castle or somewhere less pretentious, charges remain much the same: about $4 per person for the *rodizio di pasta*, a continuous round of pasta, salad and meat dishes.

Buses to Santa Felicidade can be caught on Travessa Nestor de Castro, at the intersection of Rua do Rosario, just below Curitiba's historic quarter. Take a yellow bus that goes along Avenida Manoel Ribas and it takes about 45 minutes to reach Santa Felicidade.

Lapa

Also worth visiting for culinary reasons, if for little else, is **LAPA**, a sleepy provincial town founded in 1731 on the trail linking Rio Grande do Sul to the once important cattle market in Sorocaba.

Of no great architectural interest, it's only because Lapa is one of the very few towns in Paraná's interior that has made efforts to preserve its late-eighteenth- and early-nineteenth-century buildings that the town has become a favourite place for Sunday excursions from Curitiba.

Four blocks behind the **Rodoviária**, Lapa's main church, the **Igreja Matriz de Santo Antônio**, dominates the main square, Praça General Carneiro. Built in the late eighteenth century, but reformed over subsequent years, the church's interior displays – all too typically – no original features. However, there are several small **museums** of mild interest that are worth entering, most notably the **Museu de Epoca**, an early-nineteenth-century house furnished in period style: it's on Rua XV de Novembro 67, opposite the Panteon dos Herois. The **Museu de Armas**, on the corner of Rua Barão do Rio Branco and Rua Henrique Dias, in a house of the same period, contains a poor collection of nineteenth-century weaponry.

It's to sample **Paranaense cooking**, rare in Curitiba itself, that makes Lapa really worth a visit. A few metres uphill from the *Rodoviária* is the excellent *Lipski Restaurante*, and behind the bus terminal is the cheaper, but similarly good, *Restaurante Santa Rita*, at Rua Barão do Rio Branco 1240, near the *Hotel São Carlos*.

There are ten **buses** a day between Curitiba and Lapa, but it's much more pleasant going by **train**: a steam engine covers the 80km in two and a half hours, but its schedule is restricted to departures on only the first and third Sunday of the month. Trains depart from Curitiba's railway museum – *not* the *Rodoferroviária* – at Praça Eufrasio Correia and Avenida Sete de Setembro, at 8.45am, returning at 4pm; **tickets** must be purchased in advance, no later than 8pm the day before departure.

The Parque Estadual de Vila Velha

At **Vila Velha**, carved by time and nature from glacial sandstone deposits, stand 23 rock pillars, looking from a distance like monumental, abstract sculptures. The sandstone formation is a result of sand deposited between 300 and 400 million years ago during the carboniferous period, when the region was covered by a massive ice sheet. As the glaciers moved, the soil was affected by erosion and the ice brought with it tons of rock fragments. When the ice thawed, this material remained, and as natural erosion took its course and rivers rose, these deposits were gradually worked into their current formations.

The **Parque Estadual de Vila Velha** is 97km, an hour and a half by bus, from Curitiba. From the city's *Rodoviária*, take a *semi-direito* bus (roughly every two hours) to PONTA GROSSA and ask to be let off at the park's entrance, a half-hour walk from the rock formations. If you're lucky, the driver may enter the park itself, leaving you only a few metres from the beginning of the area where you can wander between and above the fantastically shaped stones and in the partially wooded section behind. Views over the surrounding countryside from here are tremendous. There's a small entrance charge to the park, but it gets you a free, detailed map, an elevator-ride into a crater-lake, and use of the **swimming pool** – a welcome relief from the midday heat since, at an altitude of 1000m, the sun is deceptively strong.

In the park there are a couple of simple **restaurants**, but apart from a **campsite**, there's no overnight accommodation available. However, there are good late afternoon bus services back to Curitiba, so there's no chance of being left stranded. If you're travelling on to Iguaçu, there's no need to return to Curitiba: instead, take a bus (or hitch a lift) the 20km to Ponta Grossa from where you can catch an overnight bus to Foz do Iguaçu.

The Bay of Paranaguá

Sweeping down from the plateau upon which Curitiba lies, the **Serra do Mar** has long been a formidable barrier separating the coast of Paraná from the interior. Until 1885 only a narrow road (in reality often little more than a trail) connected Curitiba to the coast and the **Bay of Paranaguá**, and it took two days for carriages to cover the 75km from what was, at the time, the main port, Antonina. In 1880, work began on the construction of a **railway** between Curitiba and Paranaguá. Completed in 1885, this remains a marvel of late-nineteenth-century British engineering. Sufferers from vertigo be warned: the line grips narrow mountain ridges, traverses 41 bridges and viaducts and passes through 14 tunnels as the trains gradually wind their way down to sea level. Passing through **Morumbi State Park**, the views are absolutely spectacular, and the towering Paraná pines at the higher altitudes at the beginning of the journey and the subtropical foliage at lower levels are unforgettable.

If the fight to save the Amazon rainforest is now on, that for the **Mata Atlântica**, the Brazilian Atlantic forest, today covering barely three percent of its original area, has been all but lost. But the forbidding terrain of Paraná's Serra do Mar has provided limited natural protection from exploitation by farming and lumbering interests and, since 1986, legal protection for a wider area has been granted by the state government. In theory, the region's future development must serve the

---

GETTING THERE: TRAVEL TO THE BAY

● **Trains**: the regular train departs from Curitiba's *Rodoçerroviária* daily at 7am, arriving at 11.20am; departing Paranaguá at 4.30pm, arriving in Curitiba at 8.20pm. It's advisable to buy tickets in advance ($2 return). There's also an air-conditioned tourist train, the *Litorina*, stopping at scenic points. It departs Curitiba at 8.30am and arrives in Paranaguá at 11.20am; leaving Paranaguá at 3.30pm to arrive in Curitiba at 6.05pm. At the weekend, there's also a *Litorina* service to Antonina. Tickets for the *Litorina* ($5 return) must be purchased several days before. For the best views, sit on the left-hand side going down to the coast and on the right when returning.

● **Buses**: if timing doesn't allow you to travel by train to the coast, take a bus which follows the Graciosa road (2 daily), a route almost as beautiful as the railway's. Between Paranaguá, Antonina, Morretes and Curitiba there are constant buses, around a two-hour ride. Buses between Guaraqueçaba and Curitiba take six hours (2 daily), and between Guaraqueçaba and Paranaguá four hours (2 daily), both services going via Antonina. If travelling to or from Santa Catarina, Curitiba can be avoided by taking a bus between Paranaguá and Guaratuba (15 daily, most via Pontal do Sul for access to the Ilha do Mel), and another between Guaratuba and Joinville.

---

needs of local communities, but the regulations are being blatantly flouted, most persistently by ranchers and plantation owners in remote regions. It remains to be seen to what extent the Paranaense coastal zone will remain unspoilt.

Antonina

An important port until the mid-1940s, **ANTONINA** has all the atmosphere of a town that has long since become an irrelevance. As ships grew larger and access to Antonina's harbour was restricted by silt, the town abandoned its role as Paraná's main port and entered a long period of stagnation. Due to its decline, Antonina's eighteenth- and nineteenth-century buildings have largely been saved from the developers, leaving the town with a certain dilapidated, backwater charm. With neither masterpieces of colonial architecture, nor beaches immediately accessible, the town attracts few other than Sunday visitors from Curitiba. Nonetheless, Antonina is easily the most pleasant of Paraná's coastal towns, and is a considerably better place to stay than Paranaguá, only a 45-minute bus ride away. It also has an important Carnaval.

Arriving by bus, finding your bearings couldn't be easier as the *Rodoviária* is located right in the town centre. On leaving it, turn right onto Rua XV de Novembro, the main commercial thoroughfare, and walk two blocks, past once-elegant nineteenth-century merchants' houses, until you reach Rua Vale Porto. Continue along this road another block to Antonina's main square and evening meeting point, **Praça Coronel Macedo**, which also contains the town's principal church, **Nossa Senhora do Pilar**. Imposing rather than interesting, the church dates back to 1715 and is built in typical Portuguese colonial style. Its interior has sadly been completely remodelled and preserves no original features, removed – or so say locals – and sold abroad by the priests from the United States who are attached to the church and run the town's radio station. You can also reach the church by a couple of alternative routes: turning right from the *Rodoviária*, walk along the waterfront past the municipal market and wharf, and in about ten minutes you'll find yourself behind the church; or, if **arriving by train**, from the station turn right and right again onto Rua Cons. Alves de Araujo, which leads to Praça Coronel Macedo and the church.

Across from the church, next to Antonina's oldest house (at Praça Cel. Macedo 214), which is of late-seventeenth-century origin, is the *Hotel Regency Capela*, built amid the ruins of an eighteenth-century Jesuit mission and, at $25 for a double room, worth a splurge. If you can't be tempted, the *Hotel Cristina*, Rua XV de Novembro 285, is comfortable and much cheaper.

As for **meals**, avoid the *Regency Capela*'s extremely mediocre "international" restaurant and go instead to one serving seafood or the regional speciality, *barreado*, a dish only available on the Paranaense coast and most easily found in Antonina. **Barreado** used only to be eaten by the poor during Carnaval as it can provide food for several days and requires little attention while cooking. Traditonally, it's made of beef, bacon, onion, cumin and other spices, placed in successive layers in a large clay urn, covered and then "*barreada*" (sealed) with a paste of ash and *farinha* (manioc flour); and then slowly cooked in a wood-fired oven for twelve to fifteen hours. Today pressure cookers are often used (though not by the better restaurants), and gas or electric ovens almost always substitute for wood-fired ones. *Barreado* is served with *farinha* which you spread on a plate, place some meat and gravy on top and eat with banana and orange slices. In Antonina the best *barreado* (as well as good seafood) is found at the *Restaurante Caicara*, Rua Heitor Soares Gomes 82; but cheaper and almost as good is *Tia Rosinha*, Rua Cons. Antônio Prade 54, across from the municipal market.

If you find you must **change dollars** in Antonina, try *Betty's Presentes*, Rua XV de Novembro 203, a shop selling mainly junk souvenirs and local handicrafts.

Morretes

MORRETES, a small colonial town founded in 1721, lies sixteen kilometres inland from Antonina, at the headwater where the Nhundiaquara river meets the tidal waters of Paranaguá Bay. Buses constantly pass through Morretes on their way between Curitiba and Antonina, and Antonina and Paranaguá, but it's an unremarkable place except for its production of excellent *cachacas*. However, Morretes is a good base for visiting **Marumbi State Park**: to get there, take a bus to the village of SÃO JOÃO DE GRACIOSA, a two-kilometre walk from the park's entrance. At the entrance pick up a trail map and, if **camping** (not very pleasant because of the heavy rainfall and mosquitoes which together characterise the entire region) enquire about sites. The original **Graciosa trail**, constructed between 1646 and 1653 to link Curitiba with the coast, passes through the park alongside the newer road, and is slowly being reclaimed from the forest. There's also a network of other trails from which – on clear days at least – there are stunning views, and there's a wealth of flora and fauna. The park is open all year round.

There are three **hotels** in Morretes, the nicest of which is the *Nhundiaquara Hotel*, Rua Carneiro 13 ($8 double), picturesquely positioned on the river in the town centre. With less character, but more expensive and more comfortable, is the *Porto Real*, Rua Visconde do Rio Branco 85; and cheapest of all is the very basic *Bom Jesus*, Rua 15 de Novembro 281. The *Nhundiaquara Hotel* has Morretes' best **restaurant**, but it's only open for lunch when a very good and inexpensive *barreado* is served. Alternatively, try the *Serra do Mar*, Largo José Pereira, or the *Madalozo*, both of which also specialise in regional dishes and fish.

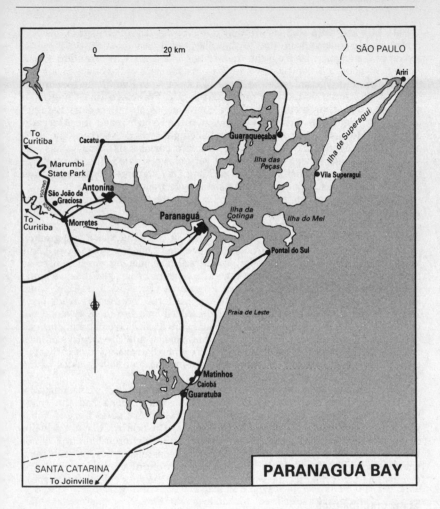

Paranaguá

Propelled into the position of Brazil's second most important port for exports within a couple of decades, **PARANAGUÁ** has lost most of its former character, becoming just another victim of the Brazilian "miracle". It was founded in 1585, and is one of Brazil's oldest cities, but only recently have measures been undertaken to preserve its colonial buildings. While Antonina boasts less of interest than Paranaguá, it has at least remained largely intact and retains an instantly accessible charm.

Paranaguá doesn't, though what is worth seeing is conveniently concentrated in quite a small area, allowing you the possibility of spending a few pleasant hours between boats, trains or buses.

Both **bus** and **train** stations are only a few blocks from Paranaguá's historic centre, and in walking from one to the other you'll pass most of what's worth seeing of the city. Across from the train station is a **tourist information kiosk** (daily 8am–noon & 2–6pm) where they have useful maps of the city. Leaving the train station, turn left and walk the three blocks or so to Rua XV de Novembro. Here, on the corner, is the very pretty **Igreja São Francisco das Chagras**, a small and simple church built in 1741 and containing eighteenth-century Baroque altars. Turn right onto Rua XV de Novembro and you'll reach the **Mercado Municipal do Café**, a turn-of-the-century building that used to serve as the city's coffee market. Today the Art Nouveau structure contains handicraft stalls and simple restaurants serving excellent and very cheap seafood. Just beyond the market, Paranaguá's most imposing building, the fortress-like **Colegio dos Jesuítas**, the old Jesuit College, overlooks the waterfront.

It has had an unfortunate history. In 1682 the Jesuits were invited by Paranaguá's citizens to establish a school for their sons, and sixteen years later construction of the college began. Because it lacked a royal permit, the authorities promptly halted work on the college until 1738, when one was at last granted and building recommenced. In 1755 the college finally opened, only to close four years later with the Jesuits' expulsion from Brazil. The building was then used as the headquarters of the local militia, then as a customs house, and today is home to the **Museu de Arqueologia e Artes Populares** (Tues–Fri 10am–5pm, Mon, Sat & Sun noon–5pm). The stone-built college has three floors and is divided into 28 rooms and a yard where, until it was destroyed by a fire in 1896, stood the chapel. None of the museum's exhibits relate to the Jesuits, concentrating instead on prehistoric archaeology, Indian culture and popular art. The displays of local artefacts are of greatest interest, and there are some fine examples of early agricultural implements and of the basketry, lace-making and fishing skills of the Tupi-Guarani Indians, early settlers and *caboclos*.

Away from the waterfront, in the area above the Jesuit College, remaining colonial buildings are concentrated on Largo Monsenhor Celso and the roads running off it. The square is dominated by a cathedral that dates from 1575 but which has since suffered innumerable reforms. On nearby Rua Conselheiro Sinimbu is the charming, little **Igreja São Benedito**, a church built in 1784 for the use of the town's slaves, and one that is unusual for not having been renovated. Beyond the church is the **Fonte Velha** or **Fontinha**, a mid-seventeenth-century fountain, primarily noteworthy for being Paranaguá's oldest monument.

Some practicalities

In the end, though, Paranaguá remains basically a place to pass through, and it is worth getting details about leaving immediately you get here, and only later setting out to explore the city. If you find you have no alternative but to spend a night, there are plenty of cheap **hotels** around Rua XV de Novembro or, for more comfort, the *Hotel Graciosa*, Avenida Gabriel de Lara 455, is not bad.

The **Rodoviária** is located on the waterfront, a few hundred metres beyond the Jesuit College, and bus timetables are also available at the tourist information kiosk (see above). For information about **boat departures** ask at the fish market below the Jesuit College. Every morning, fishermen from all around the bay land their catches in Paranaguá and it's usually possible to find boats returning to most points (see below under "Guaraqueçaba"). Keep a careful eye on the weather as storms blow up quickly, making crossings uncomfortable and, because few boats carry lifejackets, even dangerous. Apart from short tourist excursions from the new municipal market near the bus station, the only **scheduled boat service** from Paranaguá – and one which does pay heed to safety – is for Guaraqueçaba, stopping off at the Ilha das Peças; departures are in the early afternoon on Wednesday and Friday.

The Ilha do Mel and the southeast coast

To the east of Paranaguá are Paraná's main beach resorts, principally attracting visitors from Curitiba seeking open sea and all the familiar comforts of home. The surrounding countryside is relentlessly flat and the beaches can't really compare with those of Santa Catarina or, for that matter, most other parts of Brazil. There is, however, one notable exception, the Ilha do Mel, which, despite being Paraná's most beautiful island, has been protected from tourism's worst effects by being classified as an ecological protection zone – building is strictly regulated and the sale of land to outsiders forbidden.

The Ilha do Mel

The **Ilha do Mel** is reached by hourly buses from Paranaguá or Guaratuba (see below) to **PONTAL DO SUL** (there's the *Hotel Jhonny* (sic) at the bus stop if you're stuck). From here, a minibus will take you a further 3km to the beach, from where small boats depart. As there are no shops on the island and only the most basic of restaurants, it is worth coming well supplied with candles, mosquito coils, fruit and fruit juices. The **boat crossing** to Encanatada (also refered to as Prainha) or Nova Brasília, the only villages on the island, take between twenty and forty minutes, with the last boats in both directions at about 6pm. On arrival, it's compulsory to **register with the police**, where you'll be given a form to return on departure. This is no meaningless act of bureaucracy but lets the authorities know how many visitors are on the island at any one time, and when the maximum number permitted has been reached the island is closed to further visitors. Over peak holiday weekends – especially Carnaval – people are turned away; but even then it's usually only necessary to wait until late afternoon and the departure of day-trippers for permission to land.

ENCANTADA is the smaller and less developed of the two settlements. Apart from fishermen's clapboard houses, all there is to Encantada is a couple of **bars** where rather squalid accommodation is available ($3 for a double room), a campsite and a police post. In a sheltered position facing the mainland, it can feel rather claustrophobic due to the mountains all around. But only minutes' walk behind the village on the east side of the island is the **Praia de Fora** where powerful waves roll in from Africa.

Livelier than Encantada, but lacking the fishing village atmosphere, is **NOVA BRASÍLIA**, where the bulk of the island's 1200 inhabitants are concentrated. Stretched between two gently curving, sheltered bays on a narrow strip of land linking the flat western section of the island to the rugged, smaller, eastern portion, this is the area of the island where most tourist facilities are located. From the beach where boats land passengers, walk inland past the **campsite**, the ecological station, the police, medical and telephone posts, and you'll come to a beach along which are several simple **hotels** ($5–10 per person), **restaurants** and **bars** which are crowded with young people in the evenings. These are not always immediately visible, as many are either hidden along paths leading from the beach or are up to a 45-minute walk from Nova Brasília's "centre", alongside the beach out towards the ruins of the Portuguese fort (built in 1769 to guard the entrance of the Bay of Paranaguá), in the opposite direction to the lighthouse.

The most beautiful part of the island is the series of **beaches** along its mountainous southeast side, between Encantada's Praia de Fora and the lighthouse at Nova Brasília – an area of quiet coves, rocky promontories and small waterfalls. It takes about three hours to walk between the two settlements and, because of the need to clamber over rocks separating the beaches, it's easiest at low tide. Even then, however, if you have luggage, the walk is difficult. If you're carrying too much to walk between Encantada and Nova Brasília, it's usually easier and cheaper to return to the mainland and pick up another boat from there rather than wait for a boat going directly between the two settlements.

The southern Paranaense coast

In contrast to the Ilha do Mel, it's hard to find anything positive to say about the rest of the **southern Paranaense coast**, except that it's easy to get to Curitiba from, thus making it a popular location for Curitibanos' second homes. Twenty kilometres south of Pontal do Sul (from where boats leave for the Ilha do Mel) is the first such resort, **PRAIA DE LESTE**, attracting families and campers. **MATINHOS**, 20km further down the coast, is Paraná's surfing capital and, during the summer months, **hotels** here are expensive – though, in any case, they tend to be fully booked. If you're stuck, however, the *Casarão* and the *Beira-Mar*, both on Rua Reinoldo Schaffer, are the cheapest hotels in town and worth a try.

Ten kilometres further south down the coastal road, and a ten-minute ferry ride from CAIOBÁ, across the entrance of Guaratuba Bay, is **GUARATUBA** itself, Paraná's most upmarket resort. The best beaches are only accessible by car or private boat, so unless you enjoy being surrounded by luxury hotels and multistorey apartment blocks, Guaratuba offers little but the buses going to and from Santa Catarina.

Guaraqueçaba and its islands

North of Paranaguá, directly across the bay, lies **Guaraqueçaba**, Paraná's poorest and fifth largest *município*. With 55 isolated settlements, few and poor roads and a widely scattered population of only 14,000 (including a few surviving Tupi-Guarani Indians, sometimes seen by roadsides selling basketware), Guaraqueçaba's mountainous interior, coastal plain and low-lying islands give the authorities huge administrative headaches. The only town, also called **GUARAQUEÇABA**, is really only visited by the most dedicated of sports fishermen and people interested in the conservation zone which, in theory at least, encompasses ninety percent of the *município*. Guaraqueçaba is marked by a tremendous feeling of isolation, connected as it is to the outside world only by sea and an unpaved and severely potholed road, which winds about the interior for the convenience of the *latifúndios*. The owners – usually São Paulo based corporations – are illegally cutting down the forest, most of which falls within the Guaraqueçaba conservation zone, for development as buffalo pasture or banana and *palmito* plantations. Isolation apart, the town's lack of beaches, one cockroach-infested **hotel** (*Hotel Guaraqueçaba*, on the waterfront; $5 single), two very plain **restaurants** (the *Barbosa* is slightly preferable to the *Guaraqueçaba*) and rain that seems to pause only long enough to enable mosquitoes to breed, do little to encourage visitors.

None of the town's buildings bear witness to the fact that, in the seventeenth century, Guaraqueçaba was more important a port than Paranaguá. Nor, apart from the former banana producers' co-operative building (now headquarters for *APA*, the environmental protection body), do more than a few buildings remain from its heyday (between 1880 and 1930) when ships sailed from here to Europe and the River Plate laden with bananas and timber. Today, a shadow of its former self, the port is used only by local fishermen and by boats belonging to the ecological station and municipal authorities, which are used to visit otherwise inaccessible parts of the *município*.

Boats and islands

The only **scheduled boat services** are run by the *município*: precise times are available at the *Prefeitura*. If there are no municipal boats for your destination, ask at the waterfront whether a fishing boat's heading there. Alternatively, it's easy, but very expensive, to charter a boat. Though rare, good weather is of course highly desirable for exploring this, one of the more inaccessible and least spoilt parts of Brazil's coastline, but what is absolutely essential is plenty of time, patience, mosquito repellent and anti-mosquito coils for overnight stays.

Twice a week (Wed & Fri at 5am) a boat makes the crossing to Paranaguá, stopping off at the **Ilha das Peças**, where you can be let off and collected again later in the day on the boat's return journey (though confirm that the boat will in fact collect you).

The other regular service is a fortnightly boat to **ARIRI** (first and third Thursday of the month, returning the next day), a small fishing village just within Paraná on the border with São Paulo. An extremely rewarding trip, the boat stops off at **VILA FATIMA**, a tiny settlement on the northwest coast of the island of Superagui (see below), before passing through the **Canal da Varadouro**, a long, narrow mangrove-fringed channel. Ariri is only a very short boat trip from **ARAOPIRA**, a village just inside the state of São Paulo, from where another boat leaves the following day (though schedules are extremely fluid) for Cananea and Iguape.

An occasional boat service also links Guaraqueçaba with the island of **Superaqui** and its village, **VILA SUPERAQUI**, but as departures depend on the islanders' medical needs, the village is more easily reached by fishing boat from Paranaguá. In the mid-nineteenth century, Superaqui was the site of a Swiss farming colony which, not surprisingly given the subtropical climate and soil utterly unsuitable for cultivation, soon collapsed. Today, the island's inhabitants depend, rather more sensibly, on fishing for their livelihoods. By asking around, its easy to find **accommodation** with a family, but in a village where tourism is unknown, don't expect much comfort.

On the east side of the island, just a short walk from the village, is **Praia Deserta**, a beach stretching 34km and which, despite its name, has a total population of three. It's probably safe to camp on the beach, but isolation does have its risks, so unless you are in a group, ask villagers where you should pitch your tent.

West: southern central Paraná and the Ukrainians

In the late nineteenth and early twentieth centuries, European and North American companies were contracted to construct a railway line linking the state of São Paulo to Rio Grande do Sul. As part payment, large tracts of land were given to the companies and, as in the United States and the Canadian West, they subdivided their new properties for sale to land-hungry immigrants who, it was hoped, would generate traffic for the railway line. Some of the largest land grants were in southern central Paraná, which the companies quickly cleared of the valuable Paraná pine trees that dominated the territory. Settlers came from many parts of Europe, but the companies were especially successful in recruiting **Ukrainians**, and between 1895 and 1898, and 1908 and 1914 – the periods of Ukraine's so-called "Brazil fever" – over 35,000 immigrants arrived in the Ukraine's "other America".

Today, there are some 300,000 Brazilians of Ukrainian extraction, of whom eighty percent live in Paraná, largely concentrated in the southern centre of the state.

As most of the immigrants came from the western Ukraine, it's the Ukrainian Catholic rather than the Orthodox church that dominates – and dominate it certainly does. Throughout the areas where Ukrainians and their descendants are gathered, domed churches and chapels abound. While the Roman Catholic hierarchy, in general, is gradually becoming sensitive to the need to concentrate resources on social projects rather than in the building of more churches, new Ukrainian Catholic churches are proliferating in ever more lavish proportions. In Brazil, the **Ukrainian Catholic Church** is extremely wealthy, and its massive landholdings contrast greatly with the tiny properties from which the vast majority of the poverty-stricken local population eke out a living. Priests are often accused of attempting to block measures which will improve conditions: they are said to fear that educational attainment, modernisation and increased prosperity will lessen the populace's dependence on the Church for material and spiritual comfort, so reducing their own influence.

The Ukrainians' neighbours (*caboclos*, Poles, Germans and a few Italians and Dutch) frequently accuse them and their priests of maintaining an exclusiveness that is downright racist in character. While inter-communal tensions are easy to detect, the few non-Brazilian visitors to this part of Paraná are treated with the utmost civility, and if your Portuguese (or Ukrainian) is up to it you should have no problem finding people in the region's towns and hamlets who will be happy to talk about their traditions and way of life.

As none of the towns in the region are especially distinctive, it's better to use them more as bases from which to visit nearby villages and hamlets where the pioneering spirit of the inhabitants' immigrant forefathers remains. The houses, made of wood and sometimes featuring intricately carved details, are typically painted in bright colours and are usually surrounded by flower-filled gardens. Because of the ethnic mix, even small villages contain churches of several denominations; few hamlets are without at least a chapel where there'll always be someone on hand to open it up to the rare visitors.

Prudentópolis and around

The administrative centre of a *município* where 75 percent of the inhabitants are of Ukrainian origin, **PRUDENTÓPOLIS** is heralded as the capital city of Ukrainian Brazil. However, in common with the other regional urban centres, there's little in the city of Prudentópolis to indicate the ethnic background of most of its citizens. Blonde heads and pink noses do predominate, but if you're expecting plump, Tolstoyesque peasants wearing elaborately embroidered smocks and chatting to one another in Ukrainian, a skyline dominated by gold or silver domed eastern-style churches, or have a craving for cabbage rolls, borscht and *pirogies*, you'll be extremely disappointed.

At a glance, Prudentópolis is much like a thousand other nondescript small towns in the interior of southern Brazil. At the heart of the city is a large Roman (not Ukrainian) Catholic church set in a park-like square totally disproportionate in size to the town. The surrounding buildings are the usual mix of anonymous breezeblock and concrete-slab municipal buildings, houses, *lanchonetes* and small shops. Still, committed Ukrainophiles should not despair. A closer look around town will reveal some traces of the Ukraine: many of the older houses bear a resemblance to peasant cottages of eastern Europe, in particular in the style of the window frames and roofs. As throughout the region, the Ukrainian Catholic Church displays a strong presence, most visibly in the form of the **seminary**, a large mustard-coloured building located next to the Ukrainian Catholic **Cathedral** that overlooks the city centre. Across the road from the seminary is the church's printing press where Ukrainian-language propaganda is churned out on machinery that has remained unchanged since soon after the first Ukrainians arrived in Brazil. A few doors away is a stationery shop, whose Ukrainian owner sells attractive, but simple, locally produced embroidery of classic Ukrainian design.

A couple of blocks from the main square is Prudentópolis' best (and only) **hotel**, *Hotel Lopes* ($4 single), close to the town's best (and only) **restaurant**, the *Churrascaria do Penteado*, at Rua Domingos Luiz de Oliveira 1378, run by a cheerful Hawaiian-clad Ukrainian Brazilian.

It's a fairly simple matter to reach Prudentópolis: it's well served by **bus** from Curitiba (4 daily), Foz do Iguaçu (3 daily) and most nearby centres. However, as one of Paraná's largest and most sparsely populated *municípios*, travelling far beyond the city without a car, is difficult. To see some of the rural environs, though, you could always take a **local bus** (2 daily) to the village of **ESPERANSA**, where there's a large domed church and a school staffed by Ukrainian nuns; and then continue along the same road to **BARRA BONITA**, another extremely poor and overwhelmingly Ukrainian settlement.

Bairro dos Binos

While descendants of Ukrainian immigrants form the great majority of Prudentópolis' population, immigrants have arrived from elsewhere as well. Germans from Rio Grande do Sul have been buying up land vacated by Ukrainians moving into urban centres or north towards the Amazon. However, perhaps the strangest (as well as earliest) arrivals have been the **French** of **BAIRRO DOS BINOS**. In 1858, 87 French families arrived in Brazil to form a farming community in what was then – and still is – an extremely isolated part of Paraná. Within a few years the colony all but disintegrated, with only a few families remaining. Disappointingly, but not surprisingly, there remains barely the faintest trace of Bairro dos Binos' French origins – just the odd family carrying French surnames, and some uncharacteristic stone houses of the early settlers.

Getting to Bairro dos Binos is very time consuming, reached by a bus from Prudentópolis to TERESA CRISTINA (140km north), and then a 10km walk. Still, the journey to Teresa Cristina is fascinating, with the road passing through isolated communities and mountainous terrain, while Bairro dos Binos itself is quite pretty. Aim to return to Prudentópolis on the same day, but if you don't, ask the priest at Teresa Cristina's church if he can help find a bed for the night.

Irati, Mallet and around

Smaller, and with a greater ethnic diversity than Prudentópolis to the north, neither **IRATI** nor **MALLET** are especially interesting in themselves, but both are useful jumping-off points for visiting the Ukrainian villages and hamlets nearby. The two towns are very similar in character, both straddling the railway line to which they owe their existence and their growth during the first decades of the twentieth century. Mallet – smaller and generally less developed – is marginally the more attractive of the two, and its small Ukrainian Catholic Church is worth a visit, as is the railway station which dates back to 1903.

Regular **buses** link Irati and Mallet with each other, as well as União da Vitoria if travelling to or from Santa Catarina; and there are three buses a day to and from Prudentópolis, and two to and from Curitiba. On weekdays, finding **accommodation** in Irati can be a problem, but if the *Hotel Colonial* (across from the bus station; $5 per person) is full, try the *Hotel Luz* (walk downhill to the end of the road, turn left and take the second right; from $2.50 per person). In Mallet, there's always room at the *Hotel Brasil*, next to the bus station. As in Prudentópolis, **food** means meat, with *churrascarias* located near the bus stations of both towns.

Gonçalves Júnior and Serra do Tigre

From Irati, the small village of **GONÇALVES JÚNIOR** is well worth a visit if you want to get an idea of local rural traditions. Of the village's four **churches** (Lutheran, Roman Catholic, Ukrainian Catholic and Ukrainian Orthodox) the only one that deserves much attention is the Orthodox, which serves 24 local families. Built in 1934, the small church's extremely beautiful interior features Orthodox icons and a ceiling and walls bearing intricately painted traditional frescoes. From Gonçalves Júnior, take the Linha "B" road, along which there's a pretty chapel cared for by Ukrainian Catholic nuns. If walking (allow at least an hour) or hitchhiking (don't count on there being any traffic) to the chapel, try to engage in conversation with some of the *colonos* who live in the colourful wooden houses that front the dirt road. Apart from Ukrainians, I met Polish, German, Italian and Dutch-speaking peasant farmers, who were very happy to chat about their lives and those of their parents and grandparents.

Without any doubt, the most interesting and most beautiful Ukrainian Church hereabouts is in **SERRA DO TIGRE**, a small settlement near Mallet. Built in 1904, the church, spectacularly positioned high up on a mountain top where the village's core is also located, is the oldest Ukrainian Catholic church in Paraná. In traditional fashion, the church was constructed totally of wood – including, even, the roof's tiles – and both the exterior and the elaborately painted interior frescoes are being carefully maintained as a state monument.

Almost all the Serra do Tigre's inhabitants are of Ukrainian origin but, rather curiously, amongst them lives Dorothea Roepnack, a charming elderly American woman. Donna Dorothea, as everyone calls her, is making an admirable effort to preserve the forest around her home as a nature reserve, and it's one of the very few places in the area where howler monkeys still survive. If you do drop in on Donna Dorothea, watch out for her vicious guard dogs and the almost equally agressive pet orphaned howler monkeys – and, if at all possible, leave her any books that you have finished with!

Getting to Serra do Tigre is not terribly easy. Immediately on arrival in Mallet, go to the *prefeitura* and ask for a lift to Serra do Tigre on the school bus, which departs very early in the morning and then again at about noon. Alternatively, take a **bus** the 10km from Mallet to DORIZON (the *Hotel Dorizon* has good food and a natural swimming pool; $5 per person), from where it takes about an hour to walk up the very steep hill to Serra do Tigre.

Iguaçu

The **Iguaçu Falls** are, unquestionably, one of the world's great natural phenomena. To describe their beauty and power is a tall order, but for starters cast out any ideas that Iguaçu is some kind of Niagara transplanted south of the equator – compared to Iguaçu, with its total of 275 falls that cascade over a precipice 3km wide, Niagara is a ripple. But it's not the falls alone that makes Iguaçu so special. Iguaçu is part of a vast subtropical nature reserve, a forest that's home to over 2000 plant varieties, 400 bird species and innumerable insects and reptiles – a timeless haunt that even the hordes of tourists fail to destroy.

All the practicalities: arrival, orientation and accommodation

The Iguaçu Falls are a short distance from the towns of **FOZ DO IGUAÇU** in Brazil, **PUERTO IGUAZÚ** in Argentina and **CIUDAD PRESIDENTE STROESSNER** in Paraguay – which makes the practical details of getting in and out that bit trickier. Foz do Iguaçu and Puerto Iguazú are both about 20km north-west of the entrance to the National Park, while Ciudad Presidente Stroessner is 7km northwest of Foz do Iguaçu. Foz do Iguaçu is much the largest of the three towns and, featuring the most and least expensive hotels and considering its position midway between the Falls and the casinos and tax free shops in Ciudad Presidente Stroessner, most tourists choose to stay there.

Ciudad Presidente Stroessner itself is connected by bus to Ascuncion, but it's unpleasant, crowded and none too safe – best avoided.

Foz do Iguaçu

The **airport** at Foz do Iguaçu is served by flights from throughout Brazil and there are regular buses (every 35min between 6am and 7.15pm, then hourly until 11.30pm) from there to the **local bus terminal** in the centre of town on Avenida Juscelino Kubitscheck, one block east of Avenida República Argentina. Arriving by bus, Foz do Iguaçu's **Rodoviária** is, for the time being at least, located right in the centre of town behind the main street, Avenida Brasil: it's served by buses

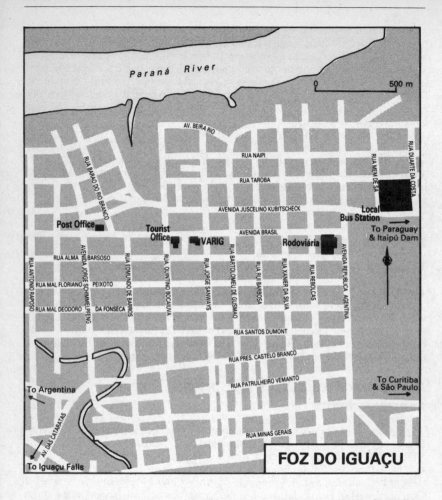

FOZ DO IGUAÇU

from throughout southern Brazil, Ascuncion in Paraguay and from as far north as Rio.

Finding a fairly cheap **hotel** in Foz do Iguaçu is easy, but it won't be comfortable. The cheapest places are in the roads immediately surrounding the *Rodoviária* with, at about $5 per person, the *Jô*, *Tropical* and *Fortaleza* bearable for a night despite being airless and noisy. During the summer months the town is often very hot, but most medium-priced hotels have air conditioning and a swimming pool: the cheapest hotels in the centre with pools are the *Foz Presidente*, Rua Xavier da Silva 918; the *Diplomata*, Avenida Brasil 678; the *San Diego*, Rua Alm. Barroso 495, and many others – around $15–20 for a double room.

For **food**, the very varied fast-food restaurant, *Centro Gastronomico Rafain*, Avenida Brasil 157, is a lively evening meeting point, and, at Avenida Brasil 531, there's a decent **vegetarian** restaurant.

SOME IGUAÇU INFORMATION

Airlines Foz do Iguaçu: *Varig/Cruzeiro*, Av. Brasil 821 (☎74-3344); *VASP*, Av. Brasil 845 (☎74-2999); *Transbrasil*, Av. Brasil 1225 (☎74-3671). Puerto Iguaźu: *Aérolineas Argentinas*, Avenida Victoria Aguirre 404.

Consulates Foz do Iguaçu: *Argentina*, Rua Dom Pedro II 28 (☎74-2877); *Paraguay*, Rua Bartolomeu de Gusmão 777 (☎74-3174/73-1499). Puerto Iguazú: *Brazil* ☎57-2601. Ciudad Presidente Stroessner: *Brazil* ☎31-2309.

Exchange Dollars (cash or travellers' cheques) can be easily changed in travel agents along Avenida Brasil in Foz do Iguaçu or at a *casa de câmbio* in Puerto Iguazú. Even if staying in Foz do Iguaçu it's a good idea to have some Argentine currency for the bus fare between Puerto Iguazú and the Falls, park entrance charges and snacks and drinks. However, *cruzados* are accepted but at a poor rate of exchange.

Post Offices Foz do Iguaçu: Praça Getúlio Vargas near Rua Barão do Rio Branco. Puerto Iguarzú: Avenida San Martín (near the main square).

Tourist Offices Foz do Iguaçu: at the airport and, in the centre, at Rua Almirante Barroso 285 and Praça Almirante Tamandaré 64. Puerto Iguazú: Avenida Victoria Aguirre 396.

Puerto Iguazú

To Puerto Iguazú, there are daily **flights** to and from Buenos Aires, Cordoba and elsewhere in Argentina. Puerto Iguazú's combined local and long distance **bus terminal** is in the town centre; several daily departures to and from Buenos Aires and Posadas.

If you want to avoid the crowds and don't object to spending a few dollars more for a room, Puerto Iguazú is the better place to stay. Near the bus terminal there are several family-run **hotels** charging about $10 for a double room: the *Residencia Paquita* is very good, or try *Los Helechos*. If you're after a pool it's necessary to pay a minimum of $15: the *Alexander* is near the bus terminal or, a few blocks beyond the central square at Avenida Tres Fronteras 434, there's *La Cabaña*. For **camping**, use the good site at PUERTO CANOAS in the National Park on the Argentine side (see "The Argentine side", below).

The Falls

The **Iguaçu Falls** are formed by the Iguaçu river, which has its source near Curitiba. Starting at an altitude of 1300 metres, the river snakes westward, picking up tributaries and increasing in size and power during its 1200-kilometre journey. About 15km before joining the Paraná river, the Iguaçu broadens out, then plunges precipitously over an eighty-metre-high cliff, the central of the 275 inter-linking cataracts that extend nearly 3km across the river. There is no "best time" to visit since the Falls are impressive and spectacularly beautiful whatever the season. That said, the rainy season is during the winter months of April to July, and at this time the volume of water is at its greatest – but then the sky is usually overcast and the air, especially near the Falls themselves, quite chilly. By the end of the summer dry season, around March, the volume of water crashing over the cliffs is reduced by a third (only once, in 1977, did the Falls dry up altogether), but even then there's no reduction in impact, with the added attraction of the rainbow effects from the splashing of falling water and the deep-blue sky.

Although many people arrive at Iguaçu in the morning and depart the same evening, the Falls should really be viewed from both the Brazilian and the Argentine sides of the river: so at least two days are needed. Crossing the **frontier** to see both sides is easy, and if you're of a nationality that normally requires a visa to visit either Argentina or Brazil, you won't need one just for a day trip. If, however, you're not returning to Foz do Iguaçu or Puerto Iguazú the same day, you'll have to go through normal **immigration** formalities on either side of the **Ponte Presidente Tancredo Neves**, the bridge that crosses the Iguaçu river between the two towns.

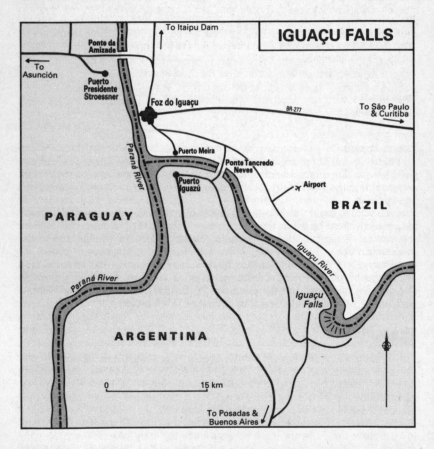

The Brazilian side

The finest overall view of the Falls is obtained from the Brazilian side, best seen in the morning when the light is much better for photography. You'll only need about half a day here, since although the view is magnificent and it's from here that you get the clearest idea as to the size of the Falls, the area from which to view them is fairly limited.

From the local bus terminal in central Foz do Iguaçu, there are **buses** every two hours (6am–9pm; hourly on Sun and public holidays) to the "Cataratas do Iguaçu", which cost around 35¢ and take about 45 minutes. Once there, entrance to the park also costs around 35¢. Buses stop on the road beneath the renowned *Hotel das Cataratas*, where, for about $6, you can have an excellent buffet lunch of typical Brazilian dishes. Once you've filled up, you're only a couple of minutes' walk from the first views of the Falls.

From the bus stop, there's a stairway which leads down to a one-and-a-half kilometre cliff-side **path** near the rim of the Falls. From spots all along the path there are excellent views, at first across the lower river at a point where it has narrowed to channel width. At the bottom of the path, where the river widens again, there's a catwalk leading out towards the Falls themselves. Depending on the force of the river, the spray can be quite heavy, so if you have a camera, be sure to carry a plastic bag. From here, you can either walk back up the path or take the elevator to the top of the cliff and the road leading to the hotel.

Every fifteen minutes or so you'll hear the slightly irritating buzzing from a **helicopter** flying overhead. It takes off from near the hotel, and offers seven-minute flights over the Falls for about $25.

The Argentine side

For more detailed views, and greater opportunities to experience the local flora and fauna at close range, Argentina offers by far the best vantage points. The Falls on the Argentine side are much more numerous and the viewing area more extensive and this, combined with the fact that many people only visit the Brazilian side, means that you'll rarely be overpowered by fellow tourists. With a good eye, toucans and other exotic birds can be spotted, and brilliantly coloured butterflies are seen all about. In warm weather, be sure to bring your bathing gear as there are some idyllic spots to cool off in, beneath cataracts, pools and in the river itself.

Getting to the Argentine side of the Falls from Foz do Iguaçu is straightforward enough, but if your time is very limited it makes sense to join an **excursion**, which most travel agencies and the better hotels organise. Otherwise, from Foz do Iguaçu's local bus terminal take a **bus to Puerto Iguazú** (50¢; departures at least every half-hour 7am–9pm; 20min). From Puerto Iguazú's bus terminal, there are connecting buses ($1) which take half an hour to reach the park. At the park's entrance there's a fee of about 70¢, and you'll be given a very useful map; the bus then continues on to the National Park's Visitors' Centre.

The **Visitors' Centre** itself makes a good first stop and there's a small but useful **museum** focusing on the region's natural history: it's here that you'll have the best chance of seeing the extremely shy, and mainly nocturnal, forest animals – though they're all stuffed. From the Centre, follow the **Circuito Inferior**, a walk that with a few interruptions to admire the scenery is likely to take a couple of hours. Despite not being as dramatic as the falls up-river, few parts of the park are more beautiful and the path passes by gentler waterfalls and dense vegetation. One of the many enchanting spots is **La Ventana**, a rock formation that's framed, as its name suggests, like a window. From here you can continue around the marked circuit but, if you are at all agile, haul yourself instead across the rocks in front and behind La Ventana where, hidden from view, is a deep natural **pool** fed by a small waterfall, allowing some relaxing swimming. Back on the main path, at the river shore, **boats** ($1.50) cross to the **Isla San Martín**, whose beaches are unfortunately marred by the streams of sand flies and mosquitoes present.

The Argentine Falls embrace a huge area, and the most spectacular spot is probably the **Garganta del Diablo** (Devil's Throat) at **PUERTO CANOAS**. The Garganta del Diablo marks a point where fourteen separate falls combine to form the world's most powerful single waterfall in terms of the volume of water flow per second. Catwalks lead into the middle of the river from where it's easy to feel that you will be swallowed by the tumbling waters. From Puerto Canoas there's no need to return to the Visitors' Centre, as there are frequent buses that link directly with Puerto Iguazú.

Itaipú

While there's complete agreement that Iguaçu is one of the great natural wonders of Brazil, there's bitter debate as to what **Itaipú** – the world's largest hydroelectricity scheme – represents. Located 19km north of Foz do Iguaçu, work on the dam began in the early 1970s and, at a cost of US$25 billion, its eighteen 700,000 kilowatt generators became fully operational in 1990. Proponents of the project argue that the rapidly growing industries of southeastern Brazil needed nothing less than Itaipú's huge electrical capacity, and that without it Brazilian development would be greatly impeded. However, critics claim that Brazil neither needs nor can afford such a massive hydroelectric scheme and that the country would have been much better served by smaller and less prestigious schemes nearer to the centres of consumption. In addition, they point to the social and environmental upheavals that have been caused by the damming of the Paraná river and the creation of a 1350-square-kilometre reservoir: 40,000 families have been forced off their land; a microclimate with as yet unknown consequences has developed; and – critics say – the much publicised animal rescue operations and financial assistance for displaced farmers barely address the complex problems that have been created.

Visiting Itaipú is easy, with hourly **buses** from Foz do Iguaçu's local bus terminal. You're dropped at the **Visitors' Centre** where a film about the project, in English and other languages, is shown, and from where **free guided tours** depart four times a day (8.30am, 10.30am, 2.30pm & 4pm), lasting about an hour. The film is extremely slick and, until you stand on the dam and look across the massive reservoir stretching into the horizon, it's easy to be convinced by Itaipú's PR machine that the project was, at worst, no more than a slight local inconvenience.

SANTA CATARINA

Santa Catarina shares a similar pattern of settlement with other parts of southern Brazil, the indigenous Indians rapidly being displaced by outsiders. In the eighteenth century the state received immigrants from the Azores who settled along the coast; cattle herders from Rio Grande do Sul spread into the higher reaches of the mountainous interior around **Lages** and **São Joaquim**; and European immigrants and their descendants made new homes for themselves in the fertile river valleys. Even today, small communities on the island of **Santa Catarina**, and elsewhere on the coast, continue a way of life that has not changed markedly over the generations. Incidentally, to prevent confusion with the name of the state (though barely succeeding at times), most people call the island of Santa Catarina **Florianópolis**, which is actually the name of the state capital – also situated on the

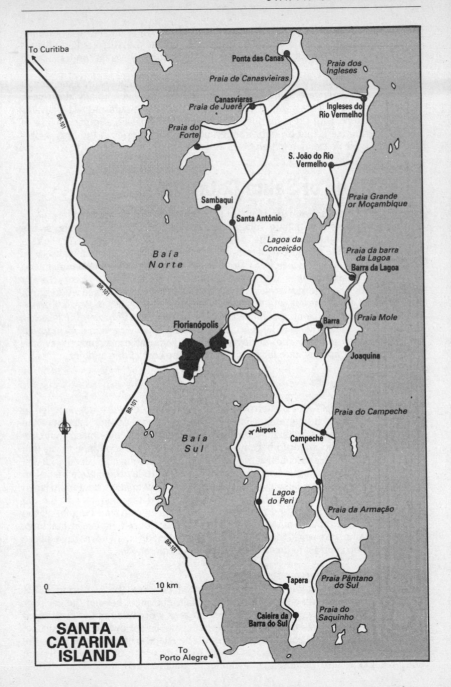

To Curitiba

Ponta das Canas
Praia de Canasvieiras
Praia dos Ingleses

Canasvieras
Praia de Juerê
Ingleses do
Rio Vermelho

Praia do
Forte

S. João do Rio
Vermelho

Sambaqui

Santa Antônio

*Praia Grande
or Moçambique*

*Lagoa da
Conceição*

*B a í a
N o r t e*

*Praia da barra
da Lagoa*
Barra da Lagoa

Florianópolis

Barra

Praia Mole

Joaquina

Praia do Campeche

Airport

Campeche

*B a í a
S u l*

*Lagoa
do Peri*

Praia da Armação

0 _____ 10 km

Tapera

*Praia Pântano
do Sul*

SANTA
CATARINA
ISLAND

Caieira da
Barra do Sul

*Praia do
Saquinho*

To
Porto Alegre

island. Elsewhere, cities such as **Blumenau** and **Joinville**, established by German immigrants, have become totally Brazilianised, but in the surrounding villages many people still speak the language of their forefathers in preference to Portuguese.

On the coast, tourism has become very important and facilities are excellent: in only a surprisingly few spots has the natural beauty been totally destroyed. **Inland**, though, visitors rarely venture, despite the good roads and widely available hotels. Here, with the minimum of discomfort, it's possible to get a sense of the pioneering spirit that brought immigrants into the interior in the first place – and keeps their descendants there.

The island of Santa Catarina

The island of **Santa Catarina** is noted throughout Brazil for its Mediterranean-like scenery, attractive fishing villages and the city of Florianópolis, the state's small and prosperous capital. The island has a subtropical climate, rarely cold in winter and with the summer heat tempered by refreshing South Atlantic breezes; and the vegetation is much softer than that further north. Joined to the mainland by two suspension bridges (the longest, British-designed and now structurally unsound, has been closed for several decades), the island is served by frequent **bus** services connecting it with the rest of the state, other parts of Brazil, Buenos Aires, Ascuncion and Santiago. Indeed, during January and February the island is extremely popular with middle- and upper-middle-class Argentine, Uruguayan and Paraguayan tourists who, during periods of favourable exchange rates, can enjoy a summer holiday here for much less than the cost of one at home.

Florianópolis

FLORIANÓPOLIS – or "Desterro" as it was originally called – was founded in 1700 and settled by immigrants from the Portuguese mid-Atlantic islands of the Azores. Since then, it's gradually developed from being a sleepy – most would say dull – provincial backwater to become a sleepy – most would continue to say dull – state capital. With the construction of the bridges linking the island with the mainland, Florianópolis as a port has all but died, and today the city thrives as an administrative, commercial and tourist centre. Land reclamation for a multi-laned highway and new bus terminals has totally eliminated the character of the old seafront and, with it, vanished much of the city's former charm. Despite all the changes, though, the late-nineteenth-century pastel-coloured, stuccoed buildings still recall faint "old world" images, while the relaxed, small-town atmosphere provides a total contrast to the excitement of São Paulo or Rio.

Arriving and changing money
Buses arrive at the modern *Rodoviária* situated between the two bridges that link the island to the mainland. Outside the main entrance, beyond the car park and dual carriageway, is the former waterfront area where one of the **municipal bus terminals** is situated. From here, frequent buses set out for most parts of the city as well as to all points in the south of the island. Otherwise, buses to the northern and eastern beach resorts depart from Rua José da Costa Moelmann and Avenida Mauro Ramos, a fifteen-minute walk around the hillside. These

buses run to a surprisingly accurate timetable (check times at the information booths) and are cheap, though generally crowded. Alternatively, from the terminal nearest to the *Rodoviária*, there are faster, more comfortable and more expensive minibuses to most of the beaches.

For **changing money**, travel agents in the *Ceisa Center*, a modern shopping mall on Rua Vidal Ramos, offer rates only slightly below those available in Rio or São Paulo for dollars and travellers' cheques. If you're planning on travelling elsewhere in the state, remember to change money in Florianópolis as, apart from the main Argentine-oriented beach resorts, you're unlikely to find anything much above the official rate for the dollar; and, west of Joaçaba, even branches of the *Banco do Brasil* may turn you away.

Finding a place to stay

Try to arrive in Florianópolis early in the day as cheap **accommodation** is snapped up quickly during the peak holiday periods, and it's especially difficult to get a bed at the well cared for **youth hostel** at Rua Duarte Schutel 59 (☎22-3781; open year round). Many of the cheapest **hotels** are located on, or just off, Rua Felipe Schmidt, only a couple of minutes from both Praça XV and the bus terminals. The *Hotel Sumare*, Rua Felipe Schmidt 53, is comfortable but at only $6 for a double room it's often full; in which case try the *Colonial*, Rua Conselheiro Mafra 45, the nearby *Majestic*, Rua Trajano 4, near the former markets (see below), and,

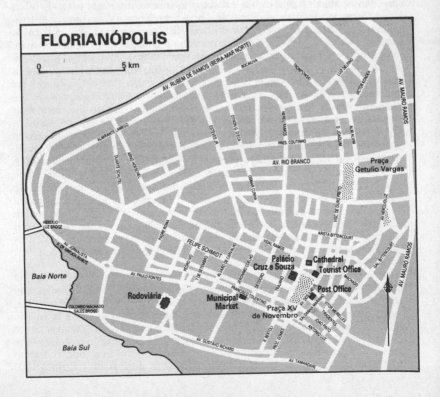

on the other side of Praça XV, the *Felipe*, Rua João Pinto (at the intersection with Rua Antônio Luz) – all of which have similar rooms at similar prices. If you have no luck (and not too strong an aversion to cockroaches), the *Dormitório da Ilha* (next to the *Colonial*) offers very basic accommodation or, in an absolute emergency, there's the *Hotel Levi*, an utter dive directly opposite the main bus terminal. Moving back up the price scale, finding accommodation around Praça XV shouldn't be a problem, and worth considering are the *Hotel Ivoram* and the *Oscar Palace*, Avenida Hercilio Luz 66 and 90 respectively, or the *Center Plaza Hotel*, Rua Felipe Schmidt 9, which all offer double rooms for $20–30.

Around the city

With the notable exception of Carnaval – rated as the country's fourth most elaborate, and certainly the liveliest south of Rio – few tourists visit the island for the limited charm and attractions of Florianópolis itself. However, being so centrally located, and with hotels much cheaper here than in the overpriced beach resorts, the city does make a good base for exploring the rest of the island, as most points are easily reached within an hour by bus. Take time, though, at least for a stroll around Florianópolis before heading out to the beaches.

On the former waterfront, you'll find the two ochre-coloured **municipal market and customs house** (*Alfândega*) buildings, now converted to contain good craft stalls, the official Ministry of Labour handicraft shop, an art gallery run by the "Association of Catarinense Artists" and snack bars. From here, there's a steep walk up to the Praia de Fora, the "new town", centred on the main, tree-filled square, **Praça XV de Novembro**. On one side of the square is Florianópolis's main post office, and across from it is the **Palácio Cruz e Souza**, an imposing pink building built between 1770 and 1780 as the seat of provincial government. It's now open to the public as the **Museu Histórico de Santa Catarina** (Tues–Fri 10am–6pm, Sat & Sun 2–6pm) and, as there's no charge for admission, it's worthwhile taking a brisk walk around the building to admire the nineteenth-century interior decoration, rather than to examine the unexciting collection of guns, swords and official scrolls. Overlooking the square from the highest point is the utterly unremarkable **Catedral Metropolitana**, originally constructed between 1753 and 1773, though having been enlarged and totally remodelled in 1922 you'd be hard pressed to identify any original features. The only church in the city centre dating back to the colonial era, and retaining some of its original Portuguese Baroque architectural character, is the **Igreja de Nossa Senhora do Rosário**, higher up from the cathedral and best approached by a flight of steep steps from Rua Marechal Guilherme. Otherwise, in the square itself, apart from Brazilian and Chilean hippies selling the usual earrings and leather items, there's a **tourist information kiosk** (summer Mon–Sat 7am–10pm, Sun 7am–7pm; rest of the year Mon–Sat 8am–6pm), where very good, free maps of the island and city are available.

That's about it as far as "culture" in the city goes. Otherwise, there are a couple of **cinemas**, which alternate between showing soft porn, Brazilian comedies and recent popular Hollywood productions, and three neglected **museums**. The **Museu de História e Arte** warrants a few minutes' attention, as it's in the old customs house, together with the state handicraft centre. On the campus of the Federal University (UFSC), twenty minutes by bus from the city centre, the **Museu de Antropologia** (Mon–Fri 9am–5pm, Sat 1–5pm) has a small collection of artefacts belonging to Santa Catarina's largely decimated Kaingang and

Xokleng forest Indians: this is worth an hour or so on a rainy day. The **Museu de Arte de Santa Catarina** (Mon–Fri 9am–noon & 1–6pm), in the Centro Integrado de Cultura (reached by buses marked *Agronomica*), hosts permanent and temporary exhibitions by local and national artists of often dubious talent, while the centre also boasts an arts cinema showing less commercial films, the programme of which is published in the *Jornal de Santa Catarina*.

Eating, drinking and nightlife

In the centre, on the roads which run off the main square in all directions, are numerous cheap, but largely uninspiring **restaurants**. There's a very pleasant Spanish restaurant, *La Taberna*, Rua Nunes Machado 21; the *Lanterna* is a fair attempt at a pizzeria, at Rua Esteves Júnior 63; and directly across the road from the *Lanterna*, the *Restaurante Nostra Damus* has a reasonable, so-called "international" menu. Good **vegetarian** meals are available at *Vida*, Rua Visconde de Ouro Preto 62 (closes daily at 8.30pm, Sat at 3pm and all day Sun), and both *Dol da Terra*, Rua Nereu Ramos 13, and *Natural Familia Doll*, Rua Vidal Ramos 43a, also serve good vegetarian meals, but close at 6pm.

Come evening, there's very little life in the commercial centre around Praça XV. Instead, people concentrate in the **bars and restaurants** that spread out along the **Beira Mar Norte** (or Avenida Rubens de Arruda Ramos as it is officially called), a dual carriageway that skirts the north of the city along reclaimed land starting at the Hercilio Luz bridge. Places move in and out of fashion rapidly and in summer you'll find that the bars – the first two of which are situated virtually under the bridge itself – are either packed solid with wealthy young people or, for no apparent reason, totally empty. Unfortunately there are no outstanding restaurants here either, but there is at least a fair choice, which is more than can be said for the commercial centre. In general, the **Italian restaurants** are disappointing, though those specialising in seafood are usually good. Towards the far end of Beira Mar Norte (take any bus which reads *via Beira Mar Norte*) there are several restaurants worth noting: on the avenue itself, the *Moçambique* is probably the best seafood restaurant in the city, and nearby there's the *Pizzeria Don Pepe*, Rua Bocaiúva 20 (closed Mon), and the *Macarronada Italiana*, Rua Bocaiúva 170, both good Italian restaurants. At no. 210 on the same road, the *Restaurante Kaffa* (closed Mon) offers huge portions of good and very reasonably priced Lebanese food, and at no. 143 the *Cida Baiana* serves acceptable attempts at Bahian dishes.

The rest of the island: the beaches

Most people arriving in Florianópolis head straight for the beaches, undoubtedly the best of which are found on the **north** and **west** coasts. With 42 beaches around the island to choose from, even the most crowded are rarely unbearably so, and they're all suited to a few days winding down. Despite the existence of a good **bus network** (see "Arriving", above), this is one place where **renting a car** (ask at any travel agency) should be considered, especially if you have limited time and want to see as much of the island as possible: the roads are excellent and drivers pretty civilised. Also, if there's one advantage of the island being so popular with Argentine tourists, it's that **hitching** lifts is easy. Once out of the city centre you'll be unlucky to have to wait for long before a family in the ubiquitous Ford Falcon stops and offers you a lift.

The north coast

The island's **north coast** offers safe swimming in calm, warm seas and, as such, is particularly popular with families. The long, gently curving bay of **CANASVIERAS** is the most fashionable of the northern resorts, largely geared towards wealthy Paulista, Argentine and Uruguayan families who camp or rent houses near to the beach. Most of the bars along the beach play Argentine and North American pop music, and serve Paraguayan or Uruguayan beer far superior to Brazilian varieties – accompanied by Argentine snacks: the tourists here are about as interested in Brazil as British tourists on the Costa del Sol are in Spain. By walking away from the concentration of bars at the centre of the beach, towards the east and Ponta das Canas, it's not too difficult to find a relatively quiet spot. Unless you're renting a house for a week or more (agencies abound), finding **accommodation** can be a problem. However, by asking in the souvenir shops and restaurants you'll eventually be directed to someone with a spare **room to rent**. Otherwise, there are plenty of well organised **campsites**, many of which – as throughout the island – rent out **cabins** suitable for two or more people. The local **restaurants** mostly offer the same menu of prawn dishes, pizza and hamburgers, with only the *Restaurante Tropical* and its Bahian dishes standing out as different.

Heading westwards, almost an extension of Canasvieras, from which it is separated by a rocky promontory, is **JURERÊ**, another long beach that also almost exclusively attracts families. Still further west, a series of coves fringed by luxuriant vegetation – reached by clambering down from the road skirting the coast, or by climbing over the rocks that separate one cove from another – link Jurerê to **DANIELA**, a smaller and less developed beach. Though it amounts to nothing special, the turquoise waters of the nearby coves are well worth the small effort needed to reach them; and **rooms** are available next to the *Lancheria Palheiro*. Roughly midway between Jurerê and Daniela, stunning views of the coast and across to the mainland can be appreciated from the ruins of the **Forte de São José** (usually refered to as Forte Jurerê), built in 1742 to guard the northern approaches to Desterro. Next to the fort there's a small eighteenth-century chapel.

The east coast

If you find the north coast too crowded and developed and the ocean too calm, head for the **east coast**, where Atlantic rollers scare away most of the families. Take extreme care yourself, though, as the undercurrents here make for dangerous swimming.

There are a couple of places to avoid. **PRAIA BRAVA** (the most northerly of the east coast beaches) is dominated by huge Argentine-owned condominium complexes that have resulted in this beautiful stretch of coast becoming the island's ugliest corner. Similarly, **INGLESES**, a little further south, is rapidly undergoing uncontrolled development and, as the sea is not too ferocious at this point, is fast becoming a downmarket alternative to Canasvieras. Instead, you're better off returning to Florianópolis and crossing the island to **LAGOA**, once a fishing hamlet but long since taken over by seafood restaurants, many of which are excellent. Lagoa is approached by a winding road from which there are truly breathtaking views across the **Lagoa da Conceição**, a large saltwater lagoon by which the village is situated. In contrast to Lagoa, **BARRA DA LAGOA**, at the entrance to the lagoon, has succeeded fairly well in allowing tourism to develop without destroying the inhabitants' traditional main activity – fishing. Azorean fishermen prepare their nets and launch their boats from the lagoon's narrow channel and Barra da Lagoa's beach, seemingly oblivious to the sunbathers and swimmers all around them. Barra da Lagoa has several **restaurants** (though not as good as Lagoa's), a good **campsite**, and there are also a couple of cheap **hotels** near the beach, a **youth hostel** (☎32-0169; open all year), and plenty of **rooms** to rent. If there's no space in the campsite or all the rooms are all occupied, walk back along the road fronting the lagoon towards Lagoa and you're sure to come across empty rooms or campsite cabins. Stretching north for kilometres, Barra da Lagoa's beach at some point merges with Praia Grande (also known as Praia da Mocambique) and you don't have to walk too far to get away from the crowds.

South of Barra da Lagoa, the road climbs steeply, passing mountain-sized sand dunes to **PRAIA MOLE**, whose beautiful beach is slightly hidden beyond sand dunes and beneath low-lying cliffs. Mole has become extremely popular with young people but, rather surprisingly, commercial activity has remained low-key. Approached by a road passing between gigantic dunes, the next beach is at **JOAQUINA**, always crowded with surfers, particularly so during the Brazilian national surf championships, held annually in the last week of January. Despite the crowds near the bars and restaurants, the beach stretches to the south, where it merges with **PRAIA DO CAMPECHE**, so by walking for fifteen minutes or so you can be almost alone. **Accommodation** hereabouts is limited and, in the two hotels by the beach itself, expensive. Cheaper is the *Estalgem das Açores*, a very pleasant medium-sized hotel with a Portuguese feel to it. On the whole the beach **restaurants** are good, though for a really superb (and expensive) meal go to the *Martim-Pescador* (closed Sun evening & Mon), on the approach road to Joaquina, which is noted for being one of the best seafood restaurants in southern Brazil.

Campeche, which merges into MORRO DAS PEDRAS and ARMACAO, is considered by many to be the most beautiful stretch of the island's coast. Due, however, to the strong current and often ferocious surf, fewer people are attracted here than to the beaches to the north. Consequently, there's been comparatively little building work and only slowly are bars and beach houses appearing. For sleeping, there's a **youth hostel** (☎22-6746; open Dec 20–Feb 25), or you'll need a **tent**. If you're sleeping under the stars, be prepared for late night thunderstorms; you're unlikely to have any hassles camping wild, at least if there's a group of you.

South again, you reach **PANTANO DO SUL**, a small fishing village at the end of a well protected bay with a mountainous backdrop. There are several restaurants, but for **accommodation** it's down to asking around for a room. The village itself is not at all attractive, but the water is calmer than elsewhere on the east coast, the views of the small, offshore, uninhabited islands are pleasant and there are some fine bars in which to while away the hours.

The west coast
The principal places of interest on the **west coast** are **SAMBAQUI** and **SANTO ANTÔNIO** to the north of Florianópolis, and Ribeiro da Ilha (see below) to the south. As the island's oldest, most attractive and least spoilt settlements, the houses in these places are almost all painted white and have dark blue sash windows – in typical Azorian style – and each village has a simple, colonial church. As was the case with most of the island's settlements, these villages were founded by immigrants from the Azores, and their present-day inhabitants – who still refer to themselves as being Azorean – retain many traditions of the islands from which their forefathers came. Fishing, rather than catering to the needs of

tourists, remains the principal activity, and it is quite a spectacle watching their boats being prepared for sailing or returning with their catch. Azorean immigrants brought their lace-making skills to Santa Catarina, too, and intricately fashioned lace tablecloths, mats and other items are displayed for sale outside many of the houses – or you'll find them for sale at the *Casa Açoriana*, Rua Conego Serpa, in Santo Antônio. Because the beaches are small and face the mainland, tourism has remained minimal, the few visitors that are about on day trips from resorts elsewhere on the island. They stay just long enough for a meal: the *Restaurante Rosemar*, outside Sambaqui towards Santo Antônio, and the *Pizzeria Lisboa*, in Santo Antônio itself, both serve excellent seafood.

Towards the southern end of Santa Catarina, **RIBEIRAO DA ILHA** is a small, pretty village of pastel-coloured houses that rarely receives visitors. From there, hugging the steep hillside as it passes tiny, deserted coves, the dreadfully potholed road leading to BARRA DO SUL runs through some of the most stunning scenery on the island. The rainfall here is extremely heavy with the result that, while discouraging tourists, there is a profusion of rich foliage, most noticeably flamboyants and bougainvillaea.

If you choose to stay in the east coast villages, **finding a room** can be quite a problem and involves, as ever, some asking around. But you'll be rewarded by complete tranquillity of a kind lost to most of the rest of the island over the course of the last couple of decades.

Near Florianópolis: the mainland

On the mainland, 30km inland and southwest of Florianópolis (4 buses daily from Praça da Bandeira), lies the small resort of **SANTO AMARO DA IMPERATRIZ**. In the late nineteenth century, Imperatriz (the name commemorating the visit in 1845 of Brazil's emperor, Dom Pedro II and his wife, the Empress Tereza Cristina) was quite a fashionable spa town. For years after it was opened to celebrate the Imperial visit, the *Hotel Caldas da Imperatriz* ($20 for a double room, including all meals) succeeded in mimicking the European idea of the "Grand Hotel", attracting wealthy Brazilians from as far away as Rio. Today most of the hotel's visitors are elderly Catarinenses and *gaúchos*, especially chronic sufferers of rheumatism and those with digestive or nervous disorders; though the baths are also open to non-guests on payment of a small fee.

A few kilometres up the narrow, tree-filled valley is another spa, the more recently developed **AGUAS MORNAS** and its luxury *Palace Hotel*, favoured by the seriously rich. The spa itself is not particularly attractive, but the approach road and general setting are delightful.

The Parque Estadual da Serra do Tabuleiro

For anyone with even a vague interest in the fauna of Santa Catarina, a visit to the nature reserve of the **Serra do Tabuleiro** is a must. Animals and birds from throughout the state live in as near to natural conditions as is possible, and endangered species are bred in the hope that they will eventually be returned to the wild. You'll see alligators, tortoises, twenty species of birds (including rheas, emus, and flamingos – and even the odd lost penguin from Patagonia), anteaters and deers and, best of all, get no feeling that you're in, essentially, a zoo.

To get to the reserve from Florianópolis, take a **bus** (*Empresa Paulo Lopez* line, or any bus heading south along the main coastal highway, the BR-101) and ask to be let off at the entrance to the "Parque da Serra". From the park's entrance, it takes about half an hour to walk to the reserve (or hitch a lift, not that there's much traffic along the side road). As the journey time there is about two hours, you'd do best to take the 7am or, at the latest, the 10.30am bus from Florianópolis; count on returning on the 2pm or 4.30pm bus (or try to beg a lift back from one of the few visitors). It's a tiring excursion, but well worth it.

The north coast: to São Francisco and Joinville

If you're going to travel on Santa Catarina's coastal highway (the BR-101) **north of Florianópolis** in the Brazilian summer you're best off keeping your eyes firmly closed. The bumper-to-bumper traffic moves at terrifying speeds, with cars, trucks and buses constantly leapfrogging one another for no apparent advantage; the wrecked cars that litter the highway are enough to make you get out of the bus and walk to your destination – something that, at times, might be faster anyway. But worse, if you don't have a car of your own, is that much of the BR-101 passes alongside absolutely stunning beaches, most of which are totally devoid of buildings and people. If you're on the bus, there's no hope of stopping for a refreshing dip, and you'll just have to make do with the idyllic images out of the window.

Porto Belo

Although the stretch immediately north of Florianópolis is probably the most beautiful part of the Catarinense coast, there's only one spot that is both easy to reach by bus and still not overrun by Argentine and Paulista tourists: the peninsula and city of **PORTO BELO**. With luck, it's less than two hours from Florianópolis, and although the local authority's claim that there are 32 beaches around Porto Belo is highly suspect, the beaches there certainly are numerous and large enough to cope with the visitors.

The "city" of Porto Belo is, in reality, just a small village containing a tourist office, post office and a couple of reasonable seafood restaurants, but from here frequent local buses fan out to beaches around the peninsula, stopping along the road to pick up passengers. The most attractive **beaches** are **Bombas** and **Bombinhas**, 5km and 8km east of Porto Belo respectively and separated from one another by a rocky promontory. The bay in which they're found is very pretty, with rich vegetation behind, and the waves here are suitable for inexperienced surfers. South of Bombinhas, for open sea and more powerful waves, the east-facing **Praia do Mariscal** is better, but should be braved by only the most expert of surfers. In complete contrast, the nearby **Praia do Canto** is ideal for anyone merely seeking a gentle swim.

All the beaches around Porto Belo are geared to **campers**, with sites mainly concentrated at Bombas and Bombinhas. Some of the campsites also rent out **cabins**, and at Bombas there are a couple of small, overpriced **hotels**, the cheapest of which is the *Bomar*. Expensive, but worth every *cruzado*, is the *Pousada do Arvoredo*, on Praia de Bombinhas, which has accommodation in individual cabins. Back in Porto Belo itself, try the *Hotel Baleia Branca*. However, at $2 a bed, the best bargain around is the **youth hostel**, about ten minutes' walk away, on the approach road to town. It has a very relaxed atmosphere, no curfew, and cooking facilities – and instant companionship if you're travelling on your own.

Balneário Camboriú

Just 20km north of Porto Belo, but a world away from it in style, lies **BALNEÁRIO CAMBORIÚ**, Brazil's answer to Benidorm. It's got the lot, though you probably won't want any of it: high-rise hotels, a towel-sized patch of beach per person, and nightclubs which celebrate "Carnaval" all summer, with dance troupes imported from the tropical, more "exotic" Brazil to the north.

Stretching for 5km along the Avenida Atlântico, Camboriú is only a few streets deep. With the mountains behind the resort plunging almost straight into the sea, it's just about possible to imagine how beautiful it once was before the developers moved in, back in the 1930s. Today, there's precious little natural beauty still in evidence, but if you do want to stick around, there's rarely a problem finding a **room**. How much you'll have to pay is totally unpredictable and depends largely on the state of the Argentine economy, the country from where the overwhelming majority of the tourists come. When the Argentine currency is strong against the Brazilian *cruzado*, hotels can demand gold as payment; in other years rooms are almost given away in the hope that guests will at least run up a bill in the hotel's bar and restaurant. In theory, however, the cheapest hotels are near the *Rodoviária* (from where buses leave for just about every city in South America south of Rio), and on the streets set back from the beach. The **tourist office**, with branches at Praça Papa João Paulo I 320 and Praça Tamandare, provides helpful information on hotel availability, a list of the phenomenal number of **restaurants** and the latest information on the constantly changing nightclub and disco scene.

Itajaí

Santa Catarina's most important port, **ITAJAÍ** is located at the mouth of the River Itajaí-Acu, 10km north of Balneário Camboriú. Although founded in the early eighteenth century, Itajaí only really started to develop in the mid-nineteenth century when surrounding parts of the state started to receive European immigrants who generated business for the port. Towards the close of that century, the town itself received a considerable influx of Italian and, to a lesser extent, German and Polish immigrants, whose – completely assimilated – descendants now make up the bulk of the population.

Despite its relative age, Itajaí looks fairly new, with few buildings dating back to before 1950 – and with nothing of any tourist interest. However, it's an important transport centre, being at the main north–south and east–west crossroads and it may not be possible to avoid the city altogether. Fortunately, most buses pass straight by it, with only a minority actually stopping to pick up and put down passengers in the city. And as there's a constant flow of buses to Blumenau, Joinville, Florianópolis, as well as further afield in all directions, there are few reasons actually to stay in Itajaí. One reason might be to catch an early morning plane from nearby Navegantes **airport**, from where you can fly to Porto Alegre and São Paulo: to get to the airport, take the ferry from Avenida Argentina, across the river, and then a taxi; or, a little more expensive, taxis will take you direct from Itajaí, via the ferry, to the airport.

Should you need a **hotel**, there are a couple clearly visible from the *Rodoviária*, or, a little better, try the *Hotel São Remo*; turn right on leaving the *Rodoviária*, left at Rua Silva and walk about five blocks to Rua Tijucas 182 – roughly midway to the city centre.

If for some reason you really can't get out of Itajaí, and have some time to spare, the city's two **beaches** aren't bad. From the local bus terminal in the city centre, near the intersection of Rua Joinville and Avenida Victor Konder, buses take about twenty minutes to reach the nearest beaches, **Atalaia** and **Geremias**, or a little longer to get to the cleaner **Praia Cabecudas**.

The Ilha de São Francisco

North of Itajaí, the highway gradually turns inland towards Joinville (see below), but 45km east of here is the **Ilha de São Francisco**, a low-lying island separated from the mainland by a narrow strait which is spanned by a causeway. As Joinville's port and the site of a major *Petrobras* oil refinery, it might be reasonable to assume that São Francisco should be avoided. However, this isn't the case. Both the port and refinery keep a discreet distance from the main town, São Francisco do Sul, and far away from the beaches, and the surprisingly few sailors that are around blend perfectly with the slightly dilapidated colonial setting.

São Francisco do Sul

The island was first visited by European sailors as early as 1504, though not until the middle of the following century was the town of **SÃO FRANCISCO DO SUL** established. It's one of the oldest settlements in the state and also one of the very few places in Santa Catarina where colonial and nineteenth-century buildings survive concentrated together. During most of its first two hundred years, São Francisco do Sul was little more than a naval outpost, its simple local economy based on fishing and sugar cane production. In the nineteenth century, with the opening of nearby areas to immigrants from Germany, the town grew in importance as a transhipment point for people and produce. Merchants established themselves in the town, building grand houses and dockside warehouses, many of which remain today – protected from demolition and gradually undergoing restoration. Dominating the city's skyline is the **Igreja Matriz**, the main church, originally built in 1665 by Indian slaves, but completely reconstructed in 1884, losing all of its original features. You might want to visit the **Museu Histórico**, on Rua Coronel Carvalho, housed in São Francisco's nineteenth-century prison building (which, incidentally, stayed in use until 1968). The former cells have been converted into small exhibition halls, the most interesting exhibits the nineteenth-century photographs of the town.

Most of the island's visitors bypass the town altogether and head straight for the beaches to the east and south. As such, even in midsummer there's rarely any difficulty in finding a **hotel** with room. Quite comfortable, and with sea views, is the *Hotel Kontiki*, at Rua Camacho 33 (near the market), which charges from

$8 double; or, slightly cheaper, there's the *Hotel Central*, Rua Rafael Pedrinho, for around $5 double. **Eating out** holds no great excitement, with the relatively luxurious *Hotel Zibamba* at Rua Fernandes Dias 27 having the best restaurant of a generally poor bunch. Alternatively, on Praça Badeira, the *Restaurante Panaroma* sports – as you might expect – very nice views across the bay, which take your mind off the totally uninspiring meals of rice, beans and fried fish.

The island's beaches

The prettiest beaches – **Paulos** and **Ingleses** – are also the nearest to town, just a couple of kilometres to the east. Both are small, and have trees to provide shade, and surprisingly few people take advantage of the protected sea, ideal for weak swimmers. On the east coast, **Praia de Ubatuba** and the adjoining **Praia de Enseada**, about 15km from town, are the island's most popular beaches, with enough surf to have fun but not enough to be dangerous. At Enseada there are a couple of **campsites** and an overpriced hotel, while Ubatuba caters mainly for families who rent or own houses that front the beach. By way of contrast, a ten-minute walk across the peninsula from the eastern end of Enseada leads to **Praia da Saude** (or just Prainha), where the waves are suitable for only the most macho *surfista*.

Buses to Enseada and Ubatuba leave from the market in the town centre, with the last buses in both directions departing at about 9.30pm. Also from the market, there are buses to the *Rodoviária*, beyond the town's limits, from where there are hourly connections to Joinville (1hr) as well as less frequent services to São Paulo (daily; 10hr) and Curitiba (3 daily; 4hr). **Travelling to Joinville**, a much more scenic, cheaper, less crowded and generally more civilised way is by **train**. Departures from the station near the town centre are at 11.50am; the train arrives in Joinville at 1pm, before continuing on inland to Corupa (for more information, see below under "Joinville").

German Santa Catarina: Joinville, Blumenau and around

In the nineteenth century, as it grew more difficult to enter the United States, land-hungry European immigrants sought new destinations, many choosing Brazil as their alternative America. Thousands made their way into the forested wilderness of Santa Catarina, attempting to become independent farmers, and of all of them, it was the **Germans** who most successfully fended off assimilationist pressures. Concentrated in areas where few non-Germans lived, there was little reason for them to learn Portuguese, and as merchants, teachers, Catholic priests and Protestant pastors arrived with the immigrants, complete communities evolved, with flourishing German cultural organisations and a varied German-language press. After Brazil's entry into World War II, restrictions on the use of German were introduced and many German organisations were proscribed, accused of being Nazi fronts. Certainly, "National Socialism" found some of its most enthusiastic followers among overseas Germans, and though the extent of **Nazi activity** in Santa Catarina is a matter of debate, for years after the collapse of the Third Reich, ex-Nazis attracted sympathy in even the most isolated forest homesteads.

Later, due to the compulsory use of Portuguese in schools, the influence of radio and television, and an influx of migrants from other parts of the state to work in the region's rapidly expanding industries, the German language appeared to be dying in Santa Catarina. As a result, in Joinville and Blumenau – the region's largest cities – German is now rarely heard. However, in outlying hamlets and villages such as Pomerode, near Blumenau, and Dona Francisca, near Joinville, German remains very much alive, spoken everywhere but in classrooms and government offices. Recently, too, the German language and Teuto-Brazilian culture have undergone a renaissance and the German government has provided financial support. Property developers are encouraged to heed supposedly traditional **German architectual styles**, resulting in a plethora of buildings that may be appropriate for alpine conditions, but look plain silly in the Brazilian subtropics. A more positive development has been the move to protect and restore the houses of the early settlers, especially those built in the most characteristic local building style, that of *enxaimel* ("Fachwerk" in German) – exposed bricks within an exposed timber frame. These houses are seen throughout the region, concentrated most heavily in the area around around Pomerode and Dona Francisca. Keen to reap benefits from the new ethnic awareness, local authorities have also initiated pseudo-German **festivals**, such as Blumenau's Munich-inspired "Oktoberfest" and Pomerode's more authentic "Festa Pomerana", both of which have rapidly become major tourist draws.

Joinville

The land on which **JOINVILLE** was settled was originally given as a dowry by Emperor Dom Pedro to his sister, who had married the Prince of Joinville, the son of Louis-Phillipe of France. A deal with Hamburg lumber merchants meant that in 1851, 191 Germans, Swiss and Norwegians arrived in Santa Catarina, to exploit the twenty-five miles of virgin forest, stake out homesteads and establish the "Colonia Dona Francisca" – later known as Joinville. As more Germans were dispatched from Hamburg, Joinville grew and prospered as it developed from an agricultural backwater into the state's foremost industrial city. This economic success has diluted much of Joinville's once solidly German character, but evidence of its ethnic origins remains: the largely Germanic architecture and the impeccably clean streets produce the atmosphere of a rather dull, small town in Germany.

Shops and services are concentrated along Rua Princesa Isabel, while Rua XV de Novembro and Rua IX de Março run parallel to each other, terminating at the river. However, the points of interest associated with Joinville's German heritage are more widely scattered. The first place to head for is the **Museu Nacional de Imigração e Colonização** at Rua Rio Branco 229, near Praça da Bandeira (Tues–Fri 9am–6pm, Sat & Sun 9am–noon & 2–6pm), an excellent introduction to the history of German immigrants in Santa Catarina in general and Joinville in particular. In the main building, once the Prince of Joinville's palace built in 1870, there are some late-nineteenth- and early-twentieth-century photographs, though the museum's most interesting features are an old barn containing farm equipment used by early *colonos*, and a typical nineteenth-century *enxaimel* farmhouse with period furnishings. If you've more than a passing interest in Joinville's history, visit the superbly organised (and German-funded) **Arquivo Histórico** (Mon–Fri 8am–noon & 2–9pm, Sat 8am–noon) as well, on Rua Rio de Janeiro, where temporary, mainly photographic, exhibitions are held.

As throughout the region, Joinville's municipal authorities are making efforts to preserve the surviving **enxaimel houses**. Although scattered throughout the city, they can be seen in some concentration along the former main approach road, the cobblestoned **Rua XV de Novembro**. On the same road, about twenty minutes' walk from the centre, is the **Cemitário do Imigrante**, the final resting place of many of Joinville's pioneer settlers. Covering a hillside from where there are fine views of the city, the cemetery has been preserved as a national monument, the tombs and headstones serving as testimony to Joinville's ethnic origins. If you have some time on the way to the cemetery, take a brief look around the **Museu de Arte**, Rua XV de Novembro 1400 (Tues–Sun 9am–noon & 2–10pm). The museum has a small collection of works by mainly local artists, hosts visiting exhibitions and has a **cinema** featuring non-commercial, often German, films.

It's also worth popping into the **Mercado Municipal**, near the local bus terminal, which sells food and some handicrafts produced by local German *colonos*. On the second Saturday of each month a **handicraft market** is held in the nearby Praça Nereu Ramos.

Arriving and information

The **Rodoviária** is 2km from the city centre, reached in five minutes by bus or in half an hour on foot by walking down Rua Ministro Calogeras and then left along Avenida Kubitschek. Bus services to neighbouring cities are excellent, with departures every hour during the day to Blumenau (2hr), São Francisco do Sul (1hr), Itajaí (1hr 30min), Florianópolis (3hr) and Curitiba (2hr 30min). There are seven buses a day to São Paulo (9hr), two to Porto Alegre (10hr) and one to Rio (15hr). The terminal for **city buses** and those to Dona Francisca (see below) is in the centre, at the end of Rua IX de Marco.

Opened in 1910, Joinville's **train station** – an imposing construction with a German half-hipped roof – is the oldest one still functioning in Santa Catarina. Today, the only passenger trains go west to Carupá (depart Joinville 1pm; return 4.05pm) and east to São Francisco do Sul (depart 8.05am; return 11.50am), most of the passengers being *colonos* travelling the short distances between otherwise isolated hamlets. Each trip takes around an hour and a half one-way, so if you wanted you could use the train for an afternoon's excursion to either place.

If you need **information**, there's a tourist information post at Praça Nereu Ramos 372 (Mon–Sat 8am–6pm).

Accommodation

Finding a comfortable, spotlessly clean and reasonably priced **hotel** is easy. In the city centre, on Rua Jeronimo Coelho near the local bus terminal, are the *Ideal* (no. 98) and the *Principe* (no. 27), both around $8 for a double room. Nearby is the slightly more expensive *Trocador*, Rua Visconde de Taunay 185, along the road from Joinville's most expensive hotel, the *Tannenhof*. But if money's no problem, stay at the *Anthurium Parque Hotel*, Rua São Jose 226, which charges $25 for a double: it's a curious building claiming to be in a "Norwegian-German" style of architecture and located in pretty grounds near the cathedral.

Further out of town and back down the price scale is the pleasant but noisy *Hotel Mattes*, at Rua XV de Novembro 811. It's $5 per person and conveniently located across the road from the Cemitário do Imigrante. A few houses along the same road, at no. 937, is an even cheaper (unnamed) hotel. Back in town, avoid the overpriced *Hotel Novo Horizonte*, unless you really need to be by the

Rodoviária, just across the road; while opposite the train station is the *Colonial*, a simple, cheap and hospitable hotel with a definite German feel to it – worth using if you're catching an early train to the coast.

Eating, drinking and entertainment

Not surprisingly **German restaurants** abound, but all are of the sausage, pig's knuckle, potato and sauerkraut level of sophistication. The *Bierkeller*, Rua XV de Novembro 497, is friendly, the *Tante Friede*, Rua Visconde de Taunay 1174 (closed Sun evening), has an excellent value buffet, and the *Juca Alemão*, Rua Jerônimo Coelho 188 (closed Mon), is reasonably priced, though with a limited menu. **Vegetarians** and other non-pork eaters should try the *Restaurante Recanto Natural*, at Rua XV de Novembro 78 (Sun–Fri 11am–10pm). Good **cakes** are found at the *Cafeteria Brunkow*, Rua 9 de Março 607.

There's a cultural institute in Joinville, the *Instituto Cultural Brasil-Alemanha* on Rua Princesa Isabel, near Rua Sergipe, and students congregate in the nearby **bars** in the evenings after classes. Otherwise, since 1937, the **Festa das Flores** has been held for ten days during the second half of November, the height of the orchid season – flower shows, German folkdancing, music and food are the main attractions.

Dona Francisca

Close to Joinville, 20km west and 45 minutes away by bus (hourly from the local bus terminal), is **VILA DONA FRANCISCA**, adminstrative centre of the *município* of the same name. Of little interest itself, the *município* on the other hand contains some of the oldest and best cared for *enxaimel* houses in Santa Catarina and, though difficult to find, they arc well worth seeking out.

Supported by the German government, the **Projeto Memória de Joinville** is slowly renovating fifty of the oldest and architecturally most significant houses. The project has an office in Dona Francisca's *prefeitura* (open Mon–Fri) and the workers are very welcoming to visitors. Thanks largely to the efforts of the project, the level of local awareness of the historic importance of the region's old buildings is high, and many people delight in showing their homes to visitors.

As the most interesting houses are scattered over a wide area and are often rather hidden in the forest, you're best off accompanied by someone who knows the area well. If you show up at the *prefeitura* early, you may be able to arrange to accompany someone from *Memória de Joinville* who's due to visit the restoration sites. Alternatively, ask for the name of a taxi driver who's familiar with the area and negotiate a price (say, about $10) for a couple of hours of back-roads driving.

On foot, head for the Estrada Dona Francisca (SC-280) by crossing the main road (BR-101) just out of town. In an old barn and *enxaimel* farmhouse, at the intersection of the BR-101 and SC-280, there's the **Museu Rural** – a museum of *colonos* life – and a shop selling local produce. From the museum, follow the SC-280 and, by keeping to the following directions, you'll see a fair amount; though be aware that the distances mentioned are only very approximate and that the summer sun is very powerful. One kilometre along the SC-280 is Dona Francisca's only **hotel**, the new and extremely comfortable *Alger Hof* ($20 double), while 2km further down the road, turn left on the Estrada Mildrau, along which you'll find the first restored *enxaimel* farmhouse. After another 3km on the SC-280, turn right on the Estrada do Pico: soon after crossing a stream, the road divides; take the right fork and continue along the road (much of the time right alongside the river) and you'll come to a perfectly restored nineteenth-century wooden, covered bridge. Along the same road for another couple of hundred metres and you'll hit the SC-280 again. From here, about 7km back, further along the SC-280, you'll come to the Estrada Quiriri, a dirt road passing through one of Dona Francisca's prettiest and most fertile valleys. Two kilometres away, on the left, is a stunning house, the bricks and timber frame of which form a particularly intricate pattern.

Traffic along these roads is very light, so allow an entire day to see something of Dona Francisca – and be prepared for blistered feet at the end of the day.

Blumenau

Despite Joinville's challenge, **BLUMENAU** has succeeded in promoting itself as the "capital" of German Santa Catarina. Picturesquely located on the right bank of the Itajaí river, Blumenau was founded in 1850 by Dr Hermann Blumenau, who served as director of the colony until returning to Germany in 1880. Blumenau always had a large Italian minority, but it was mainly settled by Germans and, as late as the 1920s, two-thirds of the population spoke German as their mother tongue. In the surrounding rural communities an even larger proportion of the population were German speakers, many of them finding it completely unnecessary to learn Portuguese. Well into this century Blumenau was isolated, with only poor river transport connections with the Brazil beyond the Itajaí Valley – something that enabled its German character to be retained for longer than was the case in Joinville.

Today, Blumenau's municipal authority never fails to miss an opportunity to remind the world of the city's German origins, the European links helping tourism and attracting outside investors. And, superficially, at least, Blumenau certainly looks, if not feels, German. The streets are sparkling clean, parking tickets are issued by wardens dressed in a uniform that Heidi would have been comfortable in, most buildings are in German architectual styles and geranium-filled window boxes are the norm. But since German is almost never heard, and the buildings (such as the half-timbered Saxon-inspired department store and the Swiss chalet-like *prefeitura*) are absurd caricatures of those found in German cities, the result is a sort of "Disneyland" interpretation of Germany.

It's easy to sneer, but Paulista tourists are impressed by Blumenau's old world atmosphere and visit in large numbers, especially during the annual **Oktoberfest**. Held, since 1984, during the second and third weeks of October, the festival is basically an advertising gimmick thought up by *Hering*, the Blumenau-based textile and agro-industrial giant. Besides vast quantities of beer and German food, the main festival attractions are the local and visiting German bands and German folkdance troupes. Performances take place at "PROEB" (Blumenau's exhibition centre), located on the city's outskirts (frequent buses during the festival period), as well as in the downtown streets and the central Biergarten.

At other times, too, local German bands perform every evening from 5pm in the **Biergarten**, the city's main meeting point, in the tree-filled Praça Hercilio Luz. In the oldest part of Blumenau, across a small bridge on the continuation of the main street, Rua XV de Novembro, the Biergarten is only a short walk from the **Museu da Família Colonial**, one of the city's few museums, at Alameda

Duque de Caxias 78 (Mon–Sat 8.30–11.30am & 1.30–5.30pm). The museum's buildings, built in 1858 and 1864 for the families of Dr Blumenau's nephew and secretary/librarian, are two of the oldest surviving *enxaimel* houses in Blumenau. Exhibits include nineteenth-century furniture and household equipment, documents relating to the foundation of the city, photographs of life in the settlement during its early years, and artefacts of the Kaingangs and Xoklengs – the indigenous population displaced by the German settlers. But it's in the beautiful forest-like garden that you'll find the most curious feature: a cemetery, the final resting place for the much loved cats of a former occupant of one of the houses!

A good half-hour walk from Praça Hercilio Luz, on the river at Rua Itajaí 2195, is the **Museu Fritz Muller** (8am–6pm), the former home of the eponymous German-born naturalist. Born in 1822, Muller lived in Santa Catarina between 1852 and 1897, and was a close collaborator of Charles Darwin; the small museum dedicated to the work of the lesser-known of the two scientists.

Arriving, transport and information

The **Rodoviária** is 7km from the city centre in the suburb of Itoupava Norte (the *Cidade Jardim* bus runs into the centre). There are hourly services to Florianópolis, Joinville and Itajaí, and frequent services to western Santa Catarina, Curitiba and São Paulo. Buses to Pomerode (see below) leave roughly hourly from Rua Paulo Zimmermann, located near the *prefeitura* and Praça Victor Konder; if in doubt, ask for the bus stop of the *Volkmann* company – last departure at 10.30pm.

Tourist information offices are found at Rua XV de Novembro 420 (at the corner of Rua Nereu Ramos; open daily), at the *Rodoviária* (daily), and in the *prefeitura* (Mon–Fri) at Praça Victor Konder. If you need official help, there's a **German consulate** at Rua Caetano Decke 20 (11th floor); and an **Italian** one at Rua Guilherme Siebert 333 (☎22-2552).

Sleeping

Centrally located hotels are plentiful so, except during the Oktoberfest, accommodation shouldn't pose a problem. At the lower end of the price range, look no further than the *Hotel Hermann* ($4 single), an early-twentieth-century *enxaimel* building in the heart of the city at Rua Floriano Peixoto 213, by the intersection with Rua Sete de Setembro. If it's full, try the similarly cheap, but characterless *Central*, Rua Sete de Setembro 1036, near the post office; the *Danubio*, Rua São Paulo 374, near the *prefeitura*; or, cheapest of all, the *Oliveira*, Alameda Duque de Caxias, opposite the Museu da Família Colonial. Blumenau's most expensive hotel is the *Plaza Hering*, Rua Sete de Setembro 818, near which, on the same road, are several other medium-priced hotels, like the *Gloria* at no. 954, and the *Rex* at no. 640 – both at $20–25 double.

Eating

The cheaper hotels don't serve **breakfast**, but a superb one – a $2 buffet affair – can be found at the *Café Haus* in the *Hotel Gloria*, around the corner from the *Hotel Hermann*. The same place also serves the best cakes in Blumenau and is an excellent spot for afternoon tea. In general, though, food in Blumenau is poor and largely takes the form of **snacks** to accompany beer.

There are several **German restaurants**, by far the most pleasant of which is the *Frohsinn* (closed Sun). The food here is not at all special, but the location – on a beautiful, cool, pine-clad hill with excellent views over the city – makes the effort to get there worthwhile. From Praça Hercilio Luz, walk for about fifteen minutes along Rua Itajaí and turn right on Rua Gertrud Sierich – the restaurant is at the top of this very steep road. Nearer to the centre, passable German food is served at the *Cavalinho Branco*, Alameda Rio Branco 165, but it's accompanied by loud Teutonic music. If you're sick of pork, try the lunch at *Cisne*, Alameda Rio Branco 238 (closed Sat).

One novel idea is to take a **dinner cruise** down the river. Trips depart at noon, 4pm and 8pm (dinner only served on this one) from Avenida Castelo Branco, near the intersection with Rua Nereu Ramos – a two-hour paddle-steamer excursion that costs from $4, the food extra.

Pomerode

It's **POMERODE**, 30km to the north of Blumenau, that probably has the best claim to be the most German city in Brazil. Not only are ninety percent of its 15,000 inhabitants descended from German immigrants, but eighty percent of the *município*'s population continue to speak the language. Unlike Blumenau, in Pomerode German continues to thrive and is spoken just about everywhere, except in schools. There are several reasons for this: almost all the immigrants – who arrived in the 1860s – came from Pomerania, and therefore did not face the problem of mixing with other immigrants speaking often mutually unintelligible dialects; ninety percent of the population are Lutheran and German was retained for the act of worship; and, until recently, Pomerode was isolated by poor roads and transport links. This isolation has all but ended, though. The road to Blumenau is now excellent, buses are frequent, car ownership is common and televisions are universal. But despite the changes, German looks more entrenched than ever. The language has been re-introduced into the local school curriculum, cultural groups thrive and, where the government has exerted pressure, it has been to encourage the language's survival.

Buses to and from Blumenau stop outside the *Hotel Schroeder* and the Lutheran Church on Rua XV de Novembro, the main street, which sprawls alongside the banks of the Rio do Testo. At no. 555 is the very helpful **tourist office** (daily 9am–noon & 2–6pm), which provides a good map and details of upcoming events. Chief of these is the **Festa Pomerana**, a celebration of local industry and culture held annually for ten days, usually around January 7–17. Most of the events take place on the outskirts of town, on Rua XV de Novembro, about 1km from the tourist office, and during the day thousands of people from neighbouring cities descend on Pomerode to sample the local food, attend the song and dance performances and visit the commercial fair. By late afternoon, though, the day-trippers leave and the *Festa Pomerana* comes alive as the *colonos* from the surrounding areas transform the festivities into a truly popular event. Local and vsiting bands play German and Brazilian music, and dancing continues long into the night.

In July, Pomerode organises the smaller, though similar, **Festa da Tradição Alema,** while every Saturday the local hunting clubs take turns to host dances. Visitors are always made to feel welcome and details of the week's venue are displayed on posters around town, or ask at the tourist office. As many of the clubs are located in the *município*'s outlying reaches, a bus is laid on and leaves from outside the post office, on Rua XV de Novembro.

Otherwise, the main activity for visitors is **walking**. Pomerode has Santa Catarina's greatest concentration of *enxaimel* buildings, the largest number found in the Wunderwald region: cross the bridge near the Lutheran Church, turn left and walk for about twenty minutes, then turn right just before a bridge across a small stream. If you get tired of walking, hitching rides is safe and easy, an excellent way to get to know the locals who, in general, are extremely friendly. Try to be taken to a **colônia**, as the farms here are still called – even if the dairy cattle look familiar and tobacco not too out of place, there aren't many places in the world where platinum blondes are found working in fields of rice.

Sleeping and eating
Accommodation is always easy to find, even during the *Festa Pomerana*. The *Schroeder*, on the main street ($10 double), is Pomerode's only hotel, but if that's full, too expensive or lacking in atmosphere, the tourist office just across the road will find you a **room** with a local family.

You can **eat** well in Pomerode, too. There's no attempt to reproduce "old world" cooking, but instead simple local dishes are prepared. Pork is, of course, ever present, but it's duck that's considered the local speciality. The *Pommerhaus* (just before the turn-off for the Testo Alto road) is, without doubt, Pomerode's best restaurant, serving typical regional food. Nearer the town centre, there are several other restaurants, the best of which is the more orthodox German *Stettiner Klause*, just across the river from the post office and opposite the unremarkable zoo.

Moving on: Jaraguá do Sul and Timbó
There are almost hourly **buses** to and from Blumenau, but as the last goes to Blumenau at 6pm and returns at 10.30pm, going into the city for an evening out is only just about possible. The roads north to **JARAGUÁ DO SUL** (take a Curitiba bus; 3 daily) and west to **TIMBÓ** (a Rio do Sul bus; 2 daily) are two of the prettiest around, but the towns they lead to are of no interest, their former German character long since eroded. To Jaraguá do Sul, the road passes through almost mountainous terrain, while that to Timbó winds its way through an incredibly fertile valley floor.

The south coast: to Laguna and Criciúma

Unlike the northern stretch of coast, heading south from Florianópolis doesn't offer as many temptations to leap off the bus and into the sea. Most of this part of the BR-101 highway is too far inland to catch even a glimpse of the sea but, in any case, south of Laguna, the beaches are less attractive and more exposed. Many of the coastal settlements were founded by Azorean immigrants in the late seventeenth century and early eighteenth century, and they've retained the fishing and lace-making traditions of their ancestors. Inland, settlement is much more recent and the inhabitants are a blend of Germans, Italians and Poles, whose forefathers were attracted in the late nineteenth century by promises of fertile land and offers of work in the region's coal mines. However, apart from surnames and scattered wooden and stone houses of the early settlers, there are few remaining traces of the immigrant heritage.

Garopaba and Imbituba

The first accessible spot worth stopping at is **GAROPABA**, a small fishing village which, despite attracting more and more people every summer, has not yet been totally overwhelmed by tourism. The beaches are excellent, but are mainly located a short distance from the village. Fifteen kilometres to the north, at GAMBOA, are some large sand dunes.

Facilities are mainly geared to campers and there are very few **restaurants**. Of Garopaba's half a dozen **hotels**, at about $10 for a double room, the cheapest are the *Pousada Casa Grande e Senzala* at Rua Dr. Elmo Kiseki 444 and, at Rua Marques Guimarães 130, the *Lobo* – but as they are small they are often full in summer. However, by asking around, there's rarely a problem in finding a room in a private house. Despite Garopaba's size, **bus** services are good, with buses to Florianópolis leaving from Rua Marques Guimarães, and those destined for points south as far as Porto Alegre leaving from Praça Silveira.

Thirty kilometres south of Garopaba, **IMBITUBA**, once one of the most attractive points along the coast, should be avoided at all costs. Imbituba's main function is that of a port serving the nearby coalfields; from here coal is sent north to the steel mills of Volta Redonda for coking. The town's beaches are polluted and, should you want putting off further, so too is the air, thanks to the carbo-chemical plant.

Laguna

LAGUNA, on the other hand, is an excellent place to break your journey; the closest Santa Catarina gets to having a near-complete colonial town. Located at the end of a narrow peninsula, at the entrance to the Lagoa Santo Antônio, Laguna feels like two distinct towns. Facing west onto the sheltered lagoon is the old port (long surpassed by Imbituba) and Lagoa's historic centre, protected as a national monument. Two kilometres away, on the far side of a granite outcrop of mountainous proportions that separates the city's two parts, is the new town, facing east onto the Atlantic Ocean.

The town

As a beach resort, Laguna's attraction is limited. The city's importance lies in its **old town** which, even during the height of the summer tourist season, attracts few people – just as well, as it's quite small and could easily be overwhelmed.

Laguna was significant as early as 1494, being the southern point of the line dividing the Americas between Spain and Portugal (the northern point at Belém), 370 leagues west of the Cape Verde Islands. A **monument**, near the *Rodoviária*, a few minutes' walk from the centre, marks the exact spot. However, a permanent settlement wasn't established until 1676, but it rapidly became the pre-eminent port of the southern fringes of the Portuguese Empire, and a base for the exploration and colonisation of what is now Rio Grande do Sul.

Although by no means all of Laguna's old town dates from the eighteenth century, its general aspect is that of a Portuguese colonial town. The oldest streets are those extending off **Praça Vidal Ramos**, the square which holds the **Igreja Santo Antônio dos Anjos**. Built in 1694, the church retains its late-eighteenth-century Baroque altars and, though simple enough, is considered the most important surviving colonial church in Santa Catarina.

On the same square as the church is the **Casa de Anita** (Tues–Sun 9am–noon & 2–4pm), a small museum dedicated to Anita Garibaldi, the Brazilian wife of Giuseppe Garibaldi, maverick military leader of the Italian unification movement. Garibaldi was employed as a mercenary in the Guerra dos Farrapos, fought between Repúblicans and Monarchists, and it was in Laguna that a short-lived Republic was declared in 1839. There are some fine photographs of nineteenth-century Laguna on display, but – oddly perhaps – there's little on Anita's life and Repúblican activities; scissors and hairbrushes that once belonged to her are typical of the exhibits. Close by, on Praça Lauro Muller, is the **Fonte da Carioca**, the oldest surviving fountain in Laguna, dating back to 1863, covered in blue and white Portuguese tiles and located next to the former slave market.

About fifteen kilometres out of town to the south, try to beg a lift to the **Farol Santa Marta**, a lighthouse (the third tallest in the Americas) which was transported piece by piece from Scotland in 1891. It's surrounded by bleak, but beautiful scenery offering wild seas (suicidal for even the strongest of swimmers) and protected beaches. If you do find a way of getting here, there's a simple **hotel**, houses renting rooms, and a couple of **restaurants**.

Staying over

The *Rodoviária* is at Rua Arcângelo Bianchini, just a couple of minutes' walk from the waterfront and the old town. Located above the old market on the waterfront is the tourist office, which provides excellent maps of Laguna and the surrounding area.

Most of Laguna's hotels and restaurants are located in the new town, alongside and parallel to the **Praia do Mar Grosso**, the city's main beach. Hotels here are large and expensive, but two moderately-priced exceptions charging about $12 for a double room are the *Mar Grosso*, Avenida Senador Galotti 644, and the *Ondao*, Avenida Beira March. The seafood **restaurants** (concentrated in the middle of of Avenida Senador Galotti) are good, if much of a muchness.

Apart from during Carnaval, which rivals that of Florianópolis, **rooms** in the **old town** are easy to find. The *Hotel Farol Palace* ($6 double), on the waterfront opposite the market, is comfortable and friendly. If you can bear a little squalor, there are a couple of extremely cheap *dormitórios* behind the hotel. **Restaurants** in this part of town are poor, the best being two pizzerias on Praça Juliana, but there's a very pleasant little *confeitaria*, the *Docelândia*, at Rua Voluntário Carper 78.

South to Criciúma

The **coastline** between Laguna and the Rio Grande do Sul border is effectively one long beach – though it's of no great beauty and can be passed with little pain. The coastal plane, which stretches inland some 30km, provides little in the way of natural attraction, and the region's two largest towns – Tubarão and Criciúma – were founded as coal-mining centres; the area remains one of Brazil's very few producers of the mineral. Should you need to stay, **CRICIÚMA** is marginally the more pleasant and least polluted of the two.

The *Rodoviária* is centrally located, on Avenida Centenário, the main artery which bisects the town, and as there are frequent buses to all points in Santa Catarina, it's unlikely that you'll have to stay the night. However, if you arrive late, there are two very good **hotels**, virtually alongside the *Rodoviária* – the luxury

Crisul and the medium-priced *Turis Center* ($15 double) – and two basic *dormitórios*. Cheap ($6 double) and comfortable, the *Cavaller Palace* is on Rua Anita Garibaldi, near the town's central square, Praça Nereu Ramos. The square is also where you'll find the **tourist office**, a five-minute walk towards the rear of the *Rodoviária*.

Killing time in Criciúma is fairly easy if you're interested in immigration history. The **Centro Cultural Teuto-Brasileiro** (reached by a bus marked *Forquilhinha*) contains a small museum related to the German settlers, while exhibits in the **Museu da Colonização**, Rua Cecília Daros Casagrande (Tues–Sun 8am–5.30pm) – take the bus marked *Bairro Comerciario* – largely relate to the Italian community. If you've only got a couple of hours to spare, a visit to the model **mine** (Tues–Sun 8–11.30am & 2–6pm) – Criciúma's prime tourist attraction – is really the best idea. It's 3km from the city centre: take a bus marked *Minha Model* from the the local bus terminal, which is next to the *Rodoviária*. Coal seams were discovered around Criciúma in 1913, and this mine entered production in 1930. Visitors are taken through the coal mine by retired miners who spiel out, in exhausting detail, information about the local geological structure and mining techniques. The squeamish should note that the mine is home to huge numbers of fruit bats which, though quite harmless, are repulsive creatures!

Central and western Santa Catarina

Until the roadbuilding programme of the 1970s, mountainous **central and western** Santa Catarina was pretty much isolated from the rest of the state. Largely settled by migrants from neighbouring states, the inhabitants of this territory are of diverse origins including Germans and Italians in the extreme west, Austrians, Italians and Ukrainians in the central Rio do Peixe Valley, and *gaúchos* – and even Japanese – in the highlands of the Serra Geral. In the more isolated areas, dominated by a single ethnic group, traditions and languages have been preserved but, as elsewhere in southern Brazil, it's debatable as to how long assimilationist pressures can be resisted.

The Serra Geral

Any route taken to reach the **Serra Geral** is spectacular, but if you enter the region directly from the coast the contrasts of landscape, vegetation and climate unfold most dramatically. From the subtropical lowlands, roads have been cut into the steep escarpment and, as the roads slowly wind their way up into the Serra, dense foliage unfolds – protected from human destruction by its ability to cling to the most precipitous of slopes. Waterfalls can be seen in every direction until suddenly you reach the *planalto*, a virtual plateau. Here, the graceful Paraná pine trees are fewer in number but much larger, their branches fanning upwards in a determined attempt to form the canopy that existed before the arrival of cattle and lumber interests.

For tourists, towns in the Serra are generally places to travel towards rather than destinations in their own right. Even if it means going a considerable distance out of the way, most **bus** services to Lages, from the coast, travel via the BR-470 – Santa Catarina's main east–west highway – before turning onto the BR-

116, that cuts north–south through the state. To and from Florianópolis, for example, it's usually much faster and more comfortable for buses to travel via Blumenau, but far more picturesque are the twice-daily services from Florianópolis to Lages via ALFREDO WAGNER. From the southern coast of Santa Catarina, the Serra can be approached by bus from Criciúma on the even more spectacular road leading up to São Joaquim, from where you can continue on to Lages.

Lages

Although founded in 1766, nothing remains in **LAGES** from the days when it was an important resting-post on the route along which cattle and mules were herded northwards to the market in Sorocaba. Nowadays, the city is a collection of anonymous post-1950s buildings and only the presence in town of visiting ranchers and cowhands, dressed in the characteristic baggy pantaloons, waist sash and poncho, reminds you that the town is at the northern edge of *gaúcho* country. Because of the presence of so many knife-carrying men, who come into town at the weekend for supplies and a good time, Lages is reputed to be the most violent town in the state. However, the general atmosphere is dull rather than menacing, and tourists are unlikely to get caught up in any truble.

The **Rodoviária** is a half-hour walk southeast from the centre, or take a bus marked *Dom Pedro*. There's a **tourist office** in the centre of town, on Praça Joao Costa (near the *prefeitura*), which distributes a good map of Lages. The office also promotes the *Turismo Rural* project, the purpose of which is to provide opportunities for people to visit typical cattle *fazendas* and catch a glimpse of life in the outlying parts of the Serra – otherwise extremely difficult for tourists to see. Only groups are catered for, so ask at the tourist office whether you can join one that has already been formed. Otherwise, the best way to get a feel of the region is to attend one of the periodic **rodeios**; again, the tourist office can provide information. Lages' great event is the *Rodeio Criola*, held over a two-week period every other January (in odd years). Much like neighbouring VACARIA's *rodeio* (held in even years), thousands of *gaúchos* from throughout southern Brazil come to watch and compete.

Hotels and food
Reasonable, modestly-priced **hotels** are easy to come by, even during the *Rodeio Criola* (when most people camp). The *Rex*, Avenida Luiz de Camoes 1380, and *Hotel Presidente*, Avenida Presidente Vargas 106, are both quite good and only minutes' walk from the cathedral and main square, Praça Waldo da Costa Avila. **Restaurants** are, of course, largely meat-orientated, the best being the *Laghões*, at Rua João de Castro 27. There are also a number of vaguely Italian restaurants, and worth a try is *Cantina d'Italia*, at Rua Francisco Furtado Ramos 122.

São Joaquim

Formerly a small ranching centre, **SÃO JOAQUIM** has only really been on the Brazilian map since the mid-1970s when apple orchards were introduced here. Within a fifteen-year period, Brazil changed from importing nearly all the apples consumed in the country to being virtually self-sufficient. At an altitude of 1360 metres (the highest town in Brazil), apples trees are in their element in São Joaquim, benefiting from the very pronounced seasonal temperature variations. Temperatures in the winter regularly dip to -15°C and, as one of the few parts of Brazil that sees regular snowfalls, there is a surprising amount of tourism in the winter in the town. Anyone with a specific interest in apples can visit the **Estação Experimental de São Joaquim**, on the outskirts of town, where research into soft fruit takes place. Or if you're just plain hungry visit the **shop**, owned by an English-speaking Israeli farmer, just below the main square, which sells a vast variety of apples.

The **Rodoviária** (good services to Lages and Criciúma) is just a couple of minutes' walk from the city centre. Opposite one another on Rua Manoel Joaquim Pinto are the town's only **hotels**, the *Nevada* and *Maristela*, both of which are quite cheap. Despite the presence of fifty Japanese apple-growing families, the only **restaurant** is a pizzeria, the *Agua na Boca* on Rua Marcos Batista.

The Rio do Peixe Valley

Immigrants were introduced to the **Peixe Valley** in around 1910 by the American-owned *Brazil Railway Company*. For completing the São Paulo–Rio Grande railway, the company received land from which they could extract valuable timber and divide for sale to homesteaders. Due to the region's isolation, war in Europe, anti-immigration legislation and the discovery that the soil was not as fertile as had been believed, fewer people than hoped moved into the area. Of those who did come, most were from neighbouring states, mainly Slavs from Paraná, and Germans and Italians from Rio Grande do Sul.

Joaçaba and around

The region's most important town is **JOAÇABA**, on the Peixe's west bank, directly across the river from the smaller town of HERVAL D'OESTE. Perhaps due to the narrowness of the valley, whose slopes rise precipitously along one entire side of town, Joaçaba has an oppressive, almost menacing, atmosphere. Although the population is dominated by people of Italian extraction, no obvious Italian influences remain, and as Joaçaba developed into an important centre of light industry and agribusiness, it lost its former frontier charm. However, if you're visiting the Rio do Peixe area, Joaçaba is difficult to avoid altogether. Buses serve all surrounding districts and towns to the west, and there are regular departures to Blumenau and Florianópolis (3 daily) and daily services to São Paulo and Foz do Iguaçu.

With the **Rodoviária** located just minutes' walk from the town centre, arriving in Joaçaba couldn't be easier. On leaving the *Rodoviária*, turn right onto Avenida XV de Novembro, the road that follows alongside the river through town; turn right again on Rua Sete de Setembro and you'll find an inexpensive **hotel**, the *Hotel Comércio* (near the *Banco do Brasil*, the only place in town to change dollars), while further along Avenida XV de Novembro, opposite the *prefeitura*, is the *Hotel Link* ($13 single). Also along this street are a couple of *churrascarias* and pizzerias.

Really though, it makes little sense to stay in Joaçaba except, possibly, to use it as a base from which to visit the surrounding area. In every direction from Joaçaba the countryside ranges from hilly to mountainous, and by selecting at random a neighbouring small town, you'll be sure to be rewarded with a bus ride through some beautiful scenery. The road to **PIRATUBA**, 50km to the south, is especially attractive and at the journey's end you can relax in the natural thermal pools there. Most of the *colonos* along this road are of Italian origin, with those around **LACERDÓPOLIS** still retaining elements of the dialects and traditions of past generations.

Treze Tilias

Of the region's ethnic groups, it is one of the smallest – the Austrians – who have been most stubborn in resisting cultural assimilation. The *município* of **TREZE TILIAS'** claim to be the "Brazilian Tyrol" is by no means a baseless one. In 1933, 82 Tyroleans led by Andreas Thaler, a former Austrian minister of agriculture, arrived in what is now Treze Tilias. As the dense forest around the settlement was gradually cleared more settlers joined the colony, but after Germany's annexation of Austria in 1936, immigration came to an end – as did funds to help support the pioneers during the difficult first years. With the onset of war, communications with Austria ceased altogether and, with no country to return to, abandoning the colony was not an option. During the immediate postwar years, contacts with Europe were minimal, but as Austria grew more prosperous, Treze Tilias began to receive assistance. The area came to specialise in dairy farming and today their milk products are sold in supermarkets throughout Santa Catarina.

Treze Tilias is only an hour from Joaçaba and Videira and it's perfectly practical to use it as a base for getting to know the wider region. All buses stop outside the *Hotel Austria* ($3 single, or $5 with a huge breakfast), the older and cheaper of the town's two **hotels**. Excellent meals, incorporating Austrian and Brazilian influences, are served at the *Austria* and the hotel is a mine of local knowledge. If you're staying there, you can ask the owner, Andreas Moser, to take you to the smallholding where all the food consumed in the hotel is produced. The other hotel, the *Tirol* ($15 double), is also good, if rather devoid of character, but its restaurant is worth trying and its *café colonial* is excellent. One place to avoid is the restaurant in the cultural centre, next to the *Banco do Brasil*: a limited menu and Brazilian food at its most uninspired.

But for the absence of snowcapped mountain peaks, the general appearance of Treze Tilas is not dissimilar to that of a small Alpine village. Walking in any direction, you'll pass through peaceful pastoral landscapes. The seven-kilometre walk to the chapel at BABENBERG is particularly rewarding, while if you set out to visit the local **waterfalls**, get very detailed directions beforehand.

In the village itself, try and visit some of the **wood carvers**, the best of whom learned their craft in Europe, and whose work is in demand throughout Brazil. Farmers and craftsmen alike respond very openly to interest in their work from outsiders.

Videira

On the eastern fringes of Treze Tilias, along the road leading to **VIDEIRA**, the population is mainly of Italian origin, descended from migrants who came from Rio Grande do Sul in the 1940s. Vines dominate the landscape, and if you visit a *colônia*, you'll probably be invited to taste their home-produced *cachaça* or the wine (an acquired taste) – it's only polite to buy a bottle before leaving. If you want to take the matter further, the small, but well organised **Museu do Vinho**, next to Videira's main church, is worth half an hour or so. The displays relate to the local winemaking skills in the early years of settlement.

Videira itself doesn't justify more than the briefest of pauses between buses which are, unfortunately, far less frequent than those from Joaçaba. If you need a **hotel**, and there's no time to go to Treze Tílias, from the *Rodoviária* walk down the hill on Avenida Dom Pedro II and at the *Shell* station turn right onto Rua Brasil (the main commercial street); the inexpensive *Hotel Savannah* and **restaurant** is the first building on the left. Alternatively, crossing the river over the bridge at the bottom of Rua Brasil, next to the local bus terminal, is Videira's luxury *Hotel San Raphael*, whose reasonably priced restaurant serves the best food in town – not that there's much competition.

The extreme west

Until the 1950s, most of the population of the **extreme west of Santa Catarina** were Kaingang Indians and semi-nomadic *caboclo erva maté* harvesters. With land availability in Rio Grande do Sul increasingly difficult, peasant farmers moved north into Santa Catarina and the area has since become the state's foremost producer of pigs and chickens.

Chapecó and around

Without an interest in agriculture, **CHAPECÓ** (or indeed any other town in the region) is unlikely to hold your attention for longer than it takes to change buses. Fortunately, Chapecó is well served with buses to points throughout Santa Catarina and Rio Grande do Sul, to Dionisio Cerqueira (for Argentina), Curitiba and Cascavel (for connections to Foz do Iguaçu) in Paraná. If you have to stick around for a while, frequent buses connect the *Rodoviária*, on the city's outskirts, with the local bus terminal, which is located virtually on the main square. There are a couple of **places to stay** near the bus terminal, and two more on the main street, Avenida Getulio Vargas.

Chapecó's self-proclaimed status as regional capital simply means that its slaughterhouses are larger than those in the surrounding towns. There's not much to delay you, though if you're stuck, browse around *Bolicho do Gauderio*, on the main square, a general outfitters aiming at fashion-conscious young *gaúchos*; it's a good place to pick up souvenirs. On a rather sadder note, souvenirs can also be purchased from forlorn-looking Kaingang Indians, who wander around town attempting to sell their brightly-coloured basket work and bows and arrows

If you do have a day to spare, head into the outlying **countryside** where the *colonos* cultivate maize, beans and manioc on even the most precipitous of mountain slopes. A typical village within an hour of Chapecó (buses from the central bus terminal) is **SAUDADES**, from where you can take another bus (or, better still, walk or hitch) to **SÃO CARLOS**, 25km south along the winding valley of the Chapecó river. From São Carlos, there are frequent buses to Chapecó (1hr) or, 3km to the east, stop off at **AGUAS DE CHAPECÓ**, a small thermal springs and beach resort beautifully located overlooking the mighty Uruguai river. There are **camping** facilities here, and two simple **hotels**.

Aberlardo Luz

Ninety kilometres north of Chapecó is **ABELARDO LUZ**, a small town near the Paranaense border. With a total population of just 15,000, in the mid-1980s Abelardo Luz briefly hit the headlines in Brazil, when thousands of landless peasants from neighbouring areas moved onto the huge estates of absentee landowners in this, one of the poorest and most sparsely populated parts of Santa Catarina.

The unrest has long since subsided and the reporters from throughout Brazil who descended on this miserable little town are now just an exciting memory for the otherwise sleepy place. However, small numbers of tourists do stop off in Abelardo Luz, on their way between eastern Santa Catarina and Rio Grande do Sul and Foz do Iguaçu. The attraction is the **Quedas do Rio Chapecó**, beautiful waterfalls a 45-minute walk from town. To reach the falls, walk up Abelardo Luz's main street and, at the top, turn left and walk until you reach an asphalted highway where you turn right. Walk along the road past the horseshoe-shaped entrance to the park, cross a bridge and continue past a hotel (very basic) until you come to signs for the *Quedas*, indicating a road to the left. You'll be charged a small entrance fee, but facilities are good; there's a **campsite**, a **restaurant** and snack bar. The **falls** themselves extend across the river and take the form of eight steps varying in breadth and width. Walkways cross parts of the waterfalls and numerous small natural pools by the side of the tourist complex. But to swim properly, you need to go three kilometres upriver to **Prainha**, a beach where there's also a campsite.

Unless you're camping, apart from the hotel on the way to the falls the only **place to stay** is a very grim, but cheap, hotel on the main street of town, across from two poor **restaurants**. Buses leave from virtually outside the hotel and there's an hourly service to Xanxere, from where there are frequent connections to points within Santa Catarina and Rio Grande do Sul. If you're travelling to or from Foz do Iguaçu, take a bus to Cascavel (Paraná) and change there.

RIO GRANDE DO SUL

Bordering Argentina and Uruguay, for many people the state of **Rio Grande do Sul** is their first or last experience of Brazil. More than most parts of the country, it has an extremely strong regional identity – to the extent that it's the only state where the possibility of independence is discussed. Central government's authority over Brazil's southernmost state has often been weak: in the colonial era, the territory was virtually a no-man's land separating the Spanish and Portuguese empires. Out of this emerged a strongly independent people, mostly pioneer farmers and the descendants of European immigrants; isolated fishing communities; and, best known, the *gaúchos*, the cowboys of southern South America whose name is now used for all inhabitants of the state, whatever their origins.

The state's **road and bus network** is excellent and it's easy to zip through the state without stopping if needs be. However, Rio Grande do Sul is as Brazilian as Bahia or Rio and it would be foolish to ignore the place. The capital, **Porto Alegre**, is southern Brazil's most important cultural and commercial centre but, like all the other cities in Rio Grande do Sul, has little to detain tourists. However, it's also the state's transportation axis and at some point you're likely to pass through the city. For a truer flavour of Rio Grande do Sul, visit the main region of Italian settlement, around the towns of **Caxias do Sul** and **Bento Gonçalves**, a couple of hours north of Porto Alegre. And for the classic image, head for the cattle country of the **Serra** and **Campanha** where old *gaúcho* traditions still linger.

Porto Alegre

The capital of Rio Grande do Sul, **PORTO ALEGRE** lies on the eastern bank of the Guaiba river, at the point where five rivers converge to form the **Lagoa dos Patos**, a giant freshwater lagoon navigable by even the largest of ships. Founded in 1755 as a Portuguese garrison, to guard against Spanish encroachment into this part of the empire, it wasn't until Porto Alegre became the port for the export of beef that it developed into Brazil's leading commercial centre south of São Paulo.

With a rather uninteresting feel to it, like a cross between a southern European and a North American city, most people will be tempted to move straight on from Porto Alegre. However, as it's a major transport centre, a stop here might be unavoidable, not that that's such a bad thing. The city has considerable life, if not much visible history, and you'll find many ways to occupy yourself.

Arriving and finding a place to stay

There's hardly an airport in southern Brazil which doesn't serve Porto Alegre, and there are international services to Buenos Aires, Montevideo and Santiago, too. The **airport** is linked by Metro to the Mercado Público, in the city centre. At other times, take the "L.05" bus, which links the airport with Praça Parobe (next to the Mercado Público). Buses from throughout Brazil and neighbouring countries stop at Porto Alegre's **Rodoviária**, which is within walking distance of the centre. However, because the *Rodoviária* is virtually ringed by a mesh of highways and overpasses, it's far less confusing, and safer, to use the Metro from there. Porto Alegre used to be a major **railway** hub but, apart from suburban routes, the only remaining services are to Santa Maria (daily except Sat), from where the line branches out to Santana do Livramento and Urugainana (3 trains weekly to and from each destination). Trains depart from the new **Ferroviária**, also accessible by Metro.

The **Metro** (Mon–Fri 5am–11pm, Sat & Sun 5am–8pm) has its city centre terminal at Mercado Público, at Praça XV de Novembro, but as the system is very limited in extent, it's only really of use when you arrive and leave Porto Alegre.

EPATUR, the city's **tourist office** (daily, office hours), has very helpful branches at the airport, the *Rodoviária*, in Praça XV de Novembro and at Travessa do Carmo 84 (Largo dos Açorianos). *CRTur*, the state tourist office, has its headquarters at Rua dos Andradas 1137 (6th floor) on Praça Senador Florencio (Mon–Fri 8–noon & 2–6pm).

Accommodation

Hotels are scattered all around the city centre. Small, clean and with a vaguely colonial character, the *Hotel Praça da Matriz* is at Largo João Amorim de Albequerque 72 and costs $12 double. Nearby, the apartment-hotel *Residence Plaza Catedral*, Rua Fernando Machado 741, is more expensive, at $20 double. Slightly more upmarket and conveniently located in the main commercial district, is the *Açores*, Rua dos Andradas 885. Of the **cheaper hotels** ($4–6 for a double room), to be found between the Mercado Público and the cathedral, the following are recommended: *Henrique*, Rua General Vitorino 182; *Metropole*, Rua Andrade Neves 59; and *Palácio*, Avenida Vigario Jose Inacio 644. Even cheaper, there's a **youth hostel**, at Rua Aurora Nunes Wagner 148, in a quiet residential suburb overlooking the city, half an hour by bus from the centre: take a bus from Rua dos Andradas, near Avenida Borges de Medeiros, going to *Morro Santa Tereza* and get off at the last stop.

Around the centre

Porto Alegre sprawls out over a series of hills with the centre spread between two levels, the older residential area on the higher level and the commercial area below. In the 1960s and 1970s the city centre underwent dramatic redevelopment with landfill schemes to improve the docks, new urban highways and ever larger office blocks. Despite the destruction accompanying the construction boom, many of Porto Alegre's nineteenth- and early-twentieth-century buildings escaped demolition, and the city has succeeded in retaining some of its former dignity. In the city centre itself, everything is within an easy walk, and a half-day or so is enough to visit most places of interest. The ochre-coloured **Mercado Público** is at the heart of the lower town, located alongside Praça Rui Barbosa and Praça XV de Novembro. Said to be a replica of Lisbon's Mercado da Figueira, this imposing building, with its intricate, typically Portuguese, stuccoed detail, has recently undergone restoration. It contains an absorbing mix of stalls selling household goods, food, a vast variety of herbs, *erva mate* of all grades of quality, and regional handicrafts. As part of the municipal authority's project to "humanise" Porto Alegre, much of the maze of streets around the market has been pedestrianised: the **bar** and restaurant on Praça XV de Novembro, formerly the meeting place of the city's artists and intellectuals, is an especially good spot from which to watch everyone pass by. To the left of the market is the **Palácio Municipal**, the old *prefeitura*, built in Neoclassical style between 1898 and 1901, its impressive proportions an indication of civic pride and self-confidence during the period when Porto Alegre was developing from being a mere southern outpost into an important city. Between about 1880 and 1930, Porto Alegre attracted large numbers of southern and eastern European immigrants and in front of the palace is a **fountain**, a gift to the city from its once considerable Spanish community.*

The streets along the steep slope, rising from the low-lying parts of the centre (Rua das Andradas, Rua General Vitorino and Avenida Senador Salgado Filho) mark Porto Alegre's main **commercial district** of clothing shops, travel agents and banks. Further up the hill are Praça da Matriz (officially called Praça Marechal Deodoro) and Largo João Amorim do Albuquerque, where the former legislative assembly and some of Porto Alegre's oldest buildings are concentrated. Despite the buildings in this part of the city having late-eighteenth- to mid-nineteenth-century origins, they have undergone so many renovations and additions over the past couple of centuries that only vaguely, if at all, do they bear any

---

*Of the descendants of the immigrant communities, only the Jews continue to identify with a particular quarter of the city. Although comparatively few members of the Jewish community still live in Bom Fim (next to Avenida Osvaldo Aranha on the northeastern side of the *Parque Farroupilha*, the city's main recreational ground), many businesses there continue to be Jewish-owned; and it's also the location of synagogues and the main community centre, the *Centro Israelita*, Rua Henrique Dias 73. As the district where earlier generations struggled during their first decades in Brazil, emotional attachments to Bom Fim linger, and the area – the background of some of the novels and short stories of the well-known author Moacyr Sclair – remains close to the heart of the community.

PORTO ALEGRE

River Guaíba

Post Off

Alfândega

RUA CALDAS JUNOR

R. CAP. MONTANNA

AV. SEP...

RUA SIQUEIRA DE CAMPOS

RUA GENERAL BENTO MARTINS

TV. ARUJI.IO RIBEIRO

RUA 7 DE SETEMBRO

PR. PE. TOME

RUA DOS ANDRADAS

RUA RIACHUELO

RUA GENERAL JOÃO MANOEL

RUA DUQUE DE CAXIAS

Palá
Farroup

Paláci
Paratin

RUA GEN. AUTO

AVENIDA JOSE LOUREIRO DA SILVA

RUA GEN. SILUSTINO

RUA GEN. VASCO ALVES

RUA GENERAL PORTINHO

RUA CORONEL FERNANDO MACH

RUA DEMETRIO RIBEIRO

RUA WASHINGTON LUIZ

AVENIDA JOSE LOUREIRO DA

AVENIDA BEIRA

0   500 m

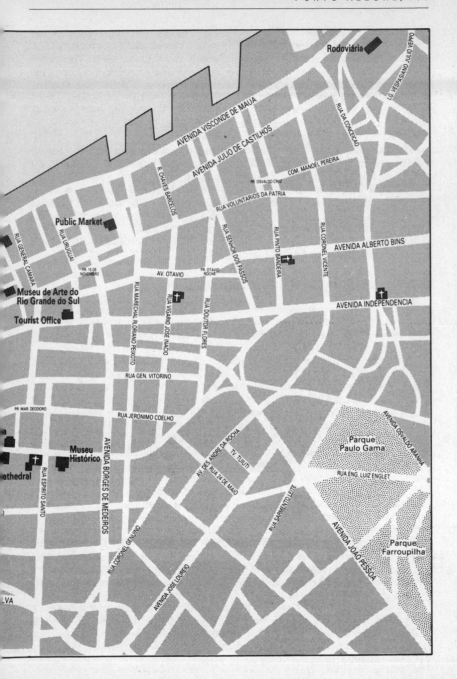

resemblance to their colonial predecessors. Though the foundations of the **Catedral Metropolitana** are built over those of a church that dates back to 1772, the present Italianate structure was only begun in 1921, and wasn't completed until 1986. Work on the former legislative assembly also started in 1772 but, likewise, it has undergone innumerable renovations over the years. The **Palácio Piratini** (the state governor's residence) dates from only 1909, while across from it, the **Teatro São Pedro** was inaugurated in 1858. Surprisingly, its Portuguese Baroque appearance has remained largely unmolested, and the theatre is an important venue for local and visiting companies.

With two exceptions, Porto Alegre's **museums** are a poor bunch. Despite suffering many losses through theft, the **Museu de Arte do Rio Grande do Sul**, Praça Barrão do Rio Branco (Tues–Sun 10am–6pm), has a reasonable collection of work by *gaúcho* national artists, while the **Museu Julio de Castilhos**, Rua Duque de Caxias 1231 (Tues–Sun 9am–5pm), covers the history of the state fairly well. A curiosity – rather than intrinsically interesting – is the **Museu da Força Expedicionária Brasileira** at Avenida João Pessoa 567 (Mon–Wed & Fri 2–5pm, Thurs 8–11.30am), where exhibits relate to the Brazilian batallions who served in the Italian campaign of World War II.

Eating, drinking and entertainment

As you'd expect, meat dominates menus here and *churrascarias* abound. However, the city centre has only a limited selection of **restaurants** of any sort, with the best located in the suburbs – which, fortunately, are not more than a $4 taxi-fare away.

With only time for one meal in Porto Alegre, go to the *Recanto do Seu Flor*, Avenida Getulio Vargas 1700, in the suburb of Menino Deus (just beneath Morro Santa Teresa), where **regional food** at its best is served. The menu is inspired by *gaúcho* traditions and concentrates on unusual stews. Serving similar, though not nearly as good, food are the *Pulperia*, Trav. do Carmo 76 (only dinner, closed Sun), and *João de Barro*, Rua da República 546 (only dinner), both a short walk from Largo João Amorim de Albuquerque. If it's **churrasco** you're seeking, the best are the *Santo Antônio*, at Rua Dr. Timoteo 465, in the suburb of Floresta, and the *Nova Bréscia*, Rua 18 de Novembro 81, further out in Navegantes. In the centre, a moderately good *churrascaria* is the *Capitão Rodrigo*, Rua Alberto Bins 514: being in the luxury *Hotel Plaza São Rafael*, it's overpriced.

Almost without exception, the numerous **Italian restaurants** are disappointing. Most are in Floresta, 3km from the centre, and the following are reputed to be acceptable: *Casa del Nono*, Rua Felix da Cunha 324; *Cantina Roma*, Rua Com. Coruja 420 (closed Mon); and *Cantina Italia*, Rua Cel. Bordini 155. Nearer the centre, the *Etruria*, Rua Santo Antônio 421 (closed Sun), in Independencia, is also well thought of. Although expensive, the *Floresta Negra*, Avenida 24 de Outubro 905 (closed Sun & all Feb), Moinhos de Vento suburb, serves **German** food at its best; other German restaurants in the city are best avoided.

Vegetarians will have a hard time in Rio Grande do Sul, and even this comparatively cosmopolitan capital is no exception. Worth trying, however, are the *Ilha Natural*, Rua Andrade Neves 42 (1st floor; Mon–Fri lunch only), and the *Associação Macrobiotica*, Rua Mal. Floriano 72 (Mon–Fri 11am–2pm & 6–7.30pm, Sat 11am–2pm).

Bars and music

Bars, some with live music and most with a predominantly young and trendy clientele, are spread out along, and just off, Avenida Osvaldo Aranha, alongside the Parque Farroupilha and near the Federal University. Favourites change constantly, but the *Doce Vicio*, Rua Vieira de Castro (off Avenida José Bonifácio at the park's southern edge), and, for dancing, the *Ocidente*, on Avenida Osvaldo Aranha itself, are usually lively. Be warned, though, that things don't get going until around 11pm.

Throughout the year, Porto Alegre's numerous *Centros de Tradição Gaúcha* organise **traditional** meals, music and dance performances. Tourist offices have only limited information on the events, but full details are available from the *Movimento Tradicionalista Gaúcho*, Rua Guilherme Schell 60 (☎23-5194).

Porto Alegre boasts a good popular **music scene** and a considerable **theatrical** tradition. Foreign performers of all kinds usually include Porto Alegre on any Brazilian or wider South American tour. It doesn't take long, either, for new American **films** to be released in Porto Alegre, while the *Instituto Goethe* regularly shows German films. To find out **what's on**, consult the monthly *Programa*, produced by the tourist office, or the events listings in the newspaper *Zero Hora*.

Listings

Airlines *Aerolineas Argentinas*, Av. Salgado Filho 267 (☎21-3300); *Air France*, Rua Sete de Setembro 1069 (☎24-6085); *British Airways*, c/o *Aerosul*, Rua Florencio Ygartua 271 (☎22-761); *Iberia*, Rua dos Andradas 1273 (☎33-6288); *KLM*, Rua dos Andradas 1535 (☎25-8666); *Lufthansa*, Praça da Alfândega 12 (☎26-9455); *Pan Am*, Av. Borges de Medeiros 464 (☎24-7147); *Swissair*, Rua Gen. Andrade Neves 100 (☎25-7045); *TAP*, Rua dos Andradas 1237 (☎26-1211); *Transbrasil*, Av. Borges de Medeiros 410 (☎25-8300); *Varig/Cruzeiro*, Rua dos Andradas 1107 (☎21-6333); *VASP*, Rua Uruguai 396 and Av. Farrapos 2059 (☎22-8522).

Boat Excursions Two-hour excursions on the Guaiba river leave from the tour-boat berth (*Doca Turistica*) on Avenida Maua, near the train station. Schedules vary seasonally, so check with the tourist office.

Consulates *Argentina*, Rua Prof. Annes Dias 112, 1st floor (☎24-6799); *Austria*, Rua Sete de Setembro 1069, cj. 1714 (☎27-1499); *Belgium*, Rua Uruguai 240, cj. 406 (☎26-0509); *Denmark*, Av. Ipiranga 321 (☎33-4600); *Finland*, Rua Com. Azevedo 224 (☎22-7188); *Italy*, Praça Mal. Deodoro 134 (☎33-4566); *Norway*, Av. Ipiranga 321 (☎33-9966); *Sweden*, Av. Sen. Salgado Filho 327, cj. 1301 (☎27-1289); *Switzerland*, Av. Viena 327, cj. 1301 (☎27-1289); *UK*, Rua Pedro Chaves Barcelos 309, cj. 12 (☎32-2745); *Uruguay*, Av. Cristovao Colombo 3133 (☎43-5756); *USA*, Rua Cel. Genuino 421 (☎26-4299); *West Germany*, Rua Prof. Annes Dias 112, 11th floor (☎24-9255).

Cultural Institutes *Instituto Cultural Brasileiro-Norte Americano*, Rua Riachuelo 1257 (☎24-4358); *Instituto Gaúcho de Tradição e Folclore*, Av. Siqueira Campos 1184, 5th Floor (☎21-5411); *Instituto Goethe*, Av. 24 de Octobro 112 (☎22-7832).

Exchange Good rates for the dollar are offered by *Turispress*, Rua dos Andradas 1089, and *Exprinter*, Av. Salgado Filho 247.

Festivals Main folklore events are the *Festa de Nossa Senhora dos Navegantes* (Feb 2), the high point of which is a procession of fishing boats; and *Semana Farroupilha* (Sept 13–20), featuring traditional local folkdancing and singing.

Medical Emergencies *Pronto-Socorro Municipal*, Av. Oswaldo Aranha at the intersection with Venâcio Aires (☎31-5900); or get advice from your consulate.

Post Office At Rua Siqueira Campos 1100, Rua Sete de Setembro 1020 and Rua General Camara, near the waterfront Avenida Maua.

Souvenirs Handicrafts from throughout the state are available at *Artesanato Rio Grande do Sul* at Av. Senador Salgado Filho 366, and the *Feira do Artesanato* on Praça da Alfândega (between Ruas da Praia and Sete de Setembro) is worth a look, too. The *Museu de Arte do Rio Grande do Sul* has a small gallery where very reasonably priced original prints and paintings by local artists are offered for sale.

Views Great views across Porto Alegre and the Guaiba estuary from the Morro de Santa Teresa; take the bus from Rua das Andradas, near Av. Borges de Medeiros.

The Serra Gaúcha

North of Porto Alegre is the **Serra Gaúcha**, a range of hills and mountains populated mainly by the descendants of German and Italian immigrants. The Germans, who settled in Rio Grande do Sul between 1824 and 1859, spread out on fairly low-lying land, establishing small farming communities, of which Nova Petrópolis is just one that still retains traces of its ethnic origins. The Italians, who arrived between 1875 and 1915, settled on more hilly land further north and, being mainly from the hills and mountains of Veneto and Trento, they adapted well and very quickly specialised in **wine production**. Caxias do Sul has developed into the region's most important administrative and industrial centre, but it is in and around smaller towns, such as Bento Gonçalves and Garibaldi, where the region's – and, in fact, Brazil's – wine production is centred.

To the **east**, and at much higher altitudes, are the resort towns of Gramado and Canela, where unspoilt landscapes, mountain trails, refreshing temperatures, *cafés coloniais* (high tea; a vast selection of cakes, jams, cheeses, meats, wine and other drinks produced by the region's *colonos*) and luxurious hotels attract visitors from cities throughout Brazil.

Nova Petrópolis

The main road north from Porto Alegre passes SÃO LEOPOLDO and NOVA HAMBURGO (Rio Grande do Sul's first two German settlements but now mere industrial satellites of the city) before entering more hilly terrain inhabited by peasant farmers. Although on some of the more outlying family farms, German-based dialects are still spoken, in the towns and villages only Portuguese is heard. However, in architecture and culture, the ethnic origins of the townsfolk are quite obvious, and considerable pride is taken in the German heritage.

In most respects thoroughly unremarkable, **NOVA PETRÓPOLIS** makes the greatest effort in promoting its German character. The municipal authorities encourage new building to be in "traditional" German architectural styles (which is why there's a plethora of Alpine chalet-like structures around), and festivals take on a distinct German flavour. Principal amongst these are the *Festa de Verão* (Jan & Feb), the *Festa do Folklore* (July) and the *Oktoberfest*, all held in the **Parque do Imigrante**. But while clearly German-inspired, the events have little in common with the popular culture of the region's *colonos*. Indeed, of rather more interest is the Parque do Imigrante itself, where a village much like many in the region during the late nineteenth century, has been created.

As you might expect of somewhere trying so hard to be German, **hotels** here are always clean and usually expensive. Carefully cultivating a European inn-like atmosphere is the *Recanto Suiço*, Avenida XV de Novembro 2195 ($35 a double room), while cheaper is the *Petrópolis*, at Rua Cel. Alfredo Steglich 81 ($17 a double). As far as **restaurants** are concerned, a good rule of thumb is to avoid those that look excessively German, and instead search out a **café colonial** where food more characteristic of the region will be served.

Gramado and Canela

Thirty-six kilometres due east of Nova Petrópolis, along a beautiful winding road, is **GRAMADO**, Brazil's most exclusive mountain resort. At 825m you're unlikely to suffer from altitude sickness, but Gramado is high enough to be refreshingly cool in summer and positively chilly in winter. **CANELA**, 8km further east, down a road bordered on both sides by hydrangeas, is slightly lower, smaller and – for the time being at least – less commercialised; but otherwise, much like its neighbour. Architectually, both towns try hard to appear Swiss, with Alpine chalets and flower-filled window boxes the norm. It's a mere affectation, though, since hardly any of Gramado's and Canela's inhabitants are of Swiss origin – and only a small minority are of German extraction.

There is, however, no doubting the beauty of this entire region, though it's extremely difficult to explore properly without a car. Gramado's attractions lie mainly within the town itself: excellent and varied restaurants and the large and very pretty **Parque Knorr** and secluded **Lago Negro**. Canela, on the other hand, offers little of particular beauty within its small urban area, but is better situated for the **Parque Estadual do Caracol**, 8km to the north. You can reach the park by bus – marked *Caracol Circular* (4 daily) – which leaves from next to the old steam engine in the centre of Canela; get off at the restaurant-tourist complex in the park. A path leads down to the foot of the waterfall that is the park's main attraction, and other paths lead to different small falls at higher levels, from where there are panoramic views into the deep canyon of the Caí river.

Gramado practicalities

Gramado can be easily reached by **bus** from Porto Alegre and Caxias do Sul; the **Rodoviária** is on the main street, right in the centre of town. The **tourist office**, at Avenida Borges de Medeiros 1674, is extremely well organised and provides several excellent maps and comprehensive lists of local hotels and restaurants.

In Gramado you're unlikely to get away with spending less than $12 for a double **room**, with the cheapest hotels the *Tia Hilda*, Avenida Borges de Medeiros 1653, and the *Dinda*, Rua Augusto Zatti 160. As far as **restaurants** are concerned, most of them claim to be "Swiss" or "Italian" and, in general, the Italian ones are cheaper and better than the Swiss. Best of all, though, is to eat at a *café colonial* where the local goodies are served.

Canela practicalities

The **Rodoviária**, again, is on the central main street and there are regular buses there from Porto Alegre and Caxias do Sul. The **tourist office**, in Praça João Correia, tries to be helpful but is less useful than the one in Gramado.

There's a friendly **youth hostel** at Rua Oswaldo Aranha 223, 100m from the *Rodoviária*, or several **hotels** that are cheaper than their Gramado equivalents: try the *Central* or the *Jubileu*, around $8 double. If **camping**, make for the Parque Estadual do Caracol, where there's a good site.

Caxias do Sul

Seventy kilometres west of Gramado and thirty-seven north of Nova Petrópolis is **CAXIAS DO SUL**, Rio Grande do Sul's third largest city. Italian immigrants arrived in Caxias (as the city is known) in 1875, but the only obvious indication of the city's ethnic origins are its *adegas*, now huge companies or co-operatives that produce some of the state's poorest wine. Caxias' most important wine producer is the *Chateau Lacave* but, 9km from town, it's not worth the effort involved in getting there. Better, in the city centre several wine producers offer **tours** of their *cantinas*, followed by free tastings: *Riograndense*, Rua 18 do Forte 2346, are especially used to receiving visitors.

If you're tempted to stay over – or too drunk to move on – inexpensive **hotels** are located just off the main square, Praça Rui Barbosa (where, incidentally, the tourist office is, too). **Food** in this "Italian" city is disappointing, and you're best off at a restaurant serving "colonial" food: try the *Alvorado*, Rua Os 18 do Forte 200, or *Cantina Pão e Vinho*, Rua Ludovico Cavinato 1757.

Caxias is a major transport centre and **buses** run to towns throughout Rio Grande do Sul, and to states to the north, from the **Rodoviária**, seven blocks from Praça Rui Barbosa. To get there, walk straight down Rua Andrade Neves, then turn right onto Avenida Julho de Castilhos.

Bento Gonçalves and around

Approach **BENTO GONÇALVES** from any direction and there's no doubting that this is the heartland of Brazil's wine producing region. On virtually every patch of land, no matter the gradient, vines are planted. Wine production entered a new era in the late 1970s as huge co-operatives developed, local *cantinas* expanded and foreign (mainly French) companies set up local operations. But the results have been somewhat mixed. In the past, the locals relied almost exclusively on North American grape varieties and produced their own distinctive wines. Gradually, though, they were encouraged to join a co-operative or agree to sell their grapes exclusively for one company. New European and, more recently, Californian vines enabled companies to produce "finer" wines of a type until then imported. All this means that the *colonos* now rarely produce more than their own family's requirements, and the hi-tech stainless steel vats and rigidly-monitored quality control has rapidly replaced the old oaken barrel tradition – the resulting wines, at best, mediocre.

Bento Gonçalves itself is a small, undistinguished looking town whose economy totally revolves around grape and wine production. There are numerous **cantinas** in the centre of town offering free tours and tastings and a **museum** documenting the history of Italian immigration and life in the area: it's at Rua Erny Dreher (Mon–Fri 8–11.45am & 1.30–5.30pm, Sat 1.30–5.30pm, Sun 9–11.30am). There's no shortage of cheap **hotels**, which are mainly found in the streets around the very helpful **tourist office**, at Rua Mal. Deodoro 70 (Mon–Fri 8–11.45am & 1.30–6pm, Sat 8–11am & 1.30–4.30pm, Sun 8–11am). With the exception of the *Casa Colonial Felicità*, a half-hour walk from the centre in the Parque da Fenavinho, which serves excellent local **food** with strong Italian influences, restaurants are generally poor, serving overcooked pasta and undercooked pizza.

The surrounding area

It's worth visiting the surrounding countryside and villages, where, on the surface at least, the way of life has changed little over the years. The calendar revolves around the grape, with weeding, planting, pruning and the maintenance of the characteristic stone walls the main activities during the year, leading up to the **harvest** in Febuary and March. An excellent way to catch a glimpse of rural life is to take the Sunday tourist **steam train** (at 9am from Bento; $5 a ticket, bought in advance from the tourist office) into the vine-dominated countryside. Along its 48-kilometre-route (formerly part of a line extending south to Porto Alegre), the train stops at some of the more scenic spots, of which the most beautiful is the view over the **Rio das Antas Valley** where the river's path takes the form of a horseshoe.

Many of the villages around Bento could, from a distance at least, be mistaken for Italian ones. One of the nicest is **MONTE BELO**, from where there are fine views in all directions. With a simple, but very cheap **hotel** whose **restaurant** serves about the most authentic *colono* food you're likely to find anywhere, Monte Belo is a fine base from which to wander along pathways and tracks between the vineyards. There are several buses a day to Monte Belo, but try to take one that goes along the **Linha Leopoldina**, a beautiful road along which there are old stone farmhouses and other farm buildings, and a chapel, the Capela das Neves. Quite unusual in an area where wine production has become so thoroughly industrialised is the *Casa Valduga*, a small winery owned and run by a local family which produces, in limited quantities, some of Brazil's best wines – wines that are otherwise only available at some of São Paulo's best restaurants.

The coast: the Litoral Gaúcho

The **coast** of Rio Grande do Sul is a virtually unbroken 500-kilometre-long beach, along which are dotted resorts popular with Uruguayans and visitors from Porto Alegre and elsewhere in the state. In winter the beaches are deserted and most of the hotels closed, but between mid-November and March it's easy to believe that the state's entire population has migrated to the resorts. The attraction of this, the **Litoral Gaúcho**, is essentially one of convenience – from Porto Alegre many of the resorts can be reached within two or three hours, making even day trips possible. But for anyone travelling to or from points north, the beaches here can easily be ignored. Those resorts that are accessible are crowded, while – due to the influence of the powerful River Plate – the water is usually murky; and, even in summer, Antarctic currents often make for chilly bathing, too.

If travelling between Torres and Chuí, it's normally necessary to go via Porto Alegre. But if time's no problem, by taking buses from village to village it's possible to travel along the narrow peninsula that protects the Lagoa dos Patos from the sea. The road is mainly unpaved, the landscape barren and windswept, but the remote fishing communities along the way have consequently been protected from the ravages of tourism.

Torres

The northernmost point on the *Litoral Gaúcho*, 197km from Porto Alegre, **TORRES** is the one spot along the coast that is actually worth going out of the way for. Considered the state's most sophisticated coastal resort, **Praia Grande** and **Prainha**, the beaches behind which the town huddles, are packed solid on summer weekends. However, by walking across the Morro do Farol (identifiable by its lighthouse) and along the almost equally crowded Praia da Cal, you come to the **Parque Estadual da Guarita**, one of the most beautiful stretches of the southern Brazilian coast.

The state park is centred on a huge basalt outcrop, with cliffs rising 35m high, straight up from the sea, and from where there are superb views up and down the coast. At several points, steps lead down from the clifftop to basalt pillars and cavern-like formations, beaten out of the cliff face over the years. Although there are areas from where it's both possible, and safe, to dive from the rocks, generally the sea is inaccessible and ferocious. Continue along the cliff top, and you'll eventually reach the **Praia da Guarita**, a fairly small beach that is never anywhere near as crowded as those nearer town. Just beyond a further, much smaller outcrop, there's another beach, this time stretching with hardly an interruption all the way to the border with Uruguay.

Torres practicalities

From the **Rodoviária** (hourly buses to Porto Alegre and to Florianópolis), walk down Avenida Jose Bonifacio to Avenida Barão do Rio Branco. Here, turn right for the centre and the beach (six blocks) or left for the **tourist office** (one block). Torres has countless **hotels** with many of the cheaper ones located on Barão do Rio Branco and the two streets running parallel to it. Even on a midsummer weekend, accommodation should be fairly easy to track down, but try to arrive early in the day. At $3 per person, you won't find a cheaper hotel than the *Medusa* on Avenida Barão do Rio Branco but, more typically, expect to pay around $10 for a double room.

All the best **restaurants** are by the river, twenty to thirty minutes' walk from the centre. Either walk along Praia Grande in the opposite direction from the lighthouse or, quicker, along Rua Sete de Setembro, a couple of streets back from the beach. Especially recommended are *O Anzol* and the *Casa de Peixe do Souza*, which serve a wide variety of seafood. In the centre, there are plenty of beachside **bars**, some serving light meals, while just off Rua XV de Novembro is a restaurant that claims to be Swiss and which offers a good *café colonial*.

With Argentine tourists in mind, scattered about the centre are a number of **câmbios** giving a good rate for the dollar.

Capão da Canoa and Tramandi

Typical of resorts popular with day-trippers and weekend visitors are **CAPÃO DA CANOA** and **TRAMANDI**, respectively 140km and 120km northeast of Porto Alegre. Unless you're spending time in Porto Alegre and want to get away briefly from the often intense summer heat, neither resort has much to recommend it. Tramandi is the larger of the two, with more hotels, more restaurants and even more people. Both share an identical lack of character, based on wide open beaches with little in the way of vegetation, and plenty in the way of beachside bars.

Cheap **hotels** in the centre of Tramandi are the *Paulinho*, the *Tupy*, the *Siri* and the *Lessini* (all charge around $8 for a double room); and in the centre of Capão da Canoa try the *Maquine*, *Johsil* or the *Kolman* (a little more expensive).

Pelotas

Rio Grande do Sul's second largest city, **PELOTAS** is situated òn the left bank of the Canal de São Goncalo which connects the Lagoa dos Patos with the Lagoa Mirim. Founded in 1812 as a port for the *charque* (dried meat) producers of the surrounding region, with the introduction of refrigeration in the late nineteenth century, demand for beef increased, and with it Pelotas' importance as a port and commercial centre. But, come the turn of the century, Rio Grande's port (see below) – able to take larger ships – had superseded it. Nevertheless, while a slow-down in investment might have been bad for the city's economy, it saved Pelotas' nineteenth-century Neoclassical centre from the developers. **Praça Coronel Pedro Osório**, the main square, is the city's heart, and most of the very elegant, stuccoed buildings with wrought-iron balconies, overlooking the square, date from that period. Nearby, on Praça Jose Bonifâcio, the **Catedral de São Francisco de Paula** is slightly unusual for these parts: while its interior has undergone reforms over the years, the exterior has not been fundamentally altered since it was built in 1832.

As a railhead, port and an important commercial centre, late-nineteenth-century Pelotas was home to a considerable British community. Bearing witness to this is an Anglican church, the **Igreja Episcopal da Redentor**, a couple of blocks from the main square on Rua XV de Novembro. Built in 1883, the ivy-covered church would go unnoticed in any English town, but in Brazil it looks completely alien. In fact, though, in Rio Grande do Sul such churches have become a normal part of the urban landscape, with 52 others dotted around the state.

Practical details
The **Rodoviária** is way out of town, with buses running into the centre every fifteen minutes. Other, long-distance, services run to Rio Grande (1hr) and Porto Alegre (3hr) almost hourly, and less frequently to Santo Angelo, Santa Maria, Uruguaiana and Montevideo. There's an unhelpful **tourist office** at Praça Coronel Pedro Osorio 6. On Praça Coronel Osorio there are several cheap **hotels**, of which the best (at $9 double) are the *Rex* and the *Grande*. In general, **restaurants** are pretty poor but, on the main commercial street, decent (if dull) German meals are available at the *Barvaria*, Rua Sete de Setembro 306, directly opposite a Chinese restaurant, the *Shangai*. Pelotas is famous for its **sweets and cakes**, and a good place to try them is *Otto Especialidades*, Rua Sete de Setembro 304. On a different note, as a supposed **gay** centre Pelotas has a reputation for being Brazil's San Francisco. If this is true, the gay community is extremely discreet since there are no obvious gay bars or clubs.

Rio Grande, São José do Norte and Cassino

At the entrance of the Lagoa dos Patos, **RIO GRANDE** was founded in 1737 at the very southern fringe of the Portuguese Empire. With the growth of the *charque* and chilled beef economy, Rio Grande's port took on an increasing importance from the mid-nineteenth century, and – rather more spread out than Pelotas – it does not share that city's instant charm. However, colonial and late-nineteenth-century buildings are to be found in the area around Rua Floriano Reixoto and **Praça Tamandare** (the main square), which is almost next to Largo Dr. Pio and the much reformed eighteenth-century cathedral.

At the **waterfront**, just moments' walk from the cathedral, there's always a lively mixture of ocean-going ships, fishing vessels and smaller boats. From here boats cross the mouth of the Lago dos Patos to the small village of **SÃO JOSÉ DO NORTE**, one of the oldest settlements in the state. Here, apart from the beaches (lagoon- and ocean-facing) there's a simple church, Nossa Senhora dos Navegantes, which was built in 1795.

As far as **beaches** are concerned, though, much more important is **CASSINO**, a resort facing the Atlantic, 25km south of Rio Grande and very popular with Uruguayans. Like most of the rest of the *Litoral Gaúcha*, the beaches here are long, low and straight and only merit a visit if you have time between buses.

Rio Grande: practical information

A few blocks from Praça Tamandare is the **Rodoviária**, from where there are bus services to most cities in Rio Grande do Sul, and up the coast to cities as far north as Rio de Janeiro. **Buses to Cassino** stop at Praça Tamandare. Though rarely open, the **tourist office** is at Rua Riachuelo 355, in front of the *Câmara de Comércio*, by the waterfront. If you need to **change money**, try to wait until Chuí (see below), or go to the *Lancheria Oriental*, Rua General Bacelar 421 – opposite the *Transbrasil* office, whose English-speaking Egyptian owner will serve you excellent Arab cakes, and may give you a good rate for dollars.

The *Paris Hotel* ($4 single), on the waterfront at Rua Marechal Floriano 112, was once *the* place to stay in Rio Grande and, with some imagination, a little of its former Grand Hotel feel remains. More expensively, more comfortable but with no character is the *Taufik*, near the cathedral at Rua General Neto 20. For **eating**, try the *Pescal*, Rua Aarechl Andrea 269 (closed Sun), which specialises in fish, and the *Angola*, Rua Benjamin Constant 163 (closed Mon), with Portuguese specialities. Unusual, very sweet **cakes** are sold at *Especialidades Milano*, Praça Tamandare 282.

Chuí

Unless you're shopping for cheap Scotch whisky or visiting the casino, there's absolutely nothing in **CHUÍ** (or "Chuy" on the Uruguayan side of the frontier) to stick around for. **Buses entering and leaving Brazil** stop at an immigration office a short distance from town for passports to be stamped. The Brazilian **Rodoviária** (frequent services to Pelotas, Rio Grande and Porto Alegre), on Rua Venezuela, is just a couple of blocks from Avenida Brasil, which divides the Brazilian and Uruguayan sides of town: you can cross back and forth quite freely. *Onda*, one of Uruguay's main bus companies, stops on the Uruguayan side of Avenida Brasil and has frequent departures for Punta del Este and Montevideo. If you are travelling **to or from western Uruguay** and Treinta Y Tres, you will have to walk 3km down Calle General Artigas (follow the signs to Montevideo) to the Uruguayan immigration post for an entry or exit stanp in your passport.

Change money at a Uruguayan *Casa de Câmbio* or bank before travelling on into Brazil as you will receive the equivalent of the best rates available in Brazilian cities. If you can, try to avoid **staying** in Chuí as hotels are overpriced and unpleasant: as a rule, those on the Brazilian side of the common avenue are cheaper, those on the Uruguayan side cleaner and more comfortable. **Restaurants** – even the most simple – are better on the Uruguayan side of the avenue. Finally, if you plan to send parcels abroad, Uruguayan postage rates are a fraction of Brazil's.

Gaúchos, grasslands and highlands

During the colonial era and well into the nineteenth century, Rio Grande do Sul's southern and western frontiers were ill-defined, with Portugal and Spain, and then independent Brazil, Argentina and Uruguay, maintaining garrisons to assert their claims to the region. Frontier clashes were frequent, with central government presence weak or non-existent. If anyone could maintain a measure of control over these border territories it was the **gaúchos**, the fabled horsemen of southern South America. The product of miscegenation between Spanish, Portuguese, Indians and escaped slaves, the *gaúchos* wandered the region on horseback, either individually or in small bands, making a living by hunting wild cattle for their hides. Alliances were formed in support of local *caudilhos* (chiefs), who fought for control of the territory on behalf of the flag of one or other competing power. With a reputation of being tough and fearless, the *gaúcho* was also said to be supremely callous – displaying the same indifference in slitting a human or a bullock's throat.

As the nineteenth century ended, so too did the *gaúcho*'s traditional way of life. International boundaries became accepted and landowners became better able to exert control over their properties. Finally, as fencing was introduced and railways arrived, cattle turned into an industry with the animals raised rather than hunted. Gradually the *gaúcho* was made redundant, reduced to the status of mere *peões* or cattlehands.

Still, more in Rio Grande do Sul than in Argentina, some *gaúcho* traditions persist, though for a visitor to get much of a picture of the present-day way of life is difficult. In general, the cities and towns of the state's interior are fairly characterless, though travelling between towns still brings forth echoes of former times, especially if you get off the beaten track. Here, in the small villages, horses are not only a tool used to herd cattle, but remain an essential means of transport. While women are no differently dressed, men appear in much the same way as their *gaúcho* predecessors: in *bombachas* (baggy trousers), linen shirt, kerchief, poncho, felt-rimmed hat, and shod in pleated boots and fancy spurs. Also associated with the interior of Rio Grande do Sul is *chimarrão* (sugarless *maté* tea), which is sipped through a *bomba* (a silver straw) from a *cuia* (a gourd). In the towns themselves, cattlemen are always to be seen, purchasing supplies or just around for a good time. But undoubtedly your best chance of getting a feel of the interior is to attend a **rodeio**, held regularly in towns and villages throughout *gaúcho* country. Branches of the state tourist office, *CRTur*, will have information about when and where *rodeios* are due to take place.

Vacaria

On the northeastern plateau, 955m above sea level, is **VACARIA**, a quiet administrative and commercial centre for the surrounding cattle country. The road to Vacaria from Caxias do Sul, 100km to the south, is extremely beautiful, rising sharply from vine-clad hill slopes before reaching the near treeless *planalto* cattle country. Normally there would be absolutely nothing to detain you in town, though once every two years Vacaria comes to life when people from throughout southern Brazil and beyond come to participate in the **Rodeio Crioulo Internacional**, one of the country's most important *rodeios*. So as not to clash with Lages' equally important biannual *rodeio*, Vacaria's is held in the last week of January in even years.

All the **events** that you'd expect are included, like lasso-throwing, horse-breaking and steer-riding competitions, in addition to the accompanying cattle and horse shows, and song and dance events. While nattily dressed urban *gaúchos* show up in impeccably tailored *bombachas* and distinguished-looking capes, Vacaria's *rodeio* is first and foremost a popular event, attended by ordinary people of the *campanha* and cattle ranching *serra*.

Huge **tents** are erected at the *rodeio* grounds on the outskirts of town (reached by constant buses from Vacaria's main square), in which most of the spectators and competitors stay, despite the often bitterly cold midsummer temperatures. There are also several simple **hotels** on, and just off, the main square, charging from around $5 per person: there's usually space, even during *rodeio* week. The best of them is the *Alvorada*, Rua Dr. Flores ($15 double), while cheaper (around $5 single) are the *Real*, Rua Ramiro Barcelos, the *Granetto*, Rua Dr. Flores, and the *Querencia*, Rua Mal. Floriano. At the *rodeio*, **food** means meat – and only meat – and at the rodeo ground's restaurants you're expected to come equipped with your own sharp knife. However, in the town centre, just off the main square, there's a pizzeria where you can retreat, having sworn never to touch another steak.

Finally, throughout the period of the *rodeio*, the state **tourist office** maintains an office just outside the gates of the exhibition grounds; it also has a detailed programme of events.

Santa Maria and around

In the centre of Rio Grande do Sul, just at the point where the *campanha* hits the escarpment leading up into the Serra, is **SANTA MARIA**, a city of some 300,000 inhabitants. An important railway junction, farming, cattle, administrative and educational centre, Santa Maria is probably the most important city west of Porto Alegre. And, with a very pleasant and relaxed atmosphere, it makes a good stopping-off point on the way in or out of Brazil.

Founded in 1797, it wasn't until the late nineteenth century, with the rise of the cattle economy and the arrival of the railway, that Santa Maria became of significance. However, while there are a number of interesting buildings dating back to about 1900, nothing much remains from before that time. On the the main square in the heart of the city is the **catedral**, Baroque in style, but built at the beginning of the twentieth century. On the same square there's another church, Anglican and – like the others in the state – built for the employees of the once-important British railway and meat exporting interests. On Rua Daudt, a few blocks from Praça Saldanha Marinho, is another typically English building, from the same period but of otherwise uncertain origin – a curious ivy-clad house set in a beautiful garden. Many of the railway engineers at the beginning of the twentieth century were from Belgium, and they were housed in the **Vila Belga**, a row of very pretty cottages on Rua Ernesto Beck, near the railway station.

The practical details

The main commercial, largely pedestrianised, streets run off, and parallel to, the main square on the side of town where the railway station, the **Ferroviária**, is located: getting there, it's straight along Avenida Rio Branco from the cathedral square; and there are three train departures a week to Santana do Livramento, three to Uruguaiana, and six to Porto Alegre. Buses to all points in Rio Grande do Sul leave from the **Rodoviária**, those for Curitiba and São Paulo depart from the

Pluma depot, next door, and those to Montevideo from *Planalto Turismo*, beside the luxury *Itaimbé Palace Hotel*. The *Rodoviária* is about fifteen minutes' walk from the city centre; cross the road and walk across the Parque Itaimbé and at the *Itaimbé Palace Hotel* turn left and walk straight on for about three blocks. There's a helpful **tourist office** on Praça Saldanha Marinho, near the main square.

There are several cheap **hotels** near the *Ferroviária*, but better (though a little more expensive) are the *Gloria*, Avenida Rio Branco 639, and the *Hotel Jantzen*, Avenida Rio Branco 917. There's quite a good pizzeria and an excellent, and not overly expensive, **restaurant** serving regional dishes in the *Itaimbé Palace Hotel*. Or, for the same regional food, try the *Fogo de Chão*, Venacio Aires 1466.

Near Santa Maria

The immediate area around Santa Maria is now mainly given over to cattle and soya. Italians from northeastern Rio Grande do Sul have had some considerable success farming the very picturesque **Vale Veneto** (take a bus to BORGES, then just wander around), about 10km from Santa Maria, but Bessarabian Jews were not so fortunate. In 1904, eighty Jewish families arrived in Santa Maria with the intention of establishing a farming colony. They were given land 15km north of the city, but it slowly became apparent that the soil would only be of use for cattle. Over a forty-year period, settlers drifted from the **COLÔNIA PHILIPPSON** – as it was known – into Santa Maria, where there survives a small and very elderly Jewish community who still maintain a synagogue (at Rua Otavio Binato 49, Santa Maria). Virtually in the middle of nowhere, on a hill surrounded by cattle pasture, is the colony's small cemetery, located within what is now the *Fazenda Philippson*: to get there, take any bus heading north on the BR-158 and, on the left, a few kilometres past the *Oasis* swimming centre (10km from Santa Maria), is the *fazenda*'s clearly marked entrance. From there, ask for directions to the cemetery.

With even just a faint interest in geology you should find a visit to **MATA** worthwhile, an hour by bus from Santa Maria. Scattered everywhere in the small town are massive petrified tree trunks. The **Museu Guido Borgomonero** (Mon–Fri 8–11.30am & 1.30–4.30pm, Sat & Sun 9–11.30am & 2–5pm) has a well catalogued collection of fossils of all kinds, and though the local Catholic church itself is unremarkable, the steps leading to the building are made entirely of fossilised wood. If you need a **hotel** in Mata, there's a very simple one by the Catholic church, and a basic **restaurant**, too.

The mission town of São Miguel

For much of the seventeenth and eighteenth centuries, the **Guarani Indians** of what is now northeastern Argentina, southeastern Paraguay and northwestern Rio Grande do Sul were only nominally within the domain of the Spanish and Portuguese empires, and instead were ruled – or protected – by the Society of Jesus, the **Jesuits**; see "History" in *Contexts*. The first **redução** – a self-governing Indian settlement based around a Jesuit mission – was established in 1610 and, within a hundred years, thirty such places were in existence. With a total population of 150,000, these mini-cities became centres of some importance, *erva maté* and cattle the mainstay of economic activity, but spinning, weaving and metallurgical cottage industries also pursued. As the seventeenth century progressed, Spain and Portugal grew increasingly concerned over the Jesuits' power, and Rome feared that the religious order was becoming too independent of Papal authority. Finally, in 1756, Spanish and Portuguese forces attacked the missions, the Jesuits were expelled and many Indians killed. The missions themselves were dissolved, either razed to the ground or abandoned to nature, surviving only as ruins.

Of the thirty former mission towns, only seven were situated in what is now Brazil, and almost all were completely levelled. The one exception is **SÃO MIGUEL**, not to be compared in significance to San Ignacio Mini in neighbouring Argentina, but still of considerable visual interest. Despite vandalism and centuries of neglect, São Miguel's ruins offer ample evidence of the sophistication of Guarani Baroque architecture, and of *redução* life generally. Founded in 1632, to the west of the Uruguai River, São Miguel moved only a few years later to escape Paulista slavers, and then a few years after that it was destroyed by a violent windstorm. After being rebuilt, its population increased rapidly and in 1687 it was relocated across the river to its present site.

The initial priority was to provide housing, so not until 1700 did work begin on the **church** whose ruins still stand. The facade is a handsome and pure example of colonial architecture. One of the church's two towers is missing, but otherwise its stone structure is reasonably complete, the lack of a vault or dome explained by the fact that these would have been finished with wood. Other aspects of the ruins are of less interest, but the outline of the *redução*'s **walls** provides a guide to the former extent of São Miguel which, at its peak, was home to over 4000 people.

Every evening (except Mon when the ruins are closed) there's a **sound and light show** which, even if you don't understand the Portuguese narrative, is well worth staying for. As the show only begins at 9pm you'll have to stay overnight in the village that surrounds the ruins, which will give you an ideal opportunity to wander the ruins early in the day before the tourist buses arrive. There's a very basic (though clean and perfectly comfortable) **hotel**, the *Brilhante* (about $2.50 per person), with a better **restaurant** than the one at the ruins' entrance.

Getting to São Miguel: Santo Ângelo

São Miguel is 55km from **SANTO ÂNGELO**, a town in a farming region inhabited predominantly by people of German origin. Santo Ângelo is served by buses from throughout Rio Grande do Sul and there's a daily bus to and from Posadas, in Argentina, if you're planning on visiting San Ignacio Mini as well. The **Rodoviária** is within just a few blocks of the main square, Praça Pinheiro Machado; and there are four buses a day to and from São Miguel, with the last going to the ruins at 5pm and returning at 7pm.

Staying in Santo Ângelo, the cheapest **hotel** is the *Brasil*, Rua Mal. Floriano 1400, while a bit more comfortable and just off the main square there's the *Turis*, Rua Antônio Mancel 726.

Heading northeast: Iraí

On the Rio Mel, a tributary of the Rio Uruguai, near the border with Santa Catarina's extreme western region, is the small spa town of **IRAÍ**, the waters of which are claimed to offer relief from rheumatism and digestive disorders. If you don't suffer from these complaints, avoid it – it's one of the most depressing places of its kind imaginable. Most of the visitors are elderly and they spend their days in the thermal pools of the **Balneário Cruz** (8–11.30am & 2.30–5.30pm), while nights are predictably quiet, with the main action found in Iraí's late-night chemist. The town's unfortunate youth hang out at a snack bar called *K-Chorrão*, located across from the cinema (expect a 1950s *Zorro* film). Having a far worse time, however, are the 150 Kaingang Indians who camp in the most miserable conditions on the banks of the Rio Mel, beneath the gardens of the *Balneário*, trying to make a living by selling "typical" Indian basketwork, bows and arrows.

If you reckon that Iraí will do you more good than harm, **accommodation** won't be a problem. The cheapest hotels are the *São Luiz* and the *Internacional* (around $8 per person), while the cheapest place with its own pool is the *Avenida* ($12 per person); all the hotels are right in the centre. Next to the *Internacional* is the **Rodoviária**, and there are mercifully frequent buses to Santa Catarina and points throughout Rio Grande do Sul.

The southern border towns

Apart from Chuí (see above), the most commonly used **border crossing** into Uruguay is at Santana do Livramento, while most buses cross into Argentina via Uruguaiana. Rarely do people remain in the border towns longer than it takes to go through immigration formalities, but if you're trying to get a taste of *gaúcho* life, check to see if there's a *rodeio* about to be held somewhere around. Alternatively, use a smaller border crossing point, like Aceguá, near Bagé, where at least your first impressions of Uruguay or Brazil will be of cattle and ranch-hands rather than duty-free shops and casinos.

Bagé and Aceguá

Of all the towns on, or very near, Rio Grande do Sul's border with Argentina and Uruguay, **BAGÉ** is the only one with any charm, remaining first and foremost a cattle and commercial centre, rather than a tourist transit point. Like all towns in the *campanha*, Bagé has its own lively events, which attract people from the surrounding cattle ranches. The most important **festival**, held in January of odd-numbered years, is the **Semana Crioula Internacional**, but the *Semana de Bagé* (a folklore festival held annually from July 10–17), or even the *Exposição* (first half of Oct), will give you a taste of the *campanha*. For an understanding of the region's history, a visit to the excellent **Museu Dom Diogo de Souza**, Avenida Guilayn 5759 (Tues–Sun 8.30–11.30am & 1.30–5.30pm), is a must.

Arriving **from the Uruguayan border** (Melo is the nearest Uruguyan town), ask to be let off at the *Polícia Federal*, a few blocks from the main square, Praça General Osório, at Rua Barão do Trunfo 1572. It's here, not at Aceguá (see below), where you'll need to have your passport stamped. Arriving in Bagé from else-where, take a *Santa Tecla* bus into the centre from the main road next to the **Rodoviária** (3 daily buses to Santa Maria and Porto Alegre, one each to Santo Ângelo and, via Curitiba, São Paulo) and, if leaving Brazil, have your passport stamped. Failing to report to the *Polícia Federal* here will mean that you're likely to have difficulties entering or leaving Brazil later on.

ACEGUÁ, 60km south and the actual frontier crossing point, is very much a back door into Brazil and Uruguay, with only a Uruguayan immigration post (remember to be stamped in or out of the country) and a few houses and shops – certainly not a place to spend a night. However, as the four buses a day in each direction between Bagé and Aceguá connect with others to and from Melo, this shouldn't be a problem – but check bus times carefully before setting out.

Changing money is best done at a *casa de câmbio* in Melo, but in Aceguá there are always plenty of men milling about offering reasonable rates for dollar bills. In Bagé, if you can't wait for the border, you may be able to change dollars at the *Casa York*, a department store on Praça General Osório. **Hotels** in Bagé are plentiful, with the clean and friendly *Mini*, Avenida Sete de Setembro, near Praça General Osório ($7 double), the centre's cheapest; and there are two inexpensive hotels in front of, and behind, the *Rodoviária*.

Santana do Livramento

Apart from Brazilians attracted to the casino and duty-free shopping in Rivera, the Uruguayan border town into which **SANTANA DO LIVRAMENTO** (or, simply, Livramento) merges, few people stay here long. Unless in pursuit of *gaúchos* and intent upon taking local buses to outlying villages, the only times when Livramento is actually worth visiting is when there's a livestock exhibition, *rodeio* or cultural event on: the most important such events are the *Charqueada da Poesia Crioula* (last two weeks in April), the *Exposição Internacional do Corriedale* (March 5–12) and the *Exposição Agropecuária* (last two weeks in Sept), but check with the tourist office, at Rua Rivadávia Correia 280, to see if there are any other smaller events due, in or around Livramento. Livramento is also a very good place to purchase *gaúcho* **clothing and accessories**, with *Correaria Gaúcha*, Rua Rivadávia Correia 184, and *Correari Nova Esperança*, Rua Duque de Caxias and Rua 24 de Maio, having good selections.

Otherwise, the only possible reason not to move straight on would be a visit to **VILA PALOMAS**, a village 20km from Livramento, the centre of the new and increasingly important wine industry. Of all Brazil's commercial wineries, *Almadén* is about the best, and their *cantina* can be visited if you give them 24 hours' notice (ring ☎242-2309 or ☎242-2343).

Before **leaving** Livramento and Rivera, you'll need a Brazilian entry or exit passport stamp from the *Polícia Federal*, Rua Uruguai 1177, near the central park, and a stamp from Uruguay's *Dirección Nacional de Migracíon*, Calle Suarez 516 (three blocks from Plaza General José Artigas, Rivera's main square). If you have problems, Brazil's consulate in Rivera is at Calle Caballos 1159 (☎244-3278), and Uruguay's is in Livramento, at Avenida Tamandaré 2110 (☎242-1452). **Change money** at a *casa de câmbio* or bank in Rivera, where exchange rates are as good as you'll find in Brazil. The **Rodoviária**, at Rua Sen. Salgado Filho 335, serves most points in Rio Grande do Sul, and from the **Ferroviária**, in Praça Castello Branco, there are three **trains** a week to Santa Maria and Porto Alegre. From Rivera's bus terminal, there are several departures a day for Montevideo.

If you need to stay, **hotels** are cheapest in Livramento. The *Laçador* near the park, at Rua Uruguai 1227, is good or try the *Livramento*, opposite the *Rodoviária*. Conversely, **restaurants** are better in Rivera: the best is the *Dan Servanda*, Calle Carambula 1132, around the corner from the immigration office.

Uruguaiana

The busiest crossing point on Rio Grande do Sul's border with Argentina, **URUGUAIANA** is also one of the state's most important cattle centres. However, unless you're around while there's a livestock show or folklore festival, there's little to remain here for: ask about festival dates at the **tourist office** (Mon–Fri 8–

noon & 2–6pm), in the *prefeitura* which is in the main square, Praça Barão de Rio Branco. The most important annual events are the *Campeira Internacional* (a festival of regional folklore) held in first half of March, *Semana Farroupilha* (another folklore festival) held September 13–20, and a huge livestock show, the *Expo-feira Agropecuária*, held in the first half of November. Otherwise, the **Museu Municipal** and the **Museu Crioulo** (both open Mon–Sat 8.30am–noon & 2–5pm), in the cultural centre on the corner of Rua Santana and Duque de Caxias (by the main square), are worth a look for their interesting collections of *gaúcho*-related items.

Some practical details

Uruguaiana is connected to Argentina and the town of Paso de los Libres by a 1400-metre-long bridge spanning the Rio Uruguai. Frequent **buses** connect the railway and bus stations, and the centres of each city, and **immigration** formalities take place on either side of the bridge. If you have problems entering Argentina, the **consulate** in Uruguaiana is at Rua Santana 2496 (☎412-1925). You're best off **changing money** in Paso de los Libres, but travel agents in Uruguaiana give reasonable rates. If you need **accommodation**, hotels in Uruguaiana are cheaper: best bargains are at the *Wamosy*, *Monte Carlo* and *Mazza Tur*, at Rua Sete de Setembro nos. 1973, 1905 and 1088 respectively. **Restaurants** (for carnivores only) are better over the border in Argentina.

Bus services from Uruguaiana are excellent and you can get to most of the important centres, from Rio southwards. From Paso de los Libres, there are equally good services to points within Argentina. Finally, there are three **trains** a week to and from Santa Maria and Porto Alegre, and Paso de los Libres is on the Buenos Aires–Posadas railway line.

travel details

Buses
From Curitiba to Blumenau (10 daily; 4hr); Florianópolis (14 daily; 5hr); Foz do Iguaçu (12 daily; 10hr); Porto Alegre (10 daily; 11hr); Paranaguá (hourly; 2hr); Guaraqueçaba (2 daily; 6hr); Prudentópolis (4 daily; 6hr); São Paulo (hourly; 6hr); Rio (9 daily; 11hr); Buenos Aires (2 daily; 37hr).
From Florianópolis to Blumenau (6 daily; 3hr); Curitiba (14 daily; 5hr); Foz do Iguaçu (2 daily; 16hr); Porto Alegre (10 daily; 7hr); Santo Amaro da Imperatriz (4 daily; 1hr); Joinville (hourly; 3hr); São Paulo (10 daily; 12hr); Rio (8 daily; 19hr); Buenos Aires (2 daily; 30hr).
From Porto Alegre to Curitiba (10 daily; 11hr); Florianópolis (10 daily; 7hr); Rio Grande (hourly; 1hr); Pelotas (hourly; 3hr); São Paulo (8 daily; 18hr); Rio (6 daily; 26hr); Montevideo (3 daily; 12hr); Buenos Aires (2 daily; 22hr).
From Foz do Iguaçu to Itaipú (hourly; 1hr); Prudentópolis (3 daily; 7hr).

From Joinville to Blumenau (hourly; 2hr); Curitiba (hourly; 2hr 30min); São Francisco do Sul (hourly; 1hr); Porto Alegre (2 daily; 10hr); Vila Dona Francesca (hourly; 45min); São Paulo (7 daily; 9hr); Rio (1 daily; 15hr).
From Blumenau to Florianópolis (hourly; 3hr); Joinville (hourly; 2hr); Itajaí (hourly; 2hr); Pomerode (hourly; 1hr).

Trains
From Curitiba to Lapa (steam train twice a month; 2hr); Paranaguá (1 daily; 4hr 20min).
From Joinville to São Francisco do Sul (1 daily; 1hr 30min); Carupa (1 daily; 1hr 30min).
From Porto Alegre to Santa Maria (daily except Sat; 7hr); Livramento (3 weekly).

Ferries
From Guaraqueçaba to Paranaguá (2 weekly; 2hr); Ariri (2 weekly; 10hr).

PART THREE

THE

CONTEXTS

HISTORY

Brazil's recorded history begins with the arrival of the Portuguese in 1500, although it had been discovered and settled by Indians many centuries before. The importation of millions of African slaves over the next four centuries completed the rich blend of European, Indian and African influences that formed modern Brazil and its people. Achieving independence from Portugal in 1822, Brazil's enormous wealth in land and natural resources underpinned a boom-and-bust cycle of economic development that continues to the present day. The eternal "Land of the Future" is still a prisoner of its past, as industrialisation turned Brazil into the economic giant of South America, but sharpened social divisions. After a twenty-year interlude of military rule, the civilian "New Republic" now has to grapple with deep-rooted economic crisis and mounting public frustration. There are no easy answers.

EARLY HISTORY

Very little is known about the thousands of years that Brazil was inhabited exclusively by **Indians**. The first chroniclers who arrived with the Portuguese – Pedro Vaz da Caminha in 1500 and Gaspar Carvajal in 1540 – saw large villages, but nothing resembling the huge Aztec and Inca cities that the Spanish encountered. The fragile material traces left by Brazil's earliest inhabitants have for the most part not

survived. The few exceptions – like the exquisitely worked glazed ceramic jars unearthed on Marajó island in the Amazon – come from cultures vanished so completely that not even a name records their passing.

The Indians fascinated the Portuguese, and many of the first Europeans to visit Brazil sent lengthy reports back home. The most vivid account was penned by a German mercenary, **Hans Staden**, who spent three nervous years among the cannibal **Tupí** after being captured in 1552. He tells how they tied his legs together, "...and I was forced to hop through the huts, at which they made merry, saying 'Here comes our food hopping towards us'". Understandably, his memoirs were one of the first bestsellers in European history, and contained much accurate description of an Indian culture still largely untouched by the colonists. The work of Staden and the first explorers and missionaries is a brief snapshot of Indian Brazil in the sixteenth century, a blurred photograph of a way of life soon to be horribly transformed.

It was unfortunate that the Portuguese first landed in the only part of Brazil where ritualised cannibalism was practised on a large scale: away from the Tupí areas it was rare. Nowhere was stone used for building, there was no use of metal or the wheel, and no centralised, state-like civilisations on the scale of Spanish America. There are arguments about how large the Indian population was: Carvajal described taking several days to pass through the large towns of the Omagua tribe on the Amazon in 1542 but, away from the abundant food sources on the coast and the banks of large rivers, **population** densities were much lower. The total number of Indians was probably around five million: today there are 200,000.

CONQUEST

The Portuguese discovery of Brazil, when **Pedro Alvares Cabral** landed in southern Bahia on April 23, 1500, was an accident, an episode in Portugal's thrust to found a seaborne empire in the East Indies during the sixteenth century. Cabral was blown off course as he steered far to the west to avoid the African doldrums on his way to Calcutta: after a cursory week exploring the coast he continued to India, where he drowned in a shipwreck a few months later. King Manuel I sent **Amerigo Vespucci** to explore further in 1501. Reserving the name of the continent for himself, he spent several months sailing along the coast, calendar in hand, baptising places after the names of Saints' Days: entering Guanabara Bay on New Year's Day 1502, he called it Rio de Janeiro. The land was called *Terra do Brasil*, after a tropical redwood that was its first export; the scarlet dye it yielded was called *brasa*, "a glowing coal".

Portugal, preoccupied with Africa and the lucrative Far East spice trade, neglected this new addition to its Empire for the first few decades. Apart from a few lumber camps and scattered stockades, the Portuguese made no attempt at settlement. Consequently, other European countries were not slow to move in, with French and English privateers using the coast as a base to raid the spice ships. Finally, in 1532, João III was provoked into action. He divided up the coastline into **sesmarias**, captaincies fifty leagues wide and extending indefinitely inland, distributing them to aristo-crats and courtiers in return for undertakings to found settlements. It was hardly a roaring success: Pernambuco, where sugar took hold, and São Vicente, gateway to the Jesuit mission station of São Paulo, were the only securely held areas.

Irritated by the lack of progress, King João repossessed the captaincies in 1548 and brought Brazil under direct royal control, send-ing out the first governor-general, **Tomé da Sousa**, to the newly designated **capital** at Salvador in 1549. The first few governors successfully rooted out the European priva-teers, and – where sugar could grow – wiped out Indian resistance: by the closing decades of the century increasing numbers of Portuguese settlers were flowing in. Slaves began to be imported from the Portuguese outposts on the African coast, as **sugar plantations** sprang up around Salvador and Olinda. Brazil, no longer seen merely as a possible staging point on the way to the Far East, became an increasingly important piece of the far-flung Portuguese Empire. When Europe's taste for sugar took off in the early seventeenth century, the Northeast of Brazil quickly became very valuable real estate – and a tempting target for the expand-ing maritime powers of northern Europe, jeal-ous of the Iberian monopoly in the New World.

WAR WITH THE DUTCH

The **Dutch**, with naval bases in the Caribbean and a powerful fleet, were the best placed to move against Brazil. A mixture of greed and pressing political motives lay behind the Dutch decision: from 1580 to 1640 Portugal was united with Spain, against whom the Dutch had fought a bitter war of independence, and they were still menaced by the Spanish presence in Flanders. Anything that distracted Spain from further designs on the fledgling United Provinces seemed like a good idea at the time. As it turned out, neither the Spanish nor the Portuguese crowns played much of a role in the war: it was fought out between the Dutch, in the mercantile shape of the Dutch West India Company, and the Portuguese settlers already in Brazil, with Indian and *mameluco* (mixed race) backing. Although the Dutch occupied much of the Northeast for thirty years, they were finally overcome by one of South America's first guerrilla campaigns, in a war made vicious by the Catholic-Protestant divide that underlay it: few prisoners were taken and both sides massacred civilians.

In 1624 a Dutch fleet appeared off Salvador, taking the governor completely by surprise, and the city by storm. After burning down the Jesuit college and killing as many priests as they could find (like the good Calvinists they were), they were pinned down by enraged settlers for nine months and finally expelled in 1625 by a hastily assembled combined Spanish and Portuguese fleet – the only direct interven-tion made by either country in the conflict. When a Dutch force was once more repulsed from Salvador in 1627, they shifted their atten-tion further north and found the going much easier: Olinda was taken in 1630, the rich sugar zones of Pernambuco were occupied, and Dutch control extended up to the mouth of the Amazon by 1641. With settlers moving in, a strong military presence and a fleet more powerful than Portugal's, Dutch control of the Northeast looked like becoming permanent.

Maurice of Nassau was sent out as governor of the new Dutch possessions in Brazil in 1630, as the Dutch founded a new capital in Pernambuco: Mauritzstaadt, now Recife. His enlightened policies of allowing the Portuguese freedom to practise their religion, and including them in the colonial government, would probably have resulted in a Dutch Brazil, were it not for the stupidity of the Dutch West India Company. They insisted on Calvinism and heavy taxes, and when Maurice resigned in disgust and returned to Holland in 1644, the settlers rose. After five years of ambushes, plantation burnings and massacres, the Brazilians pushed the Dutch back into an enclave around Recife. The Dutch poured in reinforcements by sea, but their fate was decided by two climactic battles in 1648 and 1649 at **Guararapes**, just outside Recife, where the Dutch were routed and their military power broken. Although they held on to Recife until 1654, the dream of a Dutch Empire in the Americas was over, and Portuguese control was not to be threatened again until the nineteenth century.

THE *BANDEIRANTES*: GOLD AND GOD

The expulsion of the Dutch demonstrated the toughness of the early Brazilians, which was also well to the fore in the penetration and settling of **the interior** during the seventeenth and eighteenth centuries. Every few months, expeditions set out to explore the interior, following rumours of gold and looking for Indians to enslave. They carried an identifying banner, a *bandeira*, which gave the name **bandeirantes** to the adventurers: they became the Brazilian version of the Spanish *conquistadores*. São Paulo, thanks to its position on the Tietê river, one of the few natural highways that flowed east–west into the deep interior, became the main *bandeirante* centre.

The average *bandeira* would be made up of a mixed crew of people, reflecting the many – and often conflicting – motives underlying the expedition. None travelled without a priest or two (*bandeirantes* may have been cut-throats, but they were devout Catholic cut-throats), and many *bandeiras* were backed by the Jesuits and Franciscans, to found missions and baptise the heathen. The majority combined exploration with plundering and could last for years, with occasional stops to plant and harvest crops, before returning to São Paulo – if they ever did: many towns on the Planalto Central or Mato Grosso have their origins in the remnants of a *bandeira*. The *bandeirantes* had to fight Indians, occasionally the Spanish, and also themselves: they were riven with tension between native-born Brazilians and Portuguese, which regularly erupted into fighting.

The journeys *bandeiras* made were often epic in scale, covering immense distances and overcoming natural obstacles as formidable as the many hostile Indian tribes they encountered, who were defeated more by diseases, to which they had no resistance, than by force of arms. It was the *bandeirantes* who pushed the borders of Brazil way inland, practically to the foothills of the Andes, and also supplied the geographical knowledge that now began to fill in the blanks on the maps. They explored the Amazon, Paraná and Uruguai river systems, but the most important way they shaped the future of Brazil was in locating the Holy Grail of the New World: gold.

Gold was first found by *bandeirantes* in 1695, at the spot that is now Sabará, in Minas Gerais. As towns sprang up around further gold strikes in Minas, gold was also discovered around Cuiabá, in Mato Grosso, in 1719, adding fresh impetus to the opening up of the interior. The 3500-kilometre journey to Cuiabá, down five separate river systems, took six months at the best of times: from São Paulo it was easier to travel to Europe. Along the way the *bandeirantes* had to fight off the Paiaguá Indians, who attacked in canoes and swam like fish, and then the Guaicuru, who had taken to the horse with the same enthusiasm the Plains Indians of North America were later to show. They annihilated entire *bandeiras*; others following left descriptions of ". . . rotting belongings and dead bodies on the riverbanks, and hammocks slung with their owners in them, dead. Not a single person reached Cuiabá that year."

But the Paulista hunger for riches was equal even to these appalling difficulties. By the mid-eighteenth century, the flow of gold from Brazil was keeping the Portuguese crown afloat, temporarily halting its long slide down the league table of European powers. In Brazil, the rush of migrants to the gold areas changed the regional balance, as the new interior communities drew population away from the Northeast. The gateways to the interior, Rio de Janeiro and São Paulo, grew rapidly. The shift was recognised in 1763, when the capital was transferred from Salvador to Rio, and that filthy, disease-ridden port began its transformation into one of the great cities of the world.

THE JESUITS

Apart from the *bandeirantes*, the most important agents of the colonisation of the interior were the **Jesuits**. The first Jesuit missionaries arrived in Brazil in 1549 and, thanks to the influence they held over successive Portuguese kings, they acquired power in Brazil second only to that of the Crown itself. In Salvador they built the largest Jesuit college outside Rome, and set in motion a crusade to convert the Indian population. The usual method was to congregate the Indians in **missions**, where they worked under the supervision of Jesuit fathers. From 1600 onwards, dozens of missions were founded in the interior, especially in the Amazon and in the grasslands of the southeast.

The role the Jesuits played in the conversion of the Indians was ambiguous. Mission Indians were often released by Jesuits to work for settlers, where they died like flies; and the missionaries' intrepid penetration of remote areas resulted in the spread of diseases that wiped out entire tribes. On the other hand, many Jesuits distinguished themselves in protecting Indians against the settlers, a theological as well as a secular struggle, for many Portuguese argued that the native population had no souls and could therefore be treated like animals.

The most remarkable defender of the Indians was **Antônio Vieira**, who abandoned his position as chief adviser to the king in Lisbon to become a missionary in Brazil in 1653. Basing himself in São Luís, he struggled to implement the more enlightened Indian laws that his influence over King João IV had secured, to the disgust of settlers clamouring for slaves. Vieira denied them for years, preaching a series of sermons along the way that became famous throughout Europe, as well as Brazil: "An Indian will be your slave for the few days he lives, but your soul will be enslaved for as long as God is God. All of you are in mortal sin, all of you live in a state of condemnation, and all of you are going directly to Hell!", he thundered from the pulpit in 1654, to the fury of settlers in the congregation. So high did feelings run that, in 1661, settlers forced Vieira onto a ship bound for Portugal, standing in the surf and shouting "Out! Out!".

But Vieira returned, with renewed support from the Crown, and Jesuit power in Brazil grew. It reached a peak in the remarkable theocracy of the **Guaraní missions**, where Spanish and Portuguese Jesuits founded over a dozen missions on the pampas along the Uruguayan border. Left alone for the first fifty years, they effectively became a Jesuit state, until the Treaty of Madrid in 1752 divided up the land between Spain and Portugal: the treaty ordered the missions abandoned, so that settlers could move in. The Guaraní revolted immediately, and while the Jesuit hierarchy made half-hearted efforts to get them to move, most of the priests stayed with their Guaraní flocks. Resistance was heroic but hopeless: the superior firepower of a joint Spanish-Portuguese military expedition decimated both Guaraní and Jesuits in 1756.

Jesuit involvement in the Guaraní war lent added force to the longstanding settler demands to expel them from the colony. This time, they were helped by the rise to power of the **Marquis de Pombal**, who became the power behind the Portuguese throne for much of the eighteenth century. Seeing the Jesuits as a threat to Crown control, he seized upon the Guaraní wars as an excuse to expel the order from Brazil in 1760. The Jesuits may have been imperfect protectors, but from this time on the Indians were denied even that.

INDEPENDENCE

Brazil, uniquely among South American countries, achieved a peaceful transition to independence. The odds seemed against it at one point: Brazilian resentment at their exclusion from government, and of the Portuguese monopoly of foreign trade, grew steadily during the eighteenth century. It culminated, in 1789, in the **Inconfidência Mineira**, a plot hatched by twelve prominent citizens of Ouro Preto to proclaim Brazilian independence. The rebels, however, were betrayed almost before they started – their leader, **Tiradentes**, was executed and the rest exiled. Then, just as the tension seemed to be becoming dangerous, events in Europe once again took a hand in shaping Brazil's future.

In 1807, **Napoleon** invaded Portugal. With the French army poised to take Lisbon, the British navy hurriedly evacuated **King João VI** to Rio, which was declared the temporary capital of the Portuguese Empire and seat of the government-in-exile. While **Wellington** set about driving the French from Portugal, the British were able to force the opening-up of Brazil's ports to non-Portuguese shipping, and the economic growth that followed reinforced Brazil's increasing self-confidence. João was entranced by his tropical kingdom, unable to pull himself away even after Napoleon's defeat. Finally, in 1821, he was faced by a liberal revolt in Portugal that threatened to topple the monarchy, and he was unable to delay his return any longer. In April 1822 he appointed his son, **Dom Pedro**, as prince regent and governor of Brazil; when he sailed home, his last words to his son were "Get your hands on this kingdom, before some adventurer does".

Pedro, young and arrogant, grew increasingly irritated by the strident demands of the *Côrtes*, the Portuguese assembly, that he return home to his father and allow Brazil to be ruled from Portugal once again. On September 7, 1822, Pedro was out riding on the plain of Ypiranga, near São Paulo. Buttoning himself up after an attack of diarrhoea, he was surprised by a messenger with a bundle of letters from Lisbon: reading the usual demands for him to return his patience snapped, and he declared Brazil **independent** with the cry "Independence or death!". With overwhelming popular support for the idea, he had himself crowned **Dom Pedro I**, Emperor of Brazil, on December 1, 1822. The Portuguese, preoccupied by political crises at home and demoralised by Pedro's defection, put up little resistance. Apart from an ugly massacre of Brazilian patriots in Fortaleza, and some fighting in Bahia, the Portuguese withdrawal was peaceful and by the end of 1823 no Portuguese forces remained.

EARLY EMPIRE: REVOLT IN THE REGIONS

Although independence had been easily achieved, the early decades of Empire proved much more difficult. The first problem was Dom Pedro himself: headstrong and autocratic, he became increasingly estranged from his subjects, devoting more attention to scandalous romances than affairs of state. In April 1831 he abdicated, in a fit of petulance, in favour of the heir apparent, **Dom Pedro II**, and returned to Portugal. Pedro II would later prove an enlightened ruler, but as he was only five at the time there were limits to his capacity to influence

events. With a power vacuum at the centre of the political system, long-standing tensions in the outlying provinces erupted into revolt.

There were common threads in all the **rebellions** in the provinces: slaves rebelling against masters, Indian and mixed-race resentment of white domination, Brazilians settling scores with Portuguese, and the poor rising against the rich. The first, and most serious, conflagration was the **Cabanagem Rebellion** in Pará, where a mass revolt of the dispossessed began in 1835. The rebels took Belém, where, in a great moment of retribution, the Indian Domingues Onça killed the governor of Pará. The uprising spread through the Amazon like wildfire and took a decade to put down. A parallel revolt, the **Balaiada**, began in Maranhão in 1838. Here the rebels took Caxias, the second city of the state, and held out for three years against the army. Similar risings in Pernambuco, Bahia and Rio Grande do Sul punctuated the 1830s and 1840s; the disruption was immense, with large areas ravaged by fighting which threatened to tear the country apart.

The crisis led to Dom Pedro II being declared emperor four years early, in 1840, when he was only fourteen. Precociously talented, he was a sensible, scholarly man, completely unlike his father: his instincts were conservative, but he regularly appointed liberal governments and was respected even by republicans. With government authority restored, the provincial rebellions had by 1850 either blown themselves out or been put down. And with **coffee** beginning to be planted on a large scale in Rio, São Paulo and Minas, and the flow of European immigrants rising from a trickle to a flood, the economy of southern Brazil began to take off in earnest.

THE WAR OF THE TRIPLE ALLIANCE

With the rebellions in the provinces, the **army** became increasingly important in Brazilian political life. Pedro insisted they stay out of domestic politics, but his policy of diverting the generals by allowing them to control foreign policy ultimately led to the disaster of the war with Paraguay (1864–70). Although Brazil emerged victorious, it was at a dreadful cost. The **War of the Triple Alliance** is one of history's forgotten conflicts, but it was the bloodiest war in South American history, with a casualty list almost as long as that of the American Civil War: Brazil alone suffered over 100,000 casualties.

It pitted, in unequal struggle, the landlocked republic of Paraguay, under the dictator **Francisco Lopez**, against the combined forces of Brazil, Argentina and Uruguay. Although the Paraguayans started the war, by invading Uruguay and parts of Mato Grosso in 1864, they had been sorely provoked by Brazilian meddling in Uruguay. The generals in Rio, with no more rebels to fight within Brazil, wanted to incorporate Uruguay into the Empire: Paraguay saw Brazil blocking its access to the sea and invaded to pre-empt a Brazilian takeover, dragging Argentina reluctantly into the conflict through a mutual defence pact with Brazil.

The Brazilian army and navy were confident of victory as the Paraguayans were heavily outnumbered and outgunned. Yet the Paraguayans, for the first time, demonstrated the military prowess that would mark their history: united under the able leadership of Lopez, the Paraguayan army proved disciplined and fanatically brave, always defeated by numbers but terribly mauling the opposition. It turned into a war of extermination and six terrible years were only ended by the killing of Lopez in 1870, by which time the male adult population of Paraguay is said to have been reduced (by disease and starvation as well as war) to under 20,000, from over a million in 1864.

THE END OF SLAVERY

From the seventeenth to the nineteenth century around ten million Africans were transported to Brazil as **slaves** – ten times as many as were shipped to the United States – yet the death rate in Brazil was so great that in 1860 Brazil's black population was half the size of that in the USA. Slavery was always contested: slaves fled from the cities and plantations to form refugee communities called *quilombos*; the largest, **Palmares**, in the interior of the northeastern state of Alagoas, was several thousand strong and stayed independent for almost a century.

But it was not until the nineteenth century that slavery was seriously challenged. The initial impetus came from Britain, where the abolitionist movement became a power just when Portugal was most dependent on British capital and British naval protection. Abolition

was regarded with horror by the large landowners in Brazil, and a combination of racism and fear of economic dislocation led to a determined rearguard action to preserve slavery. A complicated diplomatic waltz began between Britain and Brazil, as slavery laws were tinkered with *para inglês ver* – "for the English to see" – a phrase that survives in the language to this day, meaning doing one thing and meaning another. The object was to make the British believe slavery would be abolished, while ensuring that the letter of the law kept it legal.

British abolitionists were not deceived, and from 1832 to 1854 the Royal Navy maintained a squadron off Brazil, intercepting and confiscating slave ships, and occasionally entering Brazilian ports to seize slavers and burn their ships – one of history's more positive examples of gunboat diplomacy. The slave trade was finally **abolished** in 1854, but to the disgust of the abolitionists, slavery itself remained legal. British power had its limits and ultimately it was a passionate campaign within Brazil itself, led by the fiery lawyer **Joaquim Nabuco**, that finished slavery off. The growing liberal movement, increasingly republican and anti-monarchist, squared off against the landowners, with Dom Pedro hovering indecisively somewhere in between. Slavery became the dominant issue in Brazilian politics for twenty years. By the time full **emancipation** came, in the "Golden Law" of May 13, 1888, Brazil had achieved the shameful distinction of being the last country in the Americas to abolish slavery.

FROM EMPIRE TO REPUBLIC

The end of slavery was also the death-knell of the monarchy. Since the 1870s the intelligentsia, deeply influenced by French liberalism, had turned against the emperor and agitated for a republic. By the 1880s they had been joined by the officer corps, who blamed Dom Pedro for lack of backing during the Paraguayan war. When large landowners withdrew their support from the emperor, furious he had not prevented emancipation, the **monarchy collapsed** very suddenly in 1889.

Once again, Brazil managed a bloodless transition. The push came from the army, detachments led by **Marechal Deodoro da Fonseca** meeting no resistance when they occupied Rio on November 15, 1889. They invited the royal family to remain, but Dom Pedro insisted on exile, boarding a ship to France, where he died in penury two years later in a shabby Parisian hotel. Deodoro, meanwhile, began a Brazilian tradition of hamfisted military autocracy. Ignoring the clamour for a liberal republic, he declared himself dictator in 1891, but was forced to resign three weeks later when even the army refused to support him. His deputy, **Marechal Floriano de Peixoto**, took over, but proved even more incompetent; Rio was actually shelled in 1893 by rebellious warships, demanding Peixoto's resignation. Finally, in 1894 popular pressure led to Peixoto stepping down in favour of the first elected civilian President, **Prudente de Morais**.

COFFEE WITH MILK – AND SUGAR

The years from 1890 to 1930 were politically undistinguished, but saw Brazil rapidly transformed economically and socially by large-scale **immigration** from Europe and Japan; they were decades of swift growth and swelling cities, which saw a very Brazilian combination of a boom-bust-boom economy and corrupt pork-barrel politics.

The boom was led by **coffee** and **rubber**, which – at opposite ends of the country – had entirely different labour forces. Millions of *nordestinos* moved into the Amazon to tap rubber, but the coffee workers swarming into São Paulo in their hundreds of thousands came chiefly from Italy: between 1890 and 1930 over four million migrants arrived from Europe and another 200,000 from Japan. Most went to work on the coffee estates of southern Brazil, but enough remained to turn São Paulo into the fastest growing city in the Americas. Urban industrialisation appeared in Brazil for the first time, taking root in São Paulo to supply the voracious markets of the young cities springing up in the Paulista interior. By 1930, São Paulo had displaced Rio as the leading industrial centre.

More improbable was the transformation of **Manaus** into the largest city of the Amazon. Rubber turned Manaus from a muddy village into a rich trading city within a couple of decades: the peak of the **rubber boom**, from the 1870s to the outbreak of World War I, financed its metamorphosis into a tropical *belle epoque* outpost, complete with opera house. Rubber exports were second only to coffee, but proved much more vulnerable to competition.

Seeds smuggled out of the Amazon by Victorian adventurer Henry Wickham in 1876 ended up in Ceylon and Malaya, where – by 1914 – plantation rubber pushed wild Amazon rubber out of the world markets. The region returned to an isolation it enjoyed until the late 1950s.

Economic growth was not accompanied by political development. Although not all the early presidents were incompetent – **Rodrigues Alves** (1902–06), for example, rebuilt Rio complete with a public health system, finally eradicating the epidemics that had stunted its growth – the majority were corrupt political bosses, relying on a network of patron-client relationships, whose main ambition seemed to be to bleed the public coffers dry. Power was concentrated in the two most populous states of São Paulo and Minas Gerais, which struck a convenient deal to alternate power, rotating the presidency between them.

This way of ensuring that both sets of snouts could slurp away in the trough uninterrupted was called **"café com leite"** by its opponents, coffee from São Paulo and milk from the *mineiro* dairy herds. In fact, it was coffee with milk and sugar: the developing national habit of the sweet *cafezinho* in the burgeoning cities of the south provided a new domestic market for sugar, which ensured support from the plantation oligarchs of the Northeast. In a pattern that would repeat itself in more modern times, the economy forged ahead while politics went backwards. The saying "Brazil grows in the dark, while politicians sleep" made its first appearance.

THE REVOLUTION OF 1930

The revolution of 1930 that brought the populist **Getúlio Vargas** to power was a critical event. Vargas dominated Brazilian politics for the next quarter-century, and the Vargas years were a time of radical change, marking a decisive break with the past. Vargas had much in common with his Argentinian contemporary, Juan Peron: both were charming, but cunning and ruthless with it, and rooted their power base in the new urban working class.

It was the **working class**, combined with disillusion in the junior ranks of the military, that swept Vargas to power. Younger officers, accustomed to seeing the armed forces as the guardian of the national conscience, were disgusted by the corruption of the military hierarchy. When the **Great Depression** hit, the government spent millions protecting coffee growers by buying crops at a guaranteed price: the coffee was then burnt, as the export market had collapsed. Workers in the cities and countryside were appalled, seeing themselves frozen out while vast sums were spent on landowners, and as the economic outlook worsened the pressure started building up from other states to end São Paulo and Minas' grip on power. This time, the transition was violent.

In 1926, **Washington Luis** was made president without an election, as the elite contrived an unopposed nomination. When Luis appeared set to do the same thing in 1930, an unstoppable **mass revolution** developed, first in Vargas' home state of Rio Grande do Sul, then in Rio, then in the Northeast. There was some resistance in São Paulo, but the worst fighting was in the Northeast, where street battles left scores dead. The shock troops of the Revolution were the young army officers who led their units against the *ancien regime* in Minas and Rio, and the *gaúcho* cavalry who accompanied Vargas on his triumphant procession to Rio. Although São Paulo rose briefly against Vargas in 1932, the revolt was swiftly crushed, and Getúlio, as Brazilians affectionately knew him, embarked on the longest and most spectacular political career in modern Brazilian history.

VARGAS AND THE ESTADO NOVO

It was not just Vargas who took power in 1930, but a whole new generation of young, energetic administrators, who set about transforming the economy and the political system. Vargas played the nationalist card with great success, nationalising the oil, electricity and steel industries, and setting up a health and social welfare system that earned him unwavering working-class support which continued even after his death.

Reforms this fundamental could not be carried out under the old constitutional framework. Vargas simplified things by declaring himself **dictator** in 1937 and imprisoning political opponents – most of whom were in the trade union movement, the Communist Party, or the *Integralistas*, the Brazilian Fascists. He called his regime the "New State", the **Estado Novo**, and certainly its reforming energy was

something new. Although he cracked down hard on dissent, Vargas was never a totalitarian dictator: he was massively popular and his great political talents enabled him to outflank most opponents.

The result was both political and economic success. The ruinous coffee subsidy was abolished, industry encouraged and agriculture diversified: by 1945 São Paulo had become the largest industrial centre in South America. With the federal government increasing its powers at the expense of state rights, regional government power was wrestled out of the hands of the oligarchs for the first time.

It took **World War II** to bring Vargas down. At first Brazil stayed neutral, reaping the benefits of increased exports, but when the United States offered massive aid in return for bases and Brazilian entry into the war, Vargas joined the Allies. Outraged by German submarine attacks on Brazilian shipping, Brazil was the only country in South America to play an active part in the war. A **Brazilian Expeditionary Force**, 5000-strong, fought in Italy from 1944 until the end of the war: when they returned, the military High Command was able to exploit the renewed prestige of the army, forcing Vargas to stand down. They argued that the armed forces could hardly fight for democracy abroad and return home to a dictatorship, and, in any case, after fifteen years a leadership change was overdue. In the election that followed in 1945, Vargas grudgingly endorsed the army general **Eurico Dutra**, who duly won – but Getúlio, brooding on his ranch, was not yet finished with the presidency.

THE DEATH OF VARGAS

Dutra proved a colourless figure, and when Vargas ran for the presidency in 1950 he won a crushing victory, the old dictator "returning on the arm of the people", as he wrote later. But he had powerful enemies, in the armed forces and on the right, and his second stint in power was turbulent. Dutra had allowed inflation to climb, and Vargas proposed to raise the minimum wage and slightly increase taxation of the middle classes. In the charged climate of the Cold War this was denounced by the right as veering towards communism, and vitriolic attacks on Vargas and his government were made in the press, notably by a slippery, ambitious journalist named **Carlos Lacerda**.

Vargas' supporters reacted angrily and argument turned into crisis in 1954, when shots were fired at Lacerda, missing their target but killing an air force officer guarding him. The attempt was traced to one of Vargas' bodyguards, but Vargas himself was not implicated. Even so, the press campaign rose to a crescendo, and finally, on August 25, 1954, the military High Command demanded his resignation. Vargas received the news calmly, went into his bedroom in the Palácio de Catete in Rio, and shot himself through the heart.

He left an emotional **suicide** note to the Brazilian people: "I choose this means to be with you always... I gave you my life; now I offer my death. Nothing remains. Serenely I take the first step on the road to eternity, as I leave life and enter History." The initial popular reaction of stunned shock gave way to fury, as Vargas' supporters turned on the forces that had hounded him to death, stoning the newspaper offices and forcing Lacerda to flee the country. Eighteen months of tension followed, as an interim government marked time until the next election.

JK AND BRASILIA

Juscelino Kubitschek, "JK" to Brazilians, president from 1956 to 1961, proved just the man to fix Brazil's attention on the future rather than the past. He combined energy and imagination with integrity and great political skill, acquired in the hard school of the politics of Minas Gerais, one of the main nurseries of political talent in Brazil. Although the tensions in the political system were still there – constitutionalists in the armed forces had to stage a pre-emptive coup to allow him to take office – Kubitschek was able to serve out his full term, still the only elected civilian president to do so in modern times. And he left a permanent reminder of the most successful postwar presidency in the form of the country's new capital, Brasília, deep in the Planalto Central.

"Fifty years in five!" was his election slogan, and his economic programme lived up to its ambitious billing. His term saw a spurt in growth rates that was the platform for the "economic miracle" of the next decade; the economic boom led to wider prosperity and renewed national confidence. Kubitschek drew on both in the flight of inspired imagination that led to **the building of Brasília**.

It could so easily have been an expensive disaster, a purpose-built capital miles from anywhere, the personal brainchild of a president anxious to make his mark. But Kubitschek implanted the idea in the national imagination, by portraying it as a renewed statement of faith in the interior, a symbol of national integration and a better future for all Brazilians, not just those in the south. He brought it off with great panache, bringing in the extravagantly talented **Oscar Niemeyer**, whose brief was to come up with a revolutionary city layout, and the architecture to go with it. Kubitschek spent almost every weekend on the huge building site that became the city, consulted on the smallest details, and had the satisfaction of handing over to his successor, **Jânio Quadros**, in the newly inaugurated capital.

1964: THE ROAD TO MILITARY RULE

At the time, the **military coup of 1964** was considered a temporary hiccup in Brazil's postwar democracy, but it lasted 21 years and left a very bitter taste. The first period of military rule saw the famous economic miracle (see below), when the economy grew at an astonishing *average* annual rate of ten percent for a decade, only to come to a juddering halt after 1974, when oil price rises and the increasing burden of debt repayment pushed it off the rails. But most depressing was the effective end of democracy for over a decade, and a time – from 1969 to 1974 – when terror was used against opponents by military hardliners. Brazil, where the *desaparecidos* numbered a few hundred rather than the tens of thousands butchered in Argentina and Chile, was not the worst military regime on the continent. But it is difficult to overestimate the shock even limited repression caused: it was the first time Brazilians experienced systematic brutality by a government, and even in the years of economic success the military governments were loathed right across the political spectrum.

The coup of 1964 was years in the brewing. It had two root causes: a constitutional crisis and the deepening divides in Brazilian society. In the developed south, relations between trade unions and employers went from bad to worse, as workers struggled to protect their wages against rising inflation. But it was in the Northeast that tension was greatest, as a result of the **Peasant Leagues** movement. Despite industrial modernisation, the rural Northeast was still stuck in a timewarped land tenure system, moulded in the colonial period and in many ways unchanged since then. Peasants, under the charismatic leadership of **Francisco Julião** and the governor of Pernambuco, **Miguel Arrães**, began forming co-operatives and occupying estates to press their claim for agrarian reform: the estate owners cried communism and openly agitated for a military coup.

The crisis might still have been avoided by a more skilful president, but Kubitschek's immediate successors were not of his calibre. Quadros resigned after only six months, in August 1961, on the anniversary of Vargas' suicide: he apparently wanted popular reaction to sweep him back into office, but shrunk from suicide and ended up shooting himself in the foot rather than the heart – the masses stayed home, and the vice-president, **João Goulart**, took over.

Goulart's accession was viewed with horror by the right. He had a reputation as a leftist firebrand, having been a Minister of Labour under Vargas, and his position was weakened by the fact that he had not succeeded by direct popular vote. As political infighting began to get out of control, with the country polarising between left and right, Goulart decided to throw himself behind the trade unions and the Peasant Leagues: his nationalist rhetoric rang alarm bells in Washington, and the army began to plot his downfall, with tacit American backing.

The coup, in the tradition of Brazilian coups, was swift and bloodless. On March 31, 1964, troops from Minas Gerais moved on Rio: when the military commanders there refused to oppose them, the game was up for Goulart. After futile efforts to rally resistance in Rio Grande do Sul, he fled into exile in Uruguay, and the first in a long line of generals, **Humberto Castelo Branco**, became president.

MILITARY RULE

The military moved swiftly to dismantle democracy. Congress was dissolved, those representatives not to military taste were removed, and then reconvened with only two parties, an official government and an official opposition ("The difference", ran a joke at the time, "is that one

says Yes, and the other, Yes Sir!"). All other parties were banned. The Peasant Leagues and trade unions were repressed, with many of their leaders tortured and imprisoned, and even prominent national politicians like Arrães were thrown into jail. The ferocity of the military took aback even those on the right who had agitated for a coup. Ironically, many of them were hoist by their own petard when they voiced criticism, and found themselves gagged by the same measures they had urged against the left.

The political climate worsened steadily during the 1960s. An **urban guerrilla campaign** took off in the cities – its most spectacular success was the kidnapping of the American ambassador in 1969, released unharmed in return for over a hundred political detainees – but it only served as an excuse for the hardliners to crack down even further. General **Emílio Garrastazú Médici**, leader of the hardliners, took over the presidency in 1969 and the worst period of military rule began. Torture became routine, censorship was strict and thousands were driven into exile: this dark chapter in Brazilian history lasted for five agonising years, until he gave way to **Ernesto Geisel** in 1974. The scars Médici left behind him, literally and metaphorically, have still not completely healed.

THE ECONOMIC MIRACLE

Despite the cold winds blowing on the political front, the Brazilian economy forged ahead from the mid-1960s to 1974, the years of the **economic miracle** – and the combination of high growth and low inflation indeed seemed miraculous to later governments. The military welcomed foreign investment, and the large pool of cheap but skilled labour was irresistible: investment poured in, both from Brazil and abroad, and the boom was the longest and largest in Brazilian history. Cities swelled, industry grew, and by the mid-1970s Brazil was the economic giant of South America, São Paulo state alone having a GNP higher than any South American country.

The problem, though, was uneven development. Even miraculous growth rates could not provide enough jobs for the hordes migrating to the cities, and the squalid **favelas** expanded even faster than the economy. The problem was worst in the Northeast and the Amazon, where industry was less developed, and drought combined with land conflict to push the people of the interior into the cities. It was also the miracle years that saw the origins of the **debt crisis**, a millstone around the neck of the Brazilian economy in the 1980s and 1990s.

After 1974, a lot of petrodollars were sloshing around the world banking system, thanks to oil price rises. Anxious to set this new capital to work, international banks and South American military regimes fell over themselves in their eagerness to organise deals. Brazil had a good credit rating: its wealth of natural resources and jailed labour leaders saw to that. The military needed money for a series of huge development projects that were central to its trickle-down economic policy, like the **Itaipú dam**, the **Carajás** mining projects in eastern Amazonia, and a **nuclear power programme**. By the end of the 1970s the debt was at $50 billion: by 1990 it had risen to $120 billion, and the interest payments were crippling the economy.

OPENING UP THE AMAZON

The first step towards opening up the vast interior of the **Amazon** was taken by Kubitschek, who built a dirt highway linking Brasília to Belém. But things really got going in 1970, when Médici realised that the Amazon could be used as a huge safety valve, releasing the pressure for agrarian reform in the Northeast. "Land without people for people without land!" became the slogan, and an ambitious programme of highway construction began that was to transform Amazonia. The main links were the **Transamazônica**, running west to the Peruvian border, the **Cuiabá–Santarém** highway into central Amazonia, and the **Cuiabá–Porto Velho/Rio Branco** highway, opening access to western Amazonia.

For the military, the Amazon was empty space, overdue for filling, and a national resource to be developed. They set up an elaborate network of tax breaks and incentives to encourage Brazilian and multinational firms to invest in the region, who also saw it as empty space and proceeded either to speculate with land or cut forest down to graze cattle. The one group that didn't perceive the Amazon as empty space was, naturally enough, the millions of people who already lived there. The immediate result was a spiralling land conflict, as ranchers, rubber tappers, Brazil nut harvesters, goldminers, smallholders, Indians, multinationals

and Brazilian companies all tried to press their claims. The result was – and is – chaos.

By the late 1980s the situation in the Amazon was becoming an international controversy, with heated claims about the uncontrolled destruction of forest in huge annual burnings, and the invasion of Indian lands. Less internationally known was the **land crisis**, although a hundred people or more were dying in land conflicts in Amazonia every year. It took the assassination in 1988 of **Chico Mendes**, leader of the rubber tappers' union and eloquent defender of the forest, to bring it home. Media attention, as usual, has shed as much heat as light, but there are grounds for hope. Deforestation follows highways and, as much of the easily accessible land has now gone and the economic crisis means that no comparable highway building programme will be mounted in the future, the worst may well be about to come to an end. And for all the destruction, Amazonia is very large – there is still time for more sensible development to protect what remains. (See also "The Environment" section, following.)

THE *ABERTURA*

Growing popular resentment of the military could not be contained indefinitely, especially when the economy turned sour. By the late 1970s debt, rising inflation and unemployment were turning the economy from a success story into a joke, and the military were further embarrassed by an unsavoury chain of corruption scandals. Geisel was the first military president to plan for a return to civilian rule, in a slow relaxing of the military grip called *abertura*, the "opening-up". Yet again, Brazil managed a bloodless – albeit fiendishly complicated – transition. Slow though the process was, the return to democracy would have been delayed even longer were it not for two events along the way: the **metalworkers' strikes** in São Paulo in 1977, and the mass **campaign for direct elections** in 1983–4.

The São Paulo strikes began in the car industry and soon spread throughout the industrial belt of São Paulo, in a movement bearing many parallels with Solidarity in Poland. Led by unions that were still illegal, and the charismatic young factory worker **Lula (Luis Inácio da Silva)**, there was a tense stand-off between army and strikers, until the military realised that having São Paulo on strike would be worse for the economy than conceding the right to free trade unions. This dramatic re-emergence of organised labour was a sign that the military could not control the situation for much longer.

Reforms in the early 1980s lifted censorship, brought the exiles home and allowed normal political life to resume. But the military came up with an ingenious attempt to control the succession: their control of Congress allowed them to pass a resolution that the president due to take office in 1985 would be elected not by direct vote, but by an electoral college, made up of congressmen and senators, where the military party had the advantage.

The democratic opposition responded with a counter-amendment proposing a direct election. It needed a two-thirds majority in Congress to be passed, and a campaign began for **diretas-já**, "elections now". Even the opposition was surprised by the response, as the Brazilian people, thoroughly sick of the generals, took to the streets in their millions. The campaign culminated in huge rallies of over a million people in Rio and São Paulo, and opinion polls showed over 90 percent in favour; but when the vote came in March 1984 the amendment just failed. The military still nominated a third of Senate seats, and this proved decisive.

It looked like defeat: in fact it turned into victory. The moment found the man in **Tancredo Neves**, ex-Minister of Justice under Vargas, ex-Prime Minister, and a wise old *mineiro* fox respected across the political spectrum, who put himself forward as opposition candidate in the electoral college. By now it was clear what the public wanted, and Tancredo's unrivalled political skills enabled him to stitch together an alliance that included dissidents from the military's own party. In January 1985 he romped home in the electoral college, to great national rejoicing, and military rule came to an end. Tancredo proclaimed the civilian **Nova República** – the New Republic.

THE NEW REPUBLIC: CRISIS AND CORRUPTION

Tragically, the New Republic was orphaned at birth. The night before his inauguration, Tancredo was rushed to hospital for an emergency operation on a bleeding stomach tumour: it proved benign, but in hospital he picked up

an infection and six weeks later died of septicaemia. His funeral was the largest mass event in Brazilian history; a crowd of two million carried his coffin from the hospital where he died in São Paulo to Guarulhos airport. The vice-president, **José Sarney**, a second-league politician from Maranhão, fobbed off with a ceremonial post, suddenly found himself serving a full presidential term.

His administration was disastrous, though not all of it was his own fault: he was saddled with a ministerial team he had not chosen, and a newly powerful Congress which would have given any president a rough ride. But Sarney made matters worse by a lack of decisiveness, and wasn't helped by the sleaze that hung like a fog around his government, with **corruption** institutionalised on a massive scale. No progress was made on the economic front either. Inflation accelerated into **hyperinflation** proper by 1990, and despite spending almost $40 billion repaying interest on the foreign debt, the principal had swollen to $120 billion at the end of the decade. Popular disgust was so great that on every occasion Sarney found himself near a crowd of real people, he was greeted with a shower of bricks and curses. The high hopes of 1985 had evaporated: Sarney had brought the whole notion of civilian politics into disrepute, and achieved the near-impossible of making the military look good.

BRAZIL IN THE 1990s

Despite everything, Brazil still managed to begin the new decade on a hopeful note, with the inauguration in 1990 of **Fernando Collor de Melo**, the first properly elected president for thirty years, after a heated but peaceful campaign had managed to consolidate democracy at a difficult economic moment. In the last months of his administration, Sarney had presided over the final ascent into hyperinflation, and it was clear the new president would have to come up with fast economic answers if he was to survive.

The campaign had passed the torch to a new generation of Brazilians, as the young Collor, playboy scion of one of Brazil's oldest and richest families, had squared off against **Lula**, who had come a long way since the São Paulo strikes; now a respected – and feared – national politician, head of the Worker's Party that the strike movement had evolved into. Lula took most of the cities, but Collor's conservative rural support was enough to secure a narrow victory.

The new decade sees Brazil still struggling against the handicaps of the past – a military accustomed to having political influence, unequal land distribution, a middle class determined not to bear the brunt of austerity measures, and an economy rewarding speculators instead of producers and workers. It is on solutions to the central problems – inflation, agrarian reform, the debt, unemployment – that answers to wider questions, like social welfare and the Amazon, will depend. Unless Brazil's politicians can overcome disillusion with answers, and fast, the outlook is not good.

THE ENVIRONMENT: AMAZON ECOLOGY AND THE PLIGHT OF THE INDIAN

In the last few years Brazil has found itself at the centre of the world environmental debate. Two issues predominate: the destruction of the Amazon rainforest and the plight of the indigenous Indian population – issues which in many cases are inextricably linked. Brazilians tend to react with outrage at being lectured by North Americans and Europeans on the preservation of their environment and the protection of native peoples. These, after all, are the same people who have raped the rest of the world and who less than ten years ago were still accusing Brazil of failing to exploit the very resources they now seek to save. Justifiable as Brazilian accusations of hypocrisy may be, however, they cannot hide the fact that there is a real environmental crisis in Brazil, a reality that is finally gaining acceptance among domestic politicians.

THE AMAZON

The Amazon is larger than life. It contains one fifth of the world's fresh water, sustaining the world's largest rainforest – over six million square kilometres – which in turn supports thousands upon thousands of animal and plant species, many of them still unknown. It possesses one in five of all the birds on earth. And so on. But perhaps the most startling statistic is the extraordinary rate at which the forest has been **destroyed** over the past twenty years.

It is impossible to understand the Amazon without grasping that the rivers and the forest are essentially different aspects of the same organic whole. The Amazon rainforest has taken over fifty million years to evolve. If small clearings are made in virgin forest they may more or less regenerate within 100–150 years. But the enormous regions being decimated these days are unlikely ever to grow back as they were.

In 1983, official Brazilian statistics showed that some two to four percent of the trees had already disappeared from the Amazon region – according to Friends of the Earth it was closer to thirty percent. Even if you bear in mind their respective bias, plus the fact that secondary regenerative growth is often mistaken for true forest in satellite photos, then the real figures are probably somewhere between ten and fifteen percent for 1983. By the middle of the 1990s some figures estimate that this will reach twenty-five percent.

The rainforest is still seen by many in Brazil as a resource to be expoited until it no longer exists, much as we see fossil fuels and mineral deposits. The indigenous Indians and many of the modern forest dwellers – including rubber tappers, nut collectors and, increasingly, even peasant settlers – view the forest differently. For them it is one of nature's gifts which, like an ocean, can be harvested regularly if it is not overtaxed. One of the most **hopeful signs** in the Amazon is that this view is increasingly gaining scientific and economic credibility, as people come to realise that sensible exploitation of the forest can in the long term be more profitable than clearance. Another piece of good news is that clearance has so far followed road building: much of the land easily accessible from existing roads has already been devastated, and major new roads seem unlikely in the current economic climate.

Until the Amazon was opened up by **roads**, many areas were inhabited and exploited only by Indian tribal peoples, who had long since retreated from the main rivers. They had done so in order to escape the white man's deadly influence and to continue their traditional forms of life. When the Spanish and Portuguese first explored the Amazon they noted that a well-established, highly organised, apparently agriculturally based Indian society thrived along the banks of the main rivers. Within a hundred years this relatively sophisticated Indian culture had vanished. Although many had died from the initial effects of new diseases (flu, smallpox, measles, etc), a large proportion had escaped into more remote areas of the forest.

When a road reaches into new territories it brings with it the financial backing and interests of big agricultural and industrial companies, plus an onslaught of land-seeking settlers. These days the **areas most endangered** by roads are Rondônia (already largely devasted by the early 1990s), the areas around the Cuiabá–Santarém highway, large areas in southern Pará (notably the giant Carajás industrial scheme, where a new railway provides the transport), the whole Trans-Amazonian belt to the south of the Amazon river, a large region around Manaus, and what's left of the corridor formed by the Brasília–Belém highway.

Chico Mendes, the Brazilian rubber tappers' union leader who was shot dead in 1988, was the best-known voice on the side of the established Amazon dwellers: "the forest is our mother, our source of life," he argued. He became a victim of the oppression of forest dwellers by large land-owning interests when he was killed by hired gunmen outside his house in the state of Acre in the southwest Amazon. His "crime" had been to stand up and be vocal in the face of financial and physical attack, mainly from large cattle-ranching companies. In February 1989, a few months after Mendes was shot, over 4000 Amazonian forest people gathered in Altamira along with environmental groups, scientists and government officials to discuss the environmental and socio-cultural effects of rainforest destruction. Altamira itself is the proposed site for the Xingu hydroelectric dam complex which, with an estimated budget of $9 billion, will flood a region of over fifteen million acres of rainforest and forcibly resettle over 70,000 people.

DESTRUCTION OF THE FOREST: THE REGIONAL CONSEQUENCES

In regional terms, the most serious effects of the destruction of the Amazon rainforest are threefold:

● Climatic experts have predicted that **deserts and droughts** will be created by the disappearance of large tracts of the Amazon rainforest. This has already happened in the Northeastern coastal regions where barely any of the original forest cover survives. Drought- and poverty-stricken peasants from the Northeast form the majority of the landless settlers moving into the recently cleared areas of the Amazon today.

● The **devastation of indigenous tribal groups** is a second major problem associated with the destruction of the Amazon. The chief culprit is disease, introduced to people who have no natural resistance, but physical violence has also taken its toll, gold-miners have polluted rivers (and the water and fish therein) with mercury, and people have been forced to move from their traditional homes to areas less able to support them.

● The **loss of the forest itself** is also serious. This may sound a circuitous argument, but the fact is that as the forest goes so does an endless potential supply of rubber and other valuable gums, medicines, nuts, fruits, fish, game, skins and the like. A wide variety of ways to harvest the natural products of the forest are emerging, and, as time goes on, it seems more and more apparent that there is a greater long-term value in this approach if the forest can be saved.

THE GLOBAL CONSEQUENCES

In world terms too, the loss of the Amazon rainforest has serious consequences.

● The destruction of the forest has two effects on the earth's atmosphere. The smoke from the vast forest clearances makes a significant direct contribution to the **greenhouse effect**. Less immediately, the fewer trees there are to absorb carbon dioxide, the faster the greenhouse effect is likely to build.

● The **loss of resources** is a world problem almost as much as it is a regional one. Only a small proportion of the plants that exist in the Amazon have been studied, and there is a real danger of losing a genetic pool of vital importance. Already, as many as one in four of the chemicals or medicines found in a high street chemist originate from rainforest products, and there can be little doubt that there are many more medical breakthroughs waiting to be discovered. In 1982 a US National Academy of Sciences report estimated that an average ten square kilometres of rainforest contains 750 tree species; 125 mammal types; 400 varieties of birds; 100 different kinds of reptiles; 60 amphibians; and that a typical individual tree might support over 400 insect species.

● The potential loss of **the world's last major forest** is perhaps enough in itself to make the Amazon worth saving.

WHY IS THE FOREST GOING?

A number of reasons are put forward for the continuing destruction of the rainforest. Few of them hold much water.

● **Population and land pressures**. Perhaps the most popular theory of all, certainly in Brazil, is that an unstoppable tide of humanity is swamping the forest. In fact the invasion of the Amazon by small-scale settlers is one of the least important factors. Farming and clearance on a small scale do relatively little damage, and in any case many of the small settlers are either moving from regions like the Northeast which have already been environmentally decimated (by large-scale agriculture) or have been squeezed off their old patches by large companies wanting to ranch or mine the place.

● **Debt**. Brazil's $120 billion external debt is another popular scapegoat, but again not a particularly convincing one. In agricultural terms, few of Brazil's export crops come from the Amazon, and the beef cattle raised here are largely for domestic consumption. Many of the area's mineral resources do go for export, but on the other hand it was the development of extraction schemes like the Grande Carajás project that largely created the debt in the first place.

● **Greed**. Underlying the continuing destruction of the rainforest is greed. In Brazil this is manifested mostly by the powerful alliance between big business and the armed forces which began back in the early 1960s. The opening up of the Amazon had always been a "national dream" and, with the building of Brasília, the 1960s seemed an appropriate time to forge ahead with the vision. There were millions of dollars to be made in foreign investment, and throughout the "economic miracle" of the Sixties and Seventies plenty of cash was available to be shared around between the construction industry, the mining companies, land-speculators and the authorities. Internationally, the greed of the industrial-consumer nations, like Britain and the United States, has also played its part: both at the level of individual consumer behaviour – using tropical hardwoods rather than replantable pine, for example – and at the level of governments and financial institutions which have been only too happy to invest in environmentally damaging schemes like Grande Carajás.

● **Ignorance**. Only the "greening" of Brazil at the level of national and individual consciousness will ultimately determine how quickly, if at all, the devastation of the Amazon can be halted. It is easy to forget just how recently environmental concerns have been widespread: as little as ten years ago Brazil was being actively encouraged to exploit the Amazon "hinterland" by European and World banks. It is only the sudden global awareness of pending serious environmental problems that has caused a change of heart.

THE FUTURE

Until recently, the Brazilian **response** to foreign environmental advice has been negative. After all, why should they listen to US scientists when the States continues to push more pollutants into the atmosphere than any other nation? But in 1989, President Sarney introduced new legislation to create sanctions against unauthorised forest clearance, to create more National Reserves, to do away with incentives for large-scale cattle-ranching, and to guarantee the Yanomami Indians the right to at least some of their traditional lands. As usual, the political decisions were made too late and the political will was too small for these decisions on paper to have any lasting or noticeable effect on the real world, but they were a start.

More significantly, Sarney's successor, Collor, has committed himself in the media to the "greening" of Brazil. He has outlined a plan for an alternative to military service – **Green Soldiers**, who will work in areas of ecological importance like National Parks and Reserves. He has talked of debt-for-nature swaps and of enforcing severe punishments for "ecological crimes".

Meanwhile the infamous dry-season *queimadas*, or annual torchings of the felled forest, are still a serious threat to the planet's climate. In 1988 alone an area larger than Belgium was estimated to have been destroyed.

To try and control the *queimadas* in 1989 and 1990, Brazil's environmental protection agency, IBAMA, organised helicopter surveillance for unauthorised burning of the forest. Not used to outside control of any kind, the larger *fazendeiros* were quick to react by shooting at helicopters and torching at weekends, at dusk or on Independence Day when the helicopters were less likely to be around. An IBAMA inspector was killed in Marabá by two timber dealers and there has been a growing number of attacks on and threats to IBAMA workers.

Still, there is a growing coalition of environmentalists and forest people uniting against the destruction of the forest (and in the case of the forest people, their own destruction). Indians, rubber tappers and recent settlers have identified a common enemy in the State-backed mega-company. Together the forest people are a growing political force both within Brazil and, since the death of Chico Mendes, on the international scene. In February 1989, the first meeting of Brazil's indigenous peoples was held in Marabá to protest about the Xingu Dam scheme. In March 1989, the **Forest People's Alliance** was formed in Rio Branco to lobby for the creation of "extractive forest reserves" as the first step towards an official policy for the exploitation of Amazon rainforest which might actually be sustainable into the twenty-first century.

TRIBAL RESISTANCE: THE AMAZON INDIAN

The **Tupí** tribe was the first Brazilian "Indian nation" to come into serious conflict with the outside world. Twelve colonies had been established in Brazil by the Portuguese King, João III, to exploit trade in wood and sugar, but slavery and death were the only things that the Tupí got out of the exchange – a pattern which was to continue for the next 500 years in Brazil. Perhaps even more devastating than murder or slavery was the spread of white man's **disease**: dysentery and influenza hit within the first two years; smallpox and the plague followed. When the Jesuit missionaries attempted to gather the natives into "reduction" missions, epidemics killed hundreds of thousands of Indians in just a few decades.

The first century and a half of contact was funded by the need for cheap labour and new resources. Spreading steadily into the savannas of the Ge-speaking peoples, and the forests of Pará and the Amazon, the colonists established cattle ranches, plantations, lumber extraction regions and mining settlements – all of which were met by considerable native resistance. Later, the development of vulcanisation in the 1870s led to an international demand for **rubber**. Prices rose rapidly and,

while there was a boom which lasted for almost fifty years, Indians were killed, moved around and enslaved by the rubber barons.

Even though it had always been going on, it wasn't until 1968 that the first reports accusing the **Indian Protection Service** (the forerunner of *FUNAI*) of "corruption, torture and murder" appeared in the world press. An example is the experience of the Nambikwara tribe, who have two main areas reserved for them. One zone of semi-arid scubland lies to the east of the Cuiabá–Porto Velho highway (BR-364), an indigenous reservation since 1968; the other area is in the fertile Guaporé river valley, where most of the zone is taken over by cattle ranchers – the Indians complain of dung-polluted river waters. The progressive extermination of the tribe has been going on for years; initially with machine guns, then with *FUNAI* issuing certificates to allow cattle-ranching concessions to set up operations in Indian lands. In their attempt to save the Nambikwara from certain death, *FUNAI* tried to transfer the Indians south from the Guaporé valley to empty arid scrubland. Many Indians became sick during and after the move – measles killed all the children of one group – and bedraggled, starving Indians could be seen walking back along the highways in 1976.

The government's **Programme of National Integration** (PIN) began in 1970. Aiming to colonise Amazonia by the construction of two highways – *Transamazonica* and Cuiabá–Santarém – the intention was to relocate some 500,000 families from the overpopulated and poor Northeast. Only some 10,000 have actually moved, but these alone have caused enormous devastation (mainly through unchecked diseases) to several tribes – Araba, Parkana, Kreen Akarore and Txukarramae. Other roads and futher problems have followed. The Northern Perimeter highway (BR-210) affected the Yanomami. A road from Manaus to Caracarai (BR-17) hurt the Waimiri-Atroari people. And the Cuiabá–Porto Velho road (BR-364) – known as the *Polonoroeste* re-settlement project – not only seriously disrupted the Nambikwara Indian tribe but also severely disappointed many thousands of peasants who found the soil lasted three or four years at most and that malaria was a common problem. The latest plan is to link up the north and south Amazon roads by cutting a highway through Acre and around the borders with Peru, Ecuador and Columbia; thereby endangering more Amazonian groups at the same time as putting them under border security control.

It was not until the **1980s** that the Indians started to display their political strength and will. In 1984, a group of Txukarramae Indians from the Xingu river held the director of the Xingu park and five other *FUNAI* employees hostage to demand demarcation of their lands, which had been cut off from the rest of the park by the BR-080 highway. The Indian leader, Raoni, had inspired prolonged resistance to the road since its construction in 1971: about thirteen employees from invading agricultural companies were killed and the Txukarramae even blockaded the BR-080 and took hostages for a period. After long negotiations, and with much support from Indian figures like Mario Juruna, they eventually received their land demarcation.

Mario Juruna – a Xavante Indian chief – didn't even see a white man until 1958, when he was seventeen. Yet in 1983, he became an overnight TV celebrity by being the first Indian elected to the Brazilian Congress. A controversial figure among Indians and non-Indians alike, he lost his seat in November 1986, along with another nine unsuccessful Indian candidates. But this emergence of **self-determined Indian organisations** has been a significant feature over the last decade.

In 1986, 537 mining claims had been conceded for research in indigenous areas; 1732 other claims were being processed – altogether affecting 77 of the 302 indigenous land areas of Brazil. Uncontacted Indians live on the lands of some ten percent of the claims.

A CASE STUDY

Straddling the hilly area of rainforest on the border between Brazil and Venezuela live the **Yanomami** tribe. One of the largest Amazon Indian groups still surviving today, there are around 10,000 of the tribe living on the Brazilian side of the frontier. Traditionally inhabiting circular, walled villages of up to 200 people, the Yanomami led a way of life which was very much in balance with the natural environment, depending on a combination of hunting, gathering and gardening. Until recently, the tribe led simple, but reasonably content lives for the most part.

However, in 1987, coming in the wake of local military-built airstrips and the announcement that the Yanomami were soon to be given "official" rights to their traditional land, a trickle of **gold-miners** began to invade their territory. Sufficient gold was found in the Indians' hills to bring more and more miners, or *garimpeiros*, into the Yanomami Reserve, and by 1990 there were some 45,000 *garimpeiros* in the region – far outnumbering the Yanomami. The Indians began to suffer from newly introduced strains of malaria and mercury-poisoned rivers and are, consequently, rapidly declining in numbers, health and morale.

After much campaigning pressure from groups like Survival International, President Sarney drew up emergency measures in 1989 to deal with the worsening plight of the Yanomami. His plan was for the police and army to move the *garimpeiros* out, by force if necessary, within a sixty-day period. The plan, however, was never executed as the army refused to comply. One thing was certain: if there had been a move to evict the 45,000 *garimpeiros* (all of whom are armed), it would have resulted in a bloodbath of historic proportions. Indeed, few ever believed it would happen, so there was little surprise when, in January 1990, Justice Minister Saulo Ramos capitulated to the *garimpeiros'* demands, rather than press ahead with the eviction operation.

The really bad news for the Yanomami is that some seventy percent of their 9000-square-kilometre reservation has been designated either for mining purposes or for the movement of miners between the various valleys; the Yanomami maintaining territorial control over only 2000 square kilometres. The only concession made by the miners has been to promise not to carry weapons, and to control the use of mercury in the gold-panning process. In reality, it's hard to imagine these restrictions being enforced, let alone happening voluntarily. Yet the Justice Minister's plan directly contradicts President Sarney's order and also violates a court ruling to expel the miners from the whole area.

Underlying the entire process, which is causing irreversible harm to the Yanomami people and the forests they have been guardians of for millennia, is the long-term strategic **military plan** known as *Calha Norte*. The main aim of this strategy is to populate relatively "uninhabited" and remote international border zones to ensure Brazilian territorial and national security, and the army's favoured method is to build airstrips, establish settlements, and then fill them with patriotic Brazilian frontierspeople.

Although gold-mining — initially at least — does much less environmental damage than logging or ranching, the long-term effects of putting mercury in the rivers are frightening. And, with the airstrips, settlements and new tracks that are being opened into the Yanomami's once peaceful forests, come an increasing number of non-Indians: after the miners will come the settlers, the ranchers and an overland transport network — all of which spell doom for the Yanomami. Once the Yanomami have disappeared, there really won't be any large tribal groups left in the Brazilian Amazon.

SELF-DETERMINATION?

If Brazilian Indians were actually granted the minimal rights which they have under Brazilian law — that is, the right to their own land, and the right to protection against violence and exploitation — there would be no Indian problem. Daniel, a Pareci Indian from Rio Verde in the Mato Grosso, said, "We were born on the land, and we are children of the land. So our rights are greater than theirs (the cattle ranchers). Just as they are human beings, we too are human beings. In fact I have found that we are even more human because we place human dignity first, rather than economic interests and concern for profit-making which can lead to human destruction." He continued: "*FUNAI* (the government agency specialising in Indian affairs) plays a policing role, preventing us from holding meetings and discussing our own problems, even though we are the only ones who have a deep understanding of those problems."

The Brazilian anthropologist Professor Roberto Oliveira believes that the "most notable thing that the government could do would be to allow the Indians the freedom to decide on their own destiny. If the relations between the State and the Indian communities were conducted as a form of diplomatic exchange rather than by administrative fiat, then we could view *FUNAI* not as the National Indian Foundation but as the Foundation of Indian Nationalities, and the internal colonialism would at last give way to internal diplomacy." And another Brazilian anthropologist, Darcy Ribeiro, has said that "many Brazilians will blush with shame tomorrow for having yesterday — today, I mean — had such brutal ancestors as we. I also fear that many humane people throughout the world are already looking at us, appalled at what they see. Why so much violence against the defenceless Indians? What is the source of so much loathing for fellow men? What will become of the Yanomami?"

In February 1989, Indian tribal leaders and environmentalists from all over the world gathered in the Amazon town of **Altamira**. Coordinated by Friends of the Earth, the Altamira meeting brought together over 500 Indians from various Amazon tribes. Although much publicity was gained for their cause, however, the promising reports that giant projects — like Brazilian *Eletronorte*'s Xingu HEP Dam scheme — may be stopped or scaled down should be taken with a pinch of salt. At the end of the day, the decisions rest with the world's banking institutions, who are not noted for their sentimentality.

Only six months earlier, back in 1988, *Eletronorte* and the Brazilian government were doing their best to discredit two Indian tribal leaders who were on trial for supposedly "denigrating the image of Brazil abroad". What actually happened was that, on returning from a visit to the USA, they were blamed for influencing the World Bank in its decision to withold a US$500,000,000 loan to the Xingu project. On October 14, 1988, around 400 Kayapo Indians arrived at the courthouse in Belém to see their two leaders on trial. They were prevented from entering the court by military police, and the defendants were not allowed into the court until they dressed in a shirt and trousers — the Indian's traditional garb evidently being judged a "sign of disrespect" to the judiciary.

For **action on the side of the forest** contact:

WWF Rain Forest Appeal
Panda House
Weyside Park
Godalming
Surrey
GU7 1BP

For **action to protect the basic rights of Brazil's indigenous people**, contact:

Survival International,
310 Edgware Road,
London,
W2 1DY
☎071/723-5535

Survival International (USA)
2121 Decatur Place NW
Washington DC 20008
USA
☎(202) 265-1077

Survival International (France)
16 Rue Littre
75006 Paris
France
☎45-49-40-18

In Brazil, contacts are:

Fundação Nacional do Indio, Ministerio do Interior
SAS Quadra 1, Bloco 1,
Brasília 70070
Brazil.

NGO's *Comisão pela Ciacão do Parque Yanomami*
Rua Sao Carlos do Pinhal 345
01333 São Paulo.

Comisão Pro-Indio SP (CPI)
Rue Caiubi 126
São Paulo.

RACE IN BRAZILIAN SOCIETY

The significance of race in Brazilian society has long been a controversial topic in Brazil. Until recently, despite the country's ethnic and racial diversity, official thinking refused to acknowledge the existence of minority groups, promoting the concept of the Brazilian "racial democracy", and denying absolutely the existence of racism or racial discrimination. If, in a country where blacks and mullatos form 65 percent of the population, there are few dark-skinned people at the upper levels of society – so the theory runs – this simply reflects past disadvantages: in particular poverty and lack of education.

MYTH

No-one contributed more to the consolidation of this myth of racial brotherhood than the anthropologist **Gilberto Freyre**. In the early 1930s he advanced the view that somehow the Portuguese colonisers were immune to racial prejudice, that they intermingled freely with Indians and blacks. If **Brazilian slavery** was not entirely benevolent patriarchy, as some people liked to believe, the mullato offspring of the sexual contact between master and slave was the personification in action. The **mullato** was the archetypal social climber, transcending class boundaries, and was upheld as a symbol of Brazil and the integration of the nation's cultures and ethnic roots. "Every Brazilian, even the light-skinned and fair-haired one," wrote Freyre in his seminal work, *Casa Grande e Senzala*, "carries about him in his soul, when not in soul and body alike, the shadow or even birthmark, of the aborigine or negro. The influence of the African, either direct or remote, is everything that is a sincere reflection of our lives. We, almost all of us, bear the mark of that influence."

Accepted with, if anything, even less questioning outside Brazil than within, the concept of a racial paradise in South America was eagerly grasped. For those outside Brazil struggling against the Nazis or segregation and racial violence in the United States, it was a belief too good to pass up. Brazil was awarded an international stamp of approval – and its **international image** is still very much that of the happy, unprejudiced melting pot.

Anomalies were easily explained away. A romanticised image of the self-sufficient **Indian** could be incorporated into Brazilian nationalism as, deep in the forested interior and numbering only a quarter of a million, they posed no threat. Picturesque Indian names – Yara and Iraçema for girls, Tibiriça and Caramuru for boys – were given to children, their white parents seeing them as representing Brazil in its purest form. Afro-Brazilian religion, folklore, and art became safe areas of interest. **Candomblé**, practised primarily in the northeastern state of Bahia and perhaps the purest of African rituals, could be seen as a quaint remnant from the past, while syncretist cults, most notably **Umbanda**, combining elements of Indian, African and European religion and which have attracted mass followings in Rio, São Paulo and the South, have been taken to demonstrate the happy fusion of cultures.

AND REALITY

Many visitors to Brazil still arrive believing in the melting pot, and for that matter many leave without questioning it. It *is* undeniable that Brazil has remarkably little in the way of obvious **racial tension**; that there are no institutional forms of racial discrimination; and that on the beach the races do seem to mix freely. But it is equally undeniable that race is a key factor in determining social position.

To say this in Brazil, even now, is to risk being attacked as "un-Brazilian". Nevertheless, the idea that race has had no significant effect on social mobility and that socio-economic differentials of a century ago explain current differences between races is increasingly discredited. It is true that Brazil is a rigidly stratified society within which upward mobility is difficult for anyone. But the lighter your skin, the easier it appears to be. Clear evidence has been produced that although in general blacks and mullatos (because of the continuing cycle of poverty) have lower education levels than whites, even when they do have equal levels of education and experience whites still enjoy substantial economic benefits. The **average**

income for white Brazilians is twice that for black.

Perhaps the most surprising realisation is that, except amongst politically developed intellectuals and progressive sectors of the church, there seems little awareness or resentment of the link between colour and class. The black consciousness movement has made slow progress in Brazil, and most people continue to acquiesce before the national myth that this is the New World's fortunate land, where there's no need to organise for improved status.

BRAZILIAN
MUSIC

Brazil's talent for music is so great it amounts to a national genius. Out of a rich stew of African, European and Indian influences it has produced one of the strongest and most diverse musical cultures in the world.

Most people have heard of *samba* and *bossa nova*, or of Heitor Vila Lobos, who introduced the rhythms of Brazilian popular music to a classical audience, but they are only the tip of a very large iceberg of genres, styles, and individual talents. Music – heard in bars, on the streets, car radios, concert halls and clubs – is a constant backdrop to social life in Brazil, and Brazilians are a very musical people. Instruments help but they aren't essential: matchboxes shaken to a syncopated beat, forks tapped on glasses and hands slapped on table-tops are all that is required. And to go with the music is some of the most stunning dancing you are ever likely to see. In Brazil, no-one looks twice at a couple that would clear any European and most American dancefloors. You don't need to be an expert, or even understand the words, to enjoy Brazilian popular music, but you may appreciate it better – and find it easier to ask for the type of record you want – if you know a little about its history.

THE ROOTS:
REGIONAL BRAZILIAN MUSIC

The bedrock of Brazilian music is the apparently inexhaustible fund of "traditional" **popular music**. There are dozens of genres, most of them associated with a specific region of the country, which you can find in raw uncut form played on local radio stations, at popular festivals – Carnaval is merely the best known – impromptu recitals in squares and on street corners, and in bars and *dancetarias*, the dance halls that Brazilians flock to at the weekend. The two main centres are Rio and Salvador; there's little argument that the best Brazilian music comes from Rio, the Northeast and parts of Amazonia, with São Paulo and southern Brazil lagging a little behind. *Samba*, and later *bossa nova*, became internationally famous, but only because they both happened to get off the ground in Rio, with its high international profile and exotic image. There are, though, less famous but equally vital musical styles elsewhere in Brazil, and it's difficult to see why they remain largely unknown to audiences outside the country – especially given western music's current obsession with the Third World.

Each local musical genre is part of a **regional identity**, of which people are very proud, and there's a distinct link between geographical rivalry and the development of Brazilian music. *Nordestinos*, in particular, all seem to know their way around the scores of Northeastern musical genres and vigorously defend their musical integrity against the influences of Rio and São Paulo, which dominate TV and national radio. A lot of people regret *carioca* and *paulista* domination of the airwaves, fearing that it's making Brazilian music homogenous, but if anything it has the opposite effect. People react against southern music by turning to their local brands – which often develop some new enriching influences, picked up along the way.

SAMBA

The best known genre, **Samba**, began in the early years of this century, in the poorer quarters of Rio, as Carnaval music, and over the decades it has developed several variations. The deafening **samba de enredo** is the setpiece of Carnaval, with one or two singers declaiming a verse joined by hundreds, even thousands, of voices and drums for the chorus, as the *bloco*, the full samba school, backs up the lead singers. A *bloco* in action during Carnaval is the loudest music you're ever likely to come across, and it's all done without the aid of amplifiers: standing up close, the massed noise of the drums vibrates every part of your body. No recording technology yet devised comes close to conveying the sound, and on record the songs and music often seem repetitive. Still, every year the main Rio *samba* schools make a compilation record of the music selected for the parade, and any record with the words *Samba de Enredo* or *Escola de Samba* will contain this mass Carnaval music.

On a more intimate scale, and musically more inventive, is **samba-canção**, which is produced by one singer and a small back-up band, who play around with basic *samba* rhythms to produce anything from a (relatively) quiet love song to frenetic dance numbers. This makes the transition to record much more effectively than *samba de enredo*, and in Brazil it's especially popular with the middle-aged, who are not able to gyrate quite as energetically as they did in their youth. Reliable, high-quality records of *samba-canção* are anything by **Beth Carvalho**, acknowledged queen of the genre, **Alcione**, **Roberto Ribeiro** – with a strong African influence as well – **Agepê** and the great **Paulinho da Viola**, who always puts a least a couple of excellent *sambas* on every record he makes.

CHORO

Much less known, **choro** (literally "crying") appeared in Rio around the time of the First World War, and by the 1930s had evolved into one of the most intricate and enjoyable of all Brazilian forms of music. Unlike *samba*, which developed variations, *choro* has remained remarkably constant over the decades. It's one of the few Brazilian genres which owes anything to Spanish-speaking America, as it is clearly related to the Argentinian tango (the real River Plate versions, that is, rather than the sequined ballroom distortions that get passed off as tango outside South America). *Choro* is mainly instrumental, played by a small group: the backbone of the combo is a guitar, picked quickly and jazzily, with notes sliding all over the place, which is played off against a flute, or occasionally a clarinet or recorder, with drums and/or maracas as an optional extra. It is as quiet and intimate as *samba* is loud and public, and of all Brazilian popular music is probably the most delicate. You often find it being played as background music in bars and cafés; local

papers advertise such places. The loveliest *choros* on record are by **Paulinho da Viola**, especially a self-explanatory record called *Chorando*. After years of neglect during the postwar decades *choro* is now undergoing something of a revival, and it shouldn't be too difficult to catch a *choro conjunto* in Rio or São Paulo.

LAMBADA

In recent years a dance craze based on **lambada** has swept nightclubs in Europe and North America. *Lambada* is in fact a dance rather than a type of music, and the term as now used is simply a new name for quite long-established musical styles in Brazil. There's some argument over who originated *lambada* and where: the first big international *lambada* hit was actually Bolivian, and *lambada*-like rhythms are also a feature of music from lowland Bolivia. Nonetheless, most *lambada* that you hear on international dancefloors is Brazilian.

What often happens, and has happened in this case, is that regional styles like *carimbó* and *forró* (see below) are souped up and reissued under a new name. This means it's impossible to determine exactly what *lambada* is, as it encompasses a number of different styles. The one thing you can say is that most – and the best – *lambada* comes from northern Brazil and is a close relative of *carimbó*. You will actually find *lambada* records far easier to get hold of outside Brazil.

OTHER GENRES

A full list of other "traditional" musical genres would have hundreds of entries and could be elaborated on indefinitely. Some of the best known are **forró**, **maracatú**, **repentismo** and **frevo**, described at greater length in the *Northeast* chapter: you'll find them all over the Northeast but especially around Recife. **Baião** is a Bahian style that bears a striking resemblance to the hard acoustic blues of the American Deep South, with hoarse vocals over a guitar singing of things like drought and migration; **carimbó** is an enjoyable, lilting rhythm and dance found all over northern Brazil but especially around Belém; and **bumba-meu-boi** is one of the strangest and most powerful of all styles, the music of Maranhão state.

A good start, if you're interested, is one of the dozens of records by the late **Luiz Gonzaga**, also known as **Gonzagão**, which have extremely tacky covers but are musically very good. They have authentic renderings of at least two or three Northeastern genres per record. His version of a beautiful song called *Asa Branca* is one of the best-loved of all Brazilian tunes, a national standard, and was played at his funeral in 1989.

THE GOLDEN AGE: 1930–1960 AND THE RADIO STARS

It was the growth of radio during the 1930s that created the popular music industry in Brazil, with homegrown stars idolised by millions. The best known was **Carmen Miranda**, spotted by a Hollywood producer singing in the famous Urca casino in Rio and whisked off to film stardom in the 1940s. Although her hats made her immortal, she deserves to be remembered more as the fine singer she was. She was one of a number of singers and groups loved by older Brazilians, like **Francisco Alves**, **Ismael Silva**, **Mário Reis**, **Ataulfo Alves**, **Trio de Ouro** and **Joel e Gaúcho**. Two great songwriters, **Ary Barroso** and **Pixinguinha**, provided the raw material.

Brazilians call these early decades *a época de ouro*, and that it really was a golden age is proved by the surviving music on record. It is slower and jazzier than modern Brazilian music, but with the same rhythms and beautiful, crooning vocals. Even in Brazil it used to be difficult get hold of **records** of this era but after years of neglect there is now a widely available series of reissues called *Revivendo*, a real bargain at $2–3 each. They send catalogues abroad, if you can't make it to Brazil to buy the records: write to *Revivendo Músicas Comércio de Discos Ltda*, Rua Barão do Rio Branco 28/36 – 1. andar, Caixa Postal 122, Curitiba, Paraná, Brazil.

INTERNATIONAL SUCCESS – THE *BOSSA-NOVA*

With this wealth of music to work with, it was only a matter of time before Brazilian music burst its national boundaries, something that duly happened in the late 1950s with the phenomenon of *bossa-nova*. Several factors led to its development: the classically trained

Tom Jobim, equally in love with Brazilian popular music and American jazz, met up with fine Bahian guitarist **João Gilberto** and his wife **Astrud Gilberto**; the growth in the Brazilian record and communications industries allowed *bossa-nova* to sweep Brazil and come to the attention of people like Stan Getz in the United States; and, above all, there developed a massive market for a sophisticated urban sound among the newly burgeoning middle class in Rio, who found Jobim and Gilberto's slowing down and breaking up of what was still basically a *samba* rhythm an exciting departure. It rapidly became an international craze, and Astrud Gilberto's quavering version of one of the earliest Jobim numbers, *A Garota de Ipanema*, became the most famous of all Brazilian songs, "The Girl from Ipanema" – although the English lyric is considerably less suggestive than the Brazilian original.

Over the next few years the craze eventually peaked and fell away, though not before leaving most people with the entirely wrong impression that *bossa-nova* is a mediocre brand of muzak well suited to lifts and airports. In North America it eventually sank under the massed strings of studio producers, but in Brazil it never lost its much more delicate touch, usually with a single guitar and a crooner holding sway. Early *bossa-nova* still stands as one of the crowning glories of Brazilian music, and all the classics – you may not know the names of tunes like *Corcovado*, *Isaura*, *Chega de Saudade* and *Desafinado* but you'll recognise the melodies – are on the easily available double album compilations called *A Arte de Tom Jobim* and *A Arte de João Gilberto*; Jobim's is the better of the two.

MORE BOSSA-NOVA ARTISTS

The great Brazilian guitarist **Luiz Bonfá** also made some fine *bossa-nova* records: the ones where he accompanies Stan Getz are superb. The *bossa-nova* records of **Stan Getz and Charlie Byrd** are one of the happiest examples of inter-American co-operation, and as they're easy to find in European and American shops they make a fine introduction to Brazilian music. They had the sense to surround themselves with Brazilian musicians, notably Jobim, the Gilbertos and Bonfá, and the interplay between their jazz and the equally skillful Brazilian response is often brilliant. **Live** *bossa-nova* is rare these days, restricted to the odd bar or hotel lobby, unless you're lucky enough to catch one of the great names in concert – Tom Jobim is still a superlative musician. But then *bossa-nova* always lent itself more to records than live performance.

TROPICALISMO

The military coup in 1964 was a crucial event in Brazil. Just as the shockwaves of the cultural upheavals of the 1960s were reaching Brazilian youth, the lid went on in a big way: censorship was introduced for all song lyrics; radio and television were put under military control; and some songwriters and musicians were tortured and imprisoned for speaking and singing out – although fame was at least some insurance against being killed (though not in Chile a few years later). The result was the opposite of what the generals had intended. A movement known as *tropicalismo* developed, calling itself cultural but in fact almost exclusively a musical movement, led by a young and extravagantly talented group of musicians. Prominent amongst them were **Caetano Veloso** and **Gilberto Gil** from Bahia and **Chico Buarque** from Rio. They used traditional popular music as a base, picking and mixing genres in a way no-one had thought of doing before – stirring in a few outside influences like the Beatles and occasional electric instruments, and topping it all off with lyrics that often stood alone as poetry and delighted in teasing the censors. Oblique images and comments were ostensibly about one thing, but everyone knew what they really meant. Chico Buarque's great song, *Tanto Mar*, for example, is apparently about the end of a party, but everyone except the censor recognised it was a salute to the Portuguese revolution, the "Revolution of the Carnations", as it's known.

> It was a fine party
> I had a great time
> I've kept an old carnation as a memento
> And even though the party's been shut down
> They're bound to have forgotten a few seeds in
>   some corner of the garden

Caetano, Gil and Chico – all of Brazil is on first name terms with them – spent a few years in exile in the late 1960s and early 1970s, Caetano and Gil in London (both still speak fluent English with immaculate BBC accents) and Chico in Rome, before returning in triumph as the military regime wound down. They have made dozens of records between them: as a rule the earlier they are the better they tend to be, although Chico Buarque, uniquely of the three, has kept up the same high standards in more recent years as well. He is the weakest singer, but his dense lyrics and hauntingly beautiful melodies have kept flowing. The best records to buy are the compilations, *A Arte de...*, *O Talento de...*, or *A Personalidade de...*, collections of their back catalogues with all their most famous songs which go up to the early 1970s. Gilberto Gil's more recent work in particular has been disappointing, as he has experimented unsuccessfully with a more rock-influenced format, the kiss of death for a good Brazilian musician.

WOMEN SINGERS

Brazilian music has a strong tradition of producing excellent women singers. The best of all time was undoubtedly the great **Elis Regina**, from Rio Grande do Sul, whose magnificent voice was tragically stilled in 1984, when she was at the peak of her career, by a drugs overdose. She interpreted everything, and whatever Brazilian genre she touched she invariably cut the definitive version. Two of her songs in particular became classics, *Aguas de Março* and *Carinhoso*, the latter being arguably the most beautiful Brazilian song of all. Again, the *A Arte de Elis Regina* double album is the best bet, although there is also a superb record of Elis with Tom Jobim, called *Elis e Tom*. After her death the mantle fell on **Gal Costa**, a very fine singer although without the extraordinary depth of emotion Elis could project, whose version of *Aquarela do Brasil* inspired Terry Gilliam to the idea for the film "Brazil", and whose LP, named after the song, is highly recommended, along with the *A Arte de Gal Costa* compilation. Others worth listening to are **Maria Bethânia** and **Nana Caymmi**. A fast-rising newcomer is Bahian **Margareth Menezes**, a name for the 1990s.

CONTEMPORARY SINGERS

The number of high-quality singers and musicians in Brazilian music besides these leading figures is enormous. **Milton Nascimento** has a talent that can only be compared with the founders of *tropicalismo*, a remarkable soaring voice, a genius for composing stirring anthems, and a passion for charting and celebrating the experience of blacks in Brazil; he has become the most prominent spokesperson of black Brazilians. **Fagner** and **Alceu Valença** are modern interpreters of Northeastern music, and strikingly original singers; **Elba Ramalho** is a Northeastern woman with an excellent voice, which she too often wastes on banal rock rather than the more traditional material she excels at; **Ney Matogrosso** has a striking falsetto voice which sounds female, but he is a man – although sometimes self-indulgent he can be very good; **Jorge Ben** is a fine Rio singer who wrote the definitive Rio verse in his classic *País Tropical*:

I live in tropical country
Blessed by God with natural beauty
In February there's Carnaval
I own a guitar and drive a Beetle
I support Flamengo and have a black girlfriend
called Tereza.

Vinícius de Morães and Toquinho are (or were in the case of Vinícius) a good singer and guitarist team, and **Dorival Caymmi** at over seventy is the doyen of Bahian musicians.

Too many musicians these days, though, waste their time attempting to fuse Brazilian genres with rock-based formats. It's not that it can't be done – *tropicalismo* pulled it off several times in the 1960s – but the type of rock music currently most popular in Brazil, appalling heavy metal and stadium rock, is completely incompatible with the subtle, versatile musical imagination of Brazilians. National radio and the dominant São Paulo radio stations pump out the worst kind of British and US FM blandness, and this has spawned a host of Brazilian imitations, almost all of them embarrassingly bad. The only two worth mentioning are **Titãs**, a São Paulo punk band with a genuinely magnetic lead singer in the Johnny Rotten mould, whose jailing on heroin charges in 1989 will make it difficult for them to keep up the high standards of their first two records; and **Premeditando o Breque**, also shortened to **PMB**, whose originality defies categorisation. Their first record was called *Tubarões Voadores* – "Flying Sharks" – and was very good indeed, managing to be ominous and very funny at the same time.

The other possible criticism of Brazilian music is that while its popular roots are healthier than ever, nobody of similar stature has come up to succeed the towering figures of the 1960s and 1970s. Elis is dead, Gil is in decline (although he may yet reverse it), Caetano, Chico and Milton are still producing but are no longer young, and while younger talent abounds, there's nothing at the moment which could be called genius – a lot to demand of anyone, but it's a tribute to Brazilian music that its pedigree allows us to judge it by the highest standards.

BUYING RECORDS ... AND LIVE MUSIC

Finally, a word about **buying records**. The price varies according to how well known the recording artist is, with records by national stars being the most expensive – $8–10 – and local records being cheapest of all, down to $2–3, which means there are a lot of bargains for the discerning. At the upper end of the scale, but dependably high quality, are the *A Arte de...*, *O Talento de...* or *A Personalidade de...* series, often double albums, which are basically "Greatest Hits" compilations of the best known singers and musicians. The best place to buy any record, no matter how regional, is São Paulo, then Rio, with cities like Recife, Salvador, Belo Horizonte and Porto Alegre a long way behind. Outside Rio and São Paulo there are good record shops, but they're few and far between: look in local papers to see if there are adverts for *Loja de Disco* (record shop), with *MPB* (*música popular brasileira*) or *discos nacionais* mentioned in the advert.

If you want to see or hear **live music**, look for suggestions in this book, buy local papers with weekend listings headed *Lazer*, which should have a list of bars with music, concerts and *dancetarias*, or ask a tourist office for advice.

Local radio is often worth listening to – you won't regret taking a transistor along and whirling the dial – and there are also local TV stations that often have MPB programmes; the *TVE, Televisão Educativa* network, funded by the Catholic church and the Ministry of Culture, is worth checking – if you see the initials *FUNARTE*, it might well be a music programme.

A SELECTED DISCOGRAPHY

Apart from the *A Arte de. . .* , *O Talento de. . .* , *A Personalidade de. . .* and *Revivendo* series
mentioned on the previous page, recommended records
easily **available in Brazil** include the following; the **artists** in bold.

Agepê
Mistura Brasileira (Sigia 1984).

Araketu
Ara Ketu (Continental 1987).

Bezerra da Silva
Se não fosse o samba (RCA Victor 1989).

Chico Buarque
Ópera do malandro (Philips 1979).
Vida (Philips 1980).

Dorival Caymmi
A música de Caymmi (Continental 1981).

Elis Regina and Tom Jobim
Elis e Tom (Philips 1974).

Gal Costa
Aquarela do Brasil (Philips 1980).

Milton Nascimento
Ao vivo (Polygram do Brasil 1983).
Clube da esquina (Polygram do Brasil 1981).

Olodum
Egito-Madagáscar (Continental 1987).

Paulinho da Viola
Eu canto samba (RCA Victor 1989).
Cantando (RCA Victor 1982).
Chorando (RCA Victor 1982).

Reflexús
Reflexús da mãe Africa (EMI 1987).

Roberto Ribeiro
De Palmares ao tamborim (EMI 1984).

Vinícius de Moraes
with Marilia Medalha and Toquinho
Como dizia o poeta. . . – música nova (RGE 1971).

As for Brazilian records **available in Britain**, only the jazz/*bossa-nova* records of Getz and his Brazilian
collaborators are easily available. However, recent interest in Brazilian music has spawned a few new
compilation albums; notably *Brazil Classics: Volume 1* (a sort of Brazilian greatest hits) and *Volume 2* (a
samba collection), both on EMI and collected and presented by David Byrne; and *Forró: Music for Maids
and Taxi Drivers* (Globestyle Records), a self-explanatory and excellent introduction to the effervescent
Northeastern music. There are also a number of *lambada* compilations, jumping on the bandwagon. The
best place to buy Brazilian music in Britain is at the *HMV* megastore, 150 Oxford Street, London W1. Or
write to Globestyle Records (48–50 Steele Road, London NW10 7AS), sending an SAE for their catalogue.

BOOKS

The recent flood of books on the Amazon masks the fact that Brazil is not well covered by books in English. With some exceptions – detailed below – good books on Brazil tend to be either fairly expensive or out of print. The easily available paperbacks are given here, together with a selection of others that a good bookshop or library will have or be able to order. Even so, important areas are sparsely covered: apart from the novels of Jorge Amado, for example, the riches of Brazilian literature lie largely untranslated.

TRAVEL

Henry Bates *The Naturalist on the River Amazon* (o/p). A Victorian botanist describes his years spent collecting in the Amazon. An unknown but wonderful book, Bates' boyish scientific excitement illuminates every page; a fascinated, and very English, eye cast over the Amazon and its people.

Catherine Caulfield *In the Rainforest* (Pan £4.95). Sharp-eyed journalist travels around the Brazilian Amazon, amongst other rainforests.

Low on context but good on atmosphere: one of the best of the recent Amazon books.

Colonel P.H. Fawcett *Exploration Fawcett* (o/p). Fawcett carries his stiff upper lip in and out of some of the most disease-infested, dangerous and downright frightening parts of interior Brazil. It's a rattling good read, compiled by his son from Fawcett's diaries and letters after his disappearance. Readily available in secondhand bookshops.

Peter Fleming *Brazilian Adventure* (Penguin £6.95). Relentlessly cheery explorer makes light of appalling dangers in his travels in search of Colonel Fawcett. Funny despite – or perhaps because of – the Ripping Yarns feel to the book.

Claude Levi-Strauss *Tristes Tropiques* (Picador £7.95). The great French anthropologist describes his time spent in 1930s Brazil – the best book ever written about the country by a foreigner. There are famous descriptions of sojourns with Nambikwara and Tupi-Kawahib Indians, epic journeys, and a remarkable eyewitness account of São Paulo exploding into a metropolis. Essential reading.

Charles Wagley *An Introduction to Brazil* (Columbia University Press o/p). Three decades old but still the best introduction to Brazil and the Brazilians. Lucidly written and with the authority of a lifetime involved with the country behind it. Available in many public libraries.

POLITICS, HISTORY, AND SOCIETY

Peter Flynn *Brazil: A Political Analysis* (Benn o/p). Massively detailed and authoritative political history of Brazil from the birth of the Republic to the beginning of the *abertura*. Best bet if you really want to get to grips with Brazilian politics; you should find it in public libraries.

USEFUL ADDRESSES

Latin American Bureau, 1 Amwell Street, London EC1R 1UL (☎071/278 2829). Publishers; see book lists.

Survival International, 310 Edgeware Road, London W2 1DY (☎071/723 5535). Publishers; see book lists.

A. Burton Garbett, 35 The Green, Morden, Surrey SM4 4HJ (☎081/540 2367). A good specialist bookshop for old and new books on Brazil.

Anglo-Brazilian Society, 32 Green Street, London W1Y 3FD (☎071/493 8493).

Brazilian Contemporary Arts, Palingswick House, 241 King Street, London W6 9LP (☎081/741 9579).

E. Bradford Burns *A History of Brazil* (Columbia University Press). Long and rather dull, but the standard modern history.

J. P. Dickenson *Brazil* (Longman World's Landscapes Series £7.95). Looks like a textbook, but actually a very readable account of the part that landscape has played in shaping the country.

John Hemming *Red Gold: the Conquest of the Brazilian Indians* (Macmillan £25). The definitive history of the topic, well-written and thoroughly researched. Both passionate and scholarly, it's a basic book for anyone interested in the Indian question in Brazil. A companion volume, *Amazon Frontier* (Harvard University Press £25) brings the depressing story up-to-date.

Leslie Bethell, ed. *Colonial Brazil* (Cambridge University Press, £12.95); *Brazilian Empire and Republic 1818–1930* (CUP £10.95). The former is the best available introduction to Brazil's colonial period, scholarly but also easily accessible to the general reader. The latter, a collection of essays by leading historians, is essential reading for anyone interested in Brazilian history since independence.

Daphne Patai, *Brazilian Women Speak: Contemporary Life Stories* (Rutgers University Press, 1988, £10.95 pb, £28.95 hb). Oral testimony forms the core of this very readable work that lets ordinary women from the Northeast and Rio speak for themselves to describe the struggles, constraints and hopes of their lives.

Gordon Campbell *Brazil Struggles for Development* (Charles Knight, 1972). A short social and political history of post-war Brazil, particularly the military years.

Bernado Kucinski *Brazil: State and Struggle* (Latin American Bureau £2.95). Extremely biased (pro-PT) account of Brazilian politics up to the 1980s, but an easy-to-read introduction that gives you the basic facts.

Jacky Roddick et. al. *The Dance of the Millions: Latin America and the Debt Crisis* (Latin American Bureau £6.95). Explains a very complicated topic extremely clearly, and sets Brazil's experience against that of other Latin American countries.

João Trevisan *Perverts in Paradise* (GMP £5.95). This is a fascinating survey of Brazilian gay life ranging from the papal inquisition to pop idols, transvestite *macumba* priests, and guerrilla idols.

Alex Shoumatoff *The Capital of Hope: Brasília and its People* (University Press of New Mexico, Albuquerque, 1987, £7.95). The author talked with government officials and settlers – rich and poor – to weave a very readable account of the first 25 years of the Brazilian capital.

David P. Appleby *The Music of Brazil* (University of Texas Press, 1983). The most comprehensive study of Brazilian music in English. It provides a clear outline of the major trends that have shaped the music of Brazil over the centuries.

Charles A. Perrone *Contemporary Brazilian Song: MPB 1965–1985* (University of Texas Press, 1989). This is the only study of *Música Popular Brasileira* in English. The book's six central chapters deal with the work of six leading poet-composers.

Frederick C. Luebke *Germans in Brazil: A Comparative History of Cultural Conflict During World War I* (Louisiana State University Press, Baton Rouge, 1987, £30.90). One of the very few studies in English on Germans in Brazil. Despite the title, this social history covers the period 1818–1918, though the focus is World War I, when Brazilians of German origin began to accept that they could not remain foreigners in their own country

Katia M. de Queiros Mattoso *To be a Slave in Brazil, 1550–1888* (Rutgers University Press, 1986, £11.75 pb, £32.70 hb). A history of slavery in Brazil, unusually written from the perspective of the slave. Intended for the general reader, the author divides her excellent study into three themes: the process of enslavement, life in slavery and the escape from slavery.

R. B. Cunningham Graham *A Vanished Arcadia* (Century £5.95). Cunningham Graham's passionate and rather romanticised account of the rise and fall of the Jesuit missions in South America was first published in 1901 and has become a classic on the subject.

Eugene Harter *The Lost Colony of the Confederacy* (University Press of Mississippi £14.95). In a thoroughly entertaining way, Harter tells the story of how southern exiles in Brazil adjusted to their new country and of how for more than a century these last Confederates have maintained elements of their distinct identity.

Thomas H. Holloway *Coffee and Society in São Paulo, 1886–1934* (University of North

Carolina Press, Chapel Hill, 1980, $25). Detailed look at the labour system that evolved on the coffee plantations of São Paulo, and the experiences of two million immigrants who worked them.

Alexander Leonard *The Valley of the Latin Bear* (Victor Gollancz, London, o/p). A delightful account of everyday life in an isolated German village in Santa Catarina. Although written thirty years ago, the account remains very recognisable and it's still well worth seeking out.

LITERATURE AND ART

Although translations of the Bahian novelist, Jorge Amado, are easily found, other infinitely better writers – like Machado de Assis and Graciliano Ramos – have been neglected. There is still no widely available translation of Machado's *Posthumous Memoirs of Brás Cubas*, the finest classic Brazilian novel, or of Graciliano's *Barren Lives*, the best modern Brazilian novel. Until they are translated, as they surely must be soon, you have to content yourself with Amado and the minor works of the masters.

Jorge Amado *Gabriela, Clove and Cinnamon*; *Tereza Batista*; *Dona Flor and Her Two Husbands*; *Tieta*; *The Violent Lands* (Abacus £4.95 each). Amado is the proverbial rollicking good read, a fine choice for the beach or on long bus journeys. He's by far the best-known Brazilian writer abroad – there is even a French wine named after him. Purists might quibble that the local colour is laid on with a trowel, but Amado's formula of vividly tropical settings and steamy eroticism has him laughing all the way to the bank.

Machado de Assis *The Devil's Church and Other Stories* (University of Texas Press £8.25), *Helena* (University of California Press £11.50). These are worth going to some trouble to get hold of: good translations of Machado's great short stories. His cool, ferociously ironic style veers between black comedy and sardonic analysis of the human condition. The finest novelist Brazil has yet produced.

Graciliano Ramos *Childhood* (Owen o/p), *São Bernado* (Owen o/p). Works by the Northeastern novelist who introduced social realism into modern Brazilian fiction. Neither are as good as his masterpiece *Barren Lives*, or

as his prison memoir, *Memories of Jail* (*Memórias do Cárcere*): translations of both are apparently in the pipeline.

The South Bank Centre *Art in Latin America* (Hayward Gallery £14.95). Lavishly illustrated catalogue to the 1989 exhibition, which includes thorough coverage of all periods of Brazilian art. Pick it up at the gallery shop on London's South Bank.

THE NORTHEAST

Billy Jaynes Chandler *The Bandit King: Lampião of Brazil* (Texas University Press £14.95). Compulsive reading that seems like fiction but is well-documented fact. Based on original sources and interviews with participants and witnesses, an American historian with a talent for snappy writing reconstructs the action-packed (and myth-encrusted) life of the famous social bandit, complete with fascinating photographs.

Euclides da Cunha *Rebellion in the Backlands* (Cambridge University Press o/p). If you can get hold of it – and specialist Latin American bookshops do stock it – there is no better introduction to the *sertão*. The translation is often clumsy but the subject – the messianic rebellion of Canudos, in Bahia – is compulsive reading. Da Cunha, one of Brazil's greatest writers, accompanied the final expedition against *sertanejo* rebels: much more than a campaign diary, he alternates between horror and admiration in a riveting history of the war, the *sertão* and its people.

Gilberto Freyre *The Masters and the Slaves* (Alfred Knopf o/p). Classic history of plantation life in the Northeast, with a wealth of detail; includes index headings like "Smutty Stories and Expressions" and "Priests, Bastards of". As you see, very readable, even if Freyre's somewhat simplistic theories are now out of fashion or discredited (see the section on "Race in Brazilian Society"). His *The Mansion and the Shanties* deals with the early growth of urban Brazil.

Mario Vargas Llosa *The War of the End of the World* (Faber £9.95). Goes well with Da Cunha: the Peruvian writer produced this haunting novel based on the events of Canudos in the 1970s. The translation is good and the book's easy to get hold of.

THE AMAZON

Far more is written in English about the Amazon than the rest of the country put together. On the whole there are two types of book about the Amazon: those that deal with the politics and economics of the region, and the heavily illustrated, natural history book. What follows is a brief survey of a crowded field; and see under "Travel" and "Politics, Economics and History".

Sue Branford and Oriel Glock *The Last Frontier: Fighting for Land in the Amazon* (Zed Books £7.95). Documents the land crisis and follows up specific disputes, giving you a good idea of the human cost of land speculation.

David Cleary *Anatomy of the Amazon Gold Rush* (Macmillan £35). Clearly written introduction to an important topic – some spectacular photographs.

Shelton Davis *Victims of the Miracle* (CUP £12.95). Important book looking at the implications of the construction of the Amazon highways for the Indians who were in its way. Good maps.

Susanna Hecht and Alexander Cockburn *The Fate of the Forest* (Verso £16.95; cheaper paperback due soon). Head and shoulders above other studies of the crisis in the Amazon. Excellently written and researched – check out the footnotes – this is as good an introduction to the problem as you will find. Very strong on Amazonian history, too – essential to understanding what's going on, but often ignored by Amazon commentators.

Chico Mendes and Tony Gross *Fight for the Forest: Chico Mendes in His Own Words* (Latin American Bureau £2.95). Long, moving passages from a series of interviews the rubber tappers' union leader gave shortly before his assassination in 1988. Well translated and with useful notes giving background to the issues raised. Direct from the sharp end of the Amazon land crisis.

Charles Wagley *Amazon Town* (o/p). Classic anthropological study of an interior Amazon town in the 1940s which inspired generations of students. Written with Wagley's incisive style and complete command of his material.

Warren Dean *Brazil and the Struggle for Rubber* (CUP £27.50). Decent environmental history of the Amazon.

Brian Kelly and Mark London *Amazon* (Holt, Rheinhart 1983). Part travelogue, part serious study, and relatively easy reading.

Margaret Mee *In Search of the Flowers of the Amazon Forest* (Nonesuch £25). The best of the natural history books by some way. Mee was a British botanist who dedicated her life to travelling the Amazon and painting its plant life. She died in a car crash in 1988, and this beautiful book is a fitting tribute to her. It includes descriptions of her many journeys, good photographs, and lavish reproductions of her wonderful drawings and paintings.

Lisa Silcock *The Rainforests: a Celebration* (Barrie and Jenkins £19.95). Most of the natural history books are much of a muchness, though in this the quality of the maps and the photos is extremely high. Basically a coffee-table book, but the images are ravishing and the text much better than you'd expect; and with a foreword by Prince Charles, no less.

Sting and Jean-Pierre Dutilleux *The Fight for the Amazon* (Rainforest Foundation £8.95). Numbingly banal text, but the photos are good and the proceeds go to a worthy cause.

David Treece *Bound in Misery and Iron* (Survival International £2.95). Detailed and disturbing examination of how the huge Carajás development project in eastern Amazonia affected Indians in the region.

LANGUAGE

Outside Rio and the tourist resorts, English is not widely spoken in Brazil, and the few Brazilians who do speak languages other than Portuguese are more likely to know French. If you speak Spanish you can make yourself understood, provided you speak slowly, but you may not understand the replies. Brazilian Portuguese is grammatically very similar to Spanish, but sounds nothing like it – most people find it much more difficult to pronounce. However, Brazilians appreciate attempts to speak Portuguese and will be very encouraging when you try. And you'll be helped by the fact that Portuguese in Brazil is spoken much more slowly than in Portugal.

PRONUNCIATION

The rules of **pronunciation** are complicated. There are thirteen vowel sounds, compared to five in Spanish, and you'll find them rather nasal.

A is somewhere between the "a" sound of bat and that of father.

E has three basic variants: "ay" as in hay, "e" as in bet, or "i" as in bit. Unfortunately, no rule governs which is used when.

I is as in police.

O is as in the "o" of opera at the beginning or in the middle of a word, but as in the "u" sound in flu when it ends a word.

U is as in flu.

C is soft before "e" and "i", hard otherwise unless it has a cedilla (ç): *cerca* is pronounced "serka".

D is often softened before "e" and "i" into a "dj" sound, otherwise hard.

G is like the English "j" but softer before "e" and "i", otherwise hard.

H is always silent, but is used like the Spanish tilde (~) after n: *senhor* is pronounced "senyor".

IL at the end of a word is pronounced "iu", so *Brasil* is pronounced "Brasiu".

J is softer than an English "j".

M is as in English, though it nasalises a preceding vowel.

N acts the same as "m".

QU is like the English "k".

R is like the "h" in hard when it's the first letter, otherwise rolled. **RR** is an almost impossible guttural "r", but you can get by using the "h" pronunciation instead, as several important Brazilian accents do.

S is as in English.

T has a "tch" sound before "i", otherwise as in English.

X is as the English "sh".

Z is as in English

VOWEL COMBINATIONS

There are four vowel combinations to get used to: the nasal ones, denoted by the tilde (~) above the letter, look difficult but are easy.

ÃO is as "ow", said through the nose.

ÕE is as "oy", said through the nose.

EI is as in weigh.

OU is as the "o" in slow.

DICTIONARIES AND PHRASEBOOKS

A **dictionary** would be useful if you are travelling for any length of time, but unfortunately Portuguese is not particularly well served. There is no good Portuguese–English dictionary in paperback: the *Collins* is barely adequate, and geared to Portugal rather than Brazil. The best option is the Brazilian Portuguese–English dictionary by James L. Taylor (Harrap £15.95), but it's only available in bulky hardback. Also, as yet, there is no good **phrasebook** for Brazilian Portuguese. Harrap's *Portuguese Phrasebook* (£1.65) is reasonable but limited by also being mainly for Portugal.

A GUIDE TO BRAZILIAN PORTUGUESE

The Basics

Yes, No	*sim, não*	Open, Closed	*aberto/a, fechado/a*
Please, Thank You	*por favor, obrigado* (men)/ *obrigada* (women)	With, Without	*com, sem*
		Good, Bad	*bom, ruim*
Where, When	*onde, quando*	Big, Small	*grande, pequeno*
What, How Much	*que, quanto*	More, Less	*mais, menos*
This, That	*este, esse, aquele*	Today, Tomorrow	*hoje, amanhã*
Now, Later	*agora, mais tarde*	Yesterday	*ontem*

Greetings and Responses

Hello, Goodbye	*olá, tchau* (like the Italian "ciao")	Sorry	*desculpa*
		Excuse me	*com licença*
Good Morning	*bom dia*	How are you?	*como vai?*
Good Afternoon/Night	*boa tarde/boa noite*	Fine	*bem*

Useful Phrases

I don't understand	*não entendo*	What's your name?	*como se chama?*
Do you speak English?	*você fala inglês?*	I am English/American	*Sou inglês/americano*
I don't speak Portuguese	*não falo português*	Everything's fine	*Tudo bem*
What's the Portuguese for this?	*como se diz em português?*	OK	*Tábom*
		I feel ill	*Me sinto mal*
What did you say?	*o que disse?*	I want to see a doctor	*Quero ver um medico*
My name is...	*meu nome é'...*	What's the matter?	*Que passa?*

Hotels and Transport

I want, I'd like...	*Quero...*	the bus station	*a rodoviária*
There is (is there?)	*Há..?*	the bus stop	*a parada de ônibus*
Do you have...?	*Você tem...?*	the nearest hotel	*o hotel mais perto*
a room?	*um quarto?*	the post office	*o correio*
the time?	*as horas?*	the toilet	*o banheiro/sanitário*
with two beds/double bed	*com duas camas/ cama de casal*	Left, right, straight on	*esquerda, direita, direto*
It's for one person/two people	*é para uma pessoa/ duas pessoas*	Go straight on and turn left	*vai direto e dobra à esquerda*
It's fine, how much is it?	*Está bom, quanto é?*	Where does the bus to ... leave?	*de onde sai o ônibus para...?*
It's too expensive	*é caro demais*	Is this the bus to Rio?	*é esse o ônibus para Rio?*
Do you have anything cheaper?	*tem algo mais barato?*	Do you go to ...?	*você vai para...?*
Is there a hotel/campsite nearby?	*Tem um hotel/camping por aqui?*	I'd like a (return) ticket to..	*quero uma passagem (ida e volta) para...*
Where is..?	*Onde fica...?*	What time does it leave/arrive?	*Que horas sai/chega?*

Numbers and Days

1	*um, uma*	10	*dez*	21	*vinte e um*	200	*duzentos*	Monday	*segunda*
2	*dois, duas*	11	*onze*	30	*trinta*	300	*trezentos*	Tuesday	*terça*
3	*tres*	12	*doze*	40	*quarenta*	500	*quinhentos*	Wednesday	*quarta*
4	*quatro*	13	*treze*	50	*cinquenta*	1000	*mil*	Thursday	*quinta*
5	*cinco*	14	*quatorze*	60	*sesenta*	2000	*dois mil*	Friday	*sexta*
6	*seis*	15	*quinze*	70	*setenta*	5000	*cinco mil*	Saturday	*sábado*
7	*sete*	16	*dezesseis*	80	*oitenta*			Sunday	*domingo*
8	*oito*	17	*dezesete*	90	*noventa*				
9	*nove*	20	*vinte*	100	*cem*				

A GLOSSARY OF BRAZILIAN TERMS AND ACRONYMS

AGRESTE In the Northeast, the intermediate zone between the coast and the sertão

ALDEIA Originally a mission where Indians were converted, now any isolated hamlet

ALFÂNDEGA Customs

AMAZÔNIA The Amazon region

ARTESANATO Artesania, craft goods

AZULEJO Decorative glazed tiling

BAIRRO Neighbourhood within town or city

BANDEIRANTE Member of a group that marched under a *bandeira* (banner or flag) in early missions to open up the interior: Brazilian *conquistador*

BATUCADA Literally drumming session – music-making in general, especially impromptu

BLOCO Large Carnaval group

CAATINGA Scrub vegetation of the interior of the Northeast

CABOCLO Native of river town or rural area of Amazônia

CANDOMBLÉ Afro-Brazilian religion

CANGACEIRO Outlaws from the interior of the Northeast who flourished in the early twentieth century: the most famous was LAMPIÃO.

CARIMBÓ Music and dance style from the north

CARIOCA Someone or something from Rio de Janeiro

CARNAVAL Carnival

CHORO Musical style, largely instrumental

CONVENTO Convent

CORREIO Postal service/post office

CUT/CGT Brazilian trades union organisations

DANCETARIA Nightspot where the emphasis is on dancing

ENGENHO Sugar mill or plantation

ESTADO NOVO The period when Getúlio Vargas was effectively dictator, from mid-1930s to 1945

EUA USA

EX-VOTO Thanks offering to saint for intercession

FAVELA Shanty town, slum

FAZENDA Country estate, ranch house

FEIRA Country market

FERROVIÁRIA Railway station

FORRÓ Dance and type of music from Northeast

FREVO Frenetic musical style and dance from Recife

FUNAI Government organisation meant to protect the interests of Brazilian indians: notoriously corrupt and underfunded.

GARIMPEIRO Prospector or miner

GAÚCHO Person or thing from Rio Grande do Sul; also southern cowboy

GRINGO/A Foreigner, westerner (not derogatory)

IBAMA Government organisation for preservation of the environment: runs national parks and nature reserves

IEMANJÁ Goddess of the sea in Candomblé

IGREJA Church

LARGO Small square

LEITO Luxury express bus

LITERATURA DE CORDEL Literally "string literature" – printed ballads, most common in Northeast but also found elsewhere, named after the string they are suspended from in country markets

LITORAL Coast, coastal zone

LOURO/A Fair-haired/blonde – westerners in general

MACONHA Marijuana

MACUMBA Afro-Brazilian religion usually thought of as more authentically "African" than candomblé, most common in the north

MARGINAL Petty thief, outlaw

MATA Jungle, remote interior

MERCADO Market

MINEIRO Person or thing from Minas Gerais

MIRANTE Viewing point

MOSTEIRO Monastery

MOVIMENTADO Lively, where the action is

MPB Música Popular Brasileira, common shorthand for Brazilian music

NORDESTE Northeastern Brazil

NORDESTINO/A Inhabitant thereof

NOVA REPUBLICA The New Republic – the period since the return to civilian democracy in 1985

PARALELO The unofficial exchange rate

PAULISTA Person or thing from São Paulo state

PAULISTANO Inhabitant of the city of São Paulo

PELOURINHO Pillory or whipping-post, common in colonial town squares

PLANALTO CENTRAL Vast interior tablelands of central Brazil

POSTO Highway service station, often with basic accommodation popular with truckers

PRAÇA Square

PRAIA Beach

PREFEITURA Town Hall, and by extension city governments in general

PT Partido dos Trabhaladores or Workers' Party, the largest left-wing party in Brazil, led by Lula (see "History")

QUEBRADO Out of order

RODOVIA Highway

RODOVIÁRIA Bus station

SAMBA Type of music most associated with Carnaval in Rio

SELVA Jungle

SERTÃO Arid, drought-ridden interior of Northeast

SERTANEJO Inhabitant of sertão

SESMARIA Royal Portuguese land grant to early settlers

SOBRADO Two-storey colonial mansion

TERREIRO House where Canbomblé or Umbanda rituals and ceremonies take place

VAQUEIRO Cowboy in the north

VISTO Visa

INDEX

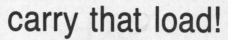

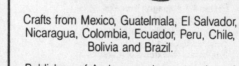
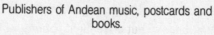